D1370933

The Complete Reference™

SAP® BusinessObjects™ BI 4.0
Third Edition

Cindi Howson
Elizabeth Newbould

New York Chicago San Francisco
Lisbon London Madrid Mexico City
Milan New Delhi San Juan
Seoul Singapore Sydney Toronto

The McGraw·Hill Companies

Cataloging-in-Publication Data is on file with the Library of Congress

McGraw-Hill books are available at special quantity discounts to use as premiums and sales promotions, or for use in corporate training programs. To contact a representative, please e-mail us at bulksales@ mcgraw-hill.com.

SAP® BusinessObjects™ BI 4.0: The Complete Reference™, Third Edition

1234567890   DOC/DOC   1098765432
ISBN   978-0-07-177312-6
MHID   0-07-177312-6

Sponsoring Editor Wendy Rinaldi	**Technical Editor** Mark Stockwell	**Production Supervisor** Jean Bodeaux
Editorial Supervisor Jody McKenzie	**Copy Editor** Marilyn Smith	**Composition** Apollo Publishing
Project Editor LeeAnn Pickrell	**Proofreader** Susie Elkind	**Illustration** Apollo Publishing, Lyssa Wald
Acquisitions Coordinator Joya Anthony	**Indexer** Rebecca Plunkett	**Art Director, Cover** Jeff Weeks

About the Authors

Cindi Howson is the founder of BI Scorecard® (www.biscorecard.com), a resource for in-depth BI product reviews, based on exclusive hands-on testing. She has been advising clients on BI tool strategies and selections for more than 20 years, and first began working with BusinessObjects in 1994. She is the author of *Successful Business Intelligence: Secrets to Making BI a Killer App* and *Business Objects XI: The Complete Reference*™. Prior to founding BI Scorecard, Cindi was a manager at Deloitte & Touche and a BI standards leader for a Fortune 500 company. She is a TDWI (The Data Warehousing Institute) faculty member, a contributing expert to *Information Week*, and has been quoted in the *Wall Street Journal*, *Irish Times*, *Forbes*, and *Business Week*. She has an MBA from Rice University. Contact Cindi at CindiHowson@biscorecard.com.

Elizabeth Newbould is the owner of Solstice Consulting Group (www.scg360.com), a premier BI and data warehousing solutions firm. She has more than 15 years of experience successfully deploying SAP BusinessObjects solutions. Elizabeth was a contributing author for *BusinessObjects XI: The Complete Reference* and the technical editor for the first edition of the book. Contact Elizabeth at enewbould@scg360.com.

About the Contributor

Clark Duey has been the chairperson for the Southern California BusinessObjects User Group and has more than 12 years of experience with SAP BusinessObjects. He is a BI Director in the retail industry.

About the Technical Editor

Mark Stockwell is Senior Principal at Myers-Holum, a premier data integration firm based in New York, specializing in all phases of data warehousing. A veteran BI/DW architect, Mark has 15 years of experience using SAP BusinessObjects and has played many roles within BI projects for the financial, pharmaceutical, and retail sectors. Contact Mark at mark.stockwell@myersholum.com.

Contents at a Glance

Contents

Acknowledgments

As with any book, I first have to thank the readers of the previous editions who helped make this third edition a worthwhile endeavor. There were multiple times in this project that I think all of us wanted to give up, but our desire both to learn the new version and to share our insights with others motivated us throughout.

I would not have been able to undertake this project without my expert coauthors, Elizabeth Newbould and Clark Duey. This is the third book Elizabeth has worked on, so I congratulate her on sticking through the evolution from tech editor to coauthor! Thank you to Mark Stockwell, whom I have enjoyed working with for years as a consultant and newly as a technical editor. Writing a book in addition to their day jobs is both a sacrifice and commitment to the community, and I thank all of them for being so dedicated.

Thank you to the McGraw-Hill team for pulling everything together, particularly Wendy Rinaldi who inherited this book midstream. Thank you to LeeAnn Pickrell for moving the book along in production and Jody McKenzie for making it all look nice in print. Thank you to the copy editor Marilyn Smith for ensuring all those product names were right, and to graphic artist Lyssa Wald who made my stick figures into something more readable.

The powerhouse of an analyst relations team at SAP—Rebecca Adams, Kate Mauser, Stephanie Marley, and Dana Dye—has supported us throughout this process by ensuring we had access to multiple software versions and in channeling dozens of questions to product marketing and management. Thank you to Ashish Morzaria who provided access to multiple versions of the software throughout the project. Thank you to those who provided the answers, particularly Pierpaolo Vezzosi on the IDT, Jacqueline Rahn, and Henry Kam. And thank you to Aundrea Lacy for helping market the book. Thank you to Jason Rose and Adam Binnie who believed in the value of an independent book and who have always accepted my criticisms ever so graciously.

As with any book, much is written at crazy times, and I once again thank my family— Keith, Megan, and Sam—for their unwavering support.

Cindi Howson

First and foremost, I want to thank Cindi Howson who I have had the opportunity and great fortune to work with on this as well as previous editions. Her professionalism and knowledge of this industry is an inspiration to me.

Thank you to Mark Stockwell for his technical scrutiny and answers to my never-ending questions. The McGraw-Hill team of Wendy Rinaldi, LeeAnn Pickrell, and Jody McKenzie was indispensable and made the whole complicated process from manuscript to production seem easy. Many thanks to them for guiding us through this process and accommodating all of our busy schedules.

I would have never made it through this project without the support of my family. Thank you to my husband Chris and my stepchildren Eric, Kathryn, and Megan for their patience and encouragement.

Elizabeth Newbould

Introduction

What's Inside

Part I, "Getting Ready for Business Intelligence," introduces SAP Business Objects the company, the history of business intelligence (BI), and key aspects of the product line. Program and project managers in particular will find Part I useful in understanding the people and communication issues that affect a BI implementation. With the myriad of product choices and deployment approaches, Part I will help you stay focused on the users and business value of your implementation while ensuring the right tool for the right user.

Part II, "Universes and the Information Design Tool," introduces the new Information Design Tool (IDT) and covers best practices in universe design. This part discusses new features, including multisource universes and universes accessing SAP BW, as well as maintenance considerations and various ways to secure the content, both through the Central Management Console and the IDT Security Editor. As you deploy SAP BusinessObjects across the enterprise, there are choices about where to build the intelligence in relational tables, MOLAP databases, the universe, and the reports. Additionally, the larger your company's deployment, the greater the need for testing and production environments, a quality assurance process, and usage monitoring. Part II explains the tools to do this. Even if you are a business user, you will want to skim sections of Part II to better drive the business requirements into the universe design.

Part III, "Reporting and Analysis," covers the business user tools: the BI Workspace, the Launch Pad portal, and Web Intelligence in depth. Part III is when you finally get the return on your BI investment as users explore and analyze data in ways never before possible. Part III covers the basics of accessing standard reports and exploring the data, as well as the advanced techniques of creating queries accessing a universe, personal data source, or BEx query, formatting documents, defining powerful report formulas, and leveraging advanced features.

Part IV, "Dashboards and More" is an all-new section covering Dashboard Design and Dashboards (previously branded Xcelsius) as well as Explorer, SAP's visual data discovery solution for casual users and iPad users. Part IV helps you design dashboards using a variety of data sources, including flat files, BEx queries, and queries from the universe. Dashboard components and their properties are discussed in detail.

Software Version and Modules Covered

We started the rewrite of this book in early 2011, initially intending the book to be focused on SAP BusinessObjects 4.0. Early chapters were written to the ramp-up version of the software and then revised against the production version released in September 2011. As Feature Pack 3 was scheduled to follow soon after, a number of chapters were written using the ramp-up version of that release, with all final technical edits done using Feature Pack 3.

The SAP BusinessObjects product line is ever evolving, with tools like Visual Intelligence and Predictive Analysis added most recently. Herein lies a dilemma with the publishing industry: *The Complete Reference*™ brand does not imply the complete SAP BusinessObjects product line, but rather, a complete reference for certain modules. To manage expectations, please be aware that the following modules are *not* covered in depth in this book: building reports with Crystal Reports (numerous other books cover this topic), Data Integrator, Analysis Edition for OLAP and for Office, and Live Office. Lack of coverage of these modules is simply a matter of scope and time. This book also does not cover conversions and migrations, installation, and performance tuning. We have tried to focus the content of the book primarily on what business application designers, business analysts, and power users need to know. Software engineers and system administrators were not the intended audience for this book.

Sample Data

Many of the examples in this book use the familiar, vendor-supplied Efashion and Island Resorts Marketing universes. Both use Microsoft Access databases. The Efashion universe is based on fictional data from a retail clothing store. It contains three years of sales and promotion costs for 211 fashion products and 13 stores. The Island Resorts Market universe contains reservation and sales information by customer and resort. In cases in which we wanted to demonstrate specific Oracle relational database management system (RDBMS) or Microsoft SQL Server capabilities, we used sample data installed as part of these RDBMSs, such as Sales History and Adventure Works.

Conventions

This book uses the following conventions:

Convention	Used For
Bold	Information you enter in a dialog box
SMALL CAPS	Keyboard keys such as DELETE or BACKSPACE
Courier font	SQL syntax, IDT, and Web Intelligence formula functions
Italics	Universe object names and input variables

CHAPTER 1

Introduction to Business Intelligence

Study the past if you would divine the future. —Confucius

Business intelligence (BI) is a way of exploring data to improve business performance, whether to drive profitability or to manage costs. It is not a technology you implement and then put in maintenance mode. It is an approach that evolves, morphs, and starts over again as the business climate changes, the users discover new opportunities to leverage information, and technology advances.

When you implement a BI platform, the focus of the project is not to finish, but rather to deliver a certain amount of value and functionality within a predefined period. As you implement SAP BusinessObjects BI, you will need to prioritize which applications and interfaces you will leverage most. Will your project be bottom-up: sort out the infrastructure to lower BI costs? Or will it be top-down: deliver dashboards and scorecards to align and measure business performance?

Much of your implementation approach will depend on where you are in the BI life cycle and whether you are completely new to SAP BusinessObjects BI or a long-time Business Objects customer. The purpose of this chapter is to provide some insight as to how BI evolved and is still evolving so that you can assess where your company is in the BI life cycle, where your users are today, and where they are heading. You'll see how SAP and SAP BusinessObjects BI have evolved with their customers and the industry, bringing the vision of BI to more users and beyond traditional corporate boundaries. In many cases, SAP BusinessObject's innovations have shaped and redefined the BI market.

The Background of Business Intelligence

The need to access information is not new. After all, people have always needed data to make informed decisions, although a number of errors in decision-making processes are still prevalent, including gut feel. As a type of technology, though, BI is relatively young; it emerged as a distinct market in the early 1990s. Before BI, it was expensive and time-consuming to get access to the right data.

If you are just starting out on the journey of BI, you may find it hard to believe there was a time when information access was more painful than it is today. There are signs that BI has not quite delivered everything we hoped it would. For example, according to BI Scorecard's annual Successful BI Survey, only 25 percent of company employees use a BI tool on a regular basis. As BI technology evolves, and with a number of recent industry innovations such as in-memory computing and mobile BI on an iPad, expect BI adoption to improve. Research firm Gartner, for example, expects BI adoption to increase to 50 percent by 2015.[1]

Prior to BI, decision makers predominantly relied on the following sources of information:

- Printed reports, generated on a periodic basis by mainframe-based systems. If a critical measure were missing from the printed report, you needed to wait months for IT to create a custom report.

- Manually populated spreadsheets, which provided a bit more flexibility than printed reports. Unlike today, when users may export data from a report, or better yet, use SAP BusinessObjects Live Office or Analysis for Microsoft Office to dynamically import data into a spreadsheet, in the late 1980s, field personnel would call in their sales figures to an analyst, who would manually enter data into a spreadsheet. This allowed for some form of analysis on monthly data at best. With manual data entry, there was enormous room for human error and a higher degree of data discrepancies, as rarely did the manually populated spreadsheet match the source system.

- Gut feel still provided the best form of decision making, as managers were close to the markets and the customers, and markets did not change at the pace they do today. If a manager had access to quantitative numbers, there was a high degree of distrust of the numbers, and rightly so. After all, the data was stale and the manual collection processes fallible.

CAUTION As you deploy SAP BusinessObjects BI, never underestimate the role and "hold" these legacy reporting systems continue to have over users. If you make SAP BusinessObjects BI more difficult to use than legacy reporting systems, your project risks failure. You are trying to change in a matter of months decision-making processes that have existed for decades.

Custom-developed decision support systems (DSSs) and executive information systems (EISs) attempted to overcome some of the limitations of these original information sources. DSSs took the data from mainframe-based transaction systems and presented the results to users in a parameterized form. Users would enter a couple of parameters, such as time period, customer, country, and product. The DSS then displayed results in a tabular format. The beauty of this was that it was easy to use, significantly more so than wading through pages of paper-based reports. If you wanted to graph something, however, you had to re-key the data into a spreadsheet.

If you wanted to view a different data subject, this was generally not possible. DSSs generally provided insight into only one subject of data at a time. Each function generally had its own custom transaction system (see Figure 1-1), making it almost impossible to

---

1. James Richardson, "The Consumerization of BI Drives Greater Adoption," Gartner, June 3, 2011.

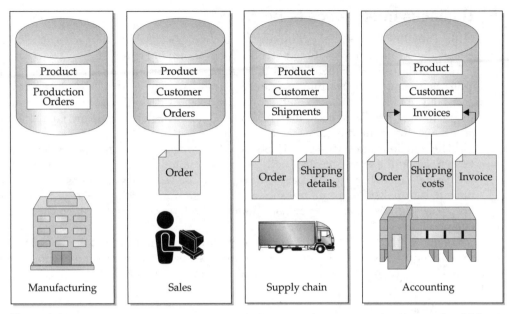

Figure 1-1   Each function had its own custom-built transaction system and corresponding DSS.

share information across functions. When a customer placed an order, the order-entry system maintained its own customer codes. To generate an invoice, the accounts receivable department would need to reenter the order into its own accounting system, which most likely used a different set of customer codes. If you wanted to combine actual sales data (accounts receivable) with shipment dates (orders), it was generally not possible.

Early DSSs, with their proprietary nature, gave way to EISs in the late 1980s. EISs were expensive to implement but provided graphical dashboards based on a broader set of information, sometimes with feeds from external data sources. At the time, products such as LightShip by Pilot Software, Inc., Forest & Trees by Platinum Technology, and Commander Decision by Comshare, Inc., were breakthrough applications and in high demand.

The fundamental problem with EISs was that *E* stood for executive. Companies soon realized that not only executives, but all decision makers, needed access to information. Some savvy marketing companies later would tout their products as *everyone's* information system. However, until organizations fixed the back-end data, the stale, silo-based information could not be actionable, regardless of how pretty it looked in a dashboard or a briefing book. At the time, data warehousing was not a generally accepted technology, so moving beyond silo-based information systems was mission impossible. It is surprising, then, that even today, more than 20 years later, one of the most often cited barriers to a successful enterprise BI deployment is lack of an integrated data architecture. Fail to address the back-end systems, and your BI initiative, will have only limited success.

Potentially, the latest approaches to dashboards, visual data discovery, mobile BI, and other innovations make the concept of *everyone's* information system a greater reality.

Business Intelligence Is Born

In the early 1990s, a number of business and technological factors merged to drive and enable the creation of a new breed of tools, BI, as shown in Figure 1-2.

Several factors drove the need for more information, faster. With the fall of the Berlin Wall, the signing of the North American Free Trade Agreement (NAFTA), the endless possibility of emerging markets, and economic prosperity, growth and globalization were the mantra for many organizations. However, to operate a global company, companies need access to global or multiregional data.

The function- and region-based DSSs could no longer satisfy users' needs. Silo-based EISs broke. At the same time, PCs were becoming common office tools. Users were increasingly analyzing data via spreadsheets or PC-based graphics programs. With this limited data analysis, users put pressure on IT to deliver more robust reports. IT could not keep pace with the demand. Personal computing both drove BI and enabled client/server computing.

Some of these same pressures apply today, particularly in the era of Big Data, in which the volume, variety, and velocity of data has increased, and an unforgiving economy. Such forces influence the demand not only for BI, but for more *self-service* BI.

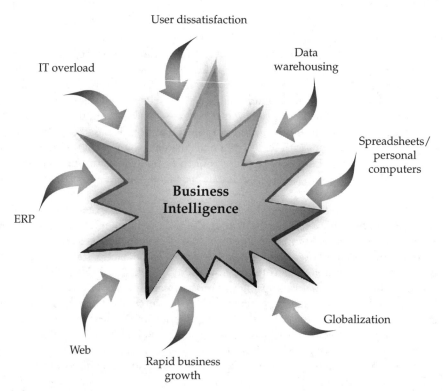

Figure 1-2   The business intelligence explosion

A number of technological advances became enablers for BI. First, large corporations began implementing enterprise resource planning (ERP) systems, often referred to as *business applications*, such as SAP, PeopleSoft, and Oracle Financials. With these implementations, companies hoped to reduce the number and complexity of custom transaction systems, meet the business demands for growth and globalization, and derive the productivity and cost benefits of business process reengineering.

With business applications, companies implement modules that share common business data (see Figure 1-3). Each module includes rules that ensure a company is following its intended business processes. For example, in generating a customer order, the shipment is not scheduled until a price has been agreed upon and inventory is available.

Modules share information with one another. The same customer information used to process the order is used to invoice the customer. When a customer places the order and the product is shipped, this information is integrated with the accounts receivable module to generate an invoice.

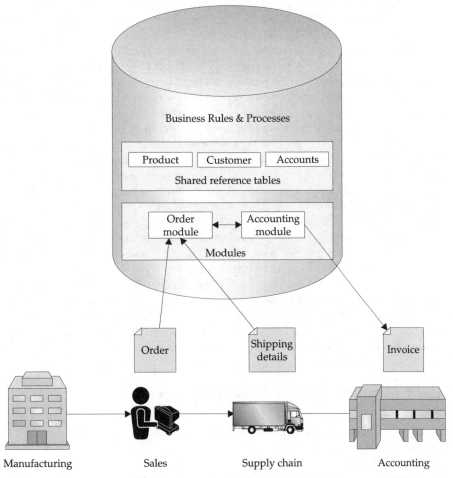

Figure 1-3   Business applications ensure data integration and adherence to standard processes.

With the proprietary transaction systems shown in Figure 1-1, data was double-entered, and customer IDs were specific to each system. With an integrated ERP system, an accountant no longer re-keys the information into a separate system; all reference data is shared across the multiple modules. (See Figure 1-3.) If the productivity and business process reengineering savings were not enough to incite companies to replace their legacy systems with an ERP system, then the threats of year 2000 issues were.

Initially, ERP vendors promised they would provide insight into a company's business. It was a false promise. ERP systems provide the infrastructure that makes the insight *possible*, but the insight comes only when BI tools and a data architecture are implemented in *conjunction with* the ERP system. System integrators and consultants, eager to assist with ERP implementations, only fueled this misconception. Some companies recognized that the newly implemented ERP system would not be able to replace all the information requirements that custom reports and DSSs provided. Although ERPs helped streamline operations and eliminate duplicate data entry, they did nothing to simplify data access. This is one reason why SAP eventually developed the Business Warehouse (BW).

The second key enabler to BI was client/server computing. With PCs on many users' desktops, companies could shift much of the processing power from mainframes to PCs, at a significantly lower cost. All of the sexy charts that made EISs so appealing could easily be rendered on a Microsoft Windows or Apple desktop. The user interface was much more intuitive than mainframe-based reports and programming languages. For the first time, companies could purchase best-of-breed products, and the components worked together. Okay, so they needed some brute force and perhaps some aggressive vendor sessions, but they did work—a shock for many who previously had single-vendor solutions.

While client/server computing placed greater demands on BI, the Web has brought BI to even more users. In some respects, the client/server computing that was once a catalyst for BI can now be an obstacle (that and a general resistance to change). With client/server computing, BI software and database connectivity had to be installed on every user's desktop. With the Web, BI users only need access to a browser.

Customers have been rethinking their corporate intranets and BI infrastructure to better leverage the Web. In some circumstances, the Web has both expedited and hindered broader BI adoption. Because many Crystal Reports consumers required little report-based interactivity, the Web became the perfect delivery vehicle for those reports.

Meanwhile, the huge installed base of SAP BusinessObjects Desktop Intelligence has slowed the adoption of Web Intelligence. Also, prior to SAP BusinessObjects XI Release 2, there was significantly more functionality in Desktop Intelligence than in Web Intelligence, a gap that SAP BusinessObjects has steadily closed with each subsequent release. Despite some strong selling points of the web-based interface, few Desktop Intelligence users were willing to give up the familiarity and robustness of the desktop tool.

Data Warehouse Speeds BI Adoption

The data warehouse was the biggest enabler for powerful reporting and BI's initial wave of success. A data warehouse extracts information from the ERP and aggregates it to allow for fast analysis of vast amounts of data.

Some initial data warehouse projects were deemed failures, costing millions of dollars and producing no measurable benefits after years of effort. Fortunately, industry consultants quickly remedied the data warehouse approach, proposing subject-oriented data marts that can be built in smaller time frames. Ideally, a central data warehouse still acts as the platform to populate the data marts.

As a technology, data marts and data warehousing allow IT to safely isolate the transaction system from the reporting system. A slow query does not halt order processing.

As a business application, data warehousing allows users to analyze broader sets of data with dimensional hierarchies. When analyzing data in either an ERP or a proprietary transaction system, the queries are still limited to a particular module or set of tables. However, SAP BusinessObjects is also widely deployed without a data warehouse, because it provides unique capabilities to report authors to circumvent constraints of reporting off a transactional data source. With Web Intelligence, report authors can query multiple subject areas and stitch the results together seamlessly, locally.

With a data warehouse, the data is combined into one subject area or business view, allowing users to perform analyses that cut across multiple business processes. This approach puts significantly less strain on the BI application and is more scalable than attempting to put so much logic within one report. As the data is aggregated, data warehouses can contain years of history, allowing users to analyze trends. ERP and transaction systems often contain only current data at the most granular level of detail, preventing any kind of trend analysis. Table 1-1 compares some of the different purposes and features of a transaction system with those of a data warehouse.

ERP/Transaction System	Data Warehouse/Data Mart
Goal is to process orders, create invoices, post journal entries	Goal is to provide access to information to improve revenues, manage costs, improve customer service, achieve strategic goals
Current information with very little history	Larger amounts of history allow multiyear trend analysis, this year versus last year comparisons
Real-time information	Information extracted on a periodic basis (hourly, daily, weekly, and so on)
Detailed data down to the line item or level of data entry	Primarily aggregated data for analysis but granular when there is an operational data store
Fast inputs, but slow queries	Read-only; tuned for fast queries
Normalized tables in thousands	Denormalized star or snowflake schemas with fewer tables
Rarely hierarchical groupings	Hierarchical groups give level of time, chart of accounts, product groupings, customer groups, and so on
Fixed reports by one detailed dimension (such as cost center, plant, order number)	Fixed or ad hoc reporting and analysis by multiple dimensions across all business functions

Table 1-1   Comparison of Transaction Systems with Data Warehouses

The Internet Influence

With the Internet boom of the late 1990s, the Web has had a dramatic impact on BI. A large deployment in a client/server system may have been in the thousands of users; in a web deployment, it's tens of thousands. What once was viewed as a departmental application is now considered an enterprise resource. In some cases, the corporate intranet is no longer the deployment boundary, as customers and suppliers can also access rich BI content from a browser.

To leverage the Web, many BI vendors re-architected their products. While the industry has embraced web delivery, authoring approaches for certain types of applications, particularly production reporting tools, continues to be debated. A browser interface is not always as intuitive or fast as a Windows environment, and may not be as integrated with development environments. For these reasons, SAP BusinessObjects continues to rely on the desktop for several of its authoring tools:

- Crystal Reports for Enterprise, for high-fidelity production-style reports, developed by professional report authors
- Dashboard Design for dashboards developed by IT or power users
- Web Intelligence Rich Client for reports that need to be accessed offline or that access personal data sources

Web Intelligence has two authoring modes: one that is purely web-based and one that is desktop-based. Both interfaces create queries and reports that can be deployed to the Web. As of SAP BusinessObjects BI 4.0, Desktop Intelligence is no longer supported.

Competing on Analytics

Many early BI implementations focused primarily on eliminating IT as the bottleneck for reporting and basic data access. These early implementations were often departmental, sponsored by visionary departmental and business unit leaders. A few factors have contributed to BI's role as a mission-critical, enterprise resource:

- Chaos and higher cost of ownership for individually implemented, departmental solutions
- Industry consolidation of smaller BI vendors into mega vendors such as SAP, IBM, and Oracle
- Greater executive awareness about the importance of analytics

In 2006, Babson Professor Tom Davenport published a *Harvard Business Review* article, "Competing on Analytics." The white paper became one of the most widely read papers of the year, later leading to a book by the same title, coauthored with Jeanne Harris of Accenture. While much of the literature on the market prior to this focused on the technical aspects of data warehousing and BI, these authors gave a much-needed business context. Case study after case study showed how smarter companies were outperforming their competitors by using data. A number of other books, such as Ian Ayres's *Super Crunchers* and Michael Lewis's

Moneyball, have reinforced the importance of competing on analytics. Admittedly, the making of *Moneyball* into a movie starring Brad Pitt has cast some stardom on BI. In 2012, business analytics and BI were once again ranked the number-one priority in a Gartner survey of more than 2,300 worldwide chief information officers (CIOs).

A Broader BI Suite

Since its inception, the BI market has been highly fragmented. The year 2007 brought significant industry consolidation, and in 2008, SAP completed the acquisition of Business Objects. In 2007, Oracle acquired Hyperion, and in 2008, IBM acquired Cognos. Vendors who were once only hardware and database partners are now competitors in BI. With this consolidation and increased move to enterprise BI, many customers thought BI standardization in the form of a single solution from a single vendor was the best path for enterprise BI.

While customers may be willing to integrate a database from one vendor with a query tool from a different vendor, they may not be willing to do the same for, say, a dashboard tool and query tool. Customers have moved from departmental, à la carte purchases of multiple BI components to centralized purchases of tightly integrated suites. The degree to which you must understand individual BI market segments depends on the stage of your implementation and your company's philosophy of seeking best-of-breed solutions versus an integrated solution.

The sections that follow describe some of the main BI market segments. Figure 1-4 shows how some of the market segments relate to components of a SAP BusinessObjects architecture.

Data Integration

Data integration or extract, transform, and load (ETL) tools used to be distinct from the BI suite, and with some vendors, they still are. Their job is to take the data from the source ERP or transaction system, and then to cleanse and aggregate it to load in a data warehouse or data mart. Simply getting the data into an online analytical processing (OLAP) database or relational database management system (RDBMS) does not in itself provide business value. As business users attempt to answer questions with the data, the ETL process often changes to extract more data, clean the data, or transform it to add robust business calculations.

In 2002, Business Objects acquired Acta Technology, a leading ETL vendor, and rebranded the product as BusinessObjects Data Integrator. SAP BusinessObjects views data quality and integrity as key to the success of any BI or Enterprise Performance Management (EPM) deployment and a component of its Enterprise Information Management (EIM) strategy.

With any BI implementation, much of the success rests with the information architecture. Provide users with bad data, and the BI tool that is the window to this bad data will take the blame; provide users with good data, and the BI tool will enjoy the credit. EIM is now central to SAP BusinessObjects business analytics portfolio. In April 2006, Business Objects acquired privately held FirstLogic as a way of improving data quality.

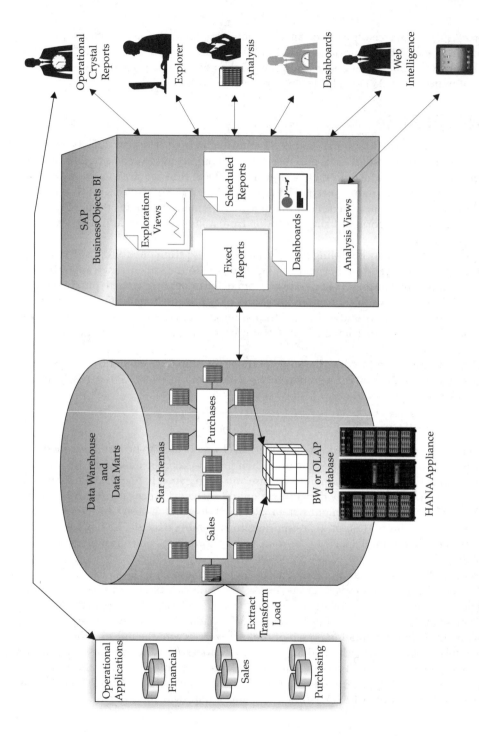

Figure 1-4 Components of a SAP BusinessObjects deployment

As an ETL solution, Data Integrator continues to compete with pure-play ETL vendors such as Informatica, as well as ETL solutions from RDBMS vendors such as Oracle Data Integrator (acquired from Sunopsis) and Microsoft Integration Services. It's perfectly reasonable to use a third-party ETL solution as part of your SAP BusinessObjects deployment.

The choice of which ETL tool to use often is made by the information architects and ETL programmers, while the BI tool choice is more in the hands of the business users. However, because SAP also owns not just the ETL piece of the BI architecture shown in Figure 1-4, but also the front-end pieces, the vendor has extended the ETL integration to the business users. In this regard, while viewing any report, a business user can see the data lineage, transformations, and business descriptions. This information is taken directly from Data Integrator and populated into the universe. This integration allows for a broader type of impact analysis. When the source information changes, an administrator can identify which data warehouse table columns, which universes, and, ultimately, which business reports are affected. In cases in which Crystal Reports instances have been used for maintaining historical data, Data Integrator can access these report instances to populate a data warehouse.

Query and Reporting

Query and reporting is the process of querying a database, and then formatting it for readability and analysis. This is the segment in which Business Objects initially was launched in the early 1990s, and its origins help explain why its SQL generation is so robust. Over the years, the prevalence of query and reporting tools has led this market segment to become synonymous with BI, even though BI encompasses so much more. With query and reporting, users may query a data mart or a data warehouse, or they may query a transaction system.

Some define "reporting" as the process of formatting a report to enable analysis, while others define reporting as the delivery and distribution of standard reports throughout an organization. In 2003, Business Objects acquired Crystal Decisions, traditionally considered an enterprise reporting vendor. Hmm, but wasn't Business Objects used for reporting as well? Yes, and herein lies a potential source of confusion that you must manage as part of your deployment. For the sake of clarity, we refer to Crystal Reports as a *production reporting tool* and Web Intelligence as a *business query tool.* But don't pigeonhole these tools as reserved only or exclusively for certain users or data sources. While there are some clear differentiators between the two, there also is potential for overlap.

The needs within production reporting are often different from the needs within business query. Yet sometimes, the needs blur and the lines cross—and just as you can use a hammer to get a screw into the wall, you can use a production reporting tool for business query and reporting. The converse, however, is rarely true; rarely can you use a business query tool to develop production-style reports. The tool may not support the pixel-perfect layouts, normalized data sources, or programmability that IT developers demand.

With business query tools, the source is more often a data warehouse (though not always) than an OLTP. Whereas IT develops production reports, power users are the primary authors of queries and reports created in a business query tool. The following table compares some additional characteristics that help distinguish production-style reports from management-style reports. These characteristics are by no means absolutes. Neither of these segments is precise. For example, Web Intelligence reports can be used individually, departmentally, or enterprise-wide. Crystal Reports reports would rarely be developed for an individual user, and are more often enterprise-wide. Similarly, bursting a report and pushing it to numerous recipients is often considered a strong point of Crystal Reports, yet this is somewhat possible with Web Intelligence reports.

Characteristic	Production-Style Report	Management-Style Query and Report
User interface	Crystal Reports	Web Intelligence
Primary author	IT developer	Power user or business user
Purpose	Complete an operational task, fulfill regulatory reporting requirement	Decision making and analysis
Report delivery	Portal, paper, or e-bill, embedded in application	Portal, e-mail
Report bursting	Burst to thousands	Schedule individually
Print quality	Pixel-perfect	Presentation quality
Number of report authors	Few	Hundreds or thousands
Number of report consumers	Tens of thousands	Hundreds or thousands
Predominant data source	OLTP—real time	Data warehouse or mart, occasionally OLTP
Level of data detail	Granular	Aggregated
Scope	Operational	Tactical, strategic
Usage	Fixed reports, with optional and limited interactivity	Fixed or interactive reports, ad hoc queries

Production-style query and reporting is the process of querying an OLTP database and then formatting it to create a document—perhaps an invoice, a bank statement, a check, a list of open orders, or a fixed report consumed by thousands of users. In creating these reports, developers often require dynamic and programmatic control over the layout. These are some reasons that Crystal Reports is embedded in so many applications, with native connectivity to dozens of data sources. When the reporting is not against the transaction system, it may be against an operational data store or detailed data within a data warehouse. An invoice looks the same month to month; users have little desire to tailor its appearance (unlike a management report). This is Crystal Reports' sweet spot.

Management-style query and reporting is intended for users who want to author their own reports. They are less concerned with the precise layout (since they aren't trying to generate an invoice), but do want charts and tables quickly and intuitively. This is Web Intelligence's sweet spot.

Most organizations have the need for both types of tools, although in smaller organizations, you may choose one or the other.

Analysis

SAP BusinessObjects provides query, reporting, and analysis in one interface, Web Intelligence, that generates a dynamic microcube based on the query results. OLAP has historically been a distinct market segment of BI. OLAP databases were often implemented as separate solutions from a query and reporting tool. With an OLAP-based universe, Web Intelligence users can analyze data in OLAP databases such as SAP BW or Microsoft Analysis Services. A new module in SAP BusinessObjects BI 4.0, referred to as Analysis (previously branded Voyager), also offers users access to OLAP databases. SAP BusinessObjects Analysis comes in two editions: an OLAP edition, which is web-based, and OLAP front end and for Office edition, which is an Excel- and PowerPoint-based front end for BW and Microsoft Analysis Services.

In its broadest sense, OLAP provides multidimensional analysis with different dimensions and different levels of detail. Capabilities such as drill-down, rotate, and swap are OLAP features. OLAP, though, has some clear definitions set forth by E.F. Codd (the father of the RDBMS) in 1993. OLAP itself can be further divided into different approaches: relational (ROLAP), multidimensional (MOLAP), hybrid (HOLAP), and dynamic (DOLAP).

NOTE DOLAP used to be an acronym for desktop OLAP because the processing initially occurred on the desktop. However, dynamic OLAP is a more appropriate term, as the processing can occur in either a desktop environment or a mid-tier application server, but in both cases, the cache is built dynamically without requiring any explicit user or administrative tasks.

These approaches differ in where the aggregations, calculations, and processing are performed. The following table compares some of the vendors and their different approaches to OLAP.

Architecture	Primary Difference	Vendor
ROLAP	Calculations done in a relational database.	SAP BW
MOLAP	Calculations performed in a server-based multidimensional database. Cubes provide write access for inputting budget data or performing what-if analysis.	Microsoft Analysis Services, Oracle Essbase
HOLAP	Aggregations in a cache but with seamless drill-through to relational.	Microsoft Analysis Services
DOLAP	Calculations performed on the desktop or Enterprise server to build a microcube. Cubes are read-only.	Web Intelligence

Given these traditional OLAP architectures, it's not surprising that many customers are not sure where to classify Web Intelligence. Web Intelligence is primarily a DOLAP solution because the cache is built dynamically, either on the desktop in the case of the Rich Client or on the Enterprise server. However, it is also a ROLAP approach because it provides automatically drill-through to detail, server-based ranking, aggregate navigation, and other capabilities, while leveraging the data storage of the RDBMS. The only architecture you can say it is not is MOLAP. You might deploy SAP BusinessObjects *instead of* a MOLAP solution or *in addition to* a MOLAP solution.

In-memory architectures, meanwhile, are challenging the notion of an OLAP database. In 2011, SAP released HANA, an in-memory engine and appliance that largely displaces MOLAP databases. As shown in Figure 1-4, HANA can be used alongside an existing data warehouse or in place of existing databases.

Analytic Applications

Henry Morris of International Data Corporation (IDC) coined the term *analytic application*. For software to be considered an analytic application, IDC says it must have the following characteristics:

- It must function independently of the transaction or source systems.
- It must extract, transform, and integrate data from multiple sources and allow for time-based analysis.
- It must automate a group of tasks related to optimizing particular business processes.

Much of what SAP has historically delivered has focused only on data stored in the SAP systems and then using SAP front-end technologies, whether the BW warehouse or Visual Composer, for example. In 2010, SAP announced a number of new analytic applications that leverage the BusinessObjects tools, Explorer, Web Intelligence, and Dashboards (formerly branded Xcelsius). Non-SAP ERP customers can now use these applications, because they are no longer reliant on BW as a data source. The data can reside in BW, a custom data warehouse, or the transaction system. The new analytic applications focus on specific industry verticals such as retail, banking, and oil and gas, as well as functional areas or lines of business such as supply chain, procurement, and human resources.

Dashboards and Scorecards

The terms *dashboard* and *scorecard* are often used interchangeably, although there is a difference. According to industry visualization expert Stephen Few, author of *Information Dashboard Design*, "a dashboard is a visual form of information display, which is used to monitor what's currently going on in the business at a glance." Any tool that can display multiple objects from multiple data sources, then, can correctly be referred to as a dashboard, including a Web Intelligence document or an interactive dashboard designed with Dashboard Design (formerly branded Xcelsius).

In its simplest terms, a dashboard is a collection of information, similar to a dashboard in your car. It might include the following:

- A map that color-codes where sales are performing well or poorly
- A gauge chart that shows if expenses are over or under budget
- A trend line that tracks stockouts

Whereas dashboards present multiple numbers in different ways, a scorecard focuses on a given metric and compares it to a target. In analyzing performance versus the target, a scorecard may provide a strategy map (see Figure 1-5) and track accountability. Scorecard products are often certified by the Balanced Scorecard Collaborative. Balanced scorecards

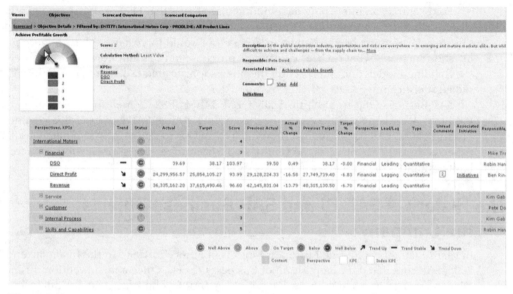

Figure 1-5   SAP BusinessObjects Strategy Management

will track KPIs according to the four dimensions of customer, financial, internal processes, and skills and capabilities.

SAP acquired Strategy Management from Pilot Software in 2007.

Visual Data Discovery

Visual data discovery is an emerging software category. The business query module and visual data discovery module both provide self-service BI. However, the former assumes the data has been modeled to some degree; the latter does not necessarily assume this. As well, a business query module may rely on a tabular data set as the starting point, whereas the visual data discovery module will render the data visually in a way that facilitates insight and pattern identification.

SAP BusinessObjects Explorer is a combination search and visual data discovery interface. An IT administrator creates an information space based on a universe. Casual users explore data via a tabular display and automatically created chart. SAP Visual Intelligence is a new desktop product intended for more sophisticated users to explore data in HANA. The vendor plans to provide connectivity to the universe in a future release.

Predictive Analytics and Data Mining

Data mining is a particular kind of analysis that discovers patterns in data using specific algorithms such as decision trees, neural networks, clustering, and so on. Data mining is used for predictive analytics and is forward-looking, whereas query and reporting tools are more typically used for analyzing current and historical data. Another difference is that, whereas standard query and reporting tools require you to ask a specific question, data mining does not.

For example, an interesting data-mining discovery is that beer and diaper sales are closely correlated (one theory: a quick stop to the store to pick up more diapers is a good time to pick up more beer). A standard query tool would force a user to ask a more precise question such as, "What do beer consumers purchase in the same store visit?"

Building models and interpreting them is a sophisticated task demanding a highly skilled statistician.

SAP Business Objects has historically OEM'd IBM SPSS Clementine as part of its Predictive Workbench. However, at the time of this writing, SAP had just released a new product called SAP BusinessObjects Predictive Analysis to ramp-up, with general availability expected in 2012. Ramp-up is the vendor's approach to releasing production software to a limited number of customers

The History of SAP BI and SAP Business Objects the Company

Bernard Liautaud cofounded Business Objects in France in 1990. In the first quarter of 2008, SAP completed the acquisition of Business Objects. Once a niche vendor, Business Objects reached one billion in revenues in 2005. SAP says business analytics now accounts for a sizable portion of its new revenues. According to industry analyst firm IDC, SAP BusinessObjects is the market leader in BI tools by a wide margin. In speaking about the company's latest BI release, SAP chief technology officer (CTO) Vishal Sikka claimed that version 4.0 is the "best release ever of BusinessObjects."

Some of the biggest improvements in SAP BusinessObjects BI 4.0 include enhanced support for SAP BW content, multisource universes, universe access for dashboards, enhanced charting across all the interfaces, and improved administration and usage monitoring. The server architecture is now 64-bit, bringing greater scalability on a single server.

While SAP BusinessObjects 4.0 is a significant product release, there have been a number of continuous improvements and innovations over the decades. Figure 1-6 provides a timeline of some of the company's major product innovations and key acquisitions.

- **1990** Patented semantic layer allows users to generate SQL using familiar business terminology.
- **1996** Business Objects introduces the microcube technology for dynamic OLAP.
- **1997** Web Intelligence thin client is first introduced.
- **1997** SAP releases first version of BW.
- **2001** Auditor is launched, allowing administrators to track use of documents, universes, and objects by users and groups.
- **2002** Acta (later rebranded as Data Integrator and Rapid Marts) is acquired by Business Objects to provide ETL capabilities and packaged data marts.
- **2003** Crystal Decisions is acquired by Business Objects for its pixel-perfect reporting solution, enterprise architecture, and huge base of OEM partners and customers.
- **2004** BusinessObjects XI Release 1 provides a new architecture that integrates Crystal Enterprise and the classic BusinessObjects suite.

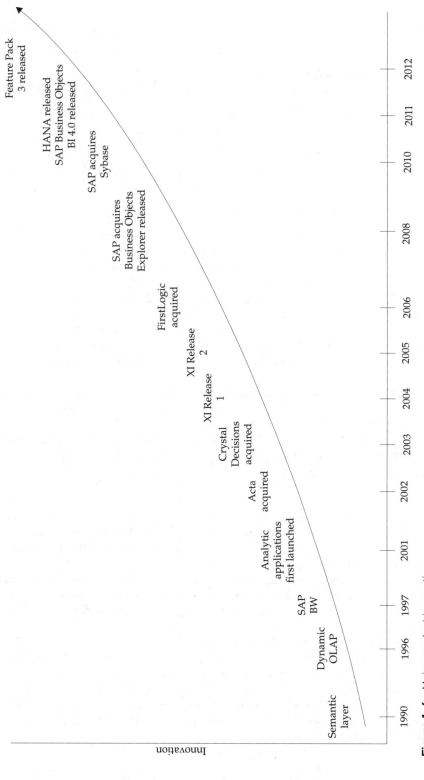

Figure 1-6 Major product innovations

- **2005**   Xcelsius is acquired from Infommersion for Flash-powered dashboards.
- **2006**   FirstLogic is acquired to embed data quality capabilities in Data Integrator.
- **2008**   SAP acquires Business Objects for $6.8 billion.
- **2008**   Explorer is released, combining search and visual exploration for casual users.
- **2010**   SAP acquires Sybase for $5.8 billion for mobile and columnar storage.
- **2011**   SAP in-memory appliance HANA is released.
- **2011**   SAP BusinessObjects BI 4.0 is released.
- **2012**   SAP BusinessObjects BI 4.0 Feature Pack 3 is released.

The Future

SAP BusinessObjects BI 4.0 was three years in the making, initially released in September 2011 with Feature Pack 3 released in June 2012. Feature Pack 3 includes enhanced capabilities such as exploration views, improvements in mobile BI, and tighter integration with HANA and SAP StreamWork.

Beyond the core capabilities, it's hard to say which technologies will most impact and accelerate BI's adoption. In-memory computing on an enterprise scale for both BI and real time is in its infancy, with SAP betting heavily on HANA. Cloud BI holds promise for companies who don't want to manage their infrastructure, yet customers are still cautious about cloud security. Social networking brings new sources of data and greater potential for collaboration.

Competing on analytics has become an aspiration for many companies. In a difficult economy and competitive landscape, BI has proved to enable the survival of the smartest.

As a set of technologies, BI is a mature software segment. However, the effective use of BI for bigger business impact is still evolving. Much of the near-term future of BI is about exploiting investments made to date, rather than about the next big innovation.

Summary

To borrow a phrase from a data warehouse vendor, BI is not a destination but a journey. While this book focuses on the company's core query and analysis products, SAP BusinessObjects now offers much more, extending its capabilities into ETL on the back end and analytic applications on the front end.

A BI implementation is a project that you will never finish. The best you can do is to provide a *starting point* for users to make more informed decisions and discover business opportunities. With so much product capability, you must stay focused on the business value of BI.

Your challenge will be to understand how the history of BI in your company influences your users' attitudes, understanding, and receptiveness toward SAP BusinessObjects. Perhaps you are still fighting some of the battles of just having implemented a new ERP. Perhaps your initial goal is to take IT out of the report-writing business and enable greater self-service BI. Perhaps your company will be one of the industry innovators that many aspire to be, using BI in ways never before anticipated, and directly contributing to your firm's market position and profitability. Enjoy the journey!

CHAPTER 2

Goals of Deploying SAP BusinessObjects

Whether you are implementing SAP BusinessObjects for the first time or expanding an existing implementation, it's important to be clear about the goals of your deployment. You may be implementing SAP BusinessObjects as part of an IT effort or as part of a specific line of a business initiative. The goals of these two groups can be quite different. The goals may be driven by the following:

- **IT** To reduce custom report development or replace a legacy reporting system.
- **A business unit** To provide access to data to manage and measure the day-to-day business activities.
- **The corporation** As part of a larger initiative to enable self-service BI and leverage data for competitive advantage.

The goals of different stakeholders may collide and impede progress or merge to make the implementation more successful. You may start out on the implementation with one set of goals, only to discover a more important goal as you proceed.

In some cases, good scope management will help the project stay on track. In other cases, recognize that BI is not as exact as other technology projects and requires a degree of flexibility. Capabilities are delivered on an iterative basis, rather than a traditional waterfall project life cycle. Often, you may feel that a BI project never ends, and in fact, it doesn't and shouldn't. However, focusing on the goals of the project will help minimize the risk that the technology and latest product innovations become all-consuming (as fun as they may be!) and ensure resources are aligned to deliver value within a defined time frame.

IT Goals

Although SAP BusinessObjects provides business insight, it is still a tool purchased primarily by the IT organization as the enabler to information access. IT controls the source systems and the data warehouse. The challenge here is in making sure the IT goals are a starting point and not an end point.

For example, let's assume that your current approach to reports is for a custom programmer to develop them against the source system. Crystal Reports may be the tool of choice for creating such custom reports. The business users are reasonably happy because each report is customized with their view of the data. It's also easy (no training required), and it's correct because the data came directly from the transaction/enterprise resource planning (ERP) system.

However, this approach to information access poses several problems:

- The report developer generally must know the detailed ERP/OLTP schema and programming language.

- The cost to develop and maintain one report is high. Because the report developer is several steps removed from the business, it may take multiple iterations to get the report right. By the time it is right, however, the user requirements change.

- Reporting directly against the OLTP can affect response time both for inputting transactions and for executing a report.

- Without a data warehouse, a significant amount of business logic is built into each individual report.

Some users, though, are not satisfied, because IT can't develop custom reports fast enough. IT has become a bottleneck. Your company decides it needs to complement the Crystal Reports deployment with Web Intelligence as an ad hoc or business query and reporting tool, with the primary goal of reducing the time and cost to develop custom reports, and ideally providing end users with more flexibility. Your company enables the Web Intelligence module and builds a few universes. You assume that users will now be able to create their own reports, and the IT department can focus on a smaller set of canned, enterprise-wide reports. Goal accomplished?

No. First, the skill set to build a universe is often quite different than the programming skills to develop an ERP-based custom report. The roles of the existing report developers must be redefined, or they will impede implementation. Is there still a need for custom reports against the ERP? Probably, yes, but ideally for a much smaller number.

Second, you just went from a business user having access to a fixed report (easy to use) to the user starting at a blank query panel with no data. Part of such a deployment effort must include an evaluation of which reports should remain as fixed reports, which should be eliminated, and which should be redeveloped as standard Web Intelligence reports. IT department members may still develop these initial Web Intelligence reports, since they know the data and current reporting requirements, or power users within the business may become the initial report authors. Don't let this step discourage you—providing standard reports is a *starting point* only.

With all the web-based interactivity in Web Intelligence, end users (not IT developers) can easily fine-tune a report to re-sort, format, filter, and drill. Creating a set of standard reports ensures that users do not perceive Web Intelligence as a step backward—theoretically empowered, but overwhelmed and with no data and certainly no business insight.

Author and researcher Jeremy Hope suggests in his book, *Reinventing the CFO* (Harvard Business Review Press, 2006), that IT is a factor in chief financial officers (CFOs) being increasingly overwhelmed. He suggests that IT has provided finance users with so much unfiltered data that CFOs should be "more wary of implementing new tools and IT systems that soak up valuable time and money but fail to provide reasonable value." At first blush, his case seems to put unfair blame on IT. IT often provides users with more unfettered access to data, because they ask for it, or because the users don't and can't adequately define their requirements.

Users must be engaged in defining BI requirements to minimize the risk of having an overwhelming amount of data but little business insight. In support of Hope's contention, IT can do much more to ensure value is provided. Standard reports are certainly a way of accomplishing this. Dashboards are yet another. In this regard, IT knows what is possible and needs to work in concert with the business to ensure both constituents achieve their goals.

Over time, as both power users and casual users work with the standard Web Intelligence reports, they can move on to modify, customize, and finally, create their own reports. It is this phase of the implementation in which IT realizes the cost benefit, and the business gains a lot of other benefits. Had your company stayed in custom development mode with only a handful of Crystal Report experts, the programmers would still be hard-coding inflexible reports, and users would see only a limited amount of data. While the goal to limiting custom report development may not sound as glorious and strategic as "competing on analytics" or "enterprise performance management," it is valid, with a measurable benefit of reduced costs and overtime, along with improved business insight.

Reporting Directly Against a Transaction System

When you implement an ad hoc or business query tool, you may reduce report development costs, but you do nothing to improve query response time or provide meaningful context to the data. In fact, you run a high risk that you will make response time significantly worse for both BI queries and transaction system inputs. The simple answer is to build a data warehouse or a data mart. After all, the fundamental difference between these two platforms is their primary purpose: automating a process versus providing business insight (see Table 1-1 in Chapter 1). Yet many companies still elect to implement SAP BusinessObjects directly against the OLTP system (or a copy of it).

Why Use OLTP Directly?

A company may decide to use SAP BusinessObjects directly against the OLTP system for several reasons, as described in the following sections.

Timing

A data warehouse may be a long-term goal, but under budget constraints, companies need to achieve immediate benefits. They don't have the time or resources to develop an enterprise information strategy. If you recently implemented a new OLTP system, then you need reports immediately, not six months from now. This kind of approach also gives you a relatively quick way of communicating the value of deploying a BI solution.

Lack of Sponsorship

A successful data warehouse project requires strong business sponsorship and agreement across departments and functions. In contrast, OLTP-based reporting is often deemed an IT responsibility, since IT programs the reports. IT can implement and control reporting in this environment, without needing to gain the buy-in necessary for a data warehouse; the politics of a data warehouse project are deferred.

Cost and Complexity

Data warehouse implementations range in price from $50,000 to millions of dollars. Poorly managed projects can take years to achieve measurable benefits, and even well-managed ones will take several months. In addition to selecting a BI tool, you will face a number of other choices in terms of architecture, servers, databases, analytic appliances, and data integration, as well as ETL tools, approach, and design.

A data warehouse is a long-term investment, but be careful not to ignore the hidden costs associated with implementing Web Intelligence against the OLTP system. Lack of dimensional or cross-functional data may limit the data's usability; data will remain just "data" and not "information." The universes will be significantly more complex and take longer to develop, as transformations normally done in the ETL process must be performed to a degree in the universe.

Real-Time Access

Real-time BI continues to generate a fair bit of hype, and buzzwords such as "operational BI" add to both hype and confusion. The real-time debate is both a technology issue and a business requirements issue: What do users need, and what technology can best meet those needs?

Certain technologies allow a data warehouse to be updated in near real time as source data changes. For some applications (such as stock traders and risk management), users indeed need access to real-time data with data feeds from multiple processes and functions.

Newer solutions such as SAP HANA (combination of in-memory and analytic appliance) and SAP Real-Time Analytics have roles to play in delivering real-time analytics. However, real-time BI also resonates with OLTP users who need flexible access to transaction-level data. ERP products may excel in business process automation, but they have generally been weak at providing intuitive reporting tools.

As long as the transaction processing time does not suffer, it makes perfect sense to integrate SAP BusinessObjects with the OLTP system, whether embedding Crystal Reports within an OLTP application or using Data Integrator and Web Intelligence against an ERP-centric data mart.

Some SAP BusinessObjects features—such as multipass SQL, derived tables, and multiple data providers per report—make real-time BI against the OLTP system achievable. However, the oft-used Free Hand SQL supported in Desktop Intelligence and widely used for OLTP data sources is no longer supported in the latest release.

Precautions for OLTP-Based Deployments

Whatever your reason for using SAP BusinessObjects directly against the OLTP system, you will need to take some precautions to ensure a successful deployment. Killer queries can cripple a system and prevent orders from being processed. It takes only a few times for this to happen before you will either fund a data warehouse or limit ad hoc access.

If SAP BusinessObjects is to become a strategic application, you do not want to limit access. However, you do want to deploy in a highly managed way, which is particularly important when you are accessing an OLTP system.

Here are some guidelines for using SAP BusinessObjects BI against an OLTP system directly:

- Pay particular attention to the universe design, ensuring optimal joins and removing the ability to use nonindexed fields as condition objects (see Chapter 7).

- Ensure the standard reports use prompts to limit the amount of data returned and to guarantee that the conditions are based on indexed fields. With custom OLTP reports, each user executes the query, placing an additional load on the OLTP system. With SAP BusinessObjects, use the public folders for users to access one pre-run, cached report.

- Use the integrated scheduling to run more resource-intensive reports during nonworking hours and possibly push certain reports to individual users.

- Ensure you use the integrated auditing capabilities to understand who is using certain reports, universes, or objects, as well as when and how they are being used (see Chapter 15).

Aligning BI to Business Goals

Regardless of whether you are starting out with a departmental implementation or with the simple goal of automating a legacy report process, the sweet spot of BI is when it is aligned with the business goals. This is when SAP BusinessObjects is not merely a productivity tool (for example, to get the same data faster), but also a strategic tool that measurably affects company profitability, competitiveness, and market share.

According to BI Scorecard's 2011 Successful BI Survey, alignment with business goals was the number one ranked organizational factor for BI success. Even if you start out implementing SAP BusinessObjects to fulfill IT cost-reduction goals, the road does not end there. Its uses will evolve, and in support of this evolution, IT must realize that much of a BI deployment is iterative.

Those initial starter reports should be modified as the business environment changes. Documents in public folders should be modified as the business uses SAP BusinessObjects more effectively, drivers of performance are measured, or the business environment changes. If these reports and/or universes remain static for an extended period of time, it may be an indication that your deployment is not closely aligned with the business needs. Arguably, there will be some universes and reports that are more operational in nature and that support work processes that may not change all that often.

If you are a project manager or sponsor, it's easier for you to keep the project aligned with the business goals. If you are a lone power user or universe developer, you may be thinking, "Not me, that's for the higher-ups to do!" Perhaps. However, as the BI expert, you are best suited to understand how the various modules can be leveraged to fulfill the business goals.

Too often, there is a disconnect between the opportunities and the technical capabilities. Keep your ear to the ground, and you will discover the opportunities. Read the company newsletters, and you will discern the company goals and come up with new ideas on how SAP BusinessObjects can help achieve those goals. Most business units have individual business plans. Take a look at them. Which reports can you design to measure the implementation of the business plan? Don't forget that some of the world's greatest innovations have come from the rank and file, not the executives!

Business Goals for BI

Given the volume and breadth of data needed to fulfill broad company goals, SAP BusinessObjects is often implemented in conjunction with a data warehouse or data mart. If the data warehouse is being implemented at the same time, many of the business goals in implementing and justifying the warehouse will be the same as those for implementing SAP BusinessObjects.

The business goals may be fairly broad, such as the following:

- Providing frontline managers with direct access to data that shows the health of the day-to-day business

- Gaining insight into what was previously a black hole, caused by a closed transaction system that lacked robust reporting capabilities

- Providing data to support company-wide initiatives such as enterprise performance management, business process reengineering, and Six Sigma

Even when the goals are this broad, to achieve measurable benefits, you need to develop more precise goals and tie them in with the BI development and implementation. Table 2-1 shows some typical goals by process. With each broad goal, as you implement SAP BusinessObjects, identify what information elements help achieve or measure the goal. If the elements are in the data warehouse, then ensure these elements are exposed in the universe along with the necessary dimensions to provide context to the data.

While the goals in Table 2-1 are company-oriented, other business goals may be more narrowly defined yet still provide a measurable benefit. As you implement SAP BusinessObjects in phases or by departments, look to align the implementation with achieving these specific business goals.

In some cases, the elements required to track these business goals may not be in the data warehouse, but you can still provide them via objects in a universe or a variable in a report. In this respect, implementing a data warehouse and SAP BusinessObjects simultaneously poses a challenge for the data warehouse not to become a constraint that limits your ability to leverage functionality provided by the BI platform.

Just because data isn't in the data warehouse, that doesn't mean you can't and shouldn't deliver data to users. If it helps achieve a business goal, do it. For example, many companies need access to external market data for benchmarking. Unless the data can be coded to conform to existing dimensions, third-party data often cannot be stored in the data warehouse. SAP BusinessObjects, on the other hand, is much more flexible. It provides a number of ways to incorporate structured or unstructured external data:

- The repository allows users to store non-SAP BusinessObjects documents, so if the data comes in the form of an Excel spreadsheet or PDF document, it can be stored in the repository.

- The Web Intelligence microcube architecture allows users to merge corporate data with external data and display the results via one report or chart.

- Universe designers can use the new multisource option to combine data warehouse and external data seamlessly for users.

- Dashboards and Explorer support loading information directly from spreadsheets into their interfaces.

Process	Goals	Measures
Sales and marketing	Improve customer loyalty	• Customer sales over time • Customers who buy both products A and B • Customer purchases by channel • Share of wallet • Customer churn
	Manage product prices	• Price trend over time • Retail price versus manufacturing costs
	Increase market share	• Revenue versus competitors • Revenue trend versus industry trend
Supply chain	On-time delivery	• Number/volume shipments shipped by requested date • Number of early, on-time, late orders over time • Inventory levels for top-selling products • Ratio of number of days of sales versus inventory to fulfill those sales (DSI)
	Low freight costs	• Orders fulfilled from most cost-effective shipping point • Freight costs • Volumes and discounts with freight suppliers
Finance	Reduce aging of accounts receivable Reduce budget variance Improve profitability	• Accounts receivable over time • Actual expense versus budget • Gross margin analysis • Cash flow analysis
Human resources	Reduce employee turnover Provide competitive pay	• Employee turnover over time • Salary versus job level, job history, market salaries

Table 2-1   Use BI to Monitor and Achieve Business Goals

Designing and building the dimensional models, ETL process, and warehouse infrastructure are resource-intensive and complex tasks. Short-staffed and nearing (or past) a project milestone, it's easy to devote 90 percent of the time spent on a BI project to delivering the physical tables or star schemas, and only 10 percent of the time to delivering universes, reports, and dashboards. For the business, though, the reports and dashboards are the primary window to the data warehouse. Make it unwieldy, and the business users will not be able to focus on analyzing data for business benefit. They'll spend an inordinate amount of time figuring out how to use the tool. Fail to provide standard reports or dashboards, and the business users may feel nothing was delivered.

For each of the business goals, you must develop a corresponding standard report or dashboard as part of the BI deployment effort. This report or dashboard may act as a template that users then refresh with their own view of the data, or it may be automatically refreshed and sent to them.

This all sounds pretty obvious, doesn't it? It should be! The issue is that while these business goals are often used to get project funding, with all the technological and organizational issues involved in delivering a BI solution, it's easy to forget why you started on this endeavor. The project team members get so focused on setting up the infrastructure that they leave it for the users to figure out what to do with these newfangled tools.

In some organizations, where data and analytic literacy is high, it may be a valid approach simply to deliver the tools. The business runs with it and exploits the value. Usually, though, users accustomed to no data or to inflexible, custom-developed reports do not immediately know how to approach a flexible BI tool. It's up to you as the BI project manager, team leader, power user, or internal expert to show them the possibilities!

BI Standardization: A Joint Goal

As BI deployments have evolved and matured over the years, both IT and the business increasingly recognize a joint goal: to reduce the number of disparate BI tools so that business users have access to one version of the truth and IT can better support a smaller number of tools. SAP BusinessObjects offers a complete tool set that serves a broad range of users' needs, all on a common platform.

Chapter 3 discusses the different user segments in a BI implementation and how you can tailor your solution, training, and promotion efforts to each of these user segments. With BI standardization, the goal is not to create a "one-size-fits-all" solution. Instead, it's to ensure that for each BI segment, there is only one standard tool that shares a common server, security, and metadata environment. For example, you might have one business query tool for power users, one dashboard interface for executives, and one production reporting tool for IT developers.

With a smaller number of tools to support, IT reaps enormous cost savings in terms of reduced software licensing and maintenance fees, lower hardware costs, and lower support costs, while still improving service levels. For the business, standardization reduces training time and ensures one version of the truth. Even when companies implement a data warehouse to achieve a single version of truth, if different BI tools access the same data in the data warehouse, measures can be recalculated and represented in each BI tool in a slightly different way.

Although BI standardization is crucial for an enterprise solution, there are often insurmountable obstacles to achieving standardization:

- Many companies still allow individual business units to purchase BI solutions themselves. Such solutions are not necessarily purchased by a central IT or purchasing department.

- When IT fails to partner with the business and views itself as the "gatekeeper" to data access rather than an enabler, the business must take matters into its own hands. At risk for IT is control and, for some, job protection. At risk for the business is competitiveness and, eventually, viability. Ideally, both stakeholders share a common goal, and those who don't will ultimately fail, causing IT to be outsourced or the business to go bankrupt.

- Standardization takes a high degree of executive sponsorship, as some users may need to make sacrifices, either in terms of shutting down other BI applications or in giving up customized or specialized functionality that may be important to a few but not to the enterprise as a whole.

With so many barriers to standardization, according to BI Scorecard's 2011 survey, 55 percent of companies now have a predominant BI standard. The operative word is "predominant," as companies may supplement a standard with specialty tools on an exception basis. This is a big shift in the minority (24 percent) who claimed they had a standard in 2005.

Measures of Success

How you measure success is determined, in part, by the goals you wish to achieve. On an intangible level, the following are some indications that your implementation is successful:

- People have heard of SAP BusinessObjects (or the name of your BI project/ application).
- The business sees IT as a partner and not as a gatekeeper who holds the key to corporate data.
- Users feel empowered to get to the information they need to do their jobs.
- Business and financial analysts feel they spend less time collecting data and more time analyzing data, using it to make informed decisions.

It's a paradox that a tool that allows quantitative measurement of business goals is seldom measured itself. In some respects, this is true of many IT projects in which the measure of success is simply whether the application is delivered on time and on budget.

In achieving IT goals, there are a number of ways to measure success:

- The number of custom OLTP reports eliminated
- Reduction in IT overtime or contract programmers for developing custom reports
- Elimination of duplicate, competing report systems
- Number of users trained versus number of users who log in to SAP BusinessObjects on a regular basis
- Number of queries executed each month
- Number of standard reports accessed

Refer to Chapter 15 for approaches to tracking SAP BusinessObjects usage.

Measuring Business Benefits

In measuring achievement of business goals, the great debate is over how much can be attributed to implementing a BI solution versus other variables that help achieve the goal. For example, one of the company's goals may be to improve market share. This can be measured by changes in revenue over time or for particular market segments. SAP BusinessObjects provides the *information* to measure progress and to do more targeted marketing. However, *achieving the goal* may require increased promotion, improved product support and innovation, better training of customer service personnel, reduced employee turnover, and so on. Exogenous change may remove a competitor from the market, allowing a company to improve market share without having taken any other action.

When several variables contribute to achieving that goal, assign a reasonable percentage for how much SAP BusinessObjects contributes toward achieving the goal, as shown in Table 2-2.

In the example in Table 2-2, SAP BusinessObjects contributed 15 percent to increased market share. Is this an exact number? No. Can it ever be precisely measured? No. It is merely one measure of success. Thus, if a $5 billion company increases its revenues by 10 percent in an otherwise flat market, you can say SAP BusinessObjects contributed $500,000 toward achieving this goal (10% × $5B × 15% = $500K).

With the more specific goals described earlier, the measure of success may be an improvement over the initial situation.

Some companies that have implemented SAP BusinessObjects can cite individual cases where BI directly affected the bottom line. For example, a manufacturing company used BusinessObjects to do a gap analysis of production costs between two similar facilities. The company identified $1 million in operating inefficiencies. Without SAP BusinessObjects, they would not have had the data to identify this opportunity for improvement. So perhaps SAP BusinessObjects is 50 percent responsible for the cost savings; the remaining 50 percent can be attributed to eliminating the inefficiencies. The beauty of this example is that the company started implementing SAP BusinessObjects as a follow-on to an ERP implementation. The goal was for IT to eliminate custom, disparate reporting systems. Now SAP BusinessObjects is a strategic asset that has helped the company achieve a number of business goals and measurable business benefit.

ROI as a Measure of Success

Return on investment (ROI) is another measure of success and one that is often used to fund the project. While it is fairly easy to measure the cost of the SAP BusinessObjects implementation (the investment portion), it is not easy to measure the return.

Action to Improve Market Share	Percent Contribution
Increased promotion and modified ad campaign	30%
Improved product line	25%
Better employee training, customer service, reduced turnover	30%
SAP BusinessObjects access to information to focus marketing efforts on most likely buyers, ensure order compliance, reduce product defects	15%

Table 2-2 Estimates for How Much Cost Savings/Revenue Improvement Can Be Attributed to the SAP BusinessObjects Implementation

As you saw in the preceding section, it's debatable how much of a revenue increase you can attribute to BI versus other factors. Even when ROI is used to fund a project, companies rarely go back and measure the actual ROI. It is a precise number derived from imprecise inputs.

IDC first published a study on the ROI for data warehouses in 1996. IDC determined the average three-year ROI was 401 percent for the 62 projects measured. The Data Warehousing Institute (TDWI) published a study in 2000, showing an ROI of 300 percent. While 47 companies participated in the study, less than a quarter measured ROI. In December 2002, IDC released another ROI study focusing on the value of business analytics, the applications that reside on top of a data warehouse. The average ROI was 431 percent, and the median was 112 percent, with less than a year payback period. Some companies had returns of more than 2,000 percent, and IDC reported that the most successful projects were when the business analytics implementation corresponded with business process improvements. More recently in 2011, Nucleus Research reported that in its ROI case studies, for every $1 spent on analytics, organizations earned an average of $10.66 on improved revenues, gross margin improvement, or expense reduction.

With ROI being such an imprecise measure, it's not surprising many companies never go back and calculate it for a BI implementation. In the 2011 Successful BI survey, only 28 percent of survey respondents (602 respondents) used ROI as a measure of success. Usage of ROI has declined from previous years.

You know your project is successful according to all the other measures of success described in the preceding sections. Nonetheless, ROI is a number that provides a basis for comparison to other BI implementations and IT initiatives. It also is a measure well understood by finance users, a significant group of SAP BusinessObjects users. In this respect, knowing your approximate ROI is a useful tool in promoting SAP BusinessObjects.

The following is the basic formula for calculating ROI over a three-year period:

$$\text{ROI} = [(\text{NPV Cost Reduction} + \text{Revenue Contribution})/\text{Initial Investment}] \times 100$$

Net present value (NPV) considers the time value of money. In simplistic terms, if the company had $1,000,000 to deposit in a bank today, next year, assuming a meager five-percent interest, it would be worth $1,050,000. The following formula calculates NPV of a three-year cost or revenue:

$$\text{NPV} = F/(1+r) + F/(1+r)^2 + F/(1+r)^3$$

F is the future cash flow from the cost reductions and revenue contributions, and r is the discount rate for your company. Five percent may be the interest a bank is willing to pay, but companies will have a different rate that takes into account the expected return for other investments and opportunity costs from investing in SAP BusinessObjects versus other capital projects.

Using the earlier example of improved market share (Table 2-2), assume the following:

- $500,000 revenue contribution each year
- $400,000 annual savings by eliminating two custom report programmers
  @ 2 × 2,000 hours × $100 an hour
- 10 percent discount rate
- $1 million initial investment in hardware, software, training, and consulting to implement SAP BusinessObjects

The projected ROI for a three-year period is calculated as follows:

$$223\% = \left[\frac{\dfrac{400{,}000 + 500{,}000}{1.10} + \dfrac{400{,}000 + 500{,}000}{1.10^2} + \dfrac{400{,}000 + 500{,}000}{1.10^3}}{1{,}000{,}000} \right] \times 100$$

Summary

You may have multiple goals in deploying SAP BusinessObjects. These goals change over time as your use of information and your BI deployment matures. Recognize that the goals of IT and business users may sometimes conflict. When IT and the business partner work together, and a BI deployment is aligned with the business objectives, expect to achieve greater success. Measuring the benefits of your implementation is useful for project funding and promoting the BI application. In absence of these measurements, look for a number of other indicators that show progress toward achieving these goals.

Right Tool for the Right User

With any BI deployment, there are different groups of users, all with distinct information and functional needs. The ways they want to access SAP BusinessObjects will also vary.

One group of users may be logged in to SAP BusinessObjects the majority of the workday, and will actively ask for more data, more resources, faster query time, and more functionality. Another group may never directly log in to SAP BusinessObjects, yet will make decisions from data delivered through SAP BusinessObjects, whether via a pushed e-mail report, a spreadsheet populated from Analysis Edition for Office, or data quoted by an analyst. Both groups of users are your BI customers, yet they will have very different needs that affect how you develop, promote, and deploy the various modules within the SAP BusinessObjects BI platform.

As you'll learn in this chapter, using the marketing concept of customer segmentation will help you identify your user groups, understand their different needs, and develop a better deployment strategy.

What Is Segmentation?

Segmentation is a way of looking at one large user base—for example, all employees in a company—and dividing it into smaller groups. Each segment, or smaller group, has similar characteristics, needs, or benefits.

In this book, we refer to two common segments: report authors and information consumers. Your company may have more than these two segments. Segmentation provides a way of better understanding your users and why their requirements are different. It will help you prioritize target user groups and provide the appropriate information and functionality to achieve the highest business value.

As you define different segments, you will want to tailor your product offering, promotion, implementation schedule, and training for each segment. You also may use the segments to define groups and permissions in the Central Management Console (see Chapter 12).

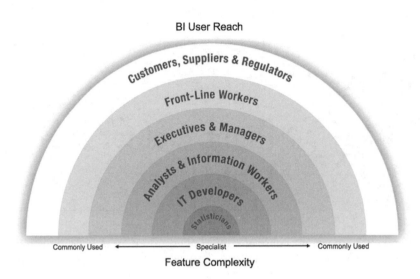

Figure 3-1   Recognize the full spectrum of potential BI users.

Figure 3-1 shows a spectrum of potential BI user segments. Often, the capabilities required for these segments are inversely related to the number of users. For example, external customers in the outer band of this spectrum may only need to refresh and view a report, whereas the handful of information workers who are power users may want to modify SQL, merge multiple data sources, and so on.

Defining BI User Segments

As you define different user segments, you need to consider the characteristics of your user groups. The following are some characteristics that will help you segment potential SAP BusinessObjects users.

Primary Versus Secondary

Some users log in to BI Launchpad to develop their own reports, refresh queries, and interactively analyze the data. These are *primary* users whom you will grant access to in the Central Management Console (CMC).

However, you will also have a *secondary* segment of users who consume the information provided by report authors and analysts. These secondary users may never log directly in to SAP BusinessObjects; in fact, they may not even know SAP BusinessObjects exists. They know only that they get a report via e-mail or a corporate intranet. For all they know, the data came directly out of one ERP screen. It will be hard for you to estimate the size of this secondary user segment, but in many instances, some of your most important customers are in this segment.

Let's say the VP of Marketing receives SAP BusinessObjects-generated PDF files via e-mail on a regular basis. These standard reports are critical for the VP. The VP's administrative assistant is the one who developed the initial reports and scheduled them via the BI Launchpad. The assistant makes sure the reports are generated and delivered as needed. Meanwhile, as more users access the system, the enterprise server is getting overloaded. Some reports run much later than requested; some fail to execute. The primary user, the administrative assistant, may be the one to shout, but it is the secondary user, the VP of Marketing, who can most likely approve funding for a more powerful server. Also, it is this secondary user—who has never logged directly in to SAP BusinessObjects—who will most likely see the business potential of products you have not yet implemented, such as Dashboards and Explorer.

Job Level

A user's job level will affect the breadth of data the user wants to access (number of reports and universes) and the level of detail.

Executive-level jobs may need a broad set of data but without a lot of detail. Analyzing the data is a minor part of these jobs. For these executives, you may want to develop a dashboard with key performance indicators, as a customized BI workspace or an interactive dashboard.

Mid-level jobs may still need a broad set of data but with more detail. The combination of broad data requirements and more detailed data may make it hard to deliver the information only with dashboards. These workers may need access to multiple folders and multiple documents, as well as ad hoc access to Web Intelligence.

Entry-level accounts payable clerks or customer service representatives may want to see only very detailed data. As their information requirements are narrow, these users may need only a few standard reports with interactive prompts. They may access SAP BusinessObjects BI often, constantly refreshing a document for a particular account, customer, date range, and so on.

Job Function

You also can segment users according to job function. For example, supply chain users will all have similar information needs, which will be different from the information needs of users in the finance department or customer service center.

Functional requirements also may vary by function. Here are some examples:

- Power users in the finance department may prefer to manipulate their data in a spreadsheet interface. This group of users may not care about dashboards as much as they care about spreadsheet integration.

- Marketing personnel will have different information requirements. With respect to functionality, they may ask for things, such as predictive analysis, that other groups have not requested.

- Administrative assistants may not be decision makers, but in many companies, their exceptional computer literacy and multitasking skills have led them to become expert users of Web Intelligence.

In many companies, certain job functions also have varying degrees of influence and power. Ideally, the degree of influence would be commensurate with the degree of value added to the company, but that's not always the case. The challenge for you as a BI expert is to do the following:

- Recognize that the different functions will have different requirements, thus demanding certain modules and capabilities more than other groups
- Prioritize fulfillment of those requirements

Degree of Analytic Job Content

Some jobs require a significant amount of data analysis. The analytic component also may relate to the job level or the job function, or sometimes to both.

For example, financial analysts may be fairly senior in a business; these jobs have a high analytic component. Statisticians and data scientists have an even greater analytic component to their jobs. These people are the number crunchers who will use BI extensively. They understand the different data nuances and even the potential data sources.

It's easy to assume that these analysts are your only users, since they may have solutions implemented first, complain loudest when something is wrong, live and die by access to information, and control the information flow to secondary users. This may in fact be you! With all your demands for access to information, the company rewarded you with being a universe designer, report author, or SAP BusinessObjects subject matter expert. Congratulations! Remember, though, that not everyone can spend all day collecting, manipulating, and exploring data.

Some users need access to standard reports simply to know what is going on. They log in to BI Launch Pad or use only a desktop widget for ten minutes a day (or week) just to make sure the business is running smoothly, to find out if there is enough inventory to fulfill an order, or to identify customers with outstanding invoices. When the information indicates a problem area, it may not be their job to sift through the data to identify the underlying cause. Instead, they may call the business or financial analyst to figure out why there is a problem.

In BI, we seem to have a tendency to want all end users to become experts. It's a profound difference to *empower* users—to provide them with easy tools to access and explore information when they need to—and an altogether different scenario to assume accessing and analyzing data is their primary job.

Users whose job content requires a fair bit of data analysis often demand more features and functions. Do not let their demands fool you into thinking all your users need these advanced capabilities. Jobs with a high analytic content may use more capabilities, such as report variables, multiple data providers, and ad hoc queries. On the other hand, users with jobs with minimal analytic content may only refresh a standard report on a periodic basis. At most, they might evolve into Web Intelligence users who take advantage of interactivity features or Explorer users.

ERP or Source System Use

Some of your users may also enter data into the transaction or ERP system. Regardless of whether your company uses SAP BusinessObjects directly against the transaction system or an ERP-populated data warehouse, these users will be more familiar with the precise meanings of individual objects.

At the same time, dimensional groupings and hierarchies that don't exist in the source system may be a completely new concept. These users may need additional explanation as to why there is a data warehouse and how the data has been transformed.

Level of Data Literacy

Data literacy and technology literacy are two entirely different things. For example, someone may be technically literate, but ask someone who is not a baseball fan to decipher the meaning of baseball statistics, such as RBIs (runs batted in), ERAs (earned run average), and SOs (strike outs), and they may not be able to. So, too, with corporate data.

Source system users and users whose jobs have a high analytic content may understand the data well and have a high level of data literacy. Certain users who work in sales may understand the finer points of "price." Is it list price, average selling price, or price net of returns? However, you cannot assume that users with high levels of data literacy have equally high technology literacy. A transaction system user may know the data but be comfortable entering data only by following the exact same screens every time. Change the user interface, and such users are lost.

An often-minimized part of a BI implementation is training users on the data. You can train users where to click to build certain queries, but training them to interpret the data and simply to know what the data is and means requires separate attention. The context panel in Web Intelligence can go a long way to helping with data literacy. Object descriptions are finally displayed to report consumers, not just to report authors. (This assumes that the universe designer has populated the object descriptions.)

Level of Spreadsheet Usage

Spreadsheet users deserve their own segment, and thus sometimes their own BI interface. They are loyal to the spreadsheet and think everything should be delivered in a spreadsheet.

SAP BusinessObjects has a couple of solutions for such users. First, users can save a report directly to Excel, which nicely preserves the charts, formatting, and breaks. Furthermore, with the integrated scheduling, you can schedule a report to be automatically exported to an Excel file format. Finally, Live Office allows users to execute queries directly from a spreadsheet. However, as of SAP BusinessObjects BI 4.0 Feature Pack 3, Live Office works only with .unv universes created with the Universe Design Tool, not .unx universes created with the new Information Design Tool (IDT). Finally, when accessing an OLAP data source such as SAP BW or Microsoft Analysis Services, there is Analysis Edition for Office.

There are a number of challenges with BI and spreadsheet integration. Volume of data is one thing. Multiple versions of the truth when the data is manipulated locally is another. So do consider why users want the spreadsheet integration at all. For a discussion of valid and less valid reasons, see the report "Spreadsheet Integration Criteria" on the BIScorecard. com web site. Regardless of such challenges, do recognize this user segment, and develop a strategy to meet the distinct needs of these users while simultaneously ensuring that the spreadsheets do not get out of hand and become mini data marts.

Amount of Travel

Certain job types require more travel than others. Some users may access the system only from their desktop or a corporate browser. Users who travel may want access via a BlackBerry, an iPhone, an iPad, or a notebook computer. They may want information broadcast to them or might want to work in offline mode, exploring previously refreshed queries and drilling in local microcubes.

Early releases of Web Intelligence and Explorer did not support disconnected or offline access. Acceptable work-arounds may have included a PDF document or spreadsheet. In SAP BusinessObjects BI 4.0, both these interfaces support offline access, but you may need to grant users that require these capabilities additional security permissions.

Implementation Phase

As you ramp up your SAP BusinessObjects implementation, you will offer different users access to the system at different points in time. Many tasks, including levels of communication, content, resource planning, and so on, will be tailored according to different user groups and their implementation phase.

Internal Versus External Users

Consider the different needs of employees of the company versus customers that you may provide information to via an extranet. Internal employees may be allowed to access whatever software module you have licensed, whereas external customers often will have more restrictions on content and functionality.

External users have different requirements from your internal users. Authentication in large extranets can be a challenge if you have thousands of potential extranet users. Do they all need a unique login, or will you use a guest login? Internal employees may have access to more data, whereas external users will only be allowed to see their data. For these users, you may use the row restrictions and object security levels in the IDT Security Editor.

Others Who Affect Implementation Efforts

In addition to your target users (either primary or secondary), you need to be aware of gatekeepers, influencers, and deciders, as illustrated in Figure 3-2. These people may or may not be eventual SAP BusinessObjects users, but they do affect project funding and your implementation efforts. For each type of stakeholder, we have provided an archetype. The individual job titles and dynamics will vary company to company. The important thing is to recognize that it is more than just the users who affect the success of your implementation and whose needs you must consider.

Gatekeepers

Gatekeepers control access to potential data sources, existing reports, or even other users. Gatekeepers can either help your implementation be a wild success or sabotage your efforts.

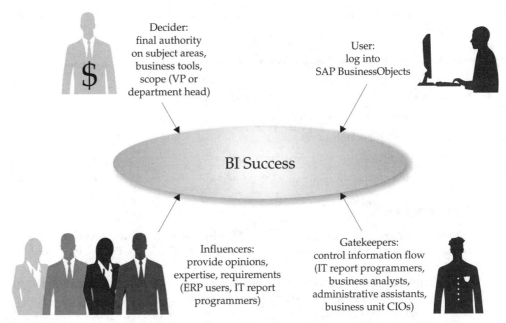

Figure 3-2   Many people besides direct users affect the success of a SAP BusinessObjects implementation.

Let's assume you want to use SAP BusinessObjects to access a central data warehouse. IT had a vision of the central data warehouse being used to populate dependent data marts. Unfortunately, due to budget constraints, lack of understanding, and political issues, your individual business unit or function never built a dependent data mart. The central data warehouse owner/project manager is a gatekeeper. The gatekeeper will either grant you ad hoc access, knowing you will only complain about the lousy response time (that's why they wanted you to sponsor a data mart!), or impede the SAP BusinessObjects implementation. Thus, the infighting begins. Ideally, the two stakeholders work together to achieve the following:

- Implement SAP BusinessObjects in a controlled way.
- Understand usage to educate users/sponsors on the value of BI.
- Analyze access patterns and problems to fund and develop the dependent data mart.

An administrative assistant, such as the type discussed earlier in the "Primary Versus Secondary" section, can also be a gatekeeper. As the BI expert, you want to better understand the information flow and business value of the reports the assistant schedules on a regular basis. A conversation with the VP of Marketing would be invaluable. The assistant sees no need for such a meeting (nor does the VP of Marketing, since the VP never uses SAP BusinessObjects directly), as the assistant can tell you everything you want to know about how the department uses the tool anyway. At this point, you can rely exclusively on the feedback the assistant gives you, or you can ask the assistant for help by having a joint conversation with both the primary and secondary users.

To make the SAP BusinessObjects implementation more successful, work with the gatekeepers:

- Understand what the gatekeepers want.
- Recognize their efforts and roles in the BI process. Look for ways to involve them or make them part of the implementation team.
- Identify the mutually exclusive goals.
- Identify the common goals.
- Build allegiances with the gatekeepers so that they work with you, not against you.
- Understand if there are any job protection issues involved here.

Influencers

Influencers are another set of people who affect how well your implementation proceeds. Influencers provide input to your users about how good the solution is, whether it will really be useful, and how it is being deployed.

The influencers often have some role in an existing reporting process and may have a vested interest in keeping the old reporting process running. They may be source system report programmers (why do we need a BI tool when we can hand-code everything?), source system experts (why do we need a data warehouse anyway?), business analysts who have developed departmental databases, or power users.

Positive influencers expedite your implementation and provide a lot of positive word-of-mouth promotion. *Negative* influencers impede your efforts by spreading fear and doubt.

Unfortunately, you may encounter a degree of job protection or "not invented here" syndrome with negative influencers. These are the hurdles to overcome. If a business analyst has spent an inordinate amount of time creating queries to populate departmental databases and spreadsheets, then the SAP BusinessObjects implementation will be perceived as a threat. It may render their data sources obsolete.

Negative influencers may slow your implementation by seeding your new users with doubt by saying, "Look how slow it is! The data is wrong!" For this reason, you need influencers on your side. If they know the data requirements, then get them to have a stake in your deployment's success. While they may be proud of the departmental system they created, they will know too well the manual processes and reconciliation time they go through to keep the data current and accurate. If they cannot be directly part of the project team, ensure they are a focal point for implementation or a designated SAP BusinessObjects expert.

Deciders

Deciders are the final decision makers. A decider may be a project sponsor, a business user, or both. Deciders are in a position of authority and can cast the final vote on funding the project, establishing an implementation strategy, or approving the initial set of modules to deploy. In the preceding examples, the decider could be the following:

- The CIO who overrules the central data warehouse project manager and allows individual business units to proceed with their own implementation efforts of certain modules, regardless of what can be supported via a BI competency center

- The VP of Marketing who requires all marketing staff to at least report consumers who log in to BI Launch Pad to retrieve their own reports, while the administrative assistant and business analyst are designated as the report authors

- The CFO who commits to phasing out the departmental spreadsheets/databases after an agreed-upon period of running SAP BusinessObjects in parallel

BI is more understood today than it was when the software segment first emerged in the 1990s. However, there are still many information boundaries in corporations. In those cases where users, gatekeepers, and influencers are resistant to BI, it helps to have a strong *decider* to champion your implementation efforts.

When to Analyze Segments

Ideally, the user segments should be identified early in the development process. User segments help you tailor deployment choices. Failure to agree on the target users or segment can derail your project.

As an example, a mid-sized maintenance supply company started out with a very clear scope: to enable senior marketing people to track monthly gross margin and sales by product, time, and region. They wanted a highly graphical tool with a dashboard. They selected a leading OLAP database and visualization tool, which was a good decision for this user segment at the time. At some point, field sellers voiced their information requirements. Field sellers needed a different level of detail than the senior marketing people, requiring daily sales figures down to the customer and order number. They didn't want graphics; they needed the detail numbers in a tabular report. Field sellers are a different user segment than senior marketing people, with different needs. Unfortunately, the scope of this project was not well managed. The right tools were used for the wrong applications and user segments. Neither user segment was satisfied with the end product. Although the project had strong business sponsorship and was driven by business goals, it failed because the target user group was not well understood.

If the user segments had been clearly defined at the project scoping stage, the project manager would have recognized the diverse needs and could have either declared the requirements out of scope or, more appropriately, matched the solution with each user segment.

Positioning the Module to the User Segment

Once you have identified your user segments, you can begin positioning the various modules in the BI platform according to those segments. The delineation for when to use a given product is not an absolute. Different user groups may overlap in requirements and therefore in product usage. Table 3-1 lists the SAP BusinessObjects modules and the corresponding primary user group.

Module in BI 4.0	Branding in 3.x	Primary User Group
Crystal Reports for Enterprise	Crystal Reports	IT developers to design pixel-perfect reports that may need to be bursted to multiple recipients or embedded within an application.
Web Intelligence	Web Intelligence, or Desktop Intelligence for full client	Business authors to design shared reports or ad hoc queries and analyses.
Dashboards	Xcelsius	Executives and managers who want an at-a-glance view of key performance indicators. The dashboard authors tend to be IT developers or sophisticated power users.
Explorer	Explorer	Casual users who want to use keyword search terms to find data and visualize results. Explorer also creates a dashboard-like interface, but the primary authors are less sophisticated users than those who would use Dashboard Design.
Analysis Edition for Office	Live Office	Power users who prefer the Excel interface.
BI Launchpad	InfoView	Information consumers who want to view and refresh standard reports and dashboards but who don't need to build their own. BI Launchpad is also the starting point for power users to create new content.
SAP Mobile	SAP Mobile	BI users who want to consume reports and dashboards on smartphones and tablet devices.
Analysis Edition for OLAP	Voyager	Analysts, executives, and managers who want to analyze data stored in an OLAP database from multiple perspectives, drilling up, down, and across hierarchies.

Table 3-1   Match the Product Module with the Needs of the User Group

Figure 3-3 adapts the spectrum graphic from Figure 3-1 to position the SAP BusinessObjects BI platform modules according to these segments. While each module may have a sweet spot, indicated with the dark dot, the concentric circles indicate that the positioning extends to other segments. For example, Web Intelligence is positioned for analysts and information workers to author reports. Executives and managers may also author reports, and will certainly consume them.

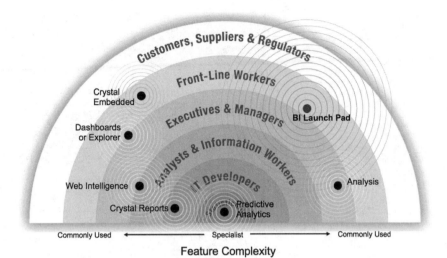

Figure 3-3 SAP BusinessObjects tool modules positioned by user segment

Project Roles

To deliver BI functionality, the project team should include both IT and business personnel. As discussed in Chapter 1, a BI project never ends, and your company's ability to leverage it to a competitive advantage is evolutionary. Therefore, many of these roles will continue beyond the project completion to provide ongoing support. You may decide to roll some of the responsibilities into a BI competency center, or conversely, you may staff certain project phases with people who are part of an existing BI competency center. A sample organizational model of a BI competency center is shown in Figure 3-4.

A project may include the following roles:

- **Sponsor(s)** When business goals drive the implementation, the sponsor is usually from the business. It may be the CFO if you are trying to measure financial performance, the VP of Marketing if you are trying to improve customer penetration and retention, the VP of Supply Chain if you are trying to improve order fulfillment and reduce inventory costs, and so on. If the goals of your implementation are IT-related (see Chapter 2), then the sponsor may be a senior person in the IT organization, such as the CIO, ERP manager, or data warehouse manager. The sponsor provides the funding for the project and resolves any scope issues the project team members cannot resolve themselves.

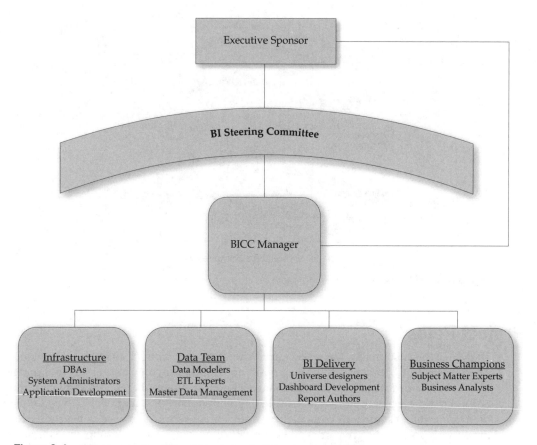

Figure 3-4   A BI organizational model includes both business and IT resources.

- **Program manager**   The program manager ensures that SAP BusinessObjects is deployed consistently across multiple projects and applications. The program manager sets the priorities for projects that vie for the same resources.

- **Project manager**   The project manager controls the budget, resources, and time to implement SAP BusinessObjects. The project manager ensures that the deliverables are within the agreed-upon scope of the project and that the project stays focused on the intended goals.

- **Security administrator**   A security administrator defines users to the CMC or to groups in the directory server and grants access to the SAP BusinessObjects modules, universes, and folders. The security function can be centralized or decentralized to allow one security administrator for each department or function. The security administrator must understand the groups, permissions, and data sources, as well as stay informed about personnel changes to revoke or add access when employees change departments. Within the CMC, you can create groups that have permissions to access certain interfaces and capabilities. These groups and permissions should correspond to the different user segments you've identified.

- **Universe designer**   The universe designer provides the business view to the relational data in a transaction system or a data warehouse. The designer must understand SQL from a query and analysis viewpoint, database performance issues, and business requirements. It can be a challenge to find one person with these diverse skill sets. Some companies will train business analysts or power users in the more technical skills, finding this an easier approach than trying to teach an IT developer the business skills. The technical aspects required to build a universe sometimes lead a DBA to become the universe designer. The role of universe designer can also be split between two people: one who physically develops the data foundation and another who ensures the universe fulfills the business requirements within the business layer of the universe.

  With larger deployments, there may be several designers across the organization, one for each business unit or function. This division has been hotly debated by customers and consultants alike. Who should own universe development—central IT or individual business units? It's clear that central IT should own the SAP BusinessObjects infrastructure. At the other end of the spectrum, it's clear that the business should own the report development (assuming the BI team provides some starter templates). The universe lies squarely in the middle. In an ideal deployment and organization in which IT and the business are closely aligned and IT is keenly focused on helping the business accomplish its goals, IT should develop the universes, with the business defining the requirements and having ultimate say over what goes in a universe and what does not. Where this centralization of the universe fails is when the universe does not meet the business requirements.

  When the universe doesn't fulfill the business requirements, it forces the users to build more report formulas, create increasingly complex reports with multiple data providers, or in the end, model their own solutions in spreadsheets and departmental databases. If the universe is monolithic and inflexible, then from a company point of view, allow individual business units to model their own universes, ideally following agreed-upon design principles. In either circumstance, it's important to have an "ultimate" designer or quality assurance process to ensure the universes are deployed consistently (see Chapter 15). The design principles and quality assurance process belong in the BI competency center, as this role continues beyond implementation.

- **Report author/pilot user**   A report author is typically a power user who both understands the data and is comfortable with software. Report authors may be business analysts who require ad hoc access to information or who previously created and maintained departmental data sources. They also may be professional developers who previously coded reports. Be careful to manage this, though. The goal is not to code complex reports, but rather to leverage the common business definitions and power built into the universe. When first deploying a new universe, pilot the universe with report authors. Only a minority of total users will be report authors.

- **Information consumers**   Information consumers, also called report readers and report recipients, access fixed reports that may include prompts to filter the data. Report authors may prepare and distribute reports to readers via e-mail, BI Launch Pad, and so on. Information consumers may not have a high degree of technology or data literacy, or the job type may have minimal information requirements. With Web Intelligence, these report readers can also dynamically sort, filter, and drill within a predefined report. While not all users will evolve into report authors, the majority of information consumers *should* evolve into interactive report consumers.

- **SAP BusinessObjects expert**   SAP BusinessObjects experts know the end-user tool sets and the different modules available, but they do not necessarily understand the data. They are good with software and technology. Report authors may become SAP BusinessObjects experts as they work more with the tool. Such experts should be part of an ongoing BI competency center.

- **Data expert**   A data expert may be a business analyst, data modeler, or source system expert who knows where the data comes from, the quality of the data, and its different meanings, and may be the champion for a metadata repository. The data expert may not necessarily use SAP BusinessObjects, but can help resolve data discrepancies that are discovered when users start analyzing it with SAP BusinessObjects. A data modeler designs the underlying star or snowflake schema in a data warehouse or data mart. That person can provide expertise on advanced business calculations and certain universe components, such as aliases, shortcut joins, how to use derived tables, and so on. When you introduce aggregate awareness into the universe, the data modeler provides the dimensions by which to aggregate.

- **Database administrator (DBA)**   A DBA may be the universe designer or may review the universe for optimal SQL. DBAs resolve query performance problems, build aggregate tables, and correct password synchronization problems between different data sources. The DBA will also help decide the technical deployment of the SAP BusinessObjects Enterprise repository.

- **Administrator or architect**   You may have a SAP BusinessObjects administrator who installs and maintains the software applications (Web Intelligence, Crystal Reports, Dashboards, Explorer, and so on). In small deployments, the SAP BusinessObjects administrator and the universe designer are often one and the same. In larger deployments, there may be multiple administrators. Whereas universe designers require a business background and SQL skills, administrators and architects require more technical skills and may be systems engineers. In addition to software issues, administrators deal with server performance and load balancing. They will decide when to deploy SAP BusinessObjects in a distributed environment, which processes to run on dedicated servers, and how to provide failover protection.

- **Trainer**   The SAP BusinessObjects trainer knows both the software and the data to a degree. Often, two people may provide the training to cover these two different aspects. Internal SAP BusinessObjects experts may train end users, or they may use an external training partner.

- **Communication/marketing specialist**   This person provides expertise on effective ways to communicate project plans, deliverables, and goals to the different user segments. The specialist may write or review articles for company newsletters, coordinate internal user conferences, design logos used in project gifts or application screens, and help ensure that key messages are stated in terms of business benefits rather than technical features.

Summary

Segmentation is a way of grouping your users according to their needs and skill sets. These groupings will help you tailor deliverables and more appropriately position BI modules accordingly. Certain user groups will want only standard reports on an intermittent basis; others will need the flexibility of ad hoc access on a daily basis. Not all users will greet SAP BusinessObjects with enthusiasm. Understanding these users' roles and objectives can help you minimize the users' disruption to your implementation efforts and enlist them as advocates to ensure a more successful deployment.

PART

II

Universes and the Information Design Tool

4 Universe Design Principles

Within the SAP BusinessObjects suite, a number of business user interfaces allow decision makers to access their data, whether via dashboards, Crystal Reports, Explorer, or Web Intelligence. Powering all these interfaces is the universe. The universe may be visible only to authors in the various interfaces. Behind the scenes, it is also key to information consumers' ability to refresh queries and have their data presented in a meaningful way.

A *universe* is a business representation of your data warehouse or transaction database. It shields query authors and dashboard designers from the underlying complexities of the database schema. The universe is sometimes referred to as the *semantic* or *metadata layer*. In all your development efforts, you must stay focused on the primary purpose of the universe as a *business* representation of the data. If your universe becomes a glorified entity-relationship model, your BI efforts will have limited success. If your universe includes every data element any user may possibly want from now to eternity, your project will fail.

Large, complex universes can be unwieldy for end users. Poorly defined joins will result in unnecessarily slow queries. Failure to define meaningful measures forces users to create their own calculations, sometimes leading to multiple versions of the truth or more frequent exports to spreadsheets. The universe is the most important component to get right. This chapter discusses concepts that will help you build a better universe and its core components.

Universe Building Blocks

SAP BusinessObjects BI 4.0 administrators build universes using either the new Information Design Tool (IDT) or the Universe Design Tool. In earlier versions of BusinessObjects, the Universe Design Tool was referred to as Designer. The Universe Design Tool is provided in version 4.0 primarily for transition purposes and is not an interface you would use in a new deployment. In version 4.0, the IDT is the primary interface for building universes.

Every universe is organized into a project. A project includes the following items:

- One or more connections that provide physical connectivity to the data sources.
- A data foundation that includes pointers to tables in the database. The data foundation also includes joins, contexts, derived tables, and aggregate navigation.

- A business layer that becomes the universe visible to end users in various modules. The business layer includes measures, dimensions, and lists of values. A business layer may contain one or more views. A view within the business layer provides a grouping of objects into subject areas such as sales or inventory.

These are the building blocks of a universe, which are introduced in this chapter. Later chapters discuss more complex components that can enhance your universe, such as contexts, hierarchies, and security.

Connections

The first step in building a universe is to define a connection to one or more data sources. SAP BusinessObjects BI 4.0 supports connecting to the following types of data sources:

- Relational data sources such as Microsoft SQL Server, Oracle, Teradata, Sybase, Salesforce.com, and Microsoft Access databases
- OLAP data sources such as SAP BW and Microsoft Analysis Services

New in SAP BusinessObjects BI 4.0 is the ability to have one universe access multiple physical data sources. For example, a universe can access enterprise sales data stored in Teradata, as well as dimensional data stored in Microsoft SQL Server and market prices stored in a departmental Microsoft Access database. When your universe needs to access data in different data sources, this is called a *multisource* universe. When creating a new universe, you must decide in advance if the universe will be based on a single data source connection or multiple connections.

Each connection includes parameters that specify the login credentials to the data source, the name and location of the database, and query limits. A connection can either be local or shared. A local connection is used only by the developer. A shared connection is stored in the enterprise repository and may be used by other developers.

Connection definitions are initially stored in a file with a .cnx extension. The extension changes to .cns when the connection is published to the repository and shared. When you use a shared connection while creating a universe, a shortcut to the shared connection is created on the local desktop.

Data Foundation

A data foundation is based on a subset of all the physical tables in the data warehouse or transaction system. A data foundation includes tables, joins, contexts, parameters, and lists of values. These are the behind-the-scenes building blocks for the universe.

Report authors never directly see these elements of a universe. As shown in Figure 4-1, universe designers use *tables* to map data from fields in the relational database to objects in the universe. *Joins* allow the use of more than one table in a report. A *context* is an optional component that resolves which join path to take when more than one path is possible. All three of these components are then combined to dynamically build SQL statements in the end-user interfaces.

Elements of the data foundation are stored in a .dfx file, as shown in the first tab at the top of Figure 4-1.

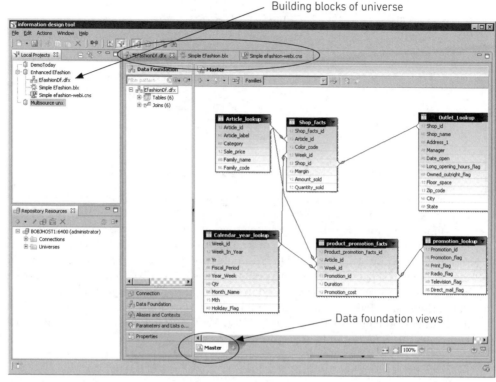

Figure 4-1   The data foundation shows the underlying physical structure of the universe.

Tables

Tables are individual database tables that provide data. A table may be a physical table in the RDBMS, or it may be a view or synonym. Within a data foundation, the IDT provides functionality to create *aliases* that are treated like tables. This eliminates the need for a DBA to create a synonym. The IDT also allows you to create *derived tables* that are SQL queries, as an alternative to a DBA creating a stored procedure or a view.

In a data warehouse or data mart environment, you will have two types of tables:

- A *fact table* that contains numeric information
- *Dimension tables* that allow a user to analyze the numeric data from different perspectives, such as product, time, or geography

The fact table can have millions of detailed rows of data, or it can be smaller, with summary numbers. One fact table together with its associated dimension tables is referred to as a *star schema*. Multiple fact tables and star schemas can exist within a universe.

Another aspect of the data foundation is its ability to support almost any physical table design. As shown in Figure 4-2, many data warehouses use star schemas to ensure fast queries. A star schema involves a fact table that includes all the measures—in this example, the ORDERS_FACT table. The dimension tables contain additional information about the

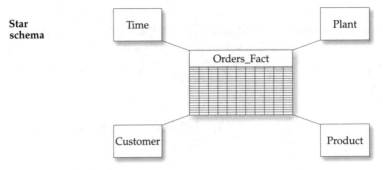

Figure 4-2   Star schemas model the business data into fact and dimension tables.

measures—in this example, customer, plant, product, and time. Most data foundations and universes will include multiple star schemas.

Dimension tables are also referred to as *lookup tables* or *reference tables*. The dimension tables can be broken into more than one table; for example, detailed material IDs may reside in a MATERIAL_ID table. The groupings and product hierarchy for the material IDs may reside in a separate table, such as PRODUCT_GROUPING. This type of structure, referred to as a *snowflake schema*, is used in some data warehouses that have extremely large dimensions. Snowflake schemas will contain many more joins between tables, but higher-level dimension tables, such as YEAR or PRODUCT_GROUPING, are inherently smaller. Figure 4-3 shows an example of a snowflake schema.

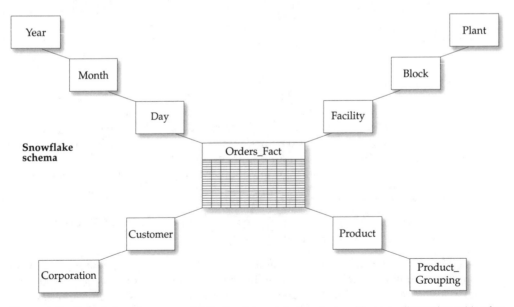

Figure 4-3   Snowflake schemas model the business data into facts with many dimension tables for each level in a hierarchy.

Transaction systems and operational data stores (ODSs) use normalized schemas to eliminate data redundancy and speed data inputs. *Normalization* refers to the degree of data replication. Third normal form (3NF) means each row in a table provides additional information about the key of the table; no data is repeated across rows.

Facts and dimensions may be spread across many physical tables in a normalized schema. For example, order information may exist in both an ORDER_HEADER table and an ORDER_LINE table, as shown in the example in Figure 4-4. Dimensions and hierarchies often do not exist in the transaction system (note in Figure 4-4 that there is no TIME or PLANT table, just a FACILITY table for the individual facility that produced the product and detailed order dates). Only the individual material IDs, customer IDs, and so on are stored with detailed records.

As shown in Figure 4-4, a normalized schema will contain many more joins than in a star schema. SAP BusinessObjects supports building data foundations and universes against normalized schemas, but creating the data foundation can be more tedious. However, the end user should never see the complexity of this data model. When you build a universe, you are not replicating any data from these sources. Instead, you are basically creating pointers to tell the query where to find the data. No data is stored in the universe itself.

Joins

Joins specify how tables, views, synonyms, or aliases relate to one another. Joins allow a user to combine information from two or more tables. For example, in the following diagram, there are joins between ORDERS_FACT and the dimension table PLANT, as well as between ORDERS_FACT and the dimension table PRODUCTS. There are no joins to

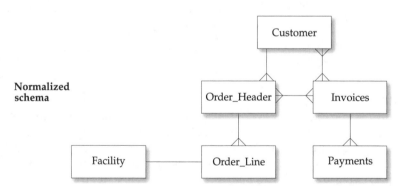

Figure 4-4 Transaction systems and ODSs often store data in third normal form to minimize data redundancy.

the SUPPLIERS table. Without this join, a user is not able to determine which suppliers provide various products. There are many types of joins, as discussed in Chapter 6.

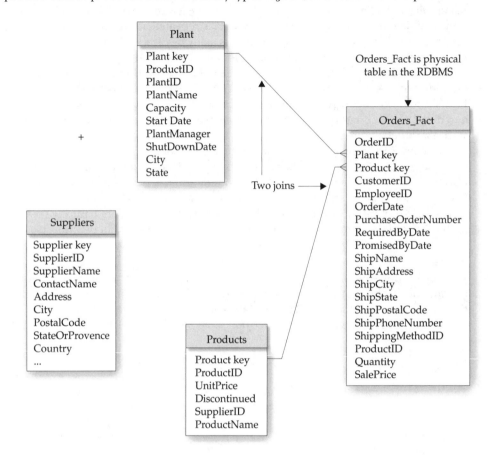

Contexts

Contexts group related joins. A context groups a set of joins together for each dimensional schema. Therefore, if your universe contains only one fact table or dimensional schema, it may not use contexts. Without contexts and when multiple dimensional schemas are involved, Web Intelligence and the various client tools would generate SQL that contained a loop. Loops generally result in incorrect queries with fewer rows returned than expected.

When a context is correctly created for multiple star schemas, Web Intelligence will automatically generate multiple SQL statements—one for each context—without prompting the user to select a context. This allows users to query multiple star schemas to create powerful business reports.

Parameters and Lists of Values

Data foundations and business layers include parameters and lists of values. The use of the term *parameters* here is unfortunate; these parameters should not be confused with connection parameters (discussed in Chapter 5). Parameters within the data foundation are variables that prompt a user for information, for example, to choose a particular year or region.

Lists of values are queries and lists that allow users to filter their data by selecting items from a list. For example, in a query for product sales, a list of values may show a product ID, product description, and product category. These values come from a query defined either in the data foundation or in the business layer. Lists of values in the data foundation may be based on custom SQL or on specific values loaded from a text file. Lists of values in the business layer are based on queries from dimensions in the business layer.

New in SAP BusinessObjects BI 4.0 is that parameters and lists of values are not explicitly connected to or created with individual universe objects. They can be used across multiple objects.

Parameters and lists of values are discussed in more detail in Chapter 8.

Data Foundation Views

By default, and as shown earlier at the bottom of Figure 4-1, the data foundation has at least one view called the Master view. Data foundation views are not to be confused with views created in the data warehouse by the DBA. A data foundation view is a way to group related tables together to ease development.

Some data foundations may have hundreds of tables. Data foundation views allow these hundreds of tables to be divided by subject area or by developer responsibility.

The use of data foundation views has no impact on query execution or on what the user ultimately sees.

Business Layer

The business layer is the representation an end user sees when creating new queries or dashboards. Regardless of how many tables, joins, and contexts are in the data foundation layer, it's critical to ensure the business layer is focused on a particular subject and optimized for a specific group of business users.

While developing the business layer, items are saved to a .blx file. For example, the second tab on the top of Figure 4-1 shows Simple Efashion.blx.

New in SAP BusinessObjects BI 4.0 is the ability to divide one business layer into multiple views. Within the IDT, this perspective is called a Business Layer view (as noted in the previous section, the default view is the Master view). Within Web Intelligence, this subset of objects is referred to as a universe view.

Folders, Dimensions, and Measures

Folders, dimensions, and measures are the main items a business user sees when building a query, as shown in Figure 4-5. Dimensions and measures become individual columns in a report; folders never appear in a report.

Folders (referred to as classes in previous releases) are a way of grouping individual objects. They do not necessarily relate to physical tables in a database. Some universe designers will mistakenly organize their folders to correspond to physical tables. This is rarely advisable. Instead, folders should represent business topics. In Figure 4-5, classes appear with a folder icon. For example, in the sample eFashion universe, the class *Product* is a more meaningful business term than *Article* and includes items from multiple tables: ARTICLE_LOOKUP and ARTICLE_COLOR_LOOKUP.

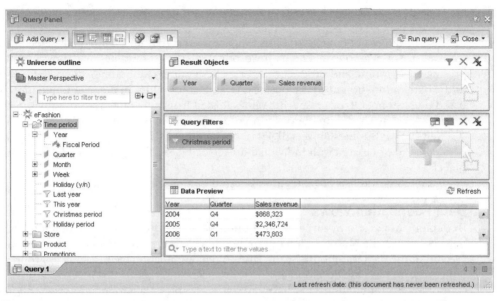

Figure 4-5 Users see folders, dimensions, and measures when building or modifying a query.

Dimensions and *measures* refer to columns of data. There are different types of objects (as explained in Chapter 7), denoted with a blue square for dimensions and an orange ruler for measures in Figure 4-5. Objects can include a significant amount of intelligence and may not relate directly to one column in the database. For example, the object Sold At (Unit Price) includes a calculation of revenue/quantity. However, to avoid divide-by-zero errors, it also includes an if-then-else statement to check for zero quantities. This is one example of why universes are so powerful and a much better alternative to providing users with direct access to tables; if-then-else statements in SQL are implemented differently for each RDBMS and are not something most users would know how to write.

The Universe

The business layer within the IDT is synonymous to the universe that authors see in Web Intelligence, Dashboard Design, and Crystal Reports. When you publish a business layer to the repository, the IDT compiles the various components—such as the connection, the data foundation, and the business layer—into a single .unx file.

Keeping It Simple

Some designers create universes that include thousands of objects and every table in the data warehouse. Such universes are difficult to maintain and, more important, are overwhelming for even expert users to use correctly. What's the result? End users create invalid queries and blame the tool for bad data. With such an overwhelming interface, authoring and modifying queries is a task reserved for only a handful of specialists.

To build a successful universe, keep the business layer simple. Changes in SAP BusinessObjects 4.0 make this vision easier to achieve. The universe should be useful for a clearly defined group of users. While the data foundation may have hundreds and sometimes thousands of objects, the business layer should not have much more than 200 objects in it. If it does, then use the new Business Layer view capability to divide the universe into particular perspectives that will be easier for users to navigate.

Target User Groups

Are there well-defined universes with more than 200 objects? Yes, but the targeted users are much more sophisticated in their knowledge of both the data and the tool. The ideal number of universe objects will vary from organization to organization. Keep in mind that bigger universes are technically feasible but not as user-friendly. Having more universes to build and maintain may result in slightly higher maintenance costs, but will significantly increase end-user productivity, satisfaction, and adoption. As your target user group expands, constantly ask yourself if the needs are distinct enough to justify a separate business layer or perspective. If some users need only a handful of additional objects, keep them in the same universe. However, if they need many additional objects, create a separate business layer.

Figure 4-6 illustrates how different user groups will need access to different information. Human resources is one group of users that needs access to salary details but does not need product sales and order information. Therefore, a Salary universe will have information from only this one fact table. Marketing people may need information about sales but will rarely need the individual order numbers. Customer service representatives need both order details and sales summaries. In this example, it may make sense to have one universe that meets the needs of both user groups (marketing and customer service representatives). A director of the marketing group is most likely a people manager, and may need salary and employee details. The director would use two universes, as including three subject areas in one big universe would potentially be overwhelming for the majority of users who don't need this information.

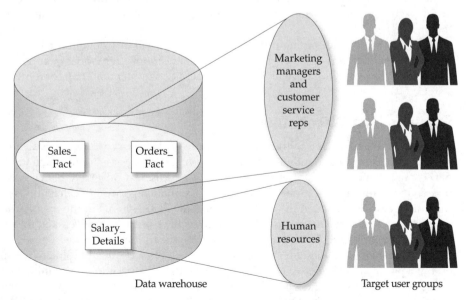

Figure 4-6 A universe is a business representation of the database based on the needs of specific user groups.

Technical Realities

Keeping it simple and aligned to a group of business users is one of the most important aspects of designing a universe. However, some technical issues may challenge this design principle.

When users want to combine data from multiple universes into a single report, it can be tedious to do so. Query authors must synchronize multiple data providers and map common dimensions, requiring a somewhat sophisticated skill set. Intending to make authoring of such queries easier to do, some designers will build bigger and bigger universes to ensure all possible business questions can be answered. An excessively large universe, however, sacrifices simplicity for the more frequent, common business queries for the occasional sophisticated queries. You might create a large universe for a handful of experts, or perhaps give them access to the Master view, while providing a smaller universe or business layer view for the majority of users.

Another argument for a bigger universe is maintenance-related, and this concern applies in particular to common dimensions used across multiple universes. For example, a product hierarchy is most likely used in several universes: inventory, accounts payable, manufacturing, sales, and so on. The same is true of a customer dimension. In SAP BusinessObjects version XI 3.x and earlier, designers might create a linked universe to reduce maintenance issues with common dimensions. However, in version 4.0, linked universes are no longer supported.

In designing your universes, it's important to constantly weigh the maintenance issues against the usability issues.

Aligning with Business Goals

As discussed in Chapter 2, a data warehouse or BI deployment should be aligned with business goals. As you develop a universe, compare how this universe helps achieve the business goals.

The process of determining universe requirements will vary depending on whether your implementation is based on an existing data warehouse, a new data warehouse developed in conjunction with an SAP BusinessObjects implementation, or a transaction system.

Existing Data Warehouse

Just because information is in the data warehouse or data mart, that doesn't mean it needs to be in either the data foundation or in the business layer. For example, data warehouses may contain dimension histories seldom used by end users. Conversely, data warehouses may contain only raw data elements that require enhancing through calculations added in the universe. In particular, don't let the physical database schema in the data warehouse constrain your universe design. Just because users have not specifically asked for something in a design session, that doesn't mean it should not be in the universe.

It's up to you as the designer to determine which objects will add value to the universe, even if a particular element was overlooked when the data warehouse was initially designed. As an example, let's assume your company has a goal for on-time delivery performance. REQUESTED_DELIVERY_DATE and SHIP_DATE may be columns in an ORDER_FACT table. In evaluating how this universe is aligned with the company's business goals, a good universe designer will know to add an object called DaysLate that calculates the difference between the requested delivery date and actual ship date. Users may not know what SQL functionality can be added to database columns. A universe designer must be well versed in SQL reporting capabilities that can make the universe more robust.

Herein lies one of the greatest challenges in designing a good universe: you must know both the business and SQL. SQL-certified experts may be proficient in creating tables, optimizing indexes, and loading volumes of data quite efficiently. This is not to say they know how to extract that same data into a report that provides business insight. This mixed skill set can be a challenge in identifying the best universe designer in a company (refer to Chapter 3 for a discussion on project roles). Often, the DBA has the SQL technical skills. A universe designed by a DBA with little knowledge of the business may be technically robust, but may lack the business functionality required. Universes designed by power users trained in SQL may have more robust business functionality, but with suboptimal joins or objects that result in slow queries. Therefore, it's important that both a DBA and a power user jointly develop and review a universe. Using agile development techniques in which the universe is designed collaboratively is highly recommended.

New Data Warehouse

If you are building a new data warehouse or data mart in conjunction with your SAP BusinessObjects implementation, ideally, your development efforts are already driven by business goals. Requirements gathering in the development stage will drive the fact table design as well as the universe design. As discussed in Chapter 13, many of the issues at this stage will be where to put the intelligence—in the fact table or in the universe.

Transaction System

When your universe is based on a transaction system, some of your universe design choices will depend not only on the business goals and user requirements, but also on minimizing the impact on the source system. For example, while users may want to search on customer name—a nonindexed field—such queries can cripple the source system (thus, many organizations implement a data mart or data warehouse).

If your company is not quite ready for a data warehouse, a quick alternative is to replicate the tables in the transaction system to a read-only instance of a database. This will better support detailed operational reporting requirements, without adversely affecting transaction processing. Even with this approach, a good designer needs to evaluate which business goals the universe is fulfilling. In our supply chain example, customer phone numbers and contact details exist in the transaction system. This information is necessary for processing orders but useless for measuring on-time shipments. (If you are building a customer-support system, then perhaps you need these details.) In building a user-friendly universe, the designer must constantly evaluate objects that fall into the category of "I might need it one day." In an initial universe, defer adding the object to the universe.

Deployments against a transaction system generally fulfill the operational needs of a company but not the strategic goals of the business, as data is seldom aggregated and may not have associated dimensional hierarchies. If the goal of deploying SAP BusinessObjects is to replace custom-developed operational reports with a purchased software package, then some of your design choices may be different and your goals more short term. In this situation, your first priority may be to reproduce fixed reports.

Evolving the Universe

For designers used to a waterfall development approach, welcome to the realities of BI: it's all iterative! Increasingly, companies are using agile development techniques in which BI capabilities are developed collaboratively between the business and IT, with new functionality delivered in weeks versus months and years.

The universe is never finished. Your first universe is version 1, which will evolve as you elicit user input, the business environment changes, the applications evolve, the source systems/data marts change, and the technology advances. After an initial deployment, there may be many enhancements as users respond to the universe and you tweak the design. Over time, the number of changes should become less frequent. Figure 4-7 illustrates how a universe evolves over time.

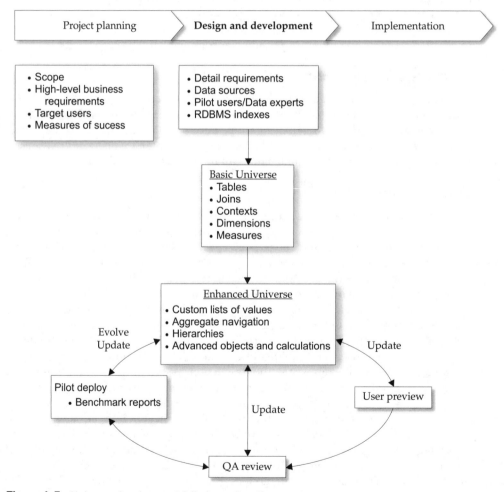

Figure 4-7 Universe development follows an iterative process.

You normally update the universe as the first users see it. Ideally, selected users will *preview* the universe as you are developing it to ensure it will fulfill the intended business goals and requirements. This can be in a formal joint application development (JAD) session, or one user might look over the designer's shoulder. At this stage, the universe is not a pilot! Until you have done a thorough quality assurance review, users should not access the universe. As a result of the quality assurance review (discussed in Chapter 15), you may make more changes, perhaps to correct errors, improve performance, or make classes and objects more meaningful. Following quality assurance, the universe goes to a pilot phase. The goal of the pilot is to identify errors and opportunities for further enhancement that you as the designer could not uncover yourself. The goal of the preview is to tell you if the universe development looks as users expect.

Users begin accessing the universe in a controlled way via a pilot. This is your first glimpse of payback for all your development efforts. If your company is new to self-service BI, be sure to choose your pilot users wisely. Casual users accustomed to static reports will be overwhelmed unless you provide them with parameterized reports. The pilot is typically accessed by a limited number of power users who understand the data and are fairly computer literate. For ad hoc access, these power users may be accountants or business analysts used to writing their own SQL. The pilot uncovers more objects that you may need to build or modify, allows you to remove hiccups in the security restrictions, and so on. Modify the universe following the pilot period and before you move to full-scale implementation.

At some point, the universe will reach a stable state. However, as often as the business environment changes, so should your universe. For example, if the business agrees on a new way of calculating customer profitability, then that new definition should be reflected in the universe. If the business acquires another company, expect the underlying data sources and/or data warehouse to accommodate the acquisition, again impacting the universe.

How the Information Design Tool Works

The IDT is a Windows client application that is installed on the developer's PC. When you first create a project, you are working locally on your computer. When you modify components of a universe, you import them to your PC and are working on a copy. When you are finished with your changes, you export your copy of the universe to a repository that end users can access.

Universe Storage During Development

When you first build a universe or after you have imported a universe from the repository, the universe is decompiled from the single .unx file into multiple individual files on your local workstation. The default directory is C:\users*username*\businessobjects\bimodeler_14\ workspace*project*, where *username* is the name of the Windows user, and *project* is the name of the project.

This folder structure is created automatically when you create your first project. In order to import existing universes, you must first create a local project to designate where you want to store the local definitions.

Universe Storage for Deployment

When you have finished designing and testing your universe, you export or publish to the repository. Publishing it to the repository is necessary to make the universe accessible to Web Intelligence, Crystal Reports, and dashboard users.

When you export the universe to the repository, several things happen:

- Entries are made in the related Central Management Server (CMS) tables in the repository to assign the universe a unique object identifier. From within the Central Management Console, you can see the file-storage location for each universe, as shown in Figure 4-8.

- The .unx file is compressed and saved to the BusinessObjects Enterprise (BOE) server file system under the Input folder. The last set of numeric folders is system-generated from the object numbers assigned in the CMS. For example, the path may be C:\Program Files\SAP BusinessObjects\BusinessObjects Enterprise XI 4.0\FileStore\Input\a_160\033\000\8608.

- The building blocks of the universe (the connection file .cns, data foundation .dfx, and business layer .blx) are compiled into a single .unx file.

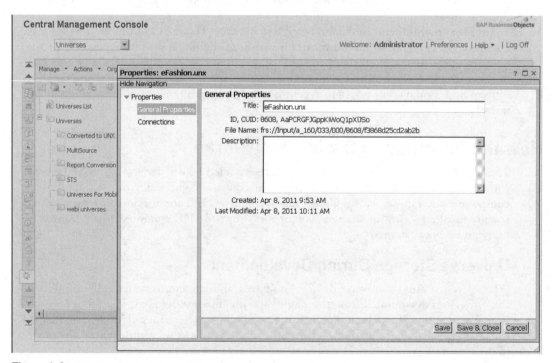

Figure 4-8   The Universe appears as a compiled .unx file in the CMC.

Crystal Business Views

For long-time Crystal developers, the universe may seem like an unnecessary bottleneck if your immediate goal is to develop a report. Indeed, the startup time is longer to develop a universe than to develop a handful of reports. The benefits are in the long-term maintenance and reusability. With a universe, measures are centrally defined and maintained. If they change, the administrator changes the calculation centrally, and these changes are propagated to any report in which the calculation is used.

The concept of business views, first introduced to Crystal Enterprise in version 10, shares some similarities and capabilities with universes. However, there are a few key differences. One important difference is in the purpose of each. Crystal business views were under development *before* Crystal Decisions was acquired by SAP BusinessObjects. The business views would have been a good competitive feature to a universe if the companies had remained separate. However, the intended user base of the two products was different before the acquisition and remains so today. Business views are primarily a way of providing developers with a library of reusable components. Universes, on the other hand, were always focused on business users who wanted to be shielded from underlying database and SQL complexities. Such a fundamental difference in purpose leads to different uses and capabilities. Crystal business views continue to be supported in SAP BusinessObjects BI 4.0, but are no longer enhanced (and the vendor has not mentioned plans to support them in subsequent releases). A business view may be required for bursting particular reports or view-time security.

Thus, while the universe as a data source is a useful integration point, it is not a substitute for all Crystal Reports developments. The integration between Crystal Reports and the universe has improved with each release. For example, with Feature Pack 3, Crystal Reports for Enterprise can now also leverage the same universe contexts that previously only Web Intelligence leveraged.

Universe Design Tool

If you are a long-time SAP BusinessObjects developer, it may be hard to let go of the well-known, familiar Designer. The Designer has changed little in the past ten years. The IDT, meanwhile, was newly developed to address some of the shortcomings of Designer. Designer is still available in version 4.0, as the Universe Design Tool, but primarily as a transition strategy.

Designers new to SAP BusinessObjects should not use the Universe Design Tool and instead use the IDT. Those who support SAP BusinessObjects 3.*x* users should use the Universe Design Tool only when necessary, as follows:

- When linked universes are involved. Linked universes are not supported in version 4.0.

- When Web Intelligence 3.*x* and Live Office are used. Live Office currently works only with Web Intelligence 3.*x* documents. If users must use Web Intelligence 3.*x*, then the universe should continue to be maintained with the Universe Design Tool.

- When stored procedures are used as a data source as the IDT does not support them.

The IDT offers the following primary benefits over universes built with the Universe Design Tool:

- It allows for multiple data sources.
- It has better support for multidimensional data sources, such as BW, Essbase, and Microsoft Analysis Services.
- Universes can be organized into views to make subsets of objects for targeted groups of users.
- New versions of the client tools such as Crystal Reports Enterprise and Dashboard Design require a .unx and cannot access 3.x universes.

Summary

The universe is core to the entire SAP BusinessObjects suite:

- Web Intelligence users access the universe to build new queries using familiar business terms.
- Crystal Reports 2011 authors may use it as an optional data source, and in Crystal Reports Enterprise, it is the default data source.
- Dashboard Design uses the universe to build dashboards.
- SAP BusinessObjects Explorer uses the universe to create information spaces used for visual data discovery.

The main building blocks of a universe are the connection to the physical data sources, the data foundation that points to the physical tables, and the business layer that is visible to end users.

In designing a better universe, understand who will be the query authors today and in the future. Ensure that the universe is simple enough not to overwhelm users, yet powerful enough to facilitate business insight.

Getting Started with the Information Design Tool

In Chapter 4, we reviewed the building blocks of a universe, the importance of aligning the universe with business goals, and techniques for iterative development. In that chapter, you learned that SAP BusinessObjects 4.0 administrators use the Information Design Tool (IDT) to build universes. For those who initially deployed on XI, the Universe Design Tool (formerly known as Designer) is also supported in version 4.0. However, the Universe Design Tool is provided primarily as a way of maintaining XI universes that you are not ready to migrate.

In this chapter, you'll learn how to work with the IDT interface and the key parameters that help you build the universe.

Launching the IDT

While much of SAP BusinessObjects is managed via a web environment and browser-based tools, the IDT must be installed locally on your PC.

1. To launch the IDT, from Windows, select Start | All Programs | SAP BusinessObjects BI platform 4.0 | SAP BusinessObjects BI platform Client Tools | Information Design Tool.

2. The IDT presents you with a login screen. After you log in, the IDT will display local projects, as shown in the following screen.

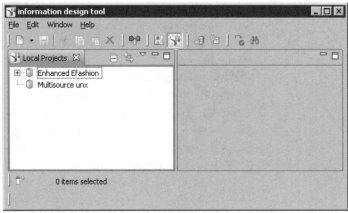

At this point, you may either work with local content or import content from the repository. To import content from the repository, follow these steps:

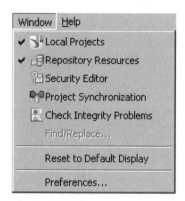

1. From the IDT, select Window | Repository Resources (ensure this menu option is checked).

2. The Repository Resources pane appears, showing your repository contents. This pane is displayed in the bottom-left area of your screen by default. You can maximize the pane or drag it to the right. Connect to the repository by clicking the Open Session button on the Repository Resources toolbar.

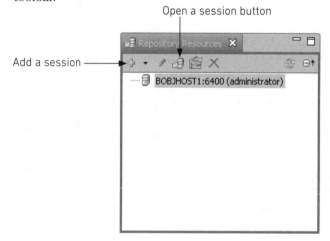

3. If your company has multiple repositories and the desired one does not immediately appear in the pane, click the Insert a Session button (the one with a plus icon) on the toolbar.

4. Select the system or server name from the drop-down box.

5. Enter your SAP BusinessObjects Enterprise username in the appropriate box. (Note that Administrator is a default username created during initial installation.) SAP BusinessObjects Enterprise usernames are not case-sensitive, but usernames in other authentication systems (such as in step 7) may be.

6. Tab to move to the Password box and enter your password. The system administrator determines the minimum length and case-sensitivity of passwords.

7. Select the authentication source for your username. This may be Enterprise for the SAP BusinessObjects Enterprise internal security or an external security system, such as LDAP, Windows Active Directory, or SAP. Security is discussed in Chapter 12. Then click OK.

If you have entered the preceding information correctly, the Repository Resource pane will display connections and universes.

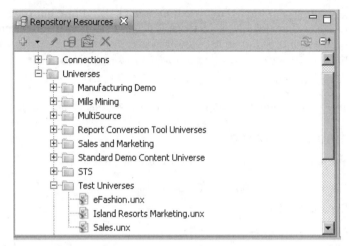

If you entered an invalid system, username, password, or authentication source, you will receive an error that clearly identifies which information is incorrect.

Retrieving and Opening a Universe

You can retrieve a universe from the repository or create a new one locally. In either situation, your first step is to create a new project. This becomes the holding place for any universes you create or retrieve.

Creating a Project

To create a project, follow these steps:

1. From the IDT pull-down menu, select File | New | Project.

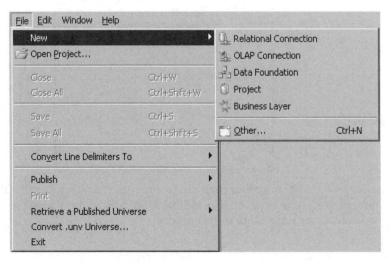

3. Enter a project name. The project name is visible only to you as the developer. It is not visible to end users. For this example, enter **First Project**.

4. You can accept the default location or click the ellipse button to select a different location. The default project location is C:\Documents and Settings*username*\\.businessobjects\bimodeler_14\workspace*project*, where *username* is the name of the Windows user, and *project* is the name of the project.

5. Click Finish to create the project.

The new project name will appear in the Local Projects pane.

Importing a Universe

To import the universe from the repository, follow these steps:

1. Navigate to the Repository Resources pane.

2. Expand the Universes folder.

3. Select the universe you would like to import.

4. Right-click the universe and select Retrieve Universe. Note that if it is an XI universe, you will be warned to first convert it.

5. Choose the project folder into which you want to import the universe. Then click OK.

The IDT will create a folder with a time stamp for when you imported the universe. The IDT will automatically create the corresponding business layer (.blx), a shortcut for the connection (.cns), and the data foundation (.dfx). In the following example, the eFashion universe has been imported into the First Project on April 15, 2011.

As discussed in the preceding chapter, it's important to remember that during universe development, you are working on a local copy. Users will not be able to see your changes until you publish the universe to the repository.

Working with the IDT Workspace and Toolbar

Figure 5-1 shows the IDT workspace, which includes panes for local projects, repository resources, and the data foundation. There are multiple tabs for each of the building blocks of the universe, including the connection shortcut and the business layer that end users ultimately see in various authoring interfaces. As you focus on particular aspects of the universe design, you may decide to resize or close certain panes.

Local projects and universe building blocks   Display panes

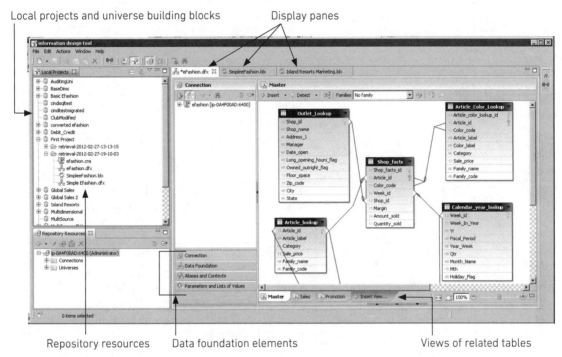

Repository resources   Data foundation elements   Views of related tables

Figure 5-1   The IDT with the data foundation displayed

To open any of the individual components, either double-click the item or select the item, right-click, and select Open from the pop up menu. For example, to open the eFashion data foundation, from the Local Projects pane, navigate to the First Project folder, position your mouse on Efashion.dfx, and double-click.

As with many Windows applications, you can perform tasks by selecting options from the pull-down menus or from the toolbar. Table 5-1 describes the purpose of each button in the IDT toolbar.

Button/Key Combo	Name	Function
or CTRL-N	New	Invokes a menu to create a new project, connection, or universe. Click the icon to launch a wizard, or click the drop-down arrow to create the item without a wizard.
or CTRL-S	Save	Saves the component to disk. Data foundation layers, connections, and business layers are saved individually. The icon is dimmed when there are no changes to be saved. This does not export the universe to the repository.
or CTRL-X	Cut	Cuts the selected item (table, join, or object).
or CTRL-C	Copy	Copies the selected item into the Windows clipboard.
or CTRL-V	Paste	Pastes the selected item.
	Delete	Deletes the selected item. The IDT will ask you to confirm that you want to permanently delete the item and will warn you if any dependent items will be impacted.
	Project Synchronization	Synchronizes projects that are codeveloped by multiple developers.
	Show/Hide Integrity Problems	Displays universe integrity issues in an additional pane. Click the icon again to hide the pane.
	Show/Hide Local Projects	Displays the Local Projects pane. Click the icon again to hide the pane.
	Show/Hide Repository Resources	Displays the Repository Resources pane. Click the icon again to hide the pane.
	Security Editor	Launches the Security Editor to control access to universe, objects, and data.
	Check Integrity	Initiates a universe integrity check and opens a new pane to display items checked or items with errors.
	Search	Invokes a Find/Replace dialog box to find an object or part of SQL.

Table 5-1 IDT Toolbar Buttons

Understanding Connections

The universe connection determines how users connect to the data warehouse or data source when they build or refresh a query. When you import a universe from the repository, the IDT creates a shortcut to the shared connection in the repository. If you are creating a brand-new universe, your first step is either to create a new connection or to import a shared connection from the repository to create the local shortcut.

The username and password used for the universe connection can be the same as those used to authenticate a user in the SAP BusinessObjects Enterprise repository, or they may be different. Often, they are the same if you use the database to control security. Certain databases, such as Teradata, also perform better when database users have their own workspace. Other databases, such as Oracle, perform better with a shared database login, as memory and resources are shared.

The IDT supports two different types of connections:

- Local connections that a designer may use during development. The local connection definition is stored on the client workstation.

- Shared connections that reside in the CMS repository in the connections folder. In order to deploy universes to end users, you must use secure connections.

The following sections describe the login parameters and connection parameters to consider when creating connections. They are followed by step-by-step instructions for creating connections.

Approaches to Login Parameters

To understand how login parameters within the universe connections work, you must first be aware of how SAP BusinessObjects is deployed and how security concerns in the various data sources, whether OLTP systems or data marts, interact. Here, we'll look at three login scenarios:

- Using database credentials
- Using a single sign-on
- Using a shared login to a data warehouse

Using Database Credentials

Let's assume that you are deploying an Orders universe directly against a transaction system. Users who enter Orders use SAP BusinessObjects to create real-time reports against the same data source. Therefore, you want the same security in the source system to apply in SAP BusinessObjects. You want SAP BusinessObjects to pass individual database logins to the Orders data source. This requires creating a set of database credentials for each individual user that will be passed on to the Orders data source.

While it would be preferable for users to have the same user ID and password for different systems, this is sometimes not the case when different system administrators are involved. As shown in the example in Figure 5-2, the user ID and password to log in to BusinessObjects Enterprise is Cindi/ASK. However, the user ID and password to log in to the Orders Transaction system is completely different: U761358/ASK1. In order to pass this second user ID through to the universe data source, an administrator defines a set of database credentials for each user (as described in Chapter 12). These database credentials will apply to any universe or connection with the option Use BusinessObjectsCredential Mapping enabled.

The following happens when a user tries to refresh a query:

1. The user supplies an SAP BusinessObjects Enterprise user ID and password—in this example, Cindi/ASK.

2. The CMS validates the user ID and password against definitions in the SAP BusinessObjects Enterprise repository and checks permissions.

3. When the user refreshes a document based on the Orders universe, the CMS checks which connection parameters to supply to the data source. For the Orders connection, the parameters are set to use SAP BusinessObjects credential mapping. The database credentials for user Cindi are defined as U761358/ASK1.

4. When the Enterprise Connection Server connects to the orders data source, the user ID U761358 is passed through to the database.

CAUTION If you enable the use of database credentials for the universe, then all users who access this universe must have a unique login ID to the data source, and the credentials must be defined via the Central Management Console (see Chapter 12). If this is missing, users will receive an error when trying to refresh a query. In Figure 5-2, the user Sam does not have database credentials defined and would receive an error.

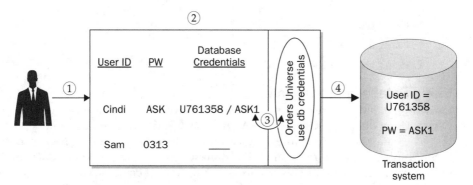

Figure 5-2   Database credentials can be different from SAP BusinessObjects Enterprise login IDs and passwords.

Using a Single Sign-On

In the previous example, the SAP BusinessObjects Enterprise user ID and the database user ID were different. However, when the user IDs and passwords are the same across the different systems, you can use a single sign-on to pass the SAP BusinessObjects Enterprise user ID through to the data source.

Using a Shared Login to a Data Warehouse

As shown in Figure 5-3, many companies use a data warehouse environment rather than accessing data directly in an OLTP. The CMS repository tables may be physically installed on the same machine as the data warehouse tables or on a separate server. However, the table owners and the database instance used are most likely different. As users execute queries against the data warehouse, the connection to the database uses the same user ID and password: BOEnterprise and BOEnterprise.

The workflow is similar to that in Figure 5-2; however, in step 3, the username and password are stored as part of the universe parameters connection and shared by multiple SAP BusinessObjects users. Database credentials for individual users are not read.

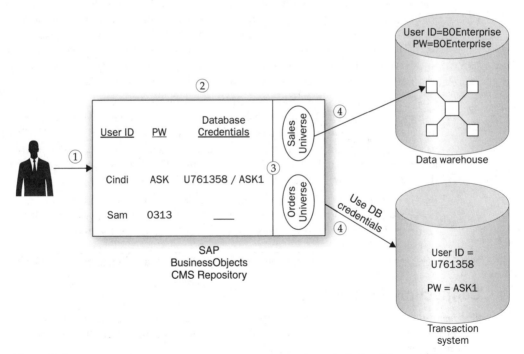

Figure 5-3   Universe connections can use a common database login for different SAP BusinessObjects Enterprise users.

Choosing Which Connection to Use in a Universe

Administrators should understand how the login user IDs and passwords interact, and carefully consider the following when creating a connection:

- **Ease of usage** If database credentials are not defined correctly, or if they become out of sync with passwords in the source system, users will blame SAP BusinessObjects for being too difficult to use or not working.

- **Security** If you define row- and column-level security in the source system, you may want to use database credentials to leverage that security. If, however, you are only concerned about access to reports in the repository, or if you use the capabilities in the IDT to control row- and object-level security, then you may want to use a common data source login.

- **Usage tracking** There are two levels of usage tracking in a SAP BusinessObjects deployment: the first is within SAP BusinessObjects, and the second is at the database level. SAP BusinessObjects Enterprise usage tracking will tell you which users access which reports and how long those queries are executing. Tracking usage at the database level lets you determine how frequently certain indexes are used and whose queries are most often doing full-table scans. If you decide to use a shared login from SAP BusinessObjects Enterprise to the source system database (see Figure 5-3), you'll find it harder to control runaway queries. The DBA sees only one user ID (BOEnterprise) logged in to the database, even though it may represent hundreds of different end users. For this reason, many companies assign user IDs and passwords at both the SAP BusinessObjects Enterprise and data source levels.

- **Cost** Another consideration in choosing between unique source system IDs or a shared one is your RDBMS licensing. If your license is by named user, it may be more cost-effective to use a shared database login for data access. You will still need to pay for the appropriate number of concurrent licenses. The IDT also enables you to set how long a database connection remains active to keep concurrency against the data source low.

- **Performance** Certain databases, such as Oracle, perform better when there is a shared login. Other databases, such as Teradata, prefer individual database credentials because of the way resources and memory are allocated.

NOTE Always, always test your connection when changing a user ID, password, or database name.

Connection Parameters

The second part of creating a new connection involves setting the connection parameters that affect users during query execution. These options and their defaults will vary depending on which database you are using.

The New Relational Connection window contains the following settings:

- **Connection Pool Mode** This offers a choice of three settings to tell the Enterprise server what to do when a query is complete:

  - **Disconnect after each transaction** This option can make repeated querying for users appear unnecessarily slow, as the login process is added to each data refresh. It does, however, keep the number of database connections open to a minimum.

- **Keep the connection active for** *NN*   This allows you to specify a time limit. If no additional queries are submitted to the database during that time, the connection is closed. A good balance is to allow the connection to be active for ten minutes, as shown in the following screen.

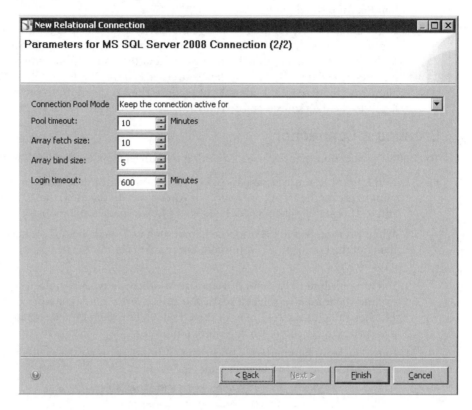

- **Keep the connection active during the whole session (local mode only)**   This means user queries are never slowed down for the source system/data warehouse login and logout process. This is great for users, but can become expensive for RDBMS licensing and Enterprise server overhead.

- **Pool timeout**   If you chose to keep the connection active for a specific period, set the number of minutes here. If you chose any other connection option for Connection Pool Mode, this box is grayed out.

- **Array fetch size**   This option determines how many rows of data can be shipped back to the client or Enterprise server in one fetch. Increasing the fetch size causes query results to return faster to the user; however, higher settings consume more memory. Response times are more greatly affected by network utilization and query performance. If you are experiencing slow fetches, try increasing the number by increments of ten. For example, in one scenario, increasing the array fetch size from 10 to 100 caused query results to return 25 percent faster.

- **Array bind size**   This setting affects how much data can be held in memory before being written to the repository. When the bind array fills, it is transmitted to the database. This setting seems to have a smaller impact on performance than the array fetch size, but a larger impact on memory used by the BOE server process that handles Web Intelligence queries.

- **Login timeout**   This setting relates to the universe connection to the data source (not between users and InfoView). As the Enterprise Connection Server connects to the data source, the user ID and password in the connection parameters are passed to the data source. Busy data sources may have slow login times. This setting allows you to increase the number of seconds the Connection Server will attempt to log in to the data source before returning an error.

Creating a Connection

To create a connection that you use in defining the universe parameters, follow these steps:

1. In the Local Resources pane, position your mouse within the project where you want to create the local connection. If you do not do this first, the IDT will prompt you to choose a project. Select File | New | Relational Connection.

2. When prompted, enter a resource name, such as Oracle Sales. This becomes the name of the connection. Optionally, enter a description for the connection. Then click Next.

3. You are presented with a list of Database Middleware types. For each type, you expand the folders to select a particular driver version. For example, to use Oracle 11, click the plus sign (+) next to the Oracle folder, then Oracle 11, and then JDBC drivers or Oracle client. Click Next to continue.

4. Enter the login parameters. Choose the authentication mode, as discussed earlier in the "Approaches to Login Parameters" section.

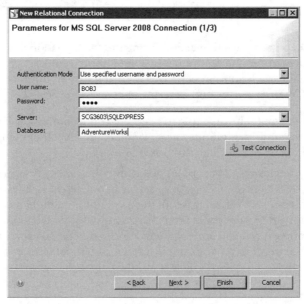

5. If you selected "Use a specified username and password" as a shared login in step 4, enter the username and password. If you choose another authentication method, these boxes will be grayed out.

6. Depending on the database type, select the name of the database and the name of the database server. Then click Test Connection. This will tell you if you have incorrectly entered a login parameter. Click Next.

7. Confirm or modify the advanced parameters, and then click Next.

8. Confirm or modify any custom parameters, and then click Finish.

When you first create a connection, it appears as a .cnx file in the local resources. In the following example, Oracle Sales.cnx is a local connection, as is sales.cnx. The other connections have a different icon, with an arrow, and end in .cns to indicate they are shortcuts to connections in the repository.

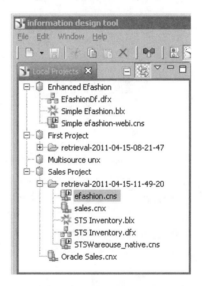

To upload and publish your newly created connection to the repository, follow these steps:

1. From within the Local Projects pane, choose the connection or .cnx file you want to publish.

2. Right-click and choose Publish to the Repository from the pop-up menu.

3. If you already have a session established with the repository, the BusinessObjects Enterprise server name will appear, and you can click Next. If you do not have a session, you will be prompted to choose a server or enter a password. Click Connect.

4. Choose the desired folder to store the connection definitions.

5. Click Finish.

6. The wizard will ask you if you want to create a local shortcut to this connection. Choose Yes. By creating a shortcut, you can reuse this connection definition in the data foundation.

Summary

This chapter introduced the IDT. You learned how to navigate it, create a project, retrieve a universe, open a data foundation, and create a connection. The next chapter discusses how to create a basic data foundation and joins between tables, aliases. and contexts.

CHAPTER 6

Data Foundation Basics

Within the data foundation, you are mainly specifying which tables you want accessible via the universe and their associated joins. *Joins* define how one or more tables relate to one another. Most of the complexities around joins occur when your universe contains multiple star schemas or when you are using SAP BusinessObjects against a transaction system with normalized data models.

This chapter explains the elements of the data foundation, join concepts, contexts, aliases, derived tables, and data foundation properties.

Creating a Data Foundation

In the previous chapter, a data foundation was automatically created when you imported the eFashion universe into your First Project folder. Within a project, you can have multiple connections, data foundations, and business layers. This is strictly for your organizational and development purposes. The business layer compiles these various elements into a single universe file when you publish it to the repository or local folder. For clarity, it may be useful for you to maintain a clean copy of the eFashion universe and create a copy or new data foundation that you can freely modify while learning the IDT.

To create a new data foundation within an existing project:

1. From within the Local Projects pane, position your mouse on your First Project folder.
2. Right-click to invoke the pop-up menu and select New | Data Foundation.
3. When prompted to enter a Resource Name, enter **Simple eFashion** and click Next.
4. When prompted for the data foundation type, choose Single Source and click Next.
5. A list of connections within the project appears. Check the box next to efashion.cns connection. Click Finish.

You can also create a new project, and then either create a new connection or create shortcut to an existing connection, and then create a data foundation. Refer to the previous chapter, Figure 5-1, for the initial view of the data foundation.

Inserting Tables

Within the Connection pane in the data foundation, you will see all the tables and views within the physical database. However, you may only want a subset of the tables in your data foundation. To add tables to the data foundation, double-click the desired table. A green checkmark appears next to the table in the Connection pane, and the table is added to the master pane on the right.

Families

Families are a way of controlling the appearance of tables within the master pane. You can create families, for example, that display all the fact tables in red and dimension tables in yellow.

1. To create a family, select Edit Families from the toolbar.

2. Click the Add button.

3. Replace the default name New Family 1 with a more meaningful name such as **Fact Tables**.

4. From the drop-down box, specify the Table Color as red.

5. Click Apply to save the changes to the family definitions.

6. From within the master pane, select the fact table that you want to apply the family color to from the Families drop-down.

Basic Joins

In the IDT, you can choose to have your joins detected automatically based on common names between tables. Alternatively, you can manually define the joins. First, you'll learn about using IDT join detection. Creating joins manually is covered in the discussion of loops and contexts later in this chapter.

Creating Joins Using Detection

When you choose to let the IDT automatically detect your joins, rather than creating them manually, it will create joins between tables based either on matching column names or key columns. A *key column* is specified by the DBA as a unique identifier for the particular table. The IDT displays a key icon next to those columns.

Using the simple eFashion data foundation, suppose you want to create three basic joins:

- From SHOP_FACTS to CALENDAR_YEAR_LOOKUP
- From SHOP_FACTS to ARTICLE_LOOKUP
- From SHOP_FACTS to OUTLET_LOOKUP

To create these joins using detection, follow these steps:

1. Insert the tables ARTICLE_LOOKUP, SHOP_FACTS, and OUTLET_LOOKUP into the data foundation by dragging them to the Data Foundation pane on the right or double-clicking in the Connection pane.

2. From the Data Foundation toolbar, click the drop-down arrow next to the Detect icon (the light bulb) and select Detect Joins from the menu.

3. Choose "Detect joins based on column names," and then click Next.

4. A dialog box will display the candidate joins. You can accept all the proposed joins or interactively select and deselect them. For this example, click Finish to accept the joins.

5. Save the data foundation.

The created joins should appear as follows:

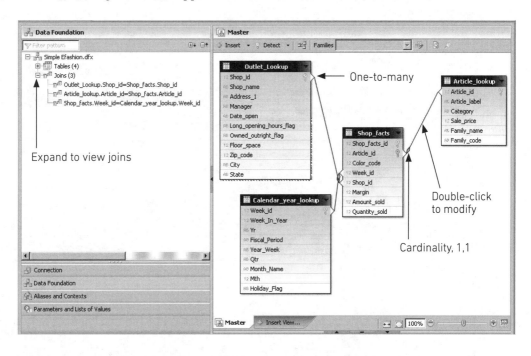

Part II

NOTE If you positioned your mouse pointer on any single table prior to detecting joins, the IDT may propose only one join statement in step 4. If you want to see all possible joins, ensure no individual tables are selected before choosing to detect joins.

The arity, or part of a diamond, indicates that the relationship between SHOP_FACTS and ARTICLE_LOOKUP is one-to-many. For every one article in ARTICLE_LOOKUP, there may be one or many sales transactions in SHOP_FACTS (for example, blazers can sell one or more times).

Modifying Joins

You can modify a join statement in several ways:

- Double-click the join line in the Data Foundation pane entity relationship diagram.
- Double-click the join line in the join list in the left pane.
- Select the join statement in either pane, right-click, and choose Edit Join from the pop-up menu.

When you use one of these methods to choose to modify the join between SHOP_FACTS and ARTICLE_LOOKUP, you are presented with the Edit Join dialog box.

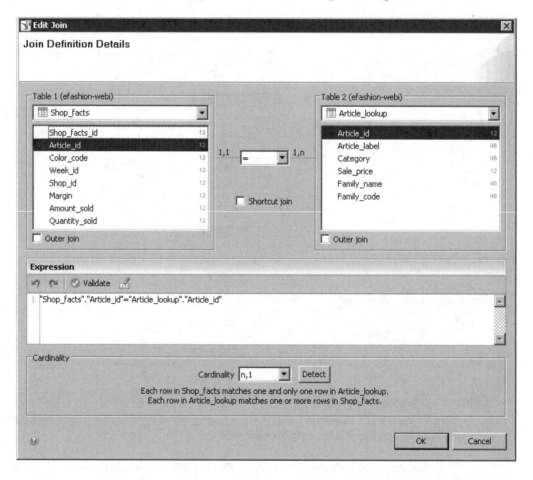

Table 1, SHOP_FACTS, appears on the left side, and Table 2, ARTICLE_LOOKUP, is on the right. In most RDBMSs, which table is on the right or left does not matter, but in older

Join Operator	Description
=	Equi-join (each data value in the left table has an equivalent value in the right table)
!=	Not equal to
>	Greater than
<	Less than
>=	Greater than or equal to
<=	Less than or equal to

Table 6-1 Join Operators

systems, it can affect how quickly a query is processed. When the IDT detects joins, it does not put the tables in any particular order, appearing to go in the order in which the table was added. Putting the larger table on the left may result in faster queries for certain databases, particularly for joins other than the default type, which is an equi-join.

The join operator defines the join type. The most common is the equi-join (=), in which two tables are related when every data value in the left table has an equivalent value in the right table. The drop-down box in the middle of the Edit Join dialog box lets you change the join operator. The join operators are listed in Table 6-1.

Getting Row Counts

Row count information helps you, as the universe designer, to understand when you are joining large tables together. Also, when generating the SQL for a query, historically the SQL generated will list the largest table first in the FROM section to make queries run faster. Databases that did not have an optimizer benefited from careful ordering of tables in the SQL statements. Newer versions of leading databases have optimizers that are less reliant on the order of the tables listed in the FROM clause.

Extracting row count information requires a full table scan against each table. The query process can be slow to generate this information for fact tables that contain millions of rows of data, as it does a SELECT COUNT(*) against the table.

To fetch the numbers, follow these steps:

1. Select the table within the Data Foundation pane by clicking the title bar that contains the table name.

2. Right-click to open the pop-up menu and select Count Rows. (Note that if your mouse cursor was positioned on an individual column within this table, you will see a different pop-up menu.)

3. A dialog box will show you the total number of rows in the table. To see the SQL used to count the rows, click Show Details.

4. Click Close to close the dialog box.

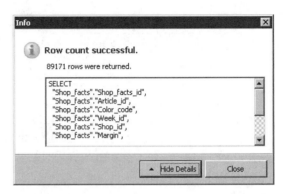

To retrieve the row count for multiple tables or to preview row counts for multiple tables at once, follow these steps:

 1. Open the Detect menu from the Data Foundation pane and choose Detect Row Count to display the Detect Row Count dialog box.

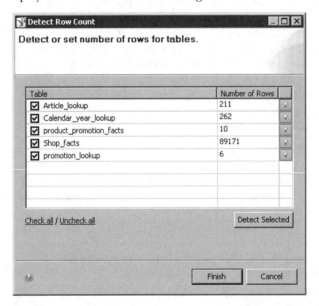

2. By default, all tables in the data foundation are selected. If your mouse was positioned on one table when you invoked the menu, then only that table has a check mark. To select multiple tables for which you want to count rows, click the checkboxes next to the desired tables.

3. Click Detect Selected. The row counts should update. If a table still shows 0 rows, click the yellow light bulb icon to refresh the count.

4. Click Finish to close the dialog box.

Detecting Cardinality

Above the join type, the cardinalities are indicated with 1,n = 1,1. *Cardinality* defines how many instances there are of each unique record in the related table: zero, one, or many.

In a typical, single-star schema, all of your relationships will be one-to-many between the dimensions and the fact table. For example, one product in the ARTICLE_LOOKUP table can have many orders in the SHOP_FACTS table.

Cardinality applies to each table in a join statement:

- **Table 1(1,n)**   One-to-many. Every item in the dimension table has one or more records in the fact table.

- **Table 2(1,1)**   One-to-one. For every record in the first table, there is one, and only one, record in the corresponding table.

- **n,n**   Many-to-many. For every record in the first table, there may be multiple facts in the corresponding table and vice versa. A good example of this is the employee-manager relationship, in which employees may report to multiple managers, and one manager will manage several employees.

Cardinality detection does not correctly identify many-to-many relationships, nor does it detect zero relationships (which would be quite useful in defining outer joins, which are discussed in the next section). According to SAP BusinessObjects product management, the detection algorithm counts rows to determine the cardinality and does not catch anomalies that may affect cardinality. This does not appear to have changed in the latest release.

If you skip cardinality detection completely, the IDT will still correctly detect loops but will not propose contexts. Therefore, you should use cardinality detection as a starting point, but be sure to override detected cardinalities based on your particular knowledge of the data.

If your data is clean, and if your universe will have multiple schemas, cardinality detection can be helpful in later detecting contexts.

Outer Joins

An *outer join* is a special join type that requires careful consideration before use. An outer join is a relationship between two tables in which records from one table do not have matching records in the other. This situation occurs frequently, particularly when your universe will access a transaction system rather than a data warehouse. For example, when a company launches a new product, sales may not yet exist for that product. So to see a report with the product listed and the sales amount displaying zero from the fact table would require an outer join.

However, it's also possible to have items in a fact table that do not have a corresponding record in the dimension table. As an example, imagine a frustrated sales clerk who keeps trying to scan a trendy new scarf for an impatient customer. The scanner does not ring up the product at the register, so the sales clerk manually enters the article code from the scarf's tag. (Of course, the scarf should have been in inventory, and it should not have been on display without existing in the product master, but it happens—unfortunately, more than businesspeople realize and more than data modelers wish.)

In an ideal world, the sales transaction would automatically have added an entry in the product master. In an almost ideal world, the data warehouse would have plugged an entry in the ARTICLE_ID field, such as 999 or XXX, to say the article description is not found. In reality (such as with a transaction system or poorly modeled data mart), you will need to use an outer join. Outer joins may not be a problem for small lookup tables, but they are best avoided for large lookup tables, because the RDBMS cannot use the index to process the query, leading to a slow query.

SAP BusinessObjects does not provide a sample universe that contains outer joins, but you can create one using the ARTICLE_LOOKUP and SHOP_FACTS tables. To try this, in the ARTICLE_LOOKUP table, add two new records: ARTICLE_ID 189480, a new Leeds United Football Club sweatshirt, and ARTICLE_ID 189481, a Green Bay Packers shirt. You know that there are no sales against the sweatshirts in the SHOP_FACTS table, because you just added the product. If a user were to run a report for the sales category Sweats, the products would not appear if the data foundation contained a default equi-join. Therefore, you need an outer join on the ARTICLE_LOOKUP table.

Article_id	Article_label	Category	Sale_price	Family_name	Family_code
186108	Vivaldi Tunic	Long sleeve	$159.00	Shirt Waist	F20
186370	Flounced Collar Shirtdress	Long sleeve	$200.00	Shirt Waist	F20
187710	Africa Zipper Cardigan	Cardigan	$231.00	Sweaters	F25
187901	Fake Leopard Skin Gloves with Lurex Trim	Hats,gloves,scarve	$852.50	Accessories	F60
187904	Denim Front Button Dress	Casual dresses	$127.50	Dresses	F80
189479	Whisky Dancer T-Shirt	T-Shirts	$214.00	Sweat-T-Shirts	F36
189480	Leeds United Football Club	T-Shirts	$150.00	Sweat-T-Shirts	F36
189481	Green Bay Packers Jersey	T-Shirts	$175.00	Sweat-T-Shirts	F36

Record: 1 of 213   No Filter   Search

New records with no corresponding record in fact table

To change the existing equi-join to an outer join, do the following:

1. Double-click the join line between SHOP_FACTS and ARTICLE_LOOKUP, or right-click and select Join Properties from the pop-up menu.
2. Under Table 2, ARTICLE_LOOKUP, select the Outer join check box.
3. Select Validate to ensure the join is valid.
4. Click OK to save the change to the join.
5. Click Save to save the changes to the data foundation.

0 means outer

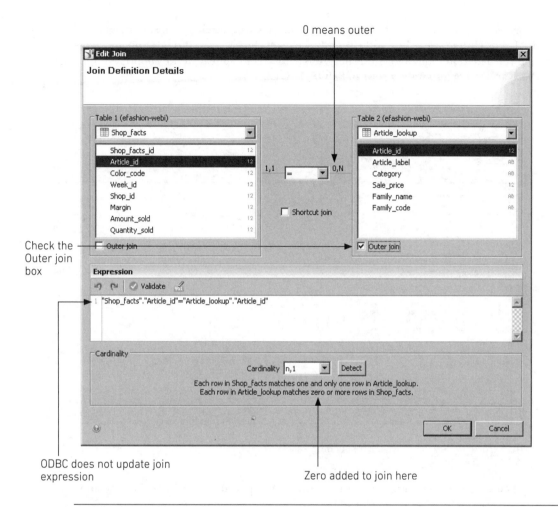

Check the
Outer join
box

ODBC does not update join
expression

Zero added to join here

NOTE The expression in the Edit Join dialog box may still appear as if it were an equi-join, but the message in the Cardinality section will now say each row in the dimension table matches zero or one rows in the fact table. When the SQL is generated in the Query panel, it will rewrite the expression as an outer join. To verify that the correct SQL is generated, create a query in the business layer that pulls two objects from the two related tables, and then select View Script to view the generated SQL statement.

When testing changes made in the data foundation, you must first refresh the business layer. To do this, choose the business layer in the Local Projects pane, right-click it, and select Refresh from the pop-up menu.

Now if you run a query in the business layer or a Web Intelligence report, you will see the Leeds United sweatshirt and Green Bay Packers jersey, even though none have been sold yet. The outer join allows this new ARTICLE_ID to appear in the report, even though there are no corresponding rows in SHOP_FACTS.

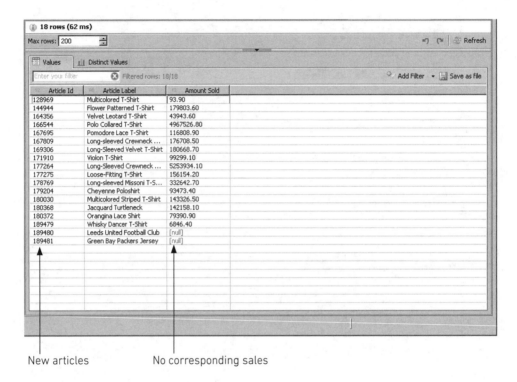

New articles   No corresponding sales

The actual SQL syntax for outer joins will vary depending on which database and driver you are using. Other RDBMSs will adjust the join expression in the dialog box. Microsoft Access SQL uses the following default syntax:

```
{ ojShop_facts RIGHT OUTER JOIN Article_lookup ON
Shop_facts.Article_id=Article_lookup.Article_id }
```

You may now be thinking that it makes sense to put outer joins on all lookup tables. For example, you may have inventory before items have sold or customers in your lead master before there are sales to those customers. However, even when you use an outer join on a small lookup table, be sure to test the response time or analyze the explain or execution plans in your RDBMS. If the response time is slow, train the users so they understand that if they want full product listings, full customer listings, or a list of customers who have not bought anything this year, they should analyze that data separately. Use of subqueries (discussed in Chapter 22) may help them answer the same questions more efficiently. Finally, in a data warehouse or data mart environment, work with the DBA and data modeler to develop approaches for minimizing the use of outer joins.

Loops and Contexts

Loops occur when there are two different paths to accomplish one join and when those joins create a circular reference between three or more tables. In the following data foundation, PRODUCT_PROMOTION_FACTS and CALENDAR_YEAR_LOOKUP have been added. If users want to analyze articles versus time, there are now two join paths.

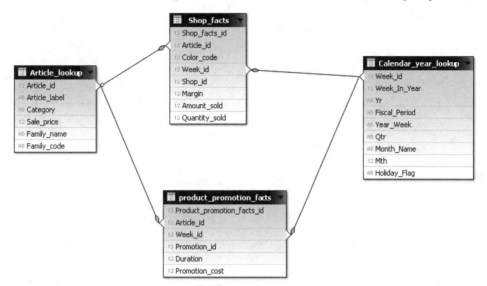

The query engine does not know which path to take: the one via SHOP_FACTS or the one via PRODUCT_PROMOTION_FACTS. Is the business question "What are *sales* by product and period?" or "What are the *promotions* by product and period?"

The circular appearance of these four joins is a loop, which can give undesired SQL results, usually returning fewer rows than expected.

There may be circumstances in which a loop is valid (see the "Are Loops a Bad Thing?" section later in this chapter), but more often, loops are the result of multiple star schemas within the data foundation. These loops should be eliminated. Contexts help break a loop into two sets of join statements, so the desired join path is always clear, and business users can answer perfectly valid business questions.

Business Questions That Demand Contexts

Following are two sample business questions that often involve multiple star schemas that require the use of contexts; without contexts, they would cause a loop.

Days Sales Inventory (DSIs)

How many days' worth of inventory do you have according to the daily sales volume? As shown in Figure 6-1, this query would involve two contexts: one with all the joins for the star schema with a SALES_FACT table and a second context with all the joins related to INVENTORY_FACT. Although certain tables appear twice in this figure (PLANT, TIME, and PRODUCT), this is strictly for conceptual purposes; they exist only once in the physical database.

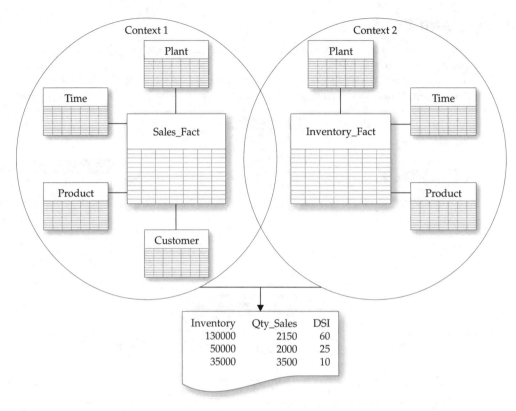

Figure 6-1 A context groups a set of tables into one star schema.

Account Balance Versus Debit/Credit

Most measures can be aggregated over time; other measures are valid at only one point in time. These are often referred to as *semi-additive* measures. Measures such as inventory, account balances, and number of customers are good examples of semi-additive measures. These measures are valid at only one particular point in time; they should be aggregated over accounts and regions but not over time. Often, though, users will want to compare them with other measures that can be aggregated over time, as shown in Table 6-2.

Semi-Additive Measures	Measures Aggregated over Time
End-of-month inventory	Movements in and out within a month
Beginning-of-month account balance	Debits and credits within a month
Number of customers at start of month	Customers gained and lost within a month

Table 6-2 Semi-Additive Measures Versus Measures Aggregated Over Time

OLAP databases such as Microsoft Analysis Services and Oracle Essbase allow an administrator to specify measures that relate to one point in time versus a period in time, but the IDT does not have built-in functionality that supports this. Contexts provide a work-around. For example, a user can run a query, selecting individual month-end balances from an ACCOUNT_FACT table, and then requesting summaries for all 30 days from a DAILY_DEBIT_CREDIT_FACT table. With contexts, SAP BusinessObjects will issue two SQL statements, and the results are again stitched together dynamically in the report.

Semi-additive measures are discussed in more detail in Chapter 7.

Inserting Contexts

1. The IDT can help you detect and resolve loops by using contexts. To enable this, you will first add the tables PRODUCT_PROMOTION_FACTS and CALENDAR_ YEAR_LOOKUP to create a loop and then resolve the loop with a context.

2. From the data foundation toolbar, choose Insert | Insert Table, or within the pane, right click and choose Insert | Insert Table from the pop-up menu.

3. From the table browser, select the PRODUCT_PROMOTION_FACTS and CALENDAR_YEAR_LOOKUP tables and click Insert.

4. Click Finish to close the Insert Table dialog box.

5. Manually insert the following joins:

    SHOP_FACTS.WEEK_ID=CALENDAR_YEAR_LOOKUP.WEEK_ID

    PRODUCT_PROMOTION_FACT.WEEK_ID=Calendar_Year_Lookup.WEEK_ID

    PRODUCT_PROMOTION_FACT.ARTICLE_ID=ARTICLE_LOOKUP.ARTICLE_ID

    To insert these joins, you may either drag a line from one table to another, or right-click and choose Insert Join. Note that if you use automatic join detection, more joins than necessary are created.

NOTE At the time of this writing for Feature Pack 3, join detection worked only when multiple new tables with matching keys were inserted into the data foundation. Join detection was not working correctly when a single table was inserted.

6. Click the Aliases and Contexts tab. Note the existence of the loop.

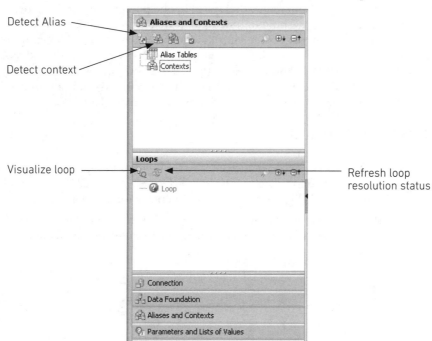

7. From the Aliases and Contexts toolbar, click Detect Contexts.

NOTE IDT will detect contexts only when the cardinalities have been set. You can set them manually or click Detect Cardinalities.

---

8. IDT will present you with a list of names as proposed contexts. These contexts include all the joins in each part of the loop or one set of joins. The proposed context name comes from whichever table name is at the center of the join path, in this case SHOP_FACTS and PRODUCTION_PROMOTION_FACTS. When you check the box for the context name, note that the related tables and joins are nicely highlighted in the Master data foundation pane as shown in Figure 6-2. Joins that will be included in the context are shown with a green plus, and those that will not be included are shown with a purple minus sign.

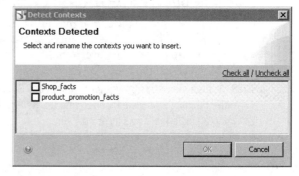

9. Click OK to create the contexts and close the Detect Contexts dialog box.

10. Click the Refresh Loop Resolution Status button on the Aliases and Contexts toolbar to ensure the loop is resolved with the two contexts.

11. Click Save on the toolbar to save your data foundation changes.

The Data Foundation pane should now appear as shown in Figure 6-2. Note that when a particular context is highlighted in the Contexts list, the join statements that belong to that context are also highlighted in the Data Foundation pane.

Congratulations! You have resolved your first loop. Unfortunately, your real-world universe may not be so easy. If your data foundation contains aggregates or is a snowflake design, the IDT may propose more contexts than necessary. Also, as you add new tables to your universe, your contexts may become incomplete.

Modifying a Context

As a best practice, universe designers leave the default context name until they have added all tables, joins, and contexts. In earlier versions, this was because the Universe Design Tool would automatically add the table to an existing context; with the Detect Contexts option, the IDT does not do that. Instead, it will create duplicate, new contexts. Therefore, after initial context creation, when you add new tables, you may decide to manually add them to the context. Once all your joins and contexts are created, you also may want to rename the context to a more meaningful name for end users.

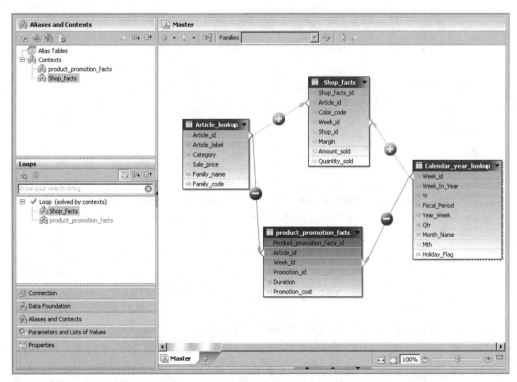

Figure 6-2   Contexts group related joins and allow users to answer valid business questions.

Follow these steps to rename the Product Promotion Fact context in our example to Promotions.

1. Select the context from the list.

2. Double-click the context you wish to edit. An Edit Context pane appears in the bottom right of the window. If the structure screen is maximized, the pane may not appear. Click the minus sign to restore to split screen.

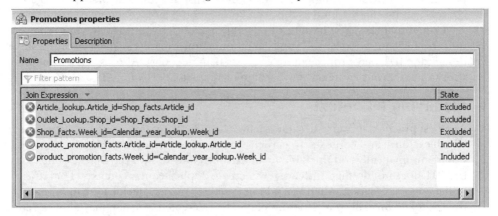

3. In the Name box, enter a business-oriented name. For this example, replace Product Promotion Facts with **Promotions**.

4. Select the Description tab and in the box, enter help text that will appear when users are prompted to select a context.

Note that joins that are part of the context appear with a green check mark and "included" designation in the join list. Joins that are part of a different context are designated "excluded," and joins that are not part of any context are designated "neutral."

Isolated Joins

Once you use contexts in a universe, you must keep using them and ensure they are complete. As you add new tables to your universe, the joins between the tables must be added to an existing context or included in a new context.

In the following example, you will add the PROMOTION_LOOKUP table to the universe to create an isolated join. The integrity check will not help you identify this problem.

1. From the Insert drop-down menu on the Aliases and Contexts pane toolbar, select Insert Tables or right-click in the Data Foundation pane and select Insert | Table.

2. From the table browser, select the PROMOTION_LOOKUP table, and then click Finish.

3. Draw a join line between PROMOTION_LOOKUP.PROMOTION_ID and PRODUCT_PROMOTION_FACTS.PROMOTION_ID.

4. From the Aliases and Context pane, expand the Contexts folder. Double-click the Promotions context. Double-click the newly added join to change the status from neutral to included.

CAUTION Once you start using contexts, you must ensure all joins are included in at least one context. If you fail to do this, user queries are split into multiple SQL statements that may lead to inaccurate results or messages such as "Incompatible combination of objects." What happens depends on whether the "Multiple SQL statements for each context" check box in the data foundation's Properties tab (in the SQL Options section) is selected (see the "Data Foundation Properties" section later in this chapter).

How Contexts Are Used

Now that you have two contexts, all user queries will be affected in one of three ways, sometimes with user prompting and sometimes without prompting.

When a user selects objects from tables purely within one context (CALENDAR_YEAR_ LOOKUP, SHOP_FACTS, and ARTICLE_LOOKUP in this example), the query engine is smart enough to know which context or join path to use to generate the SQL. The user is not prompted to choose a context.

When a user selects objects from both contexts—for example, sales and promotion costs by article and month—both contexts need to be used, and the various authoring interfaces will intelligently generate two separate SQL statements and seamlessly stitch the results together in one report. The left side of Figure 6-3 shows the first SQL statement Web Intelligence generates to retrieve sales amounts. Result 1 uses the Shop Facts context. The right side shows the second SQL statement Web Intelligence generates to retrieve the promotion costs for the *same year and article IDs*. This is very important. The dimensions form the GROUP BY section of the SELECT statement. If these are not exactly the same,

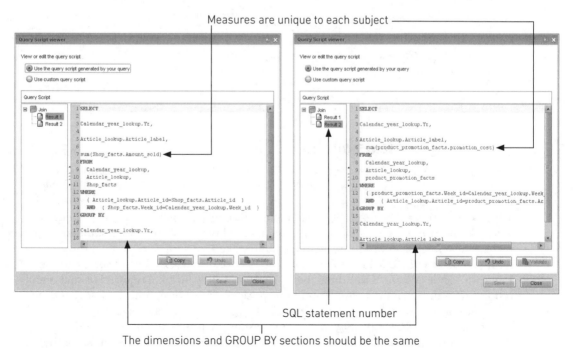

Figure 6-3 Web Intelligence automatically generates a SELECT statement for each context, without user intervention.

the query still executes, but with additional rows of data, as Web Intelligence is not clear how to synchronize the results. For example, if you added a result object named *Radio Promotion* to your query, it would appear only in the second SQL statement. The beauty of this synchronization feature is that users never see it; their business question is answered automatically and correctly.

When a user selects objects from the lookup tables without including objects from a fact table, Web Intelligence cannot determine automatically which context to use. Therefore, it prompts the user. The following shows the dialog box that appears after creating a new query that includes Article ID and Year. The query engine cannot determine if you want to know which articles sold (Shop Facts context) within a certain year or which articles had promotion costs (Product_Promotion_Facts context) within a certain year.

Processing Contexts on the RDBMS

Contexts can also be processed on the database server. In the preceding examples, when the query engine executes the separate SQL statements, each query is processed by the RDBMS sequentially. If your document contains several SQL statements, this can result in slow response times. Also, each SQL statement will return a result set that the Enterprise server then processes to present you with one merged report. If you have a summary report that calculates day sales inventory, perhaps you have ten rows for sales and ten rows of inventory data. The RDBMS sends a total of 20 rows of data across the network, and the Enterprise server synchronizes them to display 10 rows in your final report. For such small reports, the impact on the network and Enterprise server is not significant. For reports with thousands of rows (times thousands of users), the impact is naturally bigger.

The parameter JOIN_BY_SQL allows you to shift the processing from the SAP BusinessObjects Enterprise server to the RDBMS. The RDBMS server does more of the work, fewer rows travel the network, and the Enterprise server does less work. Whether this is a good thing or a bad thing depends on which aspect of your BI architecture is the bottleneck. If the load on your RDBMS is limited and it has greater processing power than the SAP BusinessObjects Enterprise server, then the JOIN_BY_SQL parameter can improve performance. If, however, the RDBMS is often the culprit for poor query performance, then using this parameter will further degrade performance.

Another consideration in using this parameter is that it allows Crystal Reports developers to build reports that access multiple contexts—a capability not previously possible. The bottom line is that you need to test the impact of using the parameter in your own real-world implementation against production data sources.

The following SQL is generated from a Microsoft SQL Server-based universe with the parameter JOIN_BY_SQL set to Yes. (Microsoft Access does not support this capability.) As you see here, the RDBMS still issues two SQL statements (or however many contexts are involved), but now the statements are joined in the database.

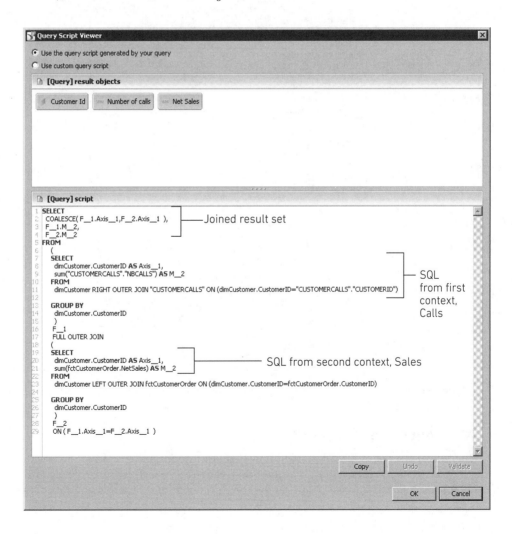

When the query is based on an Oracle data source, the SQL generated will use the NVL to display the dimensions common to both sets of queries. When the query is based on a SQL Server data source, the SQL generated will use COALESCE, as NVL is not supported. The end result is the same.

To enable this parameter in your universe, follow these steps:

1. From within the data foundation, select the Properties tab.

2. Click the Parameters button.

3. For the parameter JOIN_BY_SQL, change the default value from No to Yes.

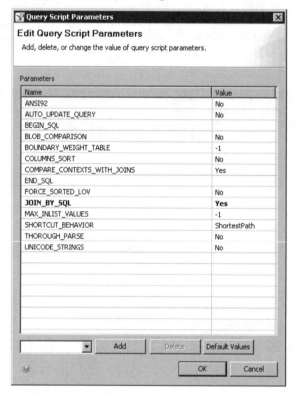

4. Click OK to apply the change.

5. Click Save to save the data foundation.

Remember to refresh the business layer before testing the impact of this change on the SQL generated.

Are Loops a Bad Thing?

The previous sections have described how to identify loops and get rid of them with contexts. In many cases, a loop is unintended, caused by poorly written SQL against complex schemas. However, loops can be the result of a valid business question if users really want to know something like which articles and weeks are common between both the promotion fact table and the sales fact table.

Look at the following two Web Intelligence reports. The articles Polo Collared T-Shirt (166544), Whisky Dancer T-Shirt (166550), and Pomodore Lace T-Shirt (167695, week 33) had promotions but no shop sales, so they appear in the table labeled "Product Promotion Context" but not in the table labeled "Loop – Fewer Rows."

Product Promotion Context

SKU number	SKU desc	Week
145404	Rounded Rectangle Brooch	30
165170	Modal Shirt	33
166544	Polo Collared T-Shirt	29
166550	Whisky Dancer T-Shirt	6
166583	Military Shirt	32
166583	Military Shirt	50
166699	Suede Stretch Dress	30
167042	Long-Sleeved Stitch Shirt	33
167695	Pomodore Lace T-Shirt	33
167695	Pomodore Lace T-Shirt	45
Count:		8

Loop - Fewer Rows

Article Id	Article Label	Year Week
145404	Rounded Rectangle Brooch	2002/30
165170	Modal Shirt	2002/33
166583	Military Shirt	2002/32
166583	Military Shirt	2002/50
166699	Suede Stretch Dress	2002/30
167042	Long-Sleeved Stitch Shirt	2002/33
167695	Pomodore Lace T-Shirt	2002/45
Count:	6	

The first table, Product Promotion Context, contains ten rows of data for eight distinct articles that had promotions during particular weeks. The second table, Loop – Fewer Rows, contains only seven rows of data, and lists six distinct articles and weeks that are common between *both* the promotion fact table and the shop fact table. There are fewer rows in this second table because not all products had both promotions and sales in the exact same week.

The following SQL is generated for a report in which the Promotions context is selected. Note that three tables are involved in the FROM portion of the query and two join statements.

```
SELECT DISTINCT
Article_lookup.Article_id,
Article_lookup.Article_label,
Calendar_year_lookup.Week_in_year
FROM
Article_lookup,
Calendar_year_lookup,
product_promotion_facts
WHERE
  ( product_promotion_facts.Week_id=Calendar_year_lookup.Week_id  )
  AND   ( Article_lookup.Article_id=product_promotion_facts.Article_id  )
```

Compare the preceding SQL with the joins from a second query that contains a loop. Note that there are now four tables in the FROM portion of the query and four join statements.

```
SELECT
Article_lookup.Article_id,
Article_lookup.article_label,
Calendar_year_lookup.Week_In_Year
FROM
Calendar_year_lookup,
Article_lookup,
product_promotion_facts,
shop_facts
WHERE
  ( Calendar_year_lookup.Week_id=product_promotion_facts.Week_id  )
  AND  ( Article_lookup.Article_id=product_promotion_facts.Article_id  )
And
  ( Calendar_year_lookup.Week_id=shop_facts.Week_id  )
  AND  ( Article_lookup.Article_id=shop_facts.Article_id  )
```

What's the bottom line? Unintentional loops are a bad thing. In earlier versions of the product, users could create queries that contained loops not resolved with contexts. In SAP BusinessObjects 4.0, users will receive a message that the query contains an incompatible combination of objects.

Chasm Traps and Contexts

Contexts allow a universe to contain multiple dimensional schemas and let users query these multiple schemas simultaneously. In addition, contexts prevent another possible join problem from occurring when you may have a common dimension table and two fact tables. In the examples in this chapter, a loop exists when the dimension tables ARTICLE_LOOKUP and CALENDAR_YEAR_LOOKUP are both referenced via either fact table. However, a loop is not present if CALENDAR_YEAR_LOOKUP is not part of the universe. The universe would pass an integrity check without this table; however, your users may get incorrect results if their query contains measures from both fact tables. Two things will go wrong.

First, promotion costs will be significantly overstated, as the one-to-many join between ARTICLE_LOOK_UP and SHOP_FACTS essentially results in a many-to-many join and Cartesian product between SHOP_FACTS and PRODUCT_PROMOTION_FACTS. If you care to test this to understand what is going on, note that there are 529 unique rows in the SHOP_FACTS table for ARTICLE_ID 145404. When the join is processed via the PRODUCT_PROMOTION_FACTS table, the one row in this fact table is repeated 529 times.

Second, just as a loop will cause rows to be dropped from a query, so will accessing two fact tables via a common dimension table. Thus, users will not get all sales for all products; instead, they will get only sales in which a corresponding ARTICLE_ID exists in the PRODUCT_PROMOTION_FACTS table. This is referred to as a *chasm trap*, as results seem to disappear into a chasm. Additionally, if there are multiple rows in the sales table, rows from the promotion table are overstated.

Figure 6-4 shows how a chasm trap causes you to lose rows, as well as overstates rows. The table on the left shows the chasm trap. The two right-hand tables show the correct results when these individual facts are used in separate queries. At first glance, the results in the left-hand table seem to answer a valid business question: "What were the promotion costs and revenues for all products?" However, because relevant options were not set correctly in the universe, users will get revenues only for those articles that had a promotion. So promotion costs are overstated (wrong value of 97,436,675 versus correct value of 60,975), and revenues for any products that do not have a corresponding promotion disappear down a chasm (understated value of 9,261,619 versus correct value of 36,387,202).

We strongly recommend that you use contexts when your universe contains multiple fact tables so that multiple SQL statements are generated for each dimensional schema. In addition to contexts, the universe parameter Multiple SQL Statements for Each Measure will also prevent this chasm trap.

CAUTION The universe integrity check will never warn you of potential chasm traps, so it's important that you view all possible joins. Keep in mind that you are developing a self-service BI environment in which business users may combine objects in ways you did not anticipate. This design approach is different from designing a single report in which you can precisely control the generated SQL.

Fan Traps and Many-to-Many Joins

Many people get confused by *fan traps* and *chasm traps*. These are two types of join problems that lead to incorrect results. How they are different matters little. In fact, we don't even like to discuss them, because if you follow the guidelines discussed in the other sections, you should never encounter either type. Furthermore, if you use these terms with SQL programmers, they will stare at you dumbfounded—*a what trap?* However, the vendor uses these terms in education courses and help text, so we describe them briefly.

As discussed in the previous section, a chasm trap occurs when you lose results by joining two fact tables to a common lookup table. With a fan trap, the opposite happens: your results are overstated (spread like a fan) because a Cartesian product occurs when aggregates go across one-to-many joins. A prime example of a fan trap is joining ORDER_HEADER to ORDER_DETAIL. This is typically a one-to-many join relationship. Freight exists in the ORDER_HEADER table, and Quantity exists in the ORDER_DETAIL table. Freight will be fanned, or overstated, by however many line items there are in the ORDER_DETAIL table.

Chasm Trap Results

Article Id	Promotion Cost	Sum of Amount So
145,404	5,025,500	435,145.8
165,170	1,320,000	474,172.3
166,544	10,348,000	4,967,526.8
166,550	11,704,000	622,943.4
166,583	10,385,650	604,034.6
166,699	41,314,000	1,412,632.5
167,042	15,142,050	511,546.7
167,695	2,197,475	233,617.8
Sum:	97,436,675	9,261,619.9

Correct Promotion Costs

Article Id	Promotion Cost
145,404	9,500
165,170	1,200
166,544	2,000
166,550	9,500
166,583	12,650
166,699	13,000
167,042	8,050
167,695	5,075
Sum:	60,975

Correct Sales

Sum of Amount Sold
36,387,202.8

Figure 6-4 Chasm traps produce incorrect query results.

Composite Keys and Complex Joins

Fact tables often have several columns that uniquely identify one row of data. In the sample Island Resorts Marketing universe, the CUST_ID and INV_ID columns uniquely identify the records in the SALES table. These two columns together are called a *composite key*.

Lookup or dimension tables also may have a composite key. Neither of the SAP BusinessObjects sample universes contain lookup tables with composite keys, and well-designed data warehouses also should not require them. However, early data warehouses often used composite keys, and transaction systems still do.

For example, to track changes in customer reference data, the month and year may be part of the composite key. To illustrate this concept, we have modified the CUSTOMER table within the sample Island Resorts Marketing database to add the month and year column as MM_YYYY. Figure 6-5 shows multiple records for the customer IDs 106, 207, and 306.

In this example, the data for these three customers has changed as follows:

- Customer 106, Baker, moved from Chicago, Illinois, to Sparta, New Jersey, in April 1997. The row from customer ID 106, MM_YYYY 04-1996 contains old data for the same customer.

- Customer 207, Dupont, divorced and reverted to her maiden name of Hayem in May 1997. The row from customer ID 207, MM_YYYY 05-1997 contains old data for the same customer.

- Customer 306, Jones, married and changed her name to Whitwell in January 2001. The row from customer ID 306, MM_YYYY 04-1996 contains old data for the same customer.

Composite key

	A	B	C	D	E	F	G	H	I
2	Customer	MM_YYYY	First Name	Customer	Address	Phone Number	Age	City	
3	106	04-1996	William	Baker	2890 Grant Avenue	(312) 555 7040	64	Chicago	
4	106	04-1997	William	Baker	71 Westgate Drive	(973) 555 1212	64	Sparta	
5	101	01-1996	Paul	Brendt	10 Jasper Blvd.	(212) 555 2146	19	New York City	
6	207	05-1996	Marie-Chantale	Dupont	37 rue Murat	46 72 23 53	72	Paris	
7	207	05-1997	Marie-Chantale	Hayem	37 rue Murat	46 72 23 53	72	Paris	
8	403	05-1997	Adolph	Durnstein	Thomashof 22	74 5464	36	Dresden	
9	301	06-1996	Caroline	Edwards	68 Downing Street	243 867945	18	London	
10	206	04-1996	Michele	Gentil	17montee des Chenes	65 62 26 13	67	Albertville	
11	105	04-1997	Tony	Goldschmidt	91 Torre drive	(619) 555 6529	55	San Diego	
12	307	05-1997	Priscilla	Hopkins	The Gables	634 634643	73	Cardiff	
13	306	04-1996	Mary	Jones	34 Apple Grove	143 546456	68	Oxford	
14	306	01-2001	Mary	Whitwell	2 Church View	143 546456	68	Oxford	
15									

MM_YYYY determines valid row   New last name   New street address   New city

Figure 6-5   This table shows that CUSTOMER_ID and MM_YYYY together uniquely identify each record, as customer names and addresses have changed over the years.

When analyzing reservations by city or by last name, the join between CUSTOMER and RESERVATIONS must now include MM_YYYY to RES_DATE, *in addition to* CUST_ID. It's technically possible to create this join by drawing two separate lines between the individual fields, as shown in the following example. However, the IDT will not be able to correctly detect cardinalities. In earlier versions of the software, Designer might interpret this as a loop. The IDT does not. It is preferable to create this as a compound via one join statement.

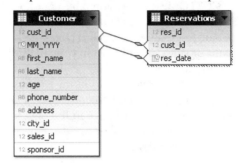

To correctly create a complex join, select the join on CUST_ID and double-click it to bring up the Edit Join dialog box. CTRL-click to select the additional join relationships between the two tables. Alternatively, in the Expression box, type **AND** at the end of the join statement. As soon as you enter AND, the IDT changes the join type to complex. Your join should read as follows:

```
Customer.cust_id=Reservations.cust_id AND Customer.MM_YYYY=Reservations.res_date
```

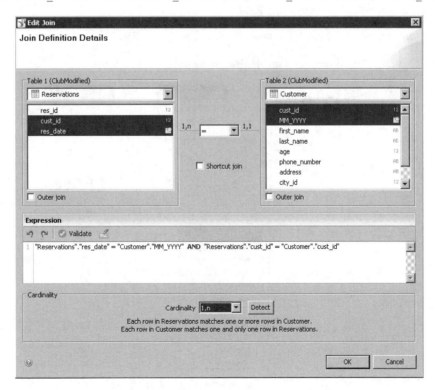

Aliases

When the IDT sees two join statements between the same two tables, it may propose an *alias* to resolve the loop. It also may not propose an alias and will only advise you that the cardinalities are confusing. If your company has multiple SQL tools accessing a data warehouse, your DBA may have resolved many of these issues by creating synonyms or views in the RDBMS. For example, one physical CUSTOMER dimension table could be joined to a fact table two times as synonyms SHIP_TO_CUSTOMER and SOLD_TO_CUSTOMER. Synonyms in the source RDBMS appear in the data foundation as physical tables, even though they behave much like aliases. If such synonyms or views do not exist in your RDBMS, create an alias to use one physical table in different ways.

When you insert a table that already exists in the universe, the IDT will prompt you to create an alias and will propose a new table name "Alias of *Duplicate Table*," where *Duplicate Table* is the physical table used more than once in the data foundation. Alternatively, you can ask the IDT to detect potential aliases, or you can consciously choose tables that you know you want to use in multiple ways.

Detecting Aliases

The sample Island Resorts Marketing universe contains information about resorts and customers who visit those resorts. Resorts can be located in different countries, and customers can be located in different countries. If you were building this universe from scratch, the IDT would have detected a join between the following tables:

```
COUNTRY.COUNTRY_ID=REGION.COUNTRY_ID
COUNTRY.COUNTRY_ID=RESORT.COUNTRY_ID
RESORT.COUNTRY_ID=REGION.COUNTRY_ID
```

Note in the following example that these joins cause a loop.

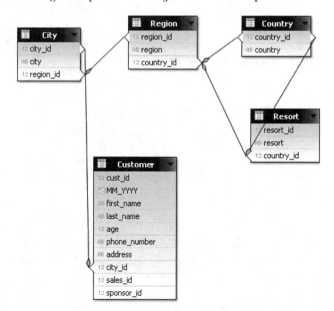

At this point, loop detection would suggest using aliases to resolve these loops. As you are a good data modeler who understands from the business rules that "country" has multiple meanings, you agree and can move directly to alias detection, as follows:

1. Create a new data foundation that includes the five tables shown in the preceding example: COUNTRY, CUSTOMER, CITY, REGION, and RESORT. The CUSTOMER and CITY tables are not necessary to create the loop. but are included to clarify how COUNTRY is used in two different ways, with two different business meanings.

2. Select the Aliases and Contexts tab.

3. Select Detect Aliases from the toolbar. The IDT suggests that an alias should be created for COUNTRY called COUNTRY_RESORT.

4. Check the box next to the table COUNTRY. Notice that a new table appears in green in the Data Foundation pane.

5. Click OK to confirm the alias creation.

As shown in Figure 6-6, a new table appears, with the physical table name in parentheses. The alias table also appears in the list on the left.

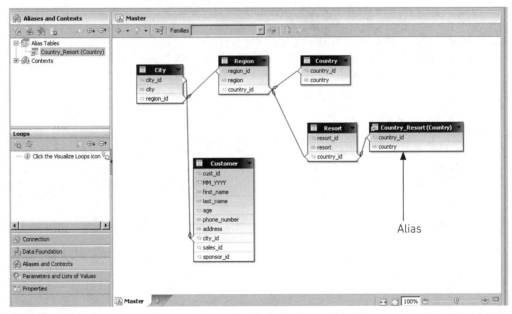

Figure 6-6   With aliases, the universe no longer contains a loop. The alias name replaces the physical table name in parentheses.

Inserting Aliases Manually

You may want to insert an alias manually if the IDT does not propose an alias that makes business sense or if you know your business meanings in advance. Here's how to create the same COUNTRY_RESORT alias discussed in the previous section manually:

1. Select the COUNTRY table from the Master structure pane on the right.
2. Right-click and select Insert | Insert Alias from the pop-up menu.
3. When prompted, accept the default name Alias of Country. You cannot change alias names in this dialog box. Click OK.
4. Expand the Alias Tables folder in the Aliases and Contexts pane on the left.
5. Select Alias of Country, right-click it, and choose Edit.
6. Replace the default name with **COUNTRY_RESORT** as the new alias name.
7. Click OK to close the dialog box.
8. Add a join between REGION.COUNTRY_ID and the new alias, COUNTRY_RESORT.COUNTRY_ID.

NOTE When you modify the alias name, only the additional part of the name is used in naming new objects in the business layer.

Aliases in SQL

In generating the SQL, the query engine will use the alias name in the column selection, join statements, and WHERE clause. In the FROM section, the query engine replaces the physical table name with the new alias name.

In the Island Resorts Marketing universe example, the alias created was COUNTRY_RESORT (based on the physical table COUNTRY). Through the use of aliases, a user can ask the question "What are the sales for our customers in Germany who wish to stay in our resorts in the United States?" This generates the following SQL:

```
SELECT
Country.country,
Resort_Country.country,  ◄——————— Alias name
  sum(Invoice_Line.days * Invoice_Line.nb_guests * Service.price)
FROM
  Country,
  Country  Resort_Country,  ◄——————— Declaring the alias here allows it to be used
Invoice_Line,                           elsewhere in the query.
  Service,
  Resort,
Service_Line,
  Sales,
  Customer,
  City,
  Region
```

```
WHERE
  ( City.city_id=Customer.city_id  )
  AND  ( City.region_id=Region.region_id  )
  AND  ( Country.country_id=Region.country_id  )
  AND  ( Resort_Country.country_id=Resort.country_id  )
  AND  ( Customer.cust_id=Sales.cust_id  )
  AND  ( Sales.inv_id=Invoice_Line.inv_id  )
  AND  ( Invoice_Line.service_id=Service.service_id  )
  AND  ( Resort.resort_id=Service_Line.resort_id  )
  AND  ( Service.sl_id=Service_Line.sl_id  )
  AND
  (
Country.country  =  'Germany'
   AND
Resort_Country.country  =  'US'
  )
GROUP BY
Country.country,
Resort_Country.country
```

Contexts Versus Aliases

In an attempt to avoid contexts, some designers will turn to aliases as a way of breaking a loop and avoiding a context. This is the wrong use of aliases.

While creating an alias might result in valid join statements, it can create an unnecessarily complicated universe and more objects (that really mean the same thing). Instead, try to understand the data from the business perspective. Use contexts to group the related schemas, and use aliases only when one table can have multiple *meanings*, such as a Sold To Customer versus a Ship To Customer or a Manager who is also an Employee.

Self-Joins and Aliases

Self-joins are a way of joining a table to itself. You may need to use one as a way of restricting rows in a table or because the same values are used in two columns in the same table. A classic example is that of employees. Employees have managers, so the employee ID in one column is also used in the manager ID in another column.

Implementing a Self-Join

The following example uses data from Microsoft SQL Server AdventureWorks schema. In this schema, every employee has a supervisor. Managers may supervise one or more employees. As shown in Figure 6-7, the employee ID is also used to indicate the manager ID in the same table. So Guy Gilbert (1) reports to or is managed by Jo Brown (16). Jo Brown manages multiple employees.

To implement the self-join, first create an alias for the VEMPLOYEE table called VEMPLOYEE_MANAGER. Next, create the join that uses the alias. By using the alias, you are self-joining the EMPLOYEE_ID field in one table to the MANAGER_ID field in the same table; the alias makes it appear as if you were joining two different tables. To get a list

Employee Id	Employee Full Name	Employee Id Manager	Last Name Manager
1	GuyGilbert	16	Brown
57	AnnikStahl	16	Brown
80	RebeccaLaszlo	16	Brown
89	MargieShoop	16	Brown
129	MarkMcArthur	16	Brown
137	BrittaSimon	16	Brown
157	BrandonHeidepriem	16	Brown
162	JoseLugo	16	Brown
175	SuchitraMohan	16	Brown
213	ChrisOkelberry	16	Brown
235	KimAbercrombie	16	Brown
247	EdDudenhoefer	16	Brown
16	JoBrown	21	Krebs

Figure 6-7 Employees report to managers, requiring a self-join using aliases.

of any employees that do not report to a manager (the CEO, for example), you may need to include an outer join on the VEMPLOYEE_MANAGER alias.

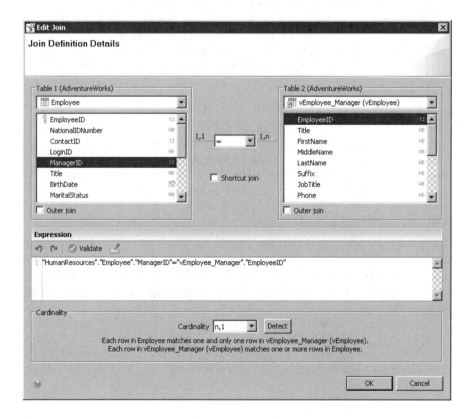

This last part is tricky. If you left the universe the way it is now, it would work fine as long as objects from EMP_MANAGER were never used in a report by itself. For example, if you tried to create a report that listed managers only, all employees would be listed on this report, as the self-join would not be activated: Guy Gilbert (1) would appear on the report, even though he is never listed in the VEMPLOYEE.MANAGER_ID column. To ensure that you get a list of managers only, you must force the self-join, as described in the next section.

Forcing a Join

To ensure the self-join is activated any time you select objects from the VEMPLOYEE_ MANAGER alias, you must include extra tables in each relevant object definition in the business layer. Some designers may try to accomplish something similar by adding the join statement in the WHERE clause of the relevant objects. However, with this approach, the WHERE statement is added to the SQL statement multiple times according to how many objects contain the condition.

To force a join, modify the relevant object definitions, click the ellipse next to the Extra Tables option, and select the additional table. (See Chapter 7 for details on how to create and modify business layer objects.)

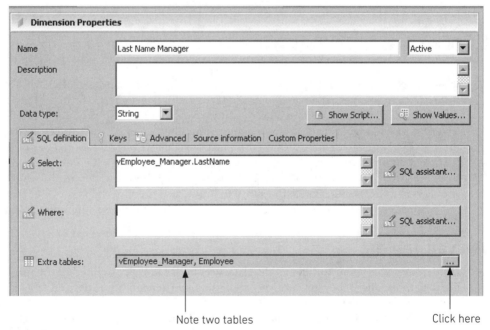

Note two tables   Click here

Shortcut Joins

Shortcut joins allow you to define an alternative, faster join path between two tables. Without the use of a shortcut join, your query would need to go through a huge fact table to create simple reference lists. To the unsuspecting user, this type of query could take hours.

To help you understand shortcut joins, consider a data foundation that includes orders, products, and plants. Products can be ordered, and plants manufacture products. Figure 6-8

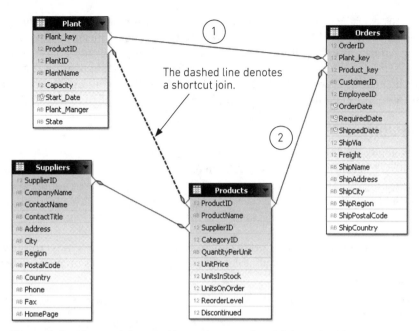

The dashed line denotes a shortcut join.

Figure 6-8 Shortcut joins provide an alternate, faster join path without creating a loop.

shows an example of a shortcut join between the PLANT table and the PRODUCTS table. If the shortcut join were a normal join, the IDT would detect a loop. If you did not define a shortcut join and users wanted a list of which plants made which products, their query would be forced to join three tables together (join lines 2 and 3) and unnecessarily go through the large 30-million-row ORDERS fact table. The shortcut join is a way of telling the query engine that this is the fastest path to use for queries in which no objects come from the ORDERS fact table. Therefore, if users create a report to determine which suppliers ship to specific plants, the shortcut join is also used.

To create a shortcut join, check the Shortcut join box in the Edit Join dialog box.

Derived Tables

Derived tables are similar to views in the database, but as they are defined in the universe in the data foundation, they give universe designers more flexibility. A derived table is a query that you can reference as a table.

As a derived table is a query and not a physical table, it's important to understand that the same performance issues that affect queries also affect derived tables:

- Do *not* use derived tables in place of aggregate tables. Aggregate tables must be physical tables built by the DBA to provide fast query performance.

- Do use derived tables that minimize the complexity of the queries users must create themselves.

- Do use derived tables in place of views and stored procedures that in the past you would have asked a DBA to create.

Derived tables may be most useful when you want to UNION two queries together (for example, a supplier and customer table combined to create a vendor table), when you want to include @Variable in the query logic, and in some cases, when you have different aggregation levels. Derived tables are often an alternative to a DBA-created stored procedure in the database.

See Chapter 9 for step-by-step instructions on creating derived tables.

Data Foundation Properties

A number of parameters that were once set in a single dialog box in the former Designer are now set either in the data foundation properties or in the business layer query options. Note that in order for this properties pane to appear, your mouse must be positioned on the *datafoundation*.dfx item and not on an individual table.

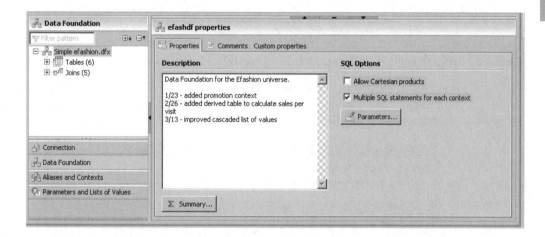

The data foundation Properties tab includes the following settings:

- **Description**   In the Description box, you can provide comments on how this data foundation will be used or revision notes. Business users will not see this text.

- **Allow Cartesian products**   Cartesian products or cross joins can occur when the join relationship is not clear, so the results are overstated. If there is no relationship between two tables, the query result will join every row in one table with every row in another table. This is generally not an intended query result, so this option should be disabled.

- **Multiple SQL statements for each context**   In most universes, you will want to enable multiple SQL statements for each context. This way, users can create queries such as those that compare sales and promotion, debits and credits, or inventory and sales in a single query. When this option is disabled, the users will receive an error stating that their query contains an incompatible combination of objects.

- **SQL Parameters**   Clicking the SQL Parameters button opens the Query Script Parameters dialog box. Parameters set here impact the way the SQL is generated. Parameters in which the default has been changed are reflected in bold. For

Parameter	Options	Default	Description
ANSI92	Yes or No	No	Determines the type of SQL generated (whether it is ANSI 92 compliant).
DISTINCT_ VALUES	GROUPBY or DISTINCT	DISTINCT	Determines how the SQL for a list of values (LOV) is generated (see Chapter 8). With the default settings, the LOV query uses SELECT DISTINCT, which can be slow against large tables.
JOIN_BY_SQL	Yes or No	No	Processes multiple SELECT statements on the RDBMS rather than on the Enterprise server. Consider enabling this option if Crystal Reports authors need to generate queries with multiple contexts.
MAX_INLIST_ VALUES	*NN* up to 256	99	Specifies the maximum values users can select when using IN LIST in query conditions.

Table 6-3   Database Parameters Configurable per Universe

example, ANSI92 has been changed from the default of No to Yes here. The full list of parameters is documented in the online help. Table 6-3 lists commonly changed parameters.

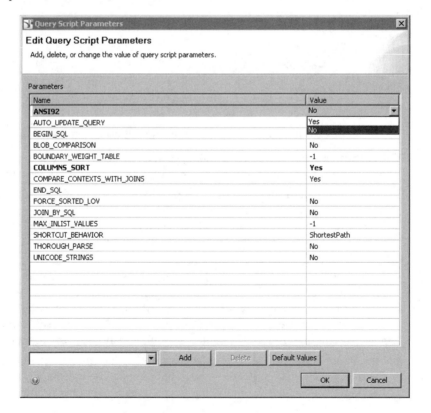

Summary

The data foundation provides information about the underlying physical structure for your universe. Joins are an important element of the data foundation, because they allow data from different tables to be used together. Contexts help group related tables and join statements together. Aliases allow the same physical table to be used in different ways and in multiple joins to the same fact table.

While users may never see joins, if the universe designer makes mistakes in the joins and related settings, then objects may not work with one another—or worse, they give users incorrect results. To define joins correctly, keep in mind the following guidelines:

- Define joins based on the actual data and not just the logical business model.
- If you start using contexts, you must keep using them and ensure all tables belong to at least one context.
- Use aliases to create multiple joins between the same two tables that have different business meanings.
- Use shortcut joins to provide faster paths between two tables that have a direct relationship, rather than forcing a join through a fact table.

CHAPTER 7

Business Layer Basics

Much of your work on the universe so far has been on the behind-the-scenes connections and data foundation elements. The business layer, meanwhile, is the part that is most visible to users.

This chapter focuses on the basics of the business layer. Chapters 8 and 9 explain how to make your universe more robust.

The Business Layer Pane

As shown in Figure 7-1, the Business Layer pane on the left is what users will see when they create a new query or insert a table or graph into an existing document. The dimensions, filters, measures, and other business layer objects are discussed in the next section.

When you first open a business layer, the universe parameters appear in the top right. As you navigate the Business Layer pane on the left, the properties for individual objects appear. For example, in Figure 7-1, the Measure Properties pane appears for the object *Promotion Cost.*

The bottom-right pane shows the data foundation associated with this business layer, and the physical table and column associated with the selected object. This is just a preview of the data foundation; you cannot make changes to the data foundation here.

You can choose to minimize, maximize, or restore the split-screen mode for the data foundation preview using the buttons above the preview, as follows:

- To hide the data foundation preview, click the downward-pointing triangle.
- To maximize the data foundation preview, click the upward-pointing triangle.
- To restore either mode to a split screen, click the horizontal line.

To modify the data foundation associated with this business layer, click the Edit Data Foundation button.

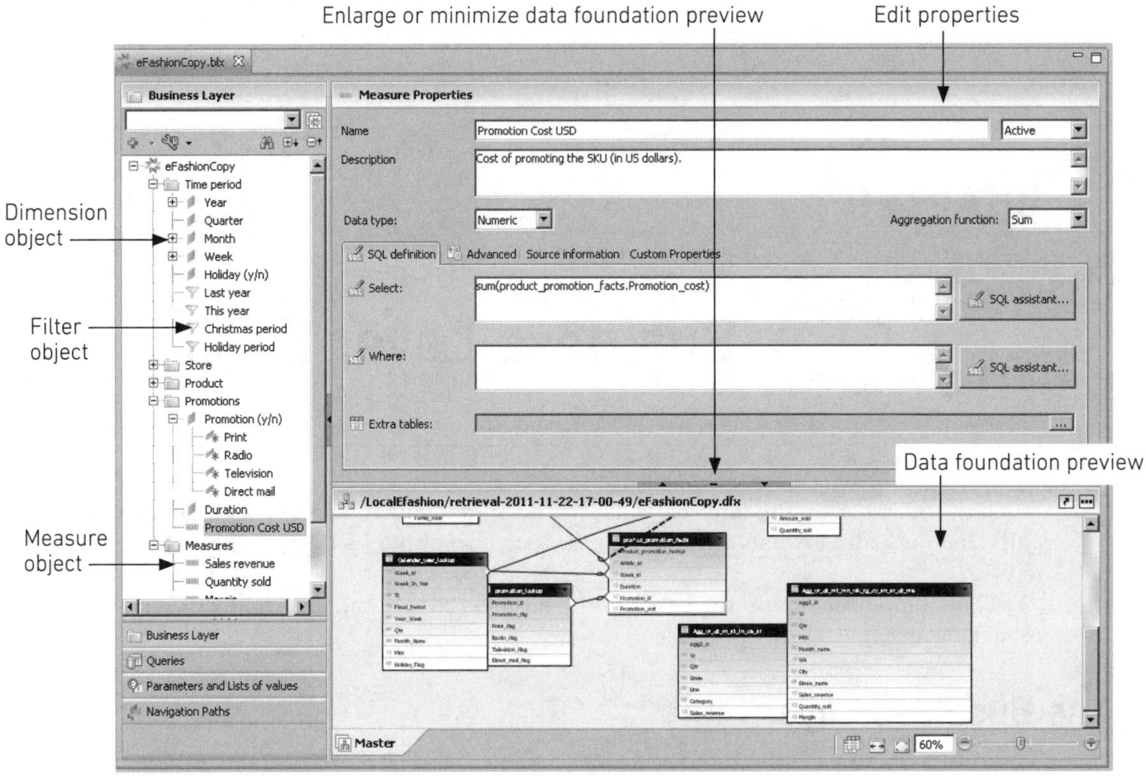

Enlarge or minimize data foundation preview   Edit properties

Dimension object

Filter object

Measure object

Data foundation preview

Figure 7-1 The business layer shows objects as they appear to users when building a query.

To navigate to particular objects within the business layer, click the plus (+) button to expand items in a folder, or click the minus (–) button to collapse the individual objects within a folder.

This table shows additional options available on the Business Layer pane toolbar.

Button	Name	Function
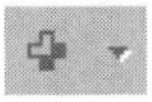	Insert	Opens the Insert menu to insert a new dimension or measure
	Display Options	Displays all objects or hides unused objects
	Show/Hide Search	Shows or hides a search panel to let you search for objects
	Manage Business Layer Views	Allows you to create views of groups of business layer objects for ease of navigation and security

Business Layer Objects

Within the business layer, folders, dimensions, and measures are the primary items a user sees when building a new query or working with an existing report. *Folders* allow you to organize objects such as measures and dimensions in much the same way as you organize documents into file folders. *Measures* and *dimensions* correspond to columns of data in a database table. These objects can be much more powerful than raw data lists, enabling you to add intelligence such as aggregations, transformations, prompts, and formatting.

   Filter and *attribute* objects are also available. The following sections describe the business layer objects.

Folder Objects

A *folder* is a way to group dimensions and measures. Folders in the IDT are synonymous with classes in the Universe Design Tool. However, the term *classes* is not generally used in the IDT, although it appears occasionally.

   You can have multiple levels of folders for folders that have a large number of objects. These groupings are purely to ease navigation for the users. If you have a lot of data elements that are not used on a regular basis, placing these objects further within a subfolder makes the universe appear less busy or difficult. However, if the information is used frequently, do not bury the dimensions, as it forces users to click more than necessary.

NOTE In the eFashion universe, the promotional media of *Print, Radio, Television,* and *DirectMail* are attributes of the base object *Promotion (y/n)* (see Figure 7-1). These details automatically become organized in a separate folder within *Promotion (y/n),* making the universe appear less cluttered. Specifying an object as an attribute rather than a dimension also means it will not be available for multidimensional analyses.

Dimension Objects

A *dimension* object, denoted by a blue cube, is typically textual information by which users analyze numeric measures, such as product, region, or month. A dimension object often comes from the lookup or reference tables within the universe. Dimensions are usually textual or date information, or numeric codes, such as product numbers and customer numbers.

   If your data warehouse uses keys for reference information, then your dimension objects will point to a lookup table. However, if your universe accesses a transaction system, or if meaningful codes and IDs are stored in your fact table, you face a decision of whether to point the dimension object to the dimension table or to the fact table.

   Some universe developers will mistakenly point the dimension object to the fact table, trying to reduce the number of joins for performance reasons. Others will duplicate the object for each occurrence in a different table. Don't make these mistakes. Create one dimension object that points to the lookup table. This makes for the simplest universe for users, who are your primary concern. Additionally, you may be able to specify keys for each object that can minimize the number of joins to process a query (see the "Dimension Keys" section later in this chapter).

TIP Have one object point to the dimension table, rather than multiple instances of similar fields/foreign key references pointing to multiple tables.

Measure Objects

A *measure* is a number that users wish to analyze. In the IDT, it is denoted with an orange ruler. Measures often come from a fact table, but measures such as number of products or number of days could come from a dimension table. Measures are almost always aggregated in some form, such as sum, count, average, min, or max.

The only measure that is not aggregated is unit price. Price is a measure, but it applies to one particular product, and it is wrong from a business viewpoint to sum prices across multiple product lines. *Average* price across multiple product lines would be a more appropriate aggregation; however, the business layer should then contain two distinct price objects to ensure users can query both unit price and average price.

Universe designers may get confused about measures that apply to one point in time, such as inventory quantity, account balances, and number of customers. Measures that should not be aggregated by time (but that may be aggregated by other dimensions such as region or product) are referred to as *semi-additive measures*. Unfortunately, Web Intelligence does not provide a solution to ensure that users do not aggregate these measures across time; they are either aggregated or not. Certain OLAP tools, such as Microsoft Analysis Services and Oracle Essbase, do provide capabilities to prevent incorrect aggregation by time. With such measures, many designers will think it too risky to allow users to make the mistake of aggregating ending inventory/balances across time.

How do users make this mistake? Figure 7-2 gives an example from a fictitious bank account. Using the data in Figure 7-2 as an example, assume that the universe references two fact tables: daily debits and credits in one fact table and daily account balances in a second fact table. If a user builds one query that accesses both tables, the user will generally insert a condition where month equals September. Web Intelligence would tell the user that the ending account balance is $129,855, rather than the correct number of $9,134 (a more attractive bank balance but not correct!).

Users might recognize an inventory or account balance that is so blatantly wrong. However, good universe designers will take extra precautions in designing a universe to guarantee correct answers, no matter how users might construct a query. Some designers will remove the SUM aggregate from all semi-additive measures, ensuring users receive a correct value for every row for each day. This is not a good solution, because now users cannot ask questions like, "What are my global inventories for a given product across all plants?" and "What is my total account balance across my various bank accounts?" As discussed in Chapter 6, the use of contexts is the first step to allowing users to pose these kinds of business questions. Chapter 9 discusses other ways to prevent users from constructing an inaccurate query, but the best practice is to include the SUM aggregate.

TIP Always use an aggregate function on a measure object, unless that measure is a unit price or other similar number.

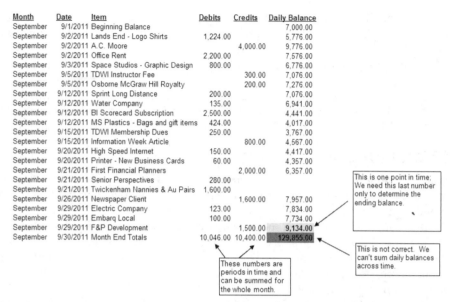

Figure 7-2   Account balances and other semi-additive measures should not be aggregated over time.

Filter Objects

Filter objects allow users to access predefined filters that the designer specifies in the WHERE clause of a query. Filter objects are denoted with a yellow filter symbol. In the example shown in Figure 7-1, the objects *Last year* and *Christmas period* are filter objects. In the Universe Design Tool, these are referred to as *condition objects*.

Attribute Objects

An attribute object provides additional information about a particular dimension. Attributes in the IDT are synonymous with details in the Universe Design Tool. In Figure 7-1, *Print, Radio, Television,* and *Direct mail* are attribute objects. Within a customer dimension, age, fax, phone number, street address, and notes are typical attributes.

Attributes may supply users with additional ways to analyze the measures, or they may be purely informational. For example, users may want to analyze sales by customer age group but rarely by customers' individual street addresses. In this respect, the street address is purely informational.

If you are using an OLAP database, Microsoft Analysis Services refers to details as *member properties*. Oracle Essbase refers to them as *attributes*.

Classifying an object as a dimension or as an attribute has no impact on the SQL generation. An object may be defined as an attribute rather than a dimension for primarily visual reasons in the folders, to ease user querying.

The main limitation with attribute objects is that they are not hierarchical. For example, if age is an attribute, then ranges within age, such as Youth, Adult, and Senior, cannot be grouped.

Attributes are denoted with a blue tilted rectangle and green asterisk in the business layer.

NOTE The Insert Attribute menu appears only when you have initially selected a dimension with which you wish to associate the attribute.

Object Ordering

When you build your business layer, you can add individual objects one at a time, or you can have the business layer automatically created from all tables and fields in the data foundation.

By default, dimensions and measures are created in the order in which they are stored in the physical tables. In earlier releases, you could choose to sort them alphabetically using the COLUMNS_SORT parameter. The default is No, which means that columns in tables appear in physical order. The vendor is deprecating this parameter, and although it appears as an option, it does not work.

The order of the columns in the table browser and the order of the objects that users see are only partially related. If you do not like either alphabetical or physical table structure order, you can manually reorder the objects by dragging and dropping them.

Notice in the following example from the Simple eFashion universe you created in Chapter 6 that objects in the *Calendar Year Lookup* folder are in the same order as in the physical table CALENDAR_YEAR_LOOKUP.

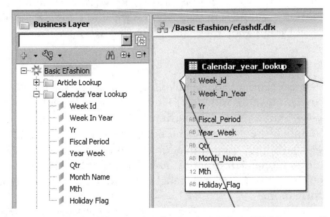

This order is really not logical from a business viewpoint. *Week* is a smaller increment than *Year*, but then *Month* appears after *Quarter*. However, alphabetical is not logical either. Therefore, you must manually re-sort the objects into incremental order by dragging and dropping.

While you are dragging an object, the mouse cursor will change to a horizontal bar to show where in the folder the object will be placed. Note that the line appears below the object that the moved object will be inserted *above* (it's somewhat misleading!).

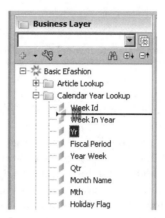

The following example shows how you want the sort order to follow time increments, running from *year* to *month* to *week*. As explained in Chapter 11, for multidimensional analysis, the larger increment or grouping should always appear at the top, and the most detailed should be at the bottom. This sort order facilitates drill-down.

Currently, the naming of these objects is not particularly helpful to the users. What is the difference between *Mth* and *Month Name?* (Naming conventions are discussed in the next section.)

Also, users will never need to access the *Week Id* object that acts as a key to the CALENDAR_YEAR_LOOKUP table. Therefore, this object should either be hidden or deleted altogether.

Object Naming Conventions

In creating your objects, it's important to develop and follow a consistent naming convention. Also, there are a few precautions you should take when renaming objects.

Naming Principles

In choosing names for your objects, use these four *Cs* as naming principles: be customer-oriented, clear, consistent, and concise.

Customer-Oriented

Your universe is for your internal and/or external customers, so you must use business terminology. Anything that reveals technical database-naming conventions does not belong in the business layer.

Clear

The object names must be clear in their meaning. *Customer* is not clear if it could potentially mean *Ship to Customer* or *Sold to Customer*.

Consider the universe design principles discussed in Chapter 4. Who is the target user group for your universe? If these users know of only one type of customer, then *Customer* alone is acceptable as a folder or dimension name. For example, supply chain personnel may only think of the ship-to customer, and accounting personnel may only think of the invoiced or sold-to customer. If these two groups of users will have separate universes, then *Customer* is acceptable. If they will share a universe, then the names must be clear and explicit.

In the Simple eFashion universe you have developed so far, the object names *Mth* and *Month Name* are not clear. For all a user knows, the object *Mth* could be Jan, 01, or January.

Consistent

Object names should be consistent in two respects:

- Use the same name when you mean the same thing. Always refer to the customer as the *customer*, and do not mix in other terminology, such as *client* or *business partner*.
- Use the same clarifiers consistently. If your universe has columns that are IDs or codes and columns that are names or descriptions, then append these clarifiers consistently, as Table 7-1 illustrates.

Concise

Object names should be concise, as they become the default column heading in a report. The bad thing about this is that a name like *Article code* can be a long column heading if most of your article codes are only four characters. In such a scenario, the abbreviated form *SKU* or *Gmid* may make for shorter and better column headings.

It would be a nice feature if the IDT allowed you to centrally rename a column heading (just as SQL does), but unfortunately, it does not. Column headings can be renamed and wrapped within individual reports. Therefore, you can consider clear business terms a higher priority than concise column headings.

Warning: Cutting and Pasting Objects and Object IDs

In early versions of BusinessObjects, object names within individual user queries and reports needed to match object names within the universe. For example, in the Simple eFashion universe, there is a *Mth* object. Unless users look at the data, they cannot be sure whether this is the month name, a number, or a three-character abbreviation. As a universe designer, you can rename *Mth* to *Month Number* in the universe, and all the user reports will automatically reflect this new object name.

Initial Object Name	Considerations	Suggested Name
Article code	This object name is consistent, assuming *article* is the generally used business term. The *code* qualifier makes it clear.	*Article code*
Article name	This object name is consistent, assuming *article* is the generally used business term. The *name* qualifier makes it clear.	*Article name*
Article	It's not clear if this object refers to an article code or a description, unless all description fields have a name or description appended at the end of the object name and, by default, everything else is a code or a number.	*Article code*
SKU	Duplicate of *Article code* and not the generally accepted business term. However, it is concise, which would make it a nice column heading in a report.	*Article code*
Product	Duplicate of *Article code* or *SKU*. Also, it's not clear if this is a code or a description object.	*Article code*
Gmid	*Gmid* is the abbreviation for global material identification as used in the OLTP system. Data-entry users know the term, but business users within the target universe group probably do not.	*Article code*

Table 7-1   Object Names Should Follow the Four Cs: Be Customer-Oriented, Clear, Consistent, and Concise

Often in renaming objects, a universe designer will make the mistake of cutting and pasting the original object, such as *Mth*, to a new object, such as one titled *MonthNumber*. This is bad practice, as it creates a different object ID, an internal mechanism the IDT uses to keep track of changes to objects. After testing the new *MonthNumber* object, the universe designer will then go back and delete the original *Mth* object. Once the original *Mth* object is deleted, all existing reports that previously used the *Mth* object will generate a meaningless error message:

Users can still view the reports, but as soon as they attempt to refresh the report, they will receive this error. (Earlier versions of the product gave a more meaningful error message indicating that an object was missing.) If the universe designer had modified the original *Mth* object, then the existing queries and reports would have automatically been updated with the new object name.

To minimize report errors, take these precautions:

- Modify existing objects when you really wish to change the name or underlying SQL. Avoid re-creating new objects to replace old ones.

- Always make a backup copy of a universe. One client we worked with deleted a number of objects accidentally. The designer thought he had fixed the problem by simply re-creating the objects with the exact same object names (which didn't work). A backup version of the universe allowed us to access and restore the original object IDs.

Creating a Business Layer

Now that you are familiar with basic object and business layer concepts, you can create a simple business layer. Follow these steps:

1. From the main IDT toolbar, click New and select Business Layer.

2. Choose the type of data source. In this example, select Relational Data Source. Then click Next.

3. When prompted, give the business layer a name. This is the name that will appear to end users as a universe. In this example, enter **Simple eFashion**.

4. Optionally, enter a description. Then click Next.

5. Choose the data foundation by clicking the ellipse button. If you followed the steps in Chapter 5, you should have a basic data foundation called Simple eFashion. Select OK to close the data foundation browser.

6. Check the box to automatically create classes (folders) and objects.

7. Click Finish to create the business layer.

8. Save the business layer file.

You can later create a new folder by dragging-and-dropping an entire table from the data foundation preview into the business layer. You can also create individual objects by dragging single fields from the data foundation preview to a particular folder.

ModifyingObjects

If you have had the IDT automatically create folders and objects, then much of your work now will be to modify names and settings for those objects. In the next example, you will modify the dimension object named *Mth* in the folder *Calendar Year Lookup*.

1. Select the object *Mth* to open the Dimension Properties pane. This pane has several tabs: SQL definition, Keys, Advanced, Source Information, and Custom Properties. The SQL definition tab contains the object name, status, data type, SQL, and description or help text.

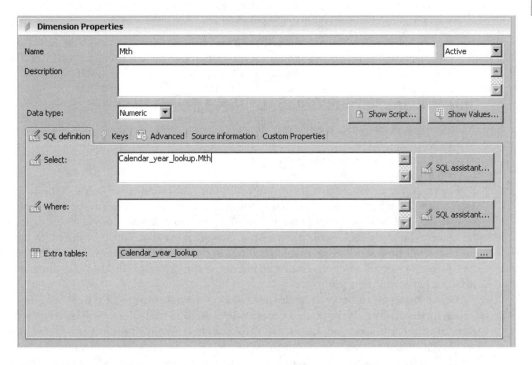

NOTE If your data foundation preview is full-screen, the related field for month is highlighted in the entity relationship diagram. To display the Dimension Properties pane, either double-click the *Mth* object or click the minimize pane icon.

2. Change the object name from *Mth* to **Month Number**.
3. The data type relates to the field format in the source database, as well as to how users will choose to manipulate the object's data in a report. Leave the Data type option set to Numeric.

4. In the Description box, enter help text that is meaningful for users. If users will use a field as part of a condition, you can give them an indication of the format. Enter the following help text: **Month Number is a numeric field that shows the month in which the sale or promotion occurred. For example, January is equal to 1**.

5. The Select box contains the SQL SELECT statement used to dynamically build the user's query. If you are creating a new object, it is best to use the SQL Assistant to select tables and columns to ensure the SQL is accurate.

6. The Where box is used to generate the WHERE clause within a SQL statement. It's important to remember that the query engine appends the WHERE clause to the entire query (assuming the particular object is used in the query). For example, suppose you have an object *Current Year Sales* with a WHERE clause of Year=2012, and a *Last Year Sales* object where Year=2011. If a user selects both objects for one report, then no data will be returned, because the two WHERE clauses are mutually exclusive. Therefore, this box is most often left blank or used for filter objects and parameters, as described in Chapter 9.

7. The Extra Tables box is used to force a join between the table required for the current object with an additional table, or if more than one table is used in the SELECT or WHERE clause. This is explained in Chapter 6 in the section on self-joins.

Object Types Versus Database Field Format

In the preceding example, you left the object type as numeric to match the data source field format. Normally, these are the same, and keeping them that way can prevent a number of errors. There is, however, one possible exception: when your source system is a number field that you will never use as a measure.

For example, product ID and customer number may be numeric fields in the source system, but you will rarely want to treat them as numbers (unless the coding has some meaningful logic that you wish to manipulate). In previous BusinessObjects versions, setting the object type to character could prevent any object misuse. However, some of the user interfaces will now generate errors depending on the type of mismatch. Therefore, editing the display format is a safer alternative to changing the data type. Table 7-2 summarizes the different types and their settings.

When you specify an object as numeric (whether or not you specify it as a measure), certain functionality in Web Intelligence is available to end users. Users will be able to do sums, divisions, averages, and so forth on these numbers. From a business point of view, these calculations make no sense against most ID fields. The only calculation that makes sense is a count: How many new products sold this month? How many customers do I have? The count aggregation is available to all objects, regardless of their types (numeric, date, or string).

For example, in the eFashion universe, from a business point of view, *Month Number* would more ideally be a date type object. This would allow users to use all the date functions within Web Intelligence formulas. However, it is a numeric field in the physical

Object Type	Description
Member	Member of a set, used for hierarchical data.
String	Fields that are character in the data source should be set to string as the object type.
Long Text	Long text fields are generally used for comments and note fields.
Numeric	Any measure objects must have the numeric object type.
Boolean	This type returns 1 or 0 or Y or N.
DateTime	This type is for the date and time.
Date	Fields that are in date format in the data source should be set to the date type in the business layer.
Blob	This type is for binary large objects (BLOBs), such as images.

Table 7-2   Object Types Correspond to Physical Database Field Formats

database, and if you specify it as a date type object in the universe, users will receive an error when executing a query. If users want to display a long month name within a report that is derived from the numeric month (for example, January instead of 1), they must use multiple report functions to convert the numeric field to character, and then to date. In Web Intelligence, the formula looks like this:

```
=Month(ToDate(FormatNumber([Month Number N];"00") ;"MM"))
```

Clearly, having users do extra conversions for what should be a simple task is poor universe design. To prevent users from needing to do extra conversions, a business-oriented universe designer may try to help users by converting the number field to a date field (or number to character, and so on) in the object's SQL SELECT statement. This might seem like a good idea in theory, but in practice, it can pose additional problems in terms of query performance. With most RDBMSs, if you change the appearance of a field, the index will not be used when the query uses such an object as a condition. Therefore, work closely with the DBA or analyze an explain plan whenever you use SQL functionality to convert field types. (See Chapter 9 for more information about creating advanced objects.)

Dimension Keys

The main purpose of keys is to generate more efficient SQL. As discussed earlier in this chapter, when users add conditions to a query, it may be more efficient to filter from the fact table than the dimension table. In earlier versions, there were problems with the key feature, as Web Intelligence generated errors, and the SQL generated sometimes caused the database to return more rows of data than necessary. The query engine in SAP BusinessObjects 4.0 seems to now correctly understand when the ID value is unique for the particular description.

Filtering on columns that contain distinct values and that are indexed columns will always be faster than filtering on columns that contain textual descriptions and that may or may not be indexed. In theory, there are two ways to accomplish this:

- Specify keys in the universe.
- Customize the list of values or parameters, as described in the next chapter.

A *primary key* is a unique identifier for each row in a given table. A *foreign key* is when that same identifier in one table is used in another table. As shown in the following example, ARTICLE_ID is the primary key to the table ARTICLE_LOOKUP. ARTICLE_ID then becomes a foreign key in the SHOP_FACTS table. The primary key to SHOP_FACTS is SHOP_FACTS_ID. SHOP_FACTS_ID is not used as a foreign key elsewhere in this schema.

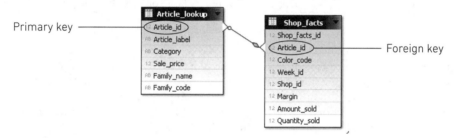

When you define these keys within the universe, you want to define them only for related description objects. It basically will tell the query engine that whenever users filter on a description object, to use the ID field instead. If you define keys on objects for other columns, it provides no benefit and may result in less efficient SQL.

For example, suppose that a user wants to analyze sales for blazers, or ARTICLE_ID 158152. The user has no idea what the article ID is, and you have not customized the list of values. The following SQL would be generated by default:

```
SELECT DISTINCT
Article_lookup.Article_label,
  sum(Shop_facts.Amount_sold)
FROM
Shop_facts,
Article_lookup
WHERE
  ( Article_lookup.Article_id=Shop_facts.Article_id  )
  AND  (
Article_lookup.Article_label  =  'Blazer'
  )
GROUP BY
Article_lookup.Article_label
```

Notice that the value Blazer is used to filter from the lookup table. However, if you specify the primary and foreign keys on the *Article Label* object, the user builds the query in the exact same way, but with the following SQL:

```
SELECT
  max(
Article_lookup.Article_label  ),
```

```
Article_lookup.Article_id,
  sum(Shop_facts.Amount_sold)
FROM
Article_lookup,
Shop_facts
WHERE
  ( Article_lookup.Article_id=Shop_facts.Article_id  )
  AND
Article_lookup.Article_id  In  ( 158152 )
GROUP BY
Article_lookup.Article_id,
Article_lookup.Article_id
```

Notice that the value 158152 is used to filter from the fact table (not the description Blazer and not from the lookup table, as in the default SQL statement).

To specify the primary and foreign keys for the *Article Label* object in this example, follow these steps:

1. From the Business Layer pane, expand the folder *Article Lookup* by clicking the plus sign (+).

2. Select the object *Article Label* to display the Dimension Properties pane.

3. Select the Keys tab.

4. For most databases, you can click the Detect button, and the IDT will automatically add the relevant primary key and foreign key to the object. With Microsoft Access databases, you must do it manually, as described next.

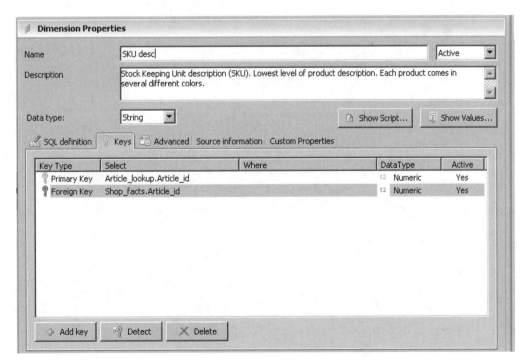

To manually add keys for an object, follow these steps:

1. In the Keys tab of the Dimension Properties pane, click the Add key button. The IDT will insert a key type of Primary Key.

2. Under the Select column, click the ellipse button to launch the SQL Expression Editor. The SELECT statement should be the *table.fieldname* of the primary key. Select ARTICLE_LOOKUP.ARTICLE_ID, or enter it manually. Click OK to close the SQL Expression editor.

3. Repeat steps 1 and 2 to insert the foreign key as SHOP_FACTS.ARTICLE_ID.

To verify the effect of these settings and see the SQL generated, use the Queries tab in the Business Layer pane to build a query that contains a condition on *Article Label.*

CAUTION When a filter value is manually entered rather than chosen from a list of values, the key field is not used. For example, if "Blazer" is entered as a constant, rather than selected from a list of values, the key field is not used.

Advanced Object Settings

The Advanced tab of an object's Properties pane controls who can access the object, where the object can be used in a query, date formats, list of value settings, and display formats.

Access Level

On the Advanced tab, security access level settings interact with other settings discussed in Chapter 12. The Public setting allows all users to access an object and is the default.

Object Can Be Used In

For each object, you can control whether the object can be used in the following:

- **Result**   A result is a column in a query or a report. Most often, all objects are allowed to be used as results. For security reasons, though, you may enable employee ID or Social Security numbers to be used as conditions but never as results that can be displayed as output next to the individual names.

- **Condition**   Conditions relate to the WHERE clause of a SQL statement. If your universe accesses an OLTP system, you may want to disallow nonindexed fields as conditions, as they may result in slow queries and bog down the source system. If you are in a data warehouse environment, we recommend allowing all objects to be used as conditions. It's true that you may want users to search on the indexed CUSTOMER_CODE, for example, but what if there are several related customers that all start with the same first few letters, such as Deloitte & Touche? They could have the forms Deloitte Consulting, Deloitte & Touche Management Solutions, Deloitte Parsippany office, and so on. If you allow *Customer Name* as a condition, a user could select everything starting with Deloitte.

- **Sort**   Sort allows users to sort results on the server rather than on the client. As with conditions, we suggest allowing this on all objects. In most cases, users will sort their results within the report once they see the data. However, if users want to select the top 10 product sales or top 100 customers, the sort must be processed on the server.

NOTE Due to concerns about response-time issues, some DBAs may disagree with our recommendations for where objects can be used, but they provide the most user flexibility. You need to weigh the risk of users creating inefficient queries and affecting system response times versus modifying these options and having an overly restrictive deployment that prevents users from asking valid business questions.

Database Format

The database format setting applies only to date fields and will be dimmed for other types of fields. For example, Americans will refer to April 1 as 04/01. A European will write April 1 as 01/04.

The format displayed in the list of values and in the report comes from either the Control Panel Regional settings (for the Web Intelligence Rich Client) or the BI Launch Pad preferences setting for Locales and Timezone (for Web Intelligence).

Meanwhile, the query engine uses the date format defined in the *database*.prm file to generate the SQL syntax when a date is used in the WHERE clause. Thus, the date you see in a list of values may be different from the date format in the SQL generated. The parameter files are located in the following directory on a Windows server: C:\Program Files (x86)\SAP BusinessObjects\SAP BusinessObjects Enterprise XI 4.0\dataAccess\connectionServer.

In the Island Resorts Marketing universe, TIME.RESERVATION_DATE is stored in Microsoft Access as *YYYY-MM-DD*. When a user places the *Reservation Date* object in the query filters pane, the query engine will automatically take the user's input and convert it to whatever input format is set in the ODBC.PRM file (*YYYY-MM-DD*). Because this format is the same as how the physical date values are stored, the user gets the correct results. However, if the object properties specified a precise time stamp that included hours and minutes or an incompatible date format, users would receive an error or no rows would be returned.

To ensure users get the correct results, specify a date format in the object's Properties pane that corresponds with the date in the physical database. In this example, {\t\s 'yyyy-mm-ddHH:mm:ss'} would be the correct database format if the reservation date also included a precise time of day. Then if a user enters 1/12/2001 as a condition value, the hours and minutes are automatically appended to the condition as Web Intelligence converts the SQL using the specified format:

```
SELECT
Reservations.res_date
FROM
  Reservations
WHERE
Reservations.res_date  =  {ts '2001-01-12 00:00:00'}
```

List of Values

List of value settings control what happens when a user applies a condition in a query and asks to be shown a list of values from which to choose. Lists of values and these settings are discussed in more detail in the next chapter.

Display Options

Display options determine how data is initially formatted within a report display. Users can override any of the default formats by formatting individual cells within a report.

Using display formats, the universe designer can centrally define a format that includes number, alignment, font, border, and shading. Object formatting is often overlooked and left at the default settings. However, for certain objects and formats, you can save hundreds of users time by applying these formats once, rather than requiring each user to change the formats in each report. Also, if you intend to display hyperlinks in a report, you need to format the object to be displayed as HTML or a hyperlink.

In the following example, you will change the object format for the *Promotion Cost* object to include dollar signs with no decimal places.

1. From the Business Layer pane, expand the *Product Promotion Facts* folder by clicking the +.

2. Select the object *Promotion Cost*.

3. The Dimension Properties pane will appear on the right. Select the Advanced tab, and then click the Create display format button in the Display section.

4. Within the Data tab, select Numeric.

5. Click the Custom Format button to open the format editor. For many numeric fields, in particular, key or ID fields, you should set the number format to drop the decimal place.

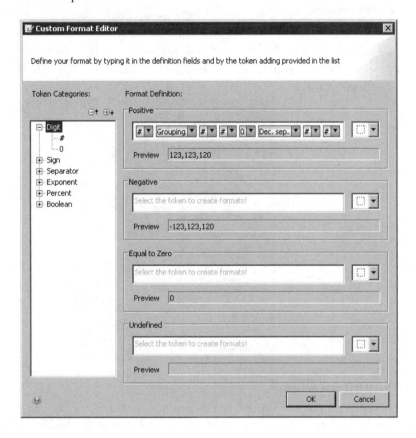

6. Click OK to apply the formatting changes, and then click OK again to close the dialog box.

Many of the formats you can apply in the IDT are also available to end users within Web Intelligence. The various options are discussed in Part III.

Object Source Information

The Source Information tab of an object's Properties pane provides information about where the data originated in the source system. SAP BusinessObjects Data Integrator automatically populates the fields in this tab to provide technical metadata, mapping of columns, and lineage from source systems. This information is currently not displayed to Web Intelligence users.

Working with Objects

You have already seen how objects can be re-sorted within a folder in the *Calendar Year Lookup* example. Objects can also be renamed, deleted, hidden, and modified. In manipulating an object, you can access these actions in a couple of ways:

- Select the item to display the item properties in the right-hand pane.
- Select the item, and then right-click to choose from various actions on the pop-up menu.

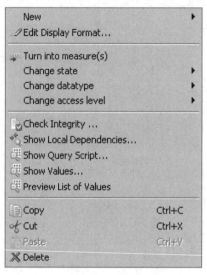

Renaming an Object

You can rename an object through its Properties pane. For example, using the Simple eFashion business layer, you can rename the folder *Calendar Year Lookup* to *Time* as follows:

1. Select the folder *Calendar Year Lookup*.
2. In the Folder Properties pane, replace the current name in the Name box with **Time**.
3. Save the business layer.

Deleting an Object

To delete a folder or object, you can select the object and choose Delete or Cut from the pop-up menu, or use the DELETE or CTRL-X (for Cut) shortcut key. The Delete option deletes the folder or object. The only way to retrieve it again is to use the Undo button. The Cut option removes the object and puts it in the Microsoft Windows clipboard. To retrieve the object, use the Paste option or press CTRL-V.

Let's imagine the worst-case scenario: you accidentally deleted an entire folder. With the Delete option, the contents are not placed in the Windows clipboard. Undo allows you to undo only the last action. If you deleted the object several steps ago, the Undo button no longer can help you. But all is not lost. As explained in Chapter 4, you are working on only a copy of the universe. There is still a universe, with all the old object definitions, stored in the repository. When you make a catastrophic mistake like this, you can reimport a copy of the universe from the repository, although you will lose all other changes you made during this session.

NOTE When you delete a folder, all the objects in that folder will also be deleted. The IDT will warn you against this.

Given that the Delete option doesn't add items to the Windows clipboard, we suggest that you use Cut as often as possible, giving you a better recovery process in case you accidentally delete something important. Keep in mind, though, that if you cut an object and recover it with the Paste option, the object will be assigned a new object ID and will generate errors in any existing user reports that reference the object.

Changing an Object's State

Objects can have one of three states:

- *Active* is the default state and makes the object usable.
- *Hidden* objects are items that appear to you as the designer in italics but that users do not see when creating queries against this universe. Some designers will hide items so that all columns within the data mart appear to the designer but not to the user. Hiding objects may also be useful when you want to hide "work in progress."
- *Deprecated* objects are also hidden to end users and not accessible by other objects. Within the IDT, these appear in italics with a line through the name. You may choose to deprecate an object that you eventually plan to delete.

Either hiding or deprecating an object gives you a transition period to ensure that the removed object will not create problems for the users. You also may want to hide an object that users will never access directly but that you as the designer may reference in WHERE or other object logic.

To change the state of an object, select the item, right-click, and choose Change State from the pop-up menu. Alternatively, from the object's Properties pane, change the default from Active to either Hidden or Deprecated in the drop-down list.

Creating an Attribute Object

You define attribute objects in much the same way that you create dimension objects. The main difference is that you must associate an attribute object with a base dimension object.

In the following example, the attribute object *Street* is associated with the dimension object *Shop Name*. Now *Street* and other related details will appear in a separate folder under *Shop Name*. These objects will not be available when users are drilling down within a report.

The object *Address_1* was created when you inserted the table OUTLET_LOOKUP into the Simple eFashion universe. By default, the IDT listed it as a dimension object. In the following example, you will create a new attribute object named *Street*.

1. From the Business Layer pane, expand the *Outlet Lookup* folder by clicking the +.

2. Position your mouse on the object *Shop Name*.

3. Click the Insert button (with the green plus icon) to add an attribute.

4. A new object named *New Attribute* is automatically created below the *Shop Name* object.

5. In the Attribute Properties pane, replace the name *Address_1* with **Street**. Notice that there is a Dimension box for the dimension object with which this attribute is associated.

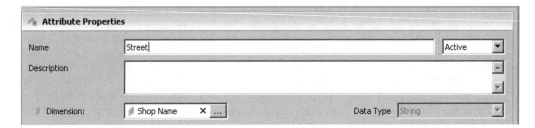

Converting a Dimension to a Measure

The preceding section discussed inserting a new object. You can also convert a dimension object to a measure or vice versa. In this section, you will add a measure object called *Promotion Cost*. This assumes that the table PRODUCT_PROMOTION_FACTS exists in the data foundation.

1. Position your mouse in the *Product Promotion Fact* folder.

2. Select the object *Promotion Cost*.

3. Right-click and select Turn into Measure from the pop-up menu.

TIP If you have several dimension objects that should be converted to measures, use CTRL-click to select multiple objects simultaneously and convert all of them into measures at once.

4. Note that the blue icon for a dimension has been replaced with an orange yardstick. In the Measure Properties pane, there is now an Aggregate function drop-down list.

5. Enter the object description as **Promotion Cost is the dollar value spent on a given radio, newspaper, or other media promotion. Promotion costs are unique for each individual product but are allocated across all stores**.

6. In the Select box of the SQL definition tab, you can either insert the SUM function or use the SQL Assistant to access the full SELECT statement and SQL functions. The functions here relate to your specific database. The SQL editor and commonly used functions are discussed in Chapter 9. Your SELECT statement should appear as follows:

```
sum(product_promotion_facts.promotion_cost)
```

7. Via the Aggregation function drop-down list, set the aggregation to Sum.

8. There is no reason to have a list of values for measure objects, so from the Advanced tab, uncheck the Associate List of Values box.

9. Click Save to save the changes made to the business layer.

About Aggregates

Two forms of aggregates are involved in measure objects: SQL functions and projection aggregates. Users can create a third aggregate called *calculations* within individual reports.

SQL Aggregates

SQL aggregates—such as SUM, MIN, and MAX—require a GROUP BY clause that the query engine automatically includes in each SQL statement.

Refer back to Figure 7-2. The sample fact table contains 23 rows of data. If a user selects debits and credits without the SQL SUM function, the report will display 23 rows. If the object uses the SUM function and requests only debit and credits by day, SQL will group the debits and credits for each day.

For example, there are four detail entries for September 12, 2011, in Figure 7-2. With the SUM function, SQL sums these into one entry for September 12, as shown in Figure 7-3. Figure 7-3 shows 10 rows of data compared to the physical 23 rows from Figure 7-2.

In this example, the number of rows returned to the client workstation or to the Enterprise server has gone from 23 to 10 through use of a SQL aggregate function. In a real-world example, this could be the difference between returning a few rows or millions of rows of data to a client. Failure to use SQL aggregates correctly can unnecessarily cause millions of rows of data to be sent across the network.

CAUTION Always use a SQL aggregate on a measure unless it involves a unit price or something similar. Otherwise, you risk overloading your servers, network, and client PCs.

Projection Aggregates

Another form of aggregate is the *projection aggregate*, used in multidimensional analysis (see Chapter 18) and when users remove dimension columns from a report or chart that still exist in the result set. In the following example, the *Date* object was deleted from the report display but not from the query itself. There are still ten rows in the result set. However, in the displayed report, Web Intelligence now does the grouping to yield one row of data for the entire month of September.

Month	Debits	Credits
September	10,046	10,400
	10,046	**10,400**

As a general rule, the SQL function you use will match the projection aggregate used on the individual object properties. As discussed earlier in the section on measure objects, price is one measure in which designers may not use a SQL aggregate; however, it would be useful to set the projection aggregate to Avg to allow further analysis. With measures such as inventory and ending balance, we recommend using the SQL SUM function but then setting the projection aggregate to None.

RowNumber	Month	Date	Debits	Credits
1	September	9/1/11		
2	September	9/2/11	3,424	4,000
3	September	9/3/11	800	
4	September	9/5/11		500
5	September	9/12/11	3,259	
6	September	9/15/11	250	800
7	September	9/20/11	210	
8	September	9/21/11	1,880	2,000
9	September	9/26/11		1,600
10	September	9/29/11	223	1,500
		Sum:	**10,046**	**10,400**

Figure 7-3 SQL SUM and GROUP BY aggregate individual rows by common dimensions, reducing the number of rows of data sent to the Enterprise server.

Universe Parameters and Query Options

Universe parameters provide information about your universe as well as allow you to change query behavior such as how long a query can run and the complexity of the SQL generated. The business layer parameters you enter here can also be overridden by settings for individual users or groups (see Chapter 12).

To access the universe parameters, from the Business Layer tab, position your mouse on the name of the universe. If you have selected an individual object such as a folder or dimension, then the properties for that object appear in the pane on the right.

From the Properties tab, you can enter a description for the universe that will appear to users when they create a report. The Query Options tab, shown in Figure 7-4, allows you to specify limits and options.

Query Limits

Query limits are sometimes referred to as *query governors*:

- **Limit Size Of Result Set To**   Prevents the Enterprise server (for Web Intelligence) or the wide area network from becoming saturated with too many rows of data. It does not reduce the load on the source system database. Therefore, leave this box unchecked or increase it to a larger number such as 200,000 rows. If you use drill-down, the number of rows in the result set can be quite large, even if the initial summary report displays only ten rows of data, for example. However, larger result sets lead to slower report generation, particularly when you have complex formatting and variables.

TIP   If you are concerned about novice users incorrectly retrieving large result sets, you can use Restriction Profiles (see Chapter 12) to tailor these settings for individual users or groups.

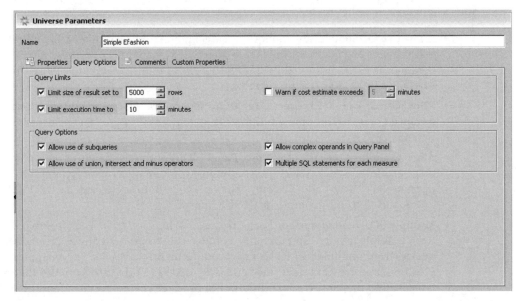

Figure 7-4   The Query Options tab allows you to control query time and complexity of SQL generated.

- **Limit Execution Time To** This is another checkbox to use carefully. This option limits the time the server connection is tied up, but it will not limit the time the database is affected. So if an administrator sets the limit to 10 minutes, the database could actually try to run the query for 60 minutes. With asynchronous connectivity, the database session becomes inactive after 10 minutes and users will receive an error message at that time. However, the query is still executing to completion on the database server, consuming resources. Also, this option refers to the time for all of the SQL statements to execute. If your query contains multiple, synchronized SQL statements (which are created when there are multiple contexts in the universe), ensure this setting is high enough for all the statements to execute.

NOTE If your queries are running this long, you should work with the DBA to do some performance tuning, or possibly modify your universe to generate more efficient SQL, or, as a last resort, encourage users to schedule long-running reports.

- **Warn If Cost Estimate Exceeds** Certain databases support the use of cost estimates when analyzing how long a query will take to execute. Although this setting suggests it relates to the query's duration, in reality, the cost is a relative measurement determined by the data source's I/O utilization, memory consumption, and CPU time.

Query Options

When deploying SAP BusinessObjects directly against a transaction system, you may want to limit complex SQL queries so they do not affect response time for inputting data. Otherwise, leave these options enabled in pure reporting databases or data warehouses. Casual users may not require these features and can ignore the options. However, if you disable advanced SQL, then power users may get frustrated. The following options allow you to limit complex queries:

- **Allow Use Of Subqueries** Subqueries are a powerful type of query that allows users to nest one query within a main query (see Chapter 22). As these queries are complex and use additional RDBMS resources, administrators can remove this capability. By default, leave it enabled.

- **Allow Use of Union, Intersect, And Minus Operators** These operators allow advanced users to combine multiple SQL statements into one data provider. By default, leave it enabled.

- **Allow Complex Operands In Query Panel** This option is similar to the preceding one but allows users to select the conditions from the query panel: Complex operands are "Both" and "Except." The operand "Both" generates an INTERSECT query, and "Except" generates a MINUS query.

- **Multiple SQL Statements For Each Measure** When you have measures that come from multiple tables within the same context, this box should always be enabled or queries from multiple fact tables may produce incorrect results. For example, in the eFashion universe, unit sales price and extended sales price are from two different tables within the same context. In order to produce correct results when these measures are used in the same query, Web Intelligence needs to issue two SELECT statements. It's also useful to check this option even if you think you have one central fact table. For example, you may later create measures such as number of days or number of products that go against dimension tables. Without this option enabled, Web Intelligence will create a Cartesian product and give incorrect information when the measures come from more than one table. The disadvantage of this option, though, is that certain queries could be processed more efficiently with one SELECT statement and still return accurate results. For example, if your query contains a COUNT DISTINCT of products from a dimension table with sales from a fact table, as long as the count object uses DISTINCT, you will get correct results. However, it will take longer and significantly more resources to process the multiple SELECT statements generated, by default, with this option set, than when using one SELECT statement without this option enabled. Correct queries are more important than fast queries. Check this option by default but monitor how many queries users create that generate multiple SELECT statements unnecessarily.

Understanding Multiple SQL Statements for Each Measure

The option Multiple SQL Statements For Each Measure has some nuances that are important to understand. First, even if this box is enabled, if the measures come from the same fact table, the query engine will issue only one SQL statement. This is a good thing, as it avoids tying up the database unnecessarily. Second, the query engine will issue only two SQL statements if the object is a measure, and it contains an aggregate function (sum, count, and so on).

When SQL joins two tables together, it repeats each row for each combination in the GROUP BY section. Figure 7-5 illustrates how this happens. The ARTICLE_LOOKUP table has only one row and shows a price of 114.55. The SHOP_FACTS table has six rows showing that this style blazer sold six times during week 8 of year 2000. When SQL joins ARTICLE_ LOOKUP with SHOP_FACTS, the 114.55 unit price is repeated six times and summed to 687.30—an incorrect result. The vendor refers to this problem as a "fan trap," but SQL experts and DBAs generically refer to it as a *Cartesian product*.

Web Intelligence prevents Cartesian products and this overstatement of results by issuing a SELECT statement for each measure coming from different tables. This is seamless to users.

NOTE This example uses the object *Extended Price* object, which includes a SUM. As a general rule, unit prices should never be summed. If anything, they can be averaged or recalculated with revenue/ quantity sold. If you wish to see another example of a fan trap, disable the option Multiple SQL Statements For Each Measure and include the two measures from two different tables, such as Store Details \Extended Sales Floor Size and Sales Revenue. These measures must contain aggregate functions such as SUM or COUNT.

The reports in Figure 7-6 show how the results depend on which option is set in the universe parameters, query options. The top report shows the correct results as the SQL is split for each measure and each table. As a control, the last column of the report uses a measure object that does not contain the SUM on price. Notice that both the *Extended Price*

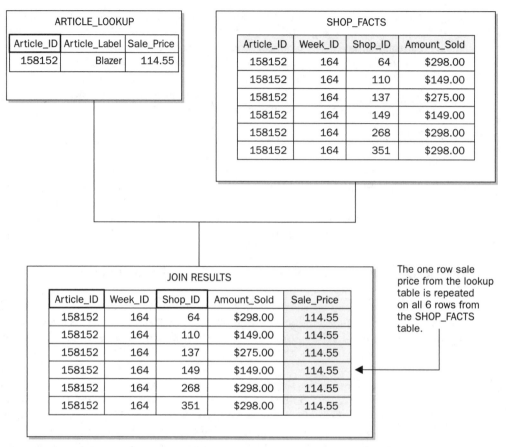

Figure 7-5 Queries produce incorrect results when aggregates are used on multiple tables. Split the SQL statements to prevent this.

object that contains the SUM and the *Unit Price* that does not contain the SUM yield the same correct results: 114.55. For the middle report, only one SQL statement is generated, as the parameter Multiple SQL Statements For Each Measure was not selected in the universe. Notice how the *Extended Price* returns grossly incorrect results, 687.30. The results have been overstated by however many rows there are in the SHOP_FACTS table.

Unfortunately, even with this setting to split the SQL, you cannot guarantee users will always get correct results, as shown in the bottom report. Although there are two SQL statements for this report, the query contains an additional result object *Year* that forces a join to SHOP_FACTS and again overstates the results. Therefore, while splitting the SQL can help in many cases, it will not resolve all problems of having measures in multiple tables. The best way to prevent such problems is to have all measures in one fact table per context. Measures that contain counts are an exception and can be resolved differently as discussed in Chapter 9.

Multiple Measures, 2 SQL Statements

SKU number	SKU desc	Sales revenue	Extended price	Unit Price - No Sum
158152	Blazer	$970,977	$114.55	$114.55

Multiple Measures, 1 SQL Statements Wrong Results

SKU number	SKU desc	Sales revenue	Extended price	Unit Price - No Sum
158152	Blazer	$1,468	$687.30	$114.55

Multiple Measures, 2 SQL Statements but WRONG Results

SKU number	SKU desc	Year	Sales revenue	Extended price	Unit Price - No Sum
158152	Blazer	2001	$290,117	$125,775.90	$114.55
158152	Blazer	2002	$666,235	$257,508.40	$114.55
158152	Blazer	2003	$14,626	$19,702.60	$114.55

Figure 7-6   Splitting the SQL ensures correct results for reports with multiple measures.

Summary

The business layer is the user interface to the physical columns in the data source. The IDT provides four main types of objects to help users differentiate between types of information more easily: folders, measures, dimensions, and attributes. This chapter covered the basics of navigating the business layer and creating different kinds of objects, and highlighted some important design principles:

- Sort dimension objects from biggest to smallest to facilitate drill-down.
- Follow the four Cs in naming objects: be customer-oriented, clear, consistent, and concise.
- Ensure object types and data field types match the type in the physical database.
- Point dimension objects to lookup tables.
- Always use SQL aggregates on measure objects.

Following these principles will make your universe powerful and ensure users consistently get correct results. In Chapters 8 and 9, you will learn how to add more intelligence to the objects.

8 Lists of Values and Parameters

The *list of values* is a powerful feature that allows users to select from a pick list when setting conditions in a query. You as a designer determine which dimensions have lists of values via the dimension properties.

Because users can select conditions from a list of values, they do not need to enter conditions manually, and therefore do not need to memorize lists of codes or guess how many leading zeros there may be in a particular field. The IDT allows you to customize the default list of values even further to present meaningful names with the codes or to shorten particularly long lists into more meaningful subsets of valid filters.

Lists of values can be based on a business layer object, a static list that you import or manually enter, or custom SQL. You can create lists of values in either the data foundation or the business layer. The main advantage of creating them in the business layer is that they are then based on business layer objects. When you convert a universe from a .unv file to a .unx file, the list of values and parameters are created in the business layer. *Parameters* are interactive objects that allow you to prompt users for additional information.

This chapter covers the details of working with lists of values and parameters.

How List of Values Works

When a user adds a condition to a query, Web Intelligence essentially launches a second query and returns a list from the dimension or lookup table in the RDBMS, as shown in Figure 8-1. In this example, the user has a query filter on City(1.)To be able to pick from a list of city names, the Enterprise server will query the data source for a list of valid cities(2.) A list of cities is displayed to the user(3,)and the user selects London(4.)The list of values ensures the query filter is valid and in the correct syntax, such as London as opposed to LONDON.

① User creates query with filter and selects values from list operand.

WHERE
CITY='London'

Web Intelligence user

④ User selects value(s) from picklist

BOE server

② a-object.lov query is sent to the RDBMS.

Dimension

Fact

③ BOE server caches results for the session and sends back to the user in the form of a picklist.

Data source

Figure 8-1   A list of values query is associated with an object in the universe. It queries the dimension tables to present users with a pick list for conditions.

In previous releases, the customized list of values was stored as an *object*.lov file, where *object* was the list filename specified in the object properties. When Web Intelligence users access a list of values, the .lovquery results are cached as part of the user session on the Web Intelligence Server. In the latest release, the name of the file is no longer *object*.lov, but rather is a system-generated filename. However, we refer to it as .lov for clarity.

The IDT automatically creates these query files whenever a universe designer enables a list of values on a universe object *and* the user requests a list of values for adding a condition to a query. Unless a designer customizes the list of values, the following SQL is always generated:

```
SELECT DISTINCT
Table.column
FROM
Table
```

Notice that the query engine adds a DISTINCT keyword to all list of values queries. This ensures that users receive only a single row for each distinct value. For example, a customer dimension table may have multiple rows for each customer ID as changes to customer information are kept and time-stamped. In setting conditions in a query, users will need to see the unique customer ID only once.

The use of the DISTINCT keyword is sensible from a user-functionality point of view, but it clearly has an impact on query response time when your list of values is directed to a large fact table. As discussed in the previous chapter, it's always preferable to have dimension objects point to a smaller dimension table. The list of values, then, should also point to the smaller dimension table and not a fact table.

TIP You can change the default setting for a list of values to use a GROUP BY rather than DISTINCT. This parameter is universe-specific and is set by selecting the business layer, Universe Parameters, SQL Parameters tab. Set the value DISTINCT_VALUES=GROUPBY. See Chapter 7 for more information on setting these parameters.

When users add a condition to a query, they must select an operand, as shown here:

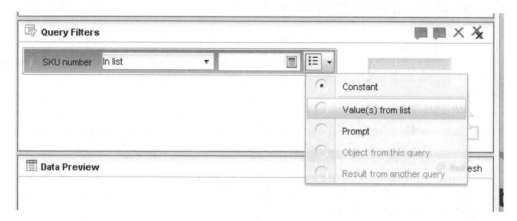

Users can either manually enter the value for the condition or select the operand Value(s) from List (step 1 in Figure 8-1). This operand will send the *object*.lov query to the dimension table in the RDBMS (step 2 in Figure 8-1). The RDBMS sends the query results back to the Web Intelligence server (or client for WebI Rich client) (step 3 in Figure 8-1). Users then select which condition value(s) they want in the original query condition (step 4 in Figure 8-1). When the user launches the main query, the .lov query is no longer involved. Also, if a user selects the operand type Constant and manually enters a filter value, then the .lov query is not involved.

Once the user session has ended, the .lov file is no longer available. For this reason, you as the designer must be particularly cognizant of long lists of values that are slow to generate. With BusinessObjects 6.5 and earlier, the way the repository was structured made exporting pregenerated lists of values to the repository exceedingly slow. A binary query file had to be extracted from the relational repository and rebuilt in the file system. With the current enterprise architecture, when you export the universe and lists of values to the repository, it's primarily copying files to the file system, a significantly faster operation than in version 6.5. With this change in architecture, longtime BusinessObjects customers have an opportunity to rethink their approach to lists of values.

Designers can customize the *object*.lov query to make it easier for users to find their relevant values by shortening the number of possible choices. For example, if you have millions of products, you may want to prompt users first to select a product category, in what is referred to as *cascading list of values*. If the users do not know the codes or spellings of the product categories, for example, then Web Intelligence may first launch a prodcat.lov query. In this respect, steps 2 and 3 in Figure 8-1 may be repeated multiple times until the user finally selects values to add to the query in step 4. The size of the *object*.lov files also may change over time as the number of products changes or as users select different product categories.

List of Values Settings

When you first create an object, the IDT enables lists of values by default on all objects. You can control particular settings via the Advanced tab of the Dimension Properties pane. Table 8-1 explains the purpose of each of the list of values check boxes.

When to Disable Lists of Values

By default, lists of values are enabled on all objects, including measures. This is slightly different behavior than with the Universe Design Tool and earlier versions. There are instances in which it is better to disable them by removing the check from the Associate List of Values check box.

Measures

As discussed in the previous chapter, all measure objects should have a SQL aggregate (SUM, COUNT, and so on) in the SELECT statement. Therefore, if you have a list of values on a measure object, the list of values will return only one row of data, since there are no dimensions in the GROUP BY clause in the SQL. If you create a new measure object, the Associate List of Values box is not enabled. However, if you convert a dimension object to a measure, this option is not explicitly disabled.

Option	Explanation
Allow users to edit this list of values	This option allowed Desktop Intelligence users to create their own custom lists, adding whatever filters, sorts, or personal data files they found most useful. We have rarely seen this used, even by power users. As Desktop Intelligence is not supported in this release, and this feature is not supported, this option appears extraneous and/or might be in place to reenable it in future releases.
Automatic refresh before use	This should rarely be checked and only for those objects in which the dimension information changes frequently. Otherwise, the users can easily refresh lists of values by request, and in most cases, the lists are refreshed when accessed. Particularly with large dimension lists or slow RDBMS response times, it is important not to force an automatic refresh.
Force users to filter values before use	With long lists of values, it's helpful to have users search for a string or set of numbers so that the pick list is smaller. When this option is checked, users must first enter a search string before the list of values is generated. So if they are looking for customers, beginning with *C,* they would enter C*.
Allow users to search values in the database	Users can search within an existing list of values result set or, when this option is set, they can search within the list of values query sent to the database.

Table 8-1 List of Value Settings

Nonindexed Fields

You might think that if you have disallowed an object to be used as a condition, that would automatically remove the list of values functionality from the object. It doesn't. So for many of the same reasons that you disallow an object to be used as a condition, you also may not want to associate a list of values.

If the field is not indexed, you may not want to associate a list of values. For example, let's assume that *Customer Name* is an object whose source system field is not indexed. It is still allowed as a condition because you may want users to be able to search for all customer names that start with a particular letter, or if they are looking for parent and subsidiary companies, parts of the name. Ideally, you want *Customer Name* to be used only for wildcard searches, and you would rather they use *Customer Code* as a condition, since it's indexed. In this case, allow the list of values on *Customer Code* and disable it on *Customer Name*.

Attributes

Rarely will users want to use attributes as conditions in queries. For example, when users are looking for customer sales, do they use attribute objects such as street address or phone number for the exact condition when it's unknown to them? No. If they know the phone number, they may use it as a condition, but then they are usually entering the phone number manually, *not* choosing it from a pick list.

However, if you look at the sample eFashion universe, it makes a lot of sense to allow a list of values for the object *ZIP code*, even though it is an attribute object. We would recommend customizing it to display the state. We would also have *ZIP code* as a dimension object, not an attribute, so that users can drill by it.

Simple List of Values Customization

A simple list of values customization may involve adding a meaningful description next to the code or adding a prompt to shorten a long list. Each customization has three main steps:

1. Associate a list of values with an object.
2. Add additional information or conditions.
3. Export the customization with the universe.

Adding a Description Object to an ID Object

Some ID and code fields may have a logical meaning with which users are familiar. For example, many accountants know the meaning of certain account ranges. Power users also may know a number of account, product, and customer codes. But in many cases, the codes are meaningless, and users will just want to use names or descriptions as conditions. However, filtering queries on nonindexed description fields can result in slow queries.

Customizing the list of values for ID fields meets the users' need of seeing a description, while also ensuring that the query is filtered on an indexed field. You also may want to include additional dimension objects in your list of values to facilitate sorting. Figure 8-2 shows that it may be meaningful to add Country, Region, and City to the Customer ID list of values.

Displaying additional information such as country can be useful

The region refers to a region within a country

Customer ID	Customer	Country of Origin	Region	City
201.00	Sartois	France	French Alps	Albertville
206.00	Gentil	France	French Alps	Albertville
204.00	Martin	France	French Alps	Grenoble
202.00	Michaud	France	French Alps	Lyon
207.00	Dupont	France	Paris	Paris
205.00	Piaget	France	Provence	Bordeaux
203.00	Robert	France	Provence	Marseilles
406.00	Tilzman	Germany	Bavaria	Augsburg
402.00	Schiller	Germany	Bavaria	Munich
405.00	Schultz	Germany	East Germany	Berlin
407.00	Reinman	Germany	East Germany	Berlin
403.00	Durnstein	Germany	East Germany	Dresden
404.00	Weimar	Germany	East Germany	Magdeburg
401.00	Diemers	Germany	Ruhr	Cologne
501.00	Arai	Japan	East Japan	Tokyo
504.00	Makino	Japan	East Japan	Tokyo
506.00	Oneda	Japan	East Japan	Tokyo
502.00	Kamata	Japan	East Japan	Yokohama
507.00	Okumura	Japan	West Japan	Kobe
505.00	Mukumoto	Japan	West Japan	Kyoto
503.00	Kamimura	Japan	West Japan	Osaka
301.00	Edwards	UK	England	London
305.00	Keegan	UK	England	London
306.00	Jones	UK	England	Oxford

Sort order by country, not by ID or name

Figure 8-2 Customers reside in cities that are part of countries. Displaying country information along with customer ID makes for a more meaningful pick list.

In the following example, you will use the Island Resorts Marketing universe. The sample universe includes a *Customer Name* object. You will first create an object that accesses an ID field that is indexed, and then customize the list to include a description. Later, you will also customize this same list to display the customer's country and city.

Creating the Dimension Object
Follow these steps to create a *Customer ID* dimension:

1. Select the *Customer* folder.

2. Select Insert Dimension by clicking the green + menu, or right-click and select New | Dimension from the pop-up menu.

3. Replace the default New Dimension with **Customer ID**. Complete the Description and SQL Select fields, as shown here:

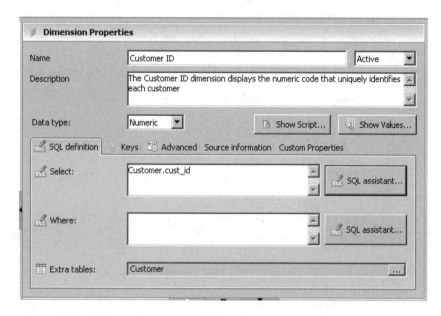

A default list of values is associated with this object.

Creating a Customized List of Values

Follow these steps to create a customized list of values:

1. Within the Business Layer pane, click the Parameters and Lists of values tab.

2. From the Lists of Values pane at the bottom left, select the Insert button, and then choose List of values based on business layer object.

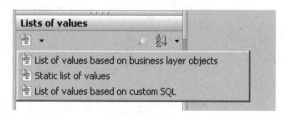

3. A Business Object LOV Properties dialog box appears with the default name New Lov. Replace this name with **CustomerIDLOV**.

4. Select Edit Query to open the Query Panel. Drag the newly created *Customer ID* and *Customer* objects to the Result Objects pane, as shown here:

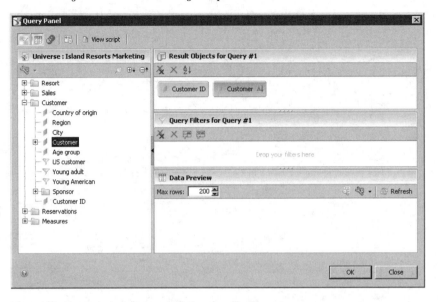

5. *Customer ID* has no sequence that is meaningful to users, so add a sort on *Customer* so that the names are sorted in alphabetical order. While *Customer* is still selected in the Result Objects pane, click the Sorts icon.

6. Click OK to return to the Business Object LOV Properties panel. The LOV definition should appear as follows (the sort order is not shown in this dialog):

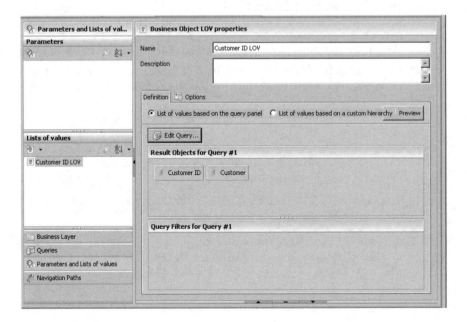

NOTE Users can now sort their own list of values.

7. Click Preview to see the results of your customized list of values. This is what users will see when accessing the list of values:

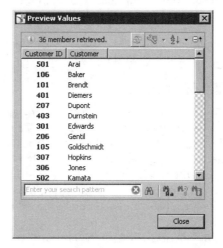

8. Click Close to close the list of values display and return to the Properties panel.

Associating the Customized List

Now that you have defined the list of values, you need to associate it with the base object *Customer ID*.

1. Click the Business Layer tab.

2. Navigate to the *Customer ID* object.

3. Select the Advanced tab.

4. Click the ellipse button to change the default list of values. You are presented with a list of all custom lists of values within this business layer. Select the newly created CustomerIDLOV.

NOTE By default, the first object in the list of values query will be used to create the WHERE clause. If you click any other columns and the check mark is changed for the mapping object, you may not have any results returned.

---

    5. Click OK. The custom list of values should now be associated with this dimension object.

As always, save the business layer. You can now test the custom list of values by creating a query, setting a query filter on the customer ID, and selecting LOV as the operand.

Cascading Lists of Values

The customer table in the Island Resorts Marketing universe is quite small (35 rows); however, for many real-world data warehouses and OLTP systems, the customer tables and product tables can be large, with many millions of rows. For this reason, universe designers should customize the list of values to reduce the number of rows presented to the user by adding a prompt. This is often referred to as a *cascading* list of values because two lists are linked to one another. There is no fixed limit to how many rows are reasonable; it's more a question of reasonable response time to generate the list of value query results and ease of navigation for the end user.

Regardless of the number of values ultimately returned in a list of values query, the list of values displayed is "chunked" according to the List of Values Batch Size setting for Web Intelligence Processing Server. For example, in Figure 8-3, the list of values batch size is set to 1,000. This means that even if your list of values returns 2,000 values, the users are presented with the first 1,000; to get to the next set of 1,000 values, they request the next page.

Figure 8-3 List of values behavior is affected by IDT customizations, but also by Web Intelligence Processing Server settings.

When cascading your list of values, you must first be familiar with the dimension tables, how they relate, and which level of prompts will give a good response time without annoying the users. If a user is simply trying to find a customer code, the user does not want to be asked five questions in advance to arrive at the customer code; one or two levels of cascades should be the most used. Whenever possible, strive to display more columns of information in the original list of values, rather than adding a prompt as your first choice. The goal of the prompt is to shorten your list to guarantee a reasonable response time and navigable size, not to generate the smallest list possible.

For a dimension such as *Customer*, there are two main ways to shorten the list. The first is to check the box "Force users to filter values before use." With this option, a user will be prompted to search for customers beginning with a certain letter or similar string. The second approach is to cascade for customers residing in a certain city or region. In looking at the sample data in Figure 8-2 (shown earlier in the chapter), for example, you may want to prompt the users to filter the customer ID list according to customers who reside within a particular country. For individual products or SKUs, including a filter on product category or line of business brings the list of values to a more manageable size.

In the following example, you will continue to work with the *Customer ID* object. First, study the dimension data. In Figure 8-2, notice in which city and country each customer resides. Additionally, each country is divided into multiple regions within the country. If your business users had not specifically told you this, or if you had not studied the dimensional data, you may have incorrectly assumed that *Region* referred to *World Region* (such as North America, Europe, and so on). Ideally, users will tell you which customizations they want, but for them, the choices may not be clear, and the business definitions may not be obvious. It's up to you as the universe designer to give them your best guess for the friendliest, fastest customization.

Next, look at the tables involved, as shown in Figure 8-4. If you decide to prompt the users on *Country of Origin,* then four tables will be joined together to present the shortened list of customer IDs. In this example, the tables are small, so the joins are not a problem. In a production implementation, carefully evaluate the impact on response time when your list of values customization involves more than one table. At this point, also see if a shortcut join is available; for example, you may want to shorten the list of product IDs according to which plants make the products (see Chapter 6). Prompting on *City* may result in a faster query, but it may not make sense from a business viewpoint if managers are organized by country.

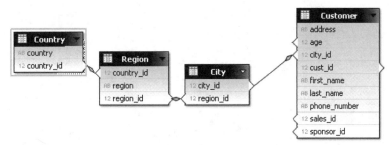

Figure 8-4   Adding Country as a prompt in the Customer ID list of values involves four tables.

To cascade the list of values for *Customer ID* by *Country,* follow these steps:

1. Select the Parameters and Lists of values tab.

2. Select the CustomerIDLOV you created earlier. From the Business Object LOV Properties panel, click the Edit Query button.

3. Drag the dimension *Country* into the Query Filters pane. Leave the default operand as Equal To. In the operand drop-down list, select Prompt.

4. Change the default Prompt Text setting to **Select the customer country**.

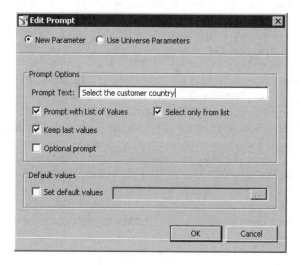

NOTE if you later decide you want to change the prompt message or options, you must remove the query filter and re-create the prompt.

---

5. Click OK to close the Edit Prompt dialog box.

6. Click OK to close the Query Panel.

7. Click Preview to see the cascaded list of values. Note that you are now first prompted to select the customer country.

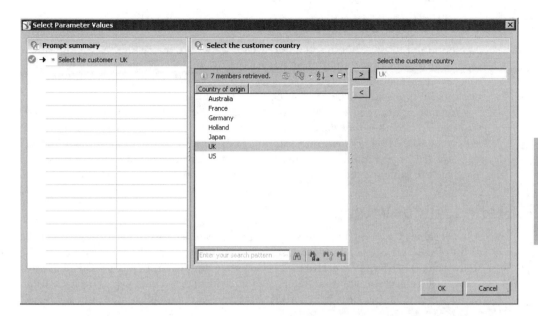

8. Select the country from the list and click > to add it to the box at the right of the Select Parameter Values dialog box.

9. Click OK to run the final list of value query with the newly selected country value. Your list should appear as follows. Note that it is a much smaller list of customers than previously shown.

9. Click Close to close the Preview Values dialog box.

As long as you used the same CustomerIDLOV that you did in the earlier example, you do not need to reassociate this list of values with the dimension object *Customer ID*.

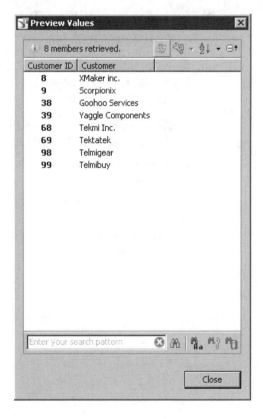

Part II

Reusable Lists of Values

As mentioned throughout this chapter, lists of values are query files. As the queries are now separate from the object definition, it is easy to use one list of values query with multiple objects. This capability is referred to as *reusable* or *shared* lists of values. Giving the lists meaningful names will make this process easier to maintain.

You may want to share the same list of values for objects used in multiple alias tables, regardless of whether they have been defined as aliases within the universe or synonyms within the RDBMS. For example, customer number may be used in both *Ship To Customer* and *Sold To Customer*. Both objects use the same underlying customer numbers, so you can associate the same named list of values with the two different dimension objects.

Static Lists of Values

A list of values based on a business layer on a query object is the most frequently used type of list of values. However, in some cases, you may want to provide users with a list based on a static data set. This can be useful if querying your dimension tables is particularly slow or if your universe accesses a transaction system and normalized database. The static list can be loaded from a flat file (text, CSV, or PRN), or you can manually enter values.

Static Lists of Values from Imported Data

In the following example, you will create a list of values based on a static list for *Article ID*. The list includes the Article ID, Article Description, and Category. First, create this static list by creating a query and saving the results to a CSV file. To do this, you can use either Web Intelligence or the Query tab within the business layer. You can also create a list of values in Excel and save it to a CSV file.

1. From within the Parameters and Lists of values tab, Select the Insert button, and then choose Static List of values.

2. A Static LOV Properties dialog box appears with the default name New Lov. Replace this name with **ArticleIDStaticLOV**.

3. Click the Import button.

4. Choose the appropriate data separator, text delimiter, and date format. If you created your CSV file from the Query tab of the business layer, use Double " as the text delimiter.

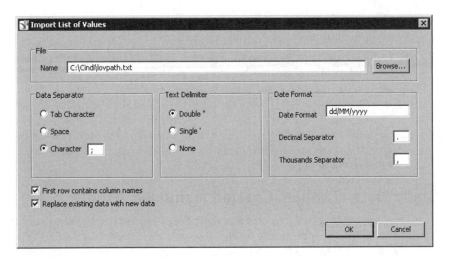

5. Check the "First row contains column names" check box if the CSV file has column headings.

6. You can either append to a list or replace existing data.

7. Click OK to close the Import List of Values dialog box. Your results should appear as follows:

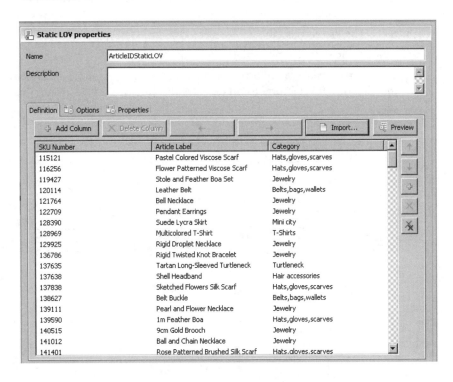

8. From within this dialog box, you can reorder, add, or delete individual rows by using the buttons on the right.

9. To have this static list of values associated with the *Article ID* dimension object, click the Business Layer tab.

10. Navigate to the *Article ID* object.

11. Select the Advanced tab.

12. Click the ellipse button to change the default list of values. You are presented with a list of all custom lists of values within this business layer. Select the newly created ArticleIDStaticLOV.

Static Lists of Values Created Manually

In some cases, you may want to create a static list of values that you manually enter into the business layer. This is appropriate when you don't have many rows of data or when you cannot otherwise generate the list from an existing data source. For example, for a *Year* object, if the SQL to create this is accessing individual order dates, it could be a slow query. There are only a few years of data, so you may manually create this list, as follows:

1. From within the Parameters and Lists of values tab, select the Insert button, and then choose Static list of values.

2. The Static LOV Properties dialog box appears with the default name New Lov. Replace this name with **YearLOV**.

3. Select the Properties tab.

4. Change the default Column0 to the name **Year**.

5. Change the Data Type to String. Note that the data type here must be the same as the data type for the dimension object with which you will associate this list of values.

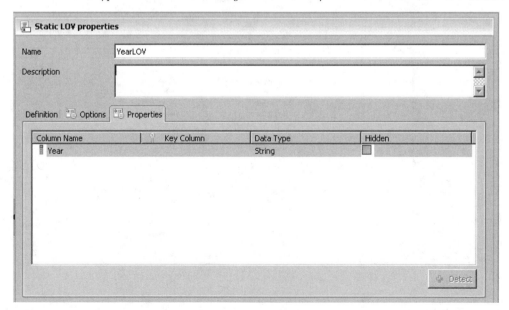

6. Select the Definition tab.

7. Click the plus button at the right to insert rows of data.

8. When the data type is numeric, the IDT will insert a default row (Row 0:0 for string, today's date for date type, or a 0 for numeric) with an initial value. Click that cell to modify the values, as in the following example:

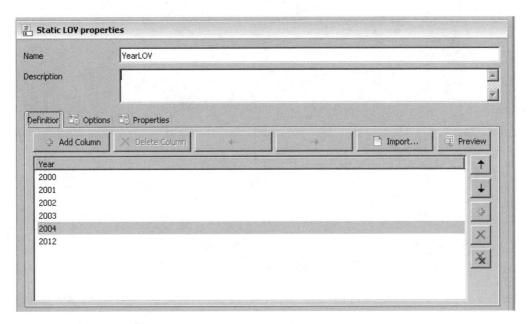

List of Values Custom Hierarchy

When you create a list of values based on a business layer object, you can choose to have the list based on a query you design via the Query Panel or based on a hierarchical display of dimension objects. When the list is based on a custom hierarchy, users are likely presented with subsets of items, rather than a tabular display, as in the earlier Country > Region > Customer ID example. However, the SQL submitted is also slightly different, with nested WHERE clauses.

To create a hierarchical list of values, follow these steps:

1. Select the Parameters and Lists of values tab.

2. From the Business Object LOV Properties dialog box, on the Definition tab, check the "List of values based on custom hierarchy" option.

3. Click the Add Dimension button. Choose the dimension objects that form the hierarchy. You can either add the dimension objects one at a time or use CTRL-click to select multiple objects.

4. Click OK to close the Add a Dimension dialog box. Use the arrow buttons so that your dimension objects are organized with the parent at the top and the most granular at the bottom. In this example, Region is first and Customer ID is the final value.

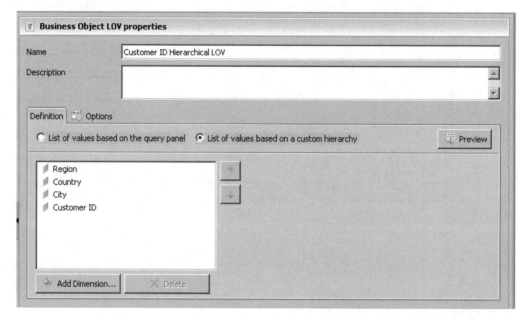

5. Click Preview to see how the list will appear to users.

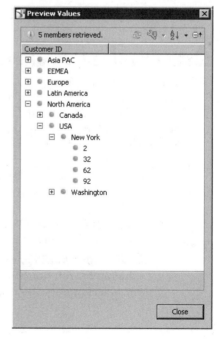

When a user selects a list of values based on a hierarchy, the following SQL WHERE clause is generated:

```
WHERE
STSWarehouse.dbo.dimCustomer.Regionname +'\'+
STSWarehouse.dbo.dimCustomer.Countryname +'\'+
STSWarehouse.dbo.dimCustomer.Cityname +'\'+
convert(char,STSWarehouse.dbo.dimCustomer.CustomerID)  =  ANY
    (
    SELECT
STSWarehouse.dbo.dimCustomer.Regionname +'\'+
STSWarehouse.dbo.dimCustomer.Countryname +'\'+
STSWarehouse.dbo.dimCustomer.Cityname +'\'+
convert(char,STSWarehouse.dbo.dimCustomer.CustomerID0029
    FROM
STSWarehouse.dbo.dimCustomer
    WHERE
    (
STSWarehouse.dbo.dimCustomer.CustomerID  =  7
      AND
STSWarehouse.dbo.dimCustomer.Cityname   =   'Marseilles'
      AND
STSWarehouse.dbo.dimCustomer.Countryname  =   'France'
      AND
STSWarehouse.dbo.dimCustomer.Regionname   =   'Europe'
    )
   )
```

Compare this to the WHERE clause generated without a custom hierarchy:

```
WHERE
STSWarehouse.dbo.dimCustomer.CustomerID  =  7
```

Parameters and Prompts

Parameters are objects that prompt users for additional information. For example, in the earlier section "Cascading Lists of Values," you created a prompt for the user to select a country. You could have created a parameter and used that as the prompt value. The main benefit to using a parameter is that it is reusable and can be referred to either as a prompt in a list of values or in measure and dimension objects.

Prompts can be useful, but they also may be annoying if the user always wants the same values. For example, if a user always wants current year data, it can be aggravating if the object prompts the user for the year each time the user refreshes the query. In such a case, it would be more appropriate to place a fixed condition in a report. Objects with prompts should be reserved for items in which some sort of condition is required, either to limit the number of rows returned or to guarantee correct results.

In Chapter 7, Figure 7-2 illustrated the risk of constructing a query that involved a single point in time (for semi-additive measures, such as account balance, ending inventory, and number of customers) and a period of time (debits and credits; movements in and out; customers acquired). One way to ensure users select one point in time for semi-additive measures is to prompt users to enter an individual date whenever they select month-end inventory, as shown in Figure 8-5. (It would be wrong to put the prompt on the *Day* object, because that would prevent users from analyzing movements in and out for more than one day.)

Notice in Figure 8-5 that the object or *TABLE.COLUMN* in the SELECT portion of the SQL can be different from the *TABLE.COLUMN* in the WHERE clause. In the figure, DEBIT_CREDIT.DAILY_BALANCE is used in the SELECT portion, but *Day* is used in the WHERE clause. Prompts are added in the WHERE clause of a new or existing object. Whenever you use a parameter in the WHERE clause, the IDT automatically adds @Prompt to the SQL.

When users now construct a query that uses the *Ending Balance* object, the query engine will always prompt them to "Select the Day for the Ending Balance."

This is appropriate when you want to be sure that users get correct balance results. However, it can also be confusing and unfriendly if the user has included the *Day* object explicitly as a query filter. From the user's viewpoint, it is nonsensical that Web Intelligence will prompt for information that the user has already included in the conditions. Also, users will be able to retrieve balances for only one day at a time, whereas it is a valid business question for them to review daily balances over a period of time. In this respect, it is important in training and object descriptions to emphasize how these objects work and when to use them.

As you build interactive objects, follow these guidelines:

- Use interactive objects only when the absence of a prompt could lead to inaccurate information or unacceptable query response times.

- If the prompts are for user-friendliness or automation, have two objects: one without a prompt for unrestricted information and one with the prompt. Differentiate between these two objects with clear names—for example, *Balance* and *Balance-Date Required*.

- Provide usage information in the object description or in training.

Figure 8-5 Create interactive objects with parameters and @Prompt.

Building a Parameter Step by Step

In the following example, you will build a parameter for *Year*. This parameter can be used to cascade a list of order dates or it can be added as a prompt in a measure object.

1. From the Parameters and Lists of values tab, select Insert a Parameter from the toolbar.

2. A Parameter Properties dialog box appears with the default name New Prompt1. Replace this name with **YearParam**. The description is optional and appears only to universe designers, not to end users.

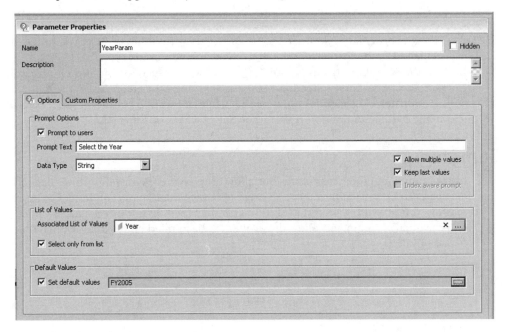

3. Check the box Prompt to users.

4. Enter the prompt text you want to appear to users to either filter the list of values or to filter the query object.

5. Set the data type. The data type must match the object type for the WHERE clause. In this example, *Year* is String.

6. If you want users to be able to enter multiple values, check this box. Note that you also will need to use the operator In List for your filter criteria.

7. Check the box Keep last values. With this option, when users refresh their query, they will not need to reenter their selection criteria. They are still prompted if they wish to change the filter values, but the last values are used by default.

8. Choose the list of values to associate with this parameter.

9. Optionally, enter default values.

Once you have created the parameter, you can refer to it in the object definitions in the WHERE clause.

Pseudo Optional Prompts

Unfortunately, there is not a simple check box to allow the prompt to be optional for the parameter.

If you do not want the prompt to be mandatory to limit the number of rows, try the following technique (originally suggested by Walter Muellner of Mercury Business Solutions in Austria). The WHERE clause uses an OR statement to allow users to either answer ALL or choose individual values from the list:

```
'ALL'  IN @prompt(YearParam)
 OR
Calendar_year_lookup.Yr=@prompt(YearParam)
```

This is a very creative approach to balancing user-friendliness with prompting. When users enter ALL, the first part of the SQL condition gets used ('ALL' IN 'ALL'). Because the condition statement uses an OR clause, the second condition is not evaluated. Conversely, if users enter individual years (or anything other than ALL), the first part of the SQL is not true, and so it does not get used, while the second condition does. Your prompt text in the parameter definition should be **Select a Year or Enter ALL**.

Summary

Lists of values and their customizations allow users to more easily filter their data. The list of values can be a dynamic query that provides a pick list at query run time. For performance reasons, you may also want a static list that can be based on imported data or values you enter manually. Parameters allow those filters to be applied either to individual objects or to lists of values.

Beyond the Basics

In the previous chapters, you created some basic dimensions and measures. In this chapter, you will add more intelligence to columns of information. The IDT provides two main categories of functionality to do this: internal IDT functions and SQL functions that are RDBMS-specific. The first part of the chapter covers functionality that is specific to the IDT but database-independent.

Certain capabilities, such as derived tables, are available in the data foundation. Others, such as aggregate awareness and advanced SQL, are accessed in the business layer. The second part of the chapter covers SQL commands that may be dependent on which RDBMS you use.

Reducing Maintenance with Base Objects and @Select

The @Select function is an internal function that allows you, as the designer, to reuse business layer objects without forcing you to repeat the entire SQL syntax. For example, consider an initial *Sales* object that provides information about revenue in U.S. dollars. You can add a number of enhancements to this object: *Sales in Local Currency, Sales in Euros, Sales Adjusted for Inflation, Sales with 10% Projected Increase,* and so on. These additional objects are not columns in the database; they are measures you create by using SQL commands. However, they all reference the same initial column in the RDBMS, such as SALES_FACT .AMOUNT, and then include further calculations for local currencies or forecasts.

When building advanced objects with the IDT, you can select either the RDBMS column or a universe object. Whenever possible, select the object. You will save time on universe maintenance. For example, suppose that six months from now, the physical field for sales (SALES_FACT.AMOUNT) in the RDBMS is renamed. If all of the related sales objects explicitly referenced the RDBMS field, that is how many objects you now must modify manually (okay, you could also use the find-and-replace approach, but manual modification is safer). However, if all the related sales objects used @Select, you need to modify only the one base object.

The syntax of @Select is as follows:

```
@Select(Folder\Object)
```

where *Folder* is the name of the folder that contains the base object—for example, *Measures*—and *Object* is the name of the object that contains the base object—for example, *Sales*.

TIP Whenever possible, use business layer objects rather than physical, individual RDBMS columns in your SQL statements. This will save you work if ever you rename an RDBMS column, as you will need to modify only the SQL of the base object. The IDT will automatically update the SQL for all other objects that use the base column.

The @Where function is similar to @Select in that you can reuse a WHERE clause from an existing object.

The SQL Expression Editor

When changing SQL statements, you can enter the SELECT statements directly in the box in the SQL definition tab, or you can use the SQL Assistant to change either the SELECT statement or the WHERE clause. The SQL Assistant also provides some help on internal IDT functions and SQL syntax.

Figure 9-1 shows the SQL Expression Editor. You launch the SQL editor by clicking the SQL Assistant button from the SQL definition tab of the object properties. As you modify the SQL for an object, you can point and click your way through it, or you can enter the functions, columns, and operators manually. Regardless of how you build the SQL statement, be sure to validate each object as you go. Validation ensures that your statement is correct and won't produce an error when a user launches a query.

In Figure 9-1, the promotional cost has been increased by 10 percent from the values stored in the database. For example, to create the measure object *Promotion Cost Increase* from the eFashion universe, as shown in Figure 9-1, follow these steps:

1. Select the object—in this example, *Promotion Cost*—from the SQL definition tab, and then click SQL Assistant to launch the SQL Expression Editor.

2. Under Functions, expand the Number functions by clicking the + sign. Scroll to sum() and double-click.

3. Position your mouse at the $1 within the newly inserted SUM function.

4. Under Tables, expand the PRODUCT_PROMOTION_FACTS table by clicking the + sign. Double-click PROMOTION_COST to insert the table and field into the statement.

5. Under Function, expand the Operators group, and then double-click the multiplication sign (*).

6. Enter **1.10**.

7. Click Validate to ensure you have built the SQL statement correctly, with the functions, operators, and parentheses in the correct positions.

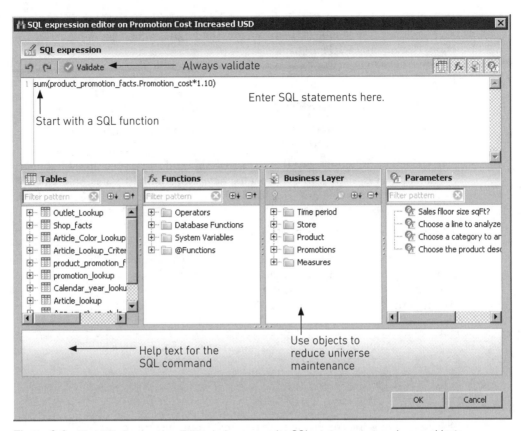

Figure 9-1   The SQL Expression Editor helps you write SQL statements to enhance objects.

Some Caveats About SQL Functions

A number of SQL commands are common to all databases. However, database vendors have
added a number of extensions to make SQL more powerful. These extensions are not
common for all databases. Some companies have development policies to keep the universe
database-agnostic, particularly when they are contemplating migrating to a new RDBMS.
OEM vendors that use SAP BusinessObjects as the reporting engine also may strive to keep
their universes database-agnostic. However, when you avoid using database-specific SQL in
the universe, you are generally forcing end users to do more work in the reports. Our
recommendation is to use your database SQL to its fullest. Your universe will be more
powerful, and you will save users time.

SQL Parameters and the PRM File

The available database-specific functions are stored in the *database*.prm file (located under
C:\Program Files (x86)\SAP BusinessObjects\SAP BusinessObjects Enterprise XI 4.0\
dataAccess\connectionServer\). The corresponding help text or function description (as

shown in Figure 9-1) is stored in a separate language-specific XML file as *RDBMSLL*.prm, where *LL* refers to the language. For example, the English language help text for Oracle functions is stored in Oracleen.prm.

SAP BusinessObjects provides a default *database*.prm file that you may want to modify, for the following reasons:

- To enable users to access SQL functions that have been disabled by default

- To improve the help text for frequently used functions, especially if your company has decentralized universe designers

- To include SQL functions that your RDBMS vendor has recently added but that do not appear by default in the provided *database*.prm file (for example, the Microsoft SQL Server .prm file does not list the RANK function, even though the database supports this)

- To add functions that your DBA created

If a command does not exist in the file, designers can also manually enter it in the SQL statement rather than changing the .prm file. When you change the *database*.prm file, you must restart the IDT for the change to take effect.

The following is a section from the Oracle.prm file on the SQL UPPERCASE function.

```
<Function Group="False" ID="Uppercase" InMacro="True" Type="String">
        <Arguments>
            <Argument Type="String"></Argument>
        </Arguments>
        <SQL>upper($1)</SQL>
    </Function>
```

The following is the corresponding help text from the Oracleen.prm file:

```
<Function Name="Uppercase">
    <Arguments>
       <Message id="1">String:</Message>
    </Arguments>
    <Message id="Name">Uppercase</Message>
    <Message id="Help">Returns a character string in upper case</Message>
```

The Arguments section provides prompts when users create their own objects. The Argument Type indicates the format required. In the preceding example, the type is String, so users will be prompted to enter a string. If we were looking at an aggregate function such as SUM, the Argument Type would be Numeric. (The Arguments section and settings are similar to TRAD in earlier versions of the .prm file.)

SQL shows the actual SQL syntax. The number of SQL parameters is indicated with ($1) and so on.

Multiple Arguments and Prompt Messages

Some SQL functions require multiple arguments. For example, SUBSTR displays a certain number of characters beginning at a certain position and counting forward so many characters (or until the end if this third argument is not supplied). So designers and users must specify at least two arguments and an optional third:

- The field or object to extract the text from (Argument Type = "String")
- Which position to start extracting from (Argument Type = "Numeric")
- Which position to stop extracting from (Argument Type = "Numeric")

As an example, assume you want to create an object called *Area Code* from the object *Phone Number.* Poorly designed, the object does not store phone numbers numerically, and the field contains parentheses and dashes, as in (973) 555-1212. To extract just the area code requires the following SQL:

```
SUBSTR(Customer.Phone,2,3)
```

The Oracle.prm file would contain the following arguments and SQL:

```
<Arguments>
<Argument Type="String"></Argument>
<Argument Type="Numeric"></Argument>
<Argument Type="Numeric"></Argument>
</Arguments>
<SQL>substr($1,$2,$3)</SQL>
```

The help text in the Oracleen.prm file appears as follows:

```
<Function Name="Substring">
    <Message id="Help">Extracts a sequence of characters from a character
string</Message>
    <Message id="Name">Substring</Message>
    <Arguments>
       <Message id="1">String:</Message>
       <Message id="2">Initial position:</Message>
       <Message id="3">Number of characters:</Message>
    </Arguments>
```

Filter Objects

Filter objects are unique objects that allow users to access predefined conditions that the designer specifies in the WHERE clause. Filter objects are denoted with a filter symbol.

The Island Resorts Marketing universe, shown next, contains several predefined filters, such as *US customer*, *Young adult*, and *Young American*. Most of these filters are fairly simple.

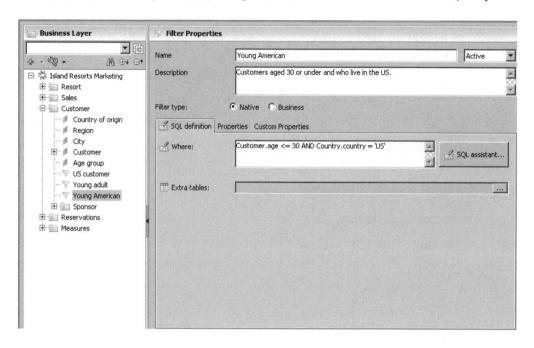

In building filter objects, you, as the designer, must evaluate if the objects add clutter or value. Filter objects can help in the following ways:

- Save users time.
- Filter groups of dimension values that may not otherwise exist in dimension tables.
- Provide consistency in how users filter data.

However, filter objects that contain only one value, such as *Year 2012*, do not provide much help; users probably could easily add the condition themselves. The object *Young American*, on the other hand, contains two conditions (`Customer.age <= 30 AND Country.country = 'US'`). Similarly, nesting conditions can be confusing and cumbersome, so an object that contains nested filters could also be very helpful to users.

Creating a Filter Object

In the following example, you will use the Island Resorts Marketing universe to create a condition object, *Platinum Customers*, for customers who generate more than $100,000 in revenue in any given year. Throughout this chapter, we will build on this example to show a number of advanced object capabilities. In this sample universe, seven customers had revenues of $100,000 or more, as shown in the following query result. You will add each of these seven customer codes to the filter object.

Customer	Customer ID	Year	Revenue
Baker	106	FY2005	150,666
Kamata	502	FY2005	128,146
Larson	104	FY2005	108,210
McCarthy	102	FY2005	135,580
Oneda	506	FY2005	143,984
Schiller	402	FY2005	127,584
Titzman	406	FY2005	145,300

1. Using the Island Resorts Marketing universe, position your cursor on the folder where you want the new object to appear—in this example, *Customer*.

2. Click the Insert Object button on the toolbar and select Filter.

3. In the Name box, enter **Platinum Customer**.

4. In the Description box, enter some meaningful help text, such as **A platinum customer is one with Revenues of $100,000 or more in any given year**.

5. Leave the filter type set as Native. A native filter allows you to choose elements from the data foundation or from tables and fields.

6. You can either manually enter the WHERE clause or use the SQL Assistant. For this example, click the SQL Assistant button. Under Tables, scroll to the table that contains the field you want to use for the WHERE clause. In this example, click the + next to CUSTOMER.

7. For response time reasons, you want the WHERE clause on the indexed CUST_ID field rather than the nonindexed CUSTOMER field. Double-click CUST_ID to add it to the WHERE statement.

8. Note that a downward arrow appears next to the selected field. Use this to invoke the Select Members dialog from which to choose the CUST_ID values.

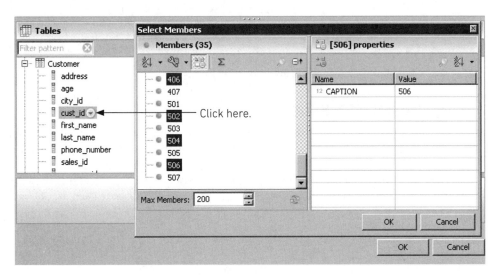

9. The selection process is a little cumbersome but less error-prone than manually entering values. Use CTRL-click to select multiple values (106, 502, 104, 102, 506, 402, and 406). Click OK to close the Select Members dialog and to insert the values in the SQL Expression Editor.

10. In the Operators box, scroll to IN and double-click to add this to the SQL statement. Enclose the list of numbers within parentheses.

11. *Always* click Validate to test the validity of the SQL statement.

12. Click OK to close the SQL Expression Editor. The filter object properties should now look like the following:

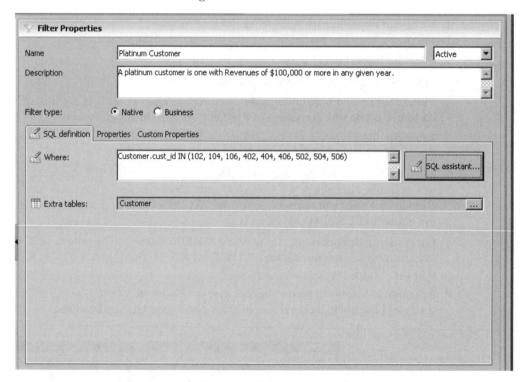

13. Click Save to save the business layer changes.

Filter Object with Subquery

The object you created in the previous section works perfectly fine and will provide the best query performance. However, what if your top customers change from quarter to quarter or year to year? In this case, you could add a subquery to the condition object so that the list of customers with a certain revenue level is generated dynamically. The following SQL would be used in the Where box of the SQL definition tab to create such an object:

```
Customer.cust_id in (
SELECT
  Customer.cust_id
```

```
FROM
  Customer,
  Sales,
  Invoice_Line,
  Service
WHERE
  ( Customer.cust_id=Sales.cust_id  )
  AND  ( Sales.inv_id=Invoice_Line.inv_id  )
  AND  ( Invoice_Line.service_id=Service.service_id  )
GROUP BY
  Customer.last_name,
  Customer.cust_id,
  'FY'+Format(Sales.invoice_date,'YYYY')
HAVING
  sum(Invoice_Line.days * Invoice_Line.nb_guests * Service.price)  >=  100000)
```

TIP In this example, consider using @Prompt to allow users to specify the revenue amount dynamically when they use this object.

Subqueries are slow, so use them with care.

Filter Object with HAVING

In previous releases of Designer, it was not possible to create condition objects based on measures (so you couldn't say Where Revenue >= 100,000), as doing so requires a different SQL clause. Filter objects with a type "native" will automatically use the WHERE clause, whereas filtering on measures requires use of a HAVING clause (explained in Chapter 22). However, the IDT allows you to create a filter object based on business layer objects.

When you set the filter type to Business when creating a filter object (rather than leaving the Native setting, as in step 5 in the previous "Creating a Filter Object" section), the SQL Where box is removed and an Edit Filter button appears. Click the Edit Filter button to choose objects from the business layer to set as filters. In this example, the measure *Revenue* is used as a filter. The query engine will correctly append the query with a HAVING clause.

NOTE Although the filter in this example generates queries for revenue greater than or equal to $100,000, keep in mind that the HAVING clause relies on whatever dimensions appear in the GROUP BY clause. So it does not strictly pertain to customers that have greater than $100,000 in revenues per year; it could also pertain to products and other items.

Filter Properties

You can require certain filters to be used automatically whenever an object from a particular folder is selected or for the entire universe. To enable this feature, follow these steps:

1. Create the filter object.
2. Navigate to the Properties tab of the filter object.
3. Select the "Use filter as mandatory in query" box.
4. Choose the desired radio button option: Apply on Universe or Apply on Folder.

Time Conditions

Filter objects involving time functions are popular. Additionally, Web Intelligence does not allow users to add calculations within the Query Panel, so filter objects become the only way that users can create rolling reports. The objects in this section's examples use SYSDATE, which returns the current date according to the RDBMS.

The following SQL creates a *One Year Ago* condition object. The comparison column is in a date format. Because SYSDATE is a date column including the day of the year, you subtract 365 days to arrive at the same date last year.

```
TIMES.END_OF_CAL_YEAR=SYSDATE-365
```

If the comparison column is not in a date format but is numeric, then you must also convert the SYSDATE calculation to numeric with TO_NUMBER. The following SQL creates a *Last Year* object in which the year is four digits. To extract only the four digits, use the TO_CHAR function.

```
TIMES.CALENDAR_YEAR=TO_NUMBER(TO_CHAR(SYSDATE-365,'YYYY'))
```

You can further nest date functions to create a *Current 3 Months* condition object. In the following example, the -3 value indicates that three months should be subtracted from the SYSDATE.

```
SH.TIMES.CALENDAR_MONTH_NUMBER BETWEEN TO_NUMBER(TO_CHAR(ADD_MONTHS(SYSDATE,-3),
'MM') ) AND TO_NUMBER(TO_CHAR(SYSDATE,'MM') )
```

NOTE The WHERE statements from each condition object and the row restrictions set through the universe security restrictions (discussed in Chapter 12) are appended to the entire SQL statement. If users combine incompatible filter objects, they may not get any rows returned.

Reusing Interactive Objects with @Variable

You can also reuse the prompt as a variable in other objects. The variable can be one that you create with @Prompt, or it can be a system variable. SAP BusinessObjects provides the following system variables:

- **BOUSER**   The SAP BusinessObjects user ID
- **DBUSER**   The database credentials used to connect to the data source
- **UNVNAME**   The name of the universe
- **DOCNAME**   The name of the document

For a full list of system variables, consult the online help.

As an example, let's assume that a hierarchical PRODUCT table contains both products and employees responsible for those products. So that users automatically see information for their products, the *My Product* object could contain the following WHERE clause:

```
PRODUCT.PRODUCT_OWNER = @Variable('BOUSER')
```

These system variables can be used in business layer objects or in the SQL query script parameters in BEGIN_SQL or END_SQL set in the data foundation. For example, for tracking purposes, you may want to append each query with a comment so the DBA can better analyze which document or user is refreshing a query. To do this, you would modify the END_SQL parameter in the data foundation to include the following:

```
/* DocumentName=@variable('DOCNAME') */
```

Reusing Interactive Objects with @Where

As mentioned previously, @Where allows you to reuse a WHERE clause in multiple objects. There are two benefits to using @Where: decreased maintenance and decreased user prompting. If a query contains multiple occurrences of the exact same prompt, Web Intelligence will prompt the user only one time.

For example, let's assume that users must filter customer information by city to ensure only a limited amount of data is returned. The dimension object *City* contains a prompt. A designer could add @Where (Customer\City) to *Customer Name*, *Customer Id*, and *Customer Age Group*. Even if a query contains all four of these objects, the user is prompted only once to select a city.

Prompts in Objects Versus Reports

Objects with prompts achieve a similar functionality as queries with prompts (discussed in Chapter 19). In Chapter 13, you will look at the pros and cons of where to put this kind of intelligence. The main difference to consider with prompts is flexibility and maintenance.

If you want to give the users flexibility, put the prompts in the query. If you want to minimize your maintenance costs, keep the prompts centralized in the universe objects.

The following table summarizes some of the key differences between prompts in objects versus prompts in a query.

Universe Object with Prompt	Query with Prompt
Designer builds into universe	User builds in query
Centralized, so cost-effective to maintain because the designer creates the prompt once	Decentralized, so expensive to maintain because users must create the prompt in every document
Users cannot remove, so it can be inflexible, but it's error-proof, as it requires an answer	Users can remove, providing flexibility

Aggregate Awareness

An *aggregate table* is a summary table that DBAs build to execute queries faster. Aggregate tables are smaller than detail tables and can be aggregated in a number of ways. Most DBAs will strive for a certain compression ratio. For example, with a 10:1 ratio, the aggregate or summary table should be ten times smaller than the detail table, or for every ten detail rows, there is one summary row.

Before you spend your time reading this section, talk to your DBA to determine if your database will automatically take advantage of aggregate tables. Customers using the newly released HANA in-memory appliance also will not need to use aggregate awareness. Newer versions of databases can automatically rewrite a query to leverage an aggregate table when it is available. The universe designer does not need to explicitly specify these aggregates. Unfortunately, it seems many organizations have been slow to take advantage of the database's query rewrite feature, so instructions are provided here on how to use IDT's aggregate awareness.

Figure 9-2 shows two sample dimensions: Time and Product. In the Time dimension, there are five years of history, with four levels going from Year to Day. Within a given year, there are 365 days. If the Time dimension contains five years of history, this results in 1,825 rows of data. The Product dimension has four levels, ranging from Total Product to individual SKU. There are 210 SKUs (this is a very small Product dimension).

A DBA may create an aggregate table summarizing data to any of these levels, across any dimension, as shown in Figure 9-3. The SALES_FACT_DAY table contains daily sales figures for five years, at the SKU level for all customers. The SALES_FACT_MONTH table aggregates sales by month and by product line. Customer is not aggregated in any way.

The following table shows the potential number of rows in such a fact table, if you have 30,000 customers. Typically, not every product sells daily, nor does every customer buy every product on a daily basis, so the potential rows represent strictly a worst-case scenario.

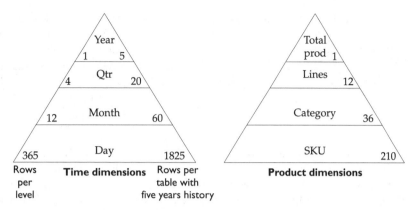

Rows
per
level

Time dimensions

Rows per
table with
five years history

Product dimensions

Figure 9-2   Two sample dimensions showing the number of potential rows at each level

These symbols show that:

• The Month table
  is smaller than
  the Day table

• Month and Prod
  columns
  aggregate

Month	Prod lines	Customer	Amount	Quantity
1/2003	Boys			
2/2003	Girls			
.				
.				
.	Men			
12/2003	Women			

Sales_Fact_Month

(1,1)

Σ   Σ

(1,1)

	SKU	Customer	Amount	Quantity
4/1/2003				
.				
.				
4/30/2003				
5/1/2003				
.				
5/30/2003				

Sales_Fact_Day

Figure 9-3   Aggregate tables are summary tables that allow for faster queries.

Part II

However, the table illustrates the purpose of using aggregate tables for faster queries. If a user wants to analyze customer or product line sales only on a monthly or quarterly basis, the queries will run much faster against a 21.6 million–row table than an 11.497 billion–row table.

	Time	Product	Customer	Potential Rows
Day, SKU	1825	210	30,000	11,497,500,000
Month, Product Line	60	12	30,000	21,600,000

The *existence* of aggregate tables does not help user queries. Users must *access* the summary tables, ideally automatically with awareness built into the RDBMS to force the query to be processed in the most efficient way. You most often will use aggregates with measures from fact tables, as shown in Figure 9-3. For extremely large dimensions, you also may have a smaller dimension table, such as one that removes dimension details lower than month and product line (as shown in Figure 9-2).

The following process outlines the key steps to enabling aggregate awareness.

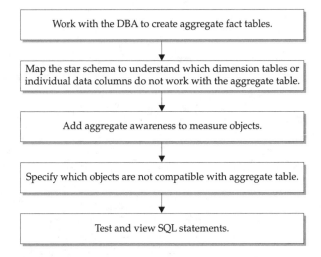

Creating Aggregate Fact Tables

There are two aggregate tables in efashion.mdb. You will focus on one table:

    AGG_YR_QT_MT_MN_WK_RG_CY_SN_SR_QT_MA

The table name reveals some information about the contents of the table:

- **AGG**   Aggregate
- **YR**   Year
- **QT**   Quarter
- **MT**   Month text

- **MN**   Month number
- **WK**   Week
- **RG**   Maybe region was intended, but it is not in the final table
- **CY**   City
- **SN**   Store name
- **SR**   Sales revenue
- **QT**   Quantity
- **MA**   Margin

Notice that the number of rows for the aggregate table is 1,982 compared to 89,171 in the detailed SHOP_FACTS table. Whenever possible, you want queries to run against the smaller AGG_YR_QT_MT_MN_WK_RG_CY_SN_SR_QT_MA table, rather than the larger SHOP_FACTS table.

The table name is a bit cumbersome, so hereafter, we will refer to it as the aggregate fact table.

Identifying Dimension Tables Irrelevant to Aggregate Tables

In Figure 9-4, notice that the aggregate table does not include any information about articles. So the dimension tables ARTICLE_LOOKUP and ARTICLE_COLOR_LOOKUP will become incompatible with the summary objects.

The fact table includes a lot of dimensional information. Time information is aggregated to the week level. You can retrieve dimensional information from either the CALENDAR_YEAR_LOOKUP table or the aggregate fact table. Outlet information is not aggregated. The aggregate table contains the store name, which is in the OUTLET_LOOKUP table, but does not contain information about the store location.

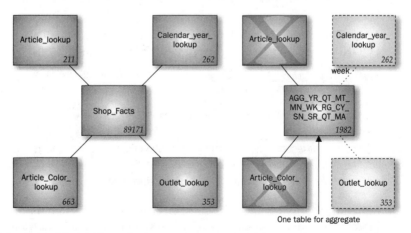

Figure 9-4   A detail fact table and a summary aggregate table may share some of the same dimension tables.

Adding Aggregate Awareness to Measure Objects

You are now ready to define aggregate awareness to the individual measure objects *Sales Revenue, Quantity Sold,* and *Margin.* Aggregate awareness uses an internal function, referencing the tables from aggregate to detail or from smallest table to biggest fact table:

```
@Aggregate_Aware(sum(smallest_table.column), sum(medium_table.column),
sum(biggest_table.column))
```

You can have multiple tables in the SELECT statement, with the smallest table first and the largest or most detailed table last. The @Aggregate_Aware function allows you to use any of the SQL aggregate commands (SUM, COUNT, AVG, MIN, and MAX); however, the aggregate command must be specified for each column. This is the correct version:

```
@Aggregate_Aware(sum(Agg_yr_qt_mt_mn_wk_rg_cy_sn_sr_qt_ma.Sales_revenue),
sum(Shop_facts.Amount_sold))
```

And this is the incorrect version:

```
@Aggregate_Aware(sum(Agg_yr_qt_mt_mn_wk_rg_cy_sn_sr_qt_ma.Sales_revenue,
Shop_facts.Amount_sold))
```

To enable aggregate navigation, you must first add the aggregate table within the data foundation, and then enable the aggregate within a measure in the business layer.

For the following example, use the Simple eFashion data foundation.

1. Insert the aggregate table into the data foundation. From within the business layer, click the Edit Data Foundation button.

2. From within the data foundation structure pane, right-click and choose Insert | Tables from the pop-up menu. Select AGG_YR_QT_MT_MN_WK_RG_CY_SN_SR_QT_MA.

3. Insert joins from the aggregate table to the two dimension tables OUTLET_LOOKUP and CALENDAR_YEAR_LOOKUP as follows:

   ```
   Agg_yr_qt_mt_mn_wk_rg_cy_sn_sr_qt_ma.Store_name=Outlet_Lookup.Shop_name

   Calendar_year_lookup.Yr=Agg_yr_qt_mt_mn_wk_rg_cy_sn_sr_qt_ma.Yr AND
   Calendar_year_lookup.Week_In_Year=Agg_yr_qt_mt_mn_wk_rg_cy_sn_sr_qt_ma.Wk
   ```

NOTE Normally, it is not recommended to join a description field from one table to a description field in another; the joins should be between indexed ID fields. However, if users want stores within a particular state, for example, you have no choice with this model.

---

4. Either draw join lines between the respective tables and columns or select Insert | Insert Join from the menu. Note that the second join is a complex join that must be entered manually.

5. Add these two new joins to a new context. If you have correctly defined the complex join, you can use the Detect Context button.

6. The IDT will propose three new contexts, creating new contexts for product promotions and shop facts, as well as for the aggregate table. You can either accept all three or only the context for the aggregate table. If you also accept the contexts for product promotions and shop facts, the new joins will specifically be excluded from these contexts, which is what you want. Otherwise, you may also modify your existing contexts, changing the status from neutral to excluded.

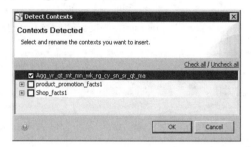

7. Save the changes to the data foundation.

Accessing the Aggregate Table

Now that the aggregate table exists in the data foundation, you can access it from the business layer as follows:

1. Refresh the business layer by pressing F5 from within the business layer. Alternatively, select the business layer from the Local Projects pane, right-click, and then select Refresh from the pop-up menu.

2. Expand the folder Test Fashion Measures.

3. Select the object *Sum of Amount Sold or Revenue.*

4. Click the SQL Assistant button to open the SQL editor.

5. If you wish to avoid re-creating the SQL for the detail SHOP_FACTS table, ensure your mouse is positioned at the start of the SQL statement.

6. Under Functions, click the + sign next to @Functions to expand the group and display the internal functions.

7. Double-click @Aggregate_Aware to insert the syntax in the SQL statement box.

8. Under Functions, click the + sign next to Database Functions, Numeric to display the SQL RDBMS functions. Scroll to sum() and double-click to insert the syntax into the SQL statement.

9. Under Tables and Columns, expand the aggregate table AGG_YR_QT_MT_MN_ WK_RG_CY_SN_SR_QT_MA and double-click SALES_REVENUE to insert the table.column within the parentheses of sum().

10. Delete the right parenthesis and move it to the end to close the statement. Your SQL statement should appear as follows:

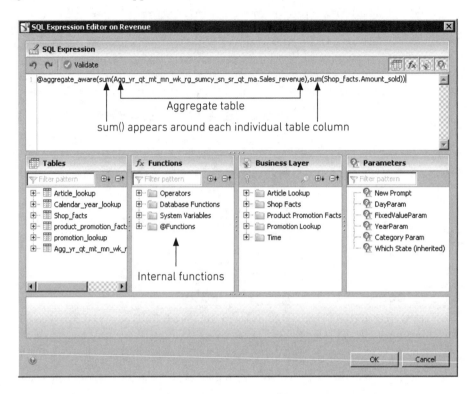

11. Click Validate to verify you have entered the correct syntax.

12. Click OK to close the SQL editor.

13. Save the business layer.

Specifying Which Objects Are Not Compatible with the Aggregate Table

The table now exists in the data foundation, and you have specified in the business layer to use this table for certain measure objects. You now need to specify that the aggregate table cannot be used when certain dimension objects exist in the query. This can be very confusing. Try to stay focused on two things:

- You are essentially telling the query engine when to use the detail table.

- You need to worry about only one context or star schema.

Referring back to Figure 9-3, notice that all article objects are incompatible with the aggregate table. If a user includes any article information in a query, it is not available in the aggregate table, and you must tell the IDT to use the detail SHOP_FACTS table.

You are only concerned with this one context and do not need to worry about the promotion objects. This second point is especially confusing, because when the IDT detects incompatibility, it unnecessarily and incorrectly marks objects from other contexts. If you mark promotion objects as incompatible here, you prevent users from constructing a query that compares sales by store (using the aggregate table) with promotions by store. For this reason, we recommend that you manually set incompatibilities. Do not use automatic detection.

NOTE You only need to mark objects that exist in the one context or star schema as incompatible.

To define incompatible objects, follow these steps:

1. From the main IDT menu, select Actions | Set Aggregate Navigation.

2. Highlight the table for which you will define incompatible objects—in this example, AGG_YR_QT_MT_MN_WK_RG_CY_SN_SR_QT_MA.

3. Under Associated Incompatible Objects, you can select entire folders or individual objects. For this example, click the *Article Lookup* folder.

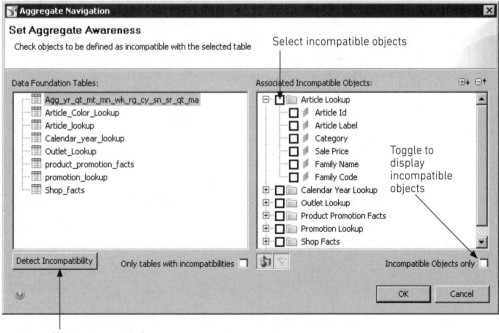

CAUTION If you toggle to display tables that contain incompatible objects, only aggregate tables should be displayed. If more than just the aggregates are displayed, you have set something incorrectly.

4. Use the toggle check box Incompatibles Objects Only to filter those objects that have been marked as incompatible against the aggregate table.

5. Click OK to close the Aggregate Navigation dialog.

6. Select File | Save from the pull-down menu or click Save to save the changes to the business layer.

Testing and Viewing SQL Statements

Now that you have defined which objects are incompatible with the aggregate fact table, you need to make sure that the query engine generates the correct SQL. To test this, use Figure 9-3 to develop a test plan, as shown in Table 9-1. Take each measure that contains @Aggregate_Aware and add a dimension object from each of the dimension tables to the query. As you create a query for each scenario, verify that the SQL generated uses the appropriate table. From within the business layer, navigate to the Queries tab to create each scenario.

Scenario	If Your Query Contains These Objects	Query Engine Should Use This Table
1	*Sum of Amount Sold*	AGG_YR_QT_MT_MN_WK_RG_CY_SN_SR_QT_MA
2	*Sum of Amount Sold, Month Name*	AGG_YR_QT_MT_MN_WK_RG_CY_SN_SR_QT_MA
3	*Sum of Amount Sold, Month Name, Shop Name*	AGG_YR_QT_MT_MN_WK_RG_CY_SN_SR_QT_MA
4	*Sum of Amount Sold, Promotion Cost, Month*	*2 SQL Select statements:* AGG_YR_QT_MT_MN_WK_RG_CY_SN_SR_QT_MA, PRODUCT_PROMOTION_FACTS
5	*Sum of Amount Sold, Month Name, Store Name, Article*	SHOP_FACTS
6	*Sum of Amount Sold, Article Color*	SHOP_FACTS
7	*Sum of Amount Sold, Number of Article Code*	SHOP_FACTS

Table 9-1 Test Plan for Aggregate Awareness

To view the SQL statement, follow these steps:

1. From within the business layer, navigate to the Queries tab.
2. Follow the test plan outlined in Table 9-1 to add the result objects to the query. The following shows a query based on scenario 3 in Table 9-1.

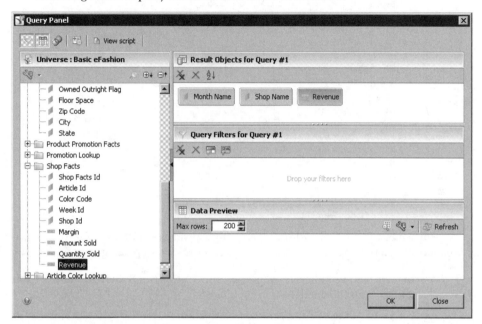

3. To verify that the correct fact table is used in the SQL, click the View script button on the Query Panel toolbar. Note that for scenario 3, the aggregate fact table was correctly used.

```
SELECT
  sum(Table__8.Sales_revenue),
  Table__2.Month_Name,
  Table__3.Shop_name
FROM
  Agg_yr_qt_mt_mn_wk_rg_cy_sn_sr_qt_ma   Table__8,
  Calendar_year_lookup   Table__2,
  Outlet_Lookup   Table__3
WHERE
  ( Table__8.Store_name=Table__3.Shop_name  )
  AND  ( Table__2.Week_In_Year = Table__8.Wk   AND   Table__2.Yr = Table__8.Yr  )
GROUP BY
  Table__2.Month_Name,
  Table__3.Shop_name
```

4. When you add *Article* to the query, as in scenario 5, the SQL engine automatically selects the SHOP_FACTS table without any user intervention.

```
SELECT
  sum(Shop_facts.Amount_sold),
  Calendar_year_lookup.Month_Name,
  Outlet_Lookup.Shop_name,
  Article_lookup.Article_code

FROM
  Shop_facts,
  Calendar_year_lookup,
  Article_lookup,
  Outlet_Lookup
WHERE
  ( Shop_facts.Article_code=Article_lookup.Article_code  )
  AND  ( Calendar_year_lookup.Week_key=Shop_facts.Week_key  )
  AND  ( Shop_facts.Shop_code=Outlet_Lookup.Shop_code  )
GROUP BY
  Calendar_year_lookup.Month_Name,
  Outlet_Lookup.Shop_name,
  Article_lookup.Article_code
```

For scenario 4 in Table 9-1, the query engine will generate two SQL statements and seamlessly stitch the results together in the report. This step can go wrong for two reasons:

- In your data foundation properties, the Multiple SQL Statements for Each Context setting is not enabled.

- You used Actions | Set Aggregate Navigation | Detect Incompatibility. In this case, the IDT incorrectly marks objects from other contexts as being incompatible with an aggregate table.

The most obvious error in this step of building aggregate awareness is if the wrong table is used in any instance. However, the ultimate goal is to get correct results. So as a final test, you should run a query to ensure that you get the same data when either the aggregate table or the detail table is used. In the preceding examples, the sales value for September 2001 is $300,848, according to both the aggregate table and the SHOP_FACTS table.

There are a few reasons why you may not get the same result for an aggregate table as for a detail table:

- One of the tables is incorrect. If the DBA has not built the aggregate table correctly, you may not be able to fix it, but you must communicate this issue to both DBAs and end users. When something is wrong, SAP BusinessObjects will be blamed, because most business users don't know and don't care which component in the information flow actually has the problem. If the summary table is incorrect in all circumstances, don't include it in the universe design. If it is correct in most circumstances, and the DBA is working to resolve one minor inconsistency, use the table but clearly explain in the object description when the data may be incorrect.

- The aggregate table contains dimensional information that is different from details in the lookup or dimension tables. As a design principle, we don't like when dimensional information is stored in the fact table. It's problematic when there is a difference between dimensional information in a fact table and a dimension table. In a perfect world, the data is clean and consistent. In the example of AGG_YR_ QT_MT_MN_WK_RG_CY_SN_SR_QT_MA, the store name exists in both this aggregate fact table and the dimension table OUTLET_LOOKUP. What if the fact table contained data for a store that did not exist in OUTLET_LOOKUP? Users would get different answers between queries that use the aggregate table and queries that use the detail table that joins to the dimension table that is missing information for a store.

- The universe contains a mistake in the join or in a dimension definition. An error in the design is completely within your control and must be resolved before deploying to end users.

Derived Tables

Derived tables are similar to views in the database, but as they are defined in the universe in the data foundation, they give universe designers more flexibility. A derived table is a query that can be referenced by a universe designer as a table.

As derived tables are queries, and not physical tables, it's important to understand that the same performance issues that affect queries also affect derived tables:

- Do *not* use derived tables in place of aggregate tables. Aggregate tables must be physical tables built by the DBA to provide fast query performance.

- Do use derived tables that minimize the complexity of the queries users need to create themselves.

- Do use derived tables in place of views and stored procedures that in the past you would have asked a DBA to create.

Derived tables may be most useful when you want to UNION two queries together (for example, a supplier and customer table to create a vendor table), when you want to include @Variable in the query logic, and in some cases, when you have different aggregation levels.

NOTE If you use derived tables to create different aggregation levels, be careful to consider the impact on joins, contexts, and many-to-many relationships. If your database supports newer analytic and report functions (see the "Ratio to Report" section later in this chapter), these functions will give you much better response time than using derived tables.

This example uses the Island Resorts Marketing universe. Earlier, in the "Filter Objects" section, you created the filter object *Platinum Customers*. A valid business question may be "How much of my business do the platinum customers account for?" To answer this, you need to get the total sales for all customers as well as the total sales for only the top customers and combine them in one query. Within the Island Resorts Marketing universe, the object *Revenue* is calculated from the INVOICE_LINES table. To define the *Top Customer Revenue* object, you create a derived table:

1. Navigate to the data foundation. From within the structure pane, right-click and select Insert | Derived Tables from the pop-up menu.

2. Within the Edit Derived Tables dialog, replace the generic Derived Table name with a meaningful table name, such as **TopCustomers**.

TIP Avoid blank spaces in table names to minimize needing to use double quotation marks when referencing the name.

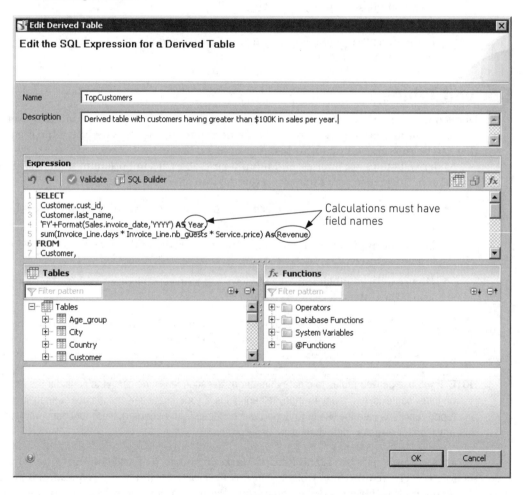

3. Enter a description for the derived table. This is seen only by the universe developer, not end users.

4. In the SQL Expression box, enter the desired SQL to create the derived table. If you have used the business layer query tab or Web Intelligence to create the initial SQL, you must ensure that each calculation is assigned a field name. For example, in the preceding example, AS Year will create the field TopCustomers.Year within the derived table.

```
SELECT
  Customer.cust_id,
  Customer.last_name,
  'FY'+Format(Sales.invoice_date,'YYYY') AS Year,
  sum(Invoice_Line.days * Invoice_Line.nb_guests * Service.price) As Revenue
FROM
  Customer,
  Sales,
  Invoice_Line,
  Service,
  { oj Customer LEFT OUTER JOIN Sales ON Customer.cust_id=Sales.cust_id },
  { oj Sales LEFT OUTER JOIN Invoice_Line ON Sales.inv_id=Invoice_Line.inv_id },
  { oj Invoice_Line LEFT OUTER JOIN Service ON Invoice_Line.service_id=Service.ser-
vice_id }
GROUP BY
  Customer.cust_id,
  Customer.last_name,
  'FY'+Format(Sales.invoice_date,'YYYY')
HAVING
  sum(Invoice_Line.days * Invoice_Line.nb_guests * Service.price)  >=  100000
```

5. Validate the SQL statement.

6. Click OK to close the Edit Derived Table dialog.

7. Add the necessary joins and include the new derived table in relevant contexts. In this example, add the join TopCustomers.cust_id=Customer.cust_id and include the table in the Sales context.

8. Create the object *Top Customer Revenue* as a measure with the following SQL that accesses the newly created derived table:

```
sum(TopCustomers.Revenue)
```

Now when a user creates a report that contains these two measures, Web Intelligence generates two SQL statements and automatically presents the results as one seamless report.

Note in the following that any data not in the derived table appears as a null value. For example, Customer 101 did not have revenues greater than 100,000.

Customer ID	Revenue	Top Customer Revenue
101	8,420	
102	400,899	400,899
103	4,380	
104	301,545	209,545
105	18,715	
106	441,594	441,594
107	10,704	
401	10,976	
402	388,524	388,524
403	4,400	
404	222,010	

With the use of derived tables, a user can easily create a report that shows that 78 percent of the total revenue comes from the top seven customers.

From derived table →

From physical table → INVOICE_LINES

Revenue	Top Customer Revenue	Percent Contribution
3,286,524	2,582,454	78.58%

Popular SQL Functions

SQL functions are powerful and limited only by your creativity, but potentially, they are more overwhelming (especially if you inadvertently put commas and parentheses in all the wrong places). In the universe design process, this is when the power users, universe designers, and DBAs must partner together to build a technically correct but business-robust universe.

There are entire books dedicated to SQL commands alone, so it is impossible to cover all of the functions here. What follows are just a few examples of some popular objects that use SQL functions to deliver business functionality.

Concatenated Objects

Concatenated objects combine information from multiple fields. A common usage is to combine a customer or employee's *First Name* and *Last Name* into a new object, *Name*. Depending on your database, you have two ways to concatenate fields:

- The CONCAT function, which is database-specific and allows you to combine two columns of data.
- An operator that allows you to combine several columns into one. Microsoft databases use +, and Oracle uses ||.

You can nest CONCAT statements to combine multiple columns, but personally, we find the nested functions harder to read than operators.

The following object uses the CONCAT function and the IDT's @Select function to reference existing objects in the universe:

```
CONCAT(@Select(Hr Employees\First Name),@Select(Hr Employees\Last Name))
```

The SQL statement will appear as follows:

```
CONCAT(HR.EMPLOYEES.FIRST_NAME,HR.EMPLOYEES.LAST_NAME)
```

The syntax for the CONCAT function in SQL Server is as follows:

```
{fn concat(HumanResources.vEmployee.FirstName, HumanResources.vEmployee.LastName)}
```

Using an operator, you can combine more than two fields plus spaces between each column:

```
( HR.EMPLOYEES.EMPLOYEE_ID ) ||' '|| ( HR.EMPLOYEES.FIRST_NAME )||' ' || (
HR.EMPLOYEES.LAST_NAME )
```

Time Objects

Many sales reports and income statements contain current period and year-to-date (YTD) information. Creating objects that include time period awareness or YTD functionality is a two-step process:

- First, you must determine what is the definition of "to-date": Is it whichever accounting month the books have closed? Is it the calendar day of today? The answer to this may depend on whether you are viewing accounting information or sales order information. Accountants may want *closed* accounting months, whereas salespeople will want the latest date possible.
- The second step involves grouping the information into columns or buckets of time periods. Grouping information into columns of data is described in the next section, "If-Then-Else Logic with CASE."

If users want to run rolling reports, you can provide them with filter objects that let them select current time periods or a rolling period. If you are looking for a closed accounting month, the best practice is to store the closed accounting month as a flag in the time dimension table. If this is not available, create an interactive object that prompts for the closed accounting month. To do this, first create a parameter to prompt the user for the latest accounting month.

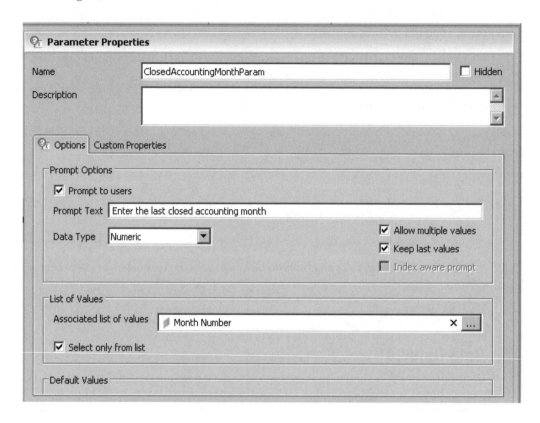

Next, use this parameter in any YTD objects. For example, *YTD Sales* would include the following in the WHERE clause:

```
@Select(Time\Fiscal Month Number)<=@Prompt (Closed Accounting Month)
```

Whenever you insert a parameter in the WHERE clause, the IDT automatically inserts @ Prompt, as shown here:

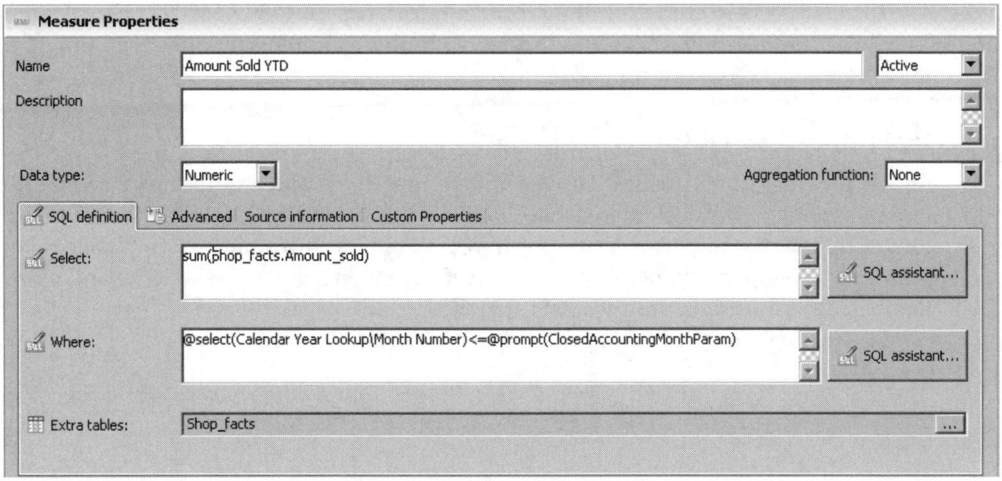

So far, you have only asked the user to specify the month and not the year. You could include the accounting year in the prompt as well, or you could get the current year from the RDBMS's system date. Users can include a current year condition in their query, or you may have a compound WHERE clause in the object *Current YTD Sales*:

```
@Select(Time\Month Number)<=@Prompt(Closed Accounting Month)
AND
@Select(Time\Year)=TO_NUMBER(TO_CHAR(SYSDATE,'YYYY') )
```

SYSDATE (for Oracle) or GETDATE() (for SQL Server) returns the system date on the RDBMS. It is a date field from which you want to extract just the year. TO_CHAR allows you to extract the four-digit year. However, your comparison object is numeric, so you must convert the character year to a numeric field using TO_NUMBER.

The following is the SQL Server equivalent to create a numeric year object:

```
Year(GetDate())
```

NOTE In using SYSDATE or GETDATE in your SELECT statement, the objects may not validate, as these fields do not physically exist. Also, be sure to use the Extra tables setting in the SQL definition tab to ensure a table is included in the SELECT statement generated by the query engine.

CAUTION Be aware that with this type of object, the *WHERE* clause gets appended to the entire query and users will not be able to have *Last Year* objects in the same report. Refer to the next section for an alternative.

To allow users to create a rolling three months, use the ADD_MONTHS SQL command to subtract three months from the SYSDATE. In this example, you only need the month, or MM, from the TO_CHAR function.

If-Then-Else Logic with CASE

Oracle provides the CASE and DECODE SQL functions, which both work like an if-then-else statement. The two functions have different syntaxes. DECODE has been around longer with earlier database versions, whereas CASE was introduced with Oracle 8, so many longtime developers still use DECODE. CASE statements are easier to write and more flexible; they also adhere to the ANSI standard.

This is the syntax for a simple CASE expression in Oracle:

```
CASE @Select(Class\ Object) when @Select(Class\ Object)='a' then 'b' else 'c' end
```

where:

- `@Select(Class\Object)` can be either the object whose value you want to change or the RDBMS *TABLE.COLUMN*.
- a is the value in the data column you wish to compare and replace.
- b is the replacement value.
- c is the alternative if there is no match for a.

The following is the syntax for DECODE:

```
DECODE (@Select(Class\Object),'if_a','then_b')
```

where `@Select(Class\Object)` can be either the object whose value you want to change or the RDBMS *TABLE.COLUMN*.

In the sample Oracle SH.CUSTOMER table, the CUST_GENDER column contains only two values: F for Female and M for Male. The gender description is not stored in a column. CASE or DECODE can help you create a description. Here is the syntax using CASE:

```
CASE
     when SH.CUSTOMERS.CUST_GENDER ='F' then 'Female'
     when SH.CUSTOMERS.CUST_GENDER = 'M' then 'Male'
     else 'Not Entered'
     End
```

And here is the syntax using DECODE:

```
decode(SH.CUSTOMERS.CUST_GENDER, 'F', 'Female', 'M', 'Male')
```

Using the SQL Server AdventureWorks schema, the syntax is as follows:

```
CASE
     when HumanResources.Employee.Gender ='F' then 'Female'
     when HumanResources.Employee.Gender = 'M' then 'Male'
     else 'Not Entered'
     End
```

Current Period and YTD Objects

CASE is also quite powerful for creating current period and YTD objects without the problem of conflicting WHERE clauses becoming appended to the entire query. To understand how to build this kind of object, first study the sample data in Figure 9-5. This is taken from the sample Oracle Sales History (SH) tables. The report shows sales amounts for this year and last, broken down by quarter. Assume the current quarter and year are the third quarter of 2005. You want to create two objects: one that retrieves the current period sales = 66,772,321 and one that retrieves the cumulative YTD sales = 217,702,751.

To determine which quarter you are in, you again use the SYSDATE and TO_CHAR commands. This time, you want the date to be in *YYYYQ* format. The sample SH.TIMES table has the year and quarter in two separate columns, so you will concatenate the two together to get the same comparison from your SYSDATE. You want to create a *Current Quarter Sales* object that says, "If the current calendar quarter matches the accounting quarter, then, for the same period in the database, show the sales; else, return zero." The objects you are trying to design look something like the table to the right:

Year	Current Quarter Sales	Current YTD Sales
2004	0	0
2005	66,772,321	217,702,752

The corresponding SQL for a *Current Quarter Sales* object using CASE is as follows:

```
sum(
CASE
When SH.TIMES.CALENDAR_YEAR=to_char(sysdate,'YYYY')
Then (CASE When
 SH.TIMES.CALENDAR_YEAR||SH.TIMES.CALENDAR_QUARTER_NUMBER
=
to_char(sysdate,'YYYYQ' )
Then SH.SALES.AMOUNT_SOLD
End)
Else 0
End
)
```

Year	Quarter Numbe	Amount Sold	YTD Sales
2004	1	61,109,170	61,109,170
	2	62,312,131	123,421,301
	3	57,156,689	180,577,990
	4	69,232,579	249,810,569
2004	**Sum:**	**249,810,569**	

Year	Quarter Numbe	Amount Sold	YTD Sales
2005	1	73,956,184	73,956,184
	2	76,974,247	150,930,430
	3	66,772,321	217,702,752
	4	51,686,766	269,389,518
2005	**Sum:**	**269,389,518**	

Figure 9-5   Quarterly sales report

You can build a similar object using DECODE. In this example, the date is fixed, rather than dynamically deciphered from the SYSDATE as in the previous CASE statement.

```
sum(decode(to_char(sysdate,'YYYYQ'),
'20053',DECODE(SH.TIMES.CALENDAR_YEAR||SH.TIMES.CALENDAR_QUARTER_NUMBER,'20053',SH
.SALES.AMOUNT_SOLD)))
```

When using CASE or DECODE in this way, it is important that the aggregate SUM function goes around the entire statement and is not nested within the CASE statement or between the DECODE statements. The following table decomposes the DECODE portion of the SQL statement:

Part	Purpose	SQL Syntax
1	If the current calendar quarter	`decode(to_char(sysdate, 'YYYYQ')`
2	Matches the accounting quarter	`'20053'`
3	Then for the same period in the database	`DECODE(SH.TIMES.CALENDAR_YEAR||SH.TIMES .CALENDAR_ QUARTER_NUMBER,'200053'`
4	Show the sales	`SH.SALES.AMOUNT_SOLD`
5	Else null	

Cumulative To-Date Objects

There are a number of ways to create a *Current YTD Sales* object that reflects the cumulative or running total for the current year (the previous example just summed one quarter). While the comparison part of your SQL (parts 1 and 2 in the preceding table) would remain the same, retrieving the values for a cumulative period in part 3 become a bit more of a challenge. You can have three sums, such as Q1+Q2+Q3, but if you ever try to create a *Current Week-To-Date* or *Current Month-To-Date* object, your SQL gets long and messy fast. What you really want is a way to retrieve a range of values or to test if the RDBMS accounting quarter is less than or equal to the SYSDATE quarter.

To create the YTD object, replace = 20053 with <= to get a cumulative total. The following SQL also contains a nested CASE statement to ensure that you add quarters from the same year.

```
sum(
     CASE
     When SH.TIMES.CALENDAR_YEAR=to_char(sysdate,'YYYY')
     Then (CASE When
SH.TIMES.CALENDAR_YEAR||SH.TIME.CALENDAR_QUARTER_NUMBER
         <=
         to_char(sysdate,'YYYYQ' )
         Then SH.SALES.AMOUNT_SOLD
         End)
```

```
      Else 0
      End
)
```

You can combine these automatic time period objects to create variances that compare sales trends between the two years or two quarters. For example, the following report uses several time period objects to determine that sales were 21 percent higher for the first three quarters of the year.

Automatic Dates					
Current Quarter Sales	Last Year Same Quarter	Current YTD Sales	Last Year YTD Sales	Variance	
66,772,321.10	57,156,688.85	217,702,751.55	180,577,989.70	21%	

One thing to be aware of with current year and YTD objects is that users do not need to enter a year as a condition. Everything is automatic. This can be great for users and for standard report maintenance, but it can be bad for the RDBMS if the queries result in a full table scan; the database will not use an index from any of the TIMES columns. If users will always select some other condition criteria, such as Product or Region, then these indexes may be used to process the query. As a work-around, you may want to include a WHERE clause in the automatic objects that includes enough years for the results to be accurate, but also for an index to be used. Alternatively, test the use of Oracle Hints if Oracle is your data source.

For example, if you have automatic objects for *Current Year*, *Last Year*, and *2 Years Ago*, then include the following as a WHERE clause for each object:

```
@Select(Time\Year) IN ('2005','2004','2003')
```

To avoid needing to update this each year, in theory, you may be able to use <= SYSDATE-(365*3); however, this assumes that the base comparison year is also a date field. In the preceding example, it is not, so you would need to convert the SYSDATE calculation using TO_CHAR.

Counting Objects

In Chapter 7, you looked at using the SQL COUNT function in measure objects to count the number of products or the number of customers. COUNT can get a little more complex than this, as what you want to count is not always obvious, and COUNT may give unexpected results.

What to Count?

The business user asks, "How many products do we have?" Easy—just count the unique PRODUCT_ID values in the dimension table! The following results show why this may not always be what the business user expects:

Prod Id	Prod Name	Supplier Id	Prod Min Price	Prod Pack Size	Prod Status
180.00	Potpourri Skirt	61.00	35.19	white paper bag	available, on stock
190.00	Potpourri Skirt	45.00	32.29	heavy duty box	available, on stock
195.00	Potpourri Skirt	77.00	32.29	brown envelope	available, on stock
200.00	Potpourri Skirt	77.00	32.29	heavy duty box	available, on stock
4,255.00	Potpourri Skirt	3.00	40.57	white paper bag	available, on stock
4,260.00	Potpourri Skirt	3.00	40.57	white paper bag	available, on stock
8,310.00	Potpourri Skirt	59.00	39.33	heavy duty box	available, on stock
8,315.00	Potpourri Skirt	105.00	39.33	heavy duty box	available, on stock
8,320.00	Potpourri Skirt	105.00	39.33	plastic bag	not available
8,325.00	Potpourri Skirt	105.00	39.33	heavy duty box	available, on stock
12,370.00	Potpourri Skirt	17.00	23.18	white paper bag	available, on stock
12,375.00	Potpourri Skirt	17.00	23.18	card box	ordered
12,390.00	Potpourri Skirt	17.00	33.53	white paper bag	available, on stock
12,395.00	Potpourri Skirt	47.00	33.53	water proof wrap	available, on stock
16,435.00	Potpourri Skirt	29.00	24.84	white paper bag	available, on stock
20,500.00	Potpourri Skirt	62.00	21.94	plastic bag	obsolete
20,515.00	Potpourri Skirt	62.00	40.99	heavy duty box	available, on stock
20,520.00	Potpourri Skirt	95.00	40.99	white paper bag	available, on stock
20,525.00	Potpourri Skirt	95.00	40.99	white paper bag	available, on stock
24,580.00	Potpourri Skirt	30.00	28.98	heavy duty box	available, on stock
24,590.00	Potpourri Skirt	83.00	36.43	plastic bag	ordered

A unique PRODUCT_ID value is created for each combination of a product description, supplier, price, packaging, and availability. Note that the only difference between PRODUCT_ID values 195 and 200 is the packaging: brown envelope versus heavy-duty box. The business definition for number of products may actually be according to the product ID, or it may be by product name. The SQL is different for each.

The following is the object definition for counting product IDs:

```
COUNT(PRODUCT_ID)
```

And this is the object definition for counting unique product names:

```
COUNT(DISTINCT PRODUCT_NAME)
```

Distinct Count

The COUNT function actually counts the number of rows returned; it does not count individual occurrences. In the preceding example, if you used COUNT(PRODUCT_NAME), you would get the same result as with COUNT(PRODUCT_ID). If you want Potpourri Skirt to count as one product regardless of the number of times it occurs in the database, you must use COUNT(DISTINCT *TABLE.COLUMN*).

Recall from Chapter 7 that a dimension object should always come from the dimension or lookup table and not the fact table, which will have multiple occurrences of the same product ID. With COUNT, this becomes even more important to guarantee correct results. There is a significant difference between counting the number of products versus the number of products sold in a particular period. The former must come from the dimension table; the latter must come from the fact table. The following report shows how each count yields different results:

COUNT - NUMBER OF PRODUCTS				
Product Category	Number of Products	Number of Product Names	Number of Products Fact	Number of Products Fact Dist
Boys	2,428.00	85.00	227,102.00	1,091.00
Girls	1,926.00	73.00	177,538.00	901.00
Men	2,594.00	193.00	238,860.00	1,278.00
Women	3,052.00	411.00	372,771.00	1,752.00

The following table shows the SQL used to generate each column of data.

Object	SQL
Number of Products	COUNT(DISTINCT PRODUCTS.PROD_ID)
Number of Product Names	COUNT(DISTINCT PRODUCTS.PROD_NAME)
Number of Products Fact	COUNT(SH.SALES.PROD_ID)
Number of Products Fact Distinct	COUNT(DISTINCT SALES.PROD_ID)

For the Boys product category, there are 2,428 unique product IDs and 85 different product names. These are both valid numbers. Users may want to see only one or both. If they want to see both, then the object name and the corresponding description must clearly convey what is being counted. Both columns come from the dimension table.

The SQL for the first object, *Number of Products,* includes the DISTINCT keyword, but only as a precaution; it is not strictly required. If the field you are counting is a unique ID or key field for the entire table, DISTINCT is not required.

CAUTION Be careful about assuming that ID fields are always unique; some IDs may have an active/inactive flag or timestamp to indicate the latest record.

The Number of Products Fact column in the report is misleading and meaningless. There are 227,102 occurrences of a PRODUCT_ID in the SALES fact table. When DISTINCT is used, there are 1,091 distinct occurrences of a PRODUCT_ID in the SALES fact table. This number has a business meaning in that 1,091 unique Boys products were sold. Users may want to see one or all three types of counts.

NOTE Always use COUNT (DISTINCT *TABLE.COLUMN*) when counting items in a fact table. Otherwise, use COUNT only against columns with unique IDs or keys.

Rank

The RANK function allows you to rank a dimension (such as customer, product, or salesperson) according to any metric (sales, profit, commission, and so on). The ranked dimension is determined by the user as result objects in the query. You, as the designer, specify the metric for the ranking.

The following is the basic syntax of RANK:

```
RANK() OVER(PARTITION BY DIMENSION_TABLE.COLUMN ORDER BY AGG(FACT_TABLE.COLUMN)
DESC
```

where:

- `PARTITION BY DIMENSION_TABLE.COLUMN` is optional and is used to rank items within a subset of data.

NOTE Depending on your database, the IDT may not display the RANK function as an option in the function pane, but you may still use it in the SELECT statement if your database supports RANK.

- `AGG(FACT_TABLE.COLUMN)` is the aggregated measure that forms the ranking. For example, products with the highest sales appear as `SUM(SALES.REVENUE)`. Customers with the highest average order price would use `AVG(SALES.ORDER_AMOUNT)`.
- `DESC` is the sort order for the rank, either `DESC` for descending or `ASC` for ascending.

The next report shows how an object built with RANK appears to users. The Amount Sold column is not required in the report but is included to show how RANK works.

Prod Category	Product Name	Amount Sold	Sales Rank
Women	Stamped Knit Skirt Set	3,232,598	1
Women	Leather Boot-Cut Trousers	2,942,222	2
Men	Fagonnable Windowpane Blazer	2,807,726	3
Men	Wiesel Keetar Jean	2,560,431	4
Women	Ukko X-Track High	2,448,324	5
Men	Dr. Mortens 809243	2,398,941	6
Men	Fagonnable Cotton Drawstring Tro	2,360,721	7
Men	Joseph Abboud Microfiber Trousei	2,260,993	8
Men	Kahala Elastic Back Chino	2,188,582	9
Women	Aff Australia Ultra Short	2,001,247	10
Women	Kenny Cool Leather Skirt	1,912,233	11
Women	Four-Piece Cotton Knit Set	1,878,582	12

The SQL for the *Sales Rank* object is as follows:

```
RANK() OVER (ORDER BY sum(SH.SALES.AMOUNT_SOLD) DESC)
```

Note that this object did not use the PARTITION BY parameter. So in the preceding report, products are ranked regardless of the product category. The following report shows both the overall ranking and the ranking within a product category.

Men

Product Id	Product Name	Amount Sold	Sales Rank	Sales Rank within Product Category
415	Joseph Abboud Microfiber Trouser	2,273,292	6	1
1,960	Ukko Track High	2,204,930	7	2
4,800	Fagonnable Windowpane Blazer	2,194,745	8	3
930	Andrew D Yahoo Jacket	2,110,218	10	4
730	Fagonnable Windowpane Blazer	2,012,829	11	5

Women

Product Id	Product Name	Amount Sold	Sales Rank	Sales Rank within Product Category
1,805	Cole Huun Ashlyn	2,919,563.5	1	1
1,250	Laundry Slim Skirt	2,714,059.8	2	2
2,185	Laundry Ostrich-Texture Leather Skirt	2,566,398.7	3	3
1,065	Ukko X-Track High	2,339,010	4	4
585	T3 Faux Fur-Trimmed Sweater	2,329,816.5	5	5

If you want to see the rankings within a product category, the SQL is as follows:

```
RANK() OVER (PARTITION BY SH.PRODUCTS.PROD_CATEGORY ORDER BY
sum(SH.SALES.AMOUNT_SOLD) DESC)
```

Similarly, if you want to rank salespeople within their respective departments, use this SQL:

```
RANK() OVER (PARTITION BY HumanResources.Department.Name ORDER BY
sum(Sales.SalesOrderHeader.TotalDue) DESC)
```

NOTE When you use the PARTITION BY option, if your SQL settings are set to generate multiple SQL statements for each measure (data foundation, properties, and SQL options), you will get two SELECT statements from the preceding report because both a dimension table and a fact table are involved in the SQL statement. Under normal circumstances, the query engine generates multiple SELECT statements only when the measures come from two different fact tables.

When using the PARTITION BY clause, the corresponding dimension must also be selected as a result object in the query. In the preceding examples, PROD_CATEGORY or DEPARTMENT_NAME must be used in the results.

If your dimension tables are set to use Index Awareness, the RANK function will not work, as the dimension name is not referenced in the GROUP BY clause. Instead, the key or ID field is substituted for the GROUP BY.

Web Intelligence users no longer need to create specific rank objects. See Chapter 18 for more information.

Ratio to Report

Certain calculations require different levels of aggregation. In the past, this was very difficult to do in SQL, so many Web Intelligence users would perform the calculations in the report. They might create variables using context operators to control the level of calculation, or they might use multiple data providers, with each data provider using a different GROUP BY clause. You also could use derived tables, as described earlier in the chapter, but you'll get much poorer response time than when using the built-in database function. The newer reporting functions allow you to provide such measures centrally, thus providing consistency of common calculations and better scalability.

To understand how this function works, suppose you were analyzing sales figures for the year 2005. You want to know how much each quarter contributed to the total sales, as shown in the following report.

Year	Quarter Number	Amount Sold	Grand Total	Percent of Total
2005	1	73,956,184	269,389,518	27.45%
2005	2	76,974,247	269,389,518	28.57%
2005	3	66,772,321	269,389,518	24.79%
2005	4	51,686,766	269,389,518	19.19%
	Sum:	269,389,518		100.00%

The following SQL will give you a grand total for the entire query:

```
sum(SUM(SH.SALES.AMOUNT_SOLD)) OVER ()
```

The OVER () indicates it should be for the whole report. Note that there are two SUM functions in this statement. If you only use one SUM function, you will get incorrect results, although the object will parse. The additional SUM function is working in conjunction with the OVER () function.

With this new *Grand Total* object, you could use the regular *Amount Sold* object to create a *Percent of Total* object:

```
@Select(Sales\Amount Sold)/@Select(Sales\Grand Total)
```

Alternatively, Oracle has a built-in RATIO_TO_REPORT function so that you do not need to first create a *Grand Total* object.

```
RATIO_TO_REPORT(sum(SH.SALES.AMOUNT_SOLD)) OVER ()
```

Summary

With the IDT's internal functions and SQL commands from your RDBMS, you can build powerful objects that make your universe more robust and business-oriented. In this part of the universe design and build process, it's important for SQL-savvy designers to have a close dialogue with the business users. Just because users did not specifically request an object, that doesn't mean they don't need the object; they simply may not realize it's possible and easy to build. Similarly, just because users can do powerful calculations in reports, they shouldn't be required to do so for routine and common business questions. Build a robust universe that promotes reusability, one version of the truth, and scalability.

While building advanced objects, you must constantly evaluate the impact on response time and user-friendliness. Certain objects may cause the RDBMS not to use a particular index to process a query. This is fine as long the RDBMS uses some other index. Objects with prompts, objects with built-in time-period intelligence, or objects that use derived tables may be incompatible with other objects and return unexpected query results. As the designer, be aware of these issues and take the necessary precautions to minimize the possibility of users building incorrect queries. As a last resort, ensure users understand when and how to use the objects to ensure accurate query results.

CHAPTER 10

Multisource Universes

Universes that support multiple data sources are a significant new feature in SAP BusinessObjects BI 4.0. Previously, customers could purchase an optional module, Data Federator, which allowed a universe to access multiple data sources. In the IDT in 4.0, federation capabilities are built into the Enterprise server. Data Federation services run on the server to distribute the queries to the different data sources and join results on the mid tier. A multiple-source universe is also used to connect to an SAP BW data source.

Multisource Concepts

In deciding whether to create a multisource universe, it's helpful to keep in mind some fundamental rules and concepts:

- Multiple data sources are defined within the data foundation. You must specify that the universe will be multisource when you initially design the data foundation. You cannot convert a single source data foundation to a multisource data foundation.

- When connecting to a relational data source that you have specified as a multisource universe, only ANSI 92 SQL syntax is supported.

- Different server processes handle queries for relational single-source universes than for multisource universes. In a relational single-source universe, the connection server routes requests to the appropriate database. In a multisource universe, the Data Federation server routes the request.

- In order to create a universe that accesses SAP BW, you must create a multisource universe (even though you may be accessing only a single BW cube), so don't let the naming of this capability distract you. Currently, SAP BusinessObjects BI 4.0 Feature Pack 3 supports SAP BW InfoCubes, Microsoft Analysis Services, and Oracle Essbase as universes (Oracle Essbase is not supported in the Analysis user interface).

- When a user connects to a SAP InfoCube or BEx query via Web Intelligence or Analysis Edition for Office, the communication is through Business Intelligence Consumer Services (BICS). When a universe connects to a SAP InfoCube, the connectivity is through JDBC. So different connections are required for universes than for client tools.

Joining large volumes of data across multiple data sources is never a good idea. One reason that companies have a data warehouse is to bring together data from different systems into a single physical database. Data Federator will attempt to process the join in whichever data source has the largest result set. For example, assume your product codes are in a small Microsoft Access database and your large sales fact table is in a Teradata database. If your query contains a filter on product, the filter will be applied to the Teradata database portion of the query. However, if you do not filter the data and rely on an equijoin between the two databases to filter your results, the full fact table will be returned to the BI Server, even though that's not what you wanted. In fact, the query may time out. The Data Federator service does not provide caching.

Creating a Universe for SAP BW

Products such as Web Intelligence, Dashboard Design, and Analysis can connect directly to BEx queries and BW InfoCubes. There is no need to create a universe to use these interfaces. However, you may wish to create a universe in the following cases:

- You want to combine data from other data sources and you don't want to force users to do this themselves in a report.
- You want to access BW via Explorer and need to create an Information Space based on the universe (see Chapter 28).
- You want to create additional calculations in the business layer.

Creating a Connection to BW

To create a universe that accesses a BW InfoCube, first create a JDBC connection to the InfoCube.

1. From within the IDT, navigate to the Repository Resources pane and select the desired folder to store the connection. Right-click and choose Insert Relational Connection from the pop-up menu.

NOTE Connections to BW can only be secure connections. You cannot first create a local connection and then publish it to the repository.

2. Enter a resource name, such as **Europe_Sales_BW_Relational.** It may be helpful in your connection naming convention to distinguish your relational BW connections from the OLAP BW connections that are used by Analysis and Web Intelligence.

3. From the Database Middleware Driver Selection dialog, expand the SAP folder and then the SAP NetWeaver BW folder. Select SAP Java Connector.

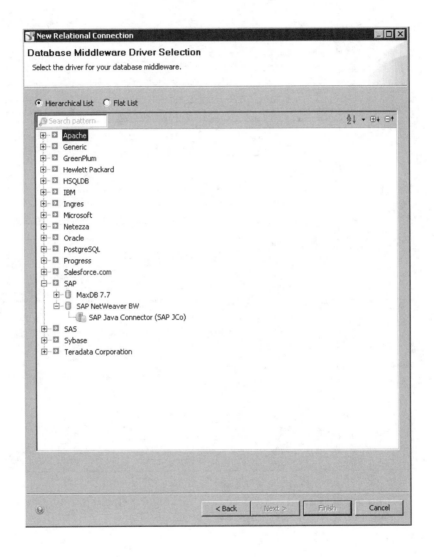

4. Complete the necessary information to access BW, as shown here:

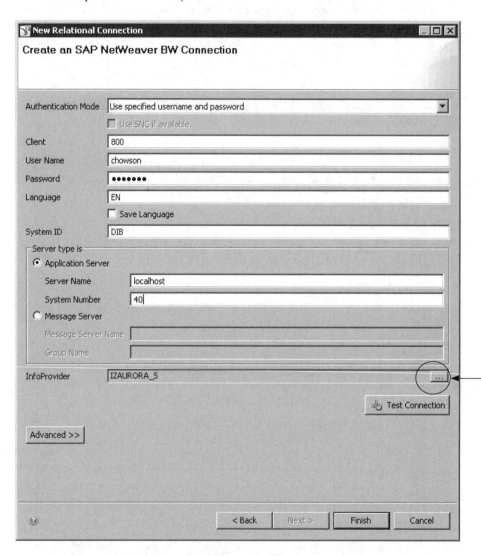

5. Choose the desired InfoProvider by clicking the ellipse button. In this example, select the Aurora Sales InfoCube, or IZAURORA_S.

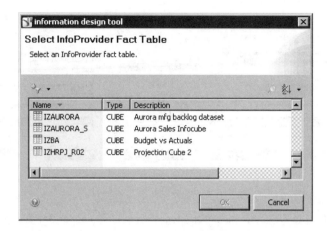

6. Test the connection to ensure you have entered the details correctly.

7. Click Finish.

Now that you have created the connection, you can create a shortcut to this connection in your local project, as described in Chapter 5.

Creating the Data Foundation

When you create a data foundation for a SAP BW InfoCube, the IDT automatically inserts the related tables and joins, and creates families for each table type, as shown in Figure 10-1. The IDT creates aliases for each of the dimension and text tables and inserts the associated joins to these alias tables.

- The fact table is prefaced with an *I* for InfoCube.
- Dimension tables are prefaced with a *D*.
- Text tables are prefaced with a *T*.

Follow these steps to create the data foundation for a multisource universe:

1. From within your local project, right-click and select New | Data Foundation from the pop-up menu.

2. Enter a resource name, such as **Sales BW**.

3. Select Multi-source Enabled, and then click Next.

4. Select the newly created BW connection, and then click Next.

5. You can either modify the color settings for the tables or accept the defaults. Then click Finish.

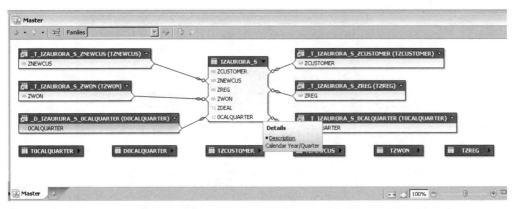

Figure 10-1   The IDT automatically creates joins and families for SAP BW InfoCubes.

At this point, you can insert a calculated column in any given table. To see more meaningful column names, hover over the individual field. For example, as shown in Figure 10-1, when you hover over the name IZAURORA_S.0CALQUARTER, you see Calendar Year/Quarter as the description. This description will become the object name in the business layer.

Creating the Business Layer

Follow these steps to create the business layer for a multisource universe:

1. From within your local project, right-click and select New | Business Layer from the pop-up menu.

2. When prompted, select Relational Data Source.

3. Enter a resource name, such as **Sales BW**.

4. Click the ellipse to select the data foundation you created in the previous section.

5. You may choose to check the box labeled "Automatically create classes (folders) and objects for SAP NetWeaver BW connections," or you may manually create them.

6. Click Finish.

NOTE As of SAP BusinessObjects BI 4.0 FP3, the vendor did not recommend having the IDT automatically create the business layer for BW cubes. This is because the dimension objects incorrectly point to the fact table, rather than the best practice of pointing to the lookup or dimension table. Depending on the size and complexity of your cube, consider if it is more efficient for you to modify such objects or to create them from scratch.

The generated business layer is shown in Figure 10-2. Notice that the longer descriptions are used for the object names and that measures from the fact table are created automatically. However, other numeric fields, such as Number of Days, are not created as measures. You can manually modify these.

Joining Data from Another Data Source

One of the most significant enhancements in SAP BusinessObjects BI 4.0 is the ability to join multiple data sources at the universe level. In the past, users could merge multiple data providers within a report. This capability still exists, so designers should consider whether to support multiple data sources within the universe or use a report, as summarized in the

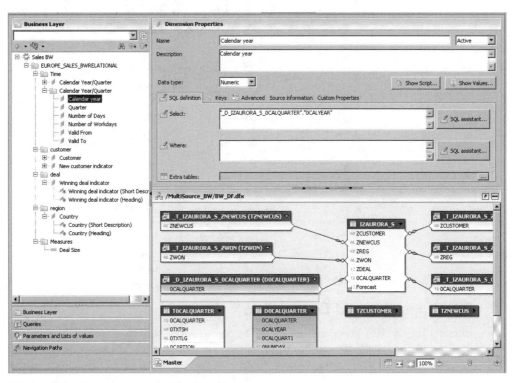

Figure 10-2 Business layer for a SAP BW universe

following table. As the Data Federator engine does not cache query results, it is not a replacement for a data mart or data warehouse for handling larger data volumes.

Consideration	Universe	Report
Who needs multiple data sources	Many users	Single report author or one time
How often does data need to be combined	Frequently recurring request	One-time analysis
Performance and scalability	SQL is processed as smaller queries	Full data sets are brought back to the server, or if Web Intelligence Rich Client, the desktop
Who maintains	Universe designer	Report author

In the following example, forecast data exists in an Excel spreadsheet. Actual data resides in the BW InfoCube. In order to correctly join data to the Excel spreadsheet, the dimensions must be conformed across the data sources.

Creating a Shared Connection

In order for the IDT and the BI Platform Server to access an Excel spreadsheet, you must first create an ODBC entry to the spreadsheet. The spreadsheet must reside on a drive that both the IDT and BI Platform Server can access, not on the universe designer's local disk.

NOTE The IDT relies on 32-bit ODBC entries, even if you are running on a 64-bit operating system. You must specifically run C:\Windows\SysWOW64\odbcad32.exe, or the IDT may not see the connection. The BI Platform Server requires 64-bit ODBC entries, so the same entries must exist on the server.

Once you have created the ODBC entry, create a shared connection in the IDT, as follows:

1. From within the IDT, navigate to the Repository Resources pane and select the desired folder to store the connection. Right-click and choose Insert Relational Connection from the pop-up menu.

2. Enter a resource name, such as **Excel_Sales_Forecast.**

3. From the Database Middleware Driver Selection dialog, expand the Microsoft folder, expand Excel Spreadsheet, and select ODBC Drivers.

4. Select the ODBC connection you created earlier.

5. Under Connection Pool Mode, set the "Disconnect after each transaction" option.

6. Test the connection to ensure you have entered the details correctly.

7. Create a shortcut and select the local project that contains the existing BW data foundation.

Adding Connections to the Data Foundation

You can either create a new data foundation or add the Excel connection to the one you created earlier. Here's how to create a new data foundation:

1. From within your local project, right-click and select New | Data Foundation from the pop-up menu.

2. Enter a resource name, such as **MultiSource_DF**.

3. Select Multi-source Enabled, and then click Next. If you are not currently logged in to the CMS, you will be prompted for credentials.

4. Click Next. Notice that you now have two connections in this project.

Data in BW

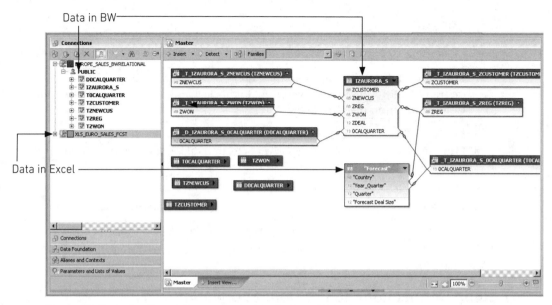

Data in Excel

Figure 10-3   A data foundation supports data from multiple data sources.

5. You can either modify the color settings for the tables or accept the defaults. Then click Finish.

As shown in Figure 10-3, the IDT automatically uses different colors for each set of tables coming from a different data source.

In order to produce the correct query results, you need to be sure that each star schema has its own context, just as you would in a data foundation that is accessing a single data source, as shown in Figure 10-4.

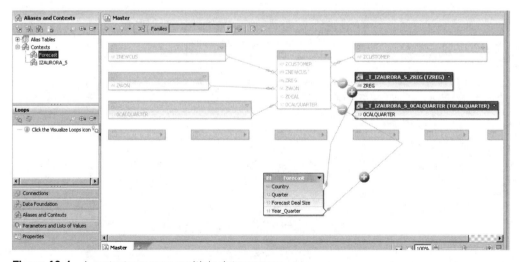

Figure 10-4   A context can span multiple data sources.

Country	Calendar Year/Quarter	Deal Size	Forecast Deal Size	Variance
BeNeLux	20,103	4,872,806	5,213,902.42	-6.54%
BeNeLux	20,104	4,101,362	4,388,457.34	-6.54%
France	20,103	9,961,868	10,459,961.4	-4.76%
France	20,104	6,679,699	7,013,683.95	-4.76%
Germany	20,103	14,465,065	14,000,000	3.32%
Germany	20,104	11,782,744	11,000,000	7.12%
Greece	20,103	8,729,880		
Greece	20,104	10,582,505		
Switzerland	20,103	10,256,545	8,205,236	25.00%
Switzerland	20,104	9,523,972	7,619,177.6	25.00%

Excel data — (label pointing to rows)

BW data — (label pointing to rows)

Local calculation — (label pointing to Variance column)

Figure 10-5   One report can span multiple data sources.

In this example, the country and time dimension tables are coming from SAP BW, and only the *Forecast* measure is coming from the spreadsheet. If a user creates a query that needs only forecast data, this example is a less efficient way to process the query than having the dimension objects come from the spreadsheet. So herein lies one of the challenges in designing a universe based on multiple data sources. From a design perspective and for query efficiency, you could have multiple time objects: one from the spreadsheet and one from the SAP BW InfoCubes. However, this would prevent users from being able to readily compare actuals data (from BW) to forecast data (coming from the spreadsheet).

NOTE When the Data Federator engine accesses data from an Excel spreadsheet, the file may become inaccessible to Excel. This depends on the connection settings you specified when initially creating the shared connection. For spreadsheets that are frequently modified, set the option "Disconnect after each transaction."

Figure 10-5 shows a report that contains data from both BW and the Excel spreadsheet, as well as a calculation that crosses both data sources, unbeknownst to the query author. In this example, the calculation is performed locally in the report, but could also have been created as a universe object. Notice that the Data Federation engine does a pseudo outer join when it merges the results. There is no forecast data for Greece in the Excel spreadsheet, so values appear as nulls.

Multisource SQL Server and Microsoft Access

In this section, we'll look at an example where dimensional information exists in a Microsoft Access database and sales information exists in a SQL Server database. As shown in the following illustration, the business would like to analyze sales according to new product groupings. The categories of Tennis, Golf, and Ski will be regrouped into Outdoor Recreation.

ID	Productnam	Category Id	Categoryname_Org	Category_NameNew	Add New Field
1	None	0	None	None	
2	Pumpit Tennis	1	Tennis	Outdoor Recreation	
3	Slamit Tennis F	1	Tennis	Outdoor Recreation	
4	SuperBounce T	1	Tennis	Outdoor Recreation	
5	Tennis cap	1	Tennis	Outdoor Recreation	
6	Berta Golf Club	2	Golf	Outdoor Recreation	
7	Clone Golf Clul	2	Golf	Outdoor Recreation	
8	Tees	2	Golf	Outdoor Recreation	
9	Golf Balls	2	Golf	Outdoor Recreation	
10	Tushuss Skis	3	Ski	Outdoor Recreation	
11	No Name Skis	3	Ski	Outdoor Recreation	
12	Ski Mask	3	Ski	Outdoor Recreation	
13	Ski Boots	3	Ski	Outdoor Recreation	
14	Pan-O Flat TVs	4	Home Theater	Electronics	
15	Pan-O Flat TVs	4	Home Theater	Electronics	
16	Pan-O Flat TVs	4	Home Theater	Electronics	
17	Pan-O Flat TVs	4	Home Theater	Electronics	
18	Sino CRT TVs	4	Home Theater	Electronics	
19	Sino CRT TVs	4	Home Theater	Electronics	
20	Sino CRT TVs	4	Home Theater	Electronics	
21	Speaker Syster	4	Home Theater	Electronics	
22	PC Systems	5	Computer	Electronics	

As shown in Figure 10-6, the data foundation contains only one star schema with the AggSalesCountryProductMonth fact table coming from SQL Server, along with the original dimProduct, dimCustomer, and dimPeriod tables. The dimProductMSACCESS table comes from a Microsoft Access database. The dimProductMSACCESS table is joined directly to the fact table. It could have also been joined to the dimProduct table.

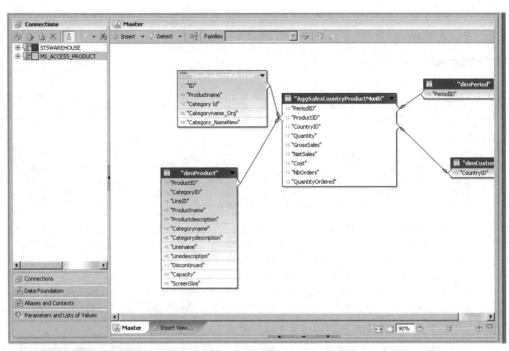

Figure 10-6   A single context or star schema can span multiple data sources.

If a user creates a query that accesses information from both tables, a single SQL statement is generated, as shown in the following example. Notice the WHERE clause for Outdoor Recreation.

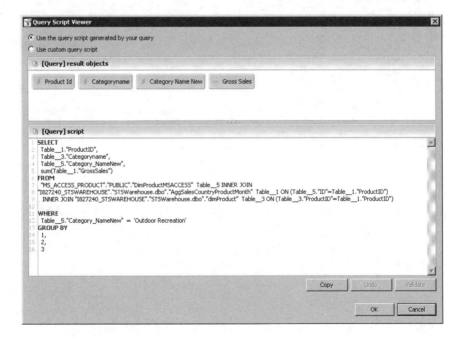

Part II

Although this is the script generated by Web Intelligence or the Query Panel within the IDT, the query submitted to SQL Server and Microsoft Access is slightly different. As shown in this trace, the SQL Server query has no corresponding filter, as there is no field for Outdoor Recreation.

```
declare @p1 int
set @p1=2
exec sp_prepare @p1 output,NULL,N'SELECT T3.C34, T3.C33, T3.C35 FROM (SELECT T2."Categoryname" AS C33, T1."ProductID" AS C34,
sum(T1."GrossSales") AS C35 FROM "STSWarehouse"."dbo"."AggSalesCountryProductMonth" T1, "STSWarehouse"."dbo"."dimProduct" T2 WHERE
(T2."ProductID" = T1."ProductID") GROUP BY T2."Categoryname", T1."ProductID") T3 ',1
select @p1
```

Trace is running.   Ln 51, Col 2   Rows: 53

This raises one of the concerns about how to approach universes with multiple data sources. In this example, the number of rows returned is not very large, so the Data Federator engine is joining two small result sets. However, if the query filter uses a field that is common to both data sources, the Data Federator engine will intelligently use the filter to create a smaller query. For example, the DimProductMSAccess.ID field contains the same values as the AggSalesCountryProductMonth.ProductID field. The following query contains a filter for DimProductMSAccess.ID=4:

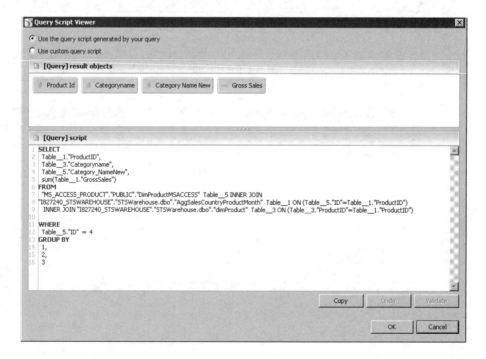

The query processed by SQL Server includes a WHERE clause for AggSalesCountryProductMonth.ProductID=4.

One way to improve performance of a query against a multisource universe is to provide the data federation engine with information about the size of the tables and number of distinct instances of particular column values. The data federation engine will use this data in its algorithms to generate the SQL in the most efficient way and in the most efficient data source. To collect these statistics:

1. From within the business layer, right-click on the business layer to invoke the pop-up menu and select Compute Statistics. Note that this menu option is not available in a single-source universe.

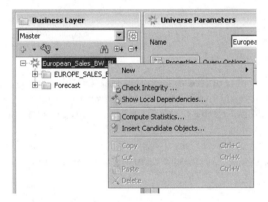

2. From the Compute Statistics dialog, you can choose to check an individual table by clicking the box next to the table. Alternatively, select Check All or Check Never Computed. Note that the SQL to gather these statistics is a COUNT DISTINCT and can be slow on large tables, so run Check All with care.

3. Once you have selected the desired tables, click Compute to see the row counts and distinct values.

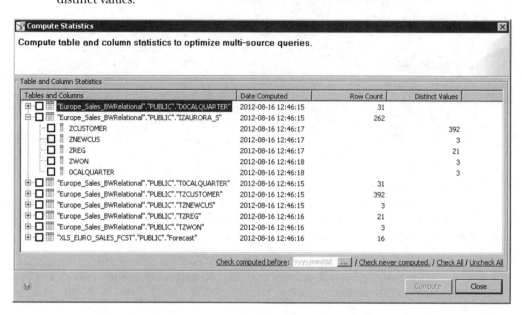

4. Click Close.

Summary

Universes that access multiple data sources are useful when users routinely need to access data stored in different physical databases. Presenting these multiple data sources seamlessly in the universe simplifies the report development process. However, this approach has performance implications for large data sources, so it should be used with caution. To improve the performance of multisource universes, compute statistics that the data federation engine can take into account when generating queries.

CHAPTER

11

Multidimensional Analysis

If you have designed a logical, business-oriented universe, designers need to do very little to provide users with multidimensional analysis capabilities. Drill capabilities are automatically available to users; there is no need to explicitly build a cube. With robust measures, users can further perform rankings, top ten queries, and so on against relational data sources.

In addition, you can also build a universe that accesses a Microsoft Analysis Services cube or Oracle Essbase. With the synchronized multiple data providers in Web Intelligence, users can create a report that spans both relational data sources and OLAP data sources. OLAP-based universes allow OLAP users to access the full range of Web Intelligence functionality, including scheduling, formatting, and formulas.

This chapter discusses multidimensional analysis for relational data sources and OLAP data sources. Multidimensional analysis is enabled in the business layer.

What Is Multidimensional Analysis?

As discussed in previous chapters, a dimension is often textual or time information by which users analyze numeric measures. Dimensional information may come from a lookup or reference table. Dimensions often have different levels or groupings associated with them called *hierarchies*. Figure 11-1 shows two sample dimensions.

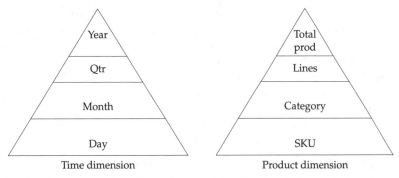

Figure 11-1   The Time and Product dimensions each has four levels that make up a hierarchy.

The levels, or hierarchies, allow users to analyze data by different groups. Some hierarchies, such as Time, are very clear-cut. As reviewed in the "Object Ordering" section in Chapter 7, time objects typically go from Year to Quarter to Month to Week to Day—a natural order. With multidimensional analysis, users may start by viewing sales for the year, and then drill down to see details by quarter or month. Users may choose to further analyze data by another dimension altogether, such as sales by product, or in combination, such as sales by product for a particular month.

Like time dimensions, geographic hierarchies may also have a predetermined order, starting with Continent, Country, and State. However, when the geography applies to a marketing region, each company may introduce its own variation. One company may group the Middle East and Africa together; another company may include Mexico as part of North America because it is part of the North American Free Trade Agreement (NAFTA). Ideally, all these groupings should be agreed upon during your data warehouse design process and built into the dimension tables. However, as the universe designer, you may find that certain business units may want to view information according to different groupings. When the groupings change, do you provide users with the old grouping, the new grouping, or both?

Within the IDT, *hierarchy* refers to hierarchies in an OLAP database, and *navigation path* refers to hierarchies in a relational data source.

Navigation Paths

A navigation path is a logical grouping of relational dimensional objects into a hierarchy. In the former Universe Design Tool, these were referred to as hierarchies. The navigation path defines the drill path available to users in Web Intelligence (refer to Chapter 18).

Default Navigation

By default, the drill or navigation path is according to the order of the dimension objects within a folder. Only dimensions (not attributes) are available for drilling. If you have ordered your objects from largest to smallest increments, as discussed in Chapter 7, you have provided users with a reasonable drill path.

Custom Navigation

The benefit of custom navigation is that you explicitly control the drill path.

When setting up your custom navigations, you also need to consider how to treat code or ID fields. If users will rarely use ID fields and most often will drill on description fields, then leave the ID fields out of custom navigations altogether. However, if your ID fields are meaningful to users, you may want two separate drill paths: one for names and one for IDs. What you don't want is for users to drill from *Product Category Name* to *Product Category ID*, for example.

In the following example, you will use the Simple eFashion business layer created in earlier chapters to set up custom navigation:

1. From within the IDT, open the Simple eFashion business layer.

2. From within the Business Layer pane, select the Navigation Paths tab.

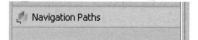

3. Click the Custom radio button, and then click the Insert Navigation Path icon.

4. Replace the default name with one that will be meaningful to users as they drill. In this example, enter **Time** as the name. Optionally, enter a description.

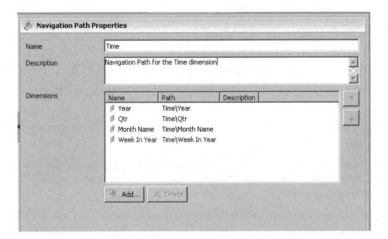

5. Click Add to select individual dimensions, organizing them from the top of a hierarchy to the most granular level of detail. In this example, select *Year.*

6. Click OK to close the Select a Dimension dialog box. Repeat steps 4 and 5 until your time objects appear as shown in the preceding screen.

TIP So that users do not drill from a name object at one level to a code object at the same level, create two navigation paths: one for name objects and one for code or ID objects.

You can organize the navigation paths in any way that makes business sense. You may choose to follow agreed-upon corporate levels or incorporate groupings that are specific to various business units. For example, perhaps some business units want the drill path to be *Family* | *Category* | *Color* | *Article Name* | *Article Code.* It's perfectly reasonable for you, as the designer, to provide multiple drill paths.

CAUTION Once you begin using custom navigation paths, you must continue to use them for all dimension objects by which users will want to drill; otherwise, they will not be available for multidimensional analysis. For example, in the preceding example, a navigation path for *Products* or *Articles* has not yet been defined. When users begin drilling, the time objects will be drillable but the article objects will not, until you create a custom navigation path.

OLAP Universes

Within a BI deployment, OLAP databases provide a way of aggregating data to provide speed of thought analysis and complex, multidimensional calculations. In SAP BusinessObjects 4.0, users can connect directly to SAP BW InfoCubes and Microsoft Analysis cubes via the web-based Analysis edition for the OLAP interface. This allows users to explore data, drill, and create charts. However, it provides limited formatting options.

To enable users to interact with Microsoft Analysis Services or Oracle Essbase cubes via Web Intelligence, you must create a business layer. This is not required for SAP BW InfoCubes, as Web Intelligence can connect to BEx queries directly, without a universe. You may still elect to create a universe for BW as discussed in the preceding chapter.

In connecting to OLAP data sources, keep in mind the various interfaces and ways of connecting to them:

- Analysis edition for OLAP can access Microsoft Analysis Services cubes or BW cubes directly. As of Feature Pack 3, Oracle Essbase is not yet supported via this interface. Within Analysis, users can export a snapshot of the data to an Analysis view.

- Web Intelligence can access BEx queries directly via the Business Intelligence Consumer Services (BICS) connectivity

- Web Intelligence can access an Analysis view, which is a snapshot of data from the Analysis edition for OLAP.

- A universe can access SAP BW InfoCube via relational connection and JDBC. These queries generate SQL. You must first create a data foundation and then a business layer.

- A universe can access Microsoft Analysis Services and Oracle Essbase. You only need to define a business layer. These queries generate Multidimensional Expressions (MDX).

In addition to the formatting options in Web Intelligence, another key benefit of an OLAP universe is that users can create one document that accesses multiple data sources and synchronize the data providers to create calculations that span relational and OLAP databases. For example, a user could have a sales query accessing an OLAP database and an inventory query accessing a relational database. As long as the product dimensions are similar in the two data sources, the user could calculate days sales inventory by product.

OLAP universes have more capabilities and menu options than business layers that access relational data sources, including the following:

- **MDX**   Whereas relational data sources use SQL to generate queries, OLAP data sources use MDX.

- **Hierarchies**   Similar in concept to navigation paths, hierarchies define the order and relationship of dimensions for drilling, such as year to quarter.

- **Analysis dimensions**   These dimensions correspond to the name of the hierarchy in the OLAP cube. They provide a folder name for the hierarchy.

- **Named sets**   Similar in concept to predefined filters, a named set contains a set of dimension members, such as top customers, new products, and so on.

- **Calculated members**   These are members of a hierarchy created through an MDX expression.

Before creating an OLAP universe, it's helpful first to understand how the database is modeled in Microsoft Analysis Services. In this example, we will use a product hierarchy from a sample STS Sales database. The Product hierarchy is organized similar to that shown earlier in Figure 11-1: *Lines | Category | Product*. Figure 11-2 shows the cube structure for this hierarchy in SQL Server Business Intelligence Development Studio. The attributes in the first pane will appear as objects in the business layer. The hierarchy in the second pane will form the hierarchy within the business layer, and items in the hierarchy will become dimension objects. The data source view represents the underlying physical table.

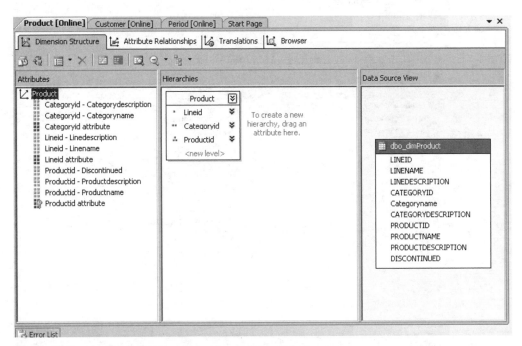

Figure 11-2   The Product hierarchy in Microsoft Analysis Services

Figure 11-3 shows the properties for the *Lineid* attribute. Two important settings here affect behavior in Web Intelligence and Analysis edition for OLAP:

- **OrderBy (Advanced category)**   Currently, items will be sorted alphabetically by the Lineid name. For certain objects, it may be preferable for the cube designer to set the sort order by ID or numeric field. This is particularly true for month numbers in a time hierarchy.
- **NameColumn (Source category)**   Notice that although the field used for filtering may be an ID field, what appears to the user will be a Name field.

From within the IDT, you can view these properties, as shown in Figure 11-4, but you cannot modify them.

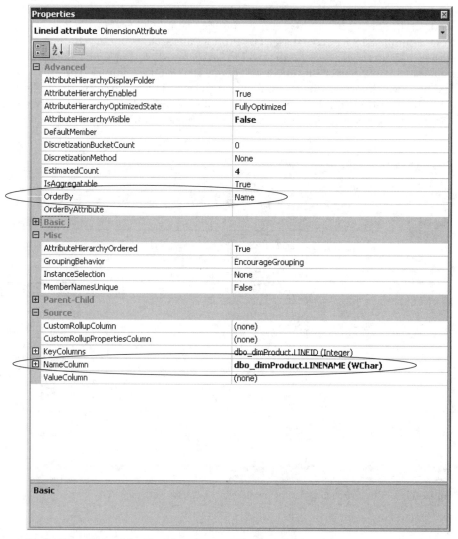

Figure 11-3   Properties of the Lineid attribute within Analysis Services

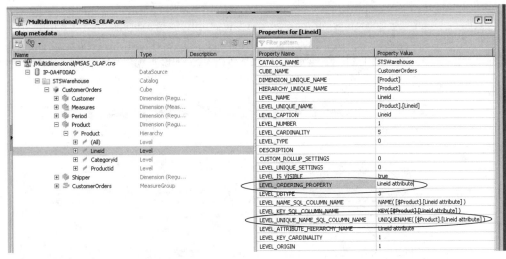

Figure 11-4   Properties of the Lineid attribute as they appear within the IDT

Creating an OLAP Connection

To create an OLAP universe, you use an OLAP database in the universe connection parameters. The following example uses the Microsoft Analysis Services Foodmart database.

1. Create a shared connection within the Repository Resources pane by right-clicking and selecting Insert OLAP connection from the pop-up menu. Alternatively, create a local connection within a project by right-clicking to invoke the pop-up menu and selecting New | OLAP connection.

2. Enter a resource name and click Next.

3. Select the OLAP Middleware driver. For this example, select Microsoft Analysis Services 2008, then XMLA. Click Next to continue.

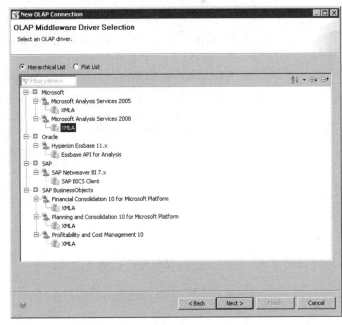

4. Enter the appropriate connection parameters, including the authentication mode, server, username, and password. (These options are discussed in Chapter 5.)

5. Specify the cube on which you would like to base the business layer. If you do not explicitly choose a cube in this step, you will be asked to choose a cube when creating the business layer. Click Finish to create the connection.

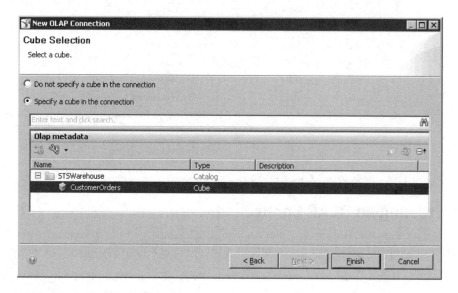

Creating a Business Layer

Once you have created the connection, you can create the business layer. Unlike with relational data sources, you do not create a data foundation first.

1. From within the IDT, in the Local Resources pane, right-click and select New | Business Layer from the pop-up menu.

2. When prompted to choose the type of data source, select OLAP Data Source. Then click Next.

3. Enter a resource name. This is the name of the universe that will appear to users. Optionally, enter a description.

4. Click the ellipse to select the OLAP connection.

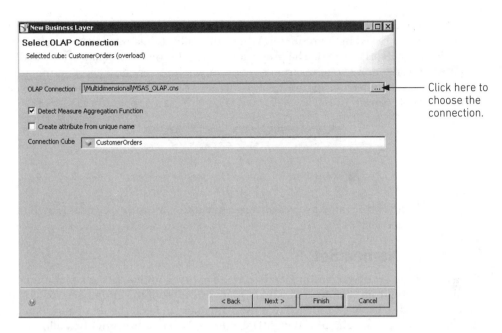

Click here to choose the connection.

5. Check the Detect Measure Aggregation Function box. Leave the Create attribute from unique name box unchecked.

6. If you explicitly selected a cube when you created a connection, then this cube automatically appears in the New Business Layer dialog box. If not, choose the appropriate cube.

7. Select Next to interactively choose which hierarchies and measures you want to include in the business layer.

8. Click Finish.

The option to detect the measure aggregation function will automatically set the projection aggregate for a particular measure. When Web Intelligence users query an OLAP data source, all relevant levels are retrieved at query execution time. Drilling is within the rows returned within the initial query. For example, in the following query, there are ten rows of data: two years plus eight quarters. The quarters for 2007 are not expanded in this screen but have been returned in the query result. In a relational query, a drill may generate a new query. As you drill by other elements in the scope of analysis, additional columns, such as for product, may be added to your report.

Time	Net Sales
⊞ 2007	841,580,393.49
⊟ 2008	1,107,105,974.87
1	210,978,968.04
2	249,454,976.04
3	297,374,684.17
4	349,297,346.62

Part II

When you drill within an OLAP report, the individual rows are expanded and collapsed based on data retrieved in the result set. When you drill within a relational report, the projection aggregates are used. The projection aggregate comes into play in an OLAP report when you remove columns from a report or when you create a chart on the subset of the data. If the projection aggregates are not set in the business layer, users will receive a #TOREFRESH error.

Time	Net Sales
⊞ 2007	#TOREFRESH
⊞ 2008	#TOREFRESH

The IDT will use the same projection aggregate in the measure object as is used in the Analysis Services cube.

Creating a Named Set

Named sets are a set of dimension members or an expression that acts as a predefined filter in a query. Recall from Chapter 9 that, in SQL, to find a list of top customers, you could either hard-code a list of customer IDs or use a subquery to fetch the list of customer IDs for sales above a certain amount. With MDX, there are built-in functions that allow you to select top (TOPCOUNT) and bottom (BOTTOMCOUNT) performers. In the following example, you will create a named set for the top five customers.

1. From within the business layer, navigate to the analysis dimension *Customers*.

2. From the business layer toolbar, select the Insert button (the green plus sign) and choose Named set. Note that if Named set does not appear, your cursor may not be positioned on an analysis dimension, and it may be on an attribute where you cannot insert a named set.

3. The Named Set Properties dialog box appears. This is similar to the measure object properties discussed in Chapter 9, except that the SQL Expression button is replaced with an MDX Assistant button.

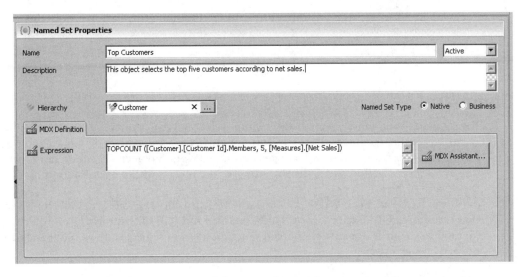

4. Replace the generic name of the named set with a meaningful name—in this example, **Top Customers**. Optionally, enter a description.

5. You may either type the MDX expression in the MDX Expression box or click the MDX Assistant button to launch the MDX Expression Editor, as done here.

6. From within the Functions pane, expand the Database Functions, Set folder, and then double-click TOPCOUNT to insert the function in the MDX Expression box.

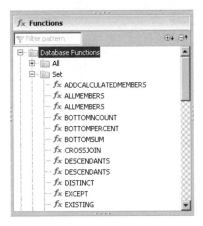

7. You may select Customer ID from either the Business Layer pane or the OLAP Metadata pane. This will insert [Customer][Customer Id] in the MDX Expression box. Manually add **.Members**, or enter the period and double-click the MEMBERS function.

8. Enter a comma, the value for the number of customers you wish to return, and a comma.

9. Select the measure for which you want to determine the filter from—in this example, *Net Sales*.

10. Click OK to close the Expression Editor.

Summary

For standard multidimensional analysis within relational data sources, designers should create custom navigation paths that determine the users' drill path. These navigation paths should ideally separate code or ID objects from description objects. If you do not create these custom navigation paths, the sort order of the objects within each folder is used as the default drill path.

If you have data in an OLAP database, the IDT provides the ability to build a universe that accesses an OLAP data source. This is enabled through the business layer. You can add hierarchies, analysis dimensions, named sets, and measures, just as you would through a normal business layer.

Securing the Data

Security is a complex topic. It requires that policies and procedures be firmly established yet flexible enough to accommodate a business's changing requirements. As you approach this chapter, then, don't dive in hoping to start clicking away. Instead, first familiarize yourself with how security works in SAP BusinessObjects and then develop a security approach that meets your company's needs. Given the complexity of this topic, this chapter uses simple scenarios to demonstrate key concepts that become the building blocks of complex implementations.

The Enterprise Environment: What Needs Securing

Figure 12-1 provides an overview of an SAP BusinessObjects Enterprise environment and the different phases of security:

- *Authentication* is the first phase. Authentication relates to user IDs and passwords—how SAP BusinessObjects recognizes you.

- *Authorization*, the second phase of security, relates to what you are allowed to access and do once you have been authenticated. In order to make the process of maintaining authorization simpler, you may use groups.

This chapter is loosely organized according to the workflow in Figure 12-1. You will first define users and groups. Then you want to grant access to users and groups to allow them to be able to access reports contained in folders. Access to universes and their connections allows users to refresh the reports. You can further restrict access at the data source, limiting the number of rows returned or the dimensional values retrieved from the database.

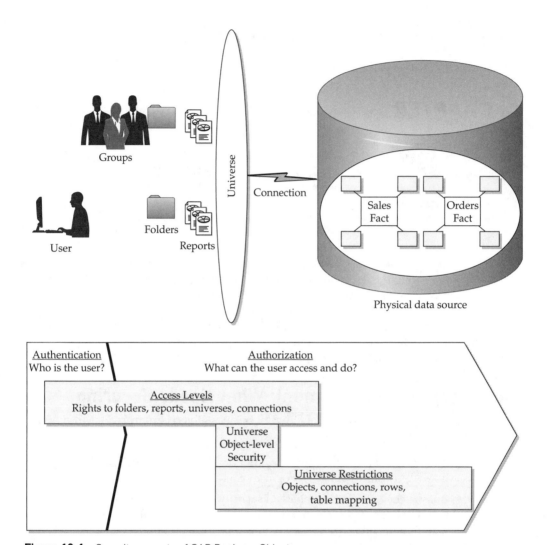

Figure 12-1   Security aspects of SAP BusinessObjects

Introducing the Central Management Console

Security is predominately handled through the Central Management Console (CMC), a web-based application that allows for control of users and repository objects, as well as servers.

NOTE Throughout this chapter, the term *object* refers to BI content stored in the repository, not to a universe object, as discussed in Chapter 7. A repository object could be a user, a group, a report, a folder, and so on.

To access the CMC, do the following:

1. From the Windows Start menu, select Programs | SAP BusinessObjects BI Platform 4 | SAP BusinessObjects BI platform | SAP BusinessObjects BI platform Central Management Console or enter the appropriate URL within a browser: http:// *BOEServer*/8080/BOE/CM, where *BOEServer* is the name of your BusinessObjects Enterprise server.

2. You will be prompted to enter a user ID and password. During an initial installation, a generic ID of Administrator is automatically created and assigned a password.

3. The default authentication type is Enterprise. Click Log On to continue. SAP BusinessObjects presents you with the main console, as shown in Figure 12-2.

Within the CMC, administrators control access to reports and universes, calendars for scheduling reports, and server settings. These tasks are divided into categories mainly to ease navigating the CMC: Organize, Define, and Manage. You also can use the scroll bar and icons on the left that represent all the tasks.

Authentication

As the number of applications and systems within organizations has continued to increase, users have been overwhelmed with multiple user IDs and passwords, different for the local area network, the transaction system, the data warehouse, and SAP BusinessObjects. To

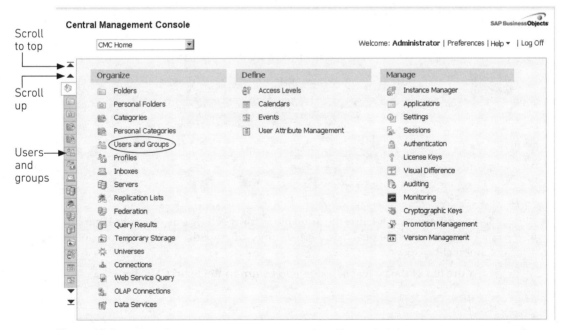

Figure 12-2   The CMC is a web-based application that allows administrators to manage security and servers.

address this issue, companies are increasingly trying to move to one central authentication system that the different applications rely on. If your company has a directory server (such as Microsoft Active Directory, Sun ONE, or Novell eDirectory), that same user ID and password can be used to log in to SAP BusinessObjects.

In discussing this with customers, we often hear concerns about the SAP BusinessObjects administrator needing to rely on a network administrator to grant access to corporate data. Clearly, a number of policy and organization issues need to be addressed before you can leverage these capabilities. However, it's important to realize that we are talking about externalizing only the *authentication*. Access to data, reports, and universes continues to be controlled within SAP BusinessObjects, even when authentication is centralized with network administrators or other security groups.

Enterprise Authentication

If your company does not have a centralized system for assigning user IDs and passwords, you can use the built-in security within SAP BusinessObjects, referred to as Enterprise authentication. With this type of deployment, you assign user IDs and passwords that are internally maintained with the CMS repository. You also specify how secure the authentication should be in terms of password length, frequency of changing passwords, and so on.

Before defining users, you should set the desired restrictions, as follows:

 1. From the main CMC Home page, select Authentication from the Manage category.

2. CMC presents you with a dialog box of authentication approaches. Double-click the first option: Enterprise.

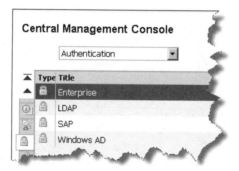

3. The Enterprise page lists the available security settings, as shown in Figure 12-3. Table 12-1 describes each of these settings. Change the settings as appropriate, and then click Update.

4. At the top of the page, click Home to return to the main CMC page.

Restriction Type	Option	Explanation
Password	Enforce mixed-case passwords	When this box is checked, users must use uppercase and lowercase letters in the password. For example, "password" would not be accepted, but "Password" would be valid.
	Must contain at least N characters	This specifies a minimum password length.
User	Must change password every N day(s)	This forces users to change their password every 90 days.
	Cannot reuse the N most recent password(s)	It's hard for users to remember passwords, and when they like to use family or pet names, they often reuse those passwords. Don't set this number too high; otherwise, users simply won't be able to log in.
	Must wait N minute(s) to change password	This determines how frequently users can change their password.
Logon	Disable account after N failed attempts to log on	If the user specifies an incorrect password more than three times, the account is disabled, and an administrator must manually reenable it, or the user can try again after so many minutes.
	Reset failed logon count after N minute(s)	This specifies how long the system keeps track of the incorrect password attempts before setting it back to 0.
	Re-enable account after N minute(s)	When a user specifies an incorrect password, the account is locked for up to 100 minutes. If you don't want the account to be automatically reenabled, set this value to 0.
Data source	Enable and update user's Data Source Credentials at logon time	This is used to synchronize database credentials with the Enterprise so that if users change their Enterprise password, the password for the data source credential is also changed. Note that this does not physically change the password in the data source.
Trusted authentication	Trusted authentication is enabled	This is used for integrating BI Launch Pad with third-party systems.

Table 12-1   Default Restrictions for Passwords and User IDs

NOTE The restrictions in Table 12-1 are valid only for Enterprise user IDs and passwords. They do not affect external user IDs and passwords.

Enterprise

Password Restrictions · N is:
☑ Enforce mixed-case passwords
☑ Must contain at least N characters: · · · · · · · · · · · · · · · · · · · [6]
User Restrictions · N is:
☐ Must change password every N day(s): · · · · · · · · · · · · · · · [30]
☑ Cannot reuse the N most recent password(s): · · · · · · · · · · [3]
☑ Must wait N minute(s) to change password: · · · · · · · · · · · · [5]
Logon Restrictions · N is:
☐ Disable account after N failed attempts to log on: · · · · · · · [3]
Reset failed logon count after N minute(s): · · · · · · · · · · · · · · · [5]
☐ Re-enable account after N minute(s): · · · · · · · · · · · · · · · · · · [0]
Synchronize Data Source Credentials with Log On
☐ Enable and update user's Data Source Credentials at logon time
Trusted Authentication · N is:
☐ Trusted Authentication is enabled
No shared secret available.
[New Shared Secret][Download Shared Secret]
    Shared Secret Validity Period (days): · · · · · · · · · · · · · · · · · · [0]
    Trusted logon request is timeout after N millisecond(s) (0 means no limit): [0]
[Update][Reset]

Figure 12-3 Enterprise security allows you to set password and logon restrictions.

Adding Users

Once you have set the global restrictions for Enterprise authentication, you can begin adding users. Here are the steps for adding a user:

1. From the CMC Home page, select Users and Groups by selecting the link within the Organize category, or click the button along the left scroll bar.

2. You are presented with a list of groups and users. If you are working with a new installation, the installation procedure automatically creates the users Administrator and Guest. Select the User List folder.

3. Click the Create New User button or right-click and select New | New User.

4. For Authentication Type, leave the default setting of Enterprise.

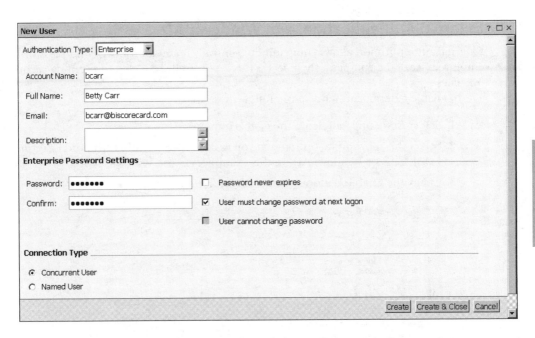

5. In the Account Name box, enter a login ID. In some organizations, this may be a numeric employee identification. This is the only required field to create a new user.

6. In the Full Name box, optionally enter a description for the login ID.

7. In the Email box, optionally enter an e-mail address to be used for scheduling reports that are automatically delivered via e-mail.

8. Optionally, enter text in the Description box.

9. In the Enterprise Password Settings section, provide the user with a default password. Alternatively, you can leave the Password box blank and check the box to ensure the user enters a password on the first login.

10. Click the Create button or the Create and Close button to create the user and exit this dialog box.

The CMC will display the newly created user with the alias name. Because SAP BusinessObjects Enterprise supports authentication against multiple directories, it uses aliases to map one Enterprise user to different user IDs in other directories. In the preceding example, the user ID Betty Carr is given the same alias name.

External Authentication with Windows AD

External authentication allows companies to centrally maintain user IDs and passwords. As employees leave the company, their access can be centrally removed, preventing security breaches.

To enable external authentication, follow these steps:

1. Select Authentication from the CMC Home page.

2. Select the appropriate option that you wish to use for authentication: Enterprise, LDAP, SAP, or Windows AD. In this example, choose Windows AD.

3. Check the Enable Windows Active Directory (AD) box.

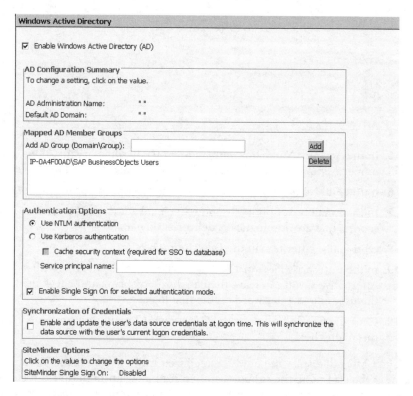

4. Click the double quotes next to AD Administrator Name to enter an administrator username and domain that can log on to Windows AD to retrieve groups and users from AD.

5. Under Mapped AD Member Groups, enter the AD groups that you wish to map to SAP BusinessObjects Enterprise, and then click Add.

6. Under Authentication Options, indicate if you wish to use NTLM or Kerberos authentication. If you're using Kerberos, you will also need to indicate a service account. If your deployment supports single sign-on, check the box to enable it.

NOTE External authentication is not synonymous with single sign-on. With single sign-on, once users are logged in to a Windows network, they do not need to specify their username or password to access SAP BusinessObjects.

7. If you are also using unique data source credentials, you can ensure that when the user logs on and changes the password for AD, it will change the credentials that SAP BusinessObjects Enterprise uses. Note that it will not go into the source system to change the password.

8. For each Windows AD user that is added to the group mapped in step 5, an alias is created within SAP BusinessObjects Enterprise. The alias is either created automatically when the user is added to the SAP BusinessObjects Users group on the Windows AD server or when the user first tries to log in to BI Launch Pad. You control this by setting one of the following update options:

   - **Assign each new AD alias to an existing User Account with the same name**   When a user is added to Windows AD, BusinessObjects Enterprise will look for the same name within the repository. If an existing BusinessObjects Enterprise account is not found, a new alias is automatically created.

   - **Create a new user account for each new AD alias**   A new alias is always created.

NOTE With either option, user aliases are automatically created. The difference is in when they are created. You can choose to have the aliases created when a user first attempts to log in to BI Launch Pad or when you schedule or run the AD update. If your deployment uses named user licensing, then it may be preferable to create the account only when a user attempts to log in the first time.

9. For each alias creation, also indicate if it should be added as a named user or concurrent user, depending on your server licensing agreement. Concurrent licensing is a newer type of license offered from the vendor.

10. Indicate if you wish to schedule the AD groups to be updated periodically or if you will update them only on demand.

NOTE When an account has been disabled within Windows Server, the user cannot log in to SAP BusinessObjects. The disabled status is unfortunately not reflected within the CMC. Also, if a user has been explicitly deleted from Windows Server, the user alias remains in the CMC until the authentication databases are synchronized. To remove the user alias from the CMC, go to the Windows AD options (from the CMC Home page, select Authentication, and then select Windows AD), select Update AD Groups and Aliases now, and then click Update.

11. When you are satisfied with the various options and settings, click Update to save your changes.

Defining Groups

SAP BusinessObjects comes with several initial groups:

- **Administrators** Members of this group can add users and control access to individual objects and folders.
- **Everyone** All users are automatically added to this group, whose rights by default allow users to view reports in all public folders.
- **QaaWS Group Designer** Members of this group can create queries as web service queries.
- **Report Conversion Tool Users** Members of this group can convert Desktop Intelligence reports to Web Intelligence.
- **Translators** Members of this group can use the Translation Manager application.
- **Universe Designer Users** Members of this group can create universes and connections.

You will most often want to grant access to groups at the folder and universe levels, and specify exceptions only at the individual user level. Users can belong to more than one group. You may give users more capabilities in one group and less in another.

To create a group, follow these steps:

1. From the CMC Home page, select Users and Groups.

2. From within the Users and Groups dialog box, click the Group List folder. You are presented with a list of the default groups or groups imported from a previous implementation.

3. Click the New Group button or right-click and select New | New Group.

4. Enter a group name (Finance in the following example) and, optionally, a description.

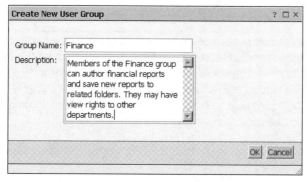

5. Click OK to create the group.

Once the group is created, you can add members to the group or create subgroups (for example, Accounts Payable and Accounts Receivable). You will want to define permissions for the group when you have published universes and created folders.

Planning for Authorization

Defining users and groups is the easy part of security. Controlling access to the BI content is more complex and demands careful planning. Before you begin the task of defining users, folders, and groups, first consider the following:

- How the company is organized; if you are using external authentication, you may be able to leverage groups defined in an external authentication system
- How you want to organize reports in a way that facilitates decision-making and minimizes duplicate analyses and report creation
- How tightly you want to control access to dashboards and reports

This section first discusses concepts within the CMC, and then provides step-by-step instructions to implement the concepts.

Understanding Your Company's Organization

Table 12-2 provides a simple scenario in which members from different groups can access content created by other groups. This table is not exhaustive of all the functional groups you may have in your organization. We have specifically kept it simple to minimize confusion.

Employee	Role	Groups				
		Everyone	Finance	Marketing	Supply Chain	Plus Individual Access
Elizabeth	Finance Director	√	√		Finance	Has full control over the top folder
Clark	Manager Accounts Payable	√	√			
Megan	VP Marketing	√		√		
Sam	Supply Chain Manager	√			√	Can view marketing content explicitly but can't modify reports or publish new ones and has full control over the Orders folder

Table 12-2 Define Groups Within CMC That Match Your Company's Organization

This example sets up access as follows:

- **Finance group**   Members of this group can access all reports contained within the Finance folder. There is a subfolder, \Finance\Internal, where everyone in the Finance group can save documents. Documents in the top Finance folder are accessible to everyone else in the company and can be refreshed but not modified. Elizabeth, as the Finance Director, is the only person who can modify reports in this top folder.

- **Marketing group**   Members of this group can access, refresh, and create new reports in the Marketing folder. Megan, as the VP of the department, can also add new users to the Marketing group.

- **Sam**   Sam is the Supply Chain Manager and occasionally may want to view some marketing and sales reports to understand order issues. He does not need to save reports to the Marketing folder, so he won't be a member of the Marketing group. Also, no other members of the Supply Chain group need this access, so permission should be granted to the individual rather than to a group.

Access Levels

SAP BusinessObjects Enterprise provides several initial access levels, starting with the most restrictive and progressing to the most permissive rights. Within the CMC, these rights relate to "objects." These objects, however, are not to be confused with universe objects (dimensions and measures), but rather collectively refer to any content, including folders, categories, reports, or spreadsheets. Table 12-3 describes the predefined access levels.

SAP BusinessObjects uses the concept of inheritance so that users inherit access by belonging to different groups. Alternatively, you may explicitly assign more permissive access or more restrictive access to a particular user or group and for a particular folder, category, or report. Explicit rights override inherited rights.

CAUTION The No Access level does not explicitly deny access, but rather sets all permissions to Not Specified. So only when this is the only access level inherited will access be denied.

Use the following formulas as a guide to understand what happens when inheritance from multiple groups overlap:

Grant + Deny + Not Specified = Deny

Grant + Not Specified = Grant

Grant + Deny = Deny

Not Specified = Denied

To use the example from the first formula, if a user belongs to two groups and permission is granted in one and denied in another, then access to the repository object will be granted. However, explicit rights always prevail. So if the user has explicit permission to modify the object, then the inherited permission to deny this right is overridden by the explicit right to modify it.

Access Level	Rights
No Access	You would think this means that the user does not see the folder, report, or universe, but in reality, this access level sets all permissions to Not Specified, which results in very different behavior when permission is granted elsewhere: the grant will take priority over those not specified. If you really want to remove access to something, do not use No Access. Instead, use Advanced and explicitly deny the access. No Access does not appear as an access level choice, but instead appears only when an access level has not been specified.
View	The user can see the folder, report, or universe. If the report contains data, the user can open the report and interact with it. If the report does not contain data, the user cannot refresh the report. By default, the user can edit the report and save it to a personal folder and refresh it there. You can explicitly prevent users from copying corporate documents to personal folders by setting an individual right that denies "Copy Objects to another folder."
Schedule	A user can schedule a report but cannot refresh it in real time.
View On Demand	A user can refresh a report in real time. When the report is a Web Intelligence document, the user also needs View On Demand access to the universe and universe connection to perform the refresh.
Full Control	A user can create new reports within a folder, modify existing reports, and delete items.
Advanced	When the preceding access levels do not meet your needs, you can provide more granular access by choosing Advanced.

Table 12-3   Access Levels Are Granted to Groups and Individual Users

When in doubt, preview the final status of an object by opening the permission explorer.

1. Select the object (such as a universe, folder, or report).

2. Right-click and select User Security.

A list of groups and users with access to the object appears, along with an indication of whether the rights were explicitly assigned or inherited.

Folders and Categories

Folders and categories provide a way of organizing documents and BI content. *Folders* provide the physical storage location of a file as well as a means to navigate content. *Categories* provide navigation only. A file must be stored in a folder; it does not need to be assigned a category.

A *group* is a way of grouping users and granting access to folders or individual reports within folders. Groups will often be associated with particular folders. Thus, you may have a Finance group that has access to documents in a Finance folder. The Finance group may have subgroups such as Accounts Payable and Accounts Receivable that can edit individual reports within the Finance folder.

At what point you create additional folders depends on the number of reports you have and how easy it is to maintain permissions to individual reports versus folders. Because folders, categories, and groups are all interrelated, it's helpful to first plan how you want to organize documents and how you want to group users to maintain permissions before you begin the task of physically defining them.

A key feature of categories is that one document can be assigned to multiple categories—a significant difference from folders, in which a document can reside in only one folder. Also, by default, if you tag a report with the Mobile category, it appears to SAP Mobile BI users. Thus, you can use folders, categories, or a combination of the two. Permissions can be applied to folders, categories, and individual files. Users navigate within BI Launch Pad using either folders or categories.

Folders and categories each have their merits, and different administrators will be most comfortable with whatever approach they've used in the past. Folders are required; categories are optional. You should provide a modest degree of folder structure before users can begin sharing content. However, when you use a combination of categories and folders and grant different permissions to each, there is potential for confusion. Therefore, we recommend using categories only for navigation purposes, not for security.

When you create a new folder, two sets of permissions are automatically assigned:

- Administrators are given the access level Full Control.
- Everyone is given the access level No Access.

CAUTION In earlier BusinessObjects versions, when you created a new folder, members of the group Everyone were assigned an access level of Schedule by default, thus enabling all users to view, open, and schedule any reports saved in the new folder. For many companies, this default access level may have been too permissive. In the latest release, whenever you create a new folder, the access level for the group Everyone is set to No Access for the newly created folder. With the permission of No Access, members of the group Everyone will not even see that the folder exists.

Table 12-4 provides some sample folders that an Administrator user could define to allow the users and groups in Table 12-3 to share content.

NOTE The access levels you grant to a user also affect which options appear to a user from within BI Launch Pad. If the user does not have View On Demand access, for example, the user's menu will lack the Refresh option.

Creating Folders and Categories

You can easily add new folders and categories with the CMC. To create a folder, do the following:

1. From the CMC Home page, select Folders under Organize.

2. The objects list shows all content in the repository, regardless of which folder the report or dashboard is stored in. All Folders presents the list of repository objects by folder. Select All Folders, and then right-click and select New | New Folder.

3. In the Folder Name box, enter a name for the folder—**Marketing** in this example.

4. Click OK.

Group	Folder	Access Level	Comments
Everyone	Top level	View	Users can view all folders and reports and schedule them to run.
	\Finance	View On Demand	Users can view and refresh all reports in this folder. They cannot make changes to the reports. Elizabeth, as the Finance Director, is the only individual who can save reports to this folder.
Finance	\Finance\ Internal	Full Control	Members of the Finance group can freely publish and modify content within this folder; other groups cannot see this content.
Marketing	\Marketing	Full Control	Members of the Marketing group can freely publish and modify content within this folder. Other groups do not see this content.
	\Orders	View On Demand	Members of the Marketing group can see reports and refresh reports within the Orders folder, but they can't save content or publish new reports. Only the individual user Sam, Supply Chain Manager, can save content to this folder.

Table 12-4   Use Folders or Categories to Organize BI Content and Grant Access

You follow a similar process to create categories, but select Categories from the CMC Home page (refer back to Figure 12-2).

Controlling Access to the Top-Level Folder

As the security in SAP BusinessObjects uses inheritance, you will first want to ensure that the security at your root, or top-level, folder is set appropriately. By default, the group Everyone is given No Access to the root. This also means that users cannot even see the individual folder names. In earlier versions, the default was Schedule.

Follow these steps to set the access for the top-level folder:

1. From the CMC Home page, select Folders.

2. From the menu, select Manage | Top-Level Security | All Folders.

3. You will be warned that you are setting top-level security. Click OK.

4. Select the group Everyone, and then click Assign Security.

5. Select Schedule from the Available Access Levels list, click > to add it to the Assigned Access Level list, and then click OK. The access level for Everyone should now show Schedule.

Controlling Access to Subfolders

When top-level security is set to the access level Schedule, the group Everyone inherits Schedule access to the Marketing folder. According to the notes in Tables 12-3 and 12-4, you want only Marketing users to be able to access and save content to this folder; users from other groups should not be able to see reports in this folder. To change the access for the group Everyone, do the following:

1. From the CMC Home page, select Folders, then Marketing.

2. Click the Manage User Security button or right-click and select User Security from the pop-up menu. The Access column indicates if a group or user's rights have been explicitly defined for this folder or if they have been inherited. In this case, the group Everyone inherited the Schedule access level from the top folder.

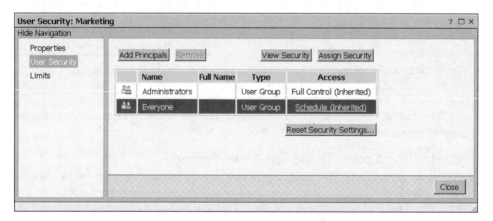

3. Select the group Everyone, and then click Assign Security.

4. Remove the check marks for Inherit from Parent Group and Inherit from Parent Folder.

5. Click OK. You will be warned that no access levels or rights have been explicitly granted, and asked if you wish to continue. Click OK.

6. The access level for Everyone should now show No Access.

To specify explicit access for the Marketing group, do the following:

1. From the User Security, Marketing folder you accessed in step 1, click Add Principals.

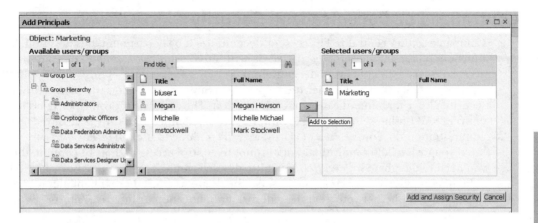

2. You may either select individual users or groups from this dialog box. The group hierarchy tree allows you to see individual members of each group. Select the Marketing group and click the > button to add the group to the Selected users/ groups list on the right.

3. Click Add and Assign Security.

4. A list of available access levels appears. Select the Full Control access level and click > to add it to the Assigned Access Levels list on the right.

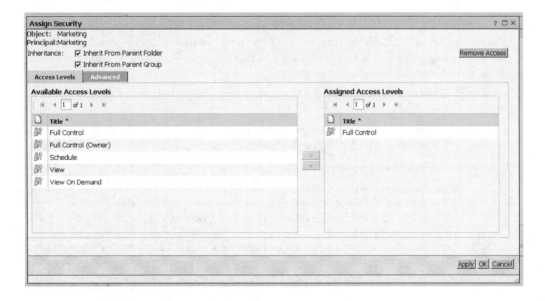

5. Click OK to apply the new security permissions.

Centralized or Decentralized Security

Companies either centralize IT access or decentralize it by department, business unit, or function. Increasingly, user *authentication* is centralized, while *authorization*, or granting access to specific BI content, is decentralized.

BusinessObjects 6 and earlier used a profile of Supervisor to allow you to decentralize security, either for authentication or authorization. The Supervisor profile per se no longer exists in SAP BusinessObjects BI 4.0; however, the capabilities to decentralize or delegate administration do. For the sake of clarity, we will continue to use the term *supervisor*.

If you wish to allow individual work groups to control access to their BI content, then you need to designate supervisors. You must also determine if these supervisors should be able to reset passwords or create new users. The desire to grant these capabilities is highly dependent on whether you are using external authentication or internal Enterprise authentication.

To demonstrate designating a supervisor for a group, we'll assign this control to Elizabeth, the Finance Director in our example (see Table 12-2). As the director of the Finance group, she will decide who is a member of the Finance group. Adding users to the Finance group is the simplest way to ensure that all users in Finance will have access to necessary content. This content may include access to documents in the \Finance folder (which Elizabeth also controls, as described in Table 12-4), to relevant universes, or to folders owned by other departments.

To allow Elizabeth to add users to this group, grant the user Elizabeth the access level of Full Control to the group Finance (different from the folder Finance), as follows:

1. From the CMC Home page, select Users and Groups.

2. In the Available Groups list, click the name of the group for which you wish to designate a supervisor—Finance in this example—right-click, and select User Security from the pop-up menu.

3. By default, you will see the Groups Administrators with Full Control. Click Add Principals.

4. Highlight the user whom you wish to designate as a supervisor—in this example, Elizabeth— and then click the > button.

5. Click Add and Assign Security.

6. At this point, you have simply added the user, Elizabeth, for specific access to the Finance group of users. However, you have not specified what additional rights Elizabeth should have. Set the level to Full Control, click >, and then click OK.

NOTE Remember that creating the user IDs and granting access to folders are two different tasks. Supervisors will be able to add users to only those groups for which they have Full Control, and thus can grant access only to the folders that the relevant user groups access.

Granting Access to Universes

So far, you've seen how to give users the ability to log in to BI Launch Pad, access content stored in folders, and in some cases, save content to these folders. This is the first part of the process in Figure 12-1. But where is this BI content coming from?

Some of the content may be from Excel spreadsheets that are saved to the repository. If the content is from Web Intelligence or dashboard documents, the users cannot *yet* refresh the data, even if they have the right "Refresh the report's data." In order for users to be able to refresh reports or create new reports, they must also have access to a universe and a universe connection.

If you want users to be able to refresh reports at any time, assign the access level View On Demand to both the universe and the universe connection. Without this setting, users may only be able to create a query with no data (with the View access level) and schedule a query (with the Schedule access level). And if you grant View On Demand access to the universe and forget to include the universe connection, users may successfully build a query, but when they try to execute the query, they receive an error message.

As with documents, you can choose to organize universes into folders and grant access to groups at the folder level. In particular, you may have test and development folders for universes that only developers or pilot users can access (unless you have completely separated these environments, as discussed in Chapter 14). If you don't have dozens of production universes, you can store these universes in the top universe folder.

CAUTION For the group Everyone, the default access to all universes and universe connections is View. This allows users only to see that the universe exists and to build a query without any data. It doesn't allow them to execute a query, either on demand or scheduled. If a designer chooses to export a universe to a specific group, then the access level is automatically changed to Full Control for the universe and Advanced for the universe connection. This potentially allows any user with access to the IDT application the ability to change a universe.

In the following example, you will allow the Marketing group to access the Sales Summary universe and Sales connection.

1. From the CMC Home page, select Universes.

2. Click the Sales and Marketing folder.

3. Right-click and select Users from the pop-up menu.

4. Click Add Principals.

5. From the Group list, select Marketing, and then click > to add this to the Selected Users/Groups list.

6. Click Add and Assign Security.

7. Change the access level for the Marketing group to View On Demand.

Repeat the preceding steps to grant access to the universe connection.

TIP If each universe has only one universe connection, consider granting the Everyone group View On Demand access to all connections. The connection alone does not provide access to the data; users need access to the universe to get to the data. If, however, your data is separated physically—for example, one Sales universe but with a connection to a European sales database and a North American sales database—then indeed you may want to control access at the connection level in addition to the universe level.

To see which connections are used within a particular universe, select the universe, right-click, and select Properties, and then choose Connections.

Further Securing the Data: Column- and Row-Level Security

In this chapter, you first created users and addressed user authentication. Through the use of folders and groups, you then managed access to reports within the folders and, ultimately, the universe and connections to allow users to refresh the reports or create new ones. This is the last phase of authorization (as shown earlier in Figure 12-1). SAP BusinessObjects offers more granular security at both the column and row levels.

There are multiple ways to implement column-level security. The first approach requires setting security levels in the business layer and then granting those levels within the CMC. This approach has existed since the early versions of BusinessObjects, but it is not widely used. A second method of controlling more granular security is via a newer tool, the Security Editor, accessed from within the IDT. The Security Editor allows you to control column-level security as well as row-level security and other security. In the next section, we provide step-by-step instructions for implementing column-level security via access levels, but we recommend that you use the Security Editor instead, as described later in the chapter.

Object-Level Security

Object-level security, often referred to as *column-level security*, allows you to control access at the individual universe object level. Do not confuse object-level security with all the references to objects in the preceding sections. Remember that objects within the repository refer to users, groups, folders, reports and so on. Objects within a universe referred to in this section relate to dimensions and measures.

In Chapter 7, you left all the object definitions set as Public. SAP BusinessObjects offers five levels of column security: Private, Confidential, Restricted, Controlled, and Public. Private is the most restrictive, and Public is the most permissive. Table 12-5 shows some sample objects for which you may want to have an object-level restriction, with the access level, priority (1 through 5 for Private through Public), and user or group.

In the examples in Table 12-5, the user Peggy processes payroll, so she needs access to Social Security numbers, designated as Private. *Salary* objects have a security access level equal to Confidential. Users with an access level of Confidential or of a higher priority (Private) can access *Salary* objects. Profit-related objects are set to Controlled. Members of the Finance and Marketing groups whose security access level is set to Controlled (in this case, anyone who has been with the firm at least three months) can access the *Profit* objects, as can any users who have a higher-priority security level (Restricted, Controlled, or Private).

Object Name	Security Access Level	Priority	User or Group
Social Security Number	Private	1	Peggy
Salary	Confidential	2	All Employee Managers
Bank Balance	Restricted	3	Finance users (but not Marketing)
Profit	Controlled	4	Finance and Marketing users
Amount Sold	Public	5	All

Table 12-5 Five Levels of Object-Level Security

When you use object-level security, three things happen if a user does not have access to the object:

- When a user creates a new query, the user never sees the object in the universe.
- When a user tries to refresh a query that contains the private object, the user receives an error message.
- When a user accesses a report that contains the private object, the user *does* see the object in the report, and if data is available, the data is also visible. In this way, object-level security is not entirely secure. Ways to overcome this breach include either publishing reports with no data or forcing a refresh on open.

You implement object-level security in two places:

- The universe's object properties, set in the business layer via the IDT
- The universe object-level security, set within the CMC

These settings can be quite tedious to maintain. If you are not using them in your universe design or if you have implemented column-level security at the database level, leave all universe settings for objects as Public.

To set the security access level on a universe object, use the IDT. Edit the business layer, select Dimension or Measure Properties, and click the Advanced tab. Choose the desired restriction level from the drop-down list. In this example, the *Salary* object has Confidential access:

Within the CMC, you need to set the security access level for both the users or groups and the respective universes. You can do this either by individual universe or for all universes. In Figure 12-4, all object-level security is set for all universes according to group membership. If you are creating groups for the primary purpose of assigning object-level security, preface the groups with a similar name, such as "Universe Objects Security," so they are clearly sorted.

NOTE   If you used object-level security from an earlier BusinessObjects implementation and imported those users, the import utility automatically created groups such as Object Level Security – Private.

To set the object-level security for all universes, follow this procedure:

1. From the CMC Home page, select Universes.

2. If you want to specify object-level security for an individual universe, user group, or user, click the desired universe. Otherwise, to apply the object-level security to all universes in the repository, right-click and select Universe Security from the pop-up menu.

3. Click Add.

4. From the Available Groups list, choose the Universe Objects Security - Confidential group and click > to add it to the list of selected users/groups. Then click OK.

5. Change the default object-level security for this group from Public to Private. Note that the levels available are listed in order of precedence.

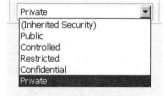

6. Click Update and ensure that the rights in the Net Security column change from Public to Private.

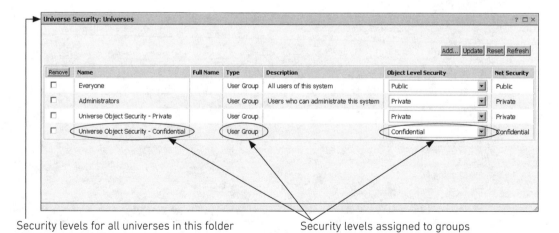

Security levels for all universes in this folder   Security levels assigned to groups

Figure 12-4   Special groups are created when object-level security is imported from earlier versions of BusinessObjects.

The Security Editor

Security you set within the CMC gives basic access to a universe. The Security Editor within the IDT allows you to assign additional levels of security to business layer views and objects, rows within the tables, and various SQL parameters. You can specify these settings either by user or groups of users, and either at the data foundation level or business layer level.

NOTE Changes within the Security Editor are not real time. If a particular user is added once you have launched the Security Editor, you will see the new user only if you refresh your view. If a new business layer perspective or object is added after you have launched the Security Editor, you also must refresh your view to see the new objects. Similarly, security changes take effect only once you save the changes.

The Security Editor allows you to create two types of security profiles:

- **Business Security**   Allows you to grant or deny access to business layer views (referred to as *perspectives* in Web Intelligence) and individual dimensions, measures, and filter objects available in the business layer.

- **Data Security**   Allows you to remap connections and tables, filter rows of data, and set SQL controls.

Business Security Profiles

Business security restrictions defined in the Security Editor can achieve similar purposes to the object-level security discussed earlier in the chapter. They have the same impact on a user's ability to create new reports containing an object or to refresh a report. However, some key differences exist between these restrictions and object-level security:

- Object-level security has multiple levels. View and object restrictions within the Security Editor are binary—either you can see the object by default or access to the object has been denied.

- Object-level security is defined both in the CMC and the universe object definitions. Object restrictions are defined only within the Security Editor in the IDT.

- Object-level security applies across multiple universes. Business layer view and object restrictions apply to specific objects within that one universe.

- You set business layer view and object restrictions within the Security Editor only; no additional settings are required in the CMC.

Here, we'll walk through creating and applying a sample business restriction.

Creating a Business Security Restriction

In our example, the user Sam works in Supply Chain. He has access to the Sales universe, so he can see the orders; however, he should not be able to see the measure object *Margin*. In setting this restriction, you first define the restriction and then apply it to the user or group. Figure 12-5 shows how the Security Editor will look after we complete this example.

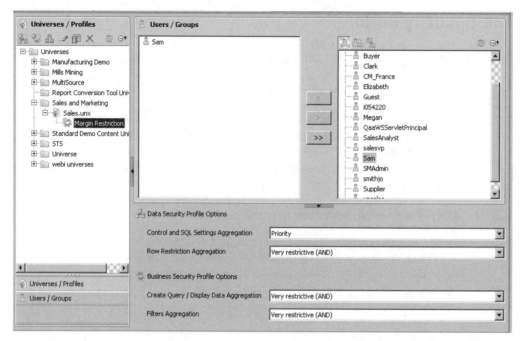

Figure 12-5 The Security Editor allows you to control access to individual data foundation and business layer elements.

Create a Business Security Restriction

To create an object restriction, follow these steps:

1. From within the IDT, choose Window | Security Editor or select Security Editor from the toolbar.

2. You will be prompted to insert a repository session. Enter your logon credentials and click OK.

3. The Security Editor displays a list of universe and groups, as shown in Figure 12-5. Navigate to the universe for which you wish to create a restriction—in this example, Sales.unx.

4. Right-click and select Insert Business Security Profile from the pop-up menu.

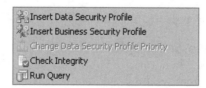

5. In the Define Business Security Profile dialog box, replace the default name of Business Security Profile with a more meaningful name, such as **Margin Restriction**.

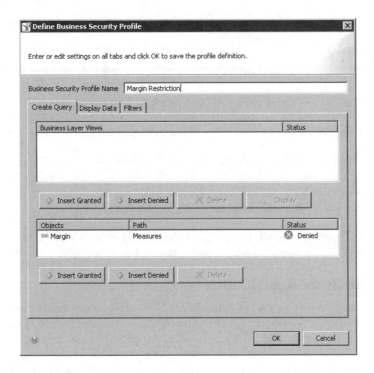

Part II

6. From this dialog box, you can either grant or remove access to particular views, objects, or filters. Beneath the Objects list at the bottom of the dialog box, click Insert Denied.

7. Choose the Margin object from the list of objects, and then click OK to close the list of objects.

8. Click OK to close the Define Business Security Profile dialog box.

Your newly created Margin Restriction profile should now appear beneath the universe name in the Security Editor, as shown in Figure 12-5.

Applying an Object Restriction

At this point, you have defined which object you want to restrict. You can now apply this restriction to the user Sam or to the group Supply Chain.

To apply an object restriction, follow these steps:

1. From the Security Editor, select the restriction, Margin Restriction.

2. From the Users/Groups list on the far right, you can scroll to individual users or navigate within the groups. For this example, locate user Sam.

NOTE All groups and users are displayed in the Security Editor, even though these groups may not have access to the universe. You want to apply object restrictions only to groups or users that have access to the universe.

3. Select the user or group—Sam in this example—and click < to add it to the list on the left, as shown in Figure 12-5.

 4. Save the changes.

NOTE Object restrictions apply to a user regardless of security access level and regardless of whether the restriction is inherited. If a user inherits access to a universe through membership in multiple groups that may allow access, the objects will still be hidden, as the object restriction applies.

When a user builds a query, the user will no longer see the restricted objects from the object list. If a user tries to refresh a query that contains a restricted object (or for which the user does not have sufficient security access), the user receives an error message that some objects are not available to the user's profile.

CAUTION If access to a business layer view or object is not explicitly granted, then it is denied by default for those users to which you have applied a business layer restriction.

Data Security Restrictions

In Chapters 5, 6, and 7, you set a number of SQL options and parameters in the Simple eFashion universe. By setting data security restrictions in the Security Editor, you can override certain options by group or by user. For example, the default result set for a universe may be 100,000 rows. With data security restrictions, you could increase this to 300,000 rows for certain power users. These are sometimes referred to as *universe overrides* because they override the default universe parameters. Keep in mind that these controls are universe-specific and would not, for example, allow power users to retrieve 300,000 rows of data from *all* universes.

You also can set a different database connection for certain users or groups. This is useful if your database is replicated on two servers (for response time or security reasons). For example, a European group could have a connection to a database with just European sales data that is physically located in Europe. A North American group could have a connection to a database with North American sales, physically located in North America.

Creating Query Controls Restrictions

Through a Data Security profile, you can define restrictions for queries. In the following example, the group Everyone can access all the reports in the \Finance folder. However, you decide that while the members of the Everyone group are allowed to execute queries that return no more than 100,000 rows, members of the Finance group should be able to return queries with 300,000 rows of data and longer execution times.

 1. From within the IDT pull-down menu, choose Window | Security Editor or select Security Editor from the toolbar.

2. You will be prompted to insert a repository session. Enter your logon credentials and click OK. The Security Editor displays a list of universe and groups, as shown earlier in Figure 12-5. Navigate to the universe for which you wish to create a restriction—in this example, Sales.unx.

3. Right-click and select Insert Data Security Profile from the pop-up menu.

4. Replace the default name of Data Security Profile with a more meaningful name, such as **Big Queries**.

5. Select the Controls tab. The Security Editor displays the default settings set in the connection, data foundation, or business layer. Any changes you make for the specific user or group are highlighted in blue. To restore the universe defaults, click Reset. For this example, increase the size of result set to 300,000 rows and the execution time to 10 minutes.

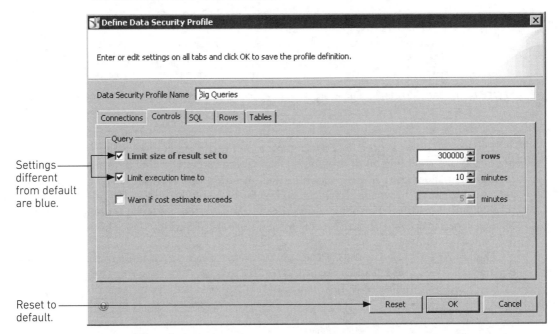

6. Select the SQL tab. You can use the options here to control how SQL is generated and which operators the individual user or group can control.

7. Click OK to save your changes to this restriction definition.

Now you can apply the Big Queries restriction definition to the Finance group, as follows:

1. Select the restriction, Big Queries.

2. From the Users/Groups list on the far right, scroll to the group Finance.

3. Select the group and click < to add the group to the list on the left.

4. Save the new restrictions.

Creating Row Restrictions

Row restrictions restrict the rows returned in a query by appending a SQL WHERE clause to every query a user runs. Multiple row restrictions are appended to the query with AND. Row restrictions are useful not only for security purposes, but also for user productivity. They save users time by automatically filtering the data according to what they need to see. Companies that have complex security requirements may elect to implement row restrictions at the database level rather than through SAP BusinessObjects.

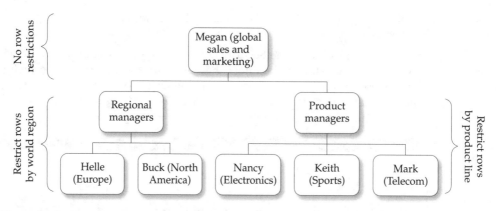

Figure 12-6 The Marketing group is organized by product and region. Row restrictions allow data to be filtered automatically.

Figure 12-6 shows a more detailed organization for the Marketing group. The group is organized by a combination of product managers who can view global information, and regional managers who can view sales information within their regions only. For example, Nancy is the Product Manager for Electronics. Nancy should be able to view all sales for this product line, regardless of which country the customer resides in. Helle is the Regional Manager for Europe; she should be able to view sales for all product lines, but only where the region is Europe.

Figure 12-7 shows all data rows available in the source system. In order to restrict which rows of data Nancy sees, you will add a restriction for `dimProduct.Linedescription= 'Electronics'`. Helle needs the restriction `dimCustomer.Regionname = 'Europe'`.

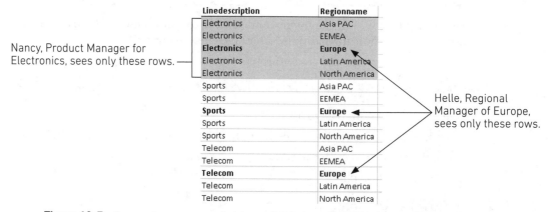

Figure 12-7 Corporate users see all data available, but a WHERE clause will filter the data for Nancy and Helle.

To apply row restrictions, follow these steps:

1. Within the Security Editor, navigate to the universe for which you want to create row restrictions. Right-click and select Insert Data Security Profile from the pop-up menu.

2. Replace the default name of Data Security Profile with a more meaningful name, such as **European Data**.

3. Select the Rows tab.

4. Click the Insert button to insert a restricted table.

5. In the Define Row Restriction dialog box, click the ellipse (...) button next to the Table box, and choose the dimCustomer table that contains the country information.

6. Enter the WHERE clause `dimCustomer. Regionname='Europe'`. Alternatively, click the ellipse (...) next to the WHERE Clause box to open the expression editor.

7. Click OK to return to the Define Data Security Profile dialog box, which will show the new restriction.

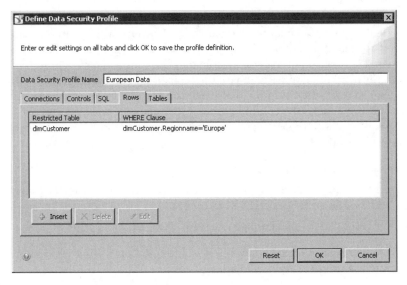

8. Click OK to close the dialog box.

You can apply the restriction definition to the user or group as in the previous sections.

Row restrictions can be quite powerful, but they also can be problematic if restrictions are applied against multiple groups. Row restrictions do not have priority levels; instead, all restrictions are used to generate the WHERE clause and, by default, are connected with AND. For example, if the Marketing group incorrectly contained a row restriction for REGION='Americas' and Helle's individual user restriction contained REGION='Europe', Helle would have no rows returned, since the two conditions are appended to the query with an AND connector. You can override this default behavior and specify the use of an OR connector by changing the Data Security Profile Options, Row Restriction Aggregation.

Database Views versus Row Restrictions

Companies that have unique logins to the data source often create views for each user or group of users to accomplish the same thing as the Security Editor's row restrictions. To implement this, the DBA creates a security table that contains each user and a column with the data values for each restriction. The security table is then joined to the fact or dimension tables to ensure users see only their own data.

There is no *best* solution for how to accomplish row-level security. Views may be easier to implement for many users with multiple security restrictions. Views are database-specific, so if your company uses more than one BI tool, the security model is open and independent of the tool. However, too many views may confuse a database optimizer, and queries may not be processed as efficiently. Unless the DBA creates an application to maintain the row restrictions, security becomes centralized with the DBA.

Table Mappings

Table mappings provide another way to implement row-level security. Table mappings allow universe designers to remap the base table in a universe with a different table name. In this way, a corporate group of users may access data in a corporate fact table, whereas a regional group may access data in a regional table that contains less data. These "tables" do not necessarily need to be physical tables; they can also be database views. In order for table mappings to work, the column names from the original table used in the universe must be exactly the same as the column names in the mapped table.

To continue with the example in Figure 12-6, you could have multiple tables, either views or physical tables:

- SALES that contains all sales data
- ELECTRONICS_SALES that contains a subset of data for dimProduct. Linedescription='Electronics'
- EURO_SALES that contains sales for dimCustomer.Regionname='Europe'

To remap a table, create a new restriction or edit an existing restriction set, and then apply it to the group or user, as follows:

1. Within the Security Editor, select the desired universe, right-click, and choose Insert Data Security Profile.

2. In the Restriction Name box, enter the name of the restriction—**EuropeanSalesFact** for this example.

3. Select the Tables tab.

4. Click Insert.

5. Click the ellipse (...) next to the Original Table Name box to select the original table name in the universe. This is the name of the table that you will be replacing.

6. Position your mouse in the Replacement Table box. Use the Select button to select the new table or enter the new table name—in this example, **AggEuroSales**.

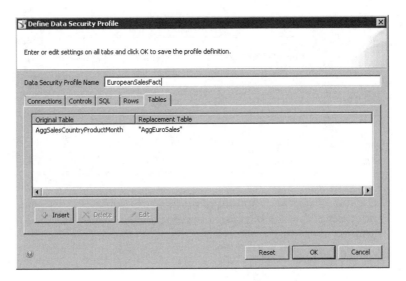

7. Click OK to return to the Define Data Security Profile dialog box, and then OK to create the profile.

8. Apply the restriction definition to the user or group as in the previous sections.

Setting Restriction Priorities

While row restrictions are all taken into consideration and connected with an OR or AND connector, for other restrictions, only one should be valid. For example, only one table mapping should take effect. You can specify which restriction should take precedence in the event that a user belongs to more than one group to which such a restriction has been applied.

In an earlier example, you increased the row limit for the Finance group. Let's assume that you also had a row restriction for the Marketing group that set the row limit to 200,000. If a user belongs to both groups, which restriction should take priority: the 300,000 row limit specified for the Finance group or the 200,000 row limit for the Marketing group?

By default, the priority goes according to the order in which the Data Security profiles were initially created and appear in the Universes/Profiles pane on the left. You can change this by manually setting the priorities, as follows:

1. Select the universe in the Universes/Profiles pane.

2. Right-click and select Change Data Security Profile Priority from the pop-up menu. Note that in order for this menu option to appear, you must have selected the .unx file and not an individual profile.

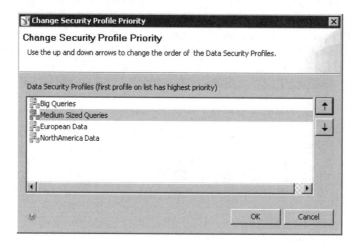

3. Use the up and down buttons to reorder the profiles. In this example, change the priorities so that the Big Queries profile appears before the Medium Sized Query profile.

4. Click OK.

Previewing Net Restrictions

When a user belongs to more than one group or when you combine multiple restrictions into one set, it's helpful to see what the net impact is: how the restrictions will be combined. To see this net effect, the Security Editor provides a Preview option.

In an earlier example, the user Sam was explicitly given an object restriction prohibiting him from seeing the *Margin* object. He also may have inherited some row restrictions by belonging to the Marketing group. To preview his net restrictions, follow this procedure:

1. Select the Users/Groups tab in the bottom left of the Security Editor.

2. Scroll to the desired user or group.

3. By default, all the universes in the repository are displayed, regardless of whether they have restriction profiles. To see only those universes with restrictions applied to the user Sam, check the box "Display only universes assigned to the selected user/group."

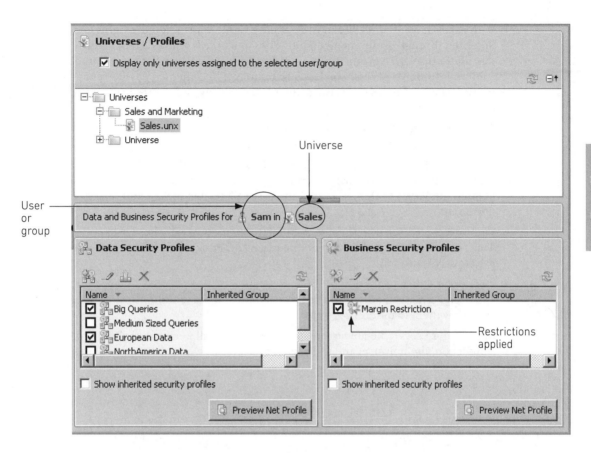

4. Click Preview Net Profile for either the Data Security profiles or the Business Security profiles.

5. The Restrictions Preview dialog box shows which restrictions affect the user, regardless of whether they were assigned via a group or an individual user.

6. Click Close to exit the preview, and then click Close again to exit the user list.

Summary

Security is implemented both in the CMC and through the IDT Security Editor. They allow for quite granular security. In planning your implementation, first understand what is possible, and then begin developing a security approach that fits your company security philosophy. Remember the following:

- Leverage external authentication and single sign-on when possible.
- Use groups and folders to simplify security administration.

- With access-level security, the most restrictive rights apply when the rights are inherited through group membership. Thus, if a user is granted view access in one folder through a group assignment and then *denied* the right to view an object (different from No Access, which translates to Not Specified) via a different group membership, the more restrictive setting takes priority and the user will not see the folder.

- Access-level security affects which menu options appear to end users within BI Launch Pad and within the individual applications.

- Explicit access takes priority over inherited access. Thus, if a user has inherited the right of denied to a particular report or folder, and then the same user is explicitly granted the View On Demand right, the user will be able to view and refresh the document.

- With object-level security (Private to Public), the most permissive right applies. Thus, if a user is granted Private in one place and Public in another place, the Private access prevails.

- Business and data restriction profiles affect universe objects, rows of data, and SQL behavior. For ease of administration, you should combine multiple settings together and apply them to different groups.

- In order for users to be able to create content, they will need access to folders, the connection, the universe, and the client application.

13 Design Principles: Where to Put the Intelligence

You have built your universe, made it more robust with advanced objects and hierarchies, and developed a security strategy. You are off to a good start. As your universe evolves, you will face a number of choices about where to put the intelligence—specifically, the *business* intelligence. This chapter focuses on the alternatives and their pros and cons. Our goal is to help you understand the cost and benefit implications of the choices as you deploy SAP BusinessObjects.

What Is Intelligence?

Intelligence is information with a *business* context. QUANTITY may be a physical column in a table. Add a time period such as month, then a business context to the time period such as order month, and multiply the column by a price, and you arrive at *Sales Revenue,* something with meaning and value to business users.

Users will rarely want to analyze straight columns of detailed data. If they did, the transaction or enterprise resource planning (ERP) system would meet their needs just fine. To provide a business context, the raw data must be combined with other information, perhaps cleansed, transformed, and aggregated. Many transformations may be critical to the project's success and known to programmers and extract, transform, and load (ETL) experts; however, they mean nothing to a business user. If a customer code is 306 in one system and 0306 in another system, the business user really doesn't care. The business user only cares and knows that this 306/0306 customer is Mrs. Whitwell. Transformations to make the data consistent are necessary to build the data warehouse or mart, but they are a given to the business user.

If the business user wants to do a promotion for newly married customers, then perhaps classifying these customers under a grouping such as newlyweds would be a form of intelligence. At first glance, you may assume that this customer grouping should exist in a dimension table. A dimension table within the database is certainly one place to put the intelligence, but the customer grouping could also go in the universe or a user's report.

Following are a few more examples of items that are considered to be more than just straight calculations or transformations; they provide BI:

- Measures that include time periods, such as *Sales YTD* and *Days Late*
- Variance analysis that compares the difference between two numbers, such as *Current Year Sales versus Last Year Sales* and *Percentage of On-time Shipments*
- Ratios, such as *Market Share, Patient Visits per Diagnosis,* and *Gross Margin*
- Dimension groupings, such as customer age, income level, product size, and type

Places for Intelligence

There are a number of places to create and store this intelligence. Often, the decision of where to build the intelligence is based on one person's knowledge of how to do it; it's assumed there is only one alternative. For example, a universe designer may naturally assume that the universe should contain all the intelligence. Power users may want report variables to contain all the intelligence. Depending on how much disk space and time a DBA has, the DBA may want the intelligence to be in the table design so that it is tool-independent. This is where a good program manager or project manager will work with the different stakeholders and determine the best place for intelligence, considering a company's resources, time, and flexibility.

Guidelines should become best practices and part of a quality assurance process. Companies can build intelligence into OLAP databases, the data warehouse, the data foundation, the business layer, and reports. If you are using SAP BusinessObjects directly against a transaction system, your alternatives may be limited to the universe and reports. Figure 13-1 shows these different places and where the intelligence is processed.

In Chapter 9, you built an object called *Current YTD Sales* as part of the universe. Stepping through Figure 13-1, you could have used an OLAP database such as Microsoft Analysis Services to include the time period awareness in the sales column (place ① in the figure). The processing for this type of object is done on the OLAP server. The intelligence also could be a physical column in an aggregate fact table.

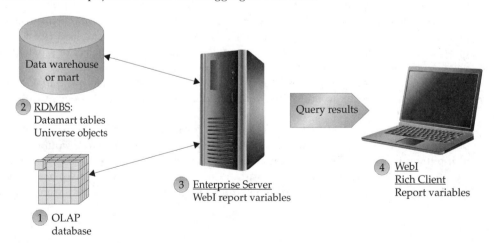

Figure 13-1 Intelligence can be built into a number of places in a SAP BusinessObjects deployment.

The information is preprocessed by the RDBMS, so when a user runs a query, it is a simple fetch (place ②in the figure). If the object exists in either the universe or a user object, the RDBMS again does the work, but does it upon query execution. The user may wait longer for the query to be processed, but the work is still done by the RDBMS. Larger-scale BI implementations will always strive to do more processing on the server, rather than on the mid-tier BI application server or, worse, on the user's desktop.

If a power user creates a report variable in Web Intelligence to calculate *Current YTD Sales,* then the RDBMS sends the detail rows to calculate that variable to either the Enterprise server when viewed from a browser or to the user's desktop if it is opened with Web Intelligence Rich Client. In a thin-client environment, the SAP BusinessObjects Enterprise server must calculate the variable and present the results to the user in HTML format (place ③in the figure). With Web Intelligence Rich Client, all the detail rows travel the network to the desktop PC that then calculates the report variable (place ④in the figure).

Evaluating the Pros and Cons of Each Alternative

Occasionally, there is a single, clear-cut choice for where to put the intelligence. The DBA is too busy to add it to the physical data warehouse, so you add it to the universe; the calculation is too complex for SQL, so you create a report variable. These are the easy answers. The not-so-easy answers are everything else in between.

The best place for intelligence is, as suggested by the consultant's annoying but valid answer, "it depends." The following sections present the pros and cons of each alternative, with examples of intelligence that are better suited to one place than another.

Each alternative has associated costs in terms of time, resources, expenses, and flexibility. The question you must answer is whether the benefits outweigh the costs and disadvantages. Building intelligence into the fact table provides faster response time and consistent results. Is this a strong enough benefit to justify the cost of redesigning the table and modifying the load routines? In some cases, absolutely. In other cases, no. You may decide you can justify the costs but that you need more flexibility or time to market.

OLAP Databases

The percentage of companies that integrate OLAP databases with SAP BusinessObjects remains small. The main benefits of OLAP databases over straight relational storage are fast response time and multidimensional analysis. However, columnar databases, such as SAP Sybase IQ, provide an alternative to OLAP. These databases have gained popularity because they provide fast response time and leverage SQL instead of MDX. In-memory processing also provides an alternative to OLAP databases, and SAP's new in-memory appliance, HANA, may make an OLAP database unnecessary. Of course, the price points, capabilities, adoption, and skills required for these alternatives are different than those for the well-established OLAP databases.

OLAP Databases As Independent Applications

Companies often treat OLAP databases as separate applications for several reasons. First, each OLAP vendor provides their own access tools. For example, later versions of Excel natively support Microsoft Analysis Services. SAP BW provides Business Explorer (BEx) as a front end to BW InfoCubes, and while SAP now recommends Web Intelligence or Analysis as alternatives, many companies have numerous BEx queries. Oracle Essbase now provides its own set of front-end tools.

Just as data marts and BI implementations can be implemented departmentally, so can OLAP databases such as Analysis Services and Oracle Essbase. SAP BW is normally implemented at an enterprise level. Unless a business sponsor and program management are in place to integrate the OLAP data source with SAP BusinessObjects, it seems rarely to happen. As these leading OLAP vendors offer their own front ends to their databases, customers often incorrectly assume that they must use the corresponding front end.

Furthermore, the vendor's approach to OLAP access has gone through many transitions, so confusion and lack of awareness abounds. With SAP BusinessObjects BI 4.0, the vendor now offers better OLAP support either via the universe for Web Intelligence users or Analysis for direct access.

Finally, Web Intelligence itself, with its microcube engine, is also considered an OLAP tool. Thus, many companies assume that they need only SAP BusinessObjects and do not need another OLAP database. This assumption is reasonable. However, because of some of the inherent limitations with the dynamic microcubes, an OLAP database can provide some significant benefits in some cases.

OLAP Databases Versus Microcubes

One of the biggest differences between the OLAP capabilities via the Web Intelligence microcube and an OLAP database is the data volume. There is no hard rule as to the size of a microcube; it could be 300 thousand rows of data. It would not be 3 million, as is the case of an OLAP database. In this respect, it is much more appropriate to think of applications such as Microsoft Analysis Services and Essbase as databases or data sources rather than as competing tools.

There also is a significant difference between drilling within a microcube and drilling against an OLAP data source. The goal with any OLAP deployment is to ensure that when users drill, it is at the speed of thought. Because an OLAP database is pre-aggregated and a subset of the data is in a data warehouse, the response times are more predictable than relational query response times. To ensure fast drilling times within the Web Intelligence microcube, report authors often cram too much information into a report. They are trying to get the microcube to act like an OLAP database. This approach is doomed to failure.

When users drill within a Web Intelligence report, they are drilling within a subset of cached data, as shown in Figure 13-2. When a user drills from year to quarter, the details for quarter already exist in the report. If not, then the user can drill through to the details and send another query to the relational database. The results are fetched and stored in the microcube. Herein lies a challenge: if your relational database is well tuned, this drill-through to detail could take a few seconds or a few minutes (hopefully not hours). And what if the majority of users never look at quarterly details? Then you have unnecessarily built a larger report than required!

Meanwhile, with an OLAP database such as SAP BW, Essbase, or Microsoft Analysis Services, the cube is built in advance of the query. When a user drills from year to quarter, the drill goes against the highly tuned OLAP database, as shown in Figure 13-3. This limits network traffic, because only the necessary results are sent to the SAP BusinessObjects Enterprise server as each user requests the details. The OLAP server performs sorts, nested rankings, cross-dimensional calculations, and more.

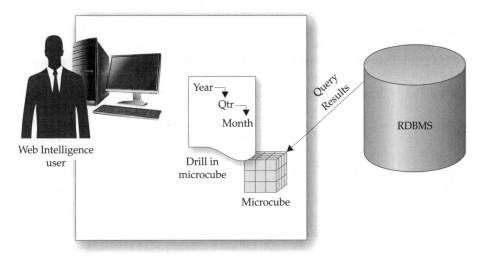

Figure 13-2   Users drill within reports.

Advantages of Building Intelligence into OLAP Databases

Clearly, for this section to have any relevance, your goal is to integrate an existing OLAP database as another data source in your SAP BusinessObjects deployment. So, when should you build intelligence into the OLAP database?

As shown earlier in Figure 13-1, when the intelligence is put in an OLAP database, the server does the work (place ①), thus minimizing network traffic. In general, building intelligence into any server-based technology will also ensure consistent business definitions (compared to varying calculations in user reports and spreadsheets).

Also, OLAP databases have a better understanding of business analysis than most SQL-based reporting tools, so a number of functions are built into the OLAP engine. For time period calculations, Essbase includes dynamic period-to-date calculations with a toggle. Period-to-date functions are native to MDX and Microsoft Analysis Services, rather than the complex SQL CASE functions presented in Chapter 9.

Recall the discussions on semi-additive measures in Chapter 7, and the issue with comparing inventories and account balances (one point in time) with material movements and debit/credits (a period of time). Web Intelligence handles this through multiple SQL statements and user training; however, OLAP databases again are aware of these issues and

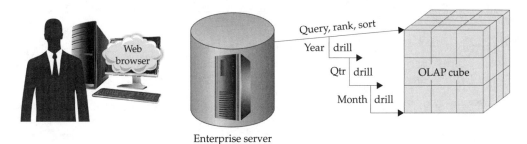

Figure 13-3   Drill within Analysis is against the OLAP database.

allow you to flag with a simple setting that such measures may be aggregated by product, for example, but not by time.

OLAP databases also provide you with more control over the calculation order, something particularly important for ratios and percentages. As an example of calculation order, look at the calculations for profit as a percent of sales, as shown in Figure 13-4. To get sales and profit totals for the fourth quarter, you correctly sum across the rows. However, for profit as a percent of sales, if you sum across, you get an incorrect percentage of 84. To calculate percentages and ratios, you need to first get the sums by quarter, and then calculate down to take profit and sales. This second calculation gives you the correct result of 28 percent.

Calculation order is also important for multidimensional and forward-looking calculations. As shown in the next example, profit and sales are at two different levels within the accounts hierarchy. To calculate profit, you must first know the subtotals for margin and total expenses. Profit is not a simple sum, but rather an aggregation of subtotal margin – subtotal expenses. To calculate profit as a percentage of sales, you must know both levels of subtotals, as well as the detail sales used to calculate the margin subtotal. The database must look "forward" to first calculate profit before it can calculate sales as a percentage of profit.

	A	B	C
1			
2			
3	Sales	184972	
4	Cost_of_Goods_Sold	75571	
5	Margin	109401	
6			
7	Marketing	14655	
8	Payroll	44185	
9	Miscellaneous	-1704	
10	Total_Expenses	57136	
11			
12	Profit	52265	
13			
14	**Profit % of Sales**	**28%**	

First subtotal (Margin 109401)

Second subtotal (Profit 52265)

= Margin – Total Expenses

= Profit/Sales: 52265/184972

This is simple for an OLAP database, which understands dimension members and levels (just say Profit % Sales!), but not so simple for SQL. Are there ways of doing this in the fact table, universe, or report? Of course! It's all a matter of the time and cost to implement and maintain the intelligence.

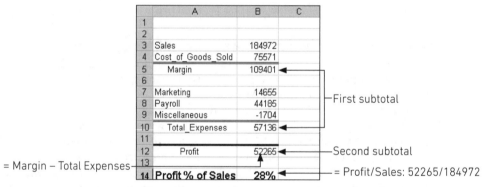

	Product	Market	Actual		
	Oct	**Nov**	**Dec**	**Q4**	
Sales	48842	62758	73372	184972	
Profit	12686	17262.2	22316.8	52265	
Profit_% of Sales	26	28	30	84	— Wrong value!

Sum across first

	Product	Market	Actual		
	Oct	**Nov**	**Dec**	**Q4**	
Sales	48842	62758	73372	184972	
Profit	12686	17262.2	22316.8	52265	
Profit_% of Sales	26	28	30	28	Calculate down (profit/sales) to correct ratios and %s

Figure 13-4   Percentages and ratios require a two-step calculation that OLAP databases handle easily.

An OLAP database is also an ideal place to store dimensional information that needs to be aggregated in different ways. As discussed early in this chapter, a customer dimension could have groupings by physical region (customers in California) or by type of customer (newly married). Users are viewing the same measures but by different groupings. OLAP tools allow dimensions to be aggregated in different ways, often without drastically increasing the size of the database.

Disadvantages of OLAP Databases

Before you rush out to implement the latest version of an OLAP database, note that its use will have some disadvantages. First, an OLAP database is another database and another data source. If your organization is strapped for IT resources, you may be forced to limit which technologies you can support. As a separate database, it is another copy of the data, so there are latency and data extraction issues. However, if the OLAP database is tightly integrated correctly with your data warehouse, it may be an alternative, smarter way to provide aggregate tables.

OLAP databases are known for ensuring consistent response times on precalculated data; however, this requires smaller data sets than what an RDBMS can handle. Some OLAP databases, such as SAP BW, allow you to store data in relational tables (referred to as ROLAP, for relational OLAP) to increase capacity, yet this will have a performance impact. OLAP databases are not well suited for list analysis, and support for attribute analysis varies greatly. For example, you might want a list of customers above a certain age or a list of products packaged a particular way, but OLAP databases generally do not support list-style reports.

OLAP Database Summary

The following table summarizes the key benefits and disadvantages to putting the intelligence in an OLAP database.

OLAP Database Benefits	OLAP Database Disadvantages
Understanding of semi-additive measures like inventory	Additional cost and expertise
Control over calculation order for ratios and percentages	Risk of duplicate, inconsistent data if not integrated with data warehouse
Multidimensional and multirow calculations	Expertise generally comes from IT
Aggregated, so fast and consistent response times	
Server-based, so consistent business definitions and minimal network traffic	
Built-in time period awareness such as year-to-date and year-over-year variances	

Relational Tables

Building the intelligence into relational tables provides many of the same benefits as OLAP databases:

- Tables are preprocessed and so are generally faster than the dynamic SQL that a universe object would use.
- Tables involve server-based processing, so only limited data is sent across the network.
- Tables are server-based, so business definitions are centralized and consistent.

Again taking the example of *Current Year To Date Sales,* a DBA could build a fact table with the following structure:

product_key	customer_key	time_key	C_Month	LY_Month	C_YTD	L_YTD
123	111	102003	500	400	5000	3850
456	111	102003	200	180	2000	1800
123	333	102003	710	300	7100	3000
123	777	102003	900	1000	8000	10000

As the data is loaded into the fact table, each column represents a "bucket" of information, with the time period intelligence built into each column. C_MONTH contains sales for just the current month. C_YTD contains sales for each month in the current year; for example, if the month is October, it contains sales from January through October.

Many analytic applications that build data marts (including SAP BW's InfoCubes) use this kind of structure. However, if your company designs and builds your own fact tables, the DBA must program this kind of intelligence into the load routines. Unlike in OLAP databases, there may not be a simple toggle to achieve time period intelligence (although newer data integration tools may assist with this). A robust ETL tool may help with the process. For example, Data Integrator has a date generation transform that will take an individual date value and create the appropriate year, quarter, and month hierarchies. Data Integrator also includes special functions to load data into fact tables to create running YTD measures, month-to-date measures, and so on.

Even with an ETL tool, however, this kind of design requires more disk space and a stronger understanding of best practices in data warehouse designs. DBAs may not have the resources or time to implement this kind of design.

Recall from the first section in this chapter that dimension groupings such as customer age, income level, and product size are also forms of intelligence. Analyzing data by dimensions is the bread and butter of most businesses.

Providing alternative groupings can help reveal previously hidden patterns. For example, for a wine merchant, users can analyze sales by type of wine and rating. Users also can see which customers buy the most wine. Now break that customer list down by corporate customers versus individual consumers, and the analysis will reveal which group of customers generates the most business. If the dimension table contained income information for each corporate customer, the wine merchant could better understand if large corporate customers are more profitable than small business owners.

The same logic applies to product information: what are sales for soft drinks in plastic bottles versus aluminum cans? Unfortunately, this kind of dimensional information is often not captured, or when it is captured, it is stored in departmental databases and spreadsheets.

While Web Intelligence users can incorporate personal data sources into their reports, such dimensional information should be stored in sources that are accessible to more users. If companies use a star or snowflake schema in data marts, then a data mart can contain both a standard customer dimension and a customer dimension with business-specific groupings and hierarchies. SAP BusinessObjects can handle multiple dimensions with alternate hierarchies in each.

Dimensional information in relational tables also allows users to create lists and easily do attribute analysis with the information. Not all OLAP databases support this type of analysis, and it's not possible when such information remains in personal workspaces only.

TIP If you do have dimensional information in a departmental database, separate from the central data warehouse, this still may be accessible via Web Intelligence. Individual users can merge personal data sources, or you can use a multisource universe to access the data, as discussed in Chapter 10.

When Not to Store Intelligence in Relational Tables

Relational tables are not a good place to physically store ratios and variances, as the ratio always needs to be recalculated with an aggregated numerator and an aggregated denominator. Continuing with the earlier example, let's say you want to calculate the percentage variance between the current YTD sales (C_YTD) and last year's YTD sales (LY_YTD). For each row in the database, you can correctly store the variance.

product_key	customer_key	time_key	C_YTD	L_YTD	% Variance
123	111	102003	5000	3850	29.87%
123	333	102003	7100	3000	136.67%
123	777	102003	8000	10000	–20.00%

However, recall that Web Intelligence users will create reports that dynamically group information by dimensions. Thus, a business user may ask for a variance analysis by product. In order to allow this, the universe designer includes the SQL SUM aggregate in the object definition. This incorrectly sums the individual variance rows, suggesting that sales are 146.54 percent higher than last year's sales. This is wrong!

product_key	customer_key	time_key	C_YTD	L_YTD	% Variance
123	111	102003	5000	3850	29.87%
123	333	102003	7100	3000	136.67%
123	777	102003	8000	10000	–20.00%
Subtotal for product 123:			20100	16850	146.54%

Wrong!

To arrive at a correct variance, you must get the subtotal for the C_YTD by product 123, and then the subtotal of L_YTD to arrive at a correct variance of sales being 19.29 percent higher than last year.

OLAP databases allow an administrator to control the calculation order; SQL tools do not. To guarantee correct results, the universe designer would ignore the variance column in the fact table and dynamically calculate the variance using a SQL statement in an object. See the "Ratio to Report" section in Chapter 9 for specific examples.

Relational Table Summary

The following table summarizes the advantages and disadvantages of storing intelligence in a fact table.

Relational Table Benefits	Relational Table Disadvantages
Precalculated in the table, so fast, consistent response times	Requires complex programming logic in the load routines
Server-based, so consistent business definitions and minimal network traffic	Fixed table design may limit flexibility
	IT/DBA must implement
	Requires additional disk space
	Not suitable for ratios and percentages

Universe

There are two places to add intelligence in a universe: the data foundation or the business layer. Compared to the earlier alternatives discussed, enabling intelligence in the universe provides a number of benefits. Of course, there are exceptions, but let's start with the arguments for putting intelligence in the universe.

Advantages of Intelligence in the Universe

Intelligence in the universe offers much more flexibility than adding intelligence either in an OLAP database or a relational table. When you add or modify a universe object, there is no need to restructure and recalculate a cube, nor to modify load routines and rebuild a table.

Because the universe is centralized, it enforces consistent business definitions, as opposed to adding intelligence in reports. Furthermore, as shown earlier in Figure 13-1, the processing is done on the database server, thus minimizing the impact on the network or SAP BusinessObjects Enterprise servers that user report formulas can overload.

The universe allows partial control of the calculation order, necessary for ratios and variance analysis, which is something relational tables cannot offer in an ad hoc reporting environment. As shown in the preceding example, if you aggregate the variance stored in a relational table, you get incorrect results. Within the universe, you use the following syntax to control the calculation order:

```
(sum(C_YTD)-sum(L_YTD)) /sum(L_YTD)
```

Alternatively, with databases that support SQL analytic functions, you can calculate ratios as follows:

```
RATIO_TO_REPORT(sum(SH.SALES.AMOUNT_SOLD)) OVER ()
```

As users build queries that analyze the percent variance by different dimensions (product, time, geography, and so on), the variance for each row returned is always recalculated with the correct numerator and denominator. Problems may arise when users add breaks and subtotals within a report, but these issues can easily be corrected with report formulas.

Intelligence in the universe also does not necessarily need to be implemented by a (typically overworked) DBA. New intelligence can be added quickly, as is critical in a changing business environment. Responsiveness and flexibility are the two main advantages of building intelligence into the universe. If the BI deployment cannot respond as quickly as the business requirements change, it will be less successful. Requirements change not simply because users overlooked something, but also often because they discovered a new or better way to explore information.

Who Designs and Maintains the Universe?

As shown in Figure 13-5, a DBA or central IT person is the predominant designer of the universe (according to the BI Scorecard Successful BI Survey, 2011). Placing the universe design responsibility within the domain of central IT is ideal, as IT staff members have the skills to understand relationships between tables, joins, and index issues. They also can write complex SQL.

NOTE Programmers and DBAs certified in SQL are not necessarily adept at SQL for business reporting and analysis. This is often a unique and hard-to-find skill set.

However, unless the IT department has a close relationship with the business and an understanding of business reporting requirements, the staff may miss opportunities to add intelligence to the universe. Users do not know SQL and do not know what objects can be built with SQL. IT knows SQL but may not realize that the business would benefit from measures such as number of customers (COUNT function), number of late orders (COUNT and DAYS_BETWEEN functions), variance analysis ((SUM1–SUM2)/SUM2), and so on.

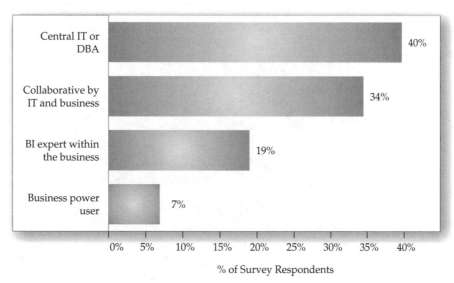

Figure 13-5 Who designs the universe?

A recurring complaint about IT maintaining the universe is lack of flexibility. Users want something, but IT may be too busy to implement it, or a minor enhancement may need to go through a lengthy maintenance prioritization, or IT might want to keep the universe general.

Figure 13-6 shows the relationship between BI success and who designs and maintains the universe. While many projects have very successful deployments when the central IT group maintains the universe, this approach shows a higher than usual rate of only slight success (43 percent), indicating that these universes may be less business-focused and more technical-focused.

As your deployment and BI organization matures, you may establish a central BI team, or BI competency center (BICC), with technically savvy business experts who either collaborate on the universe design or own the universe entirely. Another approach is to allow individual functions or business units to build and maintain their own universes. With the separation of the data foundation and business layer in the new IDT, this approach is even more possible in SAP BusinessObjects BI 4.0. For example, IT or a central BICC can maintain the data foundation, with technical experts in the business maintaining the business layer. IT should still quality-assure these universes (see the "Quality Assurance Check List" section in Chapter 15 for more information).

When a universe designer fails to build enough intelligence into the universe to satisfy the common business needs, end users are forced to build the intelligence in the report. This approach may be fine for individual needs, but it can be a maintenance challenge for reports that are widely shared, as it can significantly increase maintenance costs and the risk of inconsistent business definitions. So if a user changes a report variable that suddenly

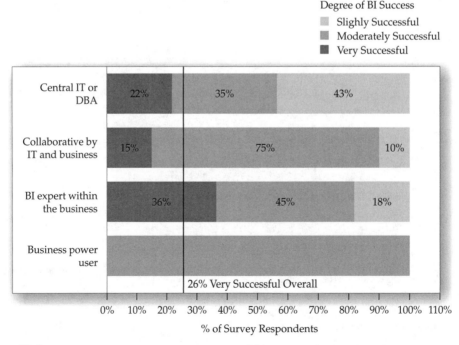

Figure 13-6 Degree of BI success is lower when the DBA alone maintains the universe.

calculates revenue in a slightly different way, there are no controls to document and identify this change. Changes in the universe at the object level are also not readily identifiable, but as a smaller group of developers are involved, they at least can be documented procedurally.

Disadvantages of Intelligence in the Universe

Even though a robust universe is ideal, there are times when the universe is not the best place for the intelligence. Advanced objects will generally use complex SQL or internal functions to create the objects. This can result in unpredictable query response times, unless you have taken the steps necessary to ensure consistent performance.

Also, as the universe becomes more complex, there is a greater risk that certain objects will not work well together. For example, if a universe contains the two objects *Sales* and *Current YTD Sales*, will users receive accurate information if they place these objects in the same query? The first object, *Sales*, does not include any time-period constraints. The user therefore adds Month=10 and Year=2012 as conditions in the report. This makes the *Current YTD Sales* information wrong (it's now one month of data versus YTD data), as Web Intelligence appends the WHERE clause to the entire query.

Users should recognize query results that are blatantly wrong; it's the not-so-obvious ones that pose a problem. In any case, a perfect universe would include only those objects that can be accurately combined together. A real-world universe accomplishes this most of the time, and supplements it with good object descriptions and training!

The following table summarizes the advantages and disadvantages of enabling intelligence in the universe.

Universe Benefits	Universe Disadvantages
Designers (IT or power users) can implement, so it is flexible	Use of complex business SQL is a unique skill
Server-based, so consistent business definitions, minimal network traffic, and better scalability	Unpredictable response times compared to fact table or OLAP database, as SQL is processed at query run time
Ratios and variances are correct	Individual objects may not be correct when combined with other objects with conflicting definitions
Leverages RDBMS analytic functions	Database-dependent

Web Intelligence Reports

With robust calculations and formulas, Web Intelligence offers users the ability to overcome many limitations in SQL. The number of functions in Web Intelligence has steadily increased with each new release (see Chapter 21). Users are familiar with formulas from spreadsheets and are comfortable building some quite powerful ones within the Web Intelligence documents. In some cases, users may have no choice but to create a formula in a report for the following reasons:

- It's an individual reporting need.
- The intelligence cannot be built with SQL.
- It's immediate and avoids the politics that accompany other alternatives.

If the report really is for individual use and the formula is not a common business one, then the intelligence does indeed belong in a report. However, too often report-based calculations are created simply because there was little dialogue between the universe designer and business users.

In some cases, it may be technically feasible to build the intelligence into a universe object, but the user needs it immediately. IT may maintain the universe and be unable to create a new object quickly enough, so the user creates a report formula for expediency. The user also may want to avoid the politics of needing to get a common buy-in for a universe modification.

OLAP solutions that support MDX overcome a number of limitations of SQL (forward calculations, time period versus point in time, and so on). However, leading database vendors have continued to provide a number of SQL extensions that make SQL more robust. Forward calculations such as rankings and percent market share that were once possible only with MDX are now possible with SQL.

Formula Functions for Reports

Web Intelligence contains a number of formula functions that may not have a SQL equivalent. Variance Percentage (VarP), Percentile, and RunningSum are just a few examples. Long before database vendors added analytic functions to SQL, Web Intelligence offered a percent of sum calculation, as well as ranking and various running aggregate functions.

Recall the particular problems that variance and ratio calculations can cause. The calculation order is very important to get the correct answer. With report formulas, users control the calculation order either by specifically inserting a formula at each break level or with calculation context operators (explained in detail in Chapter 21). To use the earlier example of the variance between C_YTD and L_YTD, look how the percent variance is correctly calculated, even for the break level by product.

product_key	customer_key	time_key	C_YTD	L_YTD	Variance
123	111	102003	5,000	3,850	29.87%
	333	102003	7,100	3,000	136.67%
	777	102003	8,000	10,000	-20.00%
123		**Sum:**	**20,100**	**16,850**	**19.29%**

Web Intelligence automatically ensures the ratios are correctly calculated at each break level by using an extended syntax in the report formula. Within the individual rows, the full syntax for the ratio in Web Intelligence is as follows:

```
=([C_YTD]-[L_YTD])/[L_YTD] ForEach ([product_key]) In ([product_
key];[customer_key];[time_key])
```

At the footer or subtotal level, the syntax is slightly different:

```
=(Sum([C_YTD])-Sum([L_YTD]))/Sum([L_YTD]) ForEach ([product_key]) In
([product_key])
```

Disadvantages of Intelligence in Reports

Too many report formulas can be problematic over time. One problem is that report variables are stored within a document and therefore are not centrally maintained. As formulas change, there is no way to track how many versions of the report have been shared and modified. Multiple versions of the formula will now exist. This problem becomes worse when the original formula creator changes jobs or leaves the company. Some statistics have shown that about 75 percent of spreadsheets contain errors. It stands to reason that report formulas may have a similarly high number of errors, or at the very least, cause a number of misunderstandings.

Another problem is that formulas contain a significant amount of intelligence that could, and should, be leveraged across the company. If a company is to ensure business consistency and capture the power of user report variables, you must develop a process to review and maintain formulas. Figure 13-7 shows one possible process:

- A user creates a standard report that contains a number of formulas (step ①).

- A report reviewer, who may be a power user or a universe designer, reviews the report and looks for formulas that are common needs (step ②).

- When they fulfill common reporting requirements, the universe designer builds the intelligence into the universe (step ③A). If it is not a broad reporting requirement but only fulfills the needs of a few users, then the intelligence will remain as a report formula.

- The report reviewer quality-assures the formula and saves the report to the public folders or corporate categories (step ③B).

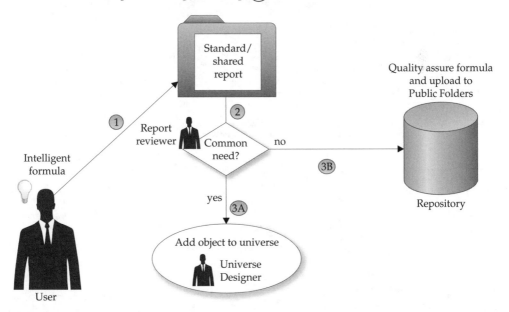

Figure 13-7   Creating a role of report reviewer can help companies minimize the risks of unnecessary and inconsistent report formulas.

Users may balk at this additional level of quality control, and the last thing a company wants to do is add barriers to sharing information. An alternative is to let users freely save documents to the public folders or corporate categories but ensure a report reviewer and/or universe designer checks the shared reports periodically. Some administrators have push backed on this idea, as they want shared folders (corporate documents in earlier releases) to be tightly controlled.

With Desktop Intelligence, users could easily use the local area network (LAN) file system to otherwise share the reports, and they may continue to do so in Web Intelligence Rich Client. In other words, if your deployment approach is an obstacle to sharing reports, users often will find their own ways to do so. When IT facilitates the sharing, though, IT can also provide some degree of control and quality assurance.

Our recommendation is to actively facilitate sharing of reports. You may want to structure folders such that there is one super-controlled area and other areas with fewer restrictions. Making the whole repository too tightly controlled may cause your deployment to be less successful in the long term.

Another major disadvantage of report variables is their effect on response time and system load. Overly complex reports consume more resources on the BI server and can be slower for users to refresh. Formulas that require detail rows may cause too much data to be sent across the network. Let's look at the example of *Last Year YTD Sales*.

The following Web Intelligence report formula looks at the Enterprise server's CurrentDate to determine which months are less than the current month. If it is less than the current month, then it displays the *Amount Sold*; otherwise, it shows zero. The year must be one year ago.

The report appears as follows (assuming the current date is April 2008). Notice that while there were sales in May, the rows for these months correctly display zeros, as it is greater than the current month.

NOTE For a detailed explanation of these formula functions, refer to Chapter 21.

Current Month: *April*   Each year goes to a separate column.

Year Number	Month Number	Linename	Net Sales	Current YTD Sale	Last YTD Sales
2007	3	Electronics	10,524,786.6	0	10,524,786.6
2007	4	Electronics	12,323,819.2	0	12,323,819.2
2007	5	Electronics	8,586,998.6	0	0
2007	6	Electronics	7,457,706.6	0	0
2008	3	Electronics	12,660,221	12,660,221	0
2008	4	Electronics	9,564,157.4	9,564,157.4	0
2008	5	Electronics	12,234,427.6	0	0
2008	6	Electronics	15,456,174	0	0

Only months < current month are used

Notice also that for every month, you need a row of data to be sent to the client. If you are analyzing sales for 20,000 products, then this kind of report requires 240,000 input rows (12 months times 20,000 products). You do not need the individual rows displayed in your final report, but as shown in the preceding report example, Web Intelligence needs the detail month rows to process the formula.

TIP Just because someone can build a complex formula in Web Intelligence, that doesn't mean it's the best place for it. Don't let someone's desire to show off their report formula talents drive the report design process. Instead, stay focused on the business needs, one version of the truth, and performance.

The following table summarizes the advantages and disadvantages of putting the intelligence in a Web Intelligence report.

Report Benefits	Report Disadvantages
Users implement	Inconsistent business definitions
Flexible within an individual report	Increased maintenance costs, as reports and formulas are not centrally maintained
No politics involved to get defined centrally in the universe, RDBMS, or OLAP database	More rows than necessary may be shipped to client, or BI server slowing response time
Easy to build!	Potential SOX compliance issues
Variables can span data providers	

Summary

This chapter first discussed what intelligence is, and then described the different places to put it. As you learned, there is no clear-cut answer as to which place is best. It all depends on the benefits you are hoping to achieve (such as robustness, flexibility, and consistent business definitions), your constraints (such as cost, skills, and technology), as well as the trade-offs (such as the time to implement, politics, maintenance effort, and costs). Figure 13-8 is a scorecard that compares the different places with the trade-offs for each alternative.

The places are represented as follows in Figure 13-8:

- If a box shows a "good" circle with a check mark, then the place is good for that criterion in deciding where to put the intelligence.

- If a box shows a "use with caution" triangle, then proceed with caution and be aware of the risks.

- If a box shows a "not recommended" stop sign, there may be significant risks.

For example, putting the intelligence in the RDBMS is great for consistency of business definitions ("good") but is not very flexible ("not recommended"); however, when compared to a universe, the maintenance effort may be somewhat higher because of the effort to redo load programs and rebuild tables ("use with caution" versus "good").

While it is important to consider these design principles in deploying SAP BusinessObjects, it's much more important that you add the intelligence *somewhere*!

Summary of Alternatives and Trade-offs				
	OLAP	RDBMS	Universe	Report
Consistent business terms	✓	✓	✓	⬢
Fast queries	✓	✓	⚠	⚠
Flexibility /implementation time	⚠	⬢	⚠	✓
User Empowerment	⚠	⬢	⚠	✓
Scalability	✓	✓	✓	⬢
Politics	⬢	⬢	⚠	✓
Cost to maintain	⚠	⚠	✓	⬢
Skills required	⚠	⬢	⚠	✓
Robustness	✓	⚠	✓ ⚠	✓

✓ : Good   ⚠ : Use with Caution   ⬢ : Problematic

Figure 13-8 Deciding where to put the intelligence is a series of trade-offs.

14 Universe Maintenance, Life Cycle Management, and Co-Development

As the number of universes in your deployment increases, you need to consider several universe maintenance and development issues:

- As users access multiple universes, built by different designers, you need to ensure that the interface is as consistent as possible. Business layer views may help somewhat, but otherwise, the concept of linked universes in the former Universe Design Tool is not supported in the new IDT.

- For large-scale deployments, you will want to establish development and test environments that are separate from production.

- Finally, project synchronization allows multiple designers to work on various components of a project in parallel.

This chapter discusses each of these issues and how to address them.

Linked Universes and Reusability

In the Universe Design Tool (UDT), linked universes allow a designer to build one master universe, called the *kernel*, which then is used to build a subsequent universe called a *derived* universe. Linked universes have been supported for several years and multiple releases, but due to bugs in various releases, they were not widely adopted. Therefore, the vendor did not carry this functionality into the new IDT, and unfortunately, there is not currently a good alternative for sharing common dimensions across universes. While elements of the data foundation can certainly be used across multiple business layers, most of the design work for object descriptions and aggregations occurs in the business layer, which cannot be reused in multiple business layers.

If you have many dimensions that are common across multiple universes, you may want to consider reverting to the UDT. However, you must also weigh the trade-offs of using this approach, including the following:

- The UDT is not currently supported by SAP BusinessObjects Dashboards 4.0 as a data source.

289

- The UDT is not currently supported by SAP BusinessObjects Explorer 4.0.
- The UDT is not the strategic tool for building new universes.

Even if you do not use universe linking in the UDT, there are a number of concepts of linked universes that you can implement as a design practice with the new IDT. This design approach will help ensure consistency in an initial build, but it does not address ongoing maintenance.

Companies generally can apply the concepts of linked universes in one of several ways.

A central universe designer builds a reference universe that contains common dimension objects, which are then imported to other universes. In the "derived" universe (which relies on content in the base, or "kernel," universe), a second designer can add universe-specific tables. For example, in Figure 14-1, the tables and corresponding objects for *Time, Products,* and *Customers* exist in the kernel universe. The data foundation in this base dimensions universe will not contain any joins or fact tables.

The designer for the Sales universe uses the kernel universe as the starting point for a new universe and imports the common dimensions. The Sales universe designer can either delete or flag as deprecated the folders and objects that sales users do not need (*Accounts* and *Employees*), and add new tables to the derived universe (SALES_FACT).

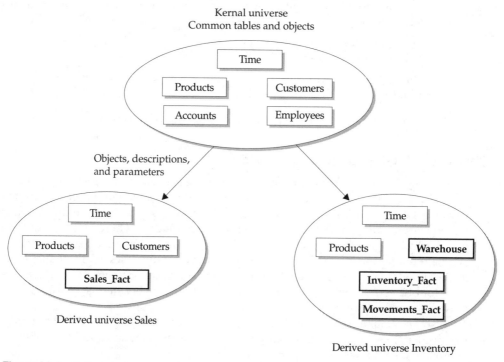

Figure 14-1   Follow design concepts to ensure consistent dimensions across multiple universes.

This approach can drastically reduce implementation time, while ensuring a consistent universe interface across multiple universes. However, as there is not a live link maintained to the kernel (base dimensions) universe, it does not help with ongoing universe maintenance.

Another approach is for a central universe designer to maintain one very large universe that contains all the star schemas in the data warehouse. Business layer designers then create smaller business layers or views within those layers, as shown in Figure 14-2.

A concern with this approach is that the base data foundation may become so large and complex that it is unwieldy to maintain. Also, much of the design work happens at the business-layer level and cannot be easily shared by multiple designers.

Approaches to Development, Test, and Production Universes

As BI deployments have matured, many companies now deploy BI across the enterprise. However, version management used extensively in software development is not quite as robust in the BI environment.

In SAP BusinessObjects 4.0, LifeCycle Manager replaced what was previously known as the Import Wizard, and in Feature Pack 3, LifeCycle Manager has been integrated with the Central Management Console (CMC) as two separate tabs: Promotion Management and Version Management.

Promotion Management uses Business Intelligence Application Resource (BIAR) files to allow you to move content from one environment to the next. A BIAR file is a type of zip or

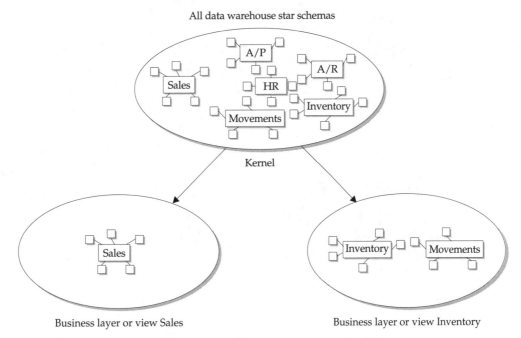

Figure 14-2   Subset a large universe into smaller business layers and views.

archive file that contains XML files for documents, universes, and other repository content. Because it is an individual file, you can incorporate the use of a BIAR file with third-party version management software, as well as the SAP Change and Transport System (CTS).

Multiple CMSs and BIAR files

Multiple CMSs allow you to have the most robust development, test, and production environments. As shown in Figure 14-3, this setup allows you to separate the following:

- Hardware components
- Software versions
- Databases with smaller, test data sets
- All the SAP BusinessObjects Enterprise repository content, such as universes, reports, and user authentication

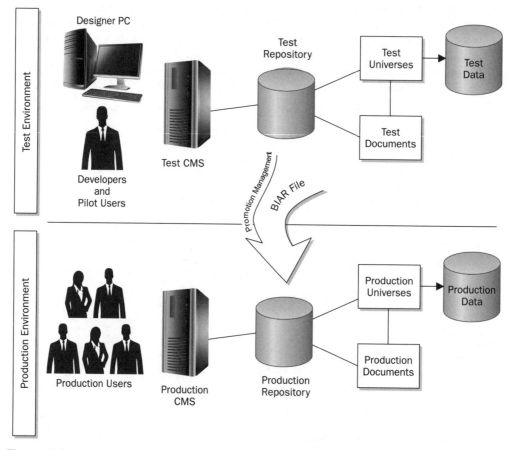

Figure 14-3 Multiple CMSs allow you to separate test and production environments.

However, this approach does have disadvantages in terms of cost and complexity. You must replicate or virtualize hardware platforms, maintain multiple systems, and license the software to run on multiple servers. For smaller implementations, the robustness of such a development environment may not be required.

Promoting Content

To promote content from a test environment to a production environment, you use Promotion Management within the CMC, as shown in Figure 14-4. Four main tasks are involved in migrating content:

- Create a job that specifies the source and destination.
- Select the repository content that you wish to migrate, such as universes and reports.
- Identify and select dependent objects.
- Execute the job, or migration of objects. If you use a BIAR file approach for migrating content, then importing the file will be an additional task.

Creating a Job

To move content from a test repository to production, you first create a job, and then you indicate the content that you wish to include in that job, as follows:

1. From the Windows Start menu, select Programs | SAP BusinessObjects BI Platform 4 | SAP BusinessObjects BI platform | SAP BusinessObjects BI platform Central Management Console. Alternatively, enter the appropriate URL within a browser: http://*BOEServer*/8080/BOE/CMC, where *BOEServer* is the name of your BusinessObjects Enterprise server.

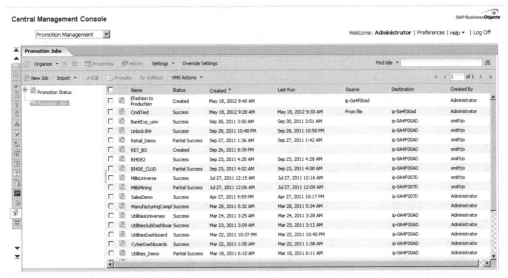

Figure 14-4   Use Promotion Management to move content from test to production environments.

2. Under the Manage category on the right, select Promotion Management. Figure 14-4 shows the initial display of Promotion Management.

3. From within Promotion Management, click New Job.

4. As shown in Figure 14-5, enter the name of this job. You can optionally enter a description and keywords.

5. In the Save Job in text box, enter the name of the folder where you wish to save the specification for this job, or use the Browse button to select a folder.

6. From the Source drop-down list, select the test repository that contains the universe, connections, and reports you wish to migrate to production.

7. From the Destination drop-down list, you can choose to create a BIAR file or select the repository that contains the production CMS.

8. Click Create to create the new job.

Specifying Objects to Migrate

When creating a new job, you are presented with a dialog box to add objects to the job. Navigate to the folder with the desired content, check the box next to the universe name you wish to add, and click Add. In adding objects to the job, there may be related content that is required. For example, a universe requires a connection object, a report requires both a universe and a connection, and so on. To see if there are any dependencies to add to the job, select Manage Dependencies.

As shown in the following example, Basic Efashion.unx is dependent on the efashion-webi connection. Promotion Management cannot tell you if that connection exists in the production repository or whether it is the most current version. Therefore, the Manage

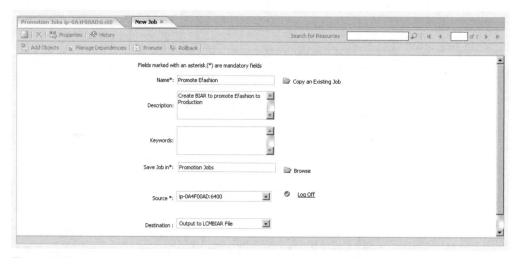

Figure 14-5   Create a job to migrate content from a test environment to production.

Dependencies dialog box is a way for you to consider if you wish to include these additional objects. If you want them included, check the box next to the dependent item.

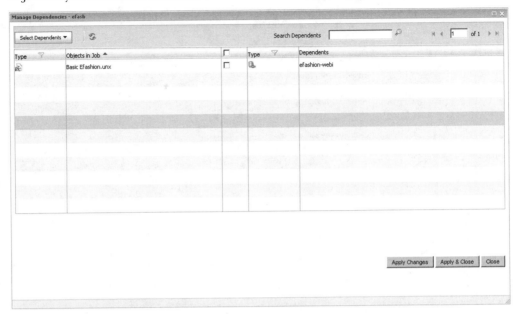

1. Click Apply & Close.
2. Select Save Job from the toolbar.

Running the Job

At this point, you have created the job and selected the objects or content to include in this job. To actually run the job and create the BIAR file, you must select Promote from the toolbar.

Figure 14-6 shows the Promote dialog box. The Summary tab provides an overview of the contents included in this job, as well as the source and destination, whether it's a CMS production repository or a BIAR file. You can choose to migrate related security settings, run a test promotion, or schedule the job to run at a later time or on a periodic basis.

To run the job now and with the default settings, click Export. You will be prompted to choose the location for the BIAR file and can specify either an FTP server or the local folder.

Importing Content in Production

You have created the BIAR file that contains the content to be imported into production. To import the new BIAR file, follow these steps:

1. Log on to the production CMC.
2. Navigate to Management | Promotion Management.
3. Select Import from the toolbar. This automatically creates a new job, similar to the one shown in Figure 14-5; however, for the source, File is selected automatically.
4. Once this job has been created, select Promote. The source will display the BIAR filename. For the destination, choose the production CMS.

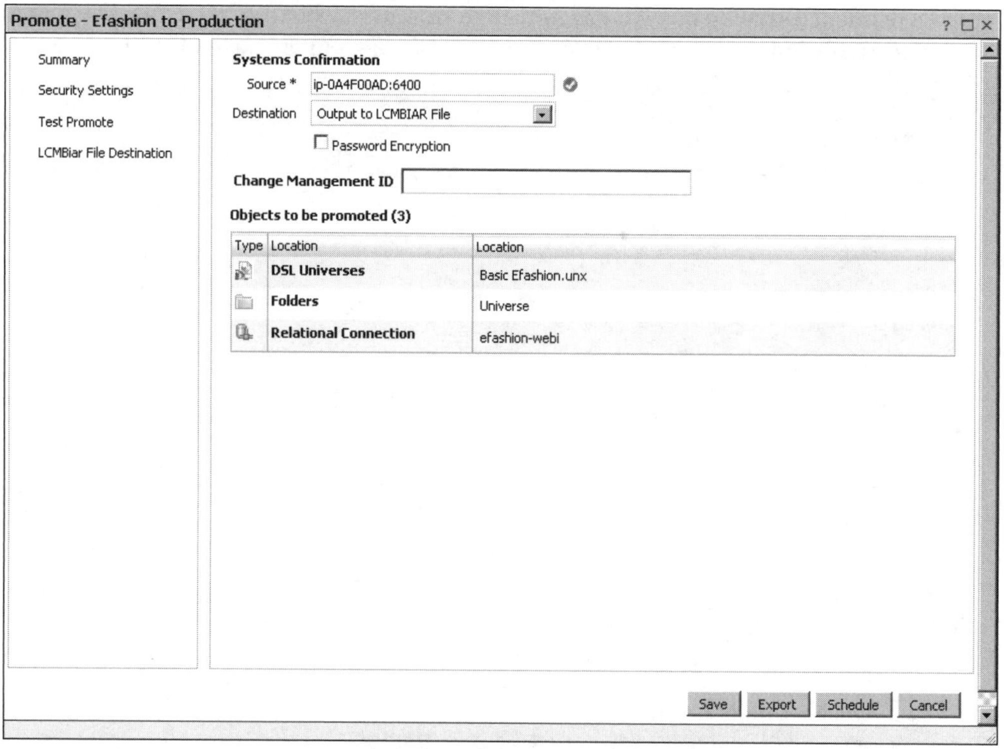

Figure 14-6 Specify job settings to migrate content from test to production.

Test Folders

The main benefit to using test folders over BIAR files is that folders are a lower-cost, lower-complexity alternative to full-blown, multiple CMS deployments. However, this approach does have limitations, so it is recommended only for smaller deployments, and it is an approach the vendor would most likely discourage.

To understand how test folders work, assume you have a Sales universe in a test folder \Test\Sales.unx. Assume you have also developed a set of reports that access \Test\Sales.unx. You now copy that universe to production, \Production\Sales.unx. When a user accesses a report, the document will look for the correct data provider using a unique ID assigned to the universe. It looks for the universe initially stored in \Test\Sales.unx. If the production users do not have access to the Test folders, then the universe is not found. In previous versions, Web Intelligence would then look using the *name* of the universe. This is no longer the case in version 4.0 Feature Pack 3, so you must manually repoint the reports to the production universe. If users try to refresh a report that has not been repointed to the production universe, they will receive an error message.

Due to these limitations, we recommend you use a test folder approach only in the following cases:

- You do not have the resources or licensing to implement multiple CMS environments.

- You use inheritance to grant access to universes at the folder level and not to individual universes.

Creating a Test Folder

There are several ways to create a test folder for universes: when you publish, via the CMC, or via the IDT Repository Resources pane. Here are the steps for using the latter approach:

1. From within the IDT, navigate to the Repository Resources pane.

2. Navigate to the Universes folder.

3. Right-click and select Insert Folder from the pop-up menu.

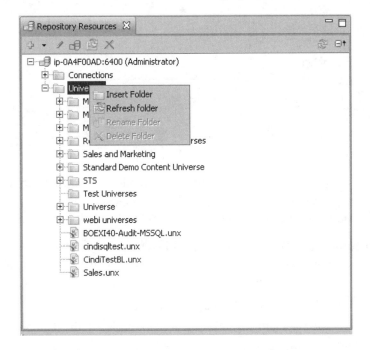

4. Enter a name for the new universe folder—**Test Universes** in this example—and press Enter.

Publishing a Universe to a Folder

After you have developed and tested your universe, you move it to production by publishing it to a folder that production users can access. This may be the root directory, or it may be a subfolder for a particular group of users. Use the IDT to publish the universe as follows:

1. From within the IDT, local resources pane, select the business layer to publish.

2. Right click to invoke the pop-up menu and select Publish | To a Repository.

3. Always publish the universe to the folder \Test Universes to ensure you maintain a copy in the repository that you can continue to use for development purposes.

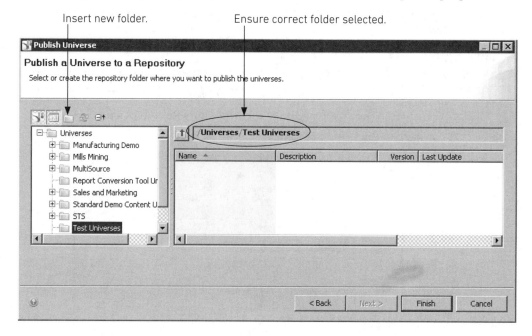

4. Publish the same universe, but this time, select the Production folder.

5. If the universe already existed in production, you will be warned that you will be overwriting an existing universe. Select Yes if you wish to proceed.

Documents in Test and Production Folders

If you created reports that access the test universe, you must manually point them to the production universe, as follows:

1. From within Web Intelligence, modify the report.

2. Click the Data button on the far right to display all the data providers.

3. Click the universe name—in this example, Sales.unx. The test folder name does not appear here. Right-click and choose Change Source.

4. Select the Specify a new data source radio button and select Universe from the drop-down menu.

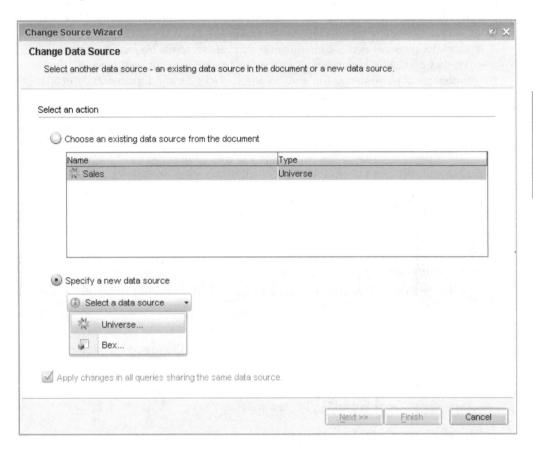

5. From the Change Universe dialog box, scroll to the production version of the universe. The name of the universe may be the same, but the folder should indicate a production folder.

6. Click Select.

7. Click Next to verify that the object names in the test universe are the same as those in the production universe. Then click Finish.

8. Save the report.

NOTE While it would seem straightforward to copy a universe from one folder to another from within the CMC, universes can only be moved from one folder to another and not copied, a difference from report objects.

Multiple Designers and Project Synchronization

When working with a repository, the IDT allows universe development and maintenance to be distributed across several designers through a locking mechanism. However, as most development work is done locally on the designer's PC, it is possible for two designers to work on local copies of the same universe and inadvertently overwrite each other's work when they export their changes. With the locking mechanism, each designer locks components of the universe for updates and unlocks it when finished making changes.

As an example, assume a global company has designers in Europe and the West Coast of the United States. There is a nine-hour time-zone difference between continental Europe and Pacific Standard Time (PST). This essentially allows a company 16 hours of development time per day.

You can either create a new project as a shared project or convert an existing one to a shared project.

Creating a New Shared Project

To create a new shared project, follow these steps:

1. Select Project Synchronization from the main toolbar, or select Window | Project Synchronization.

2. The Project Synchronization pane appears, as shown in Figure 14-7. Click New Project.

3. Enter a name for the project, such as **Global Sales**.

4. To create a local copy of this project folder, select the project name, and then click the Get Changes from Server button.

At this point, you would begin creating local connections, data foundations, and business layers, as described in the previous chapters.

Sharing an Existing Project

To convert an existing project on your local workstation to a shared project, follow these steps:

1. Select the project folder from the Local Resources pane, right-click, and select New Shared Project.

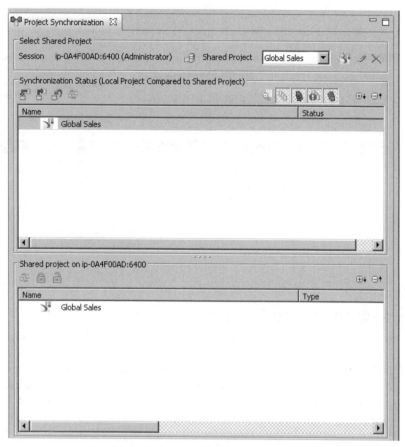

Figure 14-7   Project synchronization supports multiple universe designers.

2. When prompted, enter your credentials for opening a CMC session. Any existing content is then registered for synchronization in the CMC, and the Project Synchronization pane (shown in Figure 14-7) appears. The Project Synchronization window indicates that content has been modified locally but is not yet synchronized on the server.

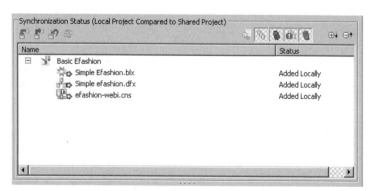

3. To upload content from your local workstation to the repository for other designers to then modify, click Save Changes on Server.

The Project Synchronization pane now indicates that all content from the local workstation and the repository is synchronized.

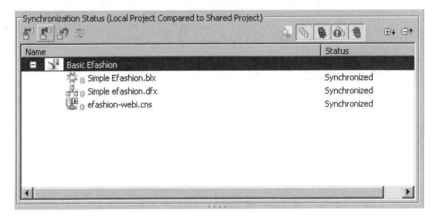

Working on Shared Projects

 As you work on the local copy of the universe, it's important to ensure you copy these elements to the server. First, refresh the display of the project synchronization.

In the example shown in Figure 14-8, the business layer has been changed locally but has not yet been synchronized with the server. The top part of the pane displays the status of local content from your workstation compared to content on the server. The bottom part of the pane displays the project components and indicates if anyone has a lock on a component. In Figure 14-8, the business layer is locked. To lock a component, select the element from the server pane, right-click, and select Lock.

When you have saved local changes to the server, you must unlock those elements to ensure the developer in the next time zone can continue working. A problem can arise if two developers make changes at the same time, without first locking those elements. In this case, a component will display a conflict, and you must resolve the problem manually.

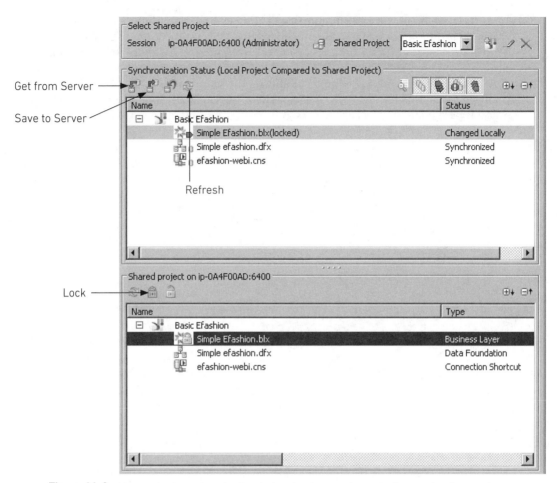

Figure 14-8 Use project synchronization to local universe elements for co- development.

Summary

As the number of universes in your deployment increases, you need to look for ways to simplify maintenance while ensuring consistency for users. Much of this can be implemented through design practices in which you have a common universe of shared elements that other designers can import.

As you develop universes and reports, you also need to establish development and test environments. Promotion Management can facilitate this via BIAR files, also allowing you to integrate changes with third-party version control software. An alternative, less robust approach is to use test folders.

When you have multiple designers modifying the same universe, the IDT offers project synchronization, which provides a check-in/check-out capability to tell you when part of a project is being modified by another designer.

CHAPTER

15

Universe Integrity, Quality Assurance, and Usage Monitoring

This is a bit of a loose-ends chapter that describes how to finalize and quality-assure the universe, prepare universe documentation, and monitor system usage. If you have had close conversations with the business users and validated universe components as you added them, you may find that some of these steps are perfunctory. If, on the other hand, you built the universe in isolation and didn't test along the way, you will find this is an intensive time to revise the universe.

Universe Integrity

As you have built the data foundation and business layer, you have done a number of integrity checks. In modifying the SQL of individual objects, you have validated each one (clicking the Validate button ensures that you have entered the SQL correctly). In building joins, you have detected cardinalities and loops to create contexts and aliases, and you may have checked the integrity of the joins in completing these steps.

The overall universe integrity check then becomes a final chance to catch anything you may have missed in earlier stages. It also will determine if anything in the data source structure has changed and made an existing object or join invalid. You may check the integrity of the data foundation, or when you check the integrity of the universe from within the business layer, it checks the integrity of both the data foundation and business layer. Within the data foundation, the integrity check validates the connection, tables, joins, and parameters and lists of values. Within the business layer, the integrity check validates these elements as well as the business layer objects.

 To check the integrity of a universe, open the business layer and navigate to the Business Layer tab. If you are within any other tab, such as Queries or Navigation Paths, the Check Integrity button appears dimmed. Also, if you have selected an individual object rather than the universe name at the top of the pane, only a subset of objects to check will appear. From the main IDT toolbar, select Check Integrity to open the Check Integrity dialog box.

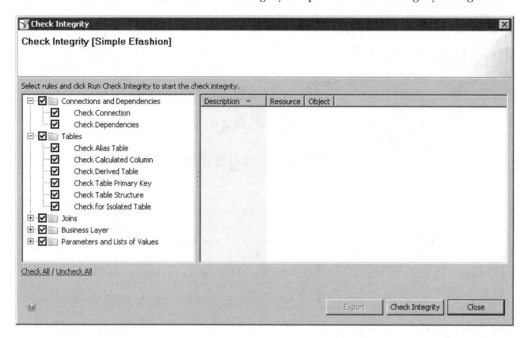

From this dialog box, you can choose Check All to have the IDT perform all possible checks, or you can choose to check the integrity of individual components. Table 15-1 explains the purpose of each check.

To perform the check, select the desired components and click Check Integrity. Figure 15-1 shows the results from Check All. Next to each component, the integrity check will display a green check mark for components that passed the check, a red *x* if there is an error, or a yellow triangle with an exclamation point to indicate a warning.

Option	Purpose
Check All	Checks all components within the universe
Connections and Dependencies	Checks that the shared connection shortcut exists in the repository
Tables	Verifies that tables defined in the data foundation exist and that all have associated joins, and verifies the syntax for any calculated columns
Joins	Checks that cardinalities are set for all joins, and that if contexts are used, all joins belong to a context
Business Layer	Verifies correct data types, that SQL is correct, and that no queries contain deleted objects
Parameters and Lists of Values	Checks that lists of values and parameters are set correctly

Table 15-1 Universe Integrity Check Options

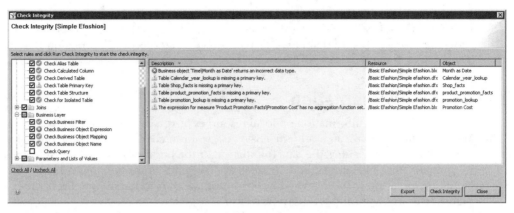

Figure 15-1   Check the universe integrity before deploying the universe.

Warnings are items that you may or may not want to resolve. For example, in Figure 15-1, there is a warning for Check Table Primary Key. A number of objects in the universe do not use a primary key. This will not create an error per se, but may not generate the most optimum SQL. On the other hand, errors need to be addressed. In the example in Figure 15-1, within the Business Layer group, Check Business Object Expression has an error: the *Month* object uses an incorrect data type of date. This will create various errors, and the object should be modified.

After running an integrity check, all errors appear in the pane on the right. You can filter the list of errors by selecting a single category on the left. You also may export the list of errors to a text file. Alternatively, to display a list of errors in a separate window while you work within the data foundation or business layer to correct the issues, select Window | Check Integrity Problems.

If there are some settings you do not use in any universes or situations that you do not want to be considered in the integrity check, you can lower the warning level of these situations. To modify such defaults, select Windows | Preferences | Information Design Tool | Check Integrity.

Universe Documentation

You can either print information on local resources or you can save content to a report. When you select to save an item (File | Save As), you can choose which elements you would like to document for either the data foundation or the business layer. When you choose to print an item (File | Print), both detailed and graphical information is printed for all components, as shown in the example of printing the data foundation in Figure 15-2. Figure 15-3 shows a printout for business layer components.

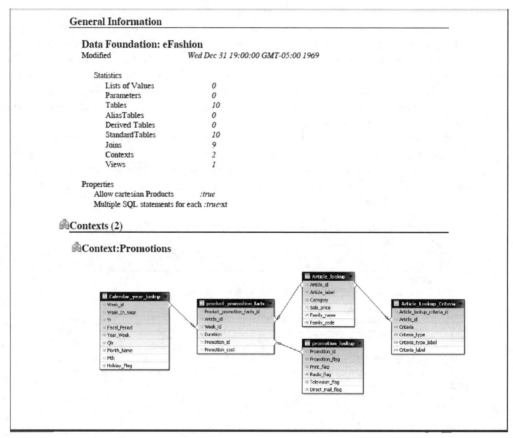

Figure 15-2   Data foundation documentation shows statistics and context definitions.

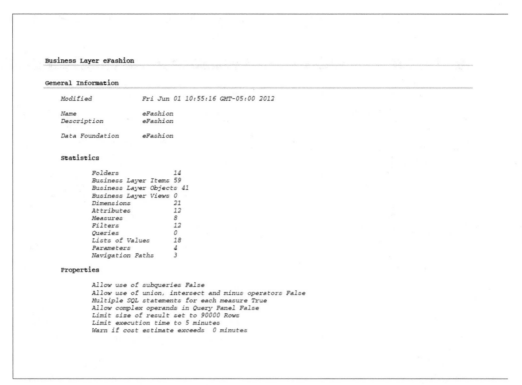

```
Business Layer eFashion

General Information

    Modified            Fri Jun 01 10:55:16 GMT-05:00 2012

    Name                eFashion
    Description         eFashion

    Data Foundation     eFashion

    Statistics

            Folders                 14
            Business Layer Items    59
            Business Layer Objects  41
            Business Layer Views    0
            Dimensions              21
            Attributes              12
            Measures                8
            Filters                 12
            Queries                 0
            Lists of Values         18
            Parameters              4
            Navigation Paths        3

    Properties

            Allow use of subqueries False
            Allow use of union, intersect and minus operators False
            Multiple SQL statements for each measure True
            Allow complex operands in Query Panel False
            Limit size of result set to 90000 Rows
            Limit execution time to 5 minutes
            Warn if cost estimate exceeds  0 minutes
```

Figure 15-3   Business layer documentation displays information on folders, dimensions, and SQL properties.

To print information, first select the item in the Local Resources pane on the left, and then choose File | Print. (When you select an item in the Data Foundation or Business Layer pane, the Print menu appears dimmed.)

NOTE To control the print orientation, from within the IDT, select Window | Preferences | Information Design Tool | Data Foundation Editor | Printing, and then choose Portrait or Landscape.

To save content to a report, follow these steps:

1. Select the item from Local Resources pane and right-click to invoke the pop-up menu.
2. Select Save As.
3. Click the ellipse to choose a location to store the PDF file and to be prompted for a filename. (The IDT does not allow you to enter a path or filename in this initial screen.)
4. In the Save As dialog box, enter a filename, and then click Save.

5. Choose the metadata elements that you want to be included in the PDF file, as described in Table 15-2, and then click Generate.

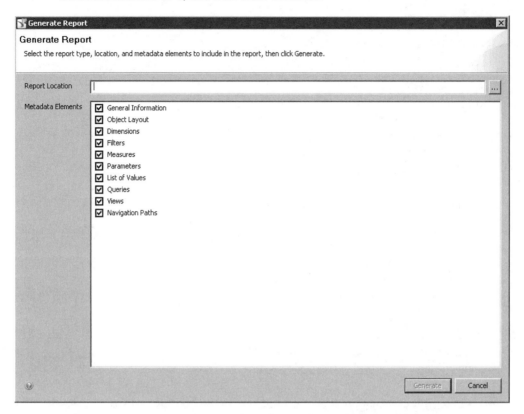

Universe Component	Metadata Element	Information Printed
Data foundation	General information	Displays statistics on the universe, including number of tables, joins, derived tables, and SQL properties such as multiple SQL statements per context. Universe-specific parameters such as the universe filename and description, revision number, total classes and objects, strategy settings, and SQL controls are set through File | Parameters. Refer to Chapter 7 for more information about these settings.
Data foundation	Contexts	Displays the context name as well as each join included in the context and which joins are excluded.

Table 15-2 Report Options to Document the Universe

Universe Component	Metadata Element	Information Printed
Data foundation	Data sources and connections	Displays the name of the data source and connections used in the data foundation and type of connection (shared or secured).
Data foundation	Families	Displays the names and settings for families used to distinguish different types of tables.
Data foundation	Joins	Lists the simple join statements, describes the cardinality between the tables, and specifies whether the join is an outer join.
Data foundation	Tables	Displays the physical table names that appear in the data foundation.
Data foundation and business layer	Views	Indicates the name of the views and associated comments. By default, each data foundation has a Master view. It does not list which tables belong to which view.
Data foundation and business layer	Parameters	Displays prompt or parameter definitions, including the message, type, index awareness, associated list of values, optional or mandatory, and so on.
Data foundation and business layer	List of Values	Displays the type of list of values (query or business layer), associated dimension, row limits, and so on.
Business layer	General information	Displays universe-specific parameters such as the universe filename and description, and total folders and objects, as well as SQL controls such as query execution time and row limits.
Business layer	Object Layout	Displays the folder and individual object names in the order in which they appear to users.
Business layer	Dimensions	Displays all the properties for each object, including object type, SELECT statement, WHERE clause, list of values settings, and so on.
Business layer	Filters	Displays the folder and object names for filter objects as well as the SQL statement.
Business layer	Navigation Paths	Displays the folder and dimension objects of any custom navigation paths that support drill-down.
Business layer	Queries	Provides the query name and result objects used in a business layer query. It does not provide the SQL generated.

Table 15-2   Report Options to Document the Universe *(continued)*

Part II

Quality Assurance Checklist

Before distributing the universe to the users, it is good to have a quality assurance session to review the universe. Table 15-3 provides a checklist that covers recommendations from the previous chapters. A spreadsheet version of this is available via various web sites (McGraw-Hill site, BusinessObjects Board (BOB), and SAP Community Network(SCN).

A quality assurance review session is different from an integrity check. The integrity check ensures that the universe is technically correct, but does little to ensure that the universe follows best practices or will be successful with the users.

Chapter	Category	Item	Date Reviewed	Comments and Exceptions
2 and 4	Overall universe	• Subject area corresponds to business goal		
3		• Target user group identified		
		• Number of objects appropriate for target user group		
		• Meaningful description		
		• Developer comments provided for major revisions		
5	Connections	• Connection synchronized with database username and password		
		• Connection timeout set for optimal user experience		
		• Connection pooling optimized for environment		
		• Array size optimized for environment		
6	Joins	• Joined fields indexed		
		• Join fields that contain nulls use an outer join		
		• All loops are resolved with a context		
		• Cardinalities set for all joins		
		• Tables with multiple meanings have an alias		
		• Joins belong to at least one context (excluding shortcut joins)		
		• Joins with composite keys are entered as complex joins		
		• Shortcut joins created for faster join paths not through fact table		
		• Query test for split SQL with multiple contexts		

Table 15-3 Quality Assurance Checklist

Chapter	Category	Item	Date Reviewed	Comments and Exceptions
7	Business layer	• Views created for targeted user groups • Folder names logical and meaningful • Folders sorted logically • Dimension objects point to lookup table • Objects not used for drill-down marked as detail objects • Column format and object type match • Measure includes SQL aggregate function • Separate measure provided for average unit price, etc. • Objects include description • Objects sorted logically within class (top to bottom for drill-down) • Object names are customer-oriented, clear, consistent, and concise • Object format is set, particularly for numeric ID fields • Unnecessary hidden objects removed or tagged as deprecated		
7 and 12		• Security access levels correctly set • Object uses make sense (recommend all enabled) • Foreign/primary keys considered for better query performance • SQL controls adequate for query results • Query test for split SQL with multiple measures		
8	List of values	• List of values disabled for measure objects • List of values disabled for nonsensical detail objects • Long lists of values customized with prompt • Meaningless ID fields customized to include name, description, or key enabled • Lists of values access dimension table not fact table • Shared list of values used for common dimension objects		

Table 15-3   Quality Assurance Checklist *(continued)*

Part II

Chapter	Category	Item	Date Reviewed	Comments and Exceptions
9	Advanced objects	• Filter objects created for common filters, particularly time • Filter objects use index or give satisfactory query performance • Objects with prompts are not overly restrictive • Prompted field is indexed or gives satisfactory query performance • Count objects point to key field or use Distinct • Ratios use sum aggregate correctly: SUM()/SUM() • Ratios in fact table recalculated in universe • Derived tables considered • Opportunities for physical columns for fact/dimension table insertion considered		
9	Aggregate objects	• Aggregate table included in universe • Aggregate table has its own context • Sum function inserted correctly within the @Aggregate_Aware function: @AGGREGATE_AWARE(SUM(AGG1)), SUM(AGG2), SUM(DETAIL)) • Incompatible objects set • Incompatible objects include only relevant context • Query test to access aggregate table and detail table as intended • Query test verifies summary answers match answers from detail table		
11	Hierarchies	• Custom navigation paths created • Navigation paths sorted from top to bottom • Separate navigation paths for ID and Description objects		
12	Universe-level security	• Object-level security matches universe object • Row restrictions do not cancel each other out • CMS groups simplify access		
15	Other	• Backup copy of universe available • Auditing enabled • Relevant documentation printed • Benchmark queries identified		

Table 15-3 Quality Assurance Checklist *(continued)*

The following people should ideally be involved in a quality assurance review:

- **DBA**   The DBA will help verify the correctness of certain SQL statements, assess their impact on response time if there are advanced SQL functions, consider join strategies to generate the fastest queries possible, and identify opportunities to create aggregate tables and to tune indexes for popular condition objects.

- **Data modeler/architect**   The data modeler or architect will help identify any possible problems with joins that arise from missing data—for example, if a particular field is not required. This person can also review business terminology, object descriptions, customized lists of values, use of derived tables and aliases (such as CUSTOMER versus CUSTOMER_SHIP_TO versus CUSTOMER_SOLD_TO). A source system expert may also be helpful in this role.

- **Power user/report authors**   Power users and report authors will provide input on the overall appearance, organization, and functionality of the universe. Did you, as the designer, actually deliver what they hoped for? Will they be able to build the reports they need using the current design of the universe? Power users will also provide input on similar items to the data modeler.

- **Other designers**   If your company has multiple universe designers, it's useful to get an objective opinion from another designer on the universe. This is an excellent way to share tips and techniques and to provide a consistent user interface across universes (as an alternative to linked universes).

As companies deploy BI as an enterprise solution, some have developed competency centers or centers of BI excellence. These competency centers maintain and add to the quality assurance checklist to ensure best practices are documented and adhered to. With the competency center, individual business units may have their own universe designers, but the competency center facilitates a quality assurance review to provide an additional level of expertise and quality control. Alternatively, designers may be staffed within the competency center, but the design review process ensures that all universe designers are adhering to best practices.

Benchmark Queries

As you make changes to the universe and extend your implementation, it is important that either the designer or the power users develop standard reports that can be used to benchmark performance. Clearly, the universe is only one component that affects performance. However, if SAP BusinessObjects is the interface that users see, it will get blamed entirely for performance issues. When a universe or report is poorly designed, or the Enterprise server is overloaded, such blame may be appropriate. However, if the database is improperly tuned, users will still lament, "BusinessObjects is slow."

There are two purposes to designating benchmark reports. The first and simplest is to ensure that when you change your universe or server settings, you do not negatively affect performance. You want to know that a query that took ten seconds to run yesterday still takes ten seconds to run today, even with all the underlying changes in the SQL settings (or better yet, maybe it now runs in one second!).

The second, more challenging purpose of identifying benchmark reports is to understand scalability. Some companies do a formal stress test during the pilot phase. Although SAP does not provide integrated load testing tools, these are available from third-party companies. For example, HP LoadRunner and Micro Focus QALoad allow customers to simulate user load on the server.

Use Cases

To understand user load and performance tuning, also recognize that different types of reports and user interactions will stress different aspects of the system. If you have different BI content types (Crystal Reports, Web Intelligence, and Dashboards), you will want to test the processing power of each of these report types. Additionally, create use cases that represent the mixed usage patterns in your deployment:

- Concurrent users viewing static reports and/or the same report, for example, to simulate when you publish an income statement that many users wish to access simultaneously (here, caching the report will help with performance)
- Concurrent users interacting (drilling, filtering, and sorting) with different reports
- Concurrent users executing simple queries
- Concurrent users executing slow-running, complex queries
- Concurrent users generating and displaying reports with complex layouts, multiple data providers, or numerous report-based calculations

Performance Bottlenecks

Figure 15-4 provides a conceptual overview of the phases of a user query, starting with the initial login and finishing with the presentation of a formatted report. The diagram is a simple deployment in which users access content via BI Launch Pad.

Particular server processes can be distributed across multiple servers. If you are *modifying* reports using Crystal Reports or Web Intelligence Rich Client, then a certain amount of processing occurs on the client PC rather than on the SAP BusinessObjects Enterprise server. *Viewing* reports, though, relies on the servers and those performance bottlenecks. Table 15-4 explains the potential bottlenecks during each of these phases in accessing, refreshing, and interacting with a report.

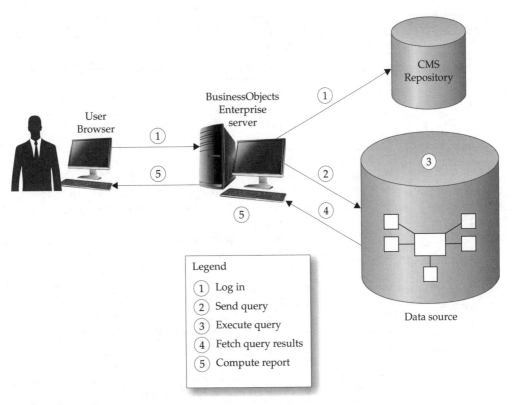

Figure 15-4   Performance bottlenecks can occur in multiple points of a BusinessObjects
implementation.

Debugging performance is a complex task. In a SAP BusinessObjects environment,
factors such as utilization of different server processes potentially distributed across
multiple machines and a mix of Web Intelligence, Crystal Reports, and Dashboard users
and processes make it harder to pinpoint bottlenecks. As the universe designer, the key
aspect within your control is the query execution time (phase 3 in Figure 15-4). While the
RDBMS may largely affect this, the SQL generated is often the culprit of poor query
performance.

When your universe contains advanced objects, as described in Chapter 9, you must
understand how these affect query performance. If users filter their queries on objects that
access nonindexed fields (because you did not define primary or foreign keys or because
you added functions on all your dimension objects), their queries will be slow, and this is
the fault of the universe designer. If your universe uses derived tables that generate
complex subqueries, query performance here may also be affected.

Phase	Description	Potential Bottlenecks
1	Log in	• CMS server load to process logins and permissions
2	Send query, connect to data source	• Universe complexity to generate the SQL, including use of security profiles • Load on the Connection server to connect to the data source (numerous slow-running queries will open numerous database connections, potentially becoming a bottleneck) • Load on the data source to process logins
3	Launch query: analyzing and executing	• Number of users concurrently logging in to RDBMS • If using row-level security within data warehouse, complexity of security model and number of views to implement • If accessing source ERP, current load on system to update transactions • Ability of RDBMS to execute SQL efficiently, using indexes whenever possible; report and universe design comes into play here, as certain SQL statements (such as subqueries, long CASE statements, and filters with dimensions that contain functions) can be slow
4	Launch query: fetching	• Network performance to deliver results from RDBMS back to the SAP BusinessObjects Enterprise server (Array fetch size option set in connection parameters)
5	Display report: Computing	• Specific servers within the BI platform to convert query results to microcube, display charts, and formatted tables, and convert to HTML or PDF

Table 15-4 Potential Bottlenecks That Affect SAP BusinessObjects Response Time

As a way of identifying performance bottlenecks, use the SQL script that you can generate within a query within the business layer to determine if the data source is the culprit for poor performance or if the culprit is load and settings within the SAP BusinessObjects Enterprise server. First, evaluate if the SQL could have been written in a more efficient way. If this is the case, then modify your universe accordingly. Next, run an explain plan to see how the database is processing the query. Full table scans are an indication that either the SQL is not generated efficiently or the database is not tuned. Lastly, assuming the query runs equally slow when submitted directly to the database, your database is the performance bottleneck, not the Enterprise server.

As a designer, you can build a simple query within the business layer Queries tab to preview the SQL generated. However, to diagnose performance issues, you most often will want to see the SQL from a query a user has built. To access the SQL from within the IDT, follow these steps:

1. Open the business layer.

2. Select the Queries tab.

 3. Click Insert New Query.

4. Drag the desired objects to the Result Objects pane.

5. Click View Script to see the SQL generated.

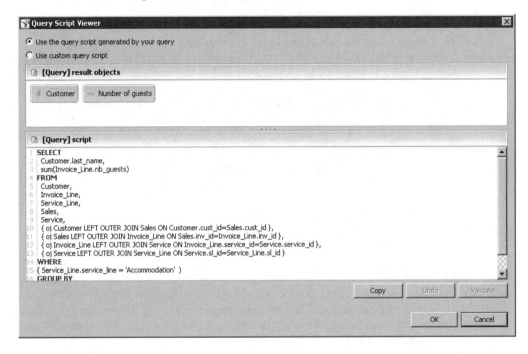

6. Click Copy to copy the SQL to the Windows clipboard and pull it into your own SQL diagnostic tools.

Monitoring User Activity

Running an enterprise BI deployment without usage monitoring is like driving at night with no headlights turned on and no dashboard gauges: it's dangerous and bound to lead to a crash! With a departmental deployment, you may not have the personnel to proactively monitor usage and system performance. You only know there is a problem when users start complaining. With critical deployments and enterprise deployments, you must be more proactive. You need to anticipate problems *before* they happen. Equally important, you must take care to evaluate that your design is meeting the needs of the users. If you've built reports and universes that are not widely used, you have a problem.

With SAP BusinessObjects BI 4.0, there are two main approaches to monitoring: real-time and historical.

Real-Time Monitoring

Real-time monitoring is provided via the CMC. There are a number of prebuilt dashboards to show current server utilization, processes, and sessions. System administrators can specify alerts to be sent when certain situations occur.

Part II

For more information about configuring real-time monitoring, consult the *SAP BusinessObjects Business Intelligence Platform Administrator's Guide.*

Auditing

Historical usage information can be captured either to a log file or to a relational database. If you wish to report off such information, it should be captured to a relational database. In contrast to monitoring, auditing is not real-time. As events occur, such as a user login or query refresh, the activity is recorded in temporary files and periodically written to the audit database. The audit database is specified in the CMC, under Manage | Auditing, as shown here:

You can determine which level of detail is captured in the audit database. Although capturing more detailed information may give you more insight into how the BI environment is used, more granular auditing can also degrade performance. Therefore, you may wish to begin your deployment with default audit settings and then optionally capture additional details on a periodic basis.

In earlier versions of SAP BusinessObjects, the vendor provided a prebuilt universe and set of reports that accessed this audit database. As of version 4.0 Feature Pack 3, such a universe and reports are no longer provided, and the structure of the audit tables has changed significantly. However, a community version is available from the SAP Community Network (SCN). This universe provides a good starting point that requires slight modification. There also are some prebuilt Crystal Reports reports. Once you have updated the universe, you can create your own Crystal Reports or Web Intelligence reports to evaluate items such as which reports are used most often or top-accessed universes. For example, in Figure 15-5, the report shows events for one particular day. To track usage of Web Intelligence, you would filter by Object Type = Web Intelligence. To track the number of logons, you would filter for Event Type=Logon, with the Object Type null.

NOTE Currently, information about Web Intelligence Rich Client document refreshes is not captured in the audit database. However, Web Intelligence Rich Client logons and logouts are captured.

Event Day	Event Type	Object Name	Object Type	Total Event Count
Jun 25 2012	Create	Product Sales June	Web Intelligence	2
Jun 25 2012	Create	Security Test	Web Intelligence	1
Jun 25 2012	Edit			2
Jun 25 2012	Logon			8
Jun 25 2012	Logout			5
Jun 25 2012	Modify	Administrator	User	2
Jun 25 2012	Modify	Product Sales June	Web Intelligence	1
Jun 25 2012	Modify	Security Test	Web Intelligence	1
Jun 25 2012	Refresh			1
Jun 25 2012	Refresh	Big query	Web Intelligence	2
Jun 25 2012	Refresh	Product Sales June	Web Intelligence	3
Jun 25 2012	Save	Product Sales June	Web Intelligence	2
Jun 25 2012	View	-1_New Document_0	Web Intelligence	1
Jun 25 2012	View	Big query	Web Intelligence	1
Jun 25 2012	View	Product Sales June	Web Intelligence	1

Figure 15-5   Web Intelligence report shows events tracked in the audit database.

Summary

In the rush to meet your BI project deadlines, it's easy to skip the steps of documentation, quality assurance, and usage monitoring. So easy, in fact, that it sometimes never happens! Yet for a mission-critical BI solution, these tasks are essential.

Quality assurance reviews help foster knowledge throughout the BI competency center and across business units that co-develop universes. Such reviews also ensure a consistent design approach across developers, which ultimately provides business users with a consistent experience.

Usage monitoring and auditing provide a mechanism for scaling your deployment in a controlled way, predicting potential performance issues, and understanding which universes and reports are most relevant.

PART

III

Reporting and Analysis

16

Navigating in
BI Launch Pad

Part I of this book lays the groundwork for implementing SAP BusinessObjects BI 4.0, and Part II provides information for universe designers and administrators to build a business-oriented solution. Part III and Part IV are for business users who need to access information to make decisions and improve business performance.

The chapters in this part of the book are organized by workflow, starting with decision makers or report consumers who access published reports. If you are a power user or report author, you may want to start with Chapter 19 to begin building new queries and Web Intelligence reports.

If you are upgrading to SAP BusinessObjects BI 4.0 from a prior version of BusinessObjects, you should be aware of the following significant changes that impact reporting and analysis:

- In prior versions of BusinessObjects, the web interface, or portal, was referred to as InfoView. In SAP BusinessObjects BI 4.0, the portal is now called BI Launch Pad.

- Desktop Intelligence and Desktop Intelligence documents have been retired in SAP BusinessObjects BI 4.0. Desktop Intelligence documents will need to be converted to Web Intelligence format documents.

The customizable page to display your own personal content formerly known as My InfoView has been replaced with BI Workspaces in SAP BusinessObjects BI 4.0. BI Launch Pad is the user interface, or portal, for SAP BusinessObjects BI 4.0. It allows you to interact with the SAP BusinessObjects BI 4.0 content and applications. This portal, coupled with the repository, allows you to access and store BI content generated by any of the applications, such as Web Intelligence, Crystal Reports, Analysis, Dashboards, and BI Workspaces, or other documents, such as Word, Excel, and PDF files. BI Launch Pad is a powerful tool for managing business performance. This chapter introduces BI Launch Pad, as well as BI Workspaces.

Logging in to BI Launch Pad

To log in to BI Launch Pad, you only need a browser and a web site address or URL. No additional software needs to be installed on your PC.

You access BI Launch Pad by entering a URL, or in some deployments, by selecting a link via a corporate intranet. The default URL is http://*webserver:portnumber*/BOE/BI, where *webserver* and *portnumber* are replaced with the values that were set up for your implementation of SAP BusinessObjects BI 4.0 Enterprise.

1. When you log in to BI Launch Pad, the server first authenticates your user ID and password. Your user ID and password may be an enterprise ID specific to SAP BusinessObjects, or it may be integrated with another authentication source such as Lightweight Directory Access Protocol (LDAP) or Microsoft Active Directory (AD). Before beginning the following login process, ensure that you know the correct authentication source. By default, you will not be asked to supply a system name. However, if you have multiple BusinessObjects implementations and you are asked to supply a system name, enter the name of the Central Management Server (CMS) in the System field.

2. Enter your username in the box provided. For most authentication methods, including LDAP, AD, and BusinessObjects Enterprise, the username is not case-sensitive.

3. Enter your password. For security purposes, asterisks (*) are displayed as you enter each character. Your password is case-sensitive and may be a combination of characters and numbers. (Enterprise passwords are discussed in more detail after the login procedure.)

SAP BusinessObjects

Log On to BI launch pad | Help

Enter your user information and click Log On.
(If you are unsure of your account information, contact your system administrator.)

System: BOBJHOST1:6400

User Name: webiuser1

Password: •••••••••

Log On

4. By default, you will not be asked to supply an authentication type. Enterprise authentication is the default authentication method. If your BusinessObjects administrator has enabled a third-party authentication type, such as LDAP or AD, you may need to select the authentication type from the Authentication list.

5. Click Log On.

If you are using Enterprise authentication, the first time you log in to BI Launch Pad, you may be prompted to change your password, as shown in the following example. You also will receive this prompt if your BusinessObjects administrator requires you to change your password on a periodic basis, such as every 90 days.

NOTE If you need to change your password at some other point, choose Preferences from the Header panel, and then select Change Password.

Enterprise password settings are determined by your SAP BusinessObjects administrator (see Chapter 12). The administrator can enforce mixed-case passwords and require that your password be a minimum length. The system may also count back a certain number to prevent you from reusing the same password.

When you enter the wrong password after a number of attempts, your account will be disabled—either permanently until you contact an administrator or for a defined period of time.

If you enter the incorrect username or password (or the correct username but against an incorrect authentication source), you will receive the error message "Account Information Not Recognized: Enterprise authentication could not log you on. Please make sure your logon information is correct. (FWB 00008)." If you eventually remember the correct username and password, and the account has been disabled, you will receive the error message "Account Information Not Recognized: The user account has been disabled. (FWB 00012)."

The BI Launch Pad Interface

BI Launch Pad has been designed to give you access to the content and applications in the SAP BusinessObjects system through an interface that consists of a Header panel and two main tabs: Home and Documents. BI Launch Pad displays the Home tab by default when you log in, as shown in Figure 16-1.

The Header Panel

The Header panel at the top of your screen displays the current user logged in and gives you access to your applications, preferences, and help. You can also log off SAP BusinessObjects and search for documents and objects contained in the repository.

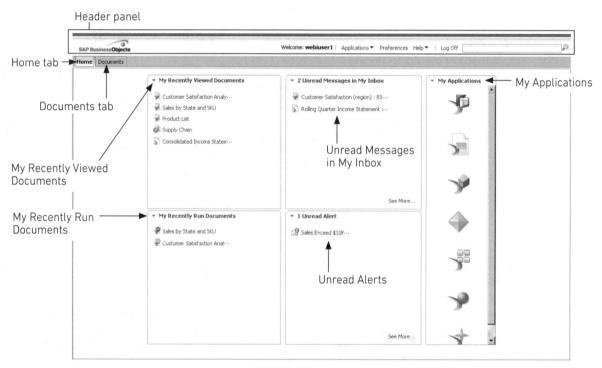

Figure 16-1   BI Launch Pad and the default Home tab

The Header panel remains visible in the window regardless of the other tabs or applications you select from BI Launch Pad.

The Home Tab

The default Home tab is designed to display the documents, content, and features of SAP BusinessObjects that you work with the most.

The Home tab is made up of the following five panels:

- **My Recently Viewed Documents**   Displays the last ten documents that you have viewed, with the most recently viewed document at the top.

- **My Recently Run Documents**   Displays the last ten documents that you have either scheduled or run, along with the status of the document instance. You can view document instances or details of failed instances from the Home tab by clicking the instance link.

- **Unread Messages in My Inbox**   Displays the last ten unread documents in your SAP BusinessObjects BI 4.0 inbox. You can view the document in your inbox by clicking the link. If you have more than ten unread documents, click the See More... link in this panel.

- **Unread Alerts**   Displays your last ten unread alert notifications. To view the alert message, click the link. If you have more than ten unread alert notifications, click the See More... link in this panel.

- **My Applications**   Provides quick access to the applications that you use and have the appropriate rights to run (granted by your administrator). To launch an application, click the application's icon.

The Documents Tab

The Documents tab is designed to display, organize, and interact with all of your documents and BI content. When you click the Documents tab, the default display does not include the Details panel. To toggle the display of the Details panel, click Details on the toolbar. Figure 16-2 shows the Documents tab with the Details panel displayed.

Part III

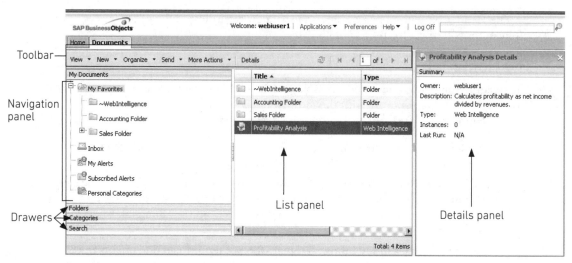

Toolbar

Navigation panel

Drawers

Figure 16-2 Documents tab

The Documents tab is made up of the following components:

- **Toolbar** The toolbar acts as your main menu within the Documents tab. The options that are enabled within the toolbar depend on whether a folder, category, document, or object is currently selected. Table 16-1 describes the options available from the toolbar.

- **Navigation panel** The Navigation panel helps you navigate through a folder or category structure, as well as to search to locate individual documents stored anywhere in the SAP BusinessObjects system.

- **Drawers** The drawers allow you to organize document content into My Documents, Folders, or Categories.

- **List panel** The List panel displays the document contents of the currently selected folder or category.

- **Details panel** The Details panel displays the folder, document, or object properties of the currently selected folder, document, or object.

Navigating in the Documents Tab

The Navigation panel of the Documents tab helps you locate individual documents in your favorite folders, personal categories, inboxes, public folders, and corporate categories. To help you easily find the content you are seeking, the Navigation panel is organized into four drawers: My Documents, Folders, Categories, and Search.

My Documents Drawer

The My Documents drawer contains documents that you have created or modified that you do not wish to share with other users. The documents in your My Documents drawer can be accessed only by you (to share one of these documents with others, you need to send it to them via their BI inbox or save it into a public folder or category).

Toolbar Option	Menu Option	Function
View	View	Allows you to view the object or document
	View Latest Instance	Allows you to view the latest instance of a document (this option will be disabled if the document does not have an instance)
	Properties	Allows you to view the properties of a folder, document, instance, or other object
New	Local Document	Uploads a new local document including formats such as Word, Excel, PDF, and JPG
	Publication	Creates a publication that allows you to design advanced batch and burst features for Web Intelligence and Crystal Reports, including the ability to define multiple source documents, dynamic recipients, and dynamic content sources
	Hyperlink	Creates a hyperlink object to any URL
	Category	Creates a new category
	Folder	Creates a new folder
Organize	Create Shortcut in My Favorites	Creates a shortcut to a document or object in your My Favorites folder
	Cut	Cuts a folder, a document, or an object
	Copy	Copies a folder, a document. or an object
	Copy Shortcut	Creates a copy of a shortcut
	Paste	Pastes a folder, a document, an object, or a shortcut
	Delete	Deletes a folder, a document, or an object
Send	BI Inbox	Sends a document or an object to a user's BusinessObjects inbox
	E-mail	Sends a document or an object to a user's e-mail address
	File Location	Sends a document or an object to a file location
	FTP Location	Sends a document or an object to a FTP server location
More Actions	Modify	Allows you to modify the document
	Schedule	Allows you to schedule a Web Intelligence or Crystal Reports document to run
	History	Displays the scheduled instance history for a Web Intelligence or Crystal Reports document
	Categories	Adds a document or an object to a category
	Document Link	Creates the document link for a document or an object
Details		Displays the Details panel

Table 16-1 Documents Tab Toolbar

Part III

When you first enter the Documents tab, the Navigation panel will display with the My Documents drawer open by default, as shown in Figure 16-2. You can modify your preference settings to show the Folders or Categories drawer open instead, as discussed in the "BI Launch Pad Preferences" section later in this chapter.

In the My Documents drawer, the My Favorites folder is open and its contents are displayed in the List panel. To expand subfolders or personal categories, click the folder or category name in the Navigation panel to display the contents of the folder or category in the List panel. You can also click the plus sign (+) next to the folder or category to expand the folder or category in the Navigation panel only (without displaying the contents in the List panel).

Documents in your inbox are reports that other users have sent to you through your BI inbox. Alerts are used to notify you when an event, such as a certain data event, has occurred. Both events that you are subscribed to (Subscribed Alerts) and events that have been triggered (My Alerts) are displayed in the My Documents drawer of the Navigation panel.

Folders Drawer

The Folders drawer contains documents organized in public folders that can be viewed and shared by other users. Public folders may be organized by department or functional area. Folders provide the physical location of a document, as well as the structure to navigate content. A document must be stored in a folder (categories are optional), and a document can reside in only a single folder. Access to folders and the documents in the folders can be restricted by your BusinessObjects administrator.

To navigate to the Folders drawer, click Folders in the Navigation panel. To expand the public folder (or any folder within it), click the folder name in the Navigation panel. The contents of the public folder will be displayed in the List panel, as shown in Figure 16-3. You can also click the + next to the folder, which will expand the folder in the Navigation panel only (and not display the contents in the List panel).

Categories Drawer

The Categories drawer contains documents organized in corporate categories that can be viewed and shared by other users. A key feature of categories is that a document can be assigned to multiple categories, making it easier to cross-reference documents. Access to categories and documents within categories can be restricted by your BusinessObjects administrator.

Click Categories in the Navigation panel to open this drawer. The contents of the corporate categories are displayed in the List panel. Click the category name in the Navigation panel to display the contents of the category in the List panel. Alternatively, click the + next to the category to expand the category in the Navigation panel only (and not display the contents in the List panel).

TIP Web Intelligence reports that are located in the "Mobile" category are available to users of the SAP BusinessObjects Mobile module.

Search Drawer

The Search drawer allows you to type in search text. Document keywords, titles, descriptions, owner information, and content will be searched for a match. As with other search engines, if no match is returned, the system will suggest alternate spellings.

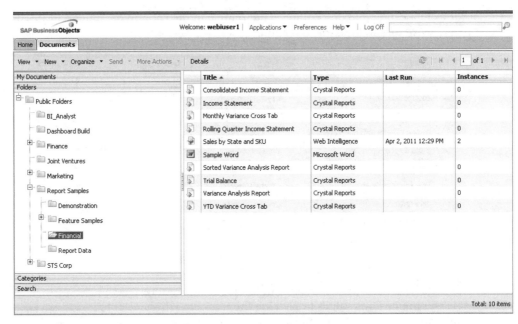

Figure 16-3   Folders drawer open in the Documents tab

To perform a search, click Search in the Navigation panel and type your search text in the input text box.

Document Display and Organization

As you learned in the previous section, the Documents tab—with its Navigation panel, List panel, and toolbar—allows you to find documents and perform actions such as viewing, creating, sending, organizing, and scheduling your BI content.

To see the contents of a folder, click the folder name within the Navigation panel. As shown in Figure 16-3, by default, the List panel displays the document title, the document type, the last run date of a scheduled instance, and the number of instances for each document in the currently selected folder or category. You can customize what information and options appear in the List panel of the Documents tab by setting your preferences, as discussed in the "BI Launch Pad Preferences" section later in this chapter.

Sorting and Filtering the List Panel

Documents in the List panel are, by default, sorted in ascending order by title. Documents can be sorted in ascending or descending order by document title, document type, or any of the other visible column heading values. Just click the column heading to toggle the sort order from ascending to descending. The triangle in the column heading indicates the current active sort and the sort direction.

Title ▲	Type	Last Run	Instances
C	Sort by Title, sorted ascending, click to sort descending		0
Income Statement	Crystal Reports		0
Monthly Variance Cross Tab	Crystal Reports		0
Rolling Quarter Income Statement	Crystal Reports		0
Sales by State and SKU	Web Intelligence	Apr 2, 2011 12:29 PM	2
Sample Word	Microsoft Word		
Sorted Variance Analysis Report	Crystal Reports		0
Trial Balance	Crystal Reports		0
Variance Analysis Report	Crystal Reports		0
YTD Variance Cross Tab	Crystal Reports		0

You can also filter the documents in the List panel by any visible column heading values by clicking the filter icon in the column heading and entering the appropriate filter value(s). When filtering on document type, the following types are available in SAP BusinessObjects:

NOTE If you set a filter, the filter will remain active throughout your entire session, even if you navigate to a different folder or category. You must select the filter and clear the filtered value if you want to display all of the documents again.

Organizing Documents

From the Documents tab, you can copy documents, move documents, or create shortcuts to documents to other folders (assuming that you have the appropriate rights). The following are some common reasons for using these options:

- You want to use an existing Web Intelligence document as a starting point, but modify it slightly to add your own sorts, filters, and calculations. You could copy the existing report document to your My Favorites folder and modify the copied version.

- You want to provide access to a document to another user who does not have security access to the same folder in which a document resides. You could copy the document to another folder where the user does have security access.

☑	All Types
☐	Administrative Tool
☐	Adobe Acrobat
☐	Advanced Analysis Workspace
☐	Agnostic
☐	Analysis View
☐	BEx Web Applications
☐	BI workspace
☐	Crystal Reports
☐	Dashboard Design
☐	Explorer Information Space
☐	Flash
☐	Folder
☐	Hyperlink
☐	Microsoft Excel
☐	Microsoft PowerPoint
☐	Microsoft Word
☐	Module
☐	Object Package
☐	Program
☐	Publication
☐	Rich Text
☐	Shortcut
☐	Text
☐	Web Intelligence
☐	Xcelsius

OK | Cancel

- You want to organize all of your frequently run report documents into a single folder to simplify navigation. You could create shortcuts to your frequently run documents in your My Favorites folder so that all of your important content is located in one place.

NOTE The list of available options in the toolbar for each document is also controlled by your permissions. If, for example, you do not have permission to delete a document, this option will not appear.

Copying Documents

To copy a document to your My Favorites folder, follow these steps:

1. Using the Navigation and List panels, find and select the document you wish to copy.

2. From the toolbar, select Organize | Copy. Alternatively, you can right-click the document name and select Organize | Copy from the pop-up menu.

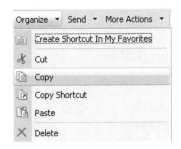

3. Navigate to the folder where you wish to copy the document. For example, you might select the My Documents drawer and the My Favorites folder.

4. From the toolbar, select Organize | Paste. Alternatively, you can right-click the List panel and select Organize | Paste.

Creating Shortcuts

Shortcuts in SAP BusinessObjects work much the same way as shortcuts in Microsoft Office. A shortcut is only a pointer to the original document, designed to make your navigation to the document simpler.

To create a shortcut in your My Favorites folder, follow these steps:

1. Using the Navigation and List panels, find and select the document you wish to create a shortcut for in your My Favorites folder.

2. From the toolbar, select Organize | Create Shortcut in My Favorites. Alternatively, right-click the document name and select Organize | Create Shortcut in My Favorites from the pop-up menu.

NOTE Deleting the shortcut will not delete the original copy of the document. Also, if the original document is deleted, any shortcuts that were created from that document will also be deleted.

BI Launch Pad Preferences

The first time you work with BI Launch Pad, you may want to modify several settings to ensure that your display and tool options are configured for your personal preferences. Some of the preferences settings available to you depend on which BusinessObjects products and interfaces your company has licensed.

To customize your preferences, follow these steps:

1. Select Preferences from the BI Launch Pad Header panel.

2. Select the Preference grouping that you would like to customize from the listing on the left.

3. If you are modifying the General preferences, you must uncheck the Use Default Settings (Administrator defined) option in order to customize your own settings.

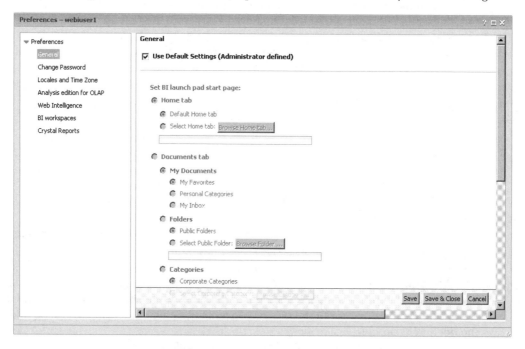

4. Specify your customized settings.

5. Click the Save & Close button.

The following sections describe the settings available in the General, Locales and Time Zone, and Web Intelligence preferences.

General

General preferences allow you to customize your starting page, the window behavior when you open and close a document, how the List panel columns appear in the Documents tab, and the number of documents that appear in the List panel.

Start Page

Your BI Launch Pad start page is the tab that will be displayed when you first log in. You can select from the following options:

- **Home tab**   The start page can be the Home tab. You can set it as either the default Home tab or a customized object that you select.

- **Documents tab**   The start page can be the Documents tab. You can specify which drawer and folder/node are open by default.

Columns Displayed in Documents Tab

You can choose which columns will display for each object in the List panel of the Documents tab. The following options are available:

- **Type**   The object type, such as Web Intelligence, Crystal Reports, Microsoft Excel, and Microsoft Word.

- **Last Run**   The date and time the last scheduled instance was run.

- **Instances**   The number of instances in history.

- **Description**   The description of the object from properties.

- **Created By**   The username that created the object.

- **Created On**   The date that the object was created.

- **Location (Categories)**   The folder in which the object is located.

- **Received On (Inbox)**   The date that the object was received in the BI inbox.

- **From (Inbox)**   The username that sent the object to your BI inbox.

Document Viewing Location

You can set how a document is displayed when it is opened or created. You can choose from two options:

- **In the BI launch pad portal as tabs**   The document will open in the same browser window as BI Launch Pad as a tab (next to the Home and Document tabs). This option keeps the navigation and actions of BI Launch Pad accessible in the same window, but makes the document workspace smaller, as it is constrained to the size of the tab available in the BI Launch Pad window.

- **In multiple full-screen browser windows, one window for each document**   The document will open in a separate browser window. This option requires you to manage multiple browser windows: one with your BI Launch Pad and one or more with your document workspace(s). The advantage is that the document workspace is larger because you have no other BI Launch Pad portal components taking up space.

Set the Maximum Number of Items per Page

You can set the number of items to appear in a given List panel document list before you need to navigate to the next page. The default is 50.

Locales and Time Zone

The Locales and Time Zone preferences allow you to set how dates, times, and numbers are formatted in reports and lists of values. These settings also determine the language used to display the screens and help in BI Launch Pad.

Product Locale

The Product Locale setting determines the language set that is used in BI Launch Pad. BI Launch Pad will be displayed using whatever language is selected, and the online help will appear in the selected language.

In the following example, Spanish was chosen as the product locale. Notice that the text on the screen is now displayed in Spanish.

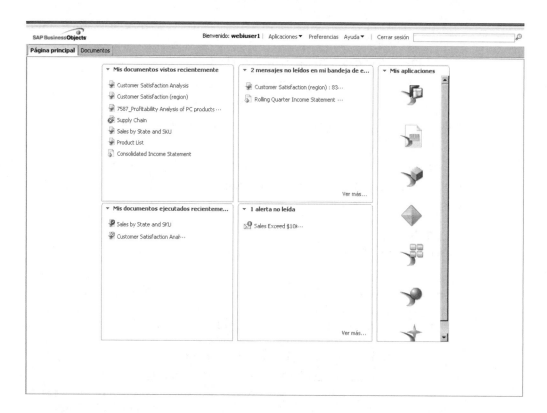

Preferred Viewing Locale

Preferred viewing locale refers to regional preferences for displaying the format for currency, date, and time. This affects how dates, times, and currency are formatted in reports and lists of values. For example, in the United States, currency is represented using a comma as the thousands separator and a period as the decimal separator (as in $9,723.00). In Europe and other regions, currency is represented using a period as the thousands separator and a comma as the decimal separator (as in €9.723,00). Additionally, preferred viewing locale determines what language a multilingual report will display in.

Current Time Zone

The current time zone settings determine how scheduled objects are processed when the web server that is running BusinessObjects Enterprise is not in the same time zone in which you are working. It is important that you set your current time zone in order for scheduled instances to run at the time scheduled in your own time zone, rather than at the time of a web server in a different time zone.

Web Intelligence

Web Intelligence preferences allow you to set options for viewing, modifying, and interacting with Web Intelligence documents.

View

The view preferences determine which interface you use to view a Web Intelligence document. You have the following choices.

- Web (no download required)
- Rich Internet Application (download required)
- Desktop (Windows only) (installation required)
- PDF

All of the viewers have the same functionality, which includes the ability to refresh the data, print, export to Excel and PDF files, drill, navigate, and filter. The only apparent differences among the viewers are the components that need to be downloaded. Therefore, it is recommended that you use a web viewer with no downloaded components for ease of upgrading and maintenance.

Modify (Creating, Editing, and Analyzing Documents)

The modify preferences determine which interface you use to modify a Web Intelligence document. Your choices are as follows:

- Web (no download required)
- Rich Internet Application (download required)
- Desktop (installation required)

All of the modification interfaces have similar functionality. The Desktop modification interface has one notable difference in that it allows for offline editing. If you would like to modify Web Intelligence documents when you cannot be connected to your network and the SAP BusinessObjects environment, you can install the Web Intelligence Desktop.

Selecting a default universe simplifies creating a new report when you work with the same universe most of the time.

When Viewing a Document   The format locale corresponds to regional settings that affect how dates and numbers are formatted in the report display, document filters, and query lists of values. For example, in Switzerland, a date is specified as *DD.MM.YY*, and the separator for thousands is an apostrophe. The following options are available:

- **Use the document locale to format the data**   When you set the format locale to use the document locale to format the data, it will override the preferred viewing locale you set in General preferences with the viewing locale set in the Web Intelligence document. The document locale for the document is set as the preferred viewing locale for the user creating the document at the time the document is created.

- **Use my preferred viewing locale to format the data** When you set the format locale to use my preferred viewing locale, it will use the preferred viewing locale that you have set in General preferences.

Drill Options

The drill options specify how the Web Intelligence interface changes when you perform a drill session. You can select from the following options:

- **Prompt when drill requires additional data** As you drill, you often will display additional levels of detail that may already exist within the document. However, in some cases, Web Intelligence may need to issue a new query to retrieve the additional details. By setting this option, you will be warned when a new query is executed. This is recommended when query response times are variable.

- **Synchronize drill on report blocks** A Web Intelligence document can contain multiple blocks, such as a chart and a crosstab. If you want a drill within a chart to be synchronized by the same drill within the corresponding crosstab, set this option.

- **Hide Drill toolbar on startup** Choosing this option hides the drill filter toolbar when you switch to Drill mode.

- **Start drill session** For drill options, you determine if you want Web Intelligence to make a copy of the report, creating another report tab when you begin drilling, or if the drill should occur in the same report tab. We recommend that you set this option to drill on a duplicate report copy, mainly as a way of preserving formatting and the initial viewpoint.

  - **On duplicate report** Starts a drill session in a copy of the report on a new report tab.

  - **On existing report** Starts a drill session on the same report.

Drilling is covered in more detail in Chapter 17.

Select a Priority for Saving to MS Excel

When scheduling or exporting a document to Excel format, the following options determine the appearance of the data in Excel:

- **Prioritize the formatting of the documents** Preserves the formatting of the data similar to working in Web Intelligence when the data is exported to Excel.

- **Prioritize easy data processing in Excel** Exports data to Excel in text format.

BI Workspaces

BI Workspaces is a dashboard, or portal page, that allows you to display the documents, dashboards, exploration views, and web sites you most frequently access. Once you have customized BI Workspaces, you can set a custom BI workspace as your starting page when you log in, or you can navigate to any of your saved BI workspaces by selecting them from the Navigation panel of the Documents tab. Figure 16-4 shows an example of a BI workspace.

Creating a New BI Workspace

Before you create a BI workspace, you should define how you want it to look, who the audience will be, and what the information requirements are. You also should gather all of the content you plan to include in your BI workspace, including Web Intelligence documents, Crystal Reports, and dashboards, as well as web sites and other text information. Take some time to plan and draw out the structure of the BI workspace.

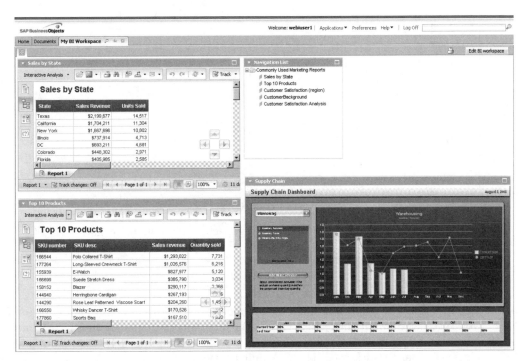

Figure 16-4   A BI workspace acts as a departmental or personal dashboard.

To create a BI workspace, follow these steps:

1. Select Applications | BI workspace from the BI Launch Pad Header panel. The BI workspace editor will launch.

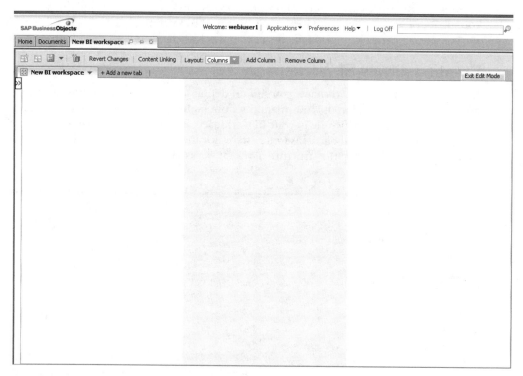

2. Click the Save icon and select Save As. The Save As dialog box will appear.

3. Select a location to save your BI workspace, enter a filename, and click OK.

4. Close your BI workspace.

Editing a BI Workspace

The BI Workspace tab in edit mode has a toolbar with options to help you design your BI workspace, as shown in Table 16-2. One of the main tools available in the BI workspace editor is the Module Library. This library allows you to access the components you will be placing in your BI workspace. These include navigation lists and web pages, as well as access to all the Web Intelligence, Crystal Reports, and dashboard content in your BusinessObjects system.

Button	Name	Function
	New	Creates a new BI workspace
	Open	Opens an existing BI workspace
	Save	Saves the latest changes made to a BI workspace
	Save As	Saves a new BI workspace
	Show Module Library	Opens the Module Library panel
Revert Changes	Revert Changes	Cancels any changes made in the current BI workspace edit session and reverts to the last saved version
Content Linking	Content Linking	Enables content linking between two modules in the BI workspace
Columns ▾	Layout	Allows you to select a layout for a BI workspace: Freeform, Template, or Columns
Exit Edit Mode	Exit Edit Mode	Exits edit mode (if you did not save changes, this will cancel modifications since the last save)

Table 16-2 BI Workspace Toolbar

To edit a BI workspace, follow these steps:

1. Navigate to your BI workspace in the Documents tab.

2. Double-click to open your BI workspace.

3. Select the Edit BI Workspace button on the right side of the tab. The BI workspace is now in edit mode.

 4. If the Module Library panel is not displayed, click the Show Module Library button on the toolbar.

5. Select your desired layout from the toolbar. For example, select Freeform.

6. From the Module Library panel, select the module type you would like to add to your BI workspace. For example, select Web Page Module and drag it to your workspace.

7. Click the wrench icon to edit the contents of the module you added to your workspace. For a web page, enter the URL you wish to be displayed in this object, such as http://www.businessobjects.com, and then click OK.

8. Drag any other modules, documents, and objects to your BI workspace.

9. Once you are satisfied with the layout of your BI workspace, click Save on the toolbar.

You can navigate to your BI workspace at any time by double-clicking the BI workspace in the Navigation panel of BI Launch Pad.

Setting Your BI Workspace As the Default Home Tab

You can set a BI workspace as your default Home tab, as follows:

1. Select Preferences from the BI Launch Pad Header panel.

2. In the General preferences, uncheck the Use Default Settings (Administrator defined) option (this allows you to customize your own settings).

3. For the "Set BI launch pad start page" option, select Home tab, select the Browse Home tab button, and navigate to your BI workspace.

4. Click Save & Close.

Summary

BI Launch Pad is your portal to all the BI content and applications within a SAP BusinessObjects 4.0 deployment. Understanding the components of the Home and Documents tabs will make organizing and navigating your BI content quick and easy. Setting your preferences lets you customize BI Launch Pad and the tools you work with to meet your needs. BI workspaces allow you to display reports and dashboards that you frequently access.

CHAPTER
17
Interacting with Documents

If you are a long-time BusinessObjects user, you have seen the query and reporting tools evolve from their full client versions (referred to as BusinessObjects classic in version 6 and earlier and Desktop Intelligence in XI versions) to both their web-based versions (referred to as Web Intelligence) and their web rich client versions (referred to as Web Intelligence Rich Client).

Web- and cloud-based computing have become more popular, and are now considered the standard for a variety of reasons, including scalability, performance, cost, maintenance, and device and location independence. It is no longer desirable for IT departments to install and maintain software loaded on each user's computer. Furthermore, users want to have access to information from a variety of devices and via the Internet so they can connect from anywhere.

Prior to BusinessObjects XI, users were not ready to give up their full client versions of query and reporting tools due to the functionality gaps between the full client and web-based tools. The result has been that BusinessObjects has needed to support multiple formats for reports: the Desktop Intelligence (full client) format and the Web Intelligence (web-based) format. With the functionality of Web Intelligence and the Web Intelligence Rich Client (introduced in BusinessObjects XI R3) now meeting and exceeding the functionality of full client report-development tools of the past, coupled with the benefits of web- and cloud-based computing, most users have converted or are ready to convert (or at least, they no longer have excuses not to convert) to the web-based world for report development.

In SAP BusinessObjects BI 4.0, there are no longer multiple report formats. The Desktop Intelligence format for reports has been retired. Web Intelligence Rich Client is a web-based rich client version of Web Intelligence and works on Web Intelligence format documents. Therefore, unlike in prior versions where Web Intelligence could not maintain Desktop Intelligence documents and vice versa, Web Intelligence documents are maintainable by Web Intelligence Rich Client and vice versa. Since the Desktop Intelligence report format is no longer supported in SAP BusinessObjects BI 4.0, you will be required to convert all Desktop Intelligence format reports to Web Intelligence format using the Report Conversion Tool.

This chapter explains how to view and work with documents in the Web Intelligence web viewer.

Working with the Web Intelligence Web Viewer

Recall from the preceding chapter that your BI Launch Pad preferences determine which Web Intelligence report viewer is used when you open a document and whether the document appears in a separate browser window or within the BI Launch Pad as a new tab. This section explains how to open a document in the web viewer and use the web viewer interface.

Opening a Document

Here, we'll assume you're opening a document using the web viewer within the BI Launch Pad as a new tab. First, locate the document you would like to open. The document could be on the Home tab as one of your recently viewed or run documents, or on the Documents tab in your My Documents drawer or Folders drawer. Next, double-click the name of the document, or right-click the document name and select View from the context menu. Your document will appear in the viewer, as shown in Figure 17-1.

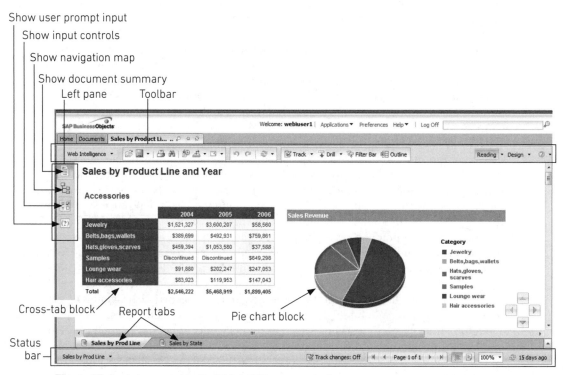

Figure 17-1   A document in the Web Intelligence web viewer

Web Viewer Status Bar

The status bar at the bottom of the web viewer has several options and displays information that is important when interacting with your documents. Figure 17-2 shows the components of the status bar.

The status bar displays whether track changes is turned on, the zoom level of the document, and the date and time the data in the document was last refreshed. Also, if only partial data results were retrieved, or if there was an error in running the query, this information will appear on the status bar.

The status bar lets you navigate between report tabs (when your document contains multiple report tabs) and between report pages.

The status bar is a selectable option. If it's not visible, right-click on the bottom of the web viewer and select the status bar to display it.

View Modes

Using the status bar, you can choose between two web viewer view modes:

- **Quick Display mode**   This mode makes it easy to view and work with your document in the viewer. It does not display the page margins, page breaks, and page footers that would appear in a printed document. Quick Display mode allows you to scroll continuously through the document, without the need to navigate from page to page. Figure 17-1 shows the document displayed in Quick Display mode.

- **Page mode**   This mode shows the document on the screen as it will appear when printed. It displays page margins, page headers and footers, and page breaks. To navigate between pages, you will need to use the page navigation buttons.

You can toggle between the view modes by selecting the Quick Display mode or Page mode button in the status bar, as shown in Figure 17-2.

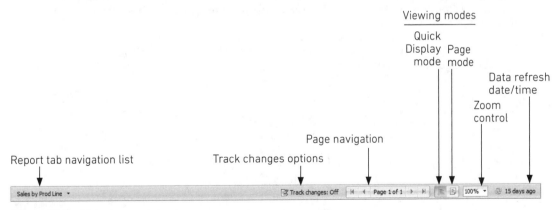

Figure 17-2   Web viewer status bar components

Page Navigation

When in Page mode, you will need to navigate between the individual pages in your document. Initially, the web viewer displays only the first page number. Use the arrows on the page navigation bar (shown in Figure 17-2) to navigate to the next, previous, or first or last page in your report. Once you have navigated to the last page in the report, the web viewer will change the page navigation bar to show a total page count.

Web Viewer Toolbar

The toolbar is located along the top of the web viewer and has several options to help you interact with your documents, as shown in Figure 17-3. The options available on the toolbar are described in Table 17-1.

Printing a Report

Before you can print a document, it must be converted to PDF format. To print a report, do the following:

 1. Select the Print button on the toolbar. The File Download dialog box will display.

 2. Click Open. The report will open in an Adobe Acrobat Reader frame.

3. Click the Print button on the Acrobat Reader toolbar.

4. Respond to the prompts for a printer and other settings, and then click OK.

5. Close the Adobe Acrobat Reader frame to return to the web viewer.

File Download

Do you want to open or save this file?

Name: Sales_by_Product_Line_and_Year.pdf
Type: Adobe Acrobat Document, 252KB
From: ec2-50-17-56-252.compute-1.amazonaws.com

[Open] [Save] [Cancel]

While files from the Internet can be useful, some files can potentially harm your computer. If you do not trust the source, do not open or save this file. What's the risk?

TIP For a quick printout that prints only the current page and does not require high-quality formatting or page breaks, you can use your browser's print capability.

Figure 17-3 Web Viewer toolbar

Button	Name	Function
	Open	Opens a document
	Save	Saves a document
	Print	Exports a document to a PDF file for printing
	Find	Finds text in tables and cells on the current page
	History	Displays a list of dates corresponding to instances of the scheduled document
	Export	Exports a document in PDF, CSV, or Excel format
	Send To…	Sends a document to an e-mail message, a user, or an FTP site
	Cut	Cuts selected elements (available only if you have rights to modify the document)
	Copy	Copies selected elements (available only if you have rights to modify the document)
	Paste	Pastes contents of the clipboard (available only if you have rights to modify the document)
	Undo	Undoes previous actions
	Redo	Redoes previous actions
	Delete	Removes the selected report elements (available only if you have rights to modify the document)
	Refresh Data	Refreshes one or all data providers
Track ▾	Track Changes	Activates or deactivates data-tracking mode
Drill ▾	Drill	Allows you to navigate the report by hierarchy
Filter Bar	Filter Bar	Shows or hides the filter bar
Outline	Outline	Shows or hides the outline, providing the option to fold or unfold report elements
Reading ▾	Reading	Switches to viewing mode in either the HTML viewer or PDF viewer

Table 17-1   Web Viewer Toolbar Buttons

Button	Name	Function
Design ▾	Design	Switches to edit mode in design mode with data, or design mode with report structure only
Data	Data	Displays data providers (available only if you have rights to edit the Web Intelligence document)
⑦	Help	Invokes help

Table 17-1 Web Viewer Toolbar Buttons *(continued)*

Using Find

The Find option is useful when you want to find a particular item, such as a customer name or individual product.

To find text or numeric values within a page, do the following:

1. Select the Find button on the toolbar. The find bar appears at the bottom of the web viewer.

2. Type the text or numeric value you want to search for in the Find text box.

3. Click the drop-down arrow next to the Find icon (the binoculars) to indicate if you would like to match case or ignore case.

4. Click Find Next or Find Previous.

If the text value is found on the document page, the matching value will be highlighted in the document, and the find bar will display the message "Found matches on current page." In the following example, **lounge wear** was entered as the text to find, and the option to ignore case was selected.

Sales by Product Line and Year

Accessories

	2004	2005	2006
Jewelry	$1,521,327	$3,600,207	$58,560
Belts,bags,wallets	$389,699	$492,931	$759,861
Hats,gloves,scarves	$459,394	$1,053,580	$37,588
Samples	Discontinued	Discontinued	$649,298
Lounge wear	$91,880	$202,247	$247,053
Hair accessories	$83,923	$119,953	$147,043
Total	$2,546,222	$5,468,919	$1,899,405

Sales Revenue

Category
- Jewelry
- Belts,bags,wallets
- Hats,gloves, scarves
- Samples
- Lounge wear
- Hair accessories

Find: lounge wear ▾ ▾ Find Next ▲ Find Previous ⓘ Found matches on current page

Sales by Prod Line | Sales by State

Note that the web viewer's Find option searches for text only within the page. (This behavior is quite different from the Find option within a Crystal Reports viewer, which will search through the entire document.) If you want to search throughout the entire document, change your view to Quick Display mode.

NOTE The Find option does not work on text within a chart legend. It also does not work when the document is in Outline mode.

Viewing Instances and Status

Once you have scheduled a document to refresh (as discussed in the "Refreshing a Document" section later in this chapter), you can see the status and history of all scheduled instances. From within the report, select the History button on the toolbar to open the History window.

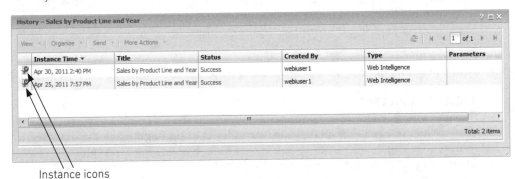

Instance icons

If you want to delete a particular instance, click the instance icon and select Organize | Delete Instance.

Exporting a Document

Exporting your document to a different format, such as to a Microsoft Excel, Adobe Acrobat, or comma-separated values (CSV) file, allows you to share your documents with users who may not have access to your SAP BusinessObjects BI 4.0 environment.

To export documents to an external format, do the following:

  1. Select the Export button on the toolbar.

2. Choose from the following options:

- **Export Document As**   The choices are PDF, Excel, and Excel 2007. This option exports all report tabs in the current document to the format selected.

- **Export Current Report As**   The choices are PDF, Excel, and Excel 2007. This option exports only the current selected report tab from the document to the format selected.

- **Export Data to CSV**   This option exports the document data to a CSV file.

3. If you select Export Data to CSV, the Save as CSV Options dialog box displays. Enter the text qualifier, the column delimiter, and the character set. Then click OK.

4. The File Download dialog box will display. Select whether you want to open the exported document file immediately or save the file to a location on disk. If you select Save, type the filename, select the location, and click OK.

Note that once a document has been exported to an external format, the data that is contained in the document is static, and the data cannot be refreshed from the data source.

Tracking Changes

Tracking changes allows you to compare data results from a document run at two different times. When you enable data tracking, the web viewer highlights changes in values, as well as insertions and deletions in the report over time. For example, you can track changes between a report run today and a report run last week, and the web viewer will highlight products that have increased in sales, products that have decreased in sales, and new products that have recent sales where there were no sales reported before.

The following example shows data tracking used with the document shown earlier in Figure 17-1. It shows that the sales of jewelry in 2006 decreased (highlighted in red); the sales of hats, gloves, and scarves in 2006 increased (highlighted in green); and the value of samples in 2005 is new (displayed in blue text).

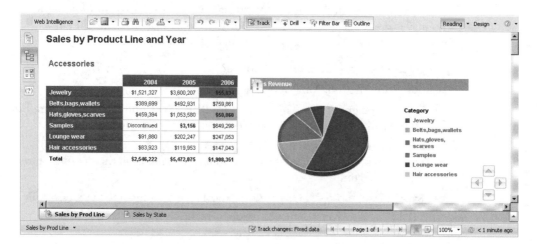

To track changes, do the following:

1. Select the Track Changes button on the toolbar. The Data Tracking dialog box will display.

2. Select tracking options to compare to the last data refresh or compare to a specific data refresh, which you choose from the drop-down list.

3. Select the reports you would like to show data tracking.

4. Optionally, select to refresh the data when you click OK to exit the Data Tracking dialog box.

5. Optionally, select the Options tab and select which changes you want to display and their format.

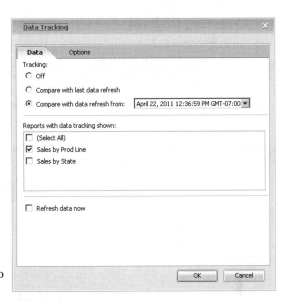

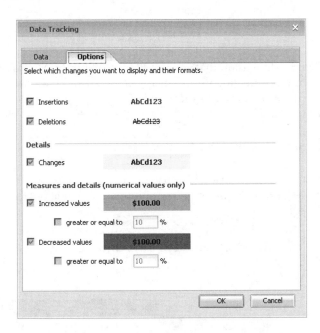

6. Click OK to close the Data Tracking dialog box and enable tracking.

Filtering Reports

The web viewer has a filter bar that allows you to filter a report on any of the dimensions that have been returned in the data provider of the report, even if those dimensions have not been used or displayed in the report tab. Filtering allows you to limit the data that is displayed in the report without modifying the query for the report. For example, you can filter the report to show only sales for a specific state.

To filter a report, do the following:

Filter Bar 1. Select the Filter Bar button on the toolbar. The filter bar will appear at the top of the report, just beneath the toolbar.

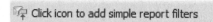

2. Click the icon to add a filter. The dimensions available to filter will display in a drop-down list.

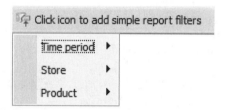

3. Select the dimension that you would like to filter by. You can select multiple dimensions. The dimension will appear as a drop-down list in the filter bar. The following example shows City and SKU desc as possible filter dimensions added to the filter bar.

City (All values) ▼ SKU desc (All values) ▼

4. Select the value for each dimension on which you wish to filter the data. The following example shows a report filtered to include only the Houston data.

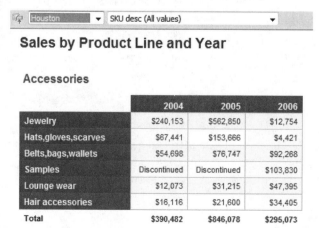

Houston ▼ SKU desc (All values) ▼

Sales by Product Line and Year

Accessories

	2004	2005	2006
Jewelry	$240,153	$562,850	$12,754
Hats,gloves,scarves	$67,441	$153,666	$4,421
Belts,bags,wallets	$54,698	$76,747	$92,268
Samples	Discontinued	Discontinued	$103,830
Lounge wear	$12,073	$31,215	$47,395
Hair accessories	$16,116	$21,600	$34,405
Total	$390,482	$846,078	$295,073

5. You can continue to change the filter values to see how the report changes, or select (All values) to return to the unfiltered version of the report at any time.

NOTE Selecting the Filter Bar button on the toolbar after you have applied a filter will hide the filter bar, but will not remove the filters. If you have an active filter, the filter will remain active for the remainder of the interactive viewer session, even after you hide the filter bar. You must reset all dimensions to (All values) in order to restore the report to its original, unfiltered version. The original report will open in the next interactive viewing session.

Viewing a Report Outline

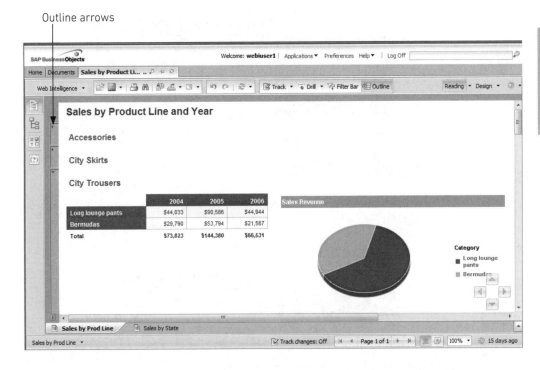

The Outline mode lets you expand and collapse sections of your report. To view a report in Outline mode, click the Outline button on the toolbar. In Outline mode, you can select the arrows on the left side of your report to expand or collapse the sections of your report.

NOTE Selecting the Outline button on the toolbar after you have collapsed sections in Outline mode will hide the outline arrow controls, but leave any collapsed sections in their collapsed state for the remainder of the web viewer session. You must reset each of the collapsed sections back to their original state. The report will open in its original state in the next web viewer session.

Drilling into a Report

You can drill into data in a report section, table, or chart to view more detailed information about summarized data. For example, if you are looking at a table that has data grouped by state, you may want to drill into that data to see the cities.

The hierarchical levels of data that define the drill paths are specified in the universe. For example, the hierarchy of State drilling to City drilling to ZIP Code is defined in the universe.

Recall from the preceding chapter that your BI Launch Pad preferences determine how your Web Intelligence session behaves during your drill session. The following steps assume that the preference is set to start the drill session on the existing report.

To start a drill session, do the following:

1. Select the Drill button on the toolbar.

2. Select a dimension or measure on your report that you would like to drill on. The following example illustrates selecting the Sales by State and Year report tab and choosing to drill on the state of Texas, which will drill down to cities in Texas.

Sales by State and Year

	2004	2005	2006
Texas	$2,199,677	$3,732,889	$4,185,098
New [Drill Down to City]	$1,667,696	$2,763,503	$3,151,022
California	$1,704,211	$2,782,680	$2,992,679
Illinois	$737,914	$1,150,659	$1,134,085
DC	$693,211	$1,215,158	$1,053,581
Colorado	$448,302	$768,390	$843,584
Florida	$405,985	$661,250	$811,924
Massachusetts	$238,819	$157,719	$887,169

3. The drilled report appears. To drill back up, select the drill up icons next to the drilled dimensions.

Sales by State and Year

	2004	2005	2006
Houston	$1,211,309	$1,990,449	$2,246,198
Austin	$561,123	$1,003,071	$1,135,479
Dallas	$427,245	$739,369	$803,421

NOTE Selecting the Drill button on the toolbar after drilling into a dimension or measure will hide the drill options and icons in the report, but will not reset the drill back to the original state. The drill will remain active for the remainder of the web viewer session even when you hide the drill options. You must drill back up to the original level to return to the undrilled state. The report will open in its original, undrilled state in the next interactive viewing session.

Web Viewer Navigation Map

The navigation map displays a list of the multiple reports within a document as well as individual sections within a report. The navigation map appears in the left pane (minimized in Figure 17-1). To display the navigation map, click the Navigation Map button in the left pane.

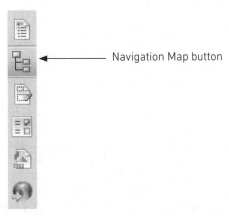

Navigation Map button

You can use the navigation map to quickly find and navigate to specific reports or sections within your document. To navigate to a report or section, just click the report or section listed in the navigation map.

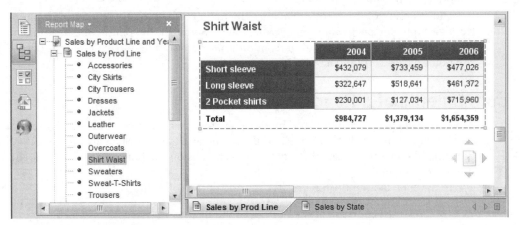

Understanding a Document's Structure

Web Intelligence documents have a flexible document structure that allows you to view and interact with different data sets in multiple ways. A document is more than just a report.

A document may contain the following components:

- One or more universes, which are typically SQL queries that extract information from a data warehouse or other data source.

- A result set in which the results of the queries are stored as a microcube that allow for drilling and slicing and dicing.

- One or more formatted reports. Figure 17-1 (shown earlier in the chapter) contains two report tabs at the bottom of the workspace: Sales by Prod Line and Sales by State. Each report may be based on a different universe or query, or they all may be based on the same query.

- Multiple blocks in each report, such as chart, table, or crosstab blocks. These blocks can all come from the same query but provide different perspectives on the data, or they may come from different universes and queries. A report may have multiple block types. For example, the Sales by Prod Line report shown in Figure 17-1 contains two blocks: a crosstab and a pie chart.

Figure 17-4 gives a conceptual overview of a document that is made up of two data sources: a universe that accesses a data warehouse and a second universe that accesses a departmental database. The document contains three reports: two tabular reports with a view to each result set and a third report that displays a chart with data from both result sets.

In many documents, you may have only one query, one result set, and one report. However, the flexibility of Web Intelligence allows you to have one query or many queries and one report or multiple reports. Each report tab may contain a view with the full data set (that is, all the variables that you included in your query) but in a different block type, such as table, crosstab, or chart. Alternatively, each report may contain a limited number of columns or rows of data, providing you with a more aggregated or targeted view as you remove variables and apply filters.

The structure of the Web Intelligence document allows you to explore information from multiple perspectives in a single document. Similarly, the microcube technology allows you to combine information from multiple data sources into one report, even if you don't have a central data warehouse.

Components of a Report

A report is one tab within the Web Intelligence document. For example, in Figure 17-1 (shown earlier in the chapter), Sales by Prod Line and Sales by State are two reports within the same document. You see these two reports as tabs on the bottom of the document or in the navigation map.

To navigate to an individual report, do one of the following:

- Click the report tab at the bottom of the main workspace.

- Click the report name in the drop-down list on the status bar.

- Click the Navigation Map button in the left pane and click the report name in the list.

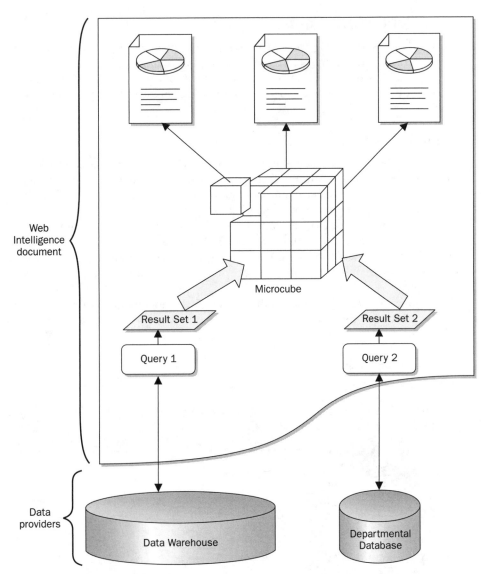

Figure 17-4 A Web Intelligence document is composed of several components.

Within a given report, several components make up its structure: a page header and footer, sections, blocks, and cells. For a consumer of a report who is exploring information within a report, distinguishing these components is not particularly important. For a designer of a report using Web Intelligence (or Web Intelligence Rich Client), it is important to understand each of these components and their corresponding data display behavior, as well as their formatting options.

Page Header and Footer

Every report has both a *page header* and *page footer*. Page headers and footers appear in only a printed report, and therefore are only visible in Page mode.

Page headers and footers typically contain the report title and page numbers. They may also include data refresh dates, logos, and other information about the report document itself.

Sections

Every report has a main *section*. Within the main section, you can have a section header and section footer; these are different from page headers and footers that appear in printed reports. Main section headers typically hold the title of the report, but also may contain a picture or logo and even grand-totaled data variables.

Reports also may have subsections if you create additional sections in the report. In Figure 17-1 (shown earlier in the chapter), there is a section for each product line (Accessories, City Skirts, and so on) that contains a crosstab and pie chart for each line. These sections are indicated with a bullet symbol in the navigation map, as shown earlier in the chapter.

Sections convert to bookmarks when you view the document as an Adobe Acrobat PDF file (for printing or for sharing documents with users who do not have a SAP BusinessObjects BI 4.0 Enterprise login ID).

Sections convert to PDF bookmarks

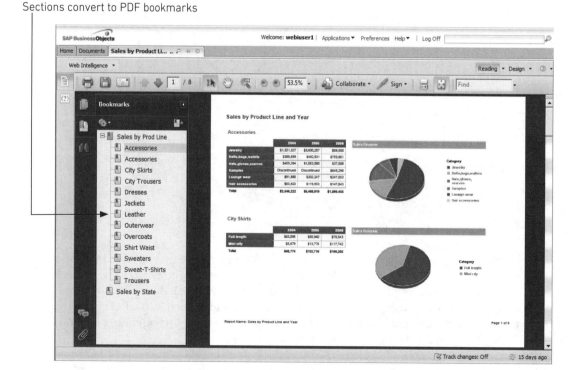

Blocks

A *block* is a set of data and is the component used to display your data in a report. Web Intelligence supports different types of blocks, such as a standard table, crosstab, or chart. A block can be sorted, filtered, and formatted.

A block is one component within a section, and a section can contain multiple blocks. Two blocks can be related or can be independent of each other. For example, you can have a crosstab block of sales with a corresponding pie chart to visually display the sales. Alternatively, you can have a crosstab of sales and a trend chart of employee satisfaction, populated from a different data provider.

Variables and Cells

A *cell* contains fixed text, pictures, formulas, hyperlinks, HTML, or data variables.

Cells that contain fixed text, such as a title or a picture, are referred to as *constants*. The contents of the cell never change, no matter which data you are viewing.

A cell whose contents can change may be either a formula or a report *variable*. Data variables are pointers to the columns of data that are returned from your query. When a report author builds a query, the author selects *objects* from the universe. These objects become data variables in a report. Three types of data variables correspond directly to how the universe designer defines an object:

- A *dimension* object is typically textual information by which you sort and analyze numeric measures. It is denoted by a blue cube. In the reports shown thus far, *Lines, State, Category,* and *Year* are dimension variables.

- A *measure* object is a number that you want to analyze. It is denoted by an orange ruler. *Sales Revenue* is a measure variable.

- An *attribute* object provides additional information about a particular dimension. It is denoted by a blue square with a green asterisk. You may want to see the information in a list report, but will not want to use it to analyze measures. Phone number and street address are typical attribute variables.

Refreshing a Document

As discussed earlier in the chapter, a document contains multiple components that make up the formatted reports and analysis. When you want to retrieve new data from a data source, you are sending a query to a database.

 To refresh a query, select the Refresh Data button on the web viewer toolbar.

NOTE A document may be set to force a query refresh as soon as you open the document. Also, the report author decides whether a shared document initially contains data or is blank.

When Web Intelligence refreshes a query, it refreshes the entire result set. For example, let's assume you have a document that shows year-to-date sales. The data source is from a data warehouse updated on a daily basis. A report author originally ran the query last week and sent you the results. So your version of the report is out of date by a week. You refresh the query. This rebuilds the entire microcube (refer back to Figure 17-4); the microcube does not incrementally add one week of data. For smaller queries, this is not important, as the results may be returned in a few seconds. Other queries, however, may take quite a long time to run.

Remember that the status bar in the web viewer displays when a data provider was last refreshed and also displays if only partial results were returned.

Canceling a Query

While a query is refreshing, the web viewer displays an alert that gives an indication of how long it should take the query to refresh. This is based on an estimate from the last query execution. If your prompt values or filter criteria have changed significantly from the last refresh, this can affect the execution time, as can changes in the server processing load at different times during the day.

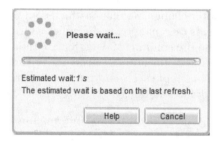

You may choose to cancel a query if you inadvertently select the wrong filters or if you decide it will take too long to refresh and you want to schedule the query. Scheduling documents is covered later in this chapter. When you cancel a query using the web viewer, the query stops, and you are presented with the last set of results.

NOTE If the universe designer has set limits for query execution time or on the number of rows of data that can be returned, you may receive only partial results for a query. When a query execution time limit interrupts a query before any rows have been returned, you may receive an erroneous error message: "No data to fetch." This is very misleading, as there may be data that would have been returned if the time limit had not been reached.

Lists of Values

When you refresh a query, you may be asked to provide additional information to customize data that is returned to you. You can enter the values yourself, or in many cases, you can choose from a list of values. Choosing from a list of values ensures you have entered the possible values correctly (either uppercase or lowercase, with or without leading zeros, valid dates, and so on), and therefore ensures you retrieve the desired results. This avoids the problem of users receiving the message "No data to fetch" simply because they have entered invalid values in a prompt.

A list of values is a pick list generated from a query the SAP BusinessObjects Enterprise server sends to the data source (for more information about how lists of values are built into the universe, refer to Chapter 8). Because the list of values is specific to each universe, even if you have similar objects, such as *Product* or *Customer*, in multiple universes, you will have multiple list of values query files. Most often, these query files are initially empty and contain no values. Therefore, the first time a user accesses a particular list of values, the user may need to refresh the query associated with the pick list. Once the list of values has been refreshed and initially populated, the results are cached in a shared area on the Enterprise server. You should periodically refresh the list of values, as values in a dimension may change—for example, as new products or customers are added.

In the following example, when you click Refresh Data to refresh the query, you are prompted to provide values for Year and Lines.

Click here to move a value
to the selected values list

Values used in prompts when document was last saved or the last prompt values entered if the document has already been refreshed during this web viewer session

List of possible values you can choose from for each prompt

Filter criteria that will be used for this prompt

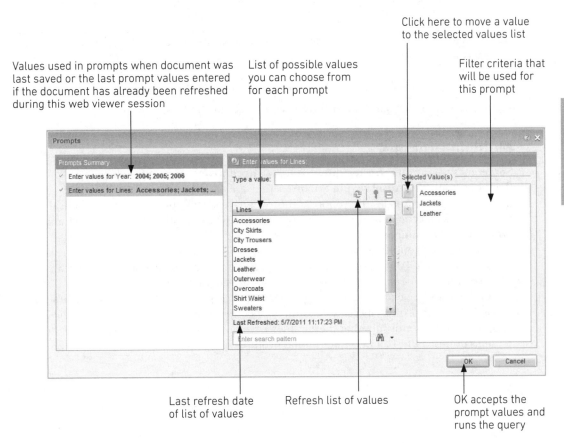

Last refresh date
of list of values

Refresh list of values

OK accepts the
prompt values and
runs the query

Follow these steps to fill in prompt values:

1. When you refresh a query for the first time during a web viewer session, the prompts will show the values entered into the document when the report author saved the report. If you have refreshed the document during the session, the last set of prompt values that you selected will be displayed in the prompts. You can OK to accept the last values used or modify the filter criteria.

2. Lists of values can become old and outdated on the server, as they are dependent on users or universe designers to keep them refreshed and up to date with current data. Notice the last refreshed date beneath the list of values. If a list of values is empty or does not contain recent data, click the Refresh Values button to update the list of values.

3. Select a prompt from the Prompts Summary pane on the left. For this example, select Enter values for Lines. The available Lines values and selected values are shown in the two lists in the pane on the right.

4. In the list of values, select filter criteria. For this example, select Sweaters.

NOTE If you know the value with the correct use of letter case, spelling, and so on, you can enter it in the box labeled "Type a value."

5. Click the > button to add Sweaters to the Selected Value(s) list.

6. When you are satisfied with your selections, click OK.

Multiple Prompts

Sometimes when you refresh a query, you may need to answer multiple prompts. By default, prompts are displayed in the order they are added to the query while the query is designed. Ideally, the report author will have sorted the prompts in a logical order, such as placing a beginning year prompt before an ending year prompt when specifying a date range.

The default prompt message also gives an indication whether you can select one value or multiple values. For example, "Enter Year" indicates you can choose only one year, whereas "Enter value(s) for State" means you can select more than one state.

In the following example, there are three required prompts. A green check mark next to the Enter Year prompt indicates a value has been entered. A red arrow next to the State and Line prompts indicates that these values have not yet been entered. The OK button remains dimmed until all the nonoptional prompts have been answered.

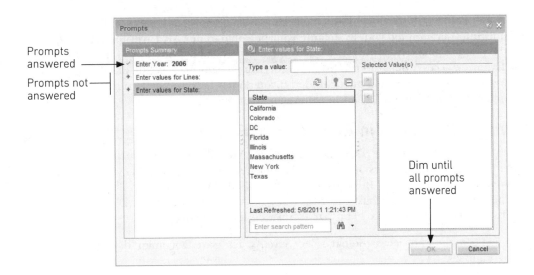

Prompts answered

Prompts not answered

Saving Documents

Once you have refreshed a document, you may want to save the document with the new set of data. To save a document to the same place from which you opened the document, click the Save button on the toolbar. To close the document without saving any changes, select the Document | Close menu item or click the X on your web intelligence document tab.

If the Save button does not appear on your main toolbar, you may not have permission to save the original document, particularly if it is stored in a public folder. In this case, select Document | Save As to save the document to another folder, such as your My Favorites folder.

NOTE Saving a document will also save any filters, drill views, or outline views that have been applied to the document.

When you use the Save As option to save the document to a different location and name, you are making a copy of the file; no link is maintained to the original report file. In the Save As dialog box, enter a document title. This will become the name of the file as it appears in the list in the BI Launch Pad documents list.

Under Folders, the folders in which you can save a document depend on the rights the administrator has granted you. By default, your personal folder, My Favorites, is selected. To see the public folders, click the + to expand the list of available folders. All folders for which you have view access appear in this list, however, you may not have create or edit rights that allow you to save a report to a public folder. If you do not have sufficient rights to save the document to a public folder, you will receive an error message.

Saving a Document in Excel or PDF Format

When you select Save As, the Save Document dialog box allows you to select a location other than your SAP BusinessObjects BI 4.0 Enterprise server. If you select your computer or a network file server, SAP BusinessObjects assumes that you want to save the document in a public format such as Microsoft Excel (.xlsx or .xls) or Adobe Acrobat (.pdf).

To save a document in Excel or PDF format, do the following:

1. From the web viewer toolbar, select Save As. The Save Document dialog box will appear.

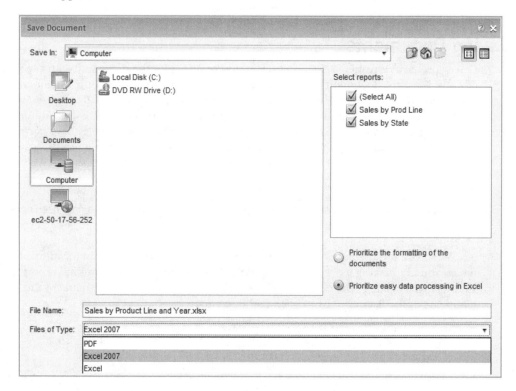

2. Enter the filename.

3. Select the file type from the Files of Type drop-down list.

4. Select the reports that you want to include in the saved document file.

5. Click the Save button.

Using Advanced Save As Options

To access the advanced Save As options, click the Advanced button in the Save Document dialog box. If you wish, enter a longer description. The description appears when you expand your document properties. Specify keywords if you want to provide additional search options for locating documents.

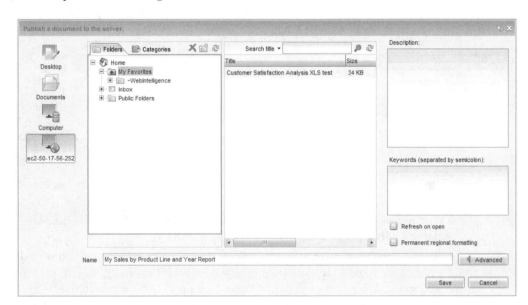

The Refresh on open option will automatically force a query refresh when you open the document. By checking the Permanent regional formatting box, you override users' personal BI Launch Pad locale settings so that formatting for dates and numeric values are stored with the document.

Scheduling a Document

If you have slow-running queries or reports that you wish to refresh on a regular basis, you can schedule them. The scheduling features are available through BI Launch Pad and for all SAP BusinessObjects Enterprise document types (Crystal Reports and Web Intelligence).

Scheduling a document creates an instance of the document that is a snapshot or a version of the document with saved data. This feature can be particularly useful if you need to track data over time. For example, you might want a monthly snapshot of financial data or a report when it is submitted to a regulatory agency.

A single document can have multiple instances. Instances can be kept in your system indefinitely or can be cleaned up by your SAP BusinessObjects administrator with settings that enable instances to automatically delete themselves after they reach a certain age limit (for example, 120 days old) or a certain number (such as more than 12 instances).

Right-click the document you wish to schedule and select Schedule. The Schedule dialog box will appear.

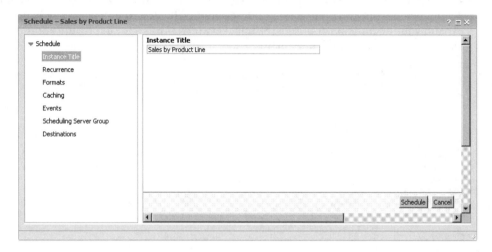

1. The instance title, by default, is the same as the document title. You can leave the default title or enter a new one.

2. Set the Recurrence parameters to specify how often the document will refresh and create an instance. Options include Now, Once, Hourly, Daily, Weekly, Monthly, and so on. The parameters depend on which option you select. In the following example, Weekly was selected, and the parameters include the days on which the document will run on a weekly basis. If you select Monthly, you will be asked to provide a number (N) representing that the object will run every N months.

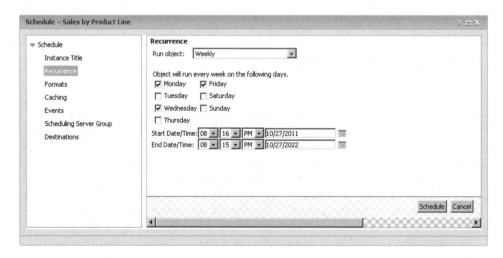

3. If your document contains prompts, you must provide the prompt values you wish the document to refresh with. (The purpose of a scheduled report is often for a

document to run unattended overnight or during nonpeak processing hours.) By default, the prompt values saved in the document will be used unless you override them. In this example, no prompts are used in the report so the prompt options are not displayed.

4. Select Formats to schedule a document to refresh as a Web Intelligence, Microsoft Excel, Adobe Acrobat, or CSV file.

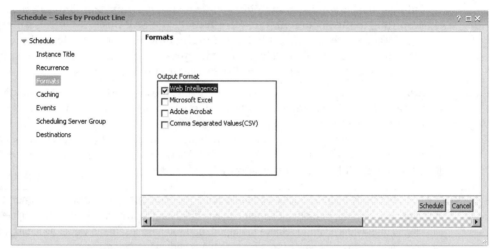

5. Select Destinations if you want to send the output to a BusinessObjects Inbox, a file location, FTP server, or e-mail address. To send a report to an e-mail recipient, select the Destination as Email, and then select Destinations Options and Settings. You can use the default settings established by the administrator by selecting Use default settings or specify your own e-mail settings.

For an e-mail destination, specify the following settings:

- **From** Enter your e-mail address using the full syntax, in the form *webiuser1@yourcompany.com.*

- **To** Enter the recipient's e-mail address. The recipient does not need to be defined on the SAP BusinessObjects Enterprise server.

- **Subject** Here, you can enter either static text or dynamic text that is populated according to the document title, refresh time, and SAP BusinessObjects Enterprise login ID. To have the subject line filled in dynamically, select the desired text from the Add placeholder drop-down list. In the preceding example, the document title will appear as the subject, as specified by the placeholder %SI_NAME%.

- **Message** Enter text to appear in the e-mail notification when the scheduled report is available. In the example, the placeholders for the document title (%SI_NAME%) and the date and time the report was scheduled (%SI_STARTTIME%) have been inserted into the message. Within the message, you can insert a hyperlink for the recipient to click to view the report via InfoView. To do so, select Viewer Hyperlink from the Add placeholder drop-down list.

NOTE When you specify a format such as Adobe Acrobat (PDF) or Excel, you can send the report as an attachment. If, however, your output format remains the default of Web Intelligence, the recipient must log in to BI Launch Pad to retrieve the report, or if you have inserted a viewer hyperlink, the recipient can click the hyperlink to go directly to the scheduled report instance.

6. After you've set all of the desired schedule options, click the Schedule button.

Logging Off

After a certain period of inactivity, your BI Launch Pad session will give you a timeout warning.

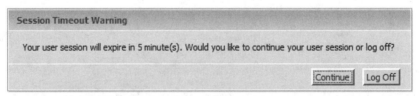

If you do not select Continue or Log Off, your session will timeout, and you will receive a session timeout message.

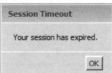

For security reasons, it is best to log out when you are finished working with SAP BusinessObjects BI 4.0. If your BI Launch Pad preferences have each document open in a separate browser window, first save and close those additional windows. Then, from the BI Launch Pad Header panel, select Log Off.

Summary

This chapter covered the basics of viewing a document using the Web Intelligence web viewer and understanding a document's components. A Web Intelligence document is much more than a report; it can contain multiple data sources and multiple report blocks to convey information from multiple perspectives. A document instance is a snapshot of the data. As data is updated in your source systems, you will need to refresh your document. For reports based on continually changing data, you may wish to schedule your documents to refresh on a periodic basis. The next chapter highlights the more powerful capabilities of interacting with a document to analyze your data.

Report-Based Analysis and Formatting

The previous chapter introduced how to interact with Web Intelligence documents using the web viewer. You learned how to open, view, refresh, navigate, print, schedule, and export Web Intelligence documents.

This chapter describes how to further explore data within an existing report to make it more meaningful. Such analysis can range from viewing information in a different block style (such as a table, crosstab, or chart), to re-sorting, adding breaks and calculations, ranking, filtering, and drilling down into the details. These report-based analysis techniques are helpful to both report consumers and power users.

In BusinessObjects XI, report consumers needed the HTML Interactive Viewer to accomplish many of these report tasks. In SAP BusinessObjects BI 4.0, the HTML Interactive Viewer no longer exists. The user interface of the web viewer has been redesigned to simplify and provide consistency between the web viewer reading mode and design mode. Thus, these actions are available using the web viewer, which seamlessly launches the Web Intelligence report design mode.

Web Intelligence Report Design Mode

In Chapter 17, we worked with the web viewer in reading mode. Figure 18-1 shows the Sales by Product Line and Year report in the web viewer in design mode. Compare this to the same report shown in Figure 17-1 in reading mode. (As in Chapter 17, we assume you are opening a document using the web viewer within the BI Launch Pad as a new tab, as set in your BI Launch Pad preferences.)

Notice that in design mode, there are now toolboxes (tabs) for modifying all objects and attributes of the report. Additionally, the left panel in design mode includes an Available Objects button, which displays all objects in the query (but perhaps not displayed in the report), and a Document Structure and Filters button, which displays all the objects (cells, tables, crosstabs, charts, and so on) and filters that are defined for the report.

Toolbar(s)　　　Toolboxes

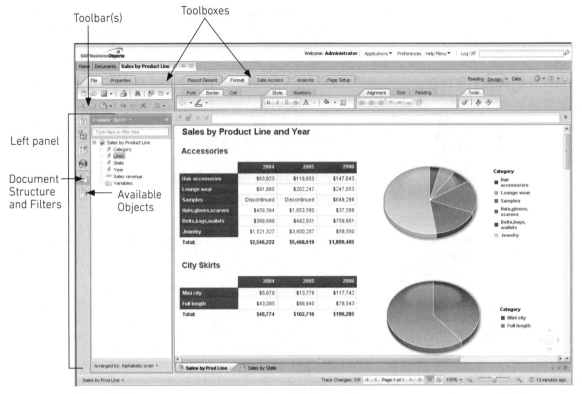

Left panel

Document
Structure
and Filters

Available
Objects

Figure 18-1 A document in the web viewer design mode

To open a document in web viewer design mode, follow these steps:

1. Locate the document you would like to open. The document could be on the Home tab as one of your recently viewed or run documents, or on the Documents tab in your My Documents drawer or Folders drawer.

2. Double-click the name of the document. Alternatively, right-click the document name and select View from the drop-down menu.

3. Click the Design option in the upper-right corner of the viewer.

Block Types

Chapter 17 introduced the different components of a Web Intelligence report and the concept of a block. A *block* is a set of data that contains column headings, row headings, and data values. Web Intelligence allows several block types: table, crosstab, form, and chart. A report can contain multiple block types. Each block can be populated from the same query or a different query.

NOTE A master/detail is a type of report, but not specifically a block type. Within a master/detail report, you specify groupings or sections of data and block type(s) to appear in each section. Figure 18-1, for example, has both a crosstab block and a chart block within each section of a master/detail report. Master/detail reports are discussed in the next section.

Table 18-1 summarizes the different block types and when to use them.

You can easily create a new block type, convert an existing block to another block type, or duplicate a block and then convert it to a new block type.

Working with Tables

When you initially create a new report, Web Intelligence uses the default block type of a vertical table. A table is a spreadsheet-style block that lists data in rows and columns.

You can easily convert a table to another block type. For example, you may want to change the following vertical table to a bar chart to further analyze the individual data values. In this example, using a chart is a good way to visually display that Texas, New York, and California stores have the highest revenues.

State	Sales revenue
California	$7,479,569
Colorado	$2,060,275
DC	$2,961,950
Florida	$1,879,159
Illinois	$3,022,968
Massachusetts	$1,283,707
New York	$7,582,221
Texas	$10,117,664

Block Type	Use When...
Table	You want to detail information in a list or spreadsheet style. You may group the list into sections with breaks. Tables can have many columns containing multiple dimensions, details, and measures. Tables can be either vertical (column headings across the top) or horizontal (column headings down the side).
Chart	You want to discover trends and patterns by exploring summary, not detail, numbers in a visual format. Charts are ideal for analyzing a limited number of measures by a limited number of dimensions.
Crosstab	You want to compare one or more measures by two or more different dimensions in a matrix style. A crosstab is a particular kind of table layout that would let you display, for example, sales (measure) by category and year (dimensions) with category listed down the side and year listed across the top.
Form	You want to see many details for a particular product, customer, or record. Instead of viewing a very wide report in which a lot of details are displayed on one row, a form lets you view the details placed throughout the page.

Table 18-1 Web Intelligence Report Block Types

To convert a table to a column chart, follow these steps:

1. Click the table.
2. Right-click, and select Turn Into | Column from the pop-up menu.

3. The data will now appear in a column chart.

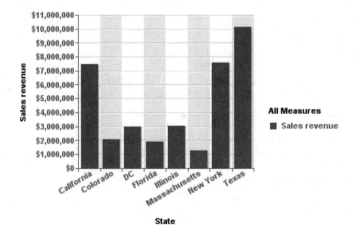

TIP Tables can also be created and maintained from the Report Elements toolbox.

Working with Crosstabs

A crosstab is the best block type for quick comparisons. It transposes what may originally be rows in a tabular report to column headings.

Crosstabs are frequently used for the following types of analysis:

- Customer sales by year, quarter, or month
- Financial measures by actual and budget
- Product sales by region

State	Year	Sales revenue
California	2004	$1,704,211
California	2005	$2,782,680
California	2006	$2,992,679
Colorado	2004	$448,302
Colorado	2005	$768,390
Colorado	2006	$843,584
DC	2004	$693,211
DC	2005	$1,215,158
DC	2006	$1,053,581
Florida	2004	$405,985
Florida	2005	$661,250
Florida	2006	$811,924
Illinois	2004	$738,224
Illinois	2005	$1,150,659
Illinois	2006	$1,134,085

To convert a block to a crosstab, follow these steps:

1. Select the block, right-click, and select Turn Into | More Transformations… from the pop-up menu to open the Turn Into dialog box. Select Tables, and then select CrossTab to display the crosstab options in the right pane.

2. Set the Horizontal Axis option to Year, the Vertical Axis option to State, and the Body Axis option to Sales Revenue.

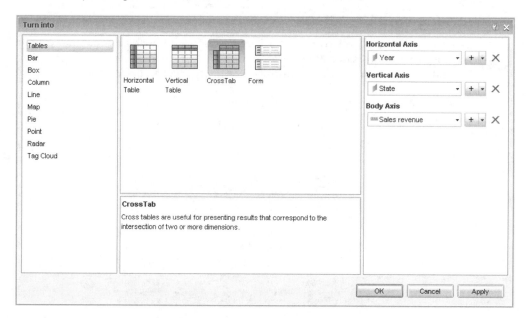

3. Click OK. The crosstab will display in the report.

	2004	2005	2006
California	$1,704,211	$2,782,680	$2,992,679
Colorado	$448,302	$768,390	$843,584
DC	$693,211	$1,215,158	$1,053,581
Florida	$405,985	$661,250	$811,924
Illinois	$738,224	$1,150,659	$1,134,085
Massachusetts	$238,819	$157,719	$887,169
New York	$1,667,696	$2,763,503	$3,151,022
Texas	$2,199,677	$3,732,889	$4,185,098

Crosstabs can have multiple dimensions for both the horizontal and vertical axes, as well as multiple measures in the body axis. To convert a block to a crosstab with multiple dimensions on an axis, follow the preceding steps, but in the Turn Into dialog box, click the plus sign (+) next to the Horizontal Axis, Vertical Axis, or Body Axis option to define additional values.

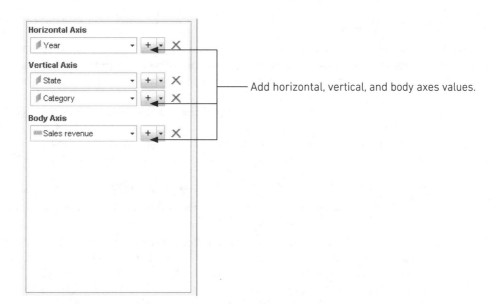

Add horizontal, vertical, and body axes values.

When you click OK, the crosstab will appear with multiple dimensions on the axis you selected.

		2004	2005	2006
California	2 Pocket shirts	$50,999	$33,103	$145,319
California	Belts,bags,wallets	$66,063	$80,787	$150,224
California	Bermudas	$5,290	$7,546	$3,245
California	Boatwear	$10,974	$6,256	$37,239
California	Cardigan	$44,294	$113,519	$2,665
California	Casual dresses	$11,240	$29,683	$24,306
California	Day wear	$46,460	$106,376	$4,401
California	Dry wear	$12,923	$26,033	$6,650
California	Evening wear	$84,664	$160,458	$70,661
California	Fancy fabric	$8,443	$15,033	$17,034
California	Full length	$10,954	$22,647	$15,686

TIP You can also drag-and-drop to define additional column (horizontal axis), row (vertical axis), and body (body axis) values.

Working with Charts

Charts are a powerful way to uncover trends and patterns in your data. They can transform a dense page of numbers into a visual that quickly highlights opportunities and problems. Web Intelligence provides numerous chart styles. Advanced charting and formatting are discussed in Chapter 20.

When you create a chart, you may want to display the detail numeric values alongside the chart, or you may need only a subset of the data that appears in a table. In these cases, we recommend using copy and paste to first create a second table and then convert it to a chart. As an example, here's how to copy a block and convert it to a pie chart:

1. Select the block that you want to convert to a chart, right-click, and select Copy.

2. Right-click in the area of the report where you would like to place the chart and select Paste.

3. If the block contains only the dimensions and measures that you want to be included in the chart, right-click, select Turn Into, and choose a chart type. For more formatting options, right-click, select Turn Into | More Transformations…, and choose the chart type. In this example, select Pie, and then choose Pie Chart from the Turn Into dialog box. Select parameters in the right pane to define the chart. For this example, set the Pie Sector Size option to Sales Revenue and the Pie Chart Selector Color option to State.

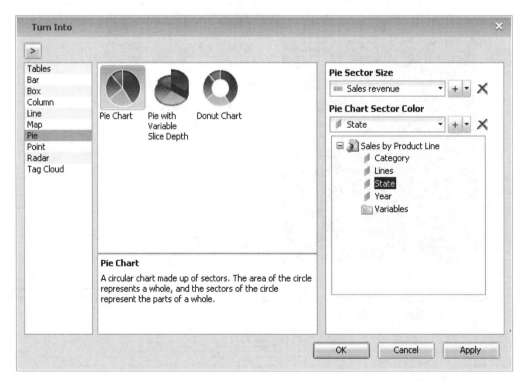

4. Click OK. The pie chart will appear in the report.

	2004	2005	2006
Belts,bags,wallets	$389,699	$492,931	$759,861
Hair accessories	$83,923	$119,953	$147,043
Hats,gloves,scarves	$459,394	$1,053,580	$37,588
Jewelry	$1,521,327	$3,600,207	$58,560
Lounge wear	$91,880	$202,247	$247,053
Samples	Discontinued	Discontinued	$649,298
Total:	**$2,546,222**	**$5,468,919**	**$1,899,405**

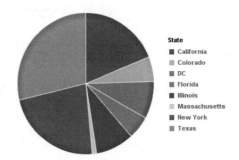

State
- California
- Colorado
- DC
- Florida
- Illinois
- Massachusetts
- New York
- Texas

Master/Detail Reports

A *master/detail report* is a particular kind of report in which a dimension value (*master*) is used to group data (*detail*) into separate sections. Master/detail reports allow you to analyze and format data for each unique master data value.

The report shown earlier in Figure 18-1 is an example of a master/detail report that contains a crosstab and a pie chart for each product line, which is the dimension that is defined as the master. The report in Figure 18-1 displays two sections on the product line: Accessories and City Skirts. Compare the layout in Figure 18-1 to the layout in Figure 18-2, in which the product lines (Accessories, City Skirts, and so on) are just in columns in the crosstab and not in separate sections.

Right-click dimension to set as section.

		2004	2005	2006
Accessories	Belts,bags,wallets	$389,699	$492,931	$759,861
Accessories	Hair accessories	$83,923	$119,953	$147,043
Accessories	Hats,gloves,scarves	$459,394	$1,053,580	$37,588
Accessories	Jewelry	$1,521,327	$3,600,207	$58,560
Accessories	Lounge wear	$91,880	$202,247	$247,053
Accessories	Samples	Discontinued	Discontinued	$649,298
City Skirts	Full length	$43,095	$88,940	$78,543
City Skirts	Mini city	$5,679	$13,776	$117,742
City Trousers	Bermudas	$29,790	$53,794	$21,587
City Trousers	Long lounge pants	$44,033	$90,586	$44,944
Dresses	Casual dresses	$63,299	$145,319	$174,085
Dresses	Evening wear	$407,860	$711,590	$400,939
Dresses	Skirts	$21,277	Discontinued	$618,540
Dresses	Sweater dresses	$57,195	$100,487	$215,031
Jackets	Boatwear	$43,070	$18,950	$183,335
Jackets	Fancy fabric	$25,281	$53,404	$76,931
Jackets	Outdoor	$77,847	$154,384	$44,415

Figure 18-2   This crosstab does not yet have a section defined to make it a master/detail report.

Part III

To change a dimension in a block to a master (section), right-click the dimension you wish to set as a section and select Set as section.

The master/detail report is displayed with sections.

Accessories

	2004	2005	2006
Belts,bags,wallets	$389,699	$492,931	$759,861
Hair accessories	$83,923	$119,953	$147,043
Hats,gloves,scarves	$459,394	$1,053,580	$37,588
Jewelry	$1,521,327	$3,600,207	$58,560
Lounge wear	$91,880	$202,247	$247,053
Samples	Discontinued	Discontinued	$649,298

City Skirts

	2004	2005	2006
Full length	$43,095	$88,940	$78,543
Mini city	$5,679	$13,776	$117,742

City Trousers

	2004	2005	2006
Bermudas	$29,790	$53,794	$21,587
Long lounge pants	$44,033	$90,586	$44,944

NOTE Sections can also be created and maintained from the Report Elements toolbox.

Sorts

Web Intelligence, by default, sorts data in a table by the leftmost column as the primary sort, the second column as the secondary sort, and so on. Sorting data within a table allows you to override this default and rearrange the rows based on any dimension or measure in the table.

A sort on a string dimension will be alphabetic, and a sort on a date dimension will be in date order. If your sort is on a measure column, the order will be numerical. For example, if you sort in descending order by a sales measure, your report will be sorted by stores with the highest sales down to stores with the lowest sales, and therefore you will be able to quickly identify which stores have the highest sales.

NOTE When you have both breaks and sorts in a table, the breaks will take sorting priority over the sorts. Breaks are discussed in the next section.

In the following example, you will sort revenue in descending order to identify which stores have the highest revenues.

1. Select the column you wish to sort within the table. For this example, select Sales Revenue. Web Intelligence highlights the selected column with a gray box.

2. Right-click Sales Revenue and select Sort | Descending from the pop-up menu.

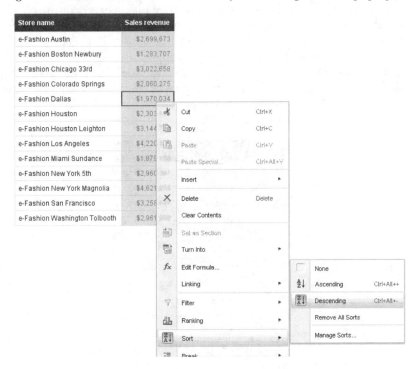

The report is now displayed in descending order by sales revenue.

NOTE Sorts can also be created and managed from the Analysis toolbox.

Managing Multiple Sorts

You can add multiple sorts to a table by following the preceding steps. Sort priority is assigned in the order that the sorts are added to the table. For example, if the first sort added is on Product Line, and the second sort added is on Product Category, then Product Line is the primary sort and Product Category is the secondary sort.

You can manage sorts and sort priorities through the Manage Sorts dialog box. To access this dialog box, select the table on which you wish to manage sorts, right-click, and select Sort | Manage Sorts…. Here, you can change the sort priority, modify the sort order (ascending or descending), and add or remove objects in the sort. Click OK to apply your changes.

Creating Custom Sorts

When you create a sort in Web Intelligence, you are asked to define the order for that sort as either ascending or descending. For example, if the object that you are using to define the sort is a string data type, then the data in the table will be sorted in either ascending (alphabetical) or descending (reverse alphabetical) order. But what if you want a different order than either ascending or descending sorting provides?

Consider the following table, which is sorted in ascending order according to the product line. Notice that the Other row appears between the Leather and Outerwear row. Suppose you would prefer to see Other at the bottom of the list. To have this arrangement, you can create a custom sort.

Lines	Sales revenue
Accessories	$9,914,546
City Skirts	$347,775
City Trousers	$284,734
Dresses	$2,915,620
Jackets	$677,616
Leather	$187,413
Other	$4,018,220
Outerwear	$1,183,083
Overcoats	$436,258
Sweaters	$2,839,035
Sweat-T-Shirts	$12,679,893
Trousers	$903,320

To create a custom sort, follow these steps:

1. Select the table on which you wish to create a custom sort, right-click, and select Sort | Manage Sorts…. to open the Manage Sorts dialog box.

2. If the table is not already sorted by the object on which you want to create a custom sort (Product Lines in this example), click the Add button. The Add Sort dialog box will appear.

3. Select Product Lines, and then click OK to return to the Manage Sorts dialog box.

4. Select Custom Order: Values…. The Custom Sort dialog box will appear.

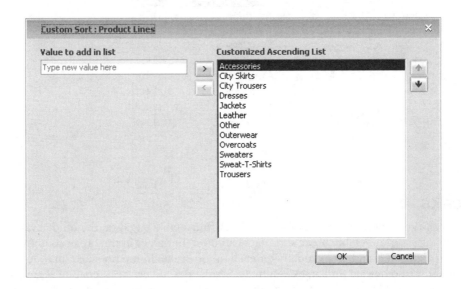

5. Select the values in the list and manually order them using the up and down arrows. For this example, move Other to the bottom of the list.

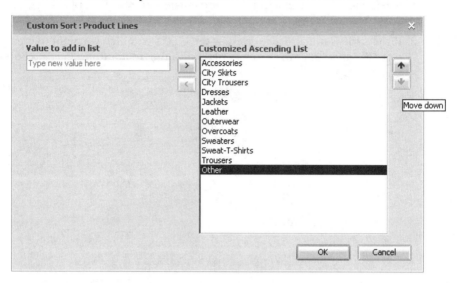

6. Click OK to return to the Manage Sorts dialog box.
7. Click OK to apply the sort and return to the report design.

Lines	Sales revenue
Accessories	$9,914,546
City Skirts	$347,775
City Trousers	$284,734
Dresses	$2,915,620
Jackets	$677,616
Leather	$187,413
Outerwear	$1,183,083
Overcoats	$436,258
Sweaters	$2,839,035
Sweat-T-Shirts	$12,679,893
Trousers	$903,320
Other	$4,018,220

Breaks

A *break* in a table creates segments or cuts within a table based on the unique values in the break column. A table break sorts data based on the values in the break column, and creates break headers and break footers for each unique value in the break column. A master/detail report is somewhat similar, except that a break does not create a separate report section. Also, a break column must exist in the table, whereas a section header in a master/detail report does not need to exist in any block (or even be displayed in the section).

Once you create a break, you can then use calculations to generate subtotals (or other aggregate calculations, including averages, maximums, minimums, and so on). The first break column becomes the primary sort order, and a break sort will override any other sorts defined on the table. Often, this is the first column in the table, but it can be another column.

Adding a Break

To add a break to a table, right-click the column in the table on which you want to create the table break (the break column) and select Break | Add Break from the menu.

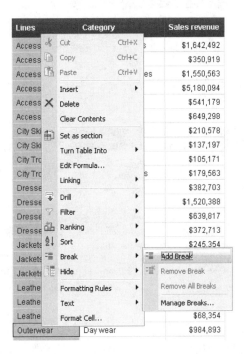

In the following example, Lines was selected as the break column, and the report displays with the breaks for each unique value in that column.

NOTE Although breaks make the data appear as if it were in separate mini-tables, Web Intelligence still treats the table as one block, an important nuance when formatting the table. In Figure 18-3, the Format Table... options will be the same for all break values, including Accessories and City Skirts.

Managing Breaks

Figure 18-3 also shows the effects of the break options, which control how the breaks display, how duplicate values are handled, and how page breaking is controlled across break values.

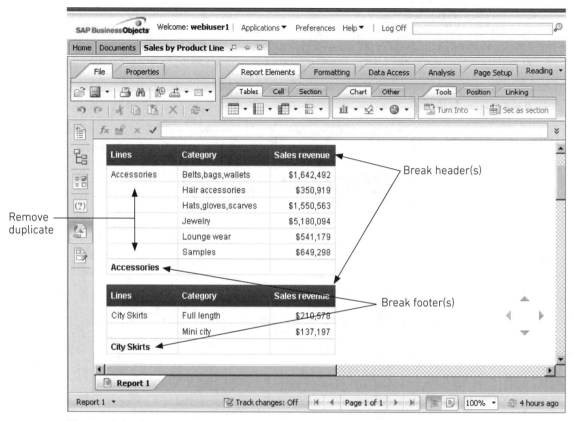

Figure 18-3 Table breaks group data based on unique values in the break column.

To modify break options, right-click the table and select Break | Manage Breaks…. The Manage Breaks dialog box will display. In this dialog box, you can set the options described in Table 18-2.

Break Option Group	Break Option Setting	Description
Display Properties	Break header	Repeats the column headings on every break value. This option can also be used to display the break column value or any other data object or formula.
	Break footer	Adds a footer for each break value. A break footer is often used to display subtotals or other aggregate calculations.
	Apply sort	Applies the default sort order for the values in the break.
Duplicate Values	Display all	Displays all the break column values, including the repeated ones.
	Display first	Displays the break column value only once on the first record of the break. Figure 18-3 shows breaks with this option selected.
	Merge	Displays the break column value once, centered on the table break with the column merged.
	Repeat first on new page	Displays the break column value on the first record of the break. However, if the break spans multiple pages, the break column value will be repeated on the first record of each page.
Page Layout	Start on a new page	Starts each break on a new page. This option is used to display only one break value per page.
	Avoid page breaks in block	Allows for multiple breaks to appear on a page. However, if a break value cannot be entirely printed prior to a page break, a page break is inserted before starting the printing of the break value.
	Repeat header on every page	Prints the row(s) of the break header on each new page if a break value is split between multiple pages.

Table 18-2   Break Options

NOTE Breaks can also be created and managed from the Analysis toolbox.

Calculations

Calculations allow you to add subtotals and other aggregate calculations (such as minimum, maximum, average, and count) to a table that contains breaks. If the table does not contain any breaks, then the calculations inserted are grand totals for the entire block. The calculations are added to the break footer as formulas.

The calculations that are available are context-sensitive, depending on the object data type (character, date, or number). For example, you may want to *count* the number of product categories that exist in a product line, but the product category object could never be *summed*. Therefore, only numeric measure objects can be used as input to the sum, average, and percentage calculations.

Web Intelligence automatically inserts the calculation you choose on all break footers and as a grand total on the table footer. You can use the page navigation buttons to scroll to the last page to see the grand totals.

You can easily add calculations to tables by using the Insert pop-up menu. For example, to insert a sum calculation and average calculation for sales revenue in the break footer, right-click the Sales Revenue column in the table and select Insert | Sum from the pop-up menu. The subtotal will appear in the break footer, as well as in the table footer.

Lines	Categories	Sales revenue
Accessories	Belts,bags,wallets	$1,642,492
	Hair accessories	$350,919
	Hats,gloves,scarves	$1,550,563
	Jewelry	$5,180,094
	Lounge wear	$541,179
	Samples	$649,298
Accessories	Sum:	**$9,914,546**

Lines	Categories	Sales revenue
City Skirts	Full length	$210,578
	Mini city	$137,197
City Skirts	Sum:	**$347,775**

Lines	Categories	Sales revenue
City Trousers	Bermudas	$105,171
	Long lounge pants	$179,563
City Trousers	Sum:	**$284,734**

TIP Consider formatting the break footer row so that your subtotals stand out.

Table 18-3 lists the calculations available via the Analysis | Functions toolbox or Insert pop-up menu, as well as the formula syntax that is automatically inserted in the break footer.

NOTE Calculations can also be created and managed from the Analys\is | Functions toolbox.

Filters

As you apply breaks, sorts, and calculations, you may find that you want to focus on one or more subsets of data within the report. Filters allow you to restrict the data displayed in one or multiple blocks in the report. For example, in Figure 18-3 (shown earlier in the chapter), the table shows several product lines. To focus only on the specific product lines,

Calculation	Description	Formula
Sum	Sums the values for a particular measure. SUM() is available only on measure objects. Used to display a subtotal value, such as total sales by product line: SUM([Sales Revenue)].	=SUM([*Measure Variable*])
Count	Counts the unique values of an object. Used to display the total number of values, such as the count of product categories in a product line: COUNT([Lines]).	=COUNT([*Dimension or Measure Variable*])
Average	Calculates the average value for a measure. Used to display the average value, such as the average sales revenue by product line: AVERAGE([Sales Revenue]). This is not a weighted average, so for calculations such as average price, you may want to create a formula to get a weighted average or use extended syntax, as discussed in Chapter 21.	=AVERAGE([*Measure Variable*])
Minimum	Displays the minimum value for a particular measure, such as the lowest sales revenue for a product category within a product line: MIN([Sales Revenue]).	=MIN([*Dimension or Measure Variable*])
Maximum	Displays the maximum value for a particular measure within the break.	=MAX([*Dimension or Measure Variable*])
Percentage	Calculates the percentage contribution a numeric value makes to the subtotal or grand total. It also inserts a new column that shows the percentage each row contributes to the individual break level. This calculation uses the ForAll context operator, which is described in Chapter 21.	=PERCENTAGE([*Measure Variable*]) ForAll (*[Dimension Variable]*)

Table 18-3 Calculation Options

you could insert a filter on the Lines column. Filters do not affect the query results; they affect only the data currently displayed in the block.

NOTE When you apply a filter, the calculations will also change to reflect only what is displayed.

Adding and Removing Filters

To add a filter to a table, follow these steps:

1. Right-click the column on which you want to filter the data (Lines in this example) and select Filter | Add Filter from the pop-up menu. The Report Filter dialog box appears.

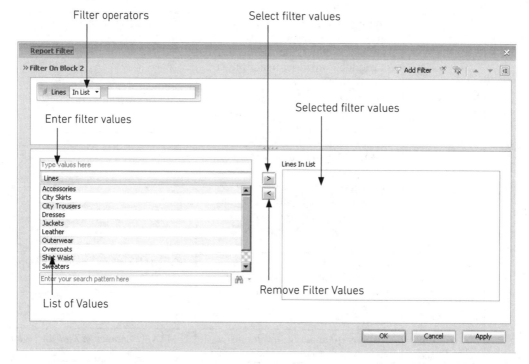

2. Select the values you wish to include in the filter to display in the block and add them to the selection box on the right, either by double-clicking the value or selecting the value and clicking the > button.

3. By default, the In List operator is used to allow you to select multiple filter values. You can change the setting to use another filter operator, such as Equal, Between, or Greater Than. Operators are discussed in Chapter 19.

4. Click OK to return to the report and see the block with the filter applied.

NOTE Filters can also be created and managed from the Analysis | Filters toolbox.

To remove a filter, right-click the data object that has the filter applied (Lines in this example) and select Filter | Remove Filter from the pop-up menu.

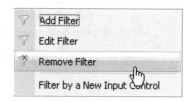

Filtering on Measure Objects

You can easily filter on measure objects in a similar fashion to filtering on dimension objects. In the following example, you'll use a measure filter to find which categories have greater than $1,000,000 in sales revenue.

To create a measure filter, follow these steps:

1. Right-click the Sales Revenue column and select Filter | Add Filter.

2. In the Report Filter dialog box, select the Greater than or Equal to operator.

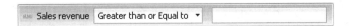

3. Note that a list of values is not available for measures. Enter the value in the input box titled "Sales revenue Greater than or Equal to." For this example, enter **1000000**.

4. Click OK to return to the report and see the block with the filter applied.

Using Report Filters

In the previous examples, filters were applied to a single block of data within a report. In this way, you can apply *different* filters to different blocks of data in a single report. If you want to apply the *same* filter to *all* blocks in a report, use a *report filter*. Report filters are global filters that apply to all blocks in a report.

To create a report filter, follow these steps:

1. Right-click in the report design panel, anywhere on the report outside a block, and select Filter | Add Filter. The Report Filter dialog box displays.

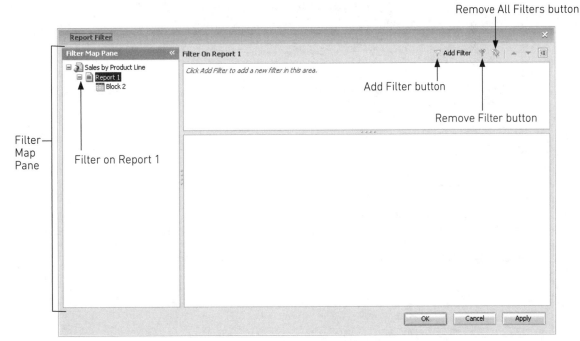

2. Click the Add Filter button and add a filter that you want to apply to the entire report. For this example, add a filter on the Lines column, using the In List operator, for the Accessories, Leather, and Sweaters values.

3. Click OK. The filter will apply for *all* blocks on the report.

NOTE Any blocks added to a report with a report filter, either before or after the report filter is defined, will be subject to the filter criteria.

Nested Filters

Nested filters are used when you need to test for more than one condition on multiple data objects. For example, suppose you have set a sales target for product categories that are in the product lines Accessories, Dresses, Sweaters, and Shirt Waist to have sales revenues greater than $500,000. For the other product categories, you set a sales revenue target of $300,000. To identify which product categories have met these targets, you can use a nested filter, as shown in Figure 18-4.

NOTE Nested filters can be used on either report filters or block filters.

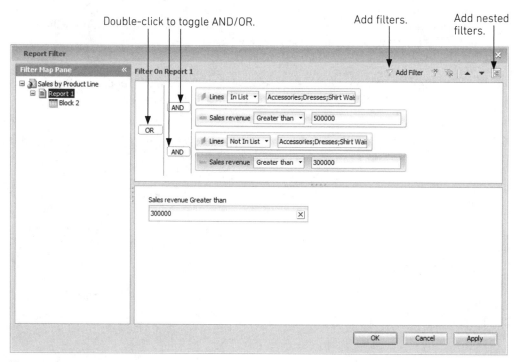

Figure 18-4 Filters can be nested.

Nesting filters can be rather tricky. You must have a clear understanding of which filters you wanted connected with an AND or an OR and how to nest your filters. There is no perfectly easy way to create nested filters. You can follow a three-step process to apply a nested filter:

- Create all of the individual filter conditions.
- Define the nesting.
- Define the AND/OR logic.

Let's look at how to use this process to apply the nested filters shown in Figure 18-4.

Creating the Filter Conditions

To create each of the individual filter conditions required for the nested condition shown in Figure 18-4, follow these steps:

1. Select the Filter button from the Analysis | Filters toolbox to open the Report Filter dialog box.
2. Click the Add Filter button and define the first filter condition. For this example, add Lines and use the In List operator. Select the Accessories, Dresses, Shirt Waist, and Sweaters values.
3. Click the Add Filter button and define the second filter condition. For this example, add Sales Revenue Greater than $500,000.
4. Click the Add Filter button and define the third filter condition. For this example, add Lines and use the Not In List operator. Choose the Accessories, Dresses, Shirt Waist, and Sweaters values.
5. Click the Add Filter button and define the fourth filter condition. For this example, add Sales Revenue Greater than $300,000. At this point, your filter definition will look like the following example.

Defining the Nesting

Follow these steps to create the nesting required for the condition displayed in Figure 18-4:

1. Click the Add Nested Filters button. An empty nesting bucket will appear.

2. Drag the appropriate filter conditions to this nesting bucket. For this example, drag the filter condition Lines In List Accessories, Dresses, Shirt Waist, Sweaters and Sales Revenue Greater than 500000 to be nested.

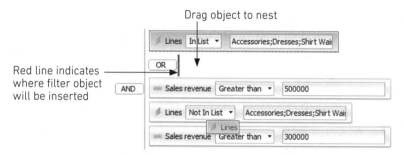

3. Make sure that you do not have any of the two filter condition objects that have already been nested selected (this would create a third-level nesting) and click the Add Nested Filters button. An empty nesting bucket will appear.

4. Drag the appropriate filter conditions to this nesting bucket. For this example, drag the filter condition Lines Not In List Accessories, Dresses, Shirt Waist, Sweaters and Sales Revenue Greater than 300000 to be nested.

Defining the AND/OR Logic

Finally, define the AND/OR logic required for the condition displayed in Figure 18-4 as follows:

1. Double-click the first-level AND to toggle it to OR.

2. Double-click each of the second-level (nested) ORs to toggle them to ANDs.

3. Click OK to apply your nested filter.

Ranking

Ranking allows you to both sort and optionally filter the rows displayed in a block according to top or bottom subtotals of measures by dimensions. As discussed earlier in this chapter, in a conventional sort, you select either a dimension or measure object in your block for sorting. The difference between ranking and conventional sorting is that in ranking, you are sorting (either ascending, bottom *n* or descending, top *n*) by a *subtotal* (or other aggregate calculation) of a measure over a dimension. Table 18-4 shows how to use ranking for some typical business questions.

The Web Intelligence ranking feature offers four different modes for ranking data:

- **Count**   Allows you to specify a fixed numeric value of dimensions, such as the top ten or the bottom three.

- **Percentage**   Allows you to specify a fixed number representing the percentage of total number of dimension values. In our example, there are 12 product lines. So if you select 50 percent, the rank will return the top six product lines (if you selected top) or the bottom six product lines (if you selected bottom).

Business Question	Measure to Rank	Dimension to Rank by
Which business units have the highest expense variance?	Expense Variance	Business Unit
What are the top-selling products?	Sales Quantity	Product
Which customers generate the most revenues?	Sales Revenue	Customer
Which warehouses have the most product on hand?	Inventory	Product
Who are the lowest selling salespeople?	Sales Amount	Salesperson

Table 18-4 Ranking for Common Business Questions

- **Cumulative Sum** Looks at the running totals for the measure object specified. For example, if you set the bottom value to 1,000,000, the rank will return the bottom four product lines.

- **Cumulative Percentage** Allows you to specify a fixed numeric value representing the cumulative percentage, such as the top 80 percent of sales revenue.

Figure 18-5 illustrates the differences between these four different modes. The tables on the left show the detailed data used for each of the modes for both a top and bottom ranking.

TOP RANKING

Product Lines	Sales Revenue	Count	Percent	Cumulative Sum	Cumulative Pct
Sweat-T-Shirts	$12,679,893	1	8.33%	$12,679,893	34.85%
Accessories	$9,914,546	2	16.67%	$22,594,439	62.09%
Shirt Waist	$4,018,220	3	25.00%	$26,612,658	73.14%
Dresses	$2,915,620	4	33.33%	$29,528,278	81.15%
Sweaters	$2,839,035	5	41.67%	$32,367,313	88.95%
Outerwear	$1,183,083	6	50.00%	$33,550,396	92.20%
Trousers	$903,320	7	58.33%	$34,453,716	94.69%
Jackets	$677,616	8	66.67%	$35,131,333	96.55%
Overcoats	$436,258	9	75.00%	$35,567,591	97.75%
City Skirts	$347,775	10	83.33%	$35,915,366	98.70%
City Trousers	$284,734	11	91.67%	$36,200,100	99.48%
Leather	$187,413	12	100.00%	$36,387,512	100.00%

Top: 3 | Mode: Count

Product Lines	Sales Revenue
Sweat-T-Shirts	$12,679,893
Accessories	$9,914,546
Shirt Waist	$4,018,220

Top: 35% | Mode: Percent

Product Lines	Sales Revenue
Sweat-T-Shirts	$12,679,893
Accessories	$9,914,546
Shirt Waist	$4,018,220
Dresses	$2,915,620

Top: 1,000,000 | Mode: Cumulative Sum

Product Lines	Sales Revenue
Sweat-T-Shirts	$12,679,893

Top: 75% | Mode: Cumulative Percent

Product Lines	Sales Revenue
Sweat-T-Shirts	$12,679,893
Accessories	$9,914,546
Shirt Waist	$4,018,220

BOTTOM RANKING

Product Lines	Sales Revenue	Count	Percent	Cumulative Sum	Cumulative Pct
Leather	$187,413	1	8.33%	$187,413	0.52%
City Trousers	$284,734	2	16.67%	$472,147	1.30%
City Skirts	$347,775	3	25.00%	$819,922	2.25%
Overcoats	$436,258	4	33.33%	$1,256,180	3.45%
Jackets	$677,616	5	41.67%	$1,933,796	5.31%
Trousers	$903,320	6	50.00%	$2,837,116	7.80%
Outerwear	$1,183,083	7	58.33%	$4,020,199	11.05%
Sweaters	$2,839,035	8	66.67%	$6,859,234	18.85%
Dresses	$2,915,620	9	75.00%	$9,774,854	26.86%
Shirt Waist	$4,018,220	10	83.33%	$13,793,074	37.91%
Accessories	$9,914,546	11	91.67%	$23,707,620	65.15%
Sweat-T-Shirts	$12,679,893	12	100.00%	$36,387,512	100.00%

Bottom: 5 | Mode: Count

Product Lines	Sales Revenue
Leather	$187,413
City Trousers	$284,734
City Skirts	$347,775
Overcoats	$436,258
Jackets	$677,616

Bottom: 25% | Mode: Percent

Product Lines	Sales Revenue
Leather	$187,413
City Trousers	$284,734
City Skirts	$347,775

Bottom: 1,000,000 | Mode: Cumul Sum

Product Lines	Sales Revenue
Leather	$187,413
City Trousers	$284,734
City Skirts	$347,775
Overcoats	$436,258

Bottom: 5% | Mode: Cumulative Pct

Product Lines	Sales Revenue
Leather	$187,413
City Trousers	$284,734
City Skirts	$347,775
Overcoats	$436,258
Jackets	$677,616

Figure 18-5 There are four calculation modes to use in ranking.

NOTE In prior versions of Web Intelligence, ranking also applied a sort on the aggregated measure value. For example, if you applied a top-three ranking on sales revenue by product line, the ranking would return the top-three product lines and sort in descending order by the subtotal of sales revenue for each product line in the top three. In SAP BusinessObjects BI 4.0, while the top three are accurately returned, the results will be displayed in the default sort order determined by the block. For example, in a standard table, the default sort order would be the leftmost column of the table. If you want the measure value for which you are determining the rank to also be the sort value, you must apply a sort to this column.

To add ranking to a block, follow these steps:

1. Right-click the block and dimension over which you wish to apply a ranking (Lines in this example) and select Ranking | Add Ranking. The same option is available on the Analysis | Filters toolbox.

2. Web Intelligence displays the Ranking dialog box. Select the calculation mode. For this example, select Count.

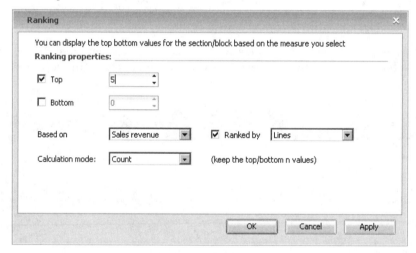

3. Select whether you would like a top or bottom sort and the number of values to display. In this example, select the Top option and set it to 5.

4. If you have more than one measure in the block you are ranking, choose the measure on which you want to base the ranking from the Ranked by drop-down list.

5. Click OK to apply the ranking.

6. Apply a sort to the measure object if you would like to sort the data in the order of your ranking.

Drilling Within Reports

So far in this chapter, you have explored many meaningful ways to analyze data in reports, including sorts, breaks, calculations, filters, and ranking. With multidimensional analysis and drilling, you look at the same data but from different viewpoints. The viewpoints may be from different levels of detail by drilling down, or from different dimensions by drilling across.

As you've learned, a *dimension* is a kind of object by which you analyze numeric measures. Dimensions often have different levels or groupings associated with them called *hierarchies. Multidimensional analysis* is the process of analyzing data by different dimensions and by different hierarchies. Within Web Intelligence, you can perform multidimensional analysis only with dimension objects, not with objects the designer has created as attribute objects.

Fixed reports often deal with standard, recurring information needs. Multidimensional analysis is more exploratory and relies on the user to discover trends and information through a drill session. For example, you may start with a standard management report that shows product sales for this year and last year. You see that sales for one product are lower this year than last year. You need to know *why*. So you begin to explore: were the sales bad for a particular region, salesperson, or quarter?

Hierarchies allow you to analyze data by different levels of detail. Some hierarchies are very clear-cut, such as Time: Year | Quarter | Month | Week | Day. There is a natural order. Geographic hierarchies are also very familiar to us: State | County | City | ZIP Code. When geographic hierarchies apply to marketing regions, however, each company introduces its own variation. For example, a company may define North, South, East, and West regions. Many of these groupings might be defined in your company's reference data and built into the enterprise resource planning (ERP) system or data warehouse. The universe designer uses these hierarchies to build the default drill paths you use for multidimensional analysis.

With Web Intelligence, you can drill *down* within a hierarchy, such as from year to quarter to month. You also can drill *across* by analyzing the current year or the past year; you are at the same level of detail (year), but you are changing the selection value that you are analyzing. You can analyze data by one dimension at a time (such as Time) or by several at once (such as Time, Geography, and Product). You can also drill against multiple report formats, including tables, crosstabs, and charts.

Web Intelligence allows you to specify several drill options through the BI Launch Pad preferences, as explained in Chapter 16. Table 18-5 summarizes each option.

Understanding the Data

You can easily get lost when drilling within a report. Therefore, it's helpful to first understand how the different universe objects relate to one another and where you are drilling from and to. Figure 18-6 shows two sample hierarchies for the eFashion universe: Time and Product. Each has four levels.

Option Type	Option	Description
Start Drill Session	On duplicate report	When first starting Drill mode, Web Intelligence will leave the current report intact and start the drill session on a copy of the report on a new report tab.
	On existing report	If you do not want a separate Drill mode report inserted, check this option. Note that when you enable Drill mode with this setting, Web Intelligence will remove all but the current block from the report. If your initial report has multiple blocks, do not use this option.
Drill Options	Prompt when drill requires additional data	As you drill through to details, check this box if you want the Extend the Scope of Analysis dialog box to be displayed to allow you to filter the data by drill filters and/or retrieve additional levels of detail in the same query.
	Synchronize drill on report blocks	If your report contains multiple blocks, such as a chart and a table, drill actions performed in one block are replicated in the other block.
	Hide drill toolbar on startup	As you drill, drill filters are automatically added in a toolbar. If you don't want the drill filter toolbar to appear, select this option.

Table 18-5 Web Intelligence Drill Options in BI Launch Pad Preferences

It's also important to understand that drilling often occurs with data that already exists within your report (or local microcube). You are not requerying the database when you drill.

Consider a simple Time hierarchy that contains Year, Quarter, and Month. When you construct a query, you first specify which columns of data you want to retrieve from the database. In this example, you would include the Year, Quarter, and Month dimensions in your query. Initially, the default report displays all columns of data. However, you can format the report, removing the Quarter and Month columns. Quarter and Month still exist in the microcube, but are not displayed in the report. This allows you to drill from Year to Quarter to Month without needing to execute a new query. However, if you want to drill down to a level of detail that does not already exist in the document—to Day, for example—then Web Intelligence will issue a new query and seamlessly display the additional level of detail. However, if Web Intelligence must run another query to get this additional level of detail, it could take a considerable amount of time, resulting in perceived application slowness.

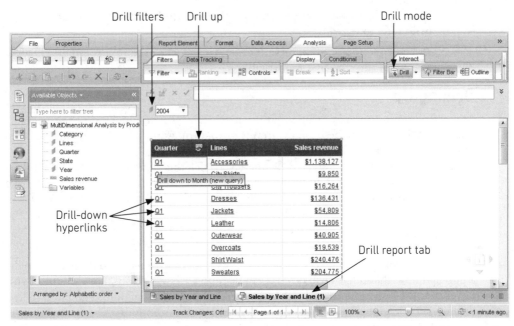

Figure 18-6   Understand the hierarchical nature of your dimensions before drilling within a report.

Drilling Down

With *drill-down*, you are looking for lower levels of detail within a hierarchy. In the following example, you will use this feature to discover which cities and stores in Texas have the highest revenues.

NOTE Be sure you have first set the desired BI Launch Pad preferences (see Table 18-5) before drilling. The following example assumes you chose to start a drill session on a duplicate report.

To drill down in a report, follow these steps:

1. Select Drill as the mode from the Analysis | Interact toolbox.

2. As shown in Figure 18-6, Web Intelligence inserts another report tab, naming it Sales by Year and Line (1). Click the Year column to drill down to Quarter.

3. From the drill filter toolbar, you can use the drop-down box to filter the current drill selection to all years or to an individual year.

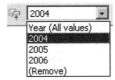

4. You can drill down from Quarter to Month or drill on another hierarchy, such as from Line to Category.

5. To return to the original version of the report, click the report tab titled Sales by Year and Line (the first report tab).

Drilling Up

As you drill down, you may decide that the particular level of detail did not provide meaningful insight into the business trends or that you want to explore details by other dimensions. You can *drill up* to the preceding summary level.

To move back up the hierarchy by one level, click the up arrow next to the dimension. For example, in Figure 18-6, to drill from Quarter back up to Year, click the up arrow next to Quarter. This will remove the detail column from the report and replace it with a column of data from one level up in the hierarchy.

Drilling By

You also can right-click while hovering the mouse cursor over a drilled dimension to display a pop-up menu that offers Drill down, Drill up, and Drill by options. For example, you might hover over the Year column and right-click to see this menu. This allows you to skip levels in drilling, such as going immediately from Year to Month without first previewing Quarter.

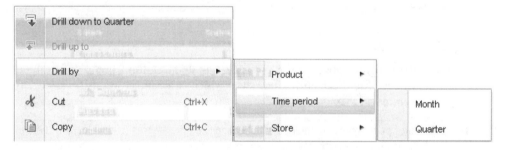

You can also use the Drill by option to explore data by other dimensions that exist in the document or microcube but that are not currently displayed in the report. In the preceding pop-up menu, Store | State would be an additional column of information that you can drill by without generating a new query. Selecting to drill by Month produces the same results as drilling down from Year to Quarter to Month. However, selecting to drill by to a dimension not yet in the report, such as State, creates an entirely new perspective on the data. Web Intelligence will automatically move the current column to the drill filter toolbar and replace it with the drill-by column, as in the following example.

State	Lines	Sales revenue
California	Accessories	$489,666
California	City Skirts	$11,072
California	City Trousers	$10,935
California	Dresses	$110,210
California	Jackets	$38,369
California	Leather	$26,912
California	Outerwear	$60,165
California	Overcoats	$22,094
California	Shirt Waist	$193,186
California	Sweaters	$70,720

The Drill by option is contextual and becomes more powerful when more details and columns of data are available in the microcube but not displayed in the report. For this reason, many Web Intelligence report authors create ever larger microcubes (*micro* would not be an appropriate term here!) in an attempt to predict report consumers' drill paths. This is a bad practice. The multidimensional analysis in Web Intelligence is not a replacement for a full-featured OLAP database such as Microsoft Analysis Services or Oracle Hyperion. You want your initial report to contain only a minimal amount of data for response time and scalability reasons. If a certain dimension does not appear in the drill by list, users can still access it by adding a drill filter or extending the scope of analysis, as described in the following sections.

Drilling Across

Drilling *across* is the process of moving within the same dimension level but changing your selection criteria or drill filter. You use the drill filter toolbar to select different values to drill across.

Dimensions can be added to the drill filter toolbar in several ways:

- As you drill down or choose to drill by different levels within the same hierarchy, the higher-level selection is added to the drill filter toolbar.
- You can drag a dimension object from the available objects list to the drill filter toolbar.

In the following example, you can drill across on Year, State, or Lines by using the drop-down menu for each.

TIP If you want to see your selected drill filters displayed on a report, you need to insert a cell in the body of the report. From the Report Elements | Cell toolbox, select the Pre-defined drop-down list, choose the Drill Filter object, and place this object on your report.

Drilling Through to Detail

As shown in Figure 18-6, the initial Drill mode display does not necessarily contain all the dimensions or levels by which you can drill; more data may exist within the microcube. Ideally, these additional drill-by details are still at a reasonably aggregated level for the most frequently performed analyses. With drill-through, you can further expand the data in the microcube by expanding the scope of analysis. In this respect, drill-through lets you expand the cube with still more detail rows or less frequently used drill-by dimensions than what were stored in the original cube.

Expanding the scope of analysis modifies the query and retrieves a new full set of data; the microcube is rebuilt. Therefore, you want to reserve drill-through for retrieving less frequently used details and dimensions.

To open the Extend the Scope of Analysis dialog box, drill down to a level of detail not immediately available in the document. Web Intelligence indicates if your drill-down will generate a new query in the pop-up menu. The following example shows drilling from Year to Quarter. Quarter does not exist in the microcube.

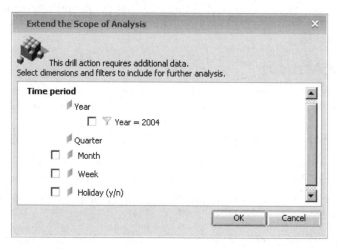

When you modify the scope of analysis, you can choose whether the query should return all rows for all selections within the dimension or if the drill filters should be translated as a condition in the query. The current drill selections are marked with filter icons. The filter values come from either the drill filter toolbar or the position of your mouse cursor within the drill table. In the preceding example, the drill-down had the Year 2004 as the filter in the drill filter toolbar. In the drill-through, you can have the query results for the quarter details filtered for Year = 2004 by checking the appropriate box in the Extend Scope of Analysis dialog box. Also, this dialog box allows you to retrieve details for Month or Week (or any other level of detail within this hierarchy), in case you will likely drill further.

Synchronized Drilling

While the previous sections describe drilling within a tabular block, you also can drill within charts. Additionally, if your report contains two block styles, such as a table and chart, you can synchronize the drill between the two blocks.

To synchronize drilling between two related blocks, in your BI Launch Pad preferences, choose to synchronize drills on report blocks (see Table 18-5).

Adding Snapshots

Snapshots allow you to save a picture of your drill at a particular level of detail or point within your exploration. Web Intelligence inserts a new report tab with the drill turned off.

To add a snapshot, from design mode select the Analysis | Interact toolbox, select the Drill drop-down and choose Snapshot.

Summary

With the newly designed Web Intelligence web viewer, the reading and design modes are more tightly integrated, allowing report consumers' full access to all the features of the report designer to analyze information in a report at the click of a mouse. Ideally, much of the formatting, sorting, breaks, and calculations have been defined for you in a shared report. However, you can fine-tune these options to suit your own analysis needs. You can change the block style from a tabular report to a chart to discover trends visually. You can re-sort the data, filter it, or insert subtotals to hone in on particular patterns or problem areas.

Use the drill functionality to explore data by additional levels of detail and different dimensions. Use the drill filter toolbar to navigate to different dimensions and select different members within a hierarchy. As you explore the data, you may find that you need additional details not within the microcube. Use drill-through to retrieve additional information from the data source and reexecute the entire query.

Part III

CHAPTER
19

Creating a New Query

There are two major panels used to create a Web Intelligence document: the Query Panel and the Report Design Panel. The Query Panel is used to return rows and columns of data from the database, and the Report Design Panel is used to take that set of data and format it and organize it so that it is not just "data," but rather, "information" to the consumer of your report. You learned about many of the features available to you in the Report Design Panel in Chapter 18.

Whether you are creating a new query or modifying an existing query, you use the Query Panel. The Query Panel lets you select result objects to display in a report and specify query filters to limit the rows returned, all without the need for you to know or understand SQL, the common language used by most relational databases. The universe's semantic layer displays the business names and dynamically generates the query in the source-specific language, for example, SQL, MDX, BICS, HiveSQL, and so on. Chapter 4 gives a more thorough discussion of how the universe accomplishes this. In this chapter, we will explore how to turn a business question into a query using the Web Intelligence Query Panel.

Formulating a Business Question

Before you begin to create a new document through Web Intelligence, it's important to formulate the business question to help you construct a query that returns the desired information. If you do not do this analysis, you run the risk of retrieving either too little or too much data, making it difficult to uncover patterns and opportunities. Without this initial planning, you may find yourself executing queries multiple times as you add or subtract objects before you achieve the desired report. With large databases, this can be inefficient and frustrating.

To formulate a business question in query terms, answer the following questions:

- Where is the data?
- Which measures do I want to analyze?
- By which dimensions do I want to analyze the measures?

- After viewing a high-level report, do I want to drill down or explore by other dimensions?
- Do I need additional dimensions for sorting, filtering, breaking, or ranking?
- How can I narrow my data results to ensure the query returns only the records I need?

As an example, assume you are a product manager. You want to analyze sales. "What are my sales?" is a fairly broad business question. Table 19-1 maps how to refine a broad question into more specific details that help you formulate a query.

Broad Question	Refined Answers	Query Component
Where is the data?	If you want to analyze sales for just your products, the data may be in a departmental data mart. If you want to compare your sales with other products, it may be in the central data warehouse. Actual sales may be in the central data warehouse; forecast sales may be in only a personal database.	Universe(s)
Which measures?	Sales could be stated in terms of revenues, quantity sold, and selling price.	Measure result object(s)
Which dimensions?	Do you want to analyze sales by product only or also by salesperson and time period?	Dimension result object(s)
Drill dimensions?	If sales for a particular product are falling or are lower than expected, do you want to drill into quarter, region, or customer to possibly identify the reason for the weak sales?	Dimension result object(s)
Additional objects for sorts, filters, breaks, or ranking	Thinking about how you will be structuring the data on your report may remind you to include additional objects in your query.	Dimension or measure result object(s)
What data do I need?	A departmental data mart may already provide a number of conditions to limit the information returned to you. You may want to limit the data by time to the current three months, current year, or last year. You may want to select only certain products. You may choose to limit results according to new salespeople or salespeople in a certain region.	Query filter(s)

Table 19-1 Refine Your Business Questions Prior to Constructing a Query

As you refine the broad "What are my sales?" business question following the guidelines in Table 19-1, it is much easier to build your query when your question looks more like the following: "What are sales by product line and by year for stores in New York for the last three years?"

Web Intelligence Versus Web Intelligence Rich Client

SAP BusinessObjects BI 4 offers two different tools to build and modify queries and report documents: Web Intelligence and Web Intelligence Rich Client. Reports developed in Web Intelligence can be modified by the Web Intelligence Rich Client tool and vice versa. The user interface and functionality in the two tools has become nearly indistinguishable as of BusinessObjects BI 4; however, there are still a few differences between the tools, as shown in Table 19-2.

This and subsequent chapters will use the Web Intelligence tool to demonstrate the functionality of building queries and report documents.

The Query Panel

From the Query Panel, you build or modify your query definitions. You run the query to retrieve the data results to display in a formatted document. In the Query Panel, you can build multiple queries, complex queries using UNION, MINUS, and INTERSECTION logic or modify the SQL generated by a universe query using custom SQL. This chapter covers the basics of creating simple queries. Chapter 22 covers complex queries.

Function	Web Intelligence	Web Intelligence Rich Client
Installation	Zero footprint, browser-based.	Requires client installation.
Data sources	Universe BEx query Analysis view	Universe BEx query Analysis view Text file Excel file Web services
Document format	Web Intelligence stores report files on the Web Intelligence server. The report file itself cannot be saved to an external file.	Files can be saved offline in a .wid file on your hard drive or file server and imported to the Web Intelligence server at a later time.

Table 19-2   Major Differences Between Web Intelligence and Web Intelligence Rich Client

Launching the Query Panel

To begin building a query in the Web Intelligence Query Panel, do the following:

1. From within BI Launch Pad, select Applications | Web Intelligence Application. Alternatively, click the Web Intelligence Application icon in the My Applications panel on the right side of the BI Launch Pad Home tab.

2. The Web Intelligence tab will open. To create a new document, select the Create a New Document button from the toolbar.

|
Open Document

Create a New Document

3. Web Intelligence prompts you to select a data source. In this example, select Universe and click OK.

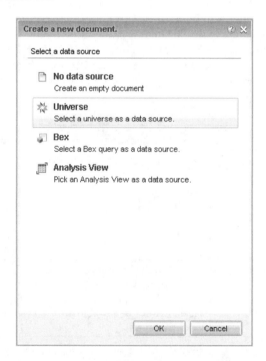

4. The list of available universes will display. Your company may have more universes, but only the ones to which you have access rights are displayed. Some companies have multiple universe folders for test and production environments or for each business unit.

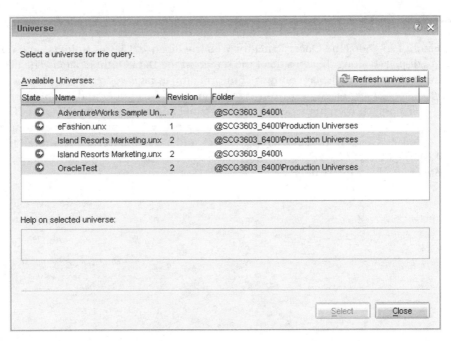

5. Select the desired universe from the desired folder, and then double-click to launch the Query Panel.

Working in the Query Panel

Figure 19-1 shows the Query Panel for Web Intelligence. Classes (folders) and objects are displayed along the left side of the screen in the Data Outline panel. The objects are available to use to display columns of information as *result objects* or to filter rows of data as *query filters*. The objects in the universe are grouped in a folder and subfolder structure.

The objects used in the Result Objects panel and those used in the Query Filters panel can be different. For example, you can create a query to display a list of customers in California. *Customer* would be a result object, and *State* would be a query filter. In Figure 19-1, the objects *Lines*, *Category*, *Year*, and *Sales revenue* are used as result objects. The object *State* is used as a query filter.

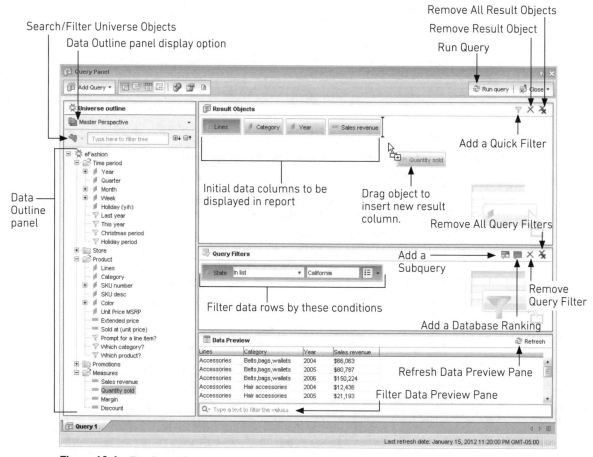

Figure 19-1   The Query Panel

Within the Data Outline panel, each object type has its own icon. Web Intelligence and the Query Panel support both universes created using the Universe Design Tool (.unv) and the new universe format created using the Information Design Tool (.unx). As described in Chapter 7, universes contain several object types, which are summarized in Table 19-3.

The Query Panel has its own buttons that allow you to modify the way the SQL is generated. Table 19-4 provides an overview of each of these buttons.

NOTE The buttons in Table 19-4 are specific to the Query Panel and not available from the Report Design Panel.

TIP As you build your query, you may want to save your query definitions without executing the query, and therefore without data. This is particularly true for complex or large queries, or queries that may be better to schedule rather than run in real time. To save the query definition without data, click Close on the Query Panel toolbar and choose Apply Changes and Close.

Creating a Simple Report

You can create a simple report in as few as three steps. First, choose the result object(s), and then click the Run Query button. Once in the Report Design Panel, your query will display the data in a standard table by default, and you can simply save your document.

Icon	Object Type (.unv)	Object Type (.unx)	Purpose
	Dimension	Dimension	A dimension object is typically string or date information by which you analyze numeric measures, such as product, region, or year.
	Measure	Measure	A measure object is a number that you wish to analyze, such as sales revenue, sales quantity, or margin.
	Detail	Attribute	A detail or attribute object provides additional information about another dimension object, like *Store*, such as a phone number or ZIP code.
	Condition	Filter	A condition object helps you filter your query data results according to a predefined set of conditions.

Table 19-3   Objects in the Data Outline Panel

Part III

Button	Name	Function
Add Query ▾	Add Query	Inserts a new query as another data provider for this document.
	Show/Hide Data Outline Panel	A toggle that shows or hides the Data Outline panel.
	Show/Hide Filter Panel	A toggle that shows or hides the Filter panel.
	Show/Hide Data Preview Panel	A toggle that shows or hides the Data Preview panel.
	Show/Hide Scope of Analysis Panel	A toggle that shows or hides the Scope of Analysis panel.
	Add a Combined Query	Creates queries that are combined with the SQL operators UNION, INTERSECT, and MINUS. These are discussed in Chapter 22.
	Query Properties	Allows you to set properties related to the query such as the query name, data limits, prompt order, contexts, and security.
	View Script	Shows the SQL script, allowing you to view, copy, or modify the SQL query.
Run query	Run Query	Executes the query and returns you to the Report Design Panel.
Close ▾	Close	Allows you to save the changes to your query and close the Query Panel without executing the query and return to the Report Design Panel. Alternatively, you can close the Query Panel without saving the changes made to the query and return to the Report Design Panel.

Table 19-4 Query Panel Toolbar Buttons

To build a query in the Web Intelligence Query Panel and save a document in the Report Design Panel, first launch the Query Panel as described earlier in the "Launching the Query Panel" section, and then follow these steps:

1. Choose the result objects (dimensions, detail or attribute, and measure objects) that will be returned as data to your report. By default, these objects will initially be displayed as columns in a standard table block.

2. Insert the appropriate query filters to retrieve only the data you want to include in your query.

NOTE You almost always need to include query filters. Most databases are large and contain massive amounts of data. For example, you may want to limit your data results to only certain periods of time or other constraints.

3. Select Run Query from the Query Panel toolbar to run the query, return the data results, and open the Report Design Panel.

4. By default, the objects that you selected as result objects are displayed in a standard table in the order that you selected the objects.

<u>Report 1</u>

Lines	Category	Year	Sales revenu
Accessories	Belts,bags,w:	2004	$66,063
Accessories	Belts,bags,w:	2005	$80,787
Accessories	Belts,bags,w:	2006	$150,224
Accessories	Hair accesso	2004	$12,436
Accessories	Hair accesso	2005	$21,193
Accessories	Hair accesso	2006	$11,939
Accessories	Hats,gloves,s	2004	$89,923
Accessories	Hats,gloves,s	2005	$206,001
Accessories	Hats,gloves,s	2006	$7,858
Accessories	Jewelry	2004	$302,352

NOTE The order of result objects in the Query Panel do not make a difference other than determining the order of the columns displayed in the table when the query is run for the first time and the default standard table is created. Subsequent changes to the order of the objects in the Query Panel or additions of new objects in the Result Objects panel have no effect.

5. Apply any desired formatting changes. Basic formatting and analysis options are discussed in Chapter 18, and advanced options are discussed in Chapter 20.

 6. Click Save from the Report Design Panel toolbar.

7. The Unsaved Changes dialog box will display. Click Yes.

Unsaved changes

Do you want to save changes to New Document ?

Yes   No   Cancel

8. The Publish a document to the server dialog box will display. Select the folder where you would like to publish your document, give your document a name, and click Save.

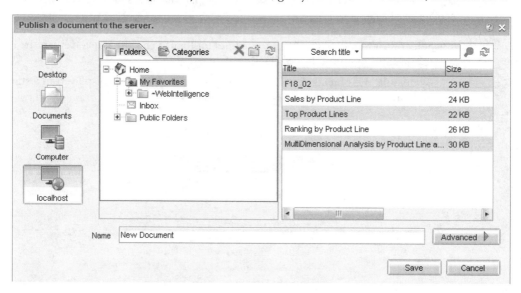

These steps will create a simple report. However, for most reports and complex business questions, there is more involved. The rest of this chapter expands on the options and functionality of the Query Panel.

Result Objects

To see individual objects within each class or folder in the Query Panel, click the + next to the class or folder. To add columns of data to the report, drag the individual object from the Data Outline panel to the Results Objects panel, or double-click the object name. When you drag an object, the cursor changes, as shown earlier in Figure 19-1, in which *Quantity sold* is being dropped into the Result Objects panel. You also can drag an entire class of objects to the Result Objects panel. Ideally, you should sort the order of the result objects from left to right by how you want them to appear in the initial report. Once you execute a query, the order of the result objects and that of the columns in a report block do not necessarily match.

To remove a result object, select the object in the Result Objects pane and click the Remove button in the upper-right corner of the Result Objects pane. Alternatively, you can drag an object from the Result Objects pane back to the Data Outline panel.

Scope of Analysis

The Query Panel Scope of Analysis button enables you to set the scope level to retrieve additional columns of data for multidimensional analysis without immediately displaying the results in the report. (The scope of analysis is discussed in Chapter 18.) The details exist in the microcube and become available when you select Drill By or Drill Down. To specify your scope of analysis settings, first ensure you understand the hierarchical nature of your data and the levels within each hierarchy. Refer to Figure 18-6 in Chapter 18 for a representation of the Time and Product Lines hierarchies. In setting the scope level, you can choose either a level number or a custom level.

Scope Levels by Number

A scope level set to *x* (a number) level allows you to automatically include data to support drilling for the next *x* number of levels before needing to requery the database based on the hierarchies *as they are defined in the universe*. For example, if *Year* is one of the result objects in your Result Objects panel, setting the scope level to one level will include *Quarter* in the query, two levels will include *Quarter* and *Month*, and so on.

NOTE A scope level of one, two, or three uses the hierarchies as they are defined in the universe. If a hierarchy was explicitly defined by the universe designer, that hierarchy will be followed. Otherwise, the physical order of the objects in the universe will define the hierarchy.

To set the scope of analysis using a scope level of one, two, or three, follow these steps:

1. Create a new Web Intelligence document. In this example, select the eFashion universe as the data source.

2. Once in the Query Panel, click the Scope of Analysis button on the Query Panel toolbar to display the Scope of Analysis panel.

3. Add *Year* and *Lines* from the Data Outline panel to the Result Objects panel. Notice that the *Year* and *Lines* objects are also added to the Scope of Analysis panel.

4. In the Scope of Analysis panel, select one level from the scope level drop-down list, as shown in Figure 19-2. Notice the Scope of Analysis panel now reflects the one-level hierarchy for both dimensions *Year - Quarter* and *Lines - Category*.

5. When you run the query, both *Quarter* and *Category* will now be included as part of the microcube and included in the Available Objects list in the Report Design Panel. On drill-down on *Year* to *Quarter* (or *Lines* to *Category*), no requery of the database will be required, and the drill response will be very fast.

The data retrieved as part of the query corresponds to both the scope level setting and the dimension result objects in your query at the time you set the scope level. If your result object is *Year*, and you change the scope level to two levels, then the query will also retrieve results for *Quarter* and *Month*. However, if your result objects were subsequently modified to include *Quarter*, then the next two levels would be *Month* and *Day*, and these objects would be automatically included in the scope of analysis.

The following table shows how the levels are relative using the Time hierarchy from Figure 18-6 in the previous chapter. For each example, assume that the scope level is set to two levels.

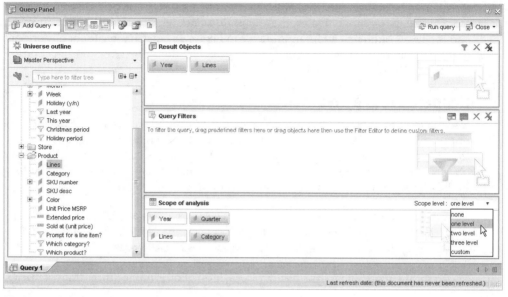

Figure 19-2 Scope of Analysis panel

If the current result object is	Then the query also retrieves
Year	Quarter, Month
Quarter	Month, Week
Month	Week, Day
Week	Day
Day	No additional columns, as it is the lowest level of detail in the hierarchy

Dimension objects added to the Result Objects panel after the scope level has been set and saved will not automatically generate additional scope level objects. For example, the query containing *Year* and *Lines* with the scope level set to one level (as shown in Figure 19-2) would maintain the same additional objects even if an additional result object, such as *State*, were added to the query.

New dimension object added to result objects

Scope level setting is changed automatically to custom

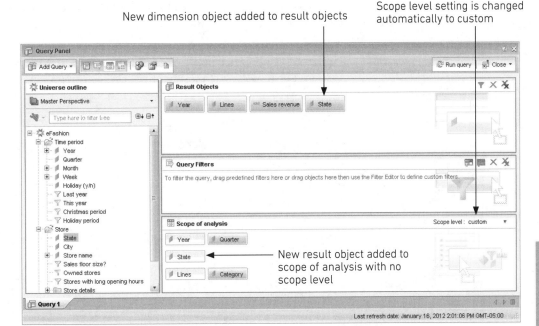

New result object added to scope of analysis with no scope level

Custom Scope Levels

A scope level set to custom allows you to control the drill path and number of drill levels based on an object hierarchy that you define, rather than the universe hierarchy. A custom scope level allows you to do the following:

- Customize the path of the universe defined hierarchy of *Year | Quarter | Month | Week | Day* to *Year | Month | Day*.

- Have different levels for each hierarchy, such as three levels on the Time hierarchy but only one level within the Product hierarchy.

- Specify a drill-by dimension that is not included as an initial result object. For example, note in the following settings that the store location or state appears in the Scope of Analysis panel but not in the Result Objects panel. Thus, when you are viewing the data and drilling, the initial table or chart will not display sales by store.

However, with the custom scope level, you can drill from product sales by year into product sales by individual state or store location.

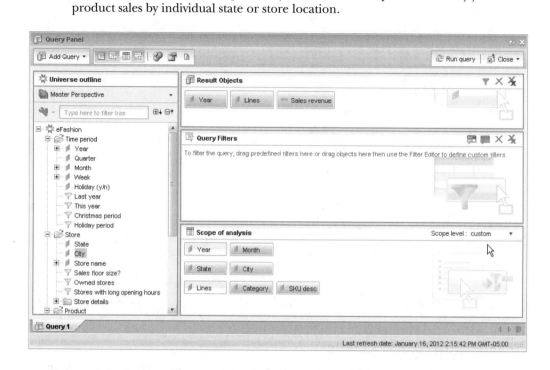

CAUTION Scope of analysis is quite powerful and allows you to pre-cache possible drill dimensions to enable you to have fast drill times. However, larger documents and larger result sets are more resource-intensive, slower to refresh, and harder to navigate. In the Scope of Analysis panel, you want only additional dimensions that are frequently accessed. If you are uncertain about retrieving a certain level of detail, you can still drill down by generating another query. If you are creating a report that other users will consume, consider using the SAP BusinessObjects BI 4 auditing capabilities to monitor how often a user must drill beyond the initial scope of analysis.

Query Filters

You use *query filters* to narrow your analysis to show information for only your particular subset of data. For example, if you are a product manager, you may limit your analysis to certain products. If you are a regional manager, you may limit your analysis to certain countries. If you are an employee supervisor, you may limit your analysis to the employees you manage. You limit your analysis by returning fewer rows of data. Query filters generate a WHERE clause in the SQL statement.

In some cases, query filters may be applied automatically through security settings in your database, in the Universe Design Tool or Information Design Tool data restriction sets, or a combination of both. For example, if the transaction system or data warehouse contains information for multiple legal entities, the DBA may restrict your access by using your ID to show you only data for the legal entity for which you are employed; you do not need to add an extra filter in your query. However, you will still need to add filters in the query to restrict your analysis to particular products, regions, employees, and so on, within your legal entity.

There are three ways to add query filters using the Query Panel: apply a quick filter, use predefined conditions, or use the Query Filters panel.

Quick Filters

You can apply a simple filter by adding an object to the Result Objects panel and then clicking the Quick Filter button. By default, quick filters use only Equal To or In List operators.

To apply a quick filter, do the following:

1. Select the *Year* object from the Result Objects panel and click the Quick Filter button.

2. The Add Quick Filter dialog box will display.

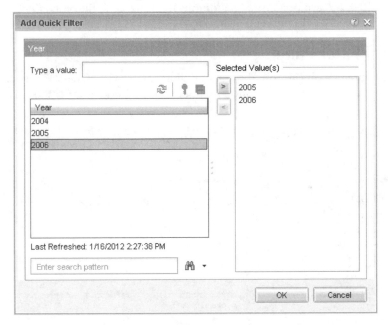

3. Select the values to include in the query filter and click OK.

4. The Query Filters panel will be updated with the result of the values selected in the Add Quick Filter dialog box.

5. Once the filter has been added to the Query Filters panel, you can modify the query filter.

Predefined Conditions

You can use a predefined condition object that is created by the universe designer. *Predefined conditions* are a particular kind of object that has built-in operators and values to restrict the number of rows returned and to display only the data you are interested in analyzing. For example, your universe may contain a predefined condition called *Current 3 Months* that automatically filters your data to retrieve the latest three months' worth of information. A predefined condition is denoted with a filter icon in the Query Filters panel.

The conditions and SQL in a predefined condition can be quite complex, performing multiple SQL translations and comparisons. See Chapter 11 for a more thorough discussion on how these are built.

To use a predefined condition as a query filter, double-click the predefined condition object in the Data Outline panel to add it to the Query Filters panel, or drag the object from the Data Outline panel to the Query Filters panel.

Multiple predefined condition objects can be added to the Query Filters panel. In Figure 19-3, the two predefined conditions have the same filtering effect as selecting Year=2011 and Weeks Between 46 and 53.

Query Filter Panel

You can drag an object from the Data Outline panel to the Query Filters panel. Using the Query Filters panel offers the most flexibility for defining query filters.

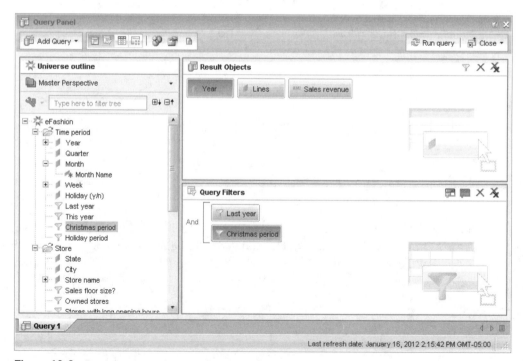

Figure 19-3   Predefined conditions are objects that are query filters defined in the universe.

When you wish to limit data in your result set by using complex operators, nesting with AND/OR logic, or by adding filters on objects that are not in the Result Objects panel, use the Query Filters panel.

To create a query filter using the Query Filters panel, do the following:

1. Create a new Web Intelligence document. For this example, select Universe as your data source and eFashion as the universe.

2. Select *Year, Lines,* and *Sales revenue* as result objects.

3. From the Stores class, select the *State* object and drag it to the Query Filters panel.

4. Web Intelligence adds the object and selects the default operator In List. In this case, leave the default.

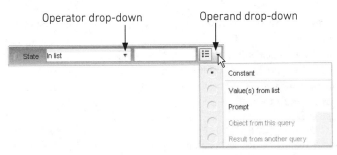

5. The default operand is a constant. You may enter the constant in the box, or you may change the operand to select Value(s) from List. In this example, use the drop-down list to change from Constant to Value(s) from List.

6. The List of Values dialog box displays. Double-click the desired state values to add them to the Selected Value(s) list. In this example, select New York and Texas.

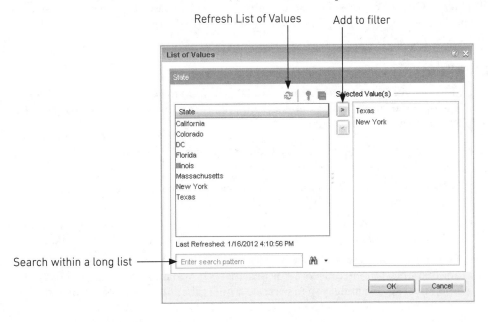

TIP Depending on your database settings, when entering constants, you may need to match the case exactly or you may not get any query results. For example, *New York* is not the same as *NEW YORK*.

---

7. Click OK to close the List of Values dialog box and return to the Query Panel. The query filter object is created with the list of values specified as the operand.

To view the SQL generated, click the View Query Script button from the Query Panel toolbar. Notice that Web Intelligence has automatically added a WHERE clause:

```
WHERE Outlet_Lookup.State  In  ( 'New York','Texas'  )
```

You can select multiple values in the List of Values dialog box. To select multiple *contiguous* values, click the first value, hold down the SHIFT key, and select the last value. All values from first to last will be selected. Now click the > button to move all items at once to the Selected Value(s) list. To select multiple *noncontiguous* values, click the first value, then while holding down the CTRL key, select each additional value. Web Intelligence uses semicolons to separate multiple values. ˋ

CAUTION When you enter multiple constants, do not put spaces between the semicolons and values. If you add a space, the SQL will contain a space in the value. For example, if you enter ' Texas' versus 'Texas', no rows will be returned.

Operators

Operators form the basis of comparison for the object and the values that you specify. As you add an object to the Query Filters panel, click the down-pointing arrow next to In List to display the Operator drop-down menu. Table 19-5 lists the available operators. Some SQL equivalents are different for specific RDBMSs. The SQL equivalents listed in Table 19-5 are based on Oracle.

Operands

Operands allow you to specify the values to which you want to compare the object. The list of available operands may change, depending on the object and the operator you specify. The following operands are available:

- **Constant**   Enables you to manually enter one or more values. If you enter multiple values, separate them with a semicolon.

- **Value(s) from list**   Allows you to choose one or more values from a pick list, if the universe designer has enabled a list of values for this particular object.

- **Prompt**   Allows you to create a prompt for shared reports in which you want users to be able to enter different operand values each time the query is executed.

- **Object from this query**   Allows you to set the operand value to the value of another object in the universe. For this operand, you may not use In List or Null operators. For example, you may create a query that filters orders in which the Order date is equal to the Ship date.

Operator	SQL Equivalent	Explanation
Equal To	=	Exactly equal to one value.
Not Equal To	<> or !=	Not equal to or different from one value.
Greater Than	>	Greater than a particular number, date, or character.
Greater Than or Equal To	>=	Greater than or equal to a particular number, date, or character.
Less Than	<	Less than a particular number, date, or character.
Less Than or Equal To	<=	Less than or equal to a particular number, date, or character.
Between	BETWEEN	Records between and including the two values—for example, Age Between 20 And 30; Price Between 100 and 150; Date Between January 1 And January 23.
Not Between	NOT BETWEEN	All values outside a particular range.
In List	IN	Equal to multiple values, generally to select multiple character values in a noncontiguous list.
Not In List	NOT IN	Different from multiple values.
Is Null	IS NULL	Rows in which no value has been entered. Null is different from zero or blank spaces.
Is Not Null	IS NOT NULL	Records that do not contain a null.
Matches Pattern	Like	Use a wildcard character such as % to find all records that contain or begin with a particular string. Use an underscore (_) to match one particular space. For example, B% is everything that starts with *B*, %B% contains a *B* somewhere in the string, and _B% has *B* as the second position. Warning: This type of query filter means an index for the particular column will not be used.
Different from Pattern	Not Like	Does not match the pattern specified. Warning: This type of query filter means an index will not be used.
Both	INTERSECT	Retrieve records in which the two values overlap (discussed in Chapter 22).
Except	MINUS	Remove records from a main query (discussed in Chapter 22).

Table 19-5   Operators Available in the Query Panel

- **Result from another query**   Allows you to set the operand value to the value(s) of an object in another query. For example, if you create one query against a separate database/universe to get all of your active customers and want to return orders from your orders universe for only those active customers, you could create a query that filters orders in which the *Customer Number* In List *Customer Number(Query 1)*.

Filters on Dates

When you use a date type dimension object as a query filter, Web Intelligence adds a calendar icon next to the constant box.

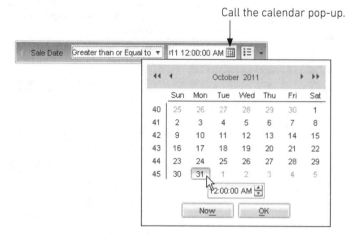

Call the calendar pop-up.

From within the calendar pop-up, you can click an individual date for the current month to add that to the constant. Today's date is highlighted with a red box. If you want to jump to a date for a different month or year, use the arrows to navigate through the calendar. Alternatively, you can enter the date in the constant box, and then click the calendar pop-up to go directly to that date.

NOTE Even though an object contains date values, if the universe designer has set this object to a character type, the calendar pop-up will not appear. As an example, in the eFashion universe, the object *Opening Date of the store* is a character data type, not a date data type, and therefore will not display a calendar.

Prompts

In Chapter 17, you saw that prompts allow you to refresh a query interactively. Prompts are useful when your query filters frequently change or if you are a report author creating a document for other users. When you set the operand to Prompt, Web Intelligence automatically creates a prompt for you, such as "Enter value(s) for *Object Name.*"

When developing prompts, follow these guidelines:

- If a list of values is available, start the prompt text with **Select**.
- If a list of values is not available, start the prompt text with **Enter**.
- When using the Equal To operator, start the prompt text with **Select value**.
- When using the In List operator, start the prompt text with **Select value(s)**.

- When prompting for data with a particular format, modify the prompt text to provide information about the format, particularly when a list of values is not present, such as **Enter Part Number as NNN-NN.**

- If a document will contain multiple queries with similar query filters, ensure you enter the prompt text exactly the same so that users are prompted only once. You can cut and paste your prompt text to ensure consistency. For example, in Figure 19-4, you see two queries within the same document that each contains a query filter on *Year*. If you use the *exact same* prompt text for each query filter object, when you refresh the document, you will be prompted to select a year only one time. Note that the prompt text is case-sensitive.

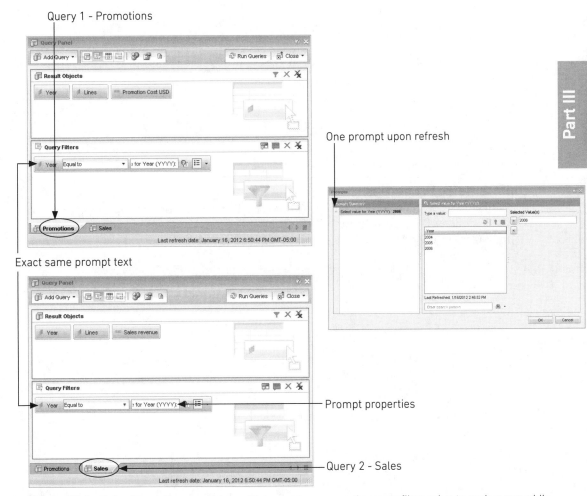

Figure 19-4   Using the same prompt in multiple queries passes the same filter value to each query while prompting the user only once.

Compare the Prompts dialog box in Figure 19-4 with the following Prompts dialog box, in which the prompt text is not consistent. When you run the query, you need to specify the year twice (even though you really want the same query filter value for year in each query).

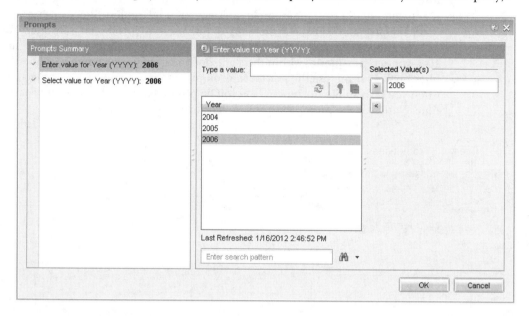

Parameter Properties

With Web Intelligence prompts, you also can specify several prompt properties. To open the Parameter Properties dialog box, click the Properties button next to the prompt message within the Query Filters panel.

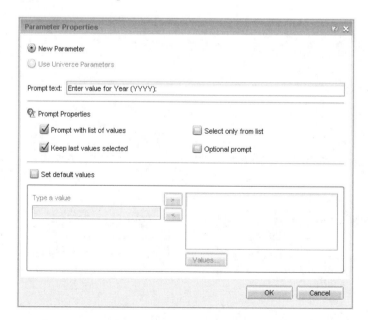

The Parameter Properties dialog box offers the following options:

- **Prompt text**   This determines the prompt message displayed to the user when the query is executed.

- **Prompt with list of values**   This will be enabled by default whenever an object has an associated list of values. If you don't want users to wait for a long list of values, then you can disable this option. We generally recommend that you disable this for all measure objects and date type objects.

- **Select only from list**   When users enter their own value, they may not get any rows returned if they enter the filter value in the wrong format or case. For this reason, you may want to force users to choose from a list of values. When you select this option, the Prompts dialog box changes slightly in that the Type a Value box will not be displayed.

- **Keep last values selected**   The last prompt values used are stored with the query. If there are prompt values that you would like prepopulated when you run the query, select this option, and the values selected for the prompt will be saved when the document is saved. This option will apply to all users when they save a version of the report (to their My Favorites folder) with their own frequently used prompt values.

- **Optional prompt**   If selected, when no value is provided in the query prompt at run-time the prompt is ignored.

- **Set default values**   This prompt property is similar to "Keep last values selected" but explicitly sets a default filter value for the report that cannot be changed by each user or each time the report is run and saved.

Creating a Prompt

To create a query filter object with a prompt, do the following:

1. Create a document using the eFashion universe.

2. Select the desired result objects.

3. Select the *Year* object and drag it to the Query Filters panel.

4. On the query filter object on *Year*, click the Operand drop-down menu and select Prompt.

5. Web Intelligence creates a default prompt message. Modify the prompt text in the operand box or in the parameter properties, or accept the default.

6. Modify any additional parameter properties or accept the defaults.

Query Properties

Query properties can be set for each individual query and are used to override certain defaults. To access the Query Properties dialog box (shown in Figure 19-5), select the Query Properties button from the Query Panel toolbar.

The Query Properties dialog box offers the following options:

- **Name** This refers to the name of the query. By default, Web Intelligence assigns the names Query 1, Query 2, and so on. You may want to specify a more meaningful query name. With more meaningful query names, it is much easier to use the Run Query button to selectively refresh individual queries within a document.

- **Universe** This refers to the universe used for this particular query.

- **Limits** These options show the default settings specified by the universe designer for the maximum number of rows and maximum retrieval time for the query. You may lower the limits for a particular query, but they may not be set higher than the default for the universe or group of users.

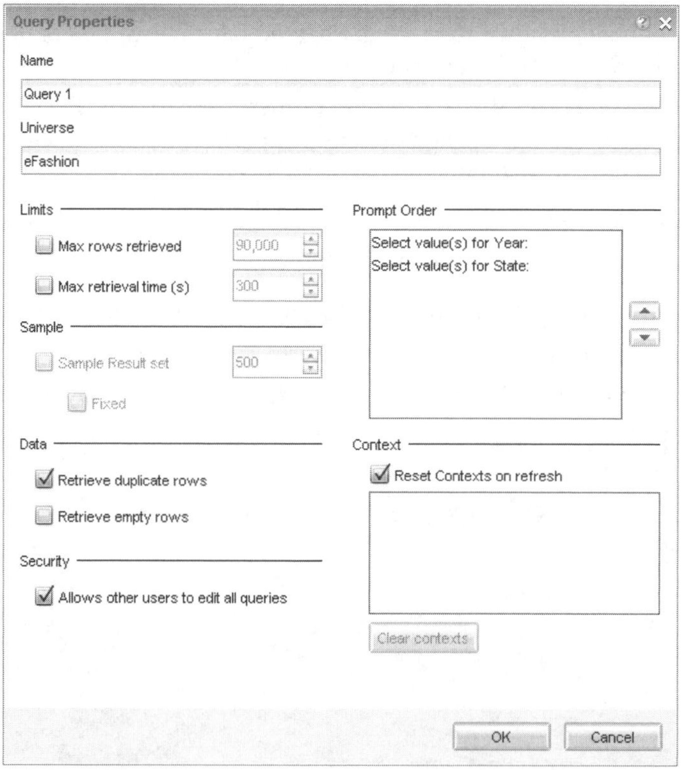

Figure 19-5 Query Properties

TIP During query design and testing, use the Limits settings to minimize the amount of data returned so that you are working with only a subset of data.

- **Sample**   These options show the default settings specified by the universe designer for retrieving the Data Preview data set.

- **Data**   These properties affect how the SQL is generated when your query does not contain a GROUP BY or aggregate. If you are accessing dimensional data in which there are multiple rows for the exact same value, uncheck the box "Retrieve duplicate rows." For example, if you have a CUSTOMER or PRODUCT table in which there are multiple records with different valid to/from dates for the same customers or products, by default, you will receive multiple rows of information in a list report. Web Intelligence generates the following SQL by default:

```
SELECT CUSTOMER.CUSTOMER_ID, CUSTOMER.CUSTOMER_NAME
FROM CUSTOMER
```

When you uncheck this setting, Web Intelligence modifies the SQL statement:

```
SELECT DISTINCT CUSTOMER.CUSTOMER_ID, CUSTOMER.CUSTOMER_NAME
FROM CUSTOMER
```

- **Security**   These settings are set by default by an administrator to determine which rights other users have for a particular folder or report. However, as the report author, you can also restrict the ability to modify a query here.

- **Prompt Order**   This allows you to specify the order in which the query prompts appear.

- **Context**   This is used when the query path is not clear, usually when you access dimension tables without explicitly choosing a measure. When the join path is not clear, you are prompted to select a context. By default, you are prompted each time you refresh the query. If you do not want to be prompted each time, and if you want to specify a default context that will be saved in the query, remove the check in "Reset Contexts on refresh" box.

Query Refresh on Open

When you save a document to a shared area of BI Launch Pad, you may want to set the document property to refresh the query on open. By default, a document is saved to the BusinessObjects BI 4 server with whatever data exists in the document at the time the document is saved. If the report is created and saved to public folders, and then accessed by a user six months later, the data in the document is at least six months old.

The Refresh on open option does the following:

- The document query is immediately launched when the document is opened. This prevents a user from opening a document and mistakenly analyzing stale data.

- If the query contains prompts, each user will be prompted to enter query filter values and will see only the relevant data.

Part III

You will not find the Refresh on Open option in the query properties. Instead, it is in the document properties. To set the document properties, do the following:

1. From the Report Design Panel, select the Properties toolbox and choose Document.

2. The Document Summary dialog box will display. Under Options, check the Refresh on open box.

BEx Queries

BEx queries are a new data source option in SAP BusinessObjects BI 4. BEx queries are created from SAP Info Cubes in a SAP BW data warehouse. A BEx query will automatically map hierarchies, attributes, dimensions, and measures into data on your data provider in your Web Intelligence report.

To create a Web Intelligence report based on a BEx query, do the following:

1. Create a new Web Intelligence document.

2. Select BEx as the data source.

3. The list of available BW BEx queries will display. Select the BW BEx query to be used in your report.

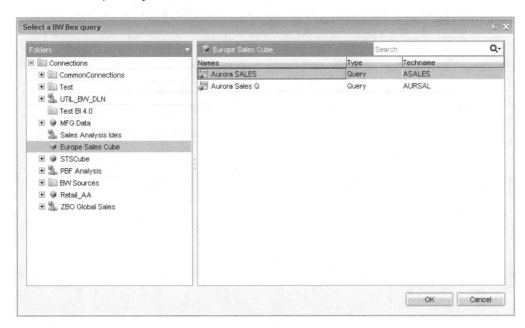

4. Select the hierarchies, dimensions, and measures to include as result objects in your query.

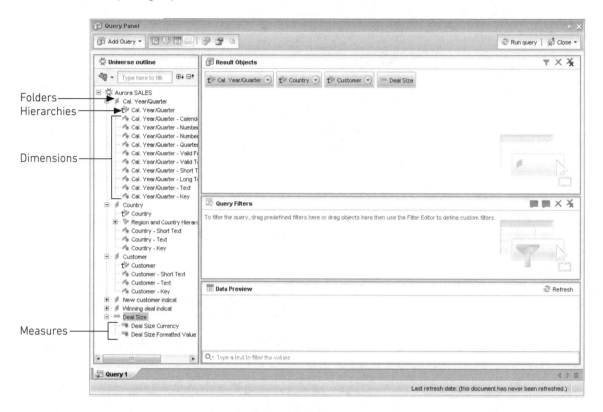

5. Select Run Query to view your results in the Web Intelligence Report Design Panel.

Hierarchy objects in the BEx query allow you to select member values that will be returned by the data provider. To restrict the member values, do the following:

1. From the Data Access toolbox, select Data Providers and choose Edit to access the Query Panel.

2. In the Result Objects panel on any hierarchy object, select the down arrow to access the Member Selector dialog box.

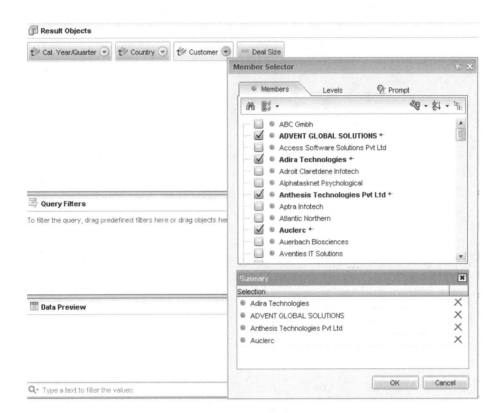

3. Click to select each value to include in your query, and then click OK.

4. Select Run Query to view your results in the Web Intelligence Report Design Panel.

Summary

The most important step in creating a new query is first formulating your business question in terms of what information you want to see and by which dimensions you want to explore (result objects). Next is identifying which subsets of data you want to analyze (query filters). If the question is too broad, you may be overwhelmed by the amount of information returned. Query filters enable you to filter the information returned to you. Predefined conditions are set by the universe designer and enable you to select predefined groupings and complex conditions. If you are building a report where the query filter values are frequently changing, use prompts to allow information consumers to select their own filters.

20 Advanced Report and Chart Formatting

When creating Web Intelligence documents, there are two distinct components that make up the report: the query and the report layout. The query defines what data is returned to the report. Queries are discussed in Chapters 19 and 22.

The report layout defines how the data is displayed and formatted in the report. Chapter 18 introduced the components of a report layout. You learned how to change basic block styles: tables, charts, and crosstabs. In this chapter, you will learn how to use some of the advanced formatting options to enhance cells, tables, charts, and crosstabs.

Formatting Components

Every component of a Web Intelligence document has formatting options. Within a Web Intelligence document, you can set individual formatting options on any of the following components:

- Document
- Report
- Report header/footer
- Page header/footer
- Block (table, crosstab, and chart)
- Block header/footer
- Table break
- Section header/footer
- Cell

Formatting a Cell

An individual cell is the lowest level of detail in a Web Intelligence report. A cell may exist in a block, such as a table or crosstab, or it may be free-standing, such as a report title. A cell may contain data values, a formula, a variable, or a constant.

By default, when you create a new report, Web Intelligence automatically puts data into a standard table. The table header cells are formatted with a font of Arial 9, bold, white text, on a blue background. The data cells are formatted with a font of Arial 9, black text. The report also contains a free-standing cell with the contents "Report Title," formatted with a font of Arial 16, underlined.

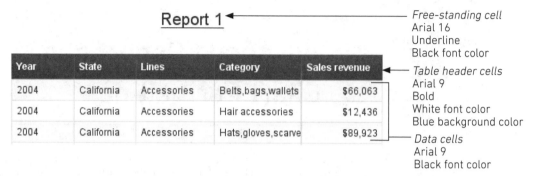

In SAP Business Objects BI 4, both the Universe Design Tool and the Information Design Tool (IDT) allow the universe designer to specify the default format for the data cells, which will override the default data cell formats. These format options are covered in Chapter 7

Regardless of whether the default formats for cells are set through the universe design or as the default settings in the Web Intelligence application, the Web Intelligence report designer can modify formats for all objects during report design. You can change the cell format through the Format toolbox and the Format Cell dialog box, accessed via the pop-up menu, as described in the following sections.

Formatting a Cell Using the Format Toolbox

The Format toolbox, accessed from the ribbon toolbar in web viewer design mode, has options for setting the font size, style, alignment, color, and other cell formatting.

For example, to format the report title cell using the Format toolbox, follow these steps:

1. To change the text from the generic "Report Title" to "Product Sales," double-click the cell to put the cell in edit mode, select the formula text =ReportName(), and replace it with **Product Sales**.

2. With the report title cell selected, select the Format toolbox from the ribbon toolbar.

3. Use the Font toolbox to change the font size from 16 points to 18 points.

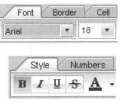

4. Use the Style toolbox to change the style: remove the underline, apply bold, and change the font color to red.

5. Use the Alignment toolbox to change the text alignment to horizontally and vertically centered.

The final cell format should appear as follows. Notice that the alignment applies only to the particular cell's contents and not to the cell's position in the report.

Product Sales

Formatting a Cell Using the Format Cell Dialog Box

The Format Cell dialog box, accessed from a cell's pop-up menu in web viewer design mode, contains all of the options available in the Format toolbox, plus some additional format options.

For example, to format the report title cell using the Format Cell dialog box, follow these steps:

1. Select the report title cell, right-click it, and select Format Cell… from the pop-up menu to open the Format Cell dialog box.

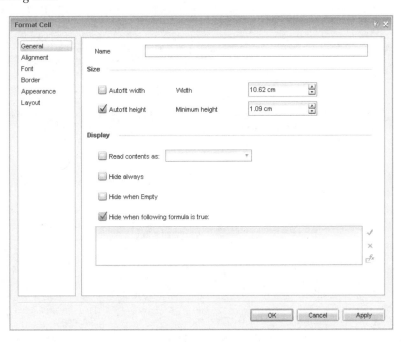

2. Select the Font category from the list box on the left side of the Format Cell dialog box. Set the font style to bold, the size to 18, and the font color to red. Under Effects, deselect Underline.

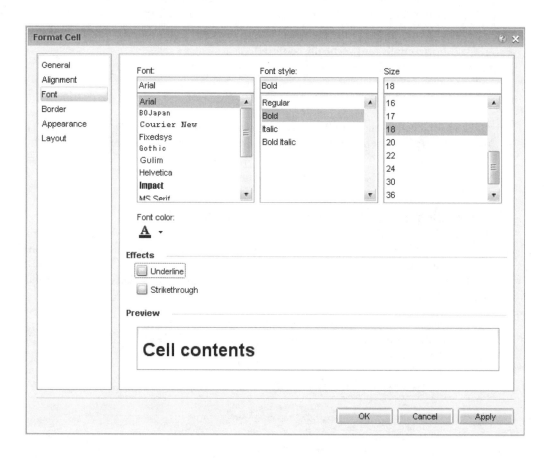

3. Select the Alignment category from the list box on the left side of the Format Cell dialog box. Set the horizontal and vertical alignment to Center.

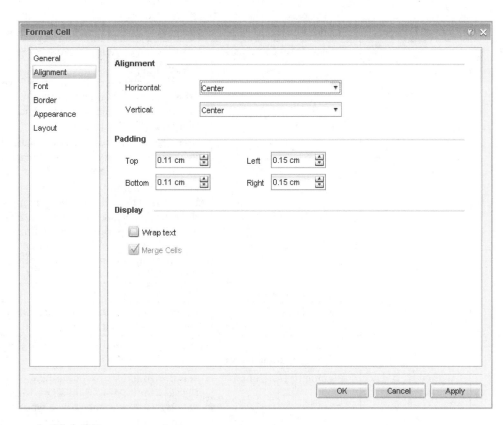

4. Click OK.

Table 20-1 lists the formatting options in the Format Cell dialog box.

Format Category	Format Option	Purpose
General	Name	Defines a name for a cell
	Size: Autofit width	Allows the cell to dynamically set the width to display the full contents of the data in the cell depending on the data that is returned from the data provider
	Size: Width	Sets a specific fixed width for a cell
	Size: Autofit height	Allows the cell to dynamically set the height to display the full contents of the data in the cell depending on the data that is returned from the data provider
	Size: Minimum height	Sets a specific fixed height for a cell

Table 20-1   Format Cell Options

Format Category	Format Option	Purpose
	Display: Read contents as	Displays cell contents in the selected format: **HTML:** Interprets cell contents as HTML. Often used in conjunction with the HTMLEncode function to dynamically build the HTML string. **Image URL:** Defines cell as an image. The image is read from a URL and must exist on the corporate server. **Hyperlink:** Defines text in a cell as a hyperlink. This will make the text in the cell a hyperlink and is best suited to access static hyperlinks such as http://www.sap.com or can be used for an OpenDocument link to open another Web Intelligence document.
	Display: Hide always	Hides the cell on the report
	Display: Hide when Empty	Hides the cell on the report only when the contents of the cell are null
	Display: Hide when following formula is true	Hides the cell on the report when the value of a formula is true
Alignment	Alignment: Horizontal	Sets horizontal alignment to Left, Center, Right, or Auto; Auto right-aligns when the data is a date or numeric data type and left-aligns when the data is a text data type
	Alignment: Vertical	Sets vertical alignment to Top, Center, Bottom, or Auto; Auto top-aligns
	Padding: Top	Sets top margin within the cell
	Padding: Left	Sets left margin within the cell
	Padding: Bottom	Sets bottom margin within the cell
	Padding: Right	Sets right margin within the cell
	Display: Wrap text	When the data within a cell exceeds the width of the cell, wraps the text rather than truncating the data on the right side of the cell; to eliminate truncating the data on the bottom of the cell, often used in conjunction with Size: Autofit height
	Display: Merge Cells	Allows multiple cells to be combined into what appears to be a single cell for formatting and data contents purposes
Font	Font	Sets the font

Table 20-1 Format Cell Options *(continued)*

Format Category	Format Option	Purpose
	Font Style	Sets the font style as Regular, Bold, Italic, or Bold Italic
	Size	Sets the font size
	Font color	Sets the font color
	Effects: Underline	Sets the text with an <u>underline</u> effect
	Effects: Strikethrough	Sets the text with a ~~strikethrough~~ effect
	Preview	Displays how your Font category settings will appear if you apply them
Border	Style	Sets the style of the line to be applied in the border as None, Dashed, Dotted, or Plain
	Thickness	Sets the thickness of the line
	Borders (left, right, top, bottom)	Allows you to independently define a left, right, top, or bottom border with independent border style and thickness settings
	Preview	Displays how your Border category settings will appear if you apply them
Appearance	Background Image: Color	Sets the background color of the cell
	Background Image: Pattern	Sets the background of the cell as an image
	Preview	Displays how your Appearance category settings will appear if you apply them
Layout	Horizontal: Start on a new page	Forces a page break (down the page) prior to displaying the cell
	Horizontal: Avoid page break	Forces a page break (down the page) prior to displaying the cell only if there is a natural page break that would split the cell
	Vertical: Start on a new page	Forces a page break (across the page) prior to displaying the cell
	Vertical: Repeat on every page	Prints the cell value on every page
	Vertical: Avoid page break	Forces a page break (across the page) prior to displaying the cell only if there is a natural page break that would split the cell
	Relative Position: Horizontal	Allows you to position a cell horizontally relative to the edges of a report, section, or block
	Relative Position: Vertical	Allows you to position a cell vertically relative to the edges of a report, section, or block

Table 20-1   Format Cell Options *(continued)*

Formatting a Cell Using the Format Number Dialog Box

The Format Number dialog box, accessible from a cell's pop-up menu in web viewer design mode, provides additional formatting options for cells containing numeric, date, or Boolean data types. For example, you can display numeric values as currency using the appropriate currency symbols (\$, £, and so on). You can also control the number of decimal places, thousands separators, and how negative numbers are displayed.

Date values can be displayed using many different format masks, from a simple date format like 6/15/2012 to a more complex format like Friday, June 15, 2012. Boolean values can be displayed as True; False or Yes; No.

NOTE Number formats can be specified by the universe designer. If numeric and date values are not formatted appropriately by default when you create a Web Intelligence report, you may want to work with your universe designer to provide meaningful defaults.

To format a numeric format for a cell using the Format Number dialog box, follow these steps:

1. Select a numeric data cell. In this example, choose Sales Revenue. Then right-click and select Format Number… from the pop-up menu to open the Format Number dialog box.

    Format Number…

NOTE The Format Number option will not be available for cells containing string data type data.

---

2. Select the Currency category on the left side of the Format Number dialog box.

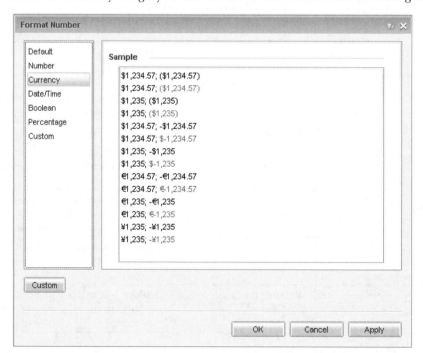

3. Select the format mask you wish to apply. Each format option has two values. The first value specifies how positive numbers will be formatted, and the second value specifies how negative numbers will be formatted.

4. Click OK.

Defining a Custom Number Format

Web Intelligence and the Format Number dialog box provide many predefined format masks. However, if you have a unique format that has not been predefined, you can use the Custom option in the Format Number dialog box, accessible from the pop-up menu in web viewer design mode.

To define a custom format for a cell using the Format Number dialog box, follow these steps:

1. For this example, select the Sales Revenue cell, right-click it, and select Format Number... from the pop-up menu to open the Format Number dialog box.

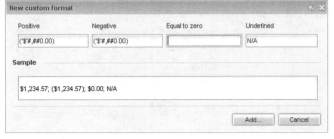

2. Click the Custom button to display the New custom format dialog box. The New custom format dialog box allows you to specify how positive, negative, equal to zero, and undefined (null values) are formatted.

For this example, enter **N/A** in the Undefined box.

3. Click Add.... The custom format will be added to the Custom category of the Format Number dialog box.

4. Click OK to apply the custom format to the cell.

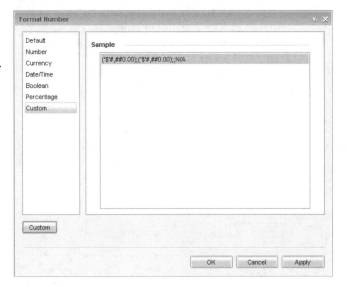

Document Summary Options

The document summary options are format settings that apply to the entire Web Intelligence document. To set the document summary options, follow these steps:

1. From the left pane of the web viewer design mode, select Document Summary and click the Edit button.

2. The Document Summary dialog box will display. Set any options you wish to change on your document. Table 20-2 lists the options and their purpose.

3. Click OK.

Document Summary Option	Purpose
Description	Allows you to enter descriptive data about the document. The description will display in the documents list when you hover the mouse over the document title.
Keywords	Allows you to enter keywords that can be used to search for a document in BI Launch Pad.
Enhanced viewing	Optimizes the document for on-screen viewing.
Refresh on open	Refreshes data providers automatically and immediately whenever the document is opened.

Table 20-2 Document Summary Options

Document Summary Option	Purpose
Permanent regional formatting	Saves the document with the format locale with which the document was saved. The users' preferred viewing locale settings in their preferences will be ignored when viewing this document.
Use query drill	Sets the document to drill in query drill mode.
Enable query stripping	Generates a query that will include only data objects that are referenced in the document. Only data considered relevant to the document will be retrieved by the query.
Hide warning icons in charts	Hides a warning from displaying when a chart cannot be generated.
Auto-merge dimensions	When multiple data providers are created in the document, automatically merges dimension objects from the same universe and with the same name.
Extend merged dimension values	When multiple data providers are merged in the document, generates a result set that will be a full outer join of both data providers; in other words, a union of both data providers. When this option is not checked, the result is an outer join of the two data providers, where all the data from data provider 1 is returned and only matching values from data provider 2 are returned.

Table 20-2 Document Summary Options *(continued)*

Default Styles

Web Intelligence uses Cascading Style Sheets (CSS) to define the presentation of your reports. The default CSS defines how the blocks and other report elements are formatted. For example, when you create a new Web Intelligence document, a standard table is created with those familiar headings on blue backgrounds, as defined in the default CSS.

CSS provides flexibility in customizing styling. In SAP Business Objects BI 4, the Document Summary Options tab allows you to customize and apply different CSS styles for each document. Most likely, you will define a few standard CSS files to create corporate standard report formats and use those CSS files. The default CSS file, located in c:\Program Files(x86)\SAP BusinessObjectsEntreprise XI\images\WebIDefaultStyleSheet.css, can be modified to be the default corporate standard.

Exporting the Default CSS File

The first step in defining custom CSS styling is to export the default CSS file, following these steps:

1. From the left panel of the web viewer design mode, select Document Summary, and then click the Edit button.

2. Select the Change Default Style... button. The Default Style dialog box will display.

> Change Default Style...

3. Click the Export Style button. The Export Default Style dialog box will display.

4. Select the directory location, type in the filename, and then click Save.

The exported CSS file can be edited to set the desired format options. Once the default CSS file is exported, anyone familiar with World Wide Web Consortium (W3C) CSS syntax can modify the CSS using any text editor to define custom formatting and standards for Web Intelligence reports.

Importing a Custom CSS File

To use a customized CSS file, follow these steps:

1. From the left pane of the web viewer design mode, select Document Summary, and then click the Edit button.

2. Select the Change Default Style… button. The Default Style dialog box will display.

3. Click the Import Style button. The Import Default Style dialog box will display.

4. Select the customized CSS file, and then click Open.

5. Click Close in the Document Summary dialog box.

NOTE To apply a CSS to a report element that has already been formatted through the Format toolbox or Format dialog box, you must first clear the format. You can clear the format of an element by selecting the formatted element and selecting Format | Clear Format from the Format toolbox. To clear the format of all the elements in a page, select the report body and select Format | Clear Format.

You must reimport the CSS file into the document every time it is modified in order for the modifications to be recognized.

Inserting and Deleting Report Tabs

A powerful Web Intelligence feature is the ability to have multiple reports within one document. Each report can display data from a different query, or it can simply be another way of viewing the same results of one query. Thus, your first report may be a crosstab, and the second report may be a chart.

To insert a new report tab, do the following:

1. Right-click the default report tab, Report 1.

2. From the pop-up menu, choose Add Report. Web Intelligence inserts a blank report named Report 2.

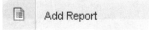

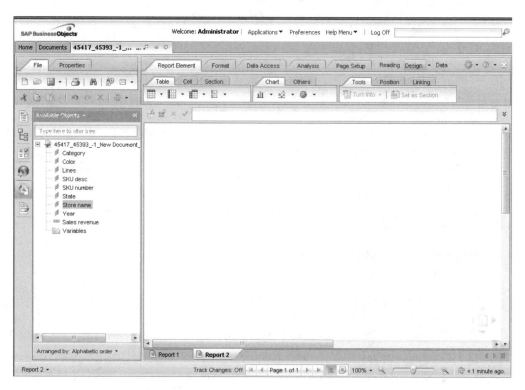

NOTE If you intend to use the same query and initial layout from Report 1, then choose Duplicate from the pop-up menu.

3. To change the name of the report, right-click the tab and select Rename from the pop-up menu. The Rename dialog box will display. In the New value box, type a meaningful name for the report, such as **Sales by State.**

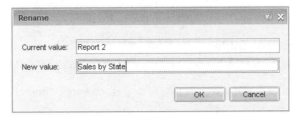

4. Click OK. This new name will now also appear in the Navigation map, as bookmarks if you convert the report to PDF format, and as worksheets if you save the report to Microsoft Excel format.

To delete a report tab, do the following:

1. Right-click the report tab you would like to delete—in this example, Report 2.

2. Select Delete Report from the pop-up menu.

Working with Table Blocks

Table blocks are commonly used to display data in Web Intelligence reports. There are three types of table blocks:

- **Vertical tables**   Default table type with the headers at the top of the table.

- **Horizontal tables**   Table format with the header row on the left side of the table.

- **Cross tables**   Matrix-style table in which dimensions are displayed on the left and top axis of the table, and measure or numeric data is displayed at the cross section of the dimensions.

Inserting a New Table Block

There are three ways to create a new table block on a report tab in a Web Intelligence document.

- Select multiple available data objects and drag-and-drop them directly onto a blank area in your report tab. A new vertical table will be created by default on the report tab with the selected data objects. This method provides the least initial flexibility.

- Select the Vertical Table, Horizontal Table, or Cross Table button from the Report Element | Table toolbox, and then click in a blank area in your report tab to insert the table. A new blank table will be created on the report tab, and you can drag data objects from the available objects list to the new table.

- Right-click your report tab and select Insert | Vertical Table, Horizontal Table, or Cross Table, and then click in a blank area in your report tab to insert the table. A new blank table will be created on the report tab, and you can drag data objects from the available objects list to the new table.

Adding a Vertical Table

To add a new vertical table using the drag-and-drop method, follow these steps:

1. Insert a new blank report tab, as described earlier in this chapter.

2. Select Available Objects from the left panel.

3. Select *State*, and while holding down the CTRL key, select *Sales revenue*. Drag-and-drop both of the data objects to the page area of Report 2.

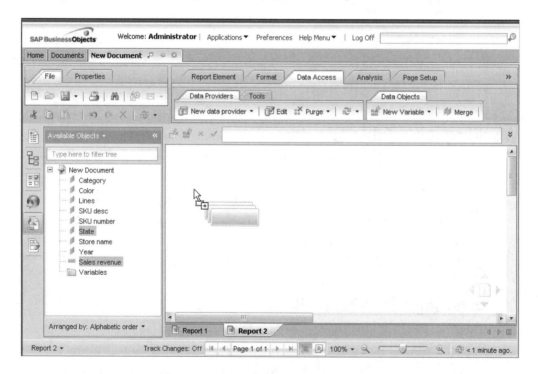

The vertical table will appear in the report tab with the columns you selected.

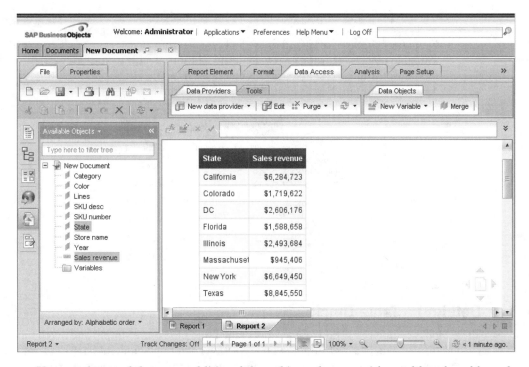

You can drag-and-drop any additional data objects that you wish to add to the table and make formatting changes to this table.

Alternatively, using either the toolbox or the pop-up menu, you may first choose the block table style, and then drag-and-drop the data objects.

Adding a Cross Table

To create a cross table block on your report tab, follow these steps:

1. Select the Cross Table button from the Report Element | Table toolbox, or right-click and select Insert | Cross Table from the pop-up menu.

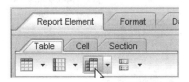

2. Drag your cursor to a blank area on the report tab. Your cursor will display as a cross table.

3. Click to place the empty cross table in the report tab.

4. From the left pane, drag-and-drop data objects from available objects list into the row heading, column heading, and body data elements for the cross table. In this example, drag *State* as the row heading, *Year* as the column heading, and *Sales revenue* as the body.

	2004	2005	2006
California	$1,704,211	$2,782,680	$2,992,679
Colorado	$448,302	$768,390	$843,584
DC	$693,211	$1,215,158	$1,053,581
Florida	$405,985	$661,250	$811,924
Illinois	$737,914	$1,150,659	$1,134,085
Massachuse	$238,819	$157,719	$887,169
New York	$1,667,696	$2,763,503	$3,151,022
Texas	$2,199,677	$3,732,889	$4,185,098

Deleting a Table Block

Table blocks can be removed from a report tab. Table blocks are simply one mechanism used to display data in a Web Intelligence report, so deleting a table block from a report tab will not remove the data from the data provider. All of the data objects in your data provider will still appear in the available objects list in the left pane, and you can add a new table, cross table, or chart to your report at any time.

To delete a table block from your report tab, follow these steps:

1. Select the table on the report tab, making sure the entire table is selected and not just a column or cell within the table.

Gray box around entire table

Selectors at each corner

	2004	2005	2006
California	$1,704,211	$2,782,680	$2,992,679
Colorado	$448,302	$768,390	$843,584
DC	$693,211	$1,215,158	$1,053,581
Florida	$405,985	$661,250	$811,924
Illinois	$737,914	$1,150,659	$1,134,085
Massachuse	$238,819	$157,719	$887,169
New York	$1,667,696	$2,763,503	$3,151,022
Texas	$2,199,677	$3,732,889	$4,185,098

2. Right-click and select Delete from the pop-up menu.

Inserting a New Column in a Table Block

There are two ways to insert a column into a table block:

- Select a data object from the list of available data objects, and then drag-and-drop it between other data objects on a table block on your report.
- Insert a blank column on your table block, and then drag a data object from the list of available objects into the blank column.

Dragging-and-Dropping a Data Object

To drag-and-drop a data object onto your table block, follow these steps:

1. Select a data object from the available objects list in the left pane of the design panel to insert into your table block. In this example, select *Category*.

2. Drag the *Category* object into the table block where you want the data field to be inserted. The small blue shading at the right side of the *State* column indicates that the new field will be inserted after the *State* column.

Year	State	Sales revenue
2004	California	$1,704,211
2004	Colorado	=[Category]
2004	DC	$693,211
2004	Florida	$405,985
2004	Illinois	$737,914
2004	Massachusetts	$238,819
2004	New York	$1,667,696

3. Drop the *Category* object to insert it.

Year	State	Category	Sales revenue
2004	California	2 Pocket shirts	$50,999
2004	California	Belts,bags,wallet:	$66,063
2004	California	Bermudas	$5,290
2004	California	Boatwear	$10,974
2004	California	Cardigan	$44,294
2004	California	Casual dresses	$11,240
2004	California	Day wear	$46,460

Inserting a Blank Column

Sometimes it can be difficult to drag-and-drop a data object exactly where you want to place it on a table block in your report. To more precisely position a data object where you want it to appear, follow these steps:

1. Position the cursor in the column next to where you want to insert a new one. Right-click and select Insert column on right (or left) from the pop-up menu.

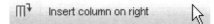

Part III

2. A new blank column will be inserted.

Year	State		Sales revenue
2004	California		$1,704,211
2004	Colorado		$448,302
2004	DC		$693,211
2004	Florida		$405,985
2004	Illinois		$737,914
2004	Massachusetts		$238,819
2004	New York		$1,667,696
2004	Texas		$2,199,677

3. Drag a data object from the available objects list in the left pane of the design panel to insert it into the new blank column in the table block. In this example, select *Category*. Notice that the blue shading covers the entire blank column, indicating that the new field will replace the contents of the blank cell.

Year	State		Sales revenue
2004	California		$1,704,211
2004	Colorado	=[Category]	302
2004	DC		$693,211
2004	Florida		$405,985
2004	Illinois		$737,914
2004	Massachusetts		$238,819
2004	New York		$1,667,696
2004	Texas		$2,199,677

4. Drop the *Category* object to insert it.

Deleting a Column in a Table Block

You can delete any columns in your table blocks. To delete a column, follow these steps:

1. Position your mouse on the column you wish to remove. Select the column. You know that the column is selected when the column is shaded.

Year	State	Category	Sales revenu
2004	California	2 Pocket shirts	$50,999
2004	California	Belts,bags,wallets	$66,063
2004	California	Bermudas	$5,290
2004	California	Boatwear	$10,974
2004	California	Cardigan	$44,294
2004	California	Casual dresses	$11,240
2004	California	Day wear	$46,460
2004	California	Dry wear	$12,923
2004	California	Evening wear	$84,664

2. Right-click to invoke the pop-up menu and select Delete.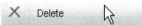

Formatting Cross Tables

Web Intelligence allows you to turn one block style into another block style. For example, you can turn a vertical table into a cross table.

When you turn a vertical table into a cross table, Web Intelligence uses the first vertical column to pivot to column headings. This is not always the best guess. So, for example, if *Lines* is your first column and *Year* is your second column, you get a really messy pivot table—one far too wide to be usable, as the product lines will become the column headings. If, however, *Year* is your first column, Web Intelligence will automatically pivot that to a column heading and use the second column, *Lines,* as the row heading.

To convert an existing vertical table to a cross table, follow these steps:

1. Select a vertical table. Be sure that a gray box appears around the entire vertical table block.

Year	State	Sales revenue
2004	California	$1,704,211
2004	Colorado	$448,302
2004	DC	$693,211
2004	Florida	$405,985
2004	Illinois	$737,914
2004	Massachusetts	$238,819
2004	New York	$1,667,696
2004	Texas	$2,199,677

2. Right-click to invoke the pop-up menu and select Turn Into | Cross Table. If Turn Into does not appear in your menu, you may have selected only one cell, rather than the entire table.

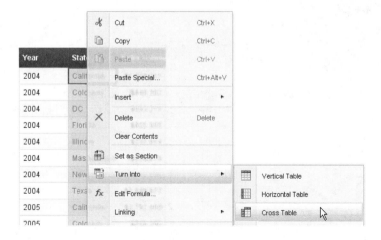

Your vertical table will display as a cross table.

	2004	2005	2006
California	$1,704,211	$2,782,680	$2,992,679
Colorado	$448,302	$768,390	$843,584
DC	$693,211	$1,215,158	$1,053,581
Florida	$405,985	$661,250	$811,924
Illinois	$737,914	$1,150,659	$1,134,085
Massachusetts	$238,819	$157,719	$887,169
New York	$1,667,696	$2,763,503	$3,151,022
Texas	$2,199,677	$3,732,889	$4,185,098

Inserting Measures in a Cross Table

A cross table can contain more than one measure object in the body. For example, a cross table can display both sales revenue and quantity sold.

To add multiple measures to a cross table block, follow these steps:

1. With your initial cross table displayed in design mode, select the Available Objects button from the left panel.

2. Drag the measure object you wish to add to your cross table—in this example, *Quantity sold*. Notice that the blue shaded rectangle is on top of the existing measure (*Sales revenue*) rather than on top of the *State* dimension, indicating that this object will be inserted as a body object rather than a row dimension object.

	2004	2005	2006
California	$1,704,211	$2,782,680	$2,992,679
Colorado	$448,302 =[Quantity sold]	$768,390	$843,584
DC	$693,211	$1,215,158	$1,053,581
Florida	$405,985	$661,250	$811,924
Illinois	$737,914	$1,150,659	$1,134,085
Massachusetts	$238,819	$157,719	$887,169
New York	$1,667,696	$2,763,503	$3,151,022
Texas	$2,199,677	$3,732,889	$4,185,098

3. Drop the measure object into the cross table to insert it.

	2004		2005		2006	
California	11,304	$1,704,211	17,001	$2,782,680	17,769	$2,992,679
Colorado	2,971	$448,302	4,700	$768,390	5,116	$843,584
DC	4,681	$693,211	7,572	$1,215,158	6,491	$1,053,581
Florida	2,585	$405,985	3,852	$661,250	4,830	$811,924
Illinois	4,713	$737,914	6,744	$1,150,659	6,519	$1,134,085
Massachusetts	1,505	$238,819	902	$157,719	5,269	$887,169
New York	10,802	$1,667,696	16,447	$2,763,503	19,109	$3,151,022
Texas	14,517	$2,199,677	22,637	$3,732,889	25,193	$4,185,098

Displaying Object Names in a Cross Table Block

Cross tables, unlike vertical and horizontal tables, do not display their object names as column headings by default.

To more clearly identify which data values are in your cross table, follow these steps:

1. Select the entire cross table block.

2. Right-click and select Format Table... from the pop-up menu.

Alternatively, you can select the Format button from the Format | Tools toolbox.

3. Check the option Show object name.

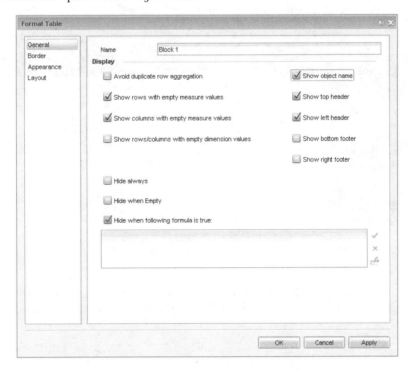

The cross table now displays object names as column headings. Admittedly, they still need some formatting.

State	2004		2005		2006	
	Quantity sold	Sales revenue	Quantity sold	Sales revenue	Quantity sold	Sales revenue
California	11,304	$1,704,211	17,001	$2,782,680	17,769	$2,992,679
Colorado	2,971	$448,302	4,700	$768,390	5,116	$843,584
DC	4,681	$693,211	7,572	$1,215,158	6,491	$1,053,581
Florida	2,585	$405,985	3,852	$661,250	4,830	$811,924
Illinois	4,713	$737,914	6,744	$1,150,659	6,519	$1,134,085
Massachusetts	1,505	$238,819	902	$157,719	5,269	$887,169
New York	10,802	$1,667,696	16,447	$2,763,503	19,109	$3,151,022
Texas	14,517	$2,199,677	22,637	$3,732,889	25,193	$4,185,098

Merging Column Titles

Now that there are two measure columns in our example cross table, this introduces another formatting challenge. The column dimension *Year* is in the cell over the *Sales revenue* measure, and it can only be aligned relative to *Sales revenue*.

To center-align the *Year* dimension over both *Sales revenue* and *Quantity sold* measures, follow these steps:

1. Use CTRL-click to select the first header cell and the second Year cell to its right. In this example, select the cell with the value 2004.

State	2004		2005		2006	
	Quantity sold	Sales revenue	Quantity sold	Sales revenue	Quantity sold	Sales revenue
California	11,304	$1,704,211	17,001	$2,782,680	17,769	$2,992,679
Colorado	2,971	$448,302	4,700	$768,390	5,116	$843,584
DC	4,681	$693,211	7,572	$1,215,158	6,491	$1,053,581
Florida	2,585	$405,985	3,852	$661,250	4,830	$811,924
Illinois	4,713	$737,914	6,744	$1,150,659	6,519	$1,134,085
Massachusetts	1,505	$238,819	902	$157,719	5,269	$887,169
New York	10,802	$1,667,696	16,447	$2,763,503	19,109	$3,151,022
Texas	14,517	$2,199,677	22,637	$3,732,889	25,193	$4,185,098

2. Right-click to invoke the pop-up menu and select Format Cell....

 Format Cell...

3. The Format Cell dialog box will display. Select the Alignment option from the right pane, and then select the Alignment: Horizontal: Center and Merge Cells options.

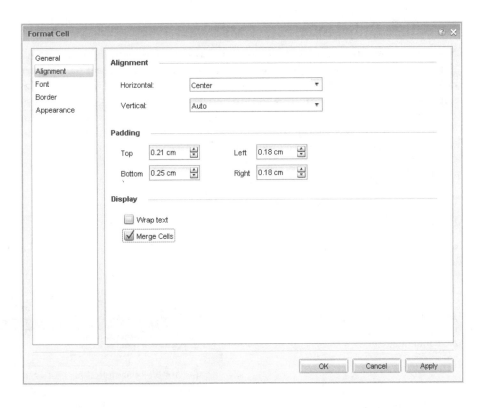

The final cross table formatting will appear, with the Year heading now centered across both the *Quantity sold* and *Sales revenue* measure objects.

State	2004		2005		2006	
	Quantity sold	Sales revenue	Quantity sold	Sales revenue	Quantity sold	Sales revenue
California	11,304	$1,704,211	17,001	$2,782,680	17,769	$2,992,679
Colorado	2,971	$448,302	4,700	$768,390	5,116	$843,584
DC	4,681	$693,211	7,572	$1,215,158	6,491	$1,053,581
Florida	2,585	$405,985	3,852	$661,250	4,830	$811,924
Illinois	4,713	$737,914	6,744	$1,150,659	6,519	$1,134,085
Massachusetts	1,505	$238,819	902	$157,719	5,269	$887,169
New York	10,802	$1,667,696	16,447	$2,763,503	19,109	$3,151,022
Texas	14,517	$2,199,677	22,637	$3,732,889	25,193	$4,185,098

Structure Only Mode

Most of the formatting you've done up until this point has been done in design mode with data. Formatting with data is helpful because you can see the impact of your formatting changes immediately. However, it can be slow when working with reports with large amounts of data or when applying multiple formatting changes at once. In these circumstances, you will have better performance if you format in *structure only* mode.

To see a report in structure only mode, click the Design drop-down from the report toolbar and select the Structure Only option.

In structure only mode, you see the cell formula contents rather than the data values.

Structure only mode shows formula references rather than data references

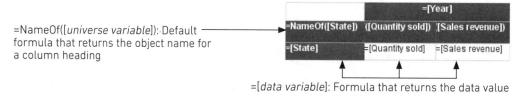

=NameOf([*universe variable*]): Default formula that returns the object name for a column heading

=[*data variable*]: Formula that returns the data value

All of the same formatting options and report design tabs and toolboxes that you have in design mode with data are also available in structure only mode.

In structure only mode, each column heading will have the following cell formula contents by default, where *Variable* is the name of the universe object:

```
=NameOf([Variable])
```

For example, the following is the column heading for *State*:

```
=NameOf([State])
```

Each data row will have the following formula contents, where *Variable* is the universe object or report variable:

```
=[data variable]
```

For example, the following is the data value for *Quantity sold*:

```
=[Quantity sold]
```

If your document contains more than one query with similar object names, then the query name precedes the object name, as in this example:

```
=[Query1].[State]
```

For more information about report variables, see Chapter 21.

To return to the data mode, click the Design drop-down from the report toolbar and select the With Data option.

Additional Table Block Formatting

Many of the formats that you apply to individual cells can also be applied to a set of cells that make up a table block. Within a table block, there are three categories of cells:

- **Header cells** Column headings that usually are object or variable names
- **Body cells** Data values from variables or universe objects
- **Footer cells** Subtotals or grand totals

You can select the individual header, footer, or body, as well as the entire table.

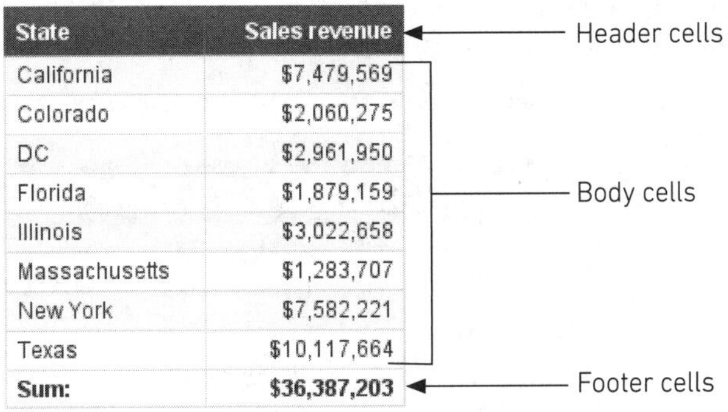
State
Sales revenue
Header cells
California
$7,479,569
Colorado
$2,060,275
DC
$2,961,950
Florida
$1,879,159
Body cells
Illinois
$3,022,658
Massachusetts
$1,283,707
New York
$7,582,221
Texas
$10,117,664
Sum:
$36,387,203
Footer cells

By default, the header cells of a table block will be the variable names of the data objects displayed in the body of the table. The header cells of a table can be formatted with your preferences for borders, colors, fonts, backgrounds, and alignment settings, as discussed earlier in this chapter. The following sections cover some special considerations when formatting header cells for table blocks.

Changing Column Names

Sometimes the variable names are longer than the data values that the column will contain. For example, if your SKU numbers are only six digits but the object name is *Product SKU Number*, the column heading would be unusually wide for a small data column.

To change the text of a column heading, follow these steps:

1. Double-click the header cell that contains the long column heading. A small formula editor will display.

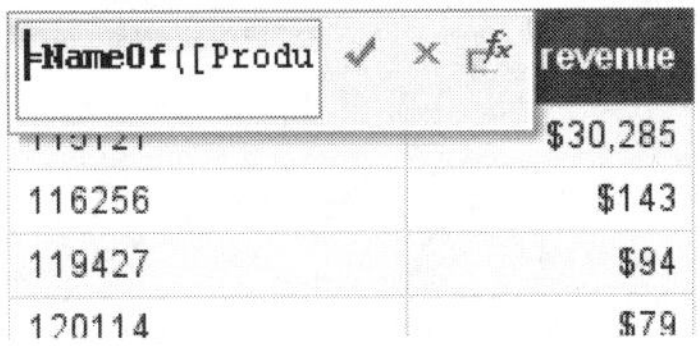
=NameOf([Produ
revenue
$30,285
116256
$143
119427
$94
120114
$79

2. Select the formula text and type in the new shorter column name. In this example, type **SKU No**. Then press ENTER or click the green check mark to validate the entry.

3. Resize the column so that it is not so wide.

SKU No	Sales revenue
115121	$30,285
116256	$143
119427	$94
120114	$79
121764	$69
122709	$533

Using Column Autofit Height and Wrapping Text

If you resize a column with a long column name to be an appropriate width for the data, the column name will, by default, truncate.

Header cell text is truncated by default when resized.

Product SK	Category	les revenue
115121	Hats,gloves,scarves	$30,285
116256	Hats,gloves,scarves	$143
119427	Jewelry	$94
120114	Belts,bags,wallets	$79
121764	Jewelry	$69
122709	Jewelry	$533
128390	Mini city	$19,786

Rather than changing the column name to make it shorter, you could choose to wrap the text and autofit the column height. These two format options often work in conjunction with one another. You would usually apply these format options to all of the header cells of a table block.

To apply the autofit height and wrap text options to table block header cells, follow these steps:

1. Select all of the header cells in the table block by clicking each individual cell while holding down the CTRL key.

2. Right-click to invoke the pop-up menu and select Format Cell....

3. The Format Cell dialog appears with the General options displayed. Within the General category, check the box for Autofit height.

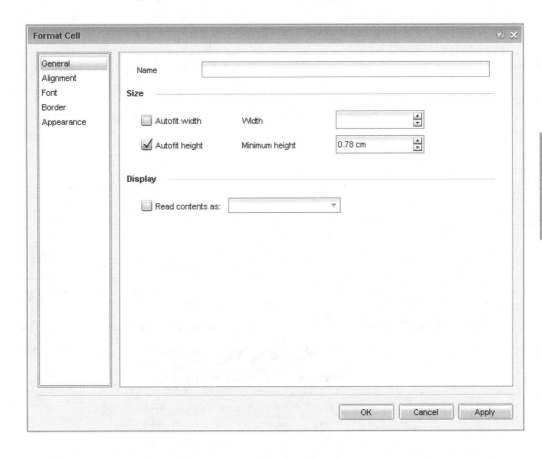

4. Select the Alignment options in the right pane. Within the Alignment category, check the box for Wrap text.

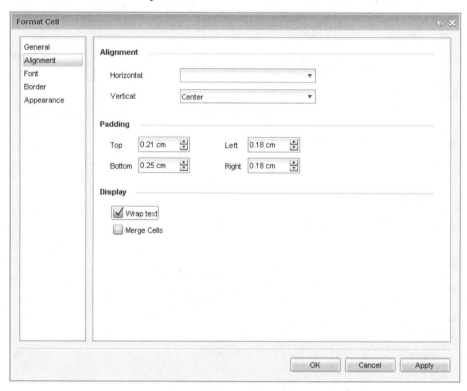

5. Click OK. The full column name will now fit in the header cell.

Product SKU No	Category	Sales revenue
115121	Hats,gloves,scarves	$30,285
116256	Hats,gloves,scarves	$143
119427	Jewelry	$94
120114	Belts,bags,wallets	$79
121764	Jewelry	$69
122709	Jewelry	$533
128390	Mini city	$19,786
128969	T-Shirts	$94

Formatting Options in the Format Table Dialog Box

In the preceding examples, you selected individual cells and components of a table. The formatting options available change dynamically depending on which object(s) you have selected. Table 20-3 outlines the options available when you select a table block and open the Format Table dialog box, as shown in Figure 20-1.

Most of the options in the Layout category of the Format Table dialog box affect how a report is printed. To see the effect of these settings, click the Page Mode button from the status bar.

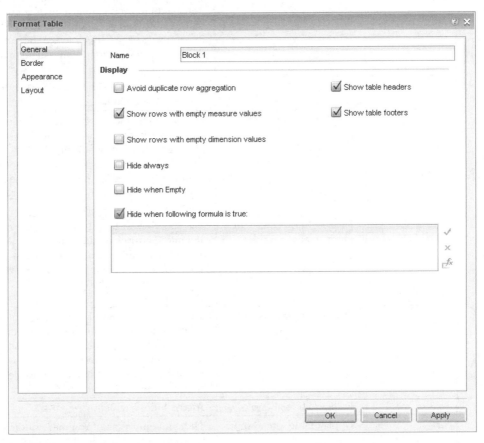

Figure 20-1   Format Table dialog box

Format Category	Format Option	Purpose
General	Name	Defines a name for a table block. The name can be useful when using the table format category Layout: Relative Position options.
	Display: Avoid duplicate row aggregation	Suppresses the display of duplicate row aggregation. When the universe designer sets an object to use a projection aggregate, Web Intelligence automatically shows the aggregate for the dimension and level of detail displayed in the table. You generally want to check this box only if you are trying to see the individual rows of a result set to identify calculation issues.
	Display: Show table headers	Displays column headings in a table block (enabled by default).
	Display: Show table footers	Displays table footers. If you add a calculation, such as a subtotal, on a measure data object, this box will be automatically checked, and the table will show an additional footer row with the subtotals. If no calculations are added and you still want to show table footer cells in your table block, you can select this option.
	Display: Show rows with empty measure values	Displays rows with null measure values. By default, if a row contains null values, Web Intelligence will suppress the row and the corresponding dimension. In some cases, you may want to select this option so that the full data set will appear.
	Display: Show rows with empty dimension values	Displays rows with null dimension values. By default, if a row contains null dimension values, Web Intelligence will suppress the row. This setting is particularly important when you are merging multiple data providers and want to see rows from both queries.
	Display: Hide always	Always hides a table.
	Display: Hide when Empty	Hides an empty table. You may want to choose this option to display a table even when no rows are present in the table.
	Display: Hide when following formula is true	Hides the table on the report when the value of a formula is true.
Appearance	Background Image: Color	Sets the background color of the table.
	Background Image: Pattern	Sets the background of the table as an image.

Table 20-3 Format Table Options

Format Category	Format Option	Purpose
	Preview	Displays all of the settings you have made from the Appearance category as they will appear if you apply them.
	Spacing and Padding: Horizontal	Sets the horizontal spacing between every column in the table.
	Spacing and Padding: Vertical	Sets the vertical spacing between every row in the table.
	Alternate Color: Frequency	Determines how often the color alternates for the table rows. For example, if the frequency is set to 2, every second row in the table will be shaded in the color set in the color setting below.
	Alternate Color: Color	Sets the color used to shade alternating rows on the table.
Border	Style	Sets the style of the line to be applied in the border as None, Dashed, Dotted, or Plain.
	Thickness	Sets the thickness of the line.
	Borders (left, right, top, bottom)	Allows you to independently define a left, right, top, or bottom border with independent border style and thickness settings.
	Preview	Displays all of the settings you have made from the Border category as they will appear if you apply them.
Layout	Horizontal: Start on a new page	Forces a page break (down the page) prior to displaying the table.
	Horizontal: Avoid page break	Forces a page break (down the page) prior to displaying the table only if there is a natural page break that would split the table.
	Vertical: Start on a new page	Forces a page break (across the page) prior to displaying the table.
	Vertical: Repeat on every page	Prints the table block on every page.
	Vertical: Avoid page break	Forces a page break (across the page) prior to displaying the table only if there is a natural page break that would split the cell.
	Relative Position: Horizontal	Allows you to position a table horizontally relative to the edges of a report, section, or block.
	Relative Position: Vertical	Allows you to position a table vertically relative to the edges of a report, section, or block.

Table 20-3   Format Table Options *(continued)*

Part III

Conditional Formatting

Conditional formatting is used to highlight rows of data. You can use different fonts, colors, styles, borders, backgrounds, or alignments to highlight a row, or you can have the conditional format display a customized message.

Figure 20-2 shows three different conditional formats:

- The first conditional format is defined to set the *Sales revenue* object to green text; bold when the value is greater than 50,000.

- The second conditional format is defined to set the *Sales revenue* object to white text; red background when the value is less than 10,000.

- The third conditional format displays a text message, "Excellent," if the value of *Sales revenue* is greater than 100,000.

Conditional formats are evaluated from top to bottom. If more than one conditional format evaluates to true, the last conditional format applied will persist. If none of the conditions are met, then the cell content and format defined for the object remain unaffected.

Working with conditional formatting requires two steps: create the conditional format rule, and then apply the conditional format rule to one or more columns.

Creating a Conditional Format

You define conditional format rules through the Formatting Rule Editor dialog box, accessible from the Analysis | Conditional toolbox.

To create the conditional formats as displayed in Figure 20-2, follow these steps:

Year	State	Category	Sales revenue
2004	California	2 Pocket shirts	$50,999
2004	California	Belts,bags,wallets	$66,063
2004	California	Bermudas	$5,290
2004	California	Boatwear	$10,974
2004	California	Cardigan	$44,294
2004	California	Casual dresses	$11,240
2004	California	Day wear	$46,460
2004	California	Dry wear	$12,923
2004	California	Evening wear	$84,664
2004	California	Fancy fabric	$8,443
2004	California	Full length	$10,954
2004	California	Hair accessories	$12,436
2004	California	Hats,gloves,scarves	EXCELLENT
2004	California	Jackets	$20,675
2004	California	Jeans	$12,981

Conditional format that formats text

Conditional format that displays text

Figure 20-2   Use conditional formatting to highlight exceptions.

1. Select the object on which you want to base your conditional format—in this example, select *Sales revenue.*

2. Click the New Rule ... button from the Analysis | Conditional toolbox. The Formatting Rule Editor dialog box appears.

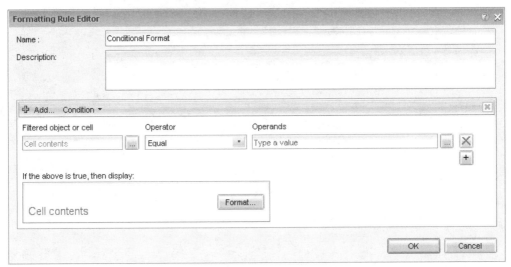

3. In the Formatting Rule Editor dialog box, enter a name and an optional description for the conditional format. In this example, give the conditional format the name **Meets Promotional Requirement.** Create the condition. In this example, set the condition to *Sales revenue* greater or equal to 50,000.

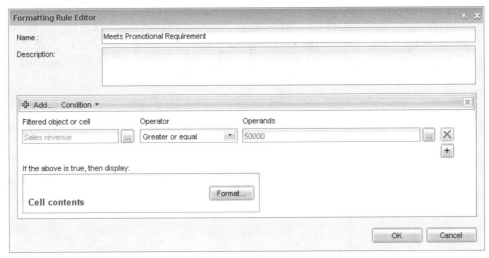

4. To set the format, when this formula evaluates to true, click the Format... button. The Formatting Rules Display dialog box will display. Click the Text category. Set the Font Style to Bold and the Font Color to Green.

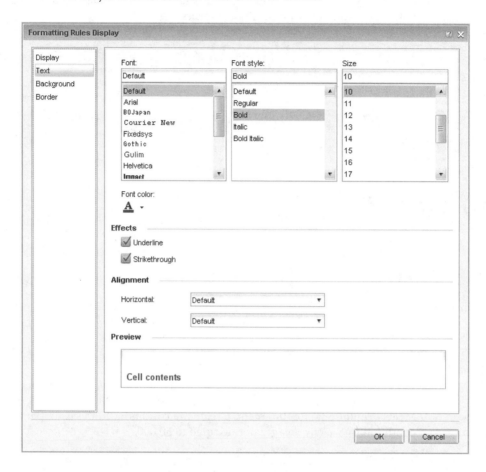

5. Click OK to return to the Formatting Rule Editor dialog box. Click OK. The Conditional Formats dialog box will display with the new formatting rule.

6. Click OK to apply the rule.

Custom Text in Conditional Formatting

In the previous section, you changed the font color and font style of the data values. Using the Formatting Rules dialog box's Display Text, Background, and Border categories, you also can change the font size, font effects, background color, alignment, and borders.

Year	State	Category	Sales revenue
2004	California	2 Pocket shirts	$50,999
2004	California	Belts,bags,wallets	$66,063
2004	California	Bermudas	$5,290
2004	California	Boatwear	$10,974
2004	California	Cardigan	$44,294
2004	California	Casual dresses	$11,240
2004	California	Day wear	$46,460

If you want your conditional format to display a text message such as "Excellent" or "Poor Sales," you can define the custom text message through the Formatting Rules dialog box's Display: Display options, as shown in Figure 20-3.

Figure 20-3 Formatting Rules dialog box Display options

Charts

Table blocks are appropriate when you want to see the actual details and numbers. However, when you are trying to identify trends, patterns, and exceptions, visually displaying your data in a chart is a more effective block style.

Inserting a New Chart

The procedure to add a chart is similar to that of adding a table, although you must first choose a chart style. Although you can always change your chart types later, before creating a chart, you will need to pick one of the available chart types: column chart, line chart, or pie chart.

To create a chart, follow these steps:

1. Select the drop-down chart type button from the Report Element | Chart toolbox. For this example, select the Insert Column Chart button.

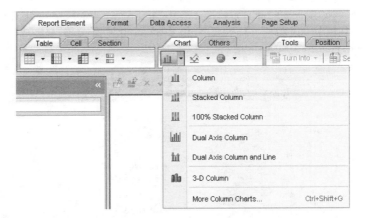

2. Select the Column option. Drag your cursor to a blank area on the report tab. Your cursor will display as a chart.

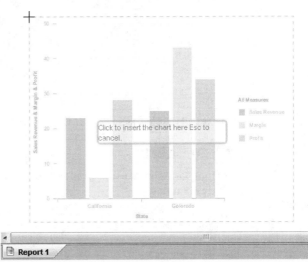

3. Click to place the chart. A blank chart is created in the report.

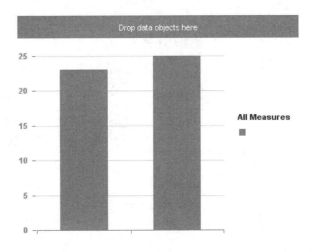

4. From the available objects list in the left pane, drag-and-drop the objects to the appropriate part of the chart. In this example, drag *State* to the X axis and *Sales revenue* to the Y axis.

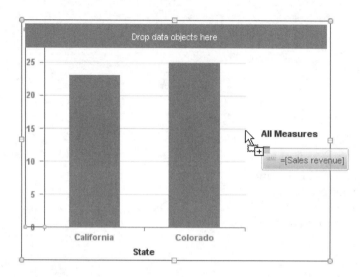

The chart will display as shown in Figure 20-4.

Formatting Charts

You can format your charts using predefined color palettes and styles, as well as through the Format Chart dialog box.

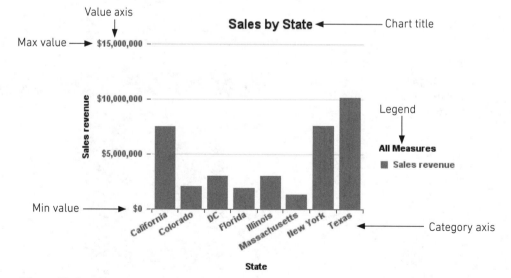

Figure 20-4 A new column chart

Using Preset Palettes and Styles

Chart colors and styles can be modified using preset color palettes and styles available through the Format | Chart Style toolbox.

To change an existing chart palette and style, follow these steps:

1. Select the chart block.

2. Select a color palette button from the Format | Chart Style toolbox. For this example, select the green button.

The chart will be updated with a green color palette.

Using the Format Chart Options

As you graph your data, you can change a number of chart properties to make the chart more visually appealing and readable. To access the chart format options, right-click a chart block and select Format Chart from the pop-up menu to display the Format Chart dialog box. Table 20-4 outlines the sections and main chart format options available.

Changing the Chart Type

You can change the chart type at anytime. To change an existing chart type, follow these steps:

1. Select the block.

2. Right-click, select Turn Into, and choose the new type from the pop-up menu. For this example, select Pie Chart.

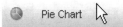

The chart will convert to a pie chart.

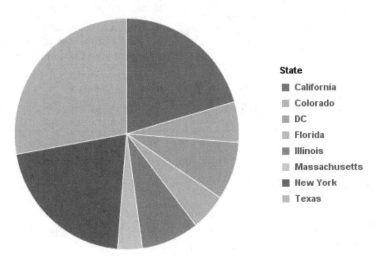

Part III

Format Category	Format Option	Purpose
Title	Visible	Specifies whether to display the chart title
	Title Label	Sets the title text to display
	Layout	Specifies the location of the title: Top, Bottom, Left, or Right
	Text: Font	Allows you to set the font, font size, style, and alignment for the title
	Text Policy	Sets the text wrap policy: No Wrap, Wrap, or Truncate
Legend	Visible	Specifies whether to display the legend
	Layout: Location	Specifies the location of the legend: Top, Bottom, Left, or Right
	Text: Font	Allows you to specify the font, font size, style, and alignment for the legend
Category Axis	Visible	Specifies whether to display the category axis
	Layout: Show Labels	Specifies whether to display the data values on the category axis
	Layout: Tick Length	Determines the length of the ticks on the category axis
	Text: Font	Allows you to specify the font, font size, and style for the category axis
Value Axis	Visible	Specifies whether to display the value axis
	Scaling: Minimum Value	Specifies the minimum value for the value axis, or can be set as automatic, which is determined from the data, or as a fixed value
	Scaling: Maximum Value	Specifies the maximum value for the value axis, or can be set as automatic, which is determined from the data, or as a fixed value
	Layout: Show Labels	Specifies whether to display the data values on the value axis
	Text: Font	Allows you to specify the font, font size, and style for the value axis

Table 20-4 Format Chart Options

Formatting Reports

In the previous sections, we have explored format options for cells, table blocks, and charts. Nearly every object in a report has format options that can be applied. The report itself also has format options.

Report Format Options

To access the Format Report dialog box, right-click any blank area of a report and select Format Report. Table 20-5 outlines the format options available for a report.

Format Category	Format Option	Purpose
General	Name	Defines a name for a report
	Page content (Quick Display mode only): Number of records per page: Vertical/ Horizontal	Sets the number of records that will display on a page in Quick Display mode
	Page layout: Page Size	Sets the page size used to lay out the printed report page (default is A4)
	Page layout: Orientation	Sets the page layout used for the printed report page (default is portrait)
	Page Scaling: Adjust to	Allows you to scale the printed page to a percentage
	Page Scaling: Fit to	Allows you to scale the printed page to a number of pages wide by a number of pages tall
	Margins: Top, Bottom, Left, Right	Allows you to set the top, bottom, left, and right margins on the printed page
Header	Show Header	Allows you to turn on or off the printed page header
	Height	Allows you to set the height of the header in centimeters or inches
Footer	Show Footer	Allows you to turn on or off the printed page footer
	Height	Allows you to set the height of the footer in centimeters or inches

Table 20-5   Report Format Options

Formatting Master/Detail Reports

As discussed in Chapter 18, master/detail reports are reports that are broken into sections. Formatting a section in a master/detail report is not that obvious, as you can clearly see the beginning and end of the section only when you are in structure only mode.

To access the Format Section dialog box, right-click any blank area of a section and select Format Section from the pop-up menu. Table 20-6 outlines the format options available for a section.

Format Category	Format Option	Purpose
General	Name	Defines a name for a section
	Display: Minimum height	Sets the minimum height of the section
	Display: Bottom Padding	Sets the amount of whitespace that will appear at the bottom of the section

Table 20-6   Format Section Options

Format Category	Format Option	Purpose
	Display: Bookmark section	Converts section cells to bookmarks when the report is converted to PDF for printing and offline viewing
	Display: Hide always	Specifies that the section will always be hidden
	Display: Hide when Empty	Specifies that the section will be hidden if there is no data in the section
	Display: Hide when following formula is true	Hides the section on the report when the value of a formula is true
Appearance	Background Image: Color	Sets the background color of the section
	Background Image: Pattern	Sets the background of the section as an image
Layout	Vertical: Start on a new page	Forces a page break prior to displaying the section
	Vertical: Repeat on every page	Repeats the section on every page
	Vertical: Avoid page break	Forces a page break prior to displaying the section only if there is a natural page break that would split the section
	Vertical: Minimum top offset	Sets the minimum height of the report section immediately above the current section (could be another section or the report header), specified in inches, centimeters, or pixels. This is the minimum height, so if there is a data block in the section above that is taller than the minimum top offset value, the height of the section will exceed the minimum top offset.
	Vertical: Top Margin	Sets the margin between the section immediately above the current section and this section specified in inches, centimeters or pixels.

Table 20-6   Format Section Options *(continued)*

Web Intelligence Options

Web Intelligence allows you to set the measurement in inches or centimeters, to optionally display grid lines for positioning report components, and to set snapping to the grid. The Web Intelligence Options button appears in the upper-right corner of the design panel. Click it to display the Web Intelligence Options dialog box, as shown in Figure 20-5.

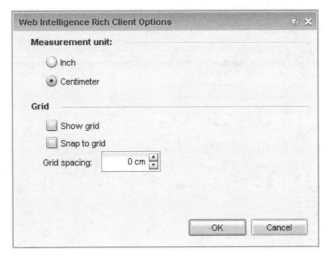

Figure 20-5   Web Intelligence Options dialog box

Summary

Web Intelligence offers formatting options for all objects in a report. The ability to add tables, cross tables, charts, and sections to your reports allows you to display data in multiple block formats. Reports, sections, blocks, and cells can all be independently formatted. Conditional formatting allows you to format data based on values within the data. All of the formatting options available offer endless flexibility for customizing how a report looks and behaves.

CHAPTER

21

Formulas and Variables

So far, you have learned how to display and manipulate objects called *universe object* variables that are returned from a data provider. Formulas provide a powerful way to enhance your reports by transforming columns of data into more meaningful information.

There are advantages and disadvantages to using user-defined formulas and variables that are created by the report designer. The key disadvantage to these user-defined formulas is that they are document-specific. In other words, they cannot be shared with other users or other documents. You must re-create the formulas in each new document. This process can be error-prone and maintenance-intensive. Differences in the way report authors create similar formulas can create multiple versions of the truth. Is it "revenue net of returns" or "revenue without returns"? For these reasons, ensure that you work with the universe designer to evaluate if the formula should be a universe object that will be available to all users and documents.

However, it is not realistic, or even possible, for the universe designer to include every conceivable calculation in the universe. Formulas allow you to create one-time and unanticipated calculations that do not exist in the universe. Another advantage to using formulas is that Web Intelligence manipulates local report data using a syntax that can overcome many limitations of SQL.

In this chapter, you'll learn how to create formulas and variables. We'll cover how to use operators and functions in formulas, and then describe the built-in functions provided by SAP BusinessObjects BI 4 Web Intelligence for you to use in your formulas.

Creating Formulas and Variables

A formula may contain any combination of universe object variables, user-defined report variables, functions, operators, calculation contexts, and numeric and string constants. Formulas can vary in complexity from basic calculations—formulas containing only universe object variables, basic operators, and constants—to very advanced formulas using complex combinations of if-then-else logic, Boolean logic, other user-defined variables, and built-in functions that Web Intelligence provides. Formulas can perform calculations on any type of data, including numeric, string, date, time, and Boolean, as shown in the examples in Table 21-1.

Type	Formula	Purpose
Numeric	=[Sales revenue]*1.10	Increases revenue by 10 percent
String	=[City] + ", " + [State]	Concatenates *City* and *State* separated by a comma into a single string
String	=Concatenation("Dear "; [Name])	Creates the salutation string that could be used for a form letter
Date	=ToDate("01/01/2005"; "MM/dd/yyyy") + 30	Converts a date string to a date data type and adds 30 days
Time	=LastExecutionTime()	Returns the last time the report data was refreshed
Boolean	=[Sales revenue] < 100000	Displays true if revenue is less than $100,000 and false if revenue is greater than or equal to $100,000
String	=If([Sales revenue]<100000; "Low Revenue"; "High Revenue")	Distinguishes between *Low Revenue* sales and *High Revenue* sales

Table 21-1   Web Intelligence Allows You to Create Different Types of Formulas

Syntax for Formulas in Web Intelligence

When creating formulas in Web Intelligence, you must follow certain syntax rules so that Web Intelligence can understand your formulas. Follow these guidelines when building a formula:

- Always start the formula with an = sign.
- When you reference a base report variable or another variable name, it must be enclosed in square brackets ([]). For example, the formula =[Sales revenue] * 1.10 contains a base report variable, [Sales revenue].
- Base report variables and user-defined variable names are case-sensitive. The base report variable [Sales revenue] is correct, but using [Sales Revenue] will return an error stating that it cannot be found.
- Function names are not case-sensitive.
- Spaces between the components of the formula can make the formula easier to read. Spaces are ignored. For example, the formula =[Sales revenue]*1.10 is the same as =[Sales revenue] * 1.10.
- Carriage returns can be added to formulas by pressing CTRL-ENTER or ALT-ENTER to make the formulas easier to read.
- String constants in formulas are always surrounded by double quotation marks. For example, to concatenate the label "Year: " to the year returned by the universe object variable, enter ="Year: " + [Year].

- Numeric constants are not surrounded by quotation marks.

- Numeric constants should be entered without any formatting such as dollar signs or thousands separators. For example, to add $500,000.00 to the `[Revenue]` universe object variable, enter `=[Revenue] + 500000`.

- Function parameter lists are separated by semicolons in Web Intelligence. For example, the formula containing the concatenation function `=Concatenation("Dear ";[Name])` requires two parameters with a semicolon separating them.

- When creating if-then-else logic in formulas, Web Intelligence provides the If function. For example, the formula `=If([Revenue]<100000; "Low Revenue"; "High Revenue")` would be used in Web Intelligence.

Creating a Formula

There are two ways to create a formula and display it in a block on your report. If you are new to creating formulas, you should start by using the Formula Editor. As you gain experience and get comfortable with Web Intelligence formula syntax, you can type the formula directly into the formula toolbar.

If the formula toolbar is not displayed below the ribbon toolbar, select the Show Formula Toolbar button from the Analysis toolbox.

Using the Formula Editor

To open the Formula Editor, click the Formula Editor button on the formula toolbar in Web Intelligence design mode. As shown in Figure 21-1, three areas of this editor contain the components you will use to create your formulas:

- **Available Objects**   Contains universe object variables and user-defined variables.

- **Available Functions**   Contains the many functions that can be used in formulas.

- **Available Operators**   Contains the operators used to perform numeric and comparison operations in your formulas.

To create a formula using the Formula Editor, do the following:

1. Insert and select a blank cell or table column in a report.

 2. Click the Formula Editor button in the formula toolbar to display the Formula Editor.

3. In the Formula Editor, you can drag, double-click, or type the components (universe object variables, user-defined variables, functions, operators). In this example, double-click the *Sales revenue* object in the Available Objects list. Note that Web Intelligence automatically inserts the equal (=) sign at the beginning of the formula. The operators that are shown in gray must be typed into the formula text directly. Also, string and numeric constants are not available in a list and must be typed in directly.

Available Objects displays the universe variables and user-defined variables that can be used in a formula

Available Functions displays all of the functions that are provided by Web Intelligence

Available Operators displays the operators used to perform numeric calculations and comparison operations in formulas

Formula text

Validate formula

Cancel formula

Universe object, function, and operator descriptions

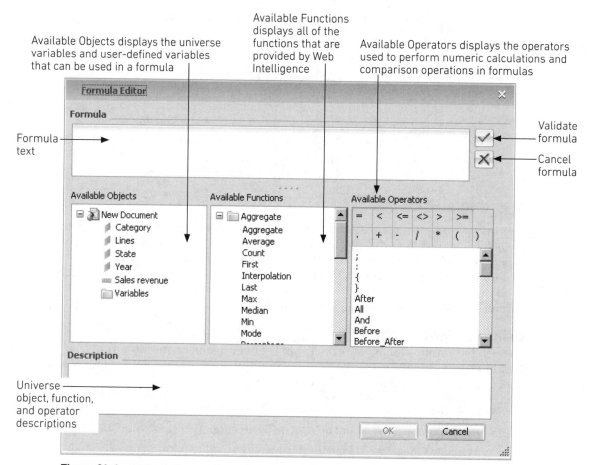

Figure 21-1   Web Intelligence Formula Editor

4. To complete the formula, place your cursor at the end of your formula in the formula text box by clicking after the *Sales revenue* object and type in the multiplication operator * and the numeric constant **1.1**.

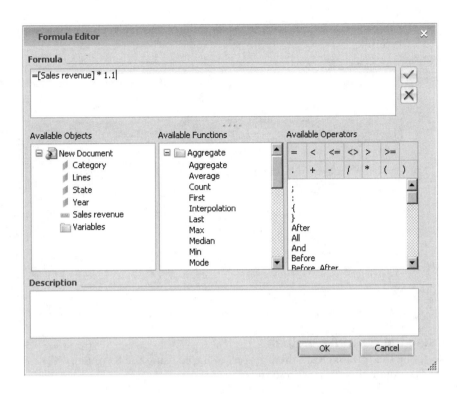

5. Click the Validate button in the Formula Editor. If there are any syntax errors in your formula, you will receive an error. If the editor lets you know the formula is defined correctly, click OK.

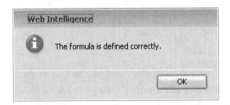

6. Click the OK button to close the Formula Editor and see the table with the new formula.

Year	State	Category	Lines	Sales revenue	
2004	California	2 Pocket shirts	Shirt Waist	$50,999	$56,099
2004	California	Belts,bags,wallets	Accessories	$66,063	$72,670
2004	California	Bermudas	City Trousers	$5,290	$5,819
2004	California	Boatwear	Jackets	$10,974	$12,071
2004	California	Cardigan	Sweaters	$44,294	$48,723
2004	California	Casual dresses	Dresses	$11,240	$12,364
2004	California	Day wear	Outerwear	$46,460	$51,106
2004	California	Dry wear	Overcoats	$12,923	$14,215
2004	California	Evening wear	Dresses	$84,664	$93,130

The formula bar shows: *fx* =[Sales revenue] * 1.1

Using the Formula Toolbar

To create the formula from the previous example using the formula toolbar, rather than the Formula Editor, follow these steps:

1. Insert and select a blank cell or table column in a report.

2. Type the formula =[Sales revenue] * 1.1 into the formula text box on the formula toolbar.

The formula bar shows: *fx* =[Sales Revenue] * 1.1

Creating a Variable

A *variable* is simply a formula with a name and a qualification. When you plan to reuse a formula throughout your document, perhaps on a different report tab or within another formula, you will want to save the formula as a variable.

Saving the formula as a variable also allows you to give the formula a meaningful name. It will be much easier to remember what the formula =[Sales revenue]*1.1 represents if it is defined as a variable with the name *Revenue w projected 10% increase*.

You can either explicitly create a formula as a variable or convert an existing formula to a variable.

Using the Variable Editor

You can create a new variable using the Create New Variable dialog box, shown in Figure 21-2. To display this editor, click the New Variable button from the Data Access | Data Objects toolbox.

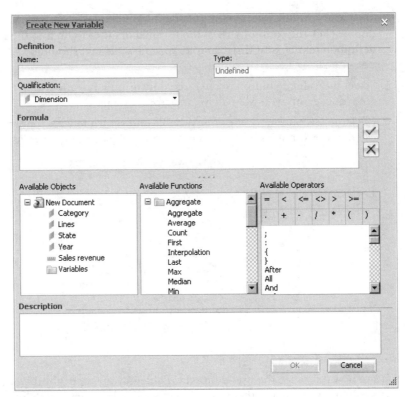

Figure 21-2   Create New Variable dialog box

To create a formula and save it as a variable, do the following:

1. Select the New Variable button from the Data Access | Data Objects toolbox to open the Create New Variable dialog box.

2. In the Name box on the right, specify a meaningful name for your variable. The variable name is used as the default column heading in your reports and will be displayed in the Variables folder in the available objects list for your report. In this example, type **Revenue with 12 pct increase**.

3. Determine and select the qualification for your variable:

   - Select Dimension for Character and Date fields.

   - Select Measure for numeric values that you will want to aggregate. This is the qualification to choose for our example.

   - Select Detail for detailed information such as phone numbers and street addresses that provide descriptive data about other dimensions and that are not useful for drilling.

NOTE You must select a qualification. Web Intelligence will always default the qualification to Dimension.

4. Type your formula into the formula definition text box. You can also drag or double-click the components of the formula to enter them into the formula definition text box. In this example, your formula text should be = [Sales revenue] * 1.12.

5. Select the Validate button to check if your formula has any syntax errors. If there are syntax errors, you will receive an error message.

6. Click the OK button to save your variable and return to your report. You will see it listed in the Variables folder of the Available Objects panel of your report.

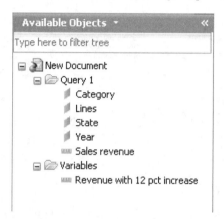

You can now reference the user-defined variable in your report by dragging it into a table as a column, referencing the user-defined variable in other user-defined variables, using the user-defined variable to define filters and alerters, and so on. This is the power of defining your formulas as variables.

Converting an Existing Formula to a Variable

If your report already contains a formula in a cell, you can convert the formula to a variable. To convert a formula in a table to a variable, do the following:

1. Select the cell in your report containing the formula that you wish to convert to a variable.

2. Click the Create Variable button on the formula toolbar. The Create New Variable dialog box will display with the formula in the formula text.

3. Type in a meaningful name and select the qualification for your variable. In this example, name the variable **Revenue with 10 pct increase** and choose the Measure qualification.

4. Click OK to close the Create New Variable dialog box and return to the report. The results of the calculation in the report will not have changed; however, the cell formula has changed to = [Revenue with 10 pct increase].

Editing and Deleting Variables

To make changes to an existing variable, on the left panel in the list of available objects, right-click the variable in the Variables folder and select Edit from the pop-up menu.

To delete a variable from your Web Intelligence document, right-click the variable on the list of available objects in the Variables folder and select Remove.

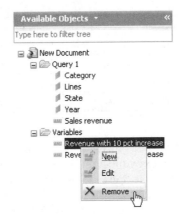

Using Operators in Formulas

Web Intelligence provides many operators for you to use in your formulas. An operator allows you to perform mathematical operations, test for conditions such as whether one value is less than another, and link multiple conditional clauses together using logical operators such as AND and OR.

Mathematical Operators

Mathematical operators allow you to perform the following basic mathematical calculations:

Operator	Description	Sample
+	Addition operator	`=[Number of guests] + [Future guests]`
-	Subtraction operator	`=[Sales revenue] – 10`
*	Multiplication operator	`=[Sales revenue] * .06`
/	Division operator	`=[Sales revenue] / [Number of guests]`

Conditional Operators

Conditional operators allow you to perform comparisons between two components of a formula, returning a true or false value. Conditional operators are most commonly used in if-then-else logic, such as = `If([Sales revenue]>50000; "Good Revenue"; "Low Revenue")`.

You can use the following conditional operators:

Operator	Description	Sample
=	Equal to	`= [Sales revenue] = 20000`
>	Greater than	`= [Sales revenue] > 50000`
<	Less than	`= [Sales revenue] < 15000`
>=	Greater than or equal to	`= [Sales revenue] >= 50000`
<=	Less than or equal to	`= [Sales revenue] <= 15000`
!=	Not equal to	`= [Sales revenue] != 20000`

Logical Operators

Logical operators allow you to connect multiple conditional clauses in your formulas, returning a single Boolean (true/false) value, or 1 for true and 0 for false. For example, = `[Sales revenue] < 50000 AND [Year] = "FY2012"` may return true or 1 for `[Sales revenue] < 50000` and false or 0 for `[Year] = "FY2012"` if you were looking at revenues from a year other than 2012. The result for the formula = `[Sales revenue] < 50000 AND [Year] = "FY2012"` would then be evaluated as =`true` (for the revenue condition) AND `false` (for the year portion), which returns false.

Operator	Description	Sample
AND	True AND True returns True True AND False returns False False AND False returns False False AND True returns False	`= [Sales revenue] < 50000 AND [Year] = "FY2012"`

Operator	Description	Sample
OR	True OR True returns True True OR False returns True False OR False returns False False OR True returns True	`= [Year] = "FY2011" OR [Year] =` `"FY2012"`
NOT	NOT True returns False NOT False returns True	`= NOT(IsNull([Year]))`

Where Operator

The Where operator allows you to specify limiting criteria on data in a formula. The Where operator is used in a formula with the following syntax:

```
= [report object] Where (Boolean expression)
```

Examples include the following:

- The Where operator could be used to return the revenue if the invoice date is in the current year using the following formula: `= [Sales revenue] Where (Year([Invoice Date]) = Year(CurrentDate()))`.

- The Where operator could be used to return the revenue if the country is US using the following formula: `= [Sales revenue] Where ([Country]="US")`.

- The Boolean expression in a formula containing a Where operator can contain other operators including AND, NOT, and OR, as in the following example: `= [Sales revenue] Where ([Country] = "US" AND [Service Line] ="Recreation")`.

Context and Function-Specific Operators

Context operators are used with calculation contexts and extended syntax. See the section "Using Context Operators in Input Contexts" later in this chapter for a discussion of context operators.

Some functions can take specific operators as arguments. These operators are function-specific and are detailed in the next section.

Using Functions in Formulas

SAP BusinessObjects BI 4 Web Intelligence provides many functions for you to use in your formulas. A function is an operation that takes zero or more input parameter values and generates a single output value. For example, `=Round(273.75;0)` returns 274. In this example, the Round function takes two input parameters—the number to be rounded (273.75) and the number of decimal places to round the number to (0)—and returns the output value (274). Input parameters can be universe object variables, user-defined variables, numeric constants, or text literals.

Functions can be added to formulas by typing them directly into the Formula Editor or by selecting them from the list of available functions when using the Formula Editor. Until you are familiar with the function syntax, select the functions from the list of available functions in the Formula Editor. When you select a function, the Formula Editor provides you with a description of the function, the syntax for the function, the data types required as input parameters, and the data type returned as the output value, as shown in Figure 21-3.

As you build your formula, pay attention to the data types required as input parameters and the data type that will be returned as the output value. Providing incorrect data types as input parameters to a function will return an error when validating or saving the formula. For example, entering the formula =Round("273.75",0) will return an error because the first input parameter is expected to be a number, not a string. The quotes around 273.75 tell Web Intelligence to treat it as a string.

The number of formula functions available in Web Intelligence has increased in SAP BusinessObjects BI 4. Table 21-2 provides a comparison of the functions from each of the various interfaces and versions. Use this table to understand when you may have report upgrade issues when converting from prior Desktop Intelligence and Web Intelligence versions to SAP BusinessObjects BI 4 Web Intelligence.

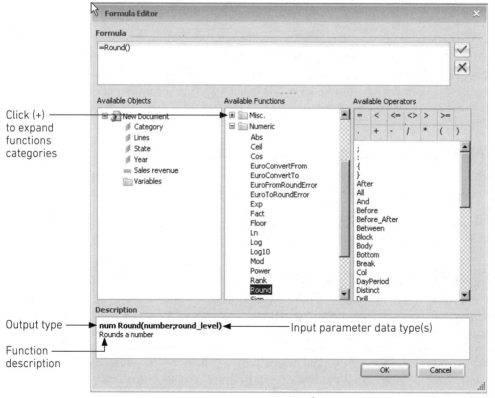

Figure 21-3 Selecting a function in theWeb Intelligence Formula Editor

Function Category	Function	DeskI 6.5	WebI 6.5	WebI XI R2	DeskI XI R2	WebI XI R3	DeskI XI R3	WebI BI 4
Aggregate	Aggregate							X
	Average	X	X	X	X	X	X	X
	Count	X	X	X	X	X	X	X
	CountAll	X			X		X	
	First					X		X
	Interpolation					X		X
	Last					X		X
	Max	X	X	X	X	X	X	X
	Median	X		X	X	X	X	X
	Min	X	X	X	X	X	X	X
	Mode					X		X
	Percentage		X	X		X		X
	Percentile	X		X	X	X	X	X
	Product	X		X	X	X	X	X
	RunningAverage	X		X	X	X	X	X
	RunningCount	X		X	X	X	X	X
	RunningMax	X		X	X	X	X	X
	RunningMin	X		X	X	X	X	X
	RunningProduct	X		X	X	X	X	X
	RunningSum	X		X	X	X	X	X
	StdDev	X		X	X	X	X	X
	StdDevP	X		X	X	X	X	X
	Sum	X	X	X	X	X	X	X
	Var	X		X	X	X	X	X
	VarP	X		X	X	X	X	X
Numeric	Abs	X	X	X	X	X	X	X
	Ceil	X	X	X	X	X	X	X

Table 21-2   Functions Available in BusinessObjects Versions

Function Category	Function	DeskI 6.5	WebI 6.5	WebI XI R2	DeskI XI R2	WebI XI R3	DeskI XI R3	WebI BI 4
	Cos	X		X	X	X	X	X
	EuroConvertFrom	X		X	X	X	X	X
	EuroConvertTo	X		X	X	X	X	X
	EuroFromRoundError	X		X	X	X	X	X
	EuroToRoundError	X		X	X	X	X	X
	Exp	X	X	X	X	X	X	X
	Fact	X	X	X	X	X	X	X
	Floor	X	X	X	X	X	X	X
	Ln	X	X	X	X	X	X	X
	Log	X	X	X	X	X	X	X
	Log10	X			X	X	X	X
	Mod	X	X	X	X	X	X	X
	Power	X	X	X	X	X	X	X
	Rank	X		X	X	X	X	X
	Round	X	X	X	X	X	X	X
	Sign	X		X	X	X	X	X
	Sin	X		X	X	X	X	X
	Sqrt	X	X	X	X	X	X	X
	Tan	X		X	X	X	X	X
	ToNumber	X	X	X	X	X	X	X
	Truncate	X	X	X	X	X	X	X
Character	Asc	X		X	X	X	X	X
	Char	X		X	X	X	X	X
	Concatenation	X		X	X	X	X	X
	Fill	X		X	X	X	X	X
	FormatDate	X	X	X	X	X	X	X
	FormatNumber	X	X	X	X	X	X	X
	Hyperlink	X			X	X	X	X
	HTMLEncode			X		X	X	X
	InitCap	X		X	X	X	X	X

Table 21-2 Functions Available in BusinessObjects Versions (*continued*)

Function Category	Function	Deskl 6.5	Webl 6.5	Webl XI R2	Deskl XI R2	Webl XI R3	Deskl XI R3	Webl BI 4
	Left	X	X	X	X	X	X	X
	LeftPad	X		X	X	X	X	X
	LeftTrim	X	X	X	X	X	X	X
	Length	X	X	X	X	X	X	X
	Lower	X		X	X	X	X	X
	Match	X	X	X	X	X	X	X
	Pos	X		X	X	X	X	X
	Replace	X	X	X		X	X	X
	Right	X	X	X		X	X	X
	RightPad	X		X		X	X	X
	RightTrim	X	X	X		X	X	X
	SubStr	X	X	X		X	X	X
	Trim	X	X	X		X	X	X
	Upper	X		X		X	X	X
	URLEncode			X		X		X
	WordCap	X		X		X	X	X
Date/Time	CurrentDate	X	X	X		X	X	X
	CurrentTime	X	X	X		X	X	X
	DayName	X	X	X		X	X	X
	DayNumberOfMonth	X	X	X		X	X	X
	DayNumberOfWeek	X	X	X		X	X	X
	DayNumberOfYear	X	X	X		X	X	X
	DaysBetween	X	X	X	X	X	X	X
	LastDayOfMonth	X		X	X	X	X	X
	LastDayOfWeek	X		X	X	X	X	X
	Month	X	X	X	X	X	X	X
	MonthNumberOfYear	X	X	X	X	X	X	X
	MonthsBetween	X	X	X	X	X	X	X
	Quarter	X	X	X	X	X	X	X

Table 21-2   Functions Available in BusinessObjects Versions *(continued)*

Function Category	Function	Deskl 6.5	Webl 6.5	Webl XI R2	Deskl XI R2	Webl XI R3	Deskl XI R3	Webl BI 4
	RelativeDate	X	X	X	X	X	X	X
	TimeDim		X	X			X	X
	ToDate	X	X	X	X	X	X	X
	Week	X	X	X	X	X	X	X
	Year	X	X	X	X	X	X	X
Logical	Even	X		X	X	X	X	X
	IsDate	X	X	X	X	X	X	X
	IsError	X	X	X	X	X	X	X
	IsLogical	X		X	X	X	X	X
	IsNull	X	X	X	X	X	X	X
	IsNumber	X	X	X	X	X	X	X
	IsString	X	X	X	X	X	X	X
	IsTime	X	X	X	X	X	X	X
	Odd	X		X	X	X	X	X
Document	BlockNumber	X			X		X	
	DocumentAuthor	X	X	X	X	X	X	X
	DocumentCreationDate					X		X
	DocumentCreationTime					X		X
	DocumentDate	X	X	X	X	X	X	X
	DocumentName	X	X	X	X	X	X	X
	DocumentOwner					X		X
	DocumentPartially Refreshed	X	X	X	X	X	X	X
	DocumentTime	X	X	X		X	X	X
	DrillFilters	X	X	X		X	X	X
	GlobalFilters	X					X	
	LastPrintDate	X		X			X	
	PageInSection	X					X	
	PromptSummary					X		X
	QuerySummary					X		X
	ReportFilter					X		X

Table 21-2 Functions Available in BusinessObjects Versions (*continued*)

Function Category	Function	DeskI 6.5	WebI 6.5	WebI XI R2	DeskI XI R2	WebI XI R3	DeskI XI R3	WebI BI 4
	ReportFilterSummary					X		X
	SectionNumber	X					X	
Data Provider	Connection	X		X		X	X	X
	DataProvider	X	X	X		X	X	X
	DataProviderKeyDate					X		X
	DataProviderKeyDateCaption					X		X
	DataProviderSQL	X		X	X	X	X	X
	DataProviderType	X			X	X	X	X
	LastExecutionDate	X	X	X	X	X	X	X
	LastExecutionDuration					X		X
	LastExecutionTime	X	X	X	X	X	X	X
	NumberOfDataProviders	X		X	X	X	X	X
	NumberOfRows	X		X	X	X	X	X
	OlapQueryDescription	X				X	X	
	RefValueDate					X		X
	RefValueUserResponse					X		X
	ServerValue	X			X		X	X
	SourceName	X			X		X	
	UniverseName	X	X	X	X	X	X	X
	UserResponse	X		X	X	X	X	X
Miscellaneous	Application Value	X			X		X	
	BlockName					X		X
	ColumnNumber	X		X	X	X	X	X
	CurrentUser	X	X	X	X	X	X	X
	Depth							X
	Else					X		X
	ElseIf					X		X
	ForceMerge					X		X
	GetContentLocale			X		X		X

Table 21-2   Functions Available in BusinessObjects Versions (*continued*)

Function Category	Function	DeskI 6.5	WebI 6.5	WebI XI R2	DeskI XI R2	WebI XI R3	DeskI XI R3	WebI BI 4
	GetDominantPreferredViewingLocale					X		X
	GetLocale		X	X		X		X
	GetLocalized					X		X
	GetPreferredViewingLocale					X		X
	GetProfileNumber	X			X		X	
	GetProfileString	X			X		X	
	If		X	X		X		X
	Key							X
	LineNumber	X		X	X	X	X	X
	MultiCube	X			X		X	
	Name							X
	NameOf	X	X	X	X	X	X	X
	NoFilter	X		X	X	X	X	X
	NumberOfPages	X		X	X	X	X	X
	Page	X		X	X	X	X	X
	Previous	X		X	X	X	X	X
	RefValue					X		X
	RelativeValue					X		X
	RepFormula							X
	ReportName					X		X
	RowIndex	X		X	X	X	X	X
	Then					X		X
	UniqueNameOf		X			X		X
Set	Ancestor							X
	Children							X
	Descendants							X
	IsLeaf							X
	Lag							X
	Parent							X
	Siblings							X

Table 21-2   Functions Available in BusinessObjects Versions *(continued)*

All Functions

The All Functions category in the Formula Editor's Available Functions list allows you to find any of the functions in Web Intelligence sorted in alphabetical order. The other categories that follow separate the functions by the type of data the function is intended to act on.

Aggregate Functions

Aggregate functions allow you to perform calculations over a collective grouping or set of data. Subtotals and grand totals using the Sum function are examples of aggregate calculations. The aggregate functions available in the Formula Editor are the same functions used when inserting calculations such as sum, count, average, minimum, maximum, and percentage in a report, as discussed in the "Calculations" section in Chapter 18.

All of the functions in the aggregate function category, by default, depend on the location or context in which they are placed to determine their values. For example, the aggregate function Sum placed in a break footer of a table will sum values only over that break or grouping of data, representing a subtotal for that break. If the aggregate function Sum were moved to the footer of the table, all values in the table would be summed, representing a grand total.

The extended syntax for the aggregate functions allows you to modify the calculation context. For example, you could calculate the grand total for a measure in the detail of the table. For a more detailed discussion of contexts, see the "Calculation Contexts and Extended Syntax" section later in this chapter. For BEx queries, the default calculation context can be overridden using the {member set} syntax.

Specifying Member Sets

Many of the aggregate functions (Aggregate, Average, Count, Max, Min, and Sum) have been expanded to include {member set} syntax, which allows you to specify which members of a custom hierarchy of a BEx query should be included in the aggregate calculation. You refer to member sets in aggregate functions with the following syntax:

```
[hierarchy]&path.function
```

Specify member sets as follows:

- Enclose member sets in { }.
- The path and function parts are optional.
- In the path, you refer to each member in square brackets.
- The names of members and levels are case-sensitive.
- Ranges of members are referred to using a colon (:) between the full path for the starting member and the full path for the ending member.

Given the hierarchy shown in Table 21-3, the following examples refer to members in the hierarchy:

- [Sales Hierarchy]&[Customer_Region].[US].[California] .Children refers to the [ABC Company], [XYZ Company], and [HKE Company] members.

- `[Sales Hierarchy].Children` refers to all members of `[Sales Hierarchy]`. This includes all companies.
- `[Sales Hierarchy]&[Customer_Type].[US].[California] .[ABC Company]; [Sales Hierarchy]&[Customer_Type].[US] .[California].[HKE Company]` refers to the two members `[ABC Company]` and `[HKE Company]`.
- `[Sales Hierarchy]&[Customer_Type].[US].[California] .[ABC Company]: [Sales Hierarchy]&[Customer_Type].[US] .[California].[HKE Company]` refers to the three members `[ABC Company]`, `[XYZ Company]`, and `[HKE Company]` in the range.

Aggregate

The Aggregate function returns the default aggregation of a `measure_variable` parameter provided in the current calculation context.

```
number Aggregate (number [measure_variable][;{member set}])
```

`[{member set}]` is an optional input parameter referring to a hierarchy in a BEx query. All member sets must be from the custom hierarchy. The `{member set}` parameter can include multiple sets separated with semicolons (;).

The following are some examples:

`Aggregate([Sales revenue])` will return the sum of all [Sales revenue] values, when sum is the default aggregation.

`Aggregate([Sales revenue]; {[Sales Hierarchy]&[Customer_ Region].[US].Children})` will return the sum of all `[Sales revenue]` values for the child members of the US, when sum is the default aggregation.

Sales Hierarchy				Sales Amount
Customer_Region				
	US			
		California		
			ABC Company	537,000
			XYZ Company	27,237
			HKE Company	77,992
		New York		
			JKR Company	678,965
			KTO Company	67,590
	Canada			
		Ontario		
			PYO Company	89,098
			RTP Company	768,000

Table 21-3 Sales Hierarchy

Average

The Average function returns the average value over the numeric object variable provided in the current calculation context. The *measure_variable* parameter can be either a universe object variable or a user-defined variable.

```
number Average (number [measure_variable] [;{member set}] [;INCLUDEEMPTY])
```

[{member set}] is an optional input parameter referring to a hierarchy in a BEx query. All member sets must be from the custom hierarchy. The {member set} parameter can include multiple sets separated with semicolons (;).

[INCLUDEEMPTY] is an optional input parameter. By default, the Average function ignores nulls when calculating the average. If the [INCLUDEEMPTY] parameter is provided, the Average function will take nulls into consideration.

The following are some examples:

Average([Sales revenue]) will return 44,666.67 when the [Sales revenue] measure contains the values (45000; 37000; 52000; <Null>). Because the default for the Average function is to ignore nulls when calculating the average, the calculation based on the preceding value is (45,000 + 37,000 + 52,000)/3.

Average([Sales revenue];IncludeEmpty) will return 33,500 when the [Sales revenue] measure contains the values (45000; 37000; 52000; <Null>). When the optional INCLUDEEMPTY parameter is provided, the average calculation becomes (45,000 + 37,000 + 52,000 + 0)/4.

Average([Sales revenue];{ [Sales Hierarchy]&[Customer_Region] .[US].[California].Children}) will return 214,076.33, which is the average of the measure values (537,000; 27,237; 77,992) for the California member set from Table 21-3.

Count

The Count function returns the count of items in an object variable provided in the current calculation context. The *object_variable* parameter can be either a universe object variable or a user-defined variable.

```
integer Count(any_datatype [object_variable][;{member set}] [;INCLUDEEMPTY]
[;DISTINCT/ALL])
```

[{member set}] is an optional input parameter referring to a hierarchy in a BEx query. All member sets must be from the custom hierarchy. The {member set} parameter can include multiple sets separated with semicolons (;).

[INCLUDEEMPTY] is an optional input parameter. By default, the Count function ignores nulls when counting the items in the object variable. If the [INCLUDEEMPTY] parameter is provided, the Count function will take nulls into consideration.

[DISTINCT/ALL] is an optional input parameter. By default, the Count function counts only distinct items in the object variable. If the [ALL] parameter is provided, the Count function will count all items in the *object_variable* parameter whether they are distinct or not. If this optional input parameter is not specified, the default is DISTINCT for dimension objects and ALL for measure objects.

The following are some examples given this sample report:

State	City	=Count([State])	=Count([State];All)	=Count([State];IncludeEmpty)	=Count([State];IncludeEmpty;All)
California	Los Angeles	1	1	1	1
California	San Francisco		2		2
Colorado	Colorado Springs	2	3	2	3
Florida	Miami	3	4	3	4
Illinois	Chicago	4	5	4	5
Massachusetts	Boston	5	6	5	6
New York	New York	6	7	6	7
Texas	Austin		8		8
Texas	Dallas	7	9	7	9
Texas	Houston		10		10
	Washington			8	11

7	=Count([State])
10	=Count([State];All)
8	=Count([State];IncludeEmpty)
11	=Count([State];IncludeEmpty;All)

Count([State]) will return 7. By default, the Count function will count only distinct items in [State].

Count([State];All) will return 10. The optional All parameter instructs the Count function to count all items in [State] whether or not they are distinct.

Count([State];IncludeEmpty) will return 8 because there is a <Null> value.

Count([State],IncludeEmpty;All) will return 11 because it counts all records in [State], including the nondistinct and <Null> values.

First

The First function returns the first value of an object variable provided in the current calculation context. The *object_variable* parameter can be either a universe object variable or a user-defined variable. The First function depends on the sort order of the data in the calculation context.

```
any_datatypeFirst(any_datatype [object_variable])
```

The following is an example given the following sample report:

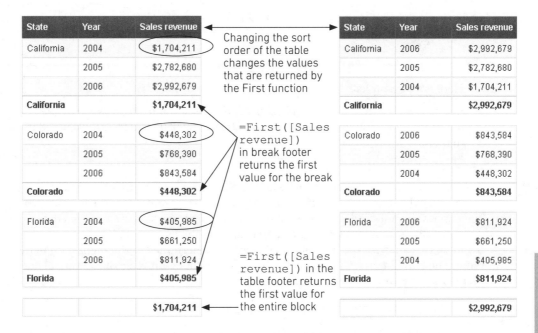

First([Sales revenue]) will return 1,704,211 when the [Sales revenue] object variable contains the values (1,704,211; 2,782,680; 2,992,679), displayed in that order.

Interpolation

The Interpolation function calculates empty measure values by interpolation. This function is most useful when plotting measure values on a graph where a measure value may contain missing values. Without the Interpolation function, the graph would contain broken and disconnected lines and points. Using this function, the graph will contain a continuous line.

```
number Interpolation(number [measure_variable][;PointToPoint|Linear]
[;NotOnBreak] [;ROW/COL])
```

[PointToPoint] interpolation calculates missing values by calculating a line equation f(x)=ax+b where passing through the two adjacent values of the missing value.

[Linear] interpolation calculates missing values by calculating a line equation f(x)=ax+b where passing through all available values of the measure.

[NotOnBreak] prevents the function from resetting on block and section breaks.

[ROW/COL] is an optional input parameter. The Interpolation function can be applied across either rows or columns.

Last

The Last function returns the last value of an object variable provided in the current calculation context. The *object_variable* parameter can be either a universe object variable or a user-defined variable. The Last function depends on the sort order of the data in the calculation context.

```
any_datatype Last(any_datatype [object_variable])
```

Here is an example:

`Last([Sales revenue])` will return 2,992,679 when the `[Sales revenue]` object variable contains the values (1,704,211; 2,782,680; 2,992,679), displayed in that order.

Max

The Max function returns the highest value found in an object variable provided in the current calculation context. If the *object_variable* parameter is a string data type, the maximum value will be determined alphabetically. If *object_variable* is a date time data type, the maximum value will be determined as the latest date. If *object_variable* is a numeric data type, the maximum value will be determined as the highest numeric value. The *object_variable* parameter can be either a universe object variable or a user-defined variable.

```
any_datatype Max(any_datatype [object_variable][;{member set}])
```

`[{member set}]` is an optional input parameter referring to a hierarchy in a BEx query. All member sets must be from the custom hierarchy. The `{member set}` parameter can include multiple sets separated with semicolons (`;`).

The following are some examples:

`Max([Sales revenue])` will return 981,210 when the `[Sales revenue]` object variable contains the values (128,100; 981,210; 277,750).

`Max([State])` will return Texas when the `[State]` object variable contains the values ("California"; "Texas"; "Colorado"; "Florida", "Illinois").

Median

The Median function returns the median value found in a numeric object variable provided in the current calculation context. The *measure variable* parameter can be either a universe object variable or a user-defined variable.

```
number Median(number [measure_variable])
```

Here is an example:

`Median([Sales revenue])` will return 552,622 when `[Sales revenue]` contains the values (503356; 552622; 570630).

Min

The Min function returns the lowest value found in an object variable provided in the current calculation context. If the *object_variable* parameter is a string data type, the minimum value will be determined alphabetically. If *object_variable* is a date time data type, the minimum value will be determined as the earliest date. If *object_* *variable* is a numeric data type, the minimum value will be determined as the lowest numeric value. The *object_variable* parameter can be either a universe object variable or a user-defined variable.

```
any_datatype Min(any_datatype [object_variable][;{member set}])
```

[{member set}] is an optional input parameter referring to a hierarchy in a BEx query. All member sets must be from the custom hierarchy. The {member set} parameter can include multiple sets separated with semicolons (;).

The following are some examples:

Min([Sales revenue]) will return 128,100 when the [Sales revenue] object variable contains the values (128100; 981210; 277750).

Min([State]) will return "California" when the [State] object variable contains the values ("California"; "Texas"; "Colorado"; "Florida", "Illinois").

Percentage

The Percentage function returns the ratio of the numeric object variable provided to the total sum of the object variable in the current calculation context.

```
number Percentage(number [object_variable];[BREAK];[ROW/COL])
```

[BREAK] is an optional input parameter and seemingly irrelevant, as in multiple tests, the aggregate will use the break level regardless of whether or not this parameter is provided. According to the vendor's online help, the Percentage function uses the total for the *object_variable* parameter over the entire table. If the [BREAK] parameter is provided, the total for *object_variable* will be calculated over the break value in the table.

[ROW/COL] is an optional input parameter. The Percentage function can be applied across either rows or columns.

Mode

The Mode function will return the most frequently occurring value found in an object variable provided in the current calculation context.

```
any_datatype Mode(any_datatype [object_variable])
```

Here is an example:

Mode([Product Line]) will return "Jackets" when the [Product Line] object variable contains the values ("Jackets"; "Trousers"; "Jackets"; "Accessories").

Percentile

The Percentile function returns the percentile based on a numeric input parameter, entered as a decimal, over a set of numbers in the *measure_variable* parameter provided in the current calculation context.

```
number Percentile(number [measure_variable];number input_parameter)
```

Product

The Product function multiplies the value of a measure.

```
number Product(number [measure_variable])
```

Here is an example:

Product([Quantity]) will return 300 when the [Quantity] object variable contains the values (10; 3; 2; 5).

RunningAverage

The RunningAverage function returns the running average for the numeric `measure_variable` parameter provided.

```
number RunningAverage(number [measure_variable][;ROW/COL] [;INCLUDEEMPTY]
[;(reset_dimension_variables)])
```

[ROW/COL] is an optional input parameter. The RunningAverage function can be applied across either rows or columns.

[INCLUDEEMPTY] is an optional parameter that tells the RunningAverage function to include null object variable values as zeros.

[reset_dimension_variables] are optional input parameters. Providing a dimension variable or a list of dimension variables tells the RunningAverage function to reset the average back to zero whenever the dimension variables change values.

The following are some examples:

RunningAverage([Sales revenue]) will return the running average of [Sales revenue] through the entire report.

RunningAverage([Sales revenue]; ([Year])) will return the running average of [Sales revenue] with a reset back to zero on the [Year] break.

RunningCount

The RunningCount function returns the running count for the `object_variable` parameter provided.

```
number RunningCount(any_datatype [object_variable] [;ROW/COL] [;INCLUDEEMPTY]
[;(reset_dimension_variables)])
```

[ROW/COL] is an optional input parameter. The RunningCount function can be applied across either rows or columns.

[INCLUDEEMPTY] is an optional parameter. This parameter tells the RunningCount function to include null object variable values in the count.

[reset_dimension_variables] are optional input parameters. Providing a dimension variable or a list of dimension variables tells the RunningCount function to reset the count back to zero whenever the dimension variables change values.

The following are some examples:

`RunningCount([State])` will return the running count of `[State]` through the entire report.

`RunningCount([State];([Year]))` will return the running count of `[State]` with a reset back to zero on the `[Year]` break.

RunningMax

The RunningMax function returns the running maximum value for the *object_variable* parameter provided.

```
any_datatype RunningMax(any_datatype [object_variable] [;ROW/COL]
[;(reset_dimension_variables)])
```

[ROW/COL] is an optional input parameter. The RunningMax function can be applied across either rows or columns.

[*reset_dimension_variables*] are optional input parameters. Providing a dimension variable or a list of dimension variables tells the RunningMax function to reset the maximum value back to <Null> whenever the dimension variables change values.

The following are some examples:

`RunningMax([Sales revenue])` will return the running maximum value of `[Sales revenue]` through the entire report.

`RunningMax([Sales revenue];([Year]))` will return the running maximum value of `[Sales revenue]` with a reset back to <Null> on the `[Year]` break.

RunningMin

The RunningMin function returns the running minimum value for the *object_variable* parameter provided.

```
any_datatype RunningMin(any_datatype [object_variable] [;ROW/COL]
[;(reset_dimension_variables)])
```

[ROW/COL] is an optional input parameter. The RunningMin function can be applied across either rows or columns.

[*reset_dimension_variables*] are optional input parameters. Providing a dimension variable or a list of dimension variables tells the RunningMin function to reset the minimum value back to <Null> whenever the dimension variables change values.

The following are some examples:

`RunningMin([State])` will return the running minimum value of `[State]` through the entire report.

`RunningMin([State];([Year]))` will return the running minimum value of `[State]` with a reset back to <Null> on the `[Year]` break.

RunningProduct

The RunningProduct function returns the running product for the numeric *measure_variable* parameter provided.

```
number RunningProduct(number [measure_variable] [;ROW/COL]
[;(reset_dimension_variables)])
```

[ROW/COL] is an optional input parameter. The RunningProduct function can be applied across either rows or columns.

[*reset_dimension_variables*] are optional input parameters. Providing a dimension variable or a list of dimension variables tells the RunningProduct function to reset the product back to zero whenever the dimension variables change values.

The following are some examples:

RunningProduct([Sales revenue]) will return the running product of[Sales revenue] through the entire report.

RunningProduct([Sales revenue];([State])) will return the running product of [Sales revenue] with a reset back to <Null> on the [State] break.

RunningSum

The RunningSum function returns the running sum for the numeric *measure_variable* parameter provided.

```
number RunningSum(number[measure_variable] [;ROW/COL] [;(reset_dimension_
variables)])
```

[ROW/COL] is an optional input parameter. The RunningSum function can be applied across either rows or columns.

[*reset_dimension_variables*] are optional input parameters. Providing a dimension variable or a list of dimension variables tells the RunningSum function to reset the sum back to zero whenever the dimension variables change values.

The following are some examples:

RunningSum([Sales revenue]) will return the running sum of [Sales revenue] through the entire report.

RunningSum([Sales revenue];([State])) will return the running sum of [Sales revenue] with a reset back to <Null> on the [State] break.

State	Product Lines	Sales revenue	=RunningSum ([Sales revenue])	=RunningSum ([Sales revenue]; ([State]))
California	City Trousers	$48,184	$48,184	$48,184
	Leather	$73,189	$121,373	$121,373
	City Skirts	$74,934	$196,307	$196,307
	Overcoats	$81,364	$277,671	$277,671
	Jackets	$152,835	$430,506	$430,506
	Outerwear	$200,696	$631,202	$631,202
	Trousers	$308,484	$939,686	$939,686
	Sweaters	$502,669	$1,442,354	$1,442,354
	Dresses	$555,253	$1,997,607	$1,997,607
	Shirt Waist	$824,658	$2,822,265	$2,822,265
	Accessories	$1,869,006	$4,691,271	$4,691,271
	Sweat-T-Shirts	$2,788,298	$7,479,569	$7,479,569
California		**$7,479,569**		
Colorado	City Trousers	$12,977	$7,492,546	$12,977
	Leather	$14,916	$7,507,462	$27,893
	City Skirts	$17,537	$7,524,999	$45,430
	Overcoats	$24,386	$7,549,385	$69,816
	Jackets	$27,371	$7,576,756	$97,187
	Outerwear	$52,644	$7,629,400	$149,831
	Trousers	$58,521	$7,687,921	$208,351

=RunningSum([Sales revenue]) is not reset over a break.

=RunningSum([Sales revenue];[State]) is reset over the [State] break.

StdDev

The StdDev function returns the standard deviation for a set of numbers in the numeric *measure_variable* parameter provided.

```
number StdDev(number [measure_variable])
```

StdDevP

The StdDevP function returns the population standard deviation for a set of numbers in the numeric *measure_variable* parameter provided.

```
number StdDevP(number [measure_variable])
```

Sum

The Sum function returns the sum of the numeric *measure_variable* parameter provided.

```
number Sum(number [measure_variable][;{member set}])
```

[{member set}] is an optional input parameter referring to a hierarchy in a BEx query. All member sets must be from the custom hierarchy. The {member set} parameter can include multiple sets separated with semicolons (;).

Here is an example:

Sum([Sales revenue]) will return 835,420 when the [Sales revenue] object variable contains (563250; 107400; 164770).

Var

The Var function returns the variance for a set of numbers in the numeric *measure_variable* parameter provided.

```
number Var(number [measure_variable])
```

VarP

The VarP function returns the population variance for a set of numbers in the numeric *measure_variable* parameter provided.

```
number VarP(number [measure_variable])
```

Character Functions

The character functions allow you to manipulate and format string data.

Asc

The Asc function returns the ASCII value of the first character value in the string input parameter provided, which can be a literal or an object variable.

```
integer Asc(string input_parameter)
```

The following are some examples:

Asc("J") returns 74.

Asc("K") returns 75.

Asc("Ka") returns 75.

Asc([State]) returns 67 when [State]= "California".

Char

The Char function returns the character associated with the ASCII value indicated in the number input parameter.

```
string Char(number input_parameter)
```

The following are some examples:

Char(74) returns J.

Char(75) returns K.

Char(10) returns a carriage return.

TIP The Char function comes in handy when you need to embed nonprintable characters, such as carriage returns, in a character string. For example, if you want to create a report header cell with your report title followed by a carriage return and the date the report was executed, use this formula:

```
="Sales Revenue Report " + Char(10) + FormatDate(LastExecutionDate();
"MM/dd/yyyy")
```

Concatenation

The Concatenation function concatenates string *input_parameter1* with string *input_parameter2*. The input parameter strings can be literals or object variables.

```
string Concatenation(string input_parameter1; string input_parameter2)
```

The following are some examples:

```
Concatenation([First Name]; [Last Name]) returns "JoeSmith" where
[First Name]= "Joe" and [Last Name]= "Smith".
```

TIP In many cases, you will want to include a space ("") between two strings when concatenating.

```
Concatenation([First Name];Concatenation(""; [Last Name])) returns
"Joe Smith" where [First Name]= "Joe" and [Last Name] = "Smith".
```

Fill

The Fill function returns a string containing the string input parameter repeated as often as specified by the numeric input parameter. The input parameter strings can be literals, constants, or object variables.

```
string Fill(string input_parameter; number input_parameter)
```

Here's an example:

Fill(".";50) returns "................ . ...". This formula could be used to create a table of contents, as with =Left([Section Title] + Fill(".";50), 50).

FormatDate

The FormatDate function takes a date input parameter value and returns a string in the format specified by the string date format.

```
string FormatDate(date input_parameter; string date_format)
```

The following date formats are available.

Date Format	Description	Sample
d	The day number in the month with no leading zeros	1; 9; 25
dd	The day number in the month with leading zeros	01; 09; 25
ddd	The abbreviated three-character day name in proper case	Mon; Tue; Wed
DDD	The abbreviated three-character day name in all uppercase	MON; TUE; WED
dddd	The full day name in proper case	Monday; Tuesday; Wednesday
DDDD	The full day name in uppercase	MONDAY; TUESDAY; WEDNESDAY
M	The month number in the year with no leading zeros	1; 6; 12
MM	The month number in the year with leading zeros	01; 06; 12
mmm	The three-character abbreviated month name in proper case	Jan; Jun; Dec
MMM	The three-character abbreviated month name in uppercase	JAN; JUN; DEC
mmmm	The full month name in proper case	January; June; December
yy	The two-digit year	87; 99; 05
yyyy	The four-digit year	1987; 1999; 2005
hh:mm	The hour and minutes with leading zeros	08:30; 09:21; 12:30
hh:mm:ss	The hour, minutes, and seconds with leading zeros	08:30:27; 09:21:59; 12:30:00
hh:mm a	The hour and minutes with leading zeros and AM or PM after the time	08:30 AM; 09:21 PM; 12:30 AM

NOTE The values provided in the date value string are case-sensitive. The string "mm" represents minutes, while the string "MM" represents the month.

The FormatDate function is used to change the data type of a date variable to a string, to do the following:

- Use date variables in functions that require string variables. For example, `Length(FormatDate(CurrentDate(); "M/d/yyyy"))` returns 8 (the length of the string value returned) when `CurrentDate() = "1/1/2012"`, and returns 9 when `CurrentDate() = "12/1/2012"`.

- Use date variables concatenated with other string data. For example, `"Current Date: " + FormatDate(CurrentDate();"mmm dd, yyyy")` returns `"Current Date: Jan 01, 2012"`.

FormatNumber

The FormatNumber function takes a number input parameter value and returns a string in the format specified by the number format string.

```
string FormatNumber(number input_parameter; string number_format)
```

The following number formats are available:

Number Format	Description	Sample
#	Displays a corresponding integer.	9999; <Null>; 1
0	Displays a corresponding integer unless there are no digits to display; in which case, a zero is displayed.	9999; 0; 1
#####	Displays a corresponding integer with no leading zeros.	9999; <Null>; 1
00000	Displays a corresponding integer unless there are fewer digits to display than indicated in the number format string; in which case, leading zeros are displayed.	09999; 00000; 00001
#,###	Displays an integer with a thousands separator.	9,999; <Null>; 1
#,##0.00	Displays a number with a thousands separator and two decimal places.	9,999.00; 0.00; 1.00
+#	Displays an integer with a plus sign.	+9999; <Null>; +1
−#	Displays an integer with a minus sign.	−9999; <Null>; −1
#.0%	Displays a number with a percentage sign.	9999.0%; .0%; 1.0%
<space> 0.0 %	A space used anywhere within the number format string will display in the number.	9999.0 %; 0.0 %; 1.0 %
<any alphanumeric character> $#,##0.00	Any alphanumeric character can be used in a number format string.	$9,999.00; $0.00; $1.00
#,###[Red]	Displays the value in the specified color. The valid colors are [Red], [Blue], [Green], [Yellow], [White], [Dark Red], [Dark Blue], and [Dark Green].	9,999; <Null>; 1

The FormatNumber function is used to change the data type of a number variable to a string. This is used to do the following:

- Use number variables in functions that are expecting string variables. For example, Length(FormatNumber([Sales revenue]; "$#,##0.00")) returns 11 when [Sales revenue]= 563250.

- Use number variables concatenated with other string data. For example, `"Your Region has revenue totaling: " + FormatNumber([Sales revenue]; "$#,##0")` returns `"Your Region has revenue totaling: $563,250"` when `[Sales revenue]`=563250.

HTMLEncode

The HTMLEncode function takes a string input parameter and returns the HTML encoded value.

```
string HTMLEncode(string input_parameter)
```

InitCap

The InitCap function takes a string input parameter and returns a character string with the first letter of the string capitalized.

```
string InitCap(string input_parameter)
```

NOTE The InitCap function capitalizes only the first letter of the first word; it does not capitalize subsequent words in the same field. Use the WordCap function when you want each word capitalized.

The following are some examples.

`InitCap("jane doe")` returns `"Jane doe"`.

`InitCap([First Name] + " " + [Last Name])` returns `"Jane doe"` where `[First Name]="JANE"` and `[Last Name]= "DOE"`.

Left

The Left function takes a string input parameter and returns the leftmost *input_num_chars* parameter.

```
string Left(string input_parameter; number input_num_chars)
```

The following are some examples:

`Left([First Name]; 1) + ". " + [Last Name]` returns `"J. Doe"`.

`Left("ABCDEFGHIJ"; 5)` returns `"ABCDE"`.

LeftPad

The LeftPad function takes string *pad_input_parameter*, number *output_length*, and string *orig _input_parameter* parameters and returns the *pad_input_parameter* parameter padded on the left with the *orig_input_parameter* parameter.

```
string LeftPad(string pad_input_parameter; number output_length; string
orig_input_parameter)
```

The following are some examples:

`LeftPad("Character Functions"; 24; ".")` returns `".....Character Functions"`.

`LeftPad("Numeric Functions"; 24; ".")` returns `".......Numeric Functions"`.

LeftTrim

The LeftTrim function takes a string input parameter and returns a string with all leading spaces removed.

```
string LeftTrim(string input_parameter)
```

Here's an example:

```
LeftTrim("  Jane Doe  ") returns " Jane Doe  ".
```

Length

The Length function takes a string input parameter and returns an integer representing the length of the character string.

```
integer Length(string input_parameter)
```

The following are some examples:

```
Length("Hawaiian Club") returns 13.
```

```
Length([Country]) returns 2 when [Country]= "US".
```

Lower

The Lower function takes a string input parameter and returns a character string converted to all lowercase.

```
string Lower(string input_parameter)
```

The following are some examples:

```
Lower("Hawaiian Club") returns "hawaiian club".
```

```
Lower([Country]) returns "us" when [Country]= "US".
```

Match

The Match function takes a string input parameter and compares it to a string pattern. If they match, the function returns a value of true; otherwise, false is returned.

```
boolean Match(string input_parameter; string pattern)
```

The string pattern can contain the wildcard character * to replace multiple characters and the wildcard character ? to replace a single character.

The following are some examples:

```
Match("Hello"; "He*") returns true (1).
```

```
Match("Hello"; "H????") returns true (1).
```

```
Match("Hello"; "H? ") returns false (0).
```

```
Match([Master Product Number]; [Supplier Product Number])
```
compares two variables to see if the product numbers are the same.

Part III

Pos

The Pos function returns an integer representing the position in the string input parameter where the string pattern input parameter is located.

```
integer Pos(string input_parameter; string pattern_input_parameter)
```

Here's an example:
```
Pos("http://www.businessobjects.com";"/" ) returns 6.
```

Replace

The Replace function takes a string input parameter and replaces all occurrences of the string *input_replace* parameter with the string *input_replace_with* parameter.

```
string Replace(string input_parameter; string input_replace; string input_
replace_with)
```

Here's an example:

```
Replace("http://www.businessobjects.com"; "http:"; "https:")
returns "https://www.businessobjects.com".
```

Right

The Right function takes a string input parameter and returns the rightmost *input_num_chars* parameter.

```
string Right(string input_parameter; number input_num_chars)
```

The following are some examples:

```
Right([Social Security Number]; 4) returns "5555" when [Social
Security Number]= "222-74-5555".
```

```
Right([Part Number]; 4) returns "7A56" when [Part Number]=
"Controller Arm: 7A56".
```

```
Right("This String",4) returns "ring".
```

RightPad

The RightPad function takes string *pad _input_parameter*, *output_length*, and string *orig _input_parameter* parameters and returns the *pad_input_parameter* parameter padded on the right with the *orig_input_parameter* parameter.

```
string RightPad(string pad_input_parameter; number output_length; string
orig_input_parameter)
```

The following are some examples:

```
RightPad("Character Functions"; 24; ".") returns "Character
Functions.....".
```

```
RightPad("Numeric Functions"; 24; ".") returns "Numeric
Functions…….".
```

RightTrim

The RightTrim function takes a string input parameter and returns a string with all trailing spaces removed.

```
string RightTrim(string input_parameter)
```

Here's an example:

```
RightTrim(" Jane Doe ") returns " Jane Doe".
```

SubStr

The SubStr function takes a string input parameter and returns a substring starting at the position indicated by the integer *start* parameter for the integer *length* parameter number of characters.

```
string SubStr(string input_parameter; integer start; integer length)
```

Here's an example:

```
SubStr("Part#7A59 Controller Arm"; 6; 4) returns "7A59".
```

Trim

The Trim function takes a string input parameter and returns a string with both the leading and trailing spaces removed.

```
string Trim(string input_parameter)
```

Here's an example:

```
Trim(" Jane Doe ") returns "Jane Doe".
```

Upper

The Upper function takes a string input parameter and returns a character string converted to all uppercase.

```
string Upper(string input_parameter)
```

The following are some examples:

```
Upper("Jane Doe") returns "JANE DOE".
```

```
Upper([Country]) returns "UNITED STATES" when [Country]=
"United States".
```

URLEncode

The URLEncode function takes a string input parameter and returns the URL-encoded value.

```
string URLEncode(string input_parameter)
```

WordCap

The WordCap function takes a string input parameter and returns a character string with the first letter of every word capitalized.

```
string WordCap(string input_parameter)
```

Here's an example:

```
WordCap([Customer Name]) returns "John Smith" when [Customer
Name]="JOHN SMITH".
```

Date and Time Functions

The date and time functions allow you to manipulate and format date and time data.

CurrentDate

The CurrentDate function returns the current system date.

```
date CurrentDate()
```

NOTE The CurrentDate function will return the system date on the server adjusted to the BI Launch Pad user's time zone as specified in BI Launch Pad preferences.

CurrentTime

The CurrentTime function returns the current system time.

```
time CurrentTime()
```

NOTE The CurrentTime function will return the system time on the server adjusted to the BI Launch Pad user's time zone.

DayName

The DayName function takes a date input parameter and returns the name of the day of the week for that date.

```
string DayName(date input_parameter)
```

The following are some examples:

DayName(CurrentDate()) returns "Wednesday" when CurrentDate()=02/01/2012.

DayName(ToDate("01/01/2012";"MM/dd/yyyy")) returns "Sunday".

DayNumberOfMonth

The DayNumberOfMonth function takes a date input parameter and returns the number of the day in the month (1–31) of a date.

```
integer DayNumberOfMonth(date input_parameter)
```

The following are some examples:

DayNumberOfMonth(CurrentDate()) returns 1 when CurrentDate()=02/01/2012.

DayNumberOfMonth(ToDate("01/28/2012";"MM/dd/yyyy")) returns 28.

DayNumberOfMonth(ToDate("02/30/2012";"MM/dd/yyyy")) returns #ERROR because 2/30/2012 is not a valid date.

DayNumberOfWeek

The DayNumberOfWeek function takes a date input parameter and returns the number of the day in the week of a date, where Monday=1, Tuesday=2, Wednesday=3, Thursday=4, Friday=5, Saturday=6, and Sunday=7.

```
integer DayNumberOfWeek(date input_parameter)
```

The following are some examples:

`DayNumberOfWeek([Invoice Date])` returns 7 when `[Invoice Date]=01/01/2012`.

`DayNumberOfWeek(ToDate("01/01/2012";"MM/dd/yyyy"))` returns 7.

DayNumberOfYear

The DayNumberOfYear function takes a date input parameter and returns the number of the day in the year (1–366) of a date.

```
integer DayNumberOfYear(date input_parameter)
```

The following are some examples:

`DayNumberOfYear(ToDate("01/01/2012";"MM/dd/yyyy"))` returns 1.

`DayNumberOfYear(ToDate("12/31/2012";"MM/dd/yyyy"))` returns 366.

DaysBetween

The DaysBetween function returns an integer representing the number of days between two dates: the date *first_input_parameter* and date *last_input_parameter* parameters.

```
integer DaysBetween(date first_input_parameter;
date last_input_parameter)
```

Here's an example:

`DaysBetween([Invoice Date]; CurrentDate())` returns 5 when `[Invoice Date]=1/2/2012` and `CurrentDate()=1/7/2012`.

LastDayOfMonth

The LastDayOfMonth function takes a date input parameter and returns the last day in the month for that date.

```
date LastDayOfMonth(date input_parameter)
```

The following are some examples:

`LastDayOfMonth(CurrentDate())` returns 1/31/2012 when `CurrentDate()=1/16/2012`.

`LastDayOfMonth([Invoice Date])` returns 4/30/2012 when `[Invoice Date]=4/1/2012`.

LastDayOfWeek

The LastDayOfWeek function takes a date input parameter and returns the last day in the week (Sunday) for that date.

```
date LastDayOfWeek(date input_parameter)
```

The following are some examples:

`LastDayOfWeek(CurrentDate())` returns 1/22/2012 when `CurrentDate()=1/16/2006`.

`LastDayOfWeek([Invoice Date])` returns 4/1/2012 when `[Invoice Date]=4/1/2012`.

Month

The Month function takes a date input parameter and returns the name of the month for that date.

```
string Month(date input_parameter)
```

The following are some examples:

`Month(CurrentDate())` returns "February" when `CurrentDate()=2/1/2012`.

`Month([Invoice Date])` returns "June" when `[Invoice Date]=6/15/2012`.

MonthNumberOfYear

The MonthNumberOfYear function takes a date input parameter and returns the number of the month (1–12) for that date.

```
integer MonthNumberOfYear(date input_parameter)
```

The following are some examples:

`MonthNumberOfYear(CurrentDate())` returns 2 when `CurrentDate()=2/1/2012`.

`MonthNumberOfYear([Invoice Date])` returns 6 when `[Invoice Date]=6/15/2012`.

MonthsBetween

The MonthsBetween function returns an integer representing the number of months between two dates: the date `first_input_parameter` parameter and the date `last_input_parameter` parameter.

```
integer MonthsBetween(date first_input_parameter; date last_input_parameter)
```

The following are some examples:

`MonthsBetween(ToDate("01/01/2012"; "MM/dd/yyyy"); ToDate("02/22/2012"; "MM/dd/yyyy"))` returns 1.

`MonthsBetween(ToDate("01/01/2012"; "MM/dd/yyyy"); ToDate("04/10/2012"; "MM/dd/yyyy"))` returns 3.

```
MonthsBetween([Invoice Date]; CurrentDate()) returns 17 when
[Invoice Date]=1/2/2011 and CurrentDate()=6/7/2012.
```

Quarter

The Quarter function takes a date input parameter and returns the number of the quarter (1–4) for that date.

```
integer Quarter(date input_parameter)
```

The following are some examples:

```
Quarter([Invoice Date]) returns 3 when [Invoice Date]=8/2/2012.

Quarter(ToDate("12/1/2012"; "MM/dd/yyyy")) returns 4.
```

RelativeDate

The RelativeDate function takes a date input parameter and returns a date that represents that date plus the *number_of_days* parameter specified.

```
date RelativeDate(date input_parameter; number_of_days)
```

The following are some examples:

```
RelativeDate(CurrentDate(); 30) returns 9/1/2012 when
CurrentDate()=8/2/2012.

RelativeDate([Invoice Date]; 45) returns 7/16/2012 when [Invoice
Date]=6/1/2012.
```

ToDate

The ToDate function takes a string input parameter that represents a date according to the string date format supplied and returns a date.

```
date ToDate(string input_parameter; string date_format)
```

NOTE If no day is provided in the string input parameter for the ToDate function, the default is 1. If no month is provided in the string input parameter, the default is 1. If no year is provided in the string input parameter, the default is 1970.

The following are some examples:

```
ToDate("01/01/2012"; "MM/dd/yyyy") returns 1/1/2012.

ToDate("Sep 1, 2012"; "Mmm d, yyyy") returns 9/1/2012.

ToDate("12";"MM") returns 12/1/1970.
```

Week

The Week function takes a date input parameter and returns the number of the week (1–53) for that date.

```
integer Week(date input_parameter)
```

The following are some examples:

`Week(ToDate("01/03/2012"; "MM/dd/yyyy"))` returns 1.

`Week(CurrentDate())` returns 31 when `CurrentDate()=8/2/2012`.

Year

The Year function takes a date input parameter and returns the number of the year for that date.

```
integer Year(date input_parameter)
```

The following are some examples:

`Year(ToDate("01/03/2012"; "MM/dd/yyyy"))` returns 2012.

`Year([Invoice Date])` returns 2012 when `[Invoice Date]=1/1/2012`.

Document Functions

Document functions allow you to access and display data related to a Web Intelligence document. Some of these functions are useful to insert in separate cells in a document header or footer,.

DocumentAuthor

The DocumentAuthor function returns the BusinessObjects Enterprise logon ID for the user who created the Web Intelligence document.

```
string DocumentAuthor()
```

DocumentCreationDate

The DocumentCreationDate function returns the date on which the document was created.

```
date DocumentCreationDate()
```

DocumentCreationTime

The DocumentCreationDate function returns the time on which the document was created.

```
date DocumentCreationTime()
```

DocumentDate

The DocumentDate function returns the date the Web Intelligence document was last saved.

```
date DocumentDate()
```

DocumentName

The DocumentName function returns the name of the Web Intelligence document.

```
string DocumentName()
```

For example, `DocumentName()` returns `"Resort Sales"` if the document is saved with a title of Resort Sales.

DocumentOwner

The DocumentOwner function returns the BI Launch Pad username that last saved the document.

```
string DocumentOwner()
```

DocumentPartiallyRefreshed

The DocumentPartiallyRefreshed function returns true if the document is partially refreshed and false if the document is fully refreshed.

```
boolean DocumentPartiallyRefreshed()
```

DocumentTime

The DocumentTime function returns the time the Web Intelligence document was last saved.

```
time DocumentTime()
```

DrillFilters

The DrillFilters function displays drill filters applied to the report and will work only when your report is in drill mode. When your report is in structure mode, the cell that contains the formula will appear empty.

```
string DrillFilters(any_datatype object_variable;
string string_separator)
```

TIP Use the DrillFilters function when you are printing a report in drill mode so that you can more readily see how the report has been filtered or its current drill level. Also, because you cannot invoke the Formula Editor while in drill mode, add the cell for this formula by selecting Templates | Free-Standing Cells | Formula and Text Cells | Drill Filters from the left panel.

PromptSummary

The PromptSummary function returns the prompt text and user response for all prompts in a document.

```
string PromptSummary()
```

For example, `PromptSummary ()` returns the following when the report contains two prompt values: "Enter value(s) for Year" and "Enter value(s) for Lines."

*** Query Name:Query 1 ***

Enter value(s) for Year 2006
Enter value(s) for Lines Dresses; Jackets; Leather

QuerySummary

The QuerySummary function returns information about a query or queries in a document.

```
string PromptSummary(dataprovider)
```

For example, QuerySummary("Query 1") returns the following for Query 1:

*** Query Name:Query 1 ***

** Query Properties:
Universe:eFashion
Last Refresh Date:5/3/12 9:20 PM
Last Execution Duration: 1
Number of rows: 39
Retrieve Duplicate Row: ON

** Query Definition:
Result Objects: Year, Opening date, State, Lines, Sales revenue
Filters (Year In List {2006 }
    AND Lines In List {Dresses;Jackets;Leather }
)

ReportFilter

The ReportFilter function takes an object variable and returns the filter values applied to that object.

```
string ReportFilter(any_datatype object_variable)
```

For example, ReportFilter([Year]) returns "FY2012" if there is a filter on [Year] restricting values to "FY2012".

ReportFilterSummary

The ReportFilterSummary function returns a summary of all report filters in a document or report.

```
string ReportFilter(report_name)
```

Data Provider Functions

The data provider functions return information about the data providers in the document.

Connection

The Connection function takes a data provider object and returns the connection information associated with that data provider.

```
string Connection(data_provider_object)
```

An example is Connection([Query1]).

DataProvider

The DataProvider function returns the name of the data provider for the object variable provided.

```
string DataProvider(any_datatype [object_variable])
```

The following are some examples:

```
DataProvider([Country]) returns "Query 1".
```

```
DataProvider([Query 2].[Revenue]) returns "Query 2".
```

DataProviderSQL

The DataProviderSQL function takes a data provider object and returns the SQL string associated with that data provider.

```
string DataProviderSQL(data_provider_object)
```

TIP The DataProviderSQL function can be useful to return the SQL string that is generated by the data provider. This SQL string can be used to troubleshoot issues and perhaps tune a report to run faster.

DataProviderType

The DataProviderType function returns "Universe" if a data provider is based on a universe or "Personal data" if a data provider is based on personal data.

```
string DataProviderType([data_provider_object])
```

Here's an example:

```
DataProviderType([Query 1]) returns "Universe".
```

LastExecutionDate

The LastExecutionDate function returns the last date a string data provider name was refreshed if that optional parameter is supplied. Without any parameters, this function returns the last date the query was refreshed.

```
date LastExecutionDate(string data_provider_name
```

data_provider_name is an optional input parameter referring to a data provider and is only required when there are multiple data providers defined in the document.

The following are some examples:

LastExecutionDate() returns 2/10/2012 if the user last refreshed this document on 2/10/2012.

LastExecutionDate([Query 1]) returns 2/10/2012 if the user last refreshed Query 1 within the document on 2/10/2012.

LastExecutionDuration

The LastExecutionDuration function returns the time taken in seconds by the last refresh of a data provider name if that optional parameter is supplied. Without any parameters, this function returns the time taken in seconds when the query was refreshed.

```
integer LastExecutionDuration(string [data_provider_name] )
```

data_provider_name is an optional input parameter referring to a data provider and is only required when there are multiple data providers defined in the document.

The following are some examples:

`LastExecutionDuration()` returns 30 if the last refresh of this document took 30 seconds.

`LastExecutionDuration([Query 1])` returns 30 if the last refresh of Query 1 within the document took 30 seconds.

LastExecutionTime

The LastExecutionTime function returns the last time a string data provider name was refreshed if that optional parameter is supplied. Without any parameters, this function returns the last time the query was refreshed.

```
time LastExecutionTime(string [data_provider_name])
```

`data_provider_name` is an optional input parameter referring to a data provider and is only required when there are multiple data providers defined in the document.

Here's an example:

`LastExecutionTime()` returns 12:32:00 AM if the user last refreshed this document at 12:32:00 A.M.

NumberofDataProviders

The NumberofDataProviders function returns a count of the data providers in a document.

```
integer NumberofDataProviders()
```

NumberofRows

The NumberofRows function returns the number of rows returned by the data provider specified.

```
integer NumberofRows([data_provider_name])
```

RefValueDate

The RefValueDate function returns the date of the reference date used for data tracking.

RefValueUserResponse

The RefValueUserResponse function returns the prompt value for the reference data set if data tracking is enabled.

Here's an example:

`RefValueUserResponse( "Which city?" )` returns `"Los Angeles"` if you entered Los Angeles in the Which city? prompt at the time when the reference data was the current data.

ServerValue

The ServerValue function will ignore all local filters applied to a dimension or hierarchy used when calculating a measure, returning the database value for the measure.

```
number ServerValue(number[measure_variable])
```

UniverseName

The UniverseName function returns the name of the universe on which a data provider_ name is based.

```
string UniverseName([data_provider_name])
```

UserResponse

The UserResponse function returns the value entered by a user into the specified string prompt name in the specified string data provider name.

```
string UserResponse(string data_provider_name; string prompt_name)
```

data_provider_name is an optional input parameter referring to a data provider and is only required when there are multiple data providers defined in the document.

prompt_name is the name of the prompt (i.e., the string that is prompted when the data provider is refreshed).

Here's an example:

UserResponse("Enter Country: ") returns "US" when a user enters **US** into a prompt named "Enter Country: ".

Miscellaneous Functions

The miscellaneous functions are all the functions that did not neatly fit into one of the other categories.

BlockName

The BlockName function returns the name of the block in which it is placed.

```
string BlockName()
```

Here's an example:

BlockName() returns "Block 1" when the formula is placed in Block 1.

ColumnNumber

The ColumnNumber function returns the number of a column in a table, starting with 1 as the leftmost column and incrementing to the right.

```
integer ColumnNumber()
```

CurrentUser

The CurrentUser function returns the name of the user who is currently logged in to InfoView and working with the Web Intelligence document.

```
string CurrentUser()
```

Here's an example:

CurrentUser() returns "Cindi" when Cindi is logged in to Web Intelligence.

Depth

The Depth function returns the depth of a member in a hierarchy, where depth is the distance from the top level of a hierarchy. The top level of a hierarchy is level 0.

```
int member.Depth
```

Here's an example:

```
[Customer_Region].[US].[California].Depth returns 2.
```

If-Then-Else

The If-Then-Else function returns a value based on whether a Boolean expression evaluates to true or false.

```
If boolean_expression Then true_value [Else false_value]
```

The following alternate syntax is also supported.

```
If(boolean_expression; any_datatype value_if_true; any_datatype value_if_
false)
```

The following are some examples:

If [Country]="US" Then [Resort] returns the value in [Resort] when [Country]= "US" and "" when [Country]<> "US".

If [Year]=2012 Then [Sales revenue] Else 0 returns the value in [Sales revenue] if the [Year]=2012 and returns 0 when the [Year]<>2012.

ElseIf

The ElseIf function can be used to nest If conditions.

```
If boolean_expression Then true_value [ElseIf boolean_expression Then
true_value Else false_value]
```

ForceMerge

The ForceMerge function includes all synchronized dimensions in measure calculations, even when the dimensions are not present in the measure's calculation context.

```
number ForceMerge(number [measure_variable])
```

Here's an example:

ForceMerge([Sales revenue]) returns the value of [Sales revenue] taking into account all synchronized dimensions even if they are not included in the same block as the [Sales revenue] measure.

GetContentLocale

The GetContentLocale function returns the locale settings for the current document.

```
string GetContentLocale()
```

The following are some examples:

`GetContentLocale()` returns `"en_US"` if the document content is English – US.

`GetContentLocale()` returns `"fr_FR"` if the document content is French.

> **NOTE** There are two locale settings available: the user session locale and the document locale. The locale is important for how dates and currencies are formatted.

GetDominantPreferredViewingLocale

The GetDominantPreferredViewingLocale function returns the dominant locale associated with the user's preferred viewing locale.

```
string GetDominantPreferredViewingLocale()
```

The dominant locales associated with each viewing locale can be found in the SAP BusinessObjects BI 4 Translation Manager Guide.

GetLocale

The GetLocale function returns the user session locale settings. This is a system setting in InfoView.

```
string GetLocale()
```

The following are some examples:

`GetLocale()` returns `"en_US"` if the locale setting is English – US.

`GetLocale()` returns `"fr_FR"` if the locale setting is French.

> **NOTE** There are two locale settings available: the user session locale and the document locale. The locale is important for how dates and currencies are formatted.

GetPreferredViewingLocale

The GetPreferredViewingLocale function returns the user's preferred locale for viewing document data as set in the BI Launch Pad preferences.

```
string GetPreferredViewingLocale()
```

Here's an example:

`GetPreferredViewingLocale()` returns `"en_US"` if the Preferred Viewing Locale setting in preferences for the user is English – US.

If

The If function evaluates a Boolean expression. If the Boolean expression is true, it returns the *value_if_true* value. If the Boolean expression is false, it returns the *value_if_false* value.

```
any_datatype If(boolean_expression; any_datatype value_if_true;
any_datatype value_if_false)
```

The following are some examples:

If([Country]="US";[Resort];"") returns the value in [Resort] when [Country]= "US" and "" when [Country]<> "US".

If([Year]=2012; [Sales revenue]; 0) returns the value in [Sales revenue] if the [Year]=2012.

Key

The Key function returns the key value of a member, where the key is the internal identifier of a member.

```
int member.Key
```

Here's an example:

[Customer_Region].[US].[California].Key returns "2CL3" if the key of the [California] member is "2CL3".

Name

The Name function returns the name of a member.

```
string member.Name
```

NameOf

The NameOf function returns the display name of the object variable provided.

```
string NameOf(any_datatype [report_variable])
```

Here's an example:

NameOf([State]) returns "State". This is the default formula used in all column headings.

NoFilter

The NoFilter function tells Web Intelligence to ignore any filters that have been applied when performing a calculation.

```
any_datatype NoFilter(calculation)
```

Here's an example:

NoFilter(Sum([Sales revenue])) returns the sum of all revenues even if there were a filter defined on the block excluding a portion of the data.

Sales ALL States

State	Sales revenue
California	$7,479,569
Colorado	$2,060,275
DC	$2,961,950
Florida	$1,879,159
Illinois	$3,022,968
Massachusetts	$1,283,707
New York	$7,582,221
Texas	$10,117,664
Total:	**$36,387,512**

Sales Top 3 States

State	Sales revenue
Texas	$10,117,664
New York	$7,582,221
California	$7,479,569
Total Top 3 States:	*$25,179,454*
Total All Other States:	*$11,208,058*
Total All States:	$36,387,512

`NoFilter(Sum([Sales revenue]))` returns the total of all `[Sales revenue]` without the ranking filter applied

NumberOfPages

The NumberOfPages function returns the total number of pages in the current report. It is most commonly used in the header or footer of a report.

```
integer NumberofPages()
```

Here's an example:

`NumberOfPages()` returns 57 if the current report contains 57 pages.

Note that the NumberOfPages function can be accessed from the Report Elements | Cell | Pre-Defined drop-down list.

Page

The Page function returns the current page number in the report. It is most commonly used in the header or footer of a report.

```
integer Page()
```

Here's an example:

`Page()` returns 3 if the current page is 3 (of 57 pages, for example).

This function can also be accessed from the Report Elements | Cell | Pre-Defined drop-down list.

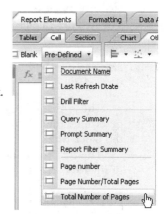

Previous

The Previous function returns the value of the object variable in the previous row of the table.

```
any_datatype Previous(any_datatype [object_variable];(reset_dimension_
variables))
```

reset_dimension_variables is an optional input parameter that allows you to reset the previous function to null.

Here's an example:

```
=Previous([Sales revenue])
```

NOTE The Previous function can be used to calculate year-to-year variances in a format different than a crosstab.

RefValue

The RefValue function returns the reference value of the object variable when data tracking is turned on.

```
any_datatype RefValue(any_datatype [object_variable])
```

RelativeValue

The RelativeValue function returns the previous or subsequent values of an object, given an offset.

```
any_datatype RelativeValue(any_datatype [object_variable]; slicing_
dimensions; offset)
```

The *slicing_dimensions* parameter provides the calculation context over which to determine the relative value of the object variable. All dimensions in the list must exist in the block where the function is placed.

The *offset* parameter is a numeric value (positive or negative) indicating the number of rows above or below the current value to return the value for the object variable.

ReportName

The ReportName function returns the name of the report.

```
string ReportName()
```

Here's an example:

```
ReportName()
```
returns "Sales Revenue Report" if the formula is placed in the Sales Revenue Report.

RowIndex

The RowIndex function returns the number of a row in a table, starting with 0 as the first row and incrementing on each subsequent data row.

```
integer RowIndex()
```

NOTE The RowIndex function is different from the LineNumber function in that it counts only the rows of data and does not include the headers and footers for the table. You will receive a `#MULTIVALUE` error if you place this function in a header or footer.

UniqueNameOf

The UniqueNameOf function returns the display name of the object variable provided. If there are multiple queries on the report containing the same object variable, the UniqueNameOf function returns the display name of the object variable along with the query name that returned the object variable.

```
string UniqueNameOf(any_datatype [object_variable])
```

The following are some examples:

`UniqueNameOf([Query 1].[Country])` returns `"Country(Query 1)"`.

`UniqueNameOf([Query 2].[Country])` returns `"Country(Query 2)"`.

`UniqueNameOf([Sales revenue])` returns `"Sales revenue"`.

Logical Functions

The Logical Functions category contains all of the boolean functions. Boolean functions return true or false values.

Even

The Even function returns a 1 for true if the number input parameter is an even number and 0 for false if the number input parameter is an odd number.

```
boolean Even(number input_parameter)
```

The following are some examples:

`Even(2)` returns true (1).

`Even([License_Number])` returns true (1) when `[License_Number]` is an even number and false (0) when `[License_Number]` is an odd number.

IsDate

The IsDate function returns true if the input parameter is a date type report variable or constant.

```
boolean IsDate(any_datatype input_parameter)
```

The following are some examples:

`IsDate([Country])` returns false (0).

`IsDate([Invoice Date])` returns true (1).

`IsDate(LastExecutionDate())` returns true (1).

`IsDate([Year])` returns false (0) where `[Year]="FY1998"`.

The IsDate function is used to determine if the data type of an object is of a date type. This is important because many functions require date type objects as inputs. If a string or numeric type is provided to a function expecting a date type object, as in =FormatDate([Year];"yyyy"), you will receive an error, as follows:

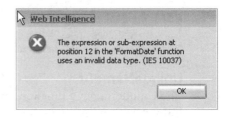

IsError

The IsError function returns true if the object variable provided returns an error, and false if the object variable provided does not return an error.

```
boolean IsError(any_datatype [object_variable])
```

The following are some examples:

IsError([Sales revenue]) returns false.

IsError(Sum([Sales revenue])/Count([Store ID])) returns true if the Count([Store ID]) ever returns a 0 because the formula would be trying to divide by 0, causing a #DIV/0 error to be returned.

IsLogical

The IsLogical function returns true if the input parameter is a Boolean data type.

```
boolean IsLogical(any_datatype input_parameter)
```

The following are some examples:

IsLogical("any") returns false (0).

IsLogical(0) returns true (1).

IsLogical([any_boolean_field]) returns true (1).

IsNull

The IsNull function returns true if the input parameter is null.

```
boolean IsNull(any_datatype input_parameter)
```

NOTE The constant string "" is not interpreted as a null.

The following are some examples:

IsNull([Address 2]) returns true (1) when there is a value populated in [Address 2] and false (0) when there is no value populated in [Address 2].

IsNull("Hello") returns false (0).

IsNumber

The IsNumber function returns true if the input parameter is a numeric data type.

```
boolean IsNumber(any_datatype input_parameter)
```

The following are some examples:

IsNumber([Country]) returns false (0).

IsNumber(125) returns true (1).

IsNumber([Sales revenue]) returns true (1).

IsString

The IsString function returns true if the input parameter is a character data type.

```
boolean IsString(any_datatype input_parameter)
```

The following are some examples:

IsString([Country]) returns true (1).

IsString("Hello") returns true (1).

IsString(LastExecutionDate()) returns false (0).

IsTime

The IsTime function returns true if the input parameter is a time data type.

```
boolean IsTime(any_datatype input_parameter)
```

The following are some examples:

IsTime([Country]) returns false (0).

IsTime(LastExecutionTime()) returns true (1).

Odd

The Odd function returns true (1) if the number input parameter is an odd number and false (0) if it is an even number.

```
boolean Odd(number input_parameter)
```

The following are some examples:

Odd(2) returns false (0).

Odd([Revenue]) returns true (1) when [Revenue] is an odd number and false (0) when [Revenue] is an even number.

Numeric Functions

The Numeric Functions category contains functions that return numeric values.

Abs

The Abs function returns the absolute value of the number input parameter provided.

```
number Abs(number input_parameter)
```

The following are some examples:

Abs (-5) returns 5.

Abs (8) returns 8.

Ceil

The Ceil function returns the number input parameter provided rounded up to the next whole number. This is different from the Round function, which will round a number either up or down.

```
integer Ceil(number input_parameter)
```

The following are some examples:

Ceil (3.999) returns 4.

Ceil (5.1) returns 6.

Cos

The Cos function returns the cosine of the number input parameter.

```
number Cos(number input_parameter)
```

Here's an example:

Cos (90) returns −.45.

EuroConvertFrom

Although the euro has been an active trading currency for many years, the European Union fixed the exchange rates for all participating countries on January 1, 1999. The euro coin and notes went into circulation later, on January 1, 2002. Not all members of the European Union agreed to participate in the euro currency; for example, Greece only began participating in mid-2001, and Great Britain still uses pounds as the official currency.

If you are accustomed to seeing measures stated in a local currency, it may not be easy to identify trends or fluctuations when viewing data in the relatively new euro. Because the exchange rates for euros are fixed, Web Intelligence can convert data to other currencies using this fixed, internal exchange rate table.

The EuroConvertFrom function converts an amount provided in the number *euro_amount_input_parameter* parameter to another currency indicated by the string *currency_code* parameter rounded to the decimal places specified by the number *decimal_places* parameter.

```
number EuroConvertFrom(number euro_amount_input_parameter; string currency_code;
number decimal_places)
```

The following are the available currency codes.

String Currency Code	Description
BEF	Belgian franc
DEM	German mark
GRD	Greek drachma
ESP	Spanish peseta
FRF	French franc
IEP	Irish punt
ITL	Italian lira
LUF	Luxembourg franc
NLG	Dutch guilder
ATS	Austrian schilling
PTS	Portuguese escudo
FIM	Finnish mark

Here's an example:

```
EuroConvertFrom(200;"DEM";2) returns 391.17.
```

EuroConvertTo

The EuroConvertTo function converts to euros an amount provided in the number *othercurrency_amount_input_parameter* parameter in the original currency indicated by the string *currency_code* parameter, with the result rounded to the decimal places specified by the number *decimal_places* parameter.

```
number EuroConvertTo(number othercurrency_amount_input_parameter;
string currency_code; number decimal_places)
```

Here's an example:

```
EuroConvertTo(391.17;"DEM";2) returns 200.00.
```

EuroFromRoundError

The EuroFromRoundError function returns the amount that is rounded off when converting to euros an amount provided in the number *othercurrency_amount_input_parameter* parameter in the original currency indicated by the string *currency_code* parameter, with the result rounded to the decimal places specified by the number *decimal_places* parameter.

```
number EuroFromRoundError(number othercurrency_amount_input_parameter; string
currency_code; number decimal_places)
```

The following are some examples:

```
EuroFromRoundError(200;"DEM";1) returns .03 because 391.17 will be rounded
```
to one decimal place, making it 391.2 with a rounding error of .03.

```
EuroFromRoundError(201;"DEM";0) returns –.12 because 393.12 will be rounded
```
to 393 with a rounding error of –.12.

EuroToRoundError

The EuroToRoundError function returns the amount that is rounded off when converting the number *euro_amount_input_parameter* parameter to another currency indicated by the string *currency_code* parameter rounded to a number *decimal_places* parameter.

```
number EuroToRoundError(number euro_amount_input_parameter;
string currency_code; number decimal_places)
```

The following are some examples:

`EuroToRoundError(393.12;"DEM";2)` returns 0 because 201.00 will be rounded to two places with a rounding error of 0.

`EuroToRoundError(500;"DEM";1)` returns –.05 because 255.65 is rounded to 255.6 with a rounding error of –.05.

Exp

The Exp function returns the constant e raised to a power.

```
number Exp(number.power)
```

Here's an example:

`Exp(3.7)` returns 40.45.

Fact

The Fact function returns the factorial of the number input parameter provided.

```
integer Fact(number input_parameter)
```

Here's an example:

`Fact(6)` returns 720.

Floor

The Floor function returns the number input parameter provided rounded down to the nearest whole number.

```
integer Floor(number input_parameter)
```

The following are some examples:

`Floor(3.999)` returns 3.

`Floor(5.1)` returns 5.

Ln

The Ln function returns the natural logarithm for the number input parameter provided.

```
number Ln(number input_parameter)
```

Log

The Log function returns the logarithm for the number input parameter provided for the number *log_base* parameter provided.

```
number Log(number input_parameter; number log_base)
```

The following are some examples:

Log(10;2) returns 3.32.

Log(16;2) returns 4.

Mod

The Mod function returns the remainder resulting from the number *input_dividend* parameter divided by the number *input_divisor* parameter.

```
number Mod(number input_dividend; number input_divisor)
```

The following are some examples:

Mod(10;3) returns 1 because 10/3 = 3 with 1 remaining.

Mod(5;3) returns 2 because 5/3 = 1 with 2 remaining.

Mod(10;2) returns 0 because 10/2 = 5 with 0 remaining.

Power

The Power function returns a number input parameter raised to a power provided in the number *power* parameter.

```
number Power(number input_parameter; number power)
```

The following are some examples:

Power(4;2) returns 16.

Power(2;5) returns 32.

Power(2;6) returns 64.

Rank

The Rank function returns the ranking for a numeric object variable as it is rolled up by the dimensions provided in the *dimension_variable* list.

```
integer Rank(number [measure_variable]; ([dimension_variable] list);
TOP|BOTTOM; ([reset_dimension_variable] list))
```

TOP|BOTTOM is an optional parameter that allows you to indicate the ranking order for the measure as either ascending (TOP) or descending (BOTTOM).

The *reset_dimension_variable* list is an optional parameter that allows you to reset the ranking back to zero when the values in the *reset_dimension_variable* list change.

By default, the Rank function resets the ranking over a table break or section.

TIP For easy ranking, use the Ranking button from the Analysis | Filters toolbox. Use the function when you wish to display the ranking position as a column in a report.

Round

The Round function returns a numeric input parameter rounded to a specified number of decimal places provided in the number *decimal_places* parameter.

```
number Round(number input_parameter; number decimal_places)
```

The following are some examples:

Round(4.499;2) returns 4.50.

Round(4.499;0) returns 4.

Round(4.75;1) returns 4.8.

Sign

The Sign function returns the sign of the number input parameter provided: –1 indicates a negative number, 0 indicates a zero, and 1 indicates a positive number.

```
number Sign(number input_parameter)
```

The following are some examples:

Sign(-23) returns –1.

Sign([Revenue]) returns 1 when the value in [Revenue] is positive.

Sin

The Sin function returns the sine of the number input parameter provided.

```
number Sin(number input_parameter)
```

Here's an example:

Sin(90) returns .89.

Sqrt

The Sqrt function returns the square root of the number input parameter provided.

```
number Sqrt(number input_parameter)
```

The following are some examples:

Sqrt(4) returns 2.

Sqrt(25) returns 5.

Sqrt(15) returns 3.87.

Tan

The Tan function returns the tangent of the number input parameter provided.

```
number Tan(number input_parameter)
```

Here's an example:

`Tan(90)` returns –2.

ToNumber

The ToNumber function returns the string input parameter as a number data type.

`number ToNumber(string `*`input_parameter`*`)`

NOTE The string input parameter provided must be a numeric value containing only numeric characters, including a decimal point. No formatting characters, such as currency signs or thousands separators, can be provided in the string input parameter.

The following are some examples:

`ToNumber("23")` returns 23.

`ToNumber("125.75")` returns 125.75.

`ToNumber("$2,250")` returns #ERROR.

`ToNumber("ABC")` returns #ERROR.

Truncate

The Truncate function returns the number input parameter truncated to a number of decimal places provided in the number *decimal_places* parameter. This function is different from the Round function in that it simply removes any numbers to the right of the decimal places specified. Truncate does not round the number.

`number Truncate(number `*`input_parameter`*`; number `*`decimal_places`*`)`

The following are some examples:

`Truncate(5.999; 1)` returns 5.9.

`Truncate(5.999; 2)` returns 5.99.

`Truncate(5.11; 1)` returns 5.1.

Set Functions

The Set Function category contains the formulas that can be used with BEx queries to return data associated with members, sets, and hierarchies.

Ancestor

The Ancestor function returns an ancestor member of a given member.

`member Ancestor(`*`member;level|distance`*`)`

Here's an example:

`Ancestor([Customer_Region].[Canada].[Ontario].[PYO Company];2)` returns "`Canada`" given the hierarchy defined in Table 21-3.

Children

The Children function returns the child members of a given member.

`member member.Children`

Here's an example:

`[Customer_Region].[US].Children` returns `[California]`, `[New York]` given the hierarchy defined in Table 21-3.

Descendants

The Descendants function returns descendant members of a given member.

`member Descendants(member[;level|distance] [;descendant_flag])`

`[level|distance]` is an optional input parameter referring to either the level of the descendants or the distance of the descendant level from the current level.

`[descendant_flag]` is an optional input parameter. The values of `descendant_flag` can be the following:

- `Self`   Returns descendants at the level specified by the `level|distance` parameter. This is the default value for the `descendant_flag` parameter.

- `Before`   Returns all members before the level specified by the `level|distance` parameter.

- `After`   Returns the current member and all members after the level specified by the `level|distance` parameter.

- `Self_Before`   Returns the current member and all members before the level specified by the `level|distance` parameter.

- `Self_After`   Returns the current member and all members after the level specified by the `level|distance` parameter.

- `Leaves`   Returns all members between the current member and the member specified by the `level|distance` parameter that do not have child members.

IsLeaf

The IsLeaf function returns true if a member has no child members and false if a member has child members.

`boolean member.IsLeaf`

The following are some examples:

`[Customer_Region].[US].IsLeaf` will return false given the hierarchy defined in Table 21-3.

```
[Customer_Region].[US].[California].[ABC Company].IsLeaf
```
will
return true given the hierarchy defined in Table 21-3.

Lag

The Lag function will return a member at the same level as the current member at a given
distance before (if *distance* is a positive value) or after (if *distance* is a negative value) it.

```
Member member.Lag(distance)
```

The following are some examples:

```
[Customer_Region].[US].[California].[XYZ Company].Lag(1)
```
returns
`[ABC Company]` given the hierarchy defined in Table 21-3.

```
[Customer_Region].[US].[California].[XYZ Company].Lag(-1)
```
returns
`[HKE Company]` given the hierarchy defined in Table 21-3.

Parent

The Parent function returns the parent member of a member.

```
Member member.Parent
```

Here's an example:

```
[Customer_Region].[US].[California].[XYZ Company].Parent
```
returns
`[California]` given the hierarchy defined in Table 21-3.

Siblings

The Siblings function returns the given member's siblings (members at the same level).

```
Member member.Siblings
```

Here's an example:

```
[Customer_Region].[US].[California].Siblings
```
returns `[New York]`
given the hierarchy defined in Table 21-3.

Calculation Contexts and Extended Syntax

When a measure object is displayed in a block on your report, it is evaluated in the *context*
of the dimensions to which it is being associated. By default, the *calculation context* will
include all of the dimensions in the block. This is called the *default calculation context*. For
example, a table that contains the dimension objects *Year* and *Quarter* and the measure
object *Sales revenue* will evaluate the measure object in the context of *Year* and *Quarter*. If the
Quarter dimension is removed, the calculation context is automatically changed to *Year*, as
shown in Figure 21-4.

The default context contains the *Year* and *Quarter* dimensions.

Year	Quarter	Sales revenue
2004	Q1	$2,660,700
2004	Q2	$2,279,003
2004	Q3	$1,367,841
2004	Q4	$1,788,580
2005	Q1	$3,326,172
2005	Q2	$2,840,651
2005	Q3	$2,879,303
2005	Q4	$4,186,120
2006	Q1	$3,742,989
2006	Q2	$4,006,718
2006	Q3	$3,953,395
2006	Q4	$3,356,041

Year	Sales revenue
2004	$8,096,124
2005	$13,232,246
2006	$15,059,143

When the *Quarter* object is removed from the table, the default context automatically changes to *Year*.

Figure 21-4 Default calculation contexts

Typically, you will not be concerned with the calculation context of a measure object or formula. Usually, the default calculation context is the context you will want to use. However, in certain circumstances, you may want to control the calculation context by using extended syntax. A measure's or formula's context is made up of two parts:

- An *input context* defines the dimensions that go into the formula. In other words, an input context defines at what level of granularity the records will be when the formula is applied.

- An *output context* defines which dimensions go into the output of the calculation, as if the calculation were placed in a break header or footer based on the dimensions specified. Think of an output context as a break.

A formula including extended syntax is written as follows:

```
=function([object_variable] In (InputContext)) In (OutputContext)
```

Using Dimensions in Input and Output Contexts

Input and output contexts may be specified by providing lists of dimension objects. In the following example, the default input context for the *Sales revenue* measure is ([Year]; [State]). However, if you wanted to calculate the percentage of sales revenue that each state represents in the total year, you must be able to change the *input context* for the *Sales revenue* measure from the default as follows:

```
=Sum([Sales revenue] In ([Year]))
```

Year	State	Sales revenue	Sales Revenue by Year	% of Sales Revenue by Year and State
2004	California	$1,704,211	$8,096,124	21.05%
	Colorado	$448,302	$8,096,124	5.54%
	DC	$693,211	$8,096,124	8.56%
	Florida	$405,985	$8,096,124	5.01%
	Illinois	$738,224	$8,096,124	9.12%
	Massachusetts	$238,819	$8,096,124	2.95%
	New York	$1,667,696	$8,096,124	20.60%
	Texas	$2,199,677	$8,096,124	27.17%
2004		**$8,096,124**		
2005	California	$2,782,680	$13,232,246	21.03%
	Colorado	$768,390	$13,232,246	5.81%
	DC	$1,215,158	$13,232,246	9.18%
	Florida	$661,250	$13,232,246	5.00%
	Illinois	$1,150,659	$13,232,246	8.70%
	Massachusetts	$157,719	$13,232,246	1.19%
	New York	$2,763,503	$13,232,246	20.88%
	Texas	$3,732,889	$13,232,246	28.21%
2005		**$13,232,246**		

Extended syntax allows you to perform complex calculations including the percentage of revenue for each state over the total year.

Sum ([Sales revenue]) has a default input context of [Year] when the formula is placed in the footer of a *Year* break.

The default input context of *Sales revenue* is ([Year]; [State]) for each detail row.

Extended syntax allows you to change the default input context: =Sum([Sales revenue] In ([Year])).

Output contexts are best demonstrated by the Min and Max functions. In the following example, the default output context for the *Revenue* measure is ([Year]; [State]). However, if you want to display the highest revenue-generating state for the year alongside each state and that state's sales revenue total for the year, you must be able to change the output context for *Sales revenue* from the default as follows:

```
=Max([Sales revenue]) In ([Year])
```

Year	State	Sales revenue	Max Sales Revenue by Year
2004	California	$1,704,211	$2,199,677
	Colorado	$448,302	$2,199,677
	DC	$693,211	$2,199,677
	Florida	$405,985	$2,199,677
	Illinois	$738,224	$2,199,677
	Massachusetts	$238,819	$2,199,677
	New York	$1,667,696	$2,199,677
	Texas	$2,199,677	$2,199,677
2004		**$8,096,124**	

```
=Max([Sales revenue])
In ([Year])
```

Year	State	Sales revenue	Max Sales Revenue by Year
2005	California	$2,782,680	$3,732,889
	Colorado	$768,390	$3,732,889
	DC	$1,215,158	$3,732,889
	Florida	$661,250	$3,732,889
	Illinois	$1,150,659	$3,732,889
	Massachusetts	$157,719	$3,732,889
	New York	$2,763,503	$3,732,889
	Texas	$3,732,889	$3,732,889
2005		**$13,232,246**	

Both input and output contexts can be combined in a single formula. The following example represents revenue calculated by year and quarter and the largest of those values output by year.

```
=Max([Sales revenue] In ([Year];[Quarter])) In ([Year])
```

Year	Quarter	Sales Person	Revenue	
FY2004	Q1	Fischer	18,240	143,244
		Galagers	56,596	143,244
		Ishimoto	56,800	143,244
	Q1		**131,636**	
	Q2	Fischer	25,346	143,244
		Galagers	43,200	143,244
		Ishimoto	42,850	143,244
		Nagata	4,700	143,244
	Q2		**116,096**	
	Q3	Fischer	21,800	143,244
		Galagers	61,892	143,244
		Ishimoto	59,552	143,244
	Q3		**143,244**	
	Q4	Fischer	13,440	143,244
		Galagers	58,674	143,244
		Ishimoto	40,266	143,244
	Q4		**112,380**	
FY2004				

```
=Max([Sales revenue]
In ([Year];[Quarter])) In
([Year])
```

Using Context Operators in Input Contexts

The previous examples use the In context operator to specify dimensions to include in the input and output contexts. Web Intelligence provides two additional context operators that can be used in extended syntax: ForEach and ForAll.

The ForEach context operator allows you to add dimensions to the current default input context. For example, if a table contains the dimensions *Year* and *Quarter* and the measure *Sales revenue*, the default context is [Year]; [Quarter]. In the following example, the ForEach context operator is used to add the *State* dimension to the context (without adding *State* to the table):

```
=Min([Sales revenue] ForEach ([State])) In ([Year])
```

This would be the same as explicitly listing all of the dimensions, as follows:

```
=Min([Sales revenue] In ([Year];[Quarter];[State])) In ([Year])
```

The ForAll context operator allows you to remove a dimension from the current default input context. For example, if a table contains the dimensions *Year, Quarter,* and *Sales Person* and the measure *Sales revenue,* the default context is [Year]; [Quarter]; [State]. In the following example, the ForAll context operator is used to remove the *State* dimension from the context (without removing *State* from the table):

```
=Min([Sales revenue] ForAll ([State])) In ([Year])
```

This would be the same as explicitly listing all of the dimensions as follows:

```
=Min([Sales revenue] In ([Year];[Quarter])) In ([Year])
```

Using Keywords in Input and Output Contexts

Web Intelligence provides keywords to help you specify the dimensions to include in the context of a formula. The use of keywords provides two benefits:

- It is a shorthand method of specifying dimensions, eliminating the need to type out the list of dimensions to include in the context.

- It allows you to add or delete dimensions to a report without needing to change the extended syntax in your formulas. Since the context does not contain a hard-coded list of dimensions, the formula will continue to work.

The keywords that can be used in extended syntax are Report, Section, Break, Block, and Body. Table 21-4 describes what data will be included when using keywords in extended syntax in different areas of a table or report.

Keyword	Within Block	Within Block Break	Within Section	Outside Any Block or Section
Report	All data in the report	All data in the report	All data in the report	All data in the report
Section	All data in the section	All data in the section	All data in the section	Not applicable
Break	Data in the block delimited by a break	Data in the block delimited by a break	Not applicable	Not applicable
Block	Data in the entire block, ignoring breaks but respecting filters	Data in the entire block, ignoring breaks but respecting filters	Not applicable	Not applicable
Body	Data in the block	Data in the block	Data in the section	Data in the report

Table 21-4 Data Included When Using Keywords in Different Areas of a Table or Report

Summary

Formulas provide a powerful way to take your reporting and analysis even further. SAP BusinessObjects BI 4.0 has added many functions to make your formulas for BEx queries very powerful.

Using functions, calculation contexts, and all the available operators allows you, the report designer, to calculate and display data to meet all the complicated demands of your report users. However, formulas and variables are document-specific, potentially posing a maintenance issue. If you are creating a formula that many documents and users will require, you may want to work with the universe designer to incorporate these formulas as universe objects.

CHAPTER
22

Complex Queries

We initially covered queries in Chapter 19. In this chapter, we will cover queries in more depth.

One of Web Intelligence's greatest strengths is the ability to create complex queries and answer complex business questions easily. The powerful semantic layer via the universe lets you create complex SQL statements, without your ever needing to know or write SQL.

We use the term *complex query* to refer to any query that has these characteristics:

- Generates SQL that is more than a straightforward SELECT and GROUP BY statement
- Leverages features that you may not necessarily use on a routine basis
- Potentially has an adverse effect on response time
- May lead you to incorrect results if you lack a clear understanding of the functionality or logic

You may not always realize when you generate a complex query; it is quite simple to add result objects to the Query Panel that come from two different star schemas or two different contexts. In other cases, you may need to define conditions in a way that gives you the desired results. For example, you may be forced to use nested conditions or subqueries that make building the query feel complex.

Multipass Queries

For certain business questions, you may need to issue multiple queries to arrive at your desired result. Web Intelligence's ability to generate multiple SQL statements and present them to you as one report is referred to as *multipass SQL*. In some cases, you, as the query author, may explicitly create two distinct queries. In other cases, Web Intelligence will do this for you automatically if your universe contains contexts or derived tables.

When Web Intelligence creates multiple SELECT statements automatically, from the report designer perspective, there is only one data provider; it appears that you are building one query. Web Intelligence automatically generates multiple SQL statements and dynamically stitches the results together. The only way you can tell there are multiple queries is to view the query script in the Query Panel.

Figure 22-1 shows how multiple queries are automatically created when measure objects from two different fact tables are combined in a single data provider. This multipass capability is one of the features that allow you to use Web Intelligence against complex data models, such as those in a transaction system, or against data warehouses that contain multiple star schemas.

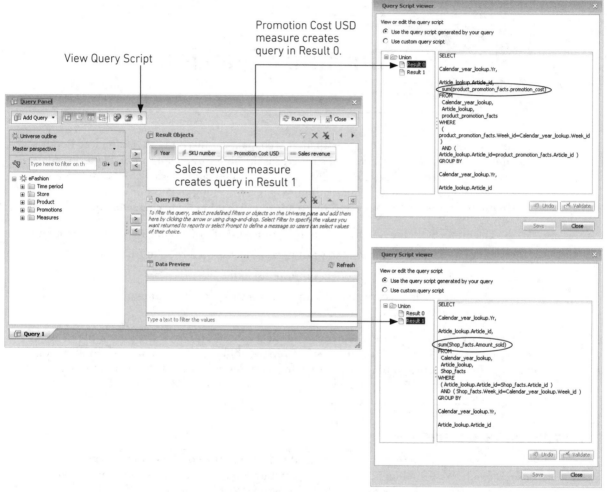

Figure 22-1   Single data provider results in multiple queries

Multipass Business Questions

The following are some sample business questions for which Web Intelligence may generate multiple SQL statements to answer. Notice that most of these involve two different metrics that may reside in two different fact tables or be stored at different levels of granularity.

Information Requirement	Explanation
Debits, credits, month-end balance	Debits and credits are aggregated over a period of time, while balances are one point in time.
Movements in/out, inventory	Material movements are aggregated over a period of time, while inventory is one point in time.
Days sales inventory (DSI)	Sales are aggregated over a period of time, while inventory is one point in time.
Product sales, promotion	Sales come from one fact table, while promotion costs come from another fact table.

In order for multipass SQL to work correctly, the universe designer must set specific SQL parameters and define contexts for each set of joins that make up a star schema. These configurations are discussed in Chapters 5 and 6, respectively.

The Two-Table Problem

From a Web Intelligence report designer viewpoint, you need to worry about multipass SQL only if you think you are getting incorrect results or if Web Intelligence unexpectedly splits your results into two tables.

For example, in Figure 22-2, there are two queries yet one table that displays *Sales revenue* and *Promotion Cost USD* by *Year* and *SKU number*. In Figure 22-3, there are two tables. The dimension object *State* (store location) was added to the query results. *State* relates only to *Sales revenue* and not *Promotion Cost*. In other words, the *State* dimension is not available in the *Promotion Cost* fact table, so the query for *Promotion Cost* that is automatically generated does not include the *State* dimension. While Web Intelligence continues to issue two SELECT statements to the data source, the two SELECT statements contain different dimensionality and cannot be joined. As a result, the data cannot be displayed in one block.

Figure 22-4 shows the two SQL statements used to generate the undesired report in Figure 22-2. The problem appears in Result 1. The dimension object *State* (OUTLET_LOOKUP.STATE) applies only to sales; it does not apply to promotions and is not defined as part of the Promotions star schema or context. Therefore, OUTLET_LOOKUP.STATE does not appear in either the SELECT or GROUP BY sections of Result 1. When a dimension does not apply to both measures, Web Intelligence automatically creates a report with two tables.

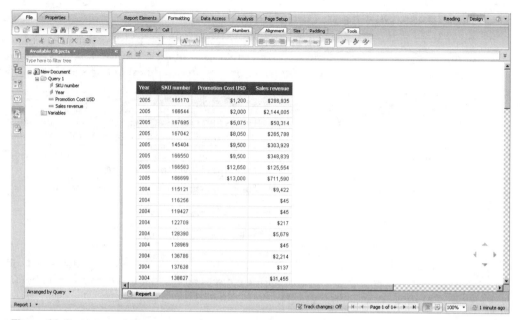

Figure 22-2 Multiple SELECT statements with common dimensionality can produce one tabular result set.

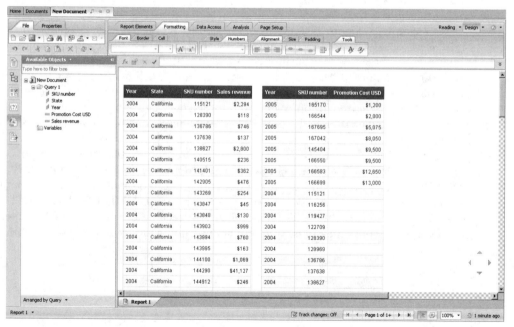

Figure 22-3 Multiple tables appear when the SELECT statements do not have the same dimensionality.

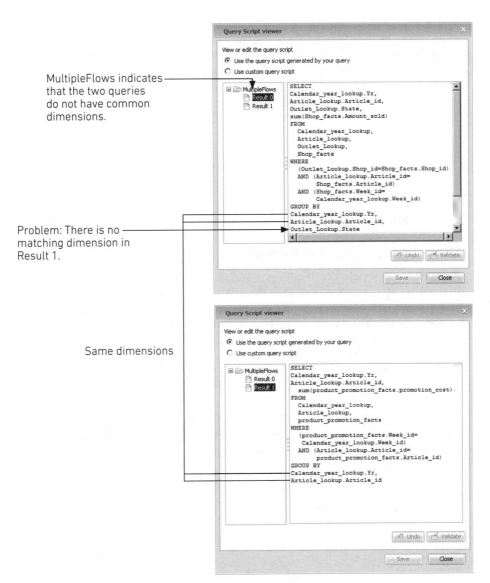

Figure 22-4   One query generates two SQL statements. Result 0 has an extra result and GROUP BY dimension.

Multiple Data Providers

In the previous section, we discussed multipass SQL, and how Web Intelligence does an automatic join of result sets by common dimensions to allow a report to have one data provider that is made up of multiple SQL statements. In developing reports, you can also manually set up multiple data providers or queries within a document. For example, you might create multiple data providers in a single document to include queries that come from different universes or that come from the same universe but with different filter criteria.

The ability to synchronize these multiple data providers is a powerful feature that allows you to combine the data from multiple data providers into a single block on your report.

With earlier versions of BusinessObjects, joining of multiple data providers happened automatically *across universes*, as long as the object names were the same. With Web Intelligence, the data providers are treated as follows:

- When the dimension object names are the same and come from the same universe, they are automatically merged.

- When the dimension object names come from different universes, you must explicitly map them to one another, in a process called *merging*.

- By default, an equi-join between the two data providers will be performed. If an outer join is desired, you must set the "Extend merged dimension values" option in the document properties.

Linking Multiple Data Providers

As an example, within the eFashion universe, Sales is in one star schema, and Promotions is in a second star schema. They both share common dimensions, such as *Time* and *Articles*. However, let's assume they are in two separate universes; you can no longer build one query or one data provider to create the report shown earlier in Figure 22-2. You need to create a query from each universe. In Web Intelligence, you must define how the dimensions in each query map to one another.

To link these multiple data providers, do the following:

1. Create a query from the first universe—in this example, eFashion—to return the *Year*, *SKU number*, and *Sales revenue* objects.

2. To insert a second data provider, from within the Web Intelligence Query Panel, select the Add Query button from the toolbox.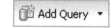

3. When prompted, select the universe to use as the data source, and then click OK. In this example, select eFashion.

4. Web Intelligence will display a blank Query Panel, with two tabs for each of the two queries at the bottom.

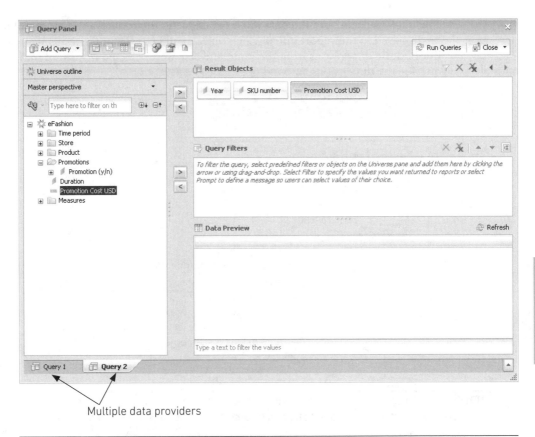

Multiple data providers

TIP You can change the generic Query 1 and Query 2 names by right-clicking the query's tab in the Query Panel and selecting Rename.

   5. Add *Year, SKU number,* and *Promotion Cost USD* as result objects.

   6. Select Run Queries from the upper-right toolbox.   <svg width="16" height="12"></svg> Run Queries

   7. If you already ran the first query, Web Intelligence asks you what you want to do with the results from the second query. Although you ultimately want to display the measure *Promotion Cost* in the same report as *Sales revenue,* for now, select "not in the report."

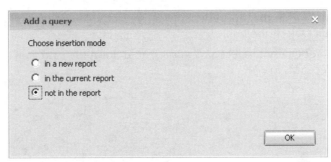

8. The query will run, and the data will be available to the report, although it will not be displayed in the report initially. The objects will be listed in the available objects list. Because dimensions from the same universe were selected in each of the queries, the dimensions auto-merge.

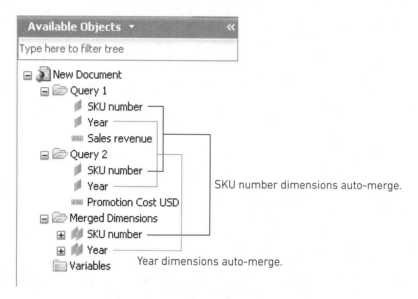

SKU number dimensions auto-merge.

Year dimensions auto-merge.

NOTE If your dimensions do not auto-merge, enable the Auto-merge dimensions setting for the document, as described in the "Setting Data Merging Options" section later in this chapter.

You can now insert the *Promotion Cost USD* measure object into a block on your report.

Manually Merging Dimensions

In order to display measures from multiple data providers in a single block on your report, you must first merge the common dimensions. If dimensions from multiple data providers have not auto-merged because they are not the same dimensions from the same universe or because the document setting Auto-merge dimensions is not checked, then you must manually merge your dimensions.

To merge dimensions across multiple data providers, follow these steps:

 1. From within the report design view, select the Merge button from the Data Access | Data Objects toolbox.

2. Under Query 1, select *SKU number*, hold down the CTRL key, and under Query 2, select *SKU number*.

3. Click OK. You will be returned to the report design view, and in the available objects list, you will see that *SKU number* is now a merged dimension.

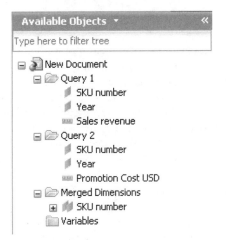

4. Repeat steps 1 through 3 until all dimensions are merged. In this example, merge the *Year* dimension.

Figure 22-5 shows the results of the merged dimensions. On the left panel in report design view, you see a Merged Dimensions folder in the available objects list. Click the + sign next to any merged dimension to see the result objects from their original queries. As a best practice, dimensions between multiple data providers should be the same, so you will notice that all dimensions from both queries have been merged.

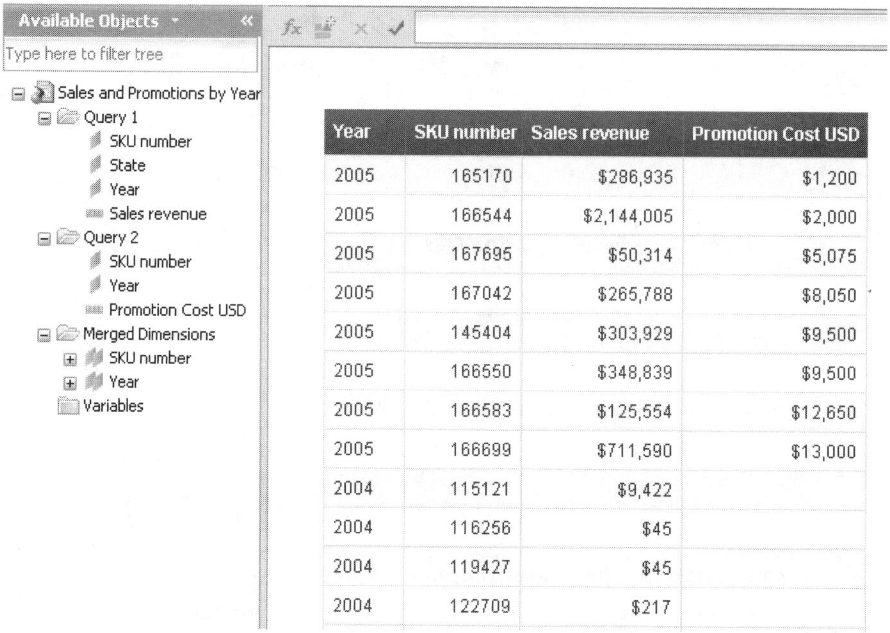

Year	SKU number	Sales revenue	Promotion Cost USD
2005	165170	$286,935	$1,200
2005	166544	$2,144,005	$2,000
2005	167695	$50,314	$5,075
2005	167042	$265,788	$8,050
2005	145404	$303,929	$9,500
2005	166550	$348,839	$9,500
2005	166583	$125,554	$12,650
2005	166699	$711,590	$13,000
2004	115121	$9,422	
2004	116256	$45	
2004	119427	$45	
2004	122709	$217	

Figure 22-5 Merged multiple data providers with matching dimensionality

In practice, you can have more dimension objects in one query than in the other query, as long as you understand the results of adding nonmerged dimensions in a tabular block on your report. For example, in Figure 22-6, we have added *State* to Query 1, which contains *Sales revenue*, but not to Query 2, because promotions are not maintained at a state level. Because both Query 1 and Query 2 do not contain the *State* dimension, this dimension cannot be merged. When *State* is added to the table, *Sales revenue* represents the state-level values, but *Promotion Cost USD* does not have state-level detail, so the promotion cost value for the SKU number is repeated for each state.

Also note in Figure 22-6 that Web Intelligence will do a pseudo–outer join when one query contains more data than the other. A null appears in the measure column for data that does not appear in the second query. By default, the outer join applies to only the second query and not the first. So for example, if there were products with promotions (the second query) and no corresponding sales revenue, these rows are dropped from the merged table. If you want all results displayed from both queries, you must set the option "Extend merged dimension values" in the document properties, as described in the next section.

Setting Data Merging Options

To set the document properties related to data merging, do the following:

1. Select Properties | Document from the toolbox on the left side of the report design view. The Document Summary dialog box will display.

2. Check the option Auto-merge dimensions to have Web Intelligence merge query results with common dimension names from the same universe.

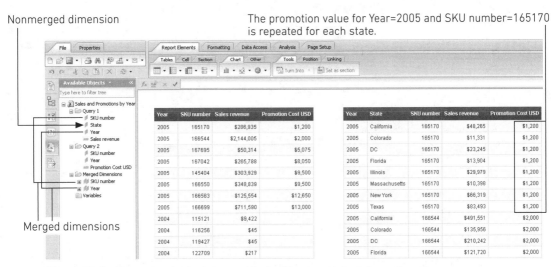

Figure 22-6 Merged multiple data providers with mismatched dimensionality

3. Check the option Extend merged dimension values. This will perform a full outer join or display results from both queries, even when only one query contains a particular dimension value.

Measure Conditions with Aggregate Functions

When you place a condition on a measure object that uses an aggregate function, Web Intelligence does not generate a WHERE clause, but instead generates a HAVING clause. The RDBMS first performs the aggregations and GROUP BY, and then returns only those results that satisfy the HAVING condition. In the following example, the query returns rows for which the SUM of SHOP_FACTS.MARGIN is less than or equal to 0.

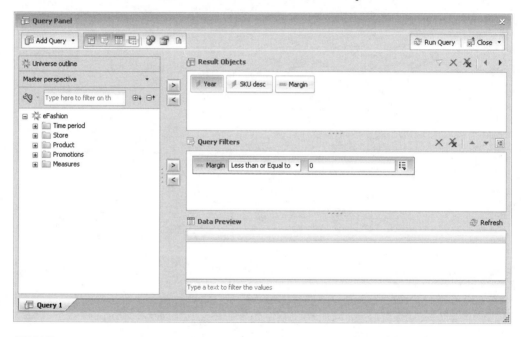

```
SELECT
Calendar_year_lookup.Yr,
Article_lookup.Article_label,
  sum(Shop_facts.Margin)
FROM
Calendar_year_lookup,
Article_lookup,
Shop_facts
WHERE
  ( Article_lookup.Article_id=Shop_facts.Article_id )
  AND  ( Shop_facts.Week_id=Calendar_year_lookup.Week_id )
GROUP BY
Calendar_year_lookup.Yr,
Article_lookup.Article_label
HAVING
  sum(Shop_facts.Margin)  <=  0
```

The problem here is that many users are deceived into thinking this is a simple query, as it returns few results. It is true that there may not be many article families/lines that have a negative margin for a particular month. However, to answer the query, the database must do a full table scan on the fact table.

In the sample database, the fact table is quite small. However, in real-world databases, the fact table can be millions of rows of data. To minimize the risk of full table scans on large fact tables, consider adding conditions on any other dimension objects that will generate a WHERE clause. For example, a condition on *Year* in addition to *Margin* will allow the database to first select only those rows for a particular year. The database then performs the GROUP BY and HAVING clauses on a smaller set of data (possibly retrieved via an index).

TIP If you use measures as conditions, ensure you include other conditions on dimension objects to improve the query processing time.

Complex Query Filters

To understand how the AND, OR, UNION, INTERSECT, and MINUS operators work, it's useful to review a bit of set theory. Figure 22-7 shows a Venn diagram with three sets of criteria: Year, State, and Product Lines.

When you add query filters to your query, the filters are joined by a default operator: AND. All conditions must be met for the query to return results. You can say this is the intersection, or solid triangle, in Figure 22-7, where all three sets of criteria are met. For example, if you set the conditions as shown in the following screen, the query will return information only for Year=2005, State=California, with Lines of Jackets or Overcoats.

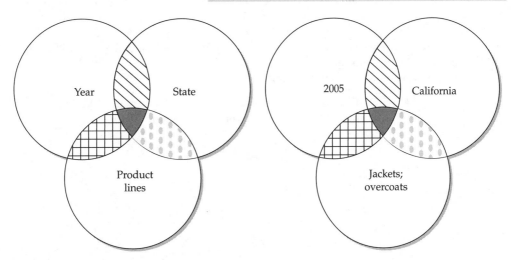

Figure 22-7   Intersection of multiple filter criteria

If *any* of the conditions could be met (an OR connector), then you can think of it as a nonoverlapping circle from Figure 22-7. If you wanted all years, regardless of state or product lines, it's the full circle. If you are trying to filter your data for years in a certain state, it's the overlap between the two criteria.

OR Operand and Nested Conditions

Sometimes the questions we ask of the data are not straightforward, and the query conditions become very complex. The complexity arises when you want to join one set of conditions with an OR and the other with an AND.

For example, suppose a sales manager wants to see only the data for the sales under his management. In 2004, he managed California, Colorado, and Texas, but in 2005 and 2006, he managed New York, Washington, D.C., Massachusetts, and Florida. If you want to analyze information for only this sales manager, you need to group your conditions in a way that is often called *nesting*. Failure to nest your conditions properly will lead to incorrect query results. In this case, you want to nest your query filters as two segments:

- Year = 2004 AND State IN (California, Colorado, Texas)

  OR

- Year IN (2005,2006) AND State IN (New York, DC, Massachusetts, Florida)

In previous versions of Web Intelligence, you could drag-and-drop objects to build and nest conditions. In SAP BusinessObjects BI 4 Web Intelligence, you cannot use the drag-and-drop technique. You must select the universe objects and then click the Nest Condition button in the Query Panel to build your query. The nesting of conditions will begin at the point you click the button.

To create a nested condition, do the following:

1. Click the Nest Condition button in the upper-right corner of the Query Panel. The query will display with a nested condition container.

2. Insert the condition objects Year=2004 And State In List (California, Colorado, Texas) within the nested condition container.

3. To insert the next nested condition objects, you must select the level at which you want to insert the nested conditions. In this example, select the OR operator, and then select the Nest Condition button. Another nested condition container will display.

4. Insert the condition objects Year In List (2005, 2006) And State In List (New York, Massachusetts, DC, Florida) within the nested condition container.

In the preceding example, the OR operator allowed you to nest or group multiple sets of criteria. You also can use OR to search for the same value across multiple fields. For example, in SAP BusinessObjects, the bill of lading may appear in several fields. With the following conditions, the OR operator allows you to search in multiple fields. By using the exact same prompt for each of the conditions, you need to enter only one bill of lading number, and it is filled in each of the conditions.

Combined Queries

In some cases, a single SQL statement will not give you the desired results. Web Intelligence supports combined queries, which extend the functionality and capability of your queries.

Combined queries are most often used to do the following:

- Combine data from different record sets where no relationship exists between the record sets into a single data provider. For example, if you were combining customer and vendor data into a single list, the first query would be a list of customers from the customer table, and the union query would be a list of vendors from the vendor table.

- Identify data that exists in one record set and does not exist in the other record set. For example, if you wanted a list of products for which there were no corresponding sales transactions, the main query would contain products from the dimension table, and the minus query would contain products from the sales fact table. The result set is a list of products for which there are no records in the sales fact table.

- Identify data that exists in both record sets. For example, if you wanted a list of vendors who have also purchased products from you, the main query would contain vendor names from the dimension table, and the intersection query would contain customer names from the sales fact table.

This table summarizes the operators used to combine queries.

Operator	Explanation
UNION	Combines the results of multiple queries. When the query contains a measure, the common rows are aggregated.
INTERSECT	Selects the rows that intersect or overlap between the two queries. This is not recommended for use with a measure as a result object. When the query contains a measure object, unless the measure values are exactly the same, there is no intersection.
MINUS	Subtracts the rows in the second query from the main query.

The following example uses the Island Resorts Marketing universe and an intersection query to identify customers who have stayed in both the Hawaiian Club resort and the French Riviera resort.

1. Create a new Web Intelligence report. For this example, when creating the data provider, select the Island Resorts Marketing universe, and *Country of Origin* and *Customer* as result objects.

2. Insert your query filter as *Resort* Equal to **Hawaiian Club**.

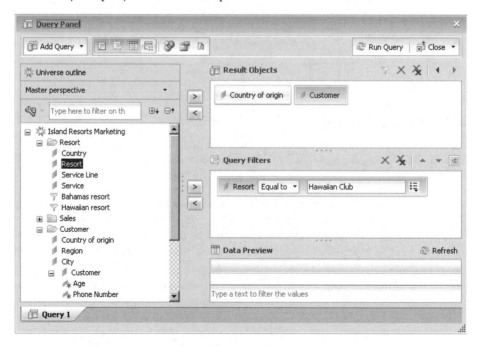

3. Select the Add a Combined Query button from the Query Panel toolbox.

4. Web Intelligence opens a Combined Query panel, as shown earlier in Figure 22-7. By default, the operator is a UNION. Double-click UNION to change it to INTERSECT. Insert your query filter as *Resort* Equal to **French Riviera**.

5. You can continue to add more queries to identify customers who have stayed at three (or more) resorts by selecting the Add Combined Query button. If at any point you need to remove a combined query, select that combined query from the Query Panel and press the DELETE key. When prompted, click

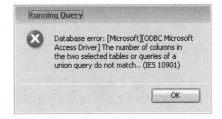

Yes to confirm that you wish to remove the combined query.

6. Once you are satisfied with each of your combined queries, select Run Query.

In combined queries, it is very important that you have the same number of result objects and that the result objects are the same data types. If you do not have the same result objects when running a combined query, you will receive an error message similar to the following:

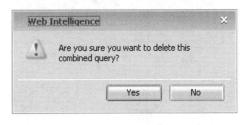

Figure 22-8 shows the results from the preceding example.

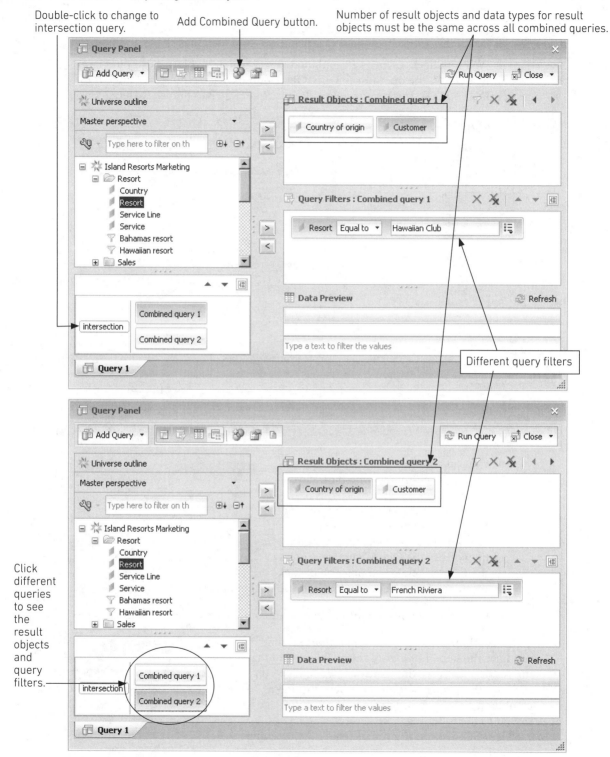

Figure 22-8   Combined query using INTERSECT

Figure 22-9 shows sample records to demonstrate how the different set operators work. The union query in this example could be accomplished by using the In List operator (Resort In List ('French Riviera', 'Hawaiian Club') in a simple query rather than a combined query. The MINUS between the two queries in Figure 22-9 shows the customers who stayed at the French Riviera minus any customers who stayed at the Hawaiian Club. The intersection between the two queries consists only of customers Schiller, Weimar, and Wilson. These are the customers who stayed at both the French Riviera and Hawaiian Club resorts.

You also can use the condition operators BOTH and EXCEPT to generate the intersection and minus queries. Remember that when using BOTH with INTERSECT, do not include the same condition objects as result objects, or no rows will be returned.

Subqueries

A subquery can be used in the WHERE clause and is a query that the main SELECT statement calls to determine the query filter values. For example, in the Island Resorts Marketing universe, you may want a listing of customers and all the resorts that the customers stayed at if the customer ever stayed at the Hawaiian Club. The problem is that if you design your query with a query filter of Resort=Hawaiian Club, you get only customers and their reservations at the resort Hawaiian Club. You will exclude their reservations at the other resorts. To get a listing of customers and *all* the resorts that the customer stayed at if the customer ever stayed at the Hawaiian Club, you can use a subquery.

Query 1			Query 1 UNION Query 2		Query 1 MINUS Query 2		Query 1 INTERSECT Query 2
Customer	**Resort**		**Customer**		**Customer**		**Customer**
Edwards	French Riviera		Edwards		Edwards		Schiller
Gentil			Gentil		Gentil		Weimar
Hopkins			Goldschmidt		Hopkins		Wilson
Jones			Hopkins		Jones		
Kamimura			Jones		Kamimura		
Keegan			Kamimura		Keegan		
McCartney			Keegan		McCartney		
Michaud			McCartney		Michaud		
Oneda			Michaud		Oneda		
Schiller			Mukumoto		Schultz		
Schultz			Oneda		Swenson		
Swenson			Reinman		Wilson		
Weimar			Schiller				
Wilson			Schultz				
			Swenson				
			Titzman				
Query 2			Weimar				
Customer	**Resort**		Wilson				
Goldschmidt	Hawaiian Club						
Mukumoto							
Reinman							
Schiller							
Titzman							
Weimar							
Wilson							

Figure 22-9   Sample data for queries using UNION, MINUS, and INTERSECT

You create a subquery by defining a query filter in a particular way. This can get a little confusing, so be sure to think carefully about which conditions apply where. In the resorts client listing example, you want to know the following:

- Customer names and all resorts that they have stayed at.
- But only where the customer name has stayed at least once at the Resort = Hawaiian Club.

In Figure 22-10, the subquery is on *Customer*. It may seem logical to put the subquery on *Resort*, but you really want to return customers where they are in a list of customers who have stayed at Resort = Hawaiian Club.

To create a subquery as in Figure 22-10, do the following:

1. Create a new Web Intelligence report and use the Island Resorts Marketing universe.

2. Select the result objects you would like to include in the report. In this example, select *Customer* and *Resort*.

3. Select the universe object on which you plan to base your subquery from the objects list in the universe outline panel. In this example, select *Customer*.

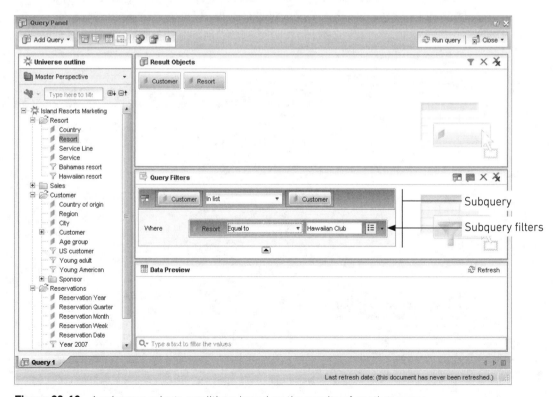

Figure 22-10 A subquery selects conditions based on the results of another query.

4. In the Query Filters panel, select the Add a Subquery button.

5. The subquery will be added to the Query Filters panel. Change the operators and add any query conditions to the subquery to meet your needs. In this example, the operator will remain In List, and you will add a query filter on Resort by dragging the *Resort* object into your subquery filters. Change the operator to Equal To and select Hawaiian Club as the operand value. Your query will look like Figure 22-10.

6. Click Run Query.

Subqueries are a powerful feature in Web Intelligence. By combining them with multiple data providers, you can answer complex business questions.

Object Equal to Object from this Query

Setting an object equal to another object from this query is a powerful capability, but as with other complex queries, you need to monitor query performance. This type of query creates a join between the tables that reference the objects (or creates a self-join when the two objects refer to the same table). You may use this capability to answer questions such as the following:

- Which orders shipped the same day the order was placed?
- Which customers traveled to a different country than the one in which they reside?
- Which invoices have the same ship-to customer ID and sold-to customer ID?

The following example looks for customers who traveled to a country different from the one in which they reside. To create a query using the object equal to an object from this query, do the following:

1. Create a Web Intelligence report using the Island Resorts Marketing universe.

2. Add the *Customer, Country of Origin, Resort*, and *Country* objects to the Result Objects pane.

3. Add the *Country of Origin* object to the Query Filters pane.

4. Select the operator. For this example, select Not Equal To.

5. Select Object from this query as the operand. The Objects and variables dialog box will display. This list of objects is not narrowed by a data type that corresponds to the object you selected in step 3. However, in order for your query to be valid, the objects must be of the same data type. If you select an object with a different data type, such as Invoice Date (which is of data type datetime), you will get an error similar to the following:

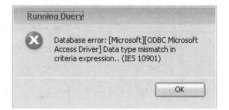

6. Select the *Resort | Country* object, and then click OK.

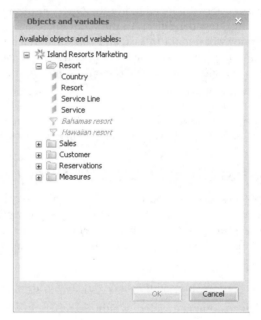

7. Click Run Query.

Summary

Much of the power in Web Intelligence lies in its robust query capabilities. It can handle complex database schemas by allowing you to generate multiple SQL statements to present one seamless report. In some cases, such as with multipass SQL, you may never realize this happens. In other queries, you may explicitly create separate queries and merge them.

As you create complex queries, be aware that the queries may run slower, and you should ideally test your query logic with small data sets. In some cases, there is no way around the performance issues—it's a complex business question answered with complex SQL. In other instances, you may be able to construct the query in ways that help the processing, or the DBA may be able to do some additional tuning in the data source.

PART

IV

Dashboards and More

CHAPTER

23

Introduction to Dashboards

As discussed in Chapter 1, dashboards present information in a way that helps managers monitor the business and align employees to common goals. According to industry visualization expert Stephen Few, author of *Information Dashboard Design,* "a dashboard is a visual form of information display, which is used to monitor what's currently going on in the business at a glance." According to Wayne Eckerson, author of *Performance Dashboards,* a performance dashboard is one that "translates the organizations strategy into objectives, metrics, initiatives, and tasks customized to each group and individual." Dashboards may be used either by managers or by operational staff. The following are some of the common benefits of dashboards:

- They give users the ability to identify both positive and negative trends at a glance, usually through a highly visual presentation.
- They allow organizations to analyze data to align business strategies and organizational goals.
- They help users identify efficiencies, opportunities, and potential problems.
- They give users the ability to quickly identify data outliers and correlations.
- They allow users to access data from multiple data sources and systems.
- They allow for quicker insight and analysis versus accessing multiple reports or navigating a dense table of numbers.

SAP BusinessObjects Dashboards 4.0 allows you to create flexible, personalized dashboards quickly and easily with a drag-and-drop interface. SAP BusinessObjects Dashboards 4.0 was formerly known as Xcelsius. This latest release introduces performance improvements and, most notably, direct data binding to the SAP BI platform, including universes and BEx queries.

New features of SAP BusinessObjects Dashboards 4.0 include the following:

- It has better scalability and performance. Two new services added are DashboardDesignCacheServer and DashboardDesignProcessingServer.

- The Query Panel allows you to connect to a universe as a data source.
- Connections to OLAP universes and SAP BW BEx queries, including support for hierarchical data, are available.
- The Query Browser panel allows you to manage your universe queries.
- Query data can be bound directly to components in your dashboard without needing to be inserted into the embedded spreadsheet.
- Components support dynamic regional date, time, number, and currency formats.
- Component text can be translated to other languages through the translation manager.
- When publishing a dashboard, both the design document (.xlf) and the Flash document (.swf) are published as a single object. This new object type can have its own object-level security.
- Alert support has been added to the combination chart and spreadsheet table components.
- A waterfall chart component has been added.

In this chapter, we will look at how to quickly create a dashboard using SAP BusinessObjects Dashboards 4.0. The remaining chapters in this section will cover the dashboard workspace, components, properties, and data connections in much greater detail.

Embedded Query Designer and Direct Data Binding: Pros and Cons

One of the most significant new features in BusinessObjects Dashboards 4.0 is the query designer and direct binding of data from universes and BEx queries to components in the dashboard, without having to insert the data into the embedded spreadsheet. While this is a significant step in the maturity of Dashboards, it is important to point out some of the pros and cons of this new feature.

The following are the advantages of the integrated query designer:

- The query designer and direct binding make dashboard development and data retrieval easier. In prior versions of Dashboard Design, the data had to be retrieved into the embedded worksheet as well as the mechanism to keep the data refreshed through Live Office or some other function. Components that are directly bound to a query can be previewed with data without requiring the developer to preview and render the dashboard.
- The new query prompt selector component is automatically bound to the list of values (LOV) for the data element. In prior versions, LOVs for selector components would have to be mapped to the embedded Excel spreadsheet, and a mechanism to refresh their values would have to be developed.

And here are the disadvantages of the embedded designer:

- Queries are executed directly against the database. At first blush, direct query execution may seem like an advantage but there are some performance risks. Dashboards 4.0 has introduced DashboardDesignCacheServer, which is designed to cache data and reduce the load from *concurrent* user queries. However, using data that has been run and saved in a scheduled report instance without direct binding can often provide better performance than using direct binding, which will execute a query against the database unless the query is found in DashboardDesignCacheServer.

- There is no aggregation engine in BusinessObjects Dashboards 4.0. Using the features and formulas in Excel and the embedded spreadsheet often allows you to return a single data set to meet the needs of multiple levels of aggregation. For example, if you have two components in your dashboard, one aggregated at the Year level and the other aggregated at the Quarter and Year level, a single data set in the embedded Excel spreadsheet can be manipulated using formulas and functions to provide data to both components. Direct data binding would require two queries to be returned: one aggregated at the Year level and one aggregated at the Quarter and Year level.

- Excel offers many features and functions when using an embedded spreadsheet that will not be available when using direct binding.

- The query designer currently supports only .unx universes, the new universe format created with the new IDT and not .unv universes created in previous versions or with the UDT.

A solution from a SAP partner, Antivia XWIS, integrates with Dashboards and addresses a number of these limitations, including native drill-down, support for both universe formats, a central calculation library, and iPad support.

Creating a Simple Dashboard

Creating a simple dashboard involves the following main steps:

- Planning the dashboard
- Populating the dashboard data
- Adding data display components
- Adding data selector components
- Applying a theme/color style
- Saving and exporting the dashboard

The following sections provide a quick overview of designing a very simple dashboard from start to finish. Chapters 24 through 27 go into much greater detail about all of the elements of dashboard design and development.

Part IV

Planning the Dashboard

Dashboards can range from a simple page of multiple visualizations to a complex application. A dashboard needs to be designed to display all of the appropriate metrics, aggregated at the appropriate level of detail to provide the business user high-level information quickly. Selectors need to be defined to allow users to interact with the data on the dashboard to quickly filter the data displayed; for example, to view specific time frames, regions, or products. Additionally, the dashboard will often provide drilling capabilities so that the user can get additional details when necessary. How users want to see and interact with the data in the dashboard should be considered before development begins.

A dashboard is often made up of multiple canvases, with each canvas containing multiple components. Understanding who will use the dashboard and how they will interact with it is important in selecting the type and number of canvases as well as the type of components. Often, mockups and prototypes are required to create an effective dashboard design.

Developing a Simple Dashboard

Once the conceptual dashboard design has been completed, you can begin developing the dashboard using SAP BusinessObjects Dashboards 4.0. The remainder of this chapter shows the steps involved with creating a very basic dashboard from start to finish.

Starting Dashboard Design

To start Dashboard Design, do the following:

1. Click the Dashboards icon on your desktop or select Start | Programs | Dashboards 4 | Dashboards.

2. By default, the start page will display. Preventing the start page from displaying when starting Dashboard Design is discussed in Chapter 24.

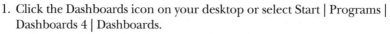

3. Under New, select Blank Model. The Dashboard Design interface will display with a blank canvas, as shown in Figure 23-1.

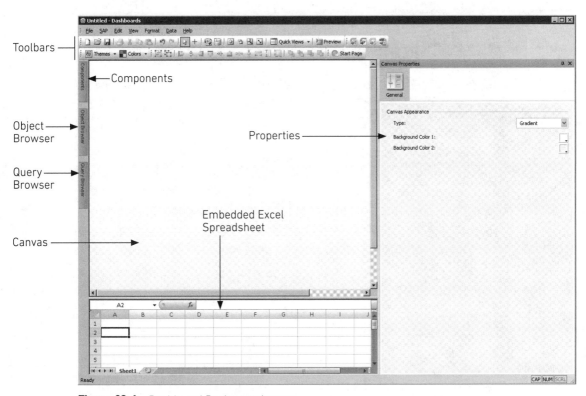

Figure 23-1   Dashboard Design workspace

Populating Data in the Dashboard Using the Query Browser

The next step is to define the data to be used in the dashboard. Dashboards 4.0 provides much more flexibility than previous versions in how data is retrieved, including the ability to directly connect to universes and BEx queries as data sources, as well as the traditional method of embedding data from Excel worksheets. In this example, the new direct connection to a universe will be used to populate the data in the dashboard.

To create a query against a universe to return data for a component in the dashboard, do the following:

1. Click the Query Browser button on the left side of the Dashboard Design window. The Query Browser panel will display.

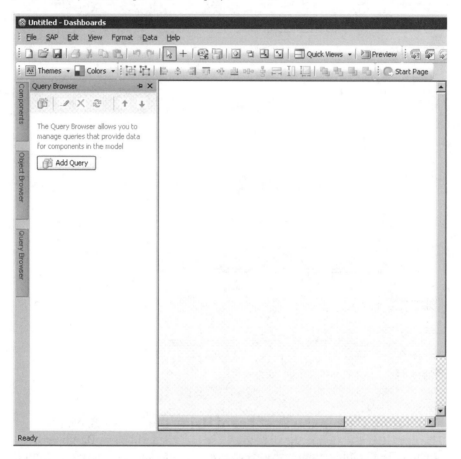

2. Click the Add Query button. The login dialog box for the SAP BusinessObjects system will display. Log in to access available universes and BEx queries.

3. Once you have successfully logged in to SAP BusinessObjects, the Add Query dialog box will display.

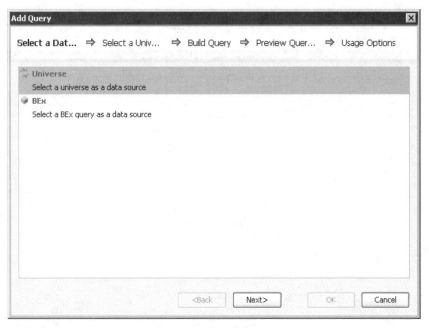

4. Select Universe and click Next. The list of available universes will display in the dialog box. Navigate through the folders and select the desired universe. In this example, select eFashion.unx and click Next.

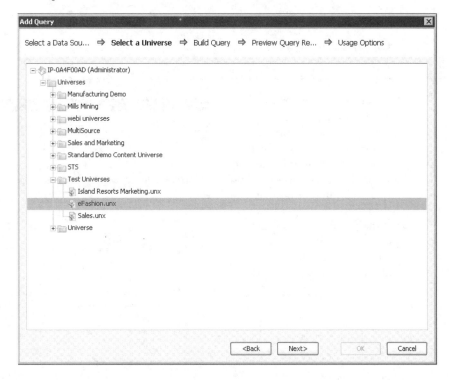

5. The Query Builder dialog box displays. Select the objects you would like to have in your query. In this example, select State and Sales revenue as Result Objects.

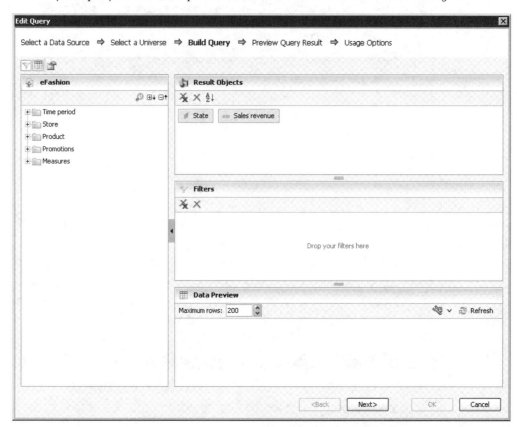

6. You will add a query prompt selector component to the dashboard in a subsequent section. So, to prepare for that, add a query condition based on a prompt to the query now. Add a query condition on State. Select the In List operator. Set the prompt options with Prompt Text=State(s), and set the default values to California;Florida;New York.

7. Your completed query should look like the following. When you are satisfied, click Next.

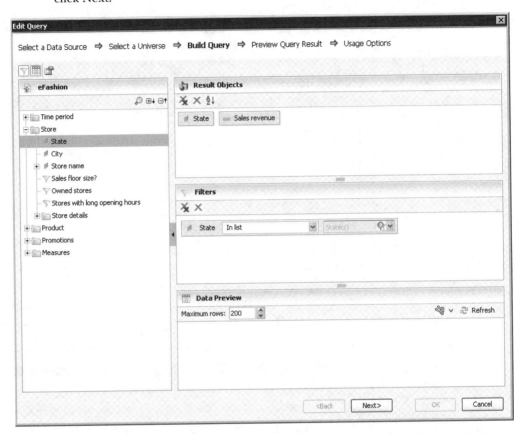

8. The Answer Prompts dialog box displays. Accept the default prompt values and click Run.

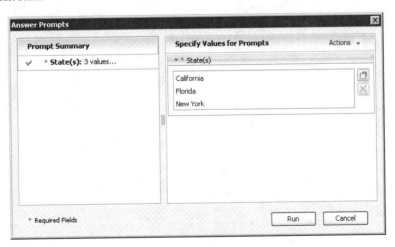

9. The Edit Query, Preview Query step displays with the results from the query. Click Next.

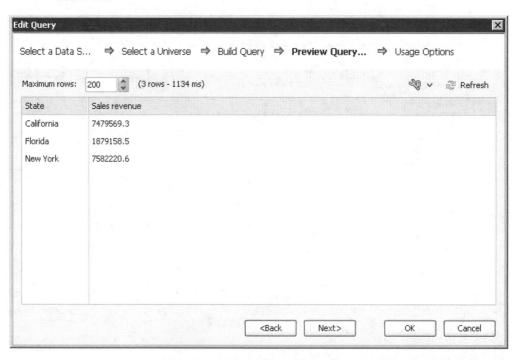

10. The Refresh Options: Refresh Before Components Are Loaded check box should be checked by default. Usage options are covered in Chapter 27. Click OK.

11. You will now be returned to the Dashboard Design window. To return to your query to see the properties, add a new query, or edit the query, click the Query Browser button in the left panel.

Adding a Component to the Canvas and Binding Data

Once data has been defined and populated, either through a direct query as created in the previous section or through the embedded spreadsheet, you can start adding components and binding data to the components on your dashboard canvas.

Components are the building blocks of your dashboard. There are nearly 200 components available in BusinessObjects Dashboards 4.0. Chapter 25 covers all the components available in Dashboard Designer.

Charts are a very common component used in dashboard design. They provide a visual representation of data. In this section, we will add a column chart component to the dashboard.

1. Click the Components button on the left side of the Dashboard Design window. The Components panel will display. From the Tree view, open the Charts folder to display the chart components.

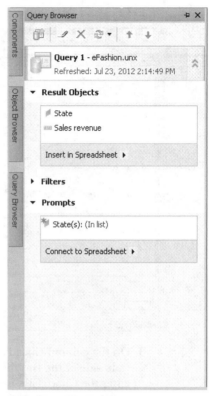

2. Click and drag the column chart component to the canvas.

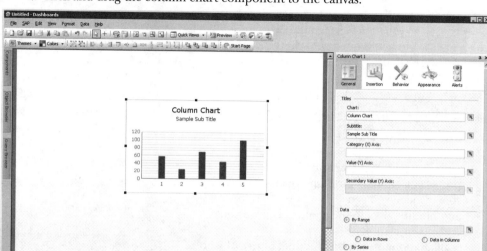

3. On the column chart Properties panel on the right side of the Dashboard Designer window, enter the Chart Title properties as **Sales Revenue**

4. On the column chart Properties panel, set the following Data properties:

- Select the By Series radio button.
- Click the plus (+) button under the series list box.
- Enter the name **Sales Revenue**.

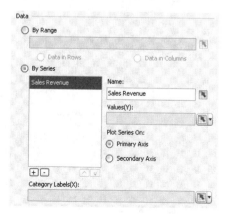

5. To bind the values data from your query to the column chart, on the column chart Properties panel, drop down the Values(Y) list and select Query Data.

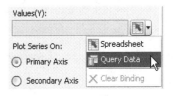

6. The Select from Query dialog box displays. Select the measure value to be bound as a chart value to the chart. In this example, select Sales revenue and click OK.

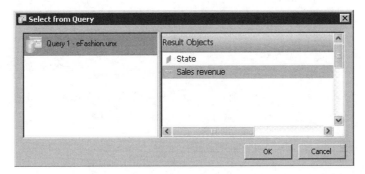

7. You will see the column chart update with the values from your query.

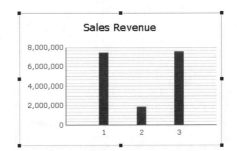

8. To bind the column category data from your query to the column chart, on the column chart Properties panel, drop down the Category Labels(X) list and select Query Data.

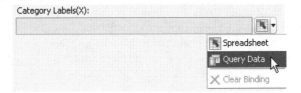

9. The Select from Query dialog box displays. Select the dimension value to be bound as a category label to the chart. In this example, select State and click OK.

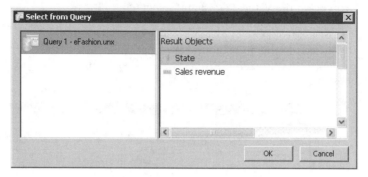

10. You will see the column chart update with X axis category labels from your query.

Adding a Selector Component

One of the features of a dashboard that makes it compelling is the ability for users to interact with it. If the column chart component that we added to the dashboard in the previous section always contained data for the same three states, a Web Intelligence report would have sufficed.

There are many selectors available, including radio buttons, check boxes, combo boxes, and so on. All of the selectors are covered in detail in Chapter 25. In this section, you will add a query prompt selector component to the dashboard that is bound to the prompt that was created in our query to allow users to dynamically select which states they would like to include in the column chart component.

The benefit of this query prompt selector component is that the LOV is dynamically created from the universe. You don't need to create an LOV in the embedded spreadsheet and create a mechanism to keep that LOV up to date.

1. Click the Components button on the left side of the Dashboard Design window. The Components panel will display. From the Tree view, open the Universe Connectivity folder to display the special universe connectivity components.

2. Click and drag the query prompt selector component to the canvas next to the column chart component.

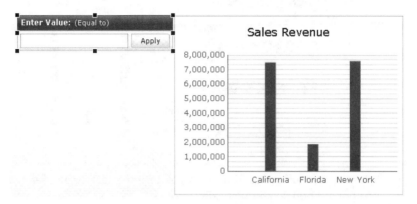

3. On the query prompt selector Properties panel on the right side of the Dashboard Designer window, set the following properties:

   - Select the Source Prompt to be the State(s): prompt entered in the query.

   - Select Refresh when Selection Changes.

4. To see the behavior of this selector component, you must preview the dashboard. Select the Preview button from the toolbar.

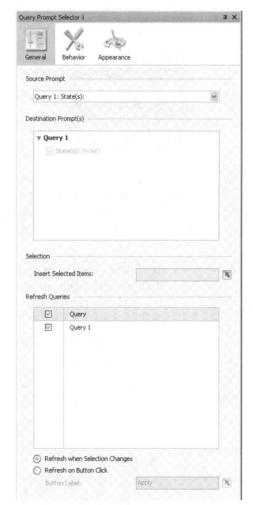

5. The dashboard is rendered and displayed on the screen.

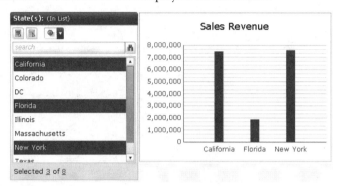

6. Select or deselect values from the query prompt selector and see the column chart component update automatically.

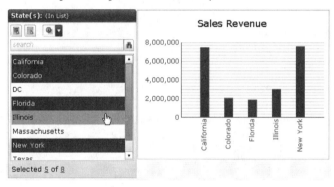

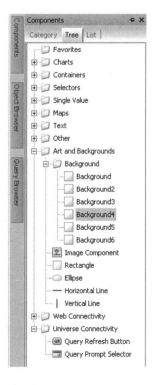

Adding Text and Graphics

Once you are satisfied with your dashboard design, you can add text and graphics to provide additional information or corporate branding.

1. Click the Components button on the left side of the Dashboard Designer window. The Components panel will display. From the Tree view, open the Art and Backgrounds/Background folder to display the background components.

2. Drag the Background4 component to the canvas.

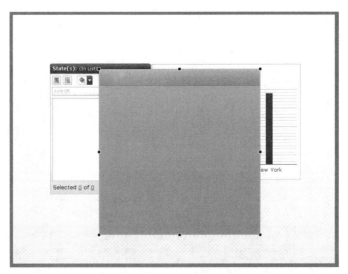

3. Right-click the background component and select Send to Back.

4. Move and size the background component on the canvas.

5. Add a text component to give the dashboard a title by clicking the Components button on the left side of the Dashboard Designer window and selecting the label component from the Text folder. Click and drag the label component to the dashboard and set the component properties. Click Preview.

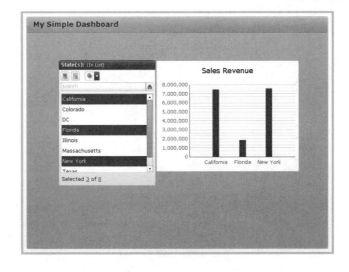

Selecting a Theme and Color Scheme

BusinessObjects Dashboards 4.0 has many built-in themes and color schemes. The themes and color schemes are available from the toolbar or the Format menu. To apply a theme, select the Theme drop-down menu on the Themes toolbar or select Format | Theme.

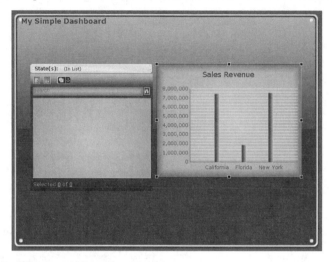

Saving your Dashboard Design Model

It is important to save your dashboard design often. Saving the dashboard design model creates an .xlf file that contains only the dashboard model design and cannot be viewed outside the Dashboard Design.

To save the .xlf file, do the following:

 1. With the dashboard design model open, select File | Save As from the menu bar. Alternatively, click the Save button from the toolbar.

2. The Save As dialog box displays. Select a folder location, type a filename for the dashboard design model, and click Save.

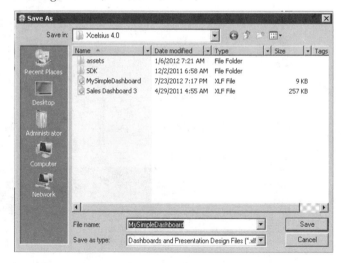

Exporting your Dashboard

Your dashboard can be exported to multiple formats for viewing. Supported formats include the following:

- SWF (Flash)
- Microsoft PowerPoint
- Microsoft Word
- Microsoft Outlook
- Adobe Acrobat PDF
- HTML
- Adobe AIR

To export your dashboard, select File | Export or choose Export Options  from the Exporting toolbar.

Summary

SAP BusinessObjects Dashboards 4.0 has been enhanced to have better scalability and performance and to support direct data binding to your universes and BEx queries. The drag-and-drop interface allows you to quickly create customized dashboards. Dashboard Design provides almost 200 components, advanced formatting capabilities, and flexible data access, which will be covered in detail in Chapters 24 through 27.

Dashboard Design Workspace and Menus

Before you start designing a dashboard or other data visualization, understanding the Dashboard Design application is needed. This chapter focuses on the basics of working with the Dashboard Design application: the menus, workspaces, icons, and toolbars. Knowing where to go for different design features before you actually begin the development process saves time and unneeded frustration.

Starting Dashboard Design

By default, when you start Dashboard Design for the first time, you see the start page (which is similar to the Crystal Reports start page), as shown in Figure 24-1. The Dashboard Design start page display New, Recent, and Open options at the top. If you're connected to a network, the bottom portion of the start page will contain tabs for Highlights, Key Resources, and eLearning. (If no network connection is available, then only the top half of the start page is visible.) This bottom section has a lot of great content to see the latest news on Dashboard Design, blogs, samples, learning options, and newsletters.

NOTE Because Dashboard Design requires Excel, an instance of Excel is executed in the background when Dashboard Design is launched. It is recommended that Excel not be running when Dashboard Design is launched. If two instances of Dashboard Design are running, only one Excel instance runs in the background. If the Dashboard Design application stops responding or ends abruptly, you may need to close the Excel instance running in the background using the Task Manager.

You can close the start page by selecting an option from the New, Open, or Recent list. To prevent the start page from appearing when you start Dashboard Design, from the Dashboard Design workspace (described in the next section), click the Start Page icon near the top of the Dashboard Design window, or open the Help menu and deselect Start Page.

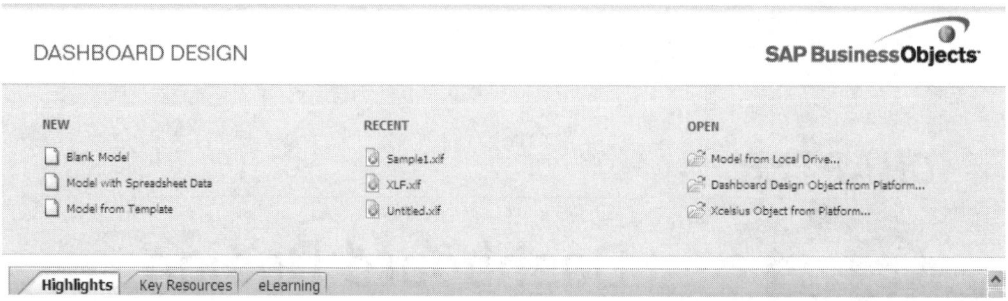

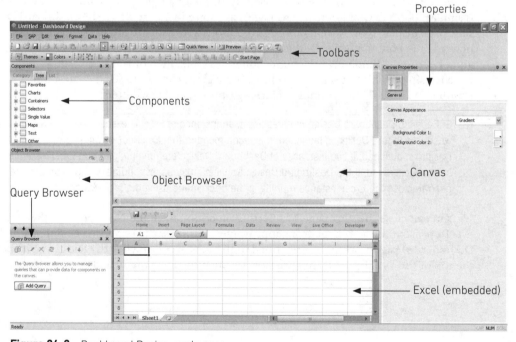

Figure 24-1   Dashboard Design start page

Dashboard Design Panels and Toolbars

The Dashboard Design workspace, shown in Figure 24-2, is where you develop a model for your dashboard. The workspace contains several toolbars, the canvas, components, embedded Excel worksheet, Object Browser, Properties, and Query Browser panels.

The Components, Object Browser, Properties, and Query Browser panels can be moved, hidden, closed, or docked as needed. Hiding and closing these panels can maximize the viewable canvas space.

The following sections describe the Dashboard Design workspace toolbars and panels, as well as how to customize the panels.

Figure 24-2   Dashboard Design workspace

Dashboard Design Toolbars

The Dashboard Design workspace offers five toolbars: Menu, Standard, Themes and Colors, Formatting, and Exporting.

Menu Toolbar

The Dashboard Design Menu toolbar contains seven menu items.

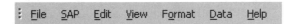

Many of these options are also available in the Standard and Formatting toolbars, as discussed in the following sections.

Standard Toolbar

The Standard toolbar contains many options, including those for creating and opening Dashboard Design files, printing models, choosing mouse selector options, adjusting the canvas size, changing the designer view, and previewing. Options for managing data connections and importing new Excel workbooks are also available on this toolbar. Table 24-1 describes the Standard toolbar buttons.

Clicking the Quick View button on the Standard toolbar presents four options:

- **Show My Workspace**   Displays the canvas and Component, Properties, Excel, Object Browser, and Query Browser panels.
- **Show Canvas Only**   Displays only the canvas.
- **Show Spreadsheet Only**   Displays only the Excel spreadsheet.
- **Show Canvas and Spreadsheet**   Displays both the canvas and the spreadsheet.

These options are extremely useful when only specific panels are needed for development. For example, if you need to modify Excel formulas, select Show Spreadsheet Only.

Themes and Colors Toolbar

The Themes and Colors toolbar offers two options to customize the look and feel of a model. Clicking the Themes drop-arrow displays a list of available themes. Each theme contains a set of default colors, components, and properties. Different themes can also contain different components.

Clicking the Colors drop-down arrow displays a list of predefined schemes of colors that can be selected for a model to change the color properties of the components. You can also add color schemes and customize them. Refer to Chapter 26 for more details.

Part IV

Button	Key Combo	Name	Function
	CTRL-N	New	Creates a new Dashboard Design model. If this is selected, the existing open model will need to be closed.
	CTRL-O	Open	Opens an existing Dashboard Design model.
	CTRL-S	Save	Saves the current model.
	CTRL-P	Print	Prints the model (the model must be in preview mode).
	CTRL-X	Cut	Cuts the selected components.
	CTRL-C	Copy	Copies the selected components.
	CTRL-V	Paste	Pastes the cut or copied components.
	CTRL-Z	Undo	Undoes the previous action(s). Undo works on only the previous ten actions and does not apply to all actions. Note that changes in the Properties panel cannot be undone with this button.
	CTRL-Y	Redo	Redoes the previous action(s).
		Selection Tool	Selects components on the canvas. This is selected by default.
+		Component Tool	Selects and adds components to the canvas. This is selected when a component is selected from the Components panel.
	CTRL-SHIFT-I	Import Spreadsheet	Imports a new Excel workbook to be embedded into the model. This will replace the existing embedded Excel file and all data.
		Manage Connections	Launches the Data Manager. This is used to manage most of the external data source connections.
		Increase Canvas	Increases the canvas by 10 pixels vertically and horizontally.
		Decrease Canvas	Decreases the canvas by 10 pixels vertically and horizontally.
		Fit Canvas to Components	Changes the canvas size to fit the components that have been added.

Table 24-1 Dashboard Design Standard Toolbar

Button	Key Combo	Name	Function
		Fit Canvas to Window	Changes the canvas size to fit the visible area of the canvas. If the Show My Workspace option is being used, the canvas will likely shrink. If the Show Canvas Only option is used, then the canvas will likely expand.
		Quick Views	Changes what is visible within Dashboard Design. The Quick View options are described after this table.
	CTRL-ENTER	Toggle Preview Mode	Creates a working preview of the Dashboard Design model.

Table 24-1   Dashboard Design Standard Toolbar *(continued)*

Formatting Toolbar

The Formatting toolbar is used to modify the size, layout, position, and grouping of components. All of these buttons require two or more components to be selected in order to be activated. See the "The Dashboard Design Canvas" section a little later in this chapter for details on how to select multiple components on the canvas.

Once you've selected more than one component, the Formatting toolbar buttons will be enabled. The order in which you select the components will determine the behavior of the formatting. The first item selected for formatting will be the one that should be used to format the others. For example, if Chart1 needs to be the same size as Chart2, then you should select Chart2 first.

The formatting options are useful when you apply dynamic visibility or layer components. If the components are not the same size or in the same location, then a flickering effect might occur when the user views the dashboard.

Table 24-2 describes the Formatting toolbar buttons.

Exporting Toolbar

The Exporting toolbar is used to export, or send, the model to another application for viewing. You can export the model to Microsoft PowerPoint, Word, and Outlook, as well as to an Adobe Acrobat PDF file. When these buttons are selected, Dashboard Design will create a new Flash file (.swf) and embed it into one of these formats.

This toolbar is primarily used to quickly export the model in these different formats to be reviewed. You can save the exported model when the embedded Flash model is open in the selected application. Table 24-3 describes the buttons on the Exporting toolbar.

Part IV

Button	Key Combo	Name	Function
	CTRL-G	Group Components	Groups the selected components. Components can be selected on the canvas or in the Object Browser.
	CTRL-SHIFT-G	Ungroup Components	Ungroups components (when grouped components are selected).
		Align Left	Aligns selected components to the left.
		Center Horizontally	Horizontally aligns components along the middle of the components.
		Align Right	Aligns selected components to the right.
		Align Top	Aligns selected components to the top.
		Center Vertically	Vertically aligns components along the middle of the components.
		Align Bottom	Aligns selected components to the bottom.
		Space Evenly Across	Evenly distributes the selected components horizontally.
		Space Evenly Down	Evenly distributes the selected components vertically.
		Make Same Width	Changes the width of the selected components based on the first component selected.
		Make Same Height	Changes the height of the selected components based on the first component selected.
		Make Same Size	Changes the height and width of the selected components based on the first component selected.
	CTRL-+	Bring to Front	Moves the selected component to the top layer on the canvas.
	CTRL-NUM – (minus)	Send to Back	Moves the selected component to the bottom layer on the canvas.
	NUM +	Bring Forward	Moves the selected component one layer up on the canvas.
	NUM –	Send Backward	Moves the selected component one layer down on the canvas.

Table 24-2 Dashboard Design Formatting Toolbar

Button	Name	Function
	Send to PowerPoint	Creates a SWF file and embeds it in a new PowerPoint slide
	Send to Microsoft Word	Creates a SWF file and embeds it in a new Word document
	Attach the SWF in Outlook	Creates a SWF file and adds it as an attachment to a new Outlook e-mail message
	Send to Adobe Acrobat PDF	Creates a SWF file and embeds it in a new Adobe Acrobat PDF file

Table 24-3   Dashboard Design Exporting Toolbar

You can also export models by selecting File | Export from the menu toolbar. The Export submenu offers three additional export options: Flash (SWF), AIR, and HTML. It also includes the option of saving the exported model and additional choices for PDF files (for example, Acrobat 6.0 or 9.0). This will be covered in more detail in the "Exporting a Dashboard Design Model" section later in this chapter.

The Dashboard Design Canvas

The canvas in Dashboard Design is where components are placed and what the users will see. During development, you add components to the canvas and rearrange them as needed.

Selecting Multiple Components
You can select multiple components on the canvas in several ways:

- Click on the canvas and select the area where components are located.
- Click the component on the canvas, press CTRL, and select another component.
- Use the Object Browser to select multiple components (using either the CTRL or SHIFT key).

Changing the Size and Appearance of the Canvas
The visual size of the canvas depends on the monitor size and resolution, and which other panels are open. You can adjust the size of the canvas to suit the needs of the model.

In the Formatting toolbar, the Increase Canvas, Decrease Canvas, Fit Canvas to Components, and Fit Canvas to Window buttons change the size of the canvas. You can also choose File | Document Properties to set the exact height and width of the canvas using the Custom option, or select from multiple size settings using the Preset Size option. To display a grid on the canvas with the option to snap to the grid, select File | Preferences. Properties and preferences are discussed later in this chapter, in the "Setting Document Properties" and "Defining Preferences" sections.

TIP To maximize the viewing area of the canvas while designing a model, use the Quick Views option Show Canvas Only. If the Fit Canvas to Components option is selected, it is good practice to also click the Increase Canvas button once or twice to add 10 to 20 pixels to the edge of the model.

Part IV

The General tab for the canvas offers the following properties to change the canvas appearance:

- **Solid Color**   Sets a single background color.
- **Gradient**   Applies a gradient effect using two background colors, from background color 1 at the top to background color 2 at the bottom, as shown in Figure 24-3.
- **Image**   Imports and embeds an image into the canvas. This image will be stretched to the canvas size.
- **None**   Displays the canvas without a background color or image.

The Components Panel

If the canvas is the foundation of a Dashboard Design model, then the components are the building blocks of a model. They are what the end users will see and interact with.

More than 190 components are available to build a model—charts, graphs, text boxes, selectors, maps, gauges, images, and containers to name a few. You select components from the Components panel and drag-and-drop them onto the canvas.

Chapter 25 provides more details about Dashboard Design components.

Figure 24-3   A gradient canvas

The Excel Panel

At the bottom of the workspace is the embedded Excel workbook. Excel is used to store and organize data (both static and dynamic data), create formulas, define events, and create mappings.

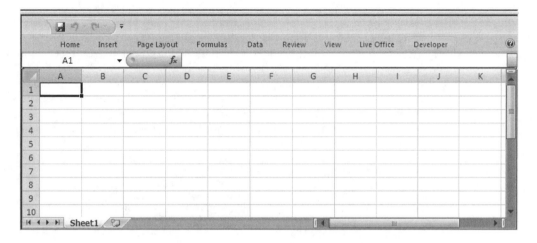

When creating a new model, the embedded Excel workbook will be blank. You can also import an existing Excel workbook into Dashboard Design. More details about the embedded Excel workbook can be found in Chapters 26 and 27.

The Object Browser

The Object Browser is often an overlooked feature when designing a dashboard. It is very useful when developing complex dashboards with multiple components because it allows you to organize the layering, visibility, grouping, naming, and locking of components.

Components are added to the Object Browser each time you place a component on the canvas. When you add a component to the canvas, it goes to the front (top) of the canvas. In the Object Browser, components listed at the top are at the bottom of the canvas, whereas components listed at the bottom of the Object Browser are at the top of the canvas.

Renaming Components

Renaming components in the Object Browser is good practice, especially when your model contains 20 or more components. This will help during the development process, documentation of the final solution, and cross-training others on the functionality of the model.

You can rename objects in the Object Browser in several ways:

- Double-click the component in the Object Browser.
- Press F2.
- Right-click the component and select Rename.

Part IV

Once a component is renamed, it can be difficult to determine the component's type (for example, a slider or label component). To avoid this problem, you should rename components using a standard naming convention, such as giving labels a prefix of LBL_ or lbl_.

When you rename objects in the Object Browser, those names are visible only in Dashboard Design. They will not be exposed to the end users viewing the Flash file.

Grouping Objects

Along with renaming components, grouping them in the Object Browser allows you to better organize and manage the components. Groups can also be part of other groups and renamed.

To group components, select the first component you want to add to the group in the Object Browser, and then select the other components while holding down either the SHIFT key (to select components that are next to each) or CTRL key (to select components anywhere in the Object Browser). Then right after the components have been selected, select rename.

When you select a component in the canvas that is part of a group, the entire group is selected. This is useful when components are layered together and need to stay in a specific alignment with other components. To select a single component in a group, you must select it within the group in the Object Browser.

To ungroup components, right-click the grouped components and select Ungroup.

Positioning, Hiding, and Locking Components

You can use the Object Browser to reposition components from the top or bottom of the canvas. To change the position of a component (or group), first select it in either the Object Browser or canvas, and then use one of the following techniques:

- Drag the component up or down in the Object Browser.

- Right-click the component and select a movement option. For example, to move the component to the very top or bottom, select Bring to Front or Send to Back.

- Click the up or down arrow at the bottom of the Object Browser.

- Press the minus (-) key to send the component backward, or press the plus (+) key to send the component forward.

- Press CTRL-plus (+) to move the component to the very top, or press CTRL-minus (-) to send it to the very bottom.

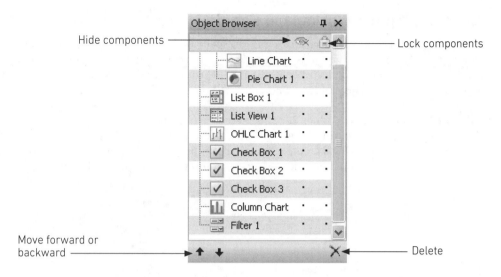

The Object Browser also has Hide and Lock buttons. The Hide button hides components on the canvas. (This does not hide them when the model is published.) Hiding objects is sometimes necessary when working with dynamic visibility or complex models. Also, you might hide a component after its design has been completed and you want to be able to see components that are beneath it.

The Lock button prevents any changes to occur to the locked components. This will help prevent objects from being modified or moved by accident.

To hide or lock a component (or multiple components), select it in the Object Browser and click the corresponding button.

The Properties Panel

The Properties panel displays the properties of the selected component. The tabs available depend on the component that has been selected. For example, the Properties panel for some chart components has an Alerts tab, as in the following example, while this tab does not appear in the panel for container components. The next chapter provides more details about component properties.

The Query Browser

The Query Browser is used to manage, create, refresh, and define sequences of queries created against a SAP BusinessObjects universe.

Query Browser is new to Dashboard Design and will be covered in more detail in Chapter 27.

Customizing the Workspace Panels

You can customize the Dashboard Design workspace in several ways: by hiding panels, closing panels, and moving panels. This makes dashboard development more efficient. Not all the panels need to be visible all the time. Customizing your work space allows you to enable and disable the panels not currently needed.

Hiding Panels

To hide a panel, click the Auto Hide button (with a pin icon) in the upper-right corner of the panel. Hiding a panel will create a bookmark on the left and right side of the workspace. You can view the hidden panel by hovering the pointer over the panel's bookmark.

To make a hidden panel visible, click the Auto Hide button again (notice that the pin icon is sideways when auto-hide has been enabled).

Closing Panels

You can also close panels. For example, you might hide a panel when you do not currently need it for development.

To close a panel, click the Close button (the X) in the upper-right corner of the panel.

You can also close panels via the View menu. For example, to close the Components panel, open the View menu and click the check mark next to its name to remove it.

Icon	Panel Position
	Pins panel to the top
	Pins panel to the right
	Pins panel to the bottom
	Pins panel to the left
	Allows the panel to be placed in a more precise location

Table 24-4   Panel Placement

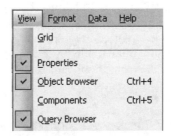

To open a closed panel, select it in the View menu.

Moving Panels

Panels can be undocked and moved to other locations. To move a panel, click the top of the panel (near its name) and drag it toward the middle of the workspace. When the panel hovers above one of the icons listed in Table 24-4, a blue box will appear where the panel will be placed when you release the mouse button.

Opening and Saving Models

You can create a new model in Dashboard Design or open an existing one. And as with any application, you should save your work frequently.

Creating a New Model

To create a new model within Dashboard Design, click the New button on the Standard toolbar, select File | New, or press CTRL-N. Another option is to choose File | New with

Spreadsheet, or press CTRL-SHIFT-N, and select an existing Excel workbook to create a model and copy the contents of that workbook into the new model. If you take this approach, it's important to remember that any changes done in the original workbook will not be reflected in the Dashboard Design model, unless that workbook is reimported.

If another model is currently open when you choose to create a new model, Dashboard Design will close that model (prompting you to save any changes that have been made) before opening the new one. Only one Dashboard Design model can be open within the same instance of Dashboard Design. However, you can run multiple instances of Dashboard Design simultaneously. This is usually done when components or data within the embedded spreadsheet need to be copied from one model to another. Note that running multiple instances is not recommended for large and complex models.

Opening an Existing Model

Dashboard Design models are saved with the file extension .xlf. These files can't be viewed or opened within SAP BusinessObjects because they are the design files for the model. Think of this file as an application that needs to be "compiled" to be used. Dashboard Design exports the model saved within the XLF file as a Flash (SWF) file.

How you open a model depends on the location of the XLF file. XLF files can be stored within a local PC, on a network drive, or even within SAP BusinessObjects. For models stored on a local or network drive, choose File | Open (or press CTRL-O).

If the XLF file is stored within the BI Launch Pad, to open it, choose File | Open from Platform | Dashboard Design Object. This opens the dialog box shown in Figure 24-4.

If Xcelsius 2008 and 4.*x* were used in the past, and the objects were stored within BusinessObjects InfoView, open the model by selecting File | Open from Platform | Xcelsius Object. When you save this model in Dashboard Design, it will be upgraded from the previous Xcelsius version to Dashboard Design.

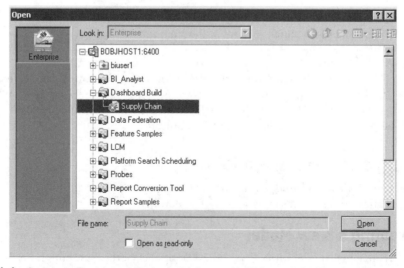

Figure 24-4   Opening a Dashboard Design model stored in BI Launch Pad

NOTE If an XLF file is renamed as a compressed file format, such as .zip or .rar, and then uncompressed, the files that make the XLF model are exposed. This will include an XML file, .xldoc (Excel workbook if it is renamed), and images and Flash files within subfolders.

You can also set a preferred folder for opening documents, as discussed in the "Defining Preferences" section later in this chapter.

Saving a Model

Saving a Dashboard Design model will result in a new or updated XLF file. Again, XLF files contain only the model design and are not visible outside the Dashboard Design application.
The following options are available for saving a model:

- Click the Save icon on the Standard toolbar (or press CTRL-S).

- Select File | Save As. Select File | Save to the Platform. This saves the model to BI Launch Pad as both the XLF model and SWF (Flash) file. Saving to the platform lets other BusinessObjects users view the Flash file, and also allows developers to open the XLF file to make modifications.

- Select File | Save to Platform as | Dashboard Design Object. This is similar to the Save As option, except the model will be saved to the platform.

- Select File | Save to Platform As | Dashboard Design Object to Replace Flash Object. This can be used to replace existing Flash files created with Xcelsius 2008 and earlier. It will update the previous Flash file with the new Dashboard Design object, maintaining any security or object rights within the dashboard.

All of these options require a name for the Dashboard Design object along with a storage location (the My Favorites or Public folder).

NOTE During the development of a Dashboard Design model, it is good practice to save often and also to occasionally use the File | Save As option to create newer versions of the model and keep the previous versions as backup or reference. As a complicated model is created and changes are made to multiple components, sometimes changes are made inadvertently to other components. Having previous Dashboard Design model files to reference can help resolve such issues.

Setting Document Properties

Each Dashboard Design model has its own set of properties, available in the Document Properties dialog box, as shown in Figure 24-5. To open this dialog box, select File | Document Properties.
You can set the following properties for each model:

- **Canvas size** Both Preset Size and Custom Size options are available. The Preset Size drop-down list offers five common sizes that can be used to develop the model. Choose Custom Size to set an exact width and height. The completed Flash file for the model will be the size defined within these settings. The Flash file will also be able to scale to the areas defined in its output (for example, a HTML web page or a widget), but it should be designed and tested to scale its final output.

Figure 24-5 Setting document properties for a model

- **Global font** These options allow you to update all the fonts used in the model to a specific font. This can either be a device font, which relies on the user's computer to render the font in the Flash file, or an embedded font (the font will be embedded into the Flash file). You might choose an embedded font when the font is not commonly used or for international deployments. Because the embedded font needs to be added into the Flash file, that file will be larger. When you select the Use Global Font option, all the components in the model and any new components added will use this selected font.

- **Loading status** The Show Loading Status option will show a high-level message on the screen when the model is being opened. This is to allow the users of the model to know what is currently occurring while the Flash file is opening.

- **Description** In the Description text box, you can enter information related to the Dashboard Design model, such as the author, created date, abd project name. This description can be viewed by developers. It will not be visible to the end users.

Defining Preferences

While the Document Properties settings define properties for a specific model, the Preferences settings affect the Dashboard Design application and its defaults. To access these settings, select File | Preferences.

The Preferences dialog box includes Document, Grid, Open, Language, Excel Options, and Accessibility sections. These preferences (especially those in the Excel Options section) should be set before creating a model to avoid potential development and performance issues. A Restore Defaults option is available for each section except Accessibility.

Document Preferences

The Document Preferences section includes options that can be changed for each model, but if you want your models to have a common size, theme/color combination, and query result settings, you should set them here.

The Document Preferences section offers the following settings:

- **Canvas size in pixels**   Includes Preset Size and Custom Size options. You can select from five preset canvas sizes or specify a custom size.
- **Components**   Includes Default Theme and Default Color Scheme options. You can select from 10 themes and one of 28 color schemes. Custom color schemes are available if these have been created. Each theme has its own color scheme, called Current Theme Color.
- **Queries**   Includes the Save Query Results with Document option, which will save the query results from universe queries. Note that depending on the size of the query results, this option can increase the saved file size.

Grid Preferences

The Grid Preferences section includes options to make a grid visible in the workspace, have objects snap to the grid, and set the grid height and width. You can use these options to help align the components on the canvas during development. When the Flash file is created from the model, the grid is no longer visible.

Open Preferences

The Open Preferences section includes an option to set the default location from which to open a model in Dashboard Design (when you choose the Open option). You can set this to be the last folder accessed from Dashboard Design or to a specific folder location.

Languages Preferences

The Languages Preferences section allows you to select both the language to be used for the Dashboard Design client and the default currency format.

To use a different language in Dashboard Design, the language options need to be selected during the installation of the application. When the languages are installed, you can select different languages. If the language is changed, Dashboard Design will need to be restarted for the changes to take effect.

The Default Currency options allow you to set a standard currency for the models. These include settings for how negative values will be displayed, the number of decimal places, and prefixes and suffixes. When you select a currency for a component's text, a Default Currency Format option is available.

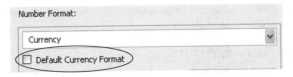

Excel Options

Excel Options is one of the most important Preferences sections when developing a model, and these settings can impact model performance. This section contains settings to enable SAP BusinessObjects Live Office, set the maximum number of rows in the model, optimize the spreadsheet, and ignore Excel formula errors.

Live Office Compatibility

Live Office is a separate download that allows the use of Microsoft Office applications to connect directly to SAP BusinessObjects. The Live Office Compatibility option allows the use of Live Office in the embedded Excel workbook during model development. This can result in quicker development and testing by bringing sample data into the model. However, enabling this option can cause some performance issues if another Excel instance is needed. You should enable Live Office only when necessary, and disable it for most development efforts.

Maximum Number of Rows

One of the common beliefs with new Dashboard Design developers is that only 512 rows of data can be used, and anything above this will cause performance issues. This is not necessarily true, as performance issues can be a result of too much data, but more frequently, these issues are related to the number of components, query execution times, and formulas. A model with 10,000 rows can perform faster than a model with 500 records. A maximum of 512 rows is the default, but this number of rows is usually too low in most situations.

When a model is exported or saved as a Flash file (or previewed), Dashboard Design converts the components, properties, and embedded spreadsheet into Flex to create a Flash file. The number of rows defined in the model will determine if the Flash file will work as designed. For example, if the limit is set to 512 rows, but 900 rows of data are used, only the first 512 records will be in the Flash file.

The maximum number of rows also determines if the formulas will work properly. Again, if the 512 row maximum is used, and a formula is designed to look at rows 1 through 800, it will not work past row 512.

Another consideration is that this maximum is cumulative across all worksheets in the embedded workbook. For example, if Sheet1 contains 200 rows and Sheet2 contains 400 rows, then the workbook has 600 rows (88 over the default limit).

NOTE Dashboard Design is designed to show aggregated data in a visual and interactive Flash model. It is not meant to display or aggregate thousands of records on the fly. This should be done with the source systems to present Dashboard Design with a small set of data to display.

Optimize Spreadsheet

The Optimize Spreadsheet option should always be enabled, as it will help with the viewing of the Flash file. This option will optimize the Flash file when it is created or previewed. This may cause some additional processing time when the Flash file is being generated, but will save time when viewing.

Ignore Excel Formula Errors

Enabling the Ignore Excel Formula Errors option helps avoid errors appearing in the model. It will replace the erroneous cell with a blank value. If this option is not enabled, the user will likely see "#N/A" in the results. If the cell includes the function ISERROR, this will likely be ignored, and a blank cell value will be supplied.

Accessibility

The Accessibility option enables the Flash model to be accessible by assistive technologies, like screen readers, so that the name of the model and a description are available. The description can contain information to help the user to understand what the model represents and what data is available, as well as other assistance, such as a person to contact.

Exporting a Dashboard Design Model

When you choose to export in model, Dashboard Design creates a Flash file from the model. The Flash file can be embedded into other application files, such as PDF, Word, or HTML file, or as a SWF Flash file. As a Flash file, the SWF can be added manually to other applications, portals, web sites, or other Flash files.

You can export a model by using the Exporting toolbar, as discussed earlier in the chapter, or by choosing File | Export.

The Export submenu offers the following options:

- **Flash (SWF)**   Creates an Adobe Flash (SWF) file from the model. Once the SWF has been created, it can be viewed in a browser, Flash viewers, and so on.

- **AIR**   Exports the model into a format that can run within Adobe AIR. Adobe AIR player is required to view the model.

- **HTML**   Creates a HTML web site with the Flash file as an embedded file. This will create at least two files: an HTML and a SWF file. Dashboard Design will create the necessary HTML code to view the Flash file in the web site.

- **PDF**   Creates an Adobe PDF file with an embedded Flash file. The PDF can then be distributed and saved for others to view. The embedded Flash file will still be interactive. The PDF file can be saved either in Acrobat 9.0 (PDF 1.8) or Acrobat 6.0 (PDF 1.5) format. The version to select depends on which version of Adobe Acrobat Reader the end users are using.

- **PowerPoint Slide**   Creates a Microsoft PowerPoint slide with an embedded Flash file. Microsoft Office 2007 does not support embedded Flash files. When the PowerPoint slide is created, it can be viewed in Slide Show mode.

- **Outlook**   Creates a Microsoft Outlook message with an attached SWF file.

- **Word**   Creates a Microsoft Word document with an embedded Flash file. The Word document will be created in the Office 97 through 2003 format. As noted, Microsoft Office 2007 does not support embedded Flash files.

All of these formats will still allow the Dashboard Design SWF to be interactive and to access external data sources (network connectivity is still needed, along with authorization).

To export a model into SAP BusinessObjects, select File | Save to Platform As. To export to SAP BW, select SAP | Publish (or Publish As).

Part IV

If other objects are embedded in the model using components, such as the image component, and they are not embedded, then another folder will be created that will contain the embedded objects.

When exporting a Dashboard Design model, you can swap out the embedded Excel workbook for another one by selecting File | Export Settings. This is useful if development is done in the embedded Excel workbook, but another one is needed for production.

The File | Export Preview option (CTRL-SHIFT-ENTER) exports the current model as a SWF file, but to a temporary location. This does not have any options to select the destination or name. This option is used to preview the model during development.

When you export a Dashboard Design model, some information about the model is stored with the Flash file. You can view this information by right-clicking the Flash file and selecting an option.

You can edit or remove the About Xcelsius option (Xcelsius was the previous name of Dashboard Design). To do this, use Notepad to open the file Ö\Xcelsius\assets\RightClick.txt. The default About line is as follows:

```
About Xcelsius, http://www.sap.com/solutions/sapbusinessobjects/sme/xcelsius/index.epx
```

Change that line to show the text to be displayed, followed by a comma, and the URL to support the text, as in this example:

```
About the Book, http://www.mcgraw-hill.com/
```

Dashboard Design Samples, Templates, and Add-ons

Dashboard Design includes several samples to help you understand how certain components and features work. The samples, along with the templates, are a great place to start learning how to build Dashboard Design models.

Viewing Samples

Dashboard Design comes with more than 30 samples. To access the Dashboard Design samples, choose File | Samples. As shown in Figure 24-6, the samples are organized by category and items.

To view a sample, select a category from the Category list and an item from the Items list. The Preview section will show what the sample looks like. Click the OK button to open the sample. You can examine the components, properties, and other settings. You can also use the sample to start a new model. The sample can't be saved (clicking Save will not overwrite the provided samples), but you can use File | Save As to save it to a new location.

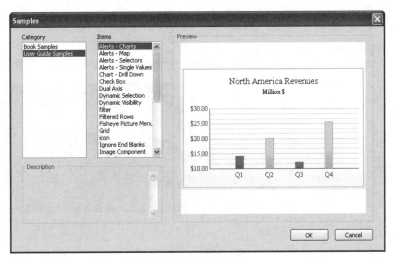

Figure 24-6   Accessing Dashboard Design samples

Dashboard Design includes samples for the category User Guide Samples. You can add other samples by creating a new folder in the path C:\SAP BusinessObjects\Xcelsius\assets\ samples\. Each sample needs to contain a SWF and an XLF file with the same name. This process is covered in the next section.

Using Templates

While the Dashboard Design samples provide examples on how to use a single component or a few components together, its templates provide fully developed Dashboard Design models. These models demonstrate several best practices, such as using multiple worksheets to organize data, documenting the model, renaming components in the Object Browser, and using color codes in the spreadsheets.

Templates are a terrific place to start exploring what and how Dashboard Design works! They also can be used as a starting point to create another model.

NOTE Templates can't be applied to an existing model. If a model is opened and a template is opened, the existing model will close.

To access the templates, select File | Templates (or press CTRL-T). As shown in Figure 24-7, 16 templates are provided, organized in six default categories (similar to the Dashboard Design samples). Select a category and item, and then click OK to open the template.

Once you've opened a template, you can save it under a different name and in another location and use it as a regular model.

You can also create your own templates and share them with other developers. This is useful if you want to use a common design with prebuilt components. Creating a new template requires the following:

1. Create a folder in C:\Program Files\SAP BusinessObjects\Xcelsius\assets\template (or use one of the existing folders). The name of this folder is used to describe the

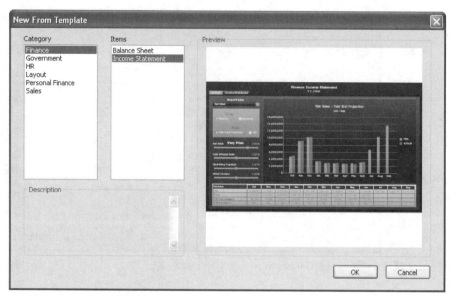

Figure 24-7 Accessing Dashboard Design templates

purpose of the dashboard (for example, Sales, Performance Metrics, or Customer Service.). The folder represents the template category.

2. Create the template and save the XLF file in the folder you set up in step 1.

3. To make your new template viewable in the Preview section of the New From Template dialog box, save a SWF version in the same directory with the same name as the XLF file.

4. To share the templates with other developers, create and save the folder from step 1 to the other developers' computer.

Managing Add-ons

Dashboard Design is a very flexible tool for creating interactive visualizations with both embedded and external data. Dashboard Design also has an SDK available to create custom components, buy components from third- party providers, or install components for other SAP products (like SAP BusinessObjects Planning and Consolidation). Eleven examples of custom components are located in C:\Program Files\SAP BusinessObjects\Xcelsius\SDK\ samples. These examples can be added into Dashboard Design, but are not necessarily intended for production use.

TIP The SAP EcoHub (http://ecohub.sdn.sap.com) contains a list of partners and third-party providers of Dashboard Design add-ons. These will likely be listed under both Xcelsius and Dashboard Design.

Before you add a new Dashboard Design add-on, it is recommended that you save and close the current model. Then select File | Manage Add-Ons to open the Add-On Manager dialog box, as shown in Figure 24-8. Click the Install Add-On button and navigate to the folder that contains the XLX file (the Dashboard Design add-on package). Select the

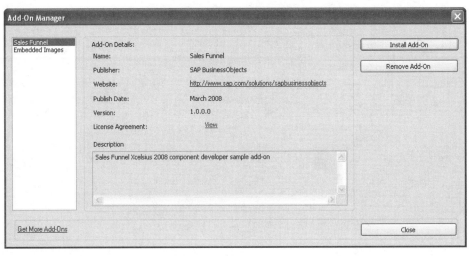

Figure 24-8   Use the Add-On Manager to install and remove add-on components.

desired XLX file, and then click the Close button in the Add-On Manager dialog box. This will require the application to restart.

Once Dashboard Design is started again, the new components will be added to the Components panel, as in the following example.

These add-on components will need to be added to each developer's computer if they are required for development.

Summary

Becoming familiar with the Dashboard Design workspace sets the foundation for successful model development. You should explore the items discussed in this chapter before beginning the development process. Also consider the use of standard templates, colors, sizes, fonts, and application behavior.

The following are some of the important points covered in this chapter:

- The Dashboard Design workspace consists of toolbars and the canvas, Components, Object Browser, Excel, Properties, and Query Browser panels.

- You can customize the size and position of the Dashboard Design panels.

- Using the Quick Views option, you can change the workspace layout to several different formats to maximize the screen space.

- The File menu contains several options to save, open, export, and set preferences for the application and model.

- You can use Dashboard Design templates and samples to jump-start the development process. These provide examples of how components can be used.

Dashboard Design Components

Components are truly the building blocks of a Dashboard Design model. They are what the users see and interact with, but they can also be used to move, calculate, and query data. Nearly 200 components are available to build extremely rich and flexible visualizations. All components have properties, which define how they look and function, along with what data to display. This chapter describes the components available in Dashboard Design.

Component Categories and Views

Dashboard Design has ten default component categories: Charts, Containers, Selectors, Single Value, Maps, Text, Other, Art and Backgrounds, Web Connectivity, and Universe Connectivity. These can all be found in the Components panel, as shown in Figure 25-1.

Figure 25-1 Tree view of components

NOTE Depending on which theme is used in Dashboard Design, some components will not be available. For example, the Nova theme has nine dial components to choose from, but the Halo theme has only two. It is good design practice to select your theme before selecting components. If you use a component that is not available in a newly selected theme, Dashboard Design will select the component that is the closest match.

The Components panel offers three different views to display the components:

- **Category** Displays categories in an accordion-type window. A medium-sized icon is displayed for each component, along with its name. This can be difficult to view on smaller screens.

- **Tree** Displays categories in a folder-type structure (see Figure 25-1). This view uses smaller icons than the Category view, but they are still visible and include the full name of the component. This is the recommended view and works well with both smaller and larger screens.

- **List** Displays all the components in an alphabetical list without any category names. Small icons, like those in the Tree view, are displayed and include the names of the components. This view is difficult to use because of the large quantity of map components, but it is useful to quickly scroll through all the components without needing to open multiple categories.

Components are primarily used to display data, but they also can allow users to interact with the data. The selector components are used to make selections. The choices can be in the form of a list, selectors, radio buttons, check boxes, and so on. Some of the other components can be used to make selections as well. For example, you might use a chart's data-insertion option, a gauge to change a value, or a table to select a row of data.

You'll also notice the Favorites category in the Components panel. This is where you should add components that are often used. To add a component to Favorites, right-click it and select Add to Favorites. To remove it, right-click the component in Favorites and select Remove from Favorites.

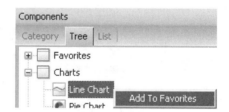

Charts

Charts are the most common category of components used in Dashboard Design models. They provide a way to display data in a visual format that is easy for users to understand.

Types of Charts

Dashboard Design includes common chart types, such as line, bar, column, pie, and area, as well as more advanced types, such as sparkline, bullet, and tree map. The chart component you should use depends on the data, the values, the dimensions, and the story that the chart should represent. For example, for sales by month data, you might choose a line, column, sparkline, or area chart. Sales by region data might be suitable for a bar, column, or pie chart. For budget versus actual by division data, you might choose a bullet chart or a line, bar, or column chart with multiple series.

Line Chart

Line charts are commonly used to show values over time. The line chart can contain multiple series of data, which will result in multiple lines. Multiple series, or lines, can use multiple axes. For example, one axis might represent sales dollars, and the other might show margin percent.

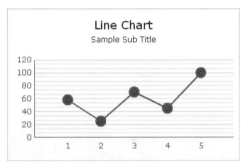

Pie Chart

Pie charts display a distribution of values across a dimension. Each slice represents a single dimension value, and the total pie chart shows the sum of all the values.

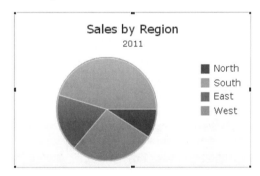

Only one dimension can be used within a pie chart, and the number of values within a pie chart should be limited. If you use a dimension with more than five values, it can be difficult to distinguish each slice. The following are some other considerations when using pie charts:

- The polarity of the values should be the same: positive or negative values.
- The values should be in the same units of measurement.
- The range of values should be similar. For example, a value of 100 will be very difficult to view when the total is 10,000.

TIP If a pie chart is going to have more than five dimension values (labels), it is useful to create a bucket called Other that groups all dimension values after the fourth or fifth value.

Part IV

OHLC Chart

An OHLC chart is used to display information that has open, close, high, and low values. A few examples are stock data, temperatures, and tides.

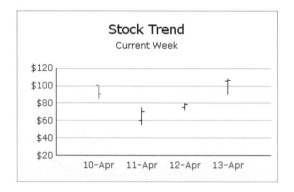

The OHLC chart represents four different values for each label. Table 25-1 shows what each line segment represents in the chart. If the value decreases between the open and close, this will be considered a negative value, which is represented by a red line (by default). If the value increases, this is a positive value, and the line will be black (by default).

Candlestick Chart

The candlestick chart type (sometimes referred to as a *box plot*) is similar to the OHLC type and has the same uses, but displays data in a box with lines protruding from the top or bottom for high and low marks. The filled boxes represent negative values, or decreases between the open and close values. The empty boxes represent positive values, or increases between the open and close values.

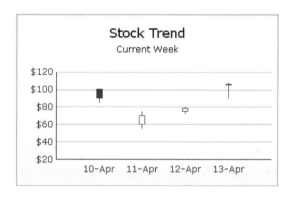

OHLC Line Segment	Value
Left tick	Open value
Right tick	Close value
High point on line	High value
Low point on line	Low value

Table 25-1 OHLC Chart Line Segments

Column and Stacked Column Charts

Column charts have nearly the same uses as line charts. They can be used to trend values over time by multiple dimensions (data series). Displaying multiple series of data allows for comparison of values over time. Two axes are available to display the different series (for example, dollars versus margin percent or number of orders versus dollar amount of shipped items).

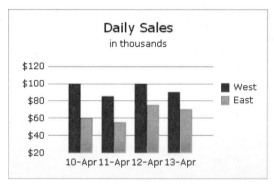

Stacked column charts show both the cumulative total, or distribution, and a trend over time. The full column height represents the total for each series (or dimension) for the time period. As with pie charts, stacked column charts should not include a large number of dimensions, the values should be close in range, and the values should use the same units of measure.

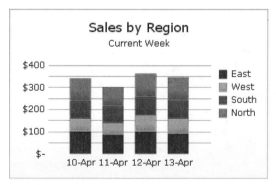

Bar and Stacked Bar Charts

Bar charts are similar to column charts, but they are typically used to compare data or distribution of data. Unlike column charts, bar charts usually are not used for time series analysis.

Stacked bar charts are used for the same purposes as bar charts, but include additional dimensionality. As with a column chart, the length of the entire bar chart is the sum of each series for each label. Stacked bar charts show the individual parts that make the whole and are useful when comparing dimension values. The number of divisions in a stacked bar chart should be limited to four or five; using more can make the chart difficult to read.

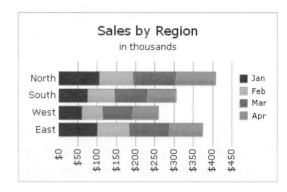

Combination Chart

A combination chart is a good choice when data should be represented as a column chart that also includes a line to show a trend. Combination charts usually have dual axes to display data with different number formats. For example, a chart may show sales in dollars and margins in percentages.

XY Chart

An XY chart shows a value in an XY axis. Each axis can represent two different sets of values, such as sales and quantity. Each data point represents a series value along the X and Y axes.

Whereas most charts show a dimension with two values with two series, the XY chart shows two values in a single point. This is useful for finding patterns in data, such as higher prices corresponding to lower average quantities sold.

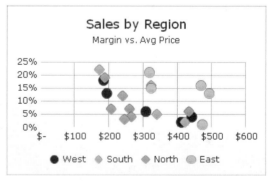

Bubble Chart

Bubble charts are like XY charts, but they include one more value for the size of the bubble—the larger the value, the larger the bubble on the chart.

As with other charts that show distribution of values, the size of the bubble will depend on range of the other values. The range of the values needs to be considered along with the position. If a larger bubble is on top of a smaller bubble, the smaller bubble will not be visible. Bubble charts are often used to convey social, economic, medical, or other scientific data and relationships.

Area and Stacked Area Charts

An area chart is similar to a line chart, but the area under the line is filled. Area charts are useful for displaying a trend over time. The number of dimensions should be limited to about three or four at the most. You also should consider the colors used, because if a dark-colored series appears over a lighter-colored series, the lighter color can be difficult to see.

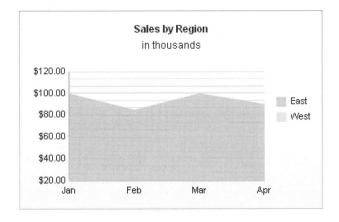

Stacked area charts are similar to stacked bar and stacked column charts, in that they show an aggregate total of all the series stacked on top of each other. A stacked area chart allows users to see a trend over time as a whole, as well as how each series is represented.

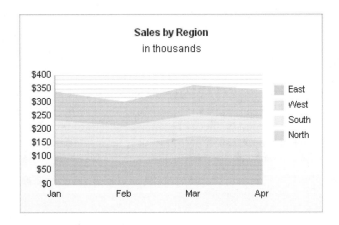

Radar and Filled Radar Charts

Radar charts are used to display data in a radial view. The radial view can make outliers more visible and easier to identify. When you use this type of chart, you should limit the number of dimensions and labels.

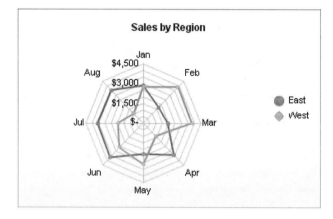

In filled radar charts, the series toward the middle of the chart is filled in. This can be difficult to read when two or more sets of series are used.

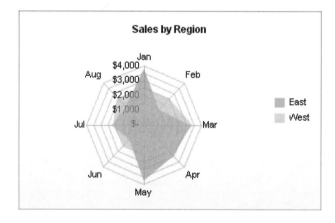

Tree Map

Tree map charts can be useful to show multiple data points in a small space. Two sets of values are used in the tree map: one for size and another for color intensity. Large values for the size are represented by bigger boxes, and large values for the color intensity are displayed as a lighter color. You can use multiple series of data, as well as different colors to represent the intensity.

Horizontal and Vertical Bullet Charts

Horizontal bullet charts display data in a gauge-type view but add measures for comparative analysis. This type of chart takes performance, comparative, and scale values. For example, a horizontal bullet chart can show sales, actual, planned, and previous period data. This will allow the users to see what is currently happening, as well as what has happened and what is expected.

Vertical bullet charts have the same uses and features as horizontal type, except they display the data in columns instead of bars.

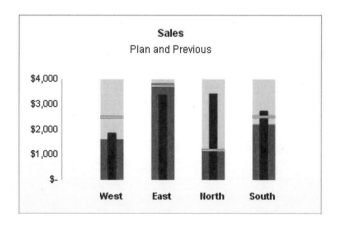

Sparkline Chart

Sparkline charts display small line charts for each series. This is a powerful charting option that allows for more data to be displayed visually in a smaller amount of space. Sparkline charts can also display data such as high, low, open, and close values.

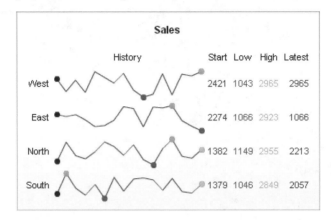

Containers

Each Dashboard Design model has one canvas by default, but sometimes more canvases are needed to organize or control multiple components at the same time. A container can hold additional canvases or act like another canvas that contains multiple components. For example, you might use a container as another canvas for help text, prompt options, or "about" information. You can also make the visibility of the containers dynamic.

You can add components to a container either by dragging them into the container on the canvas or by moving a component in the Object Browser. Dragging-and-dropping a component into a container does take some practice, but when you drag a component, its outline will turn light blue. When you move a container component, the components in the container are also moved. If you delete a container component, the components within the container are also deleted.

Types of Containers

Three types of containers are available: canvas, panel, and tab set. The container components act like a canvas or a group when they are added to the model, as shown in Figure 25-2.

Canvas Container

The canvas container acts as a new canvas, but with limited options. It differs from the model's canvas in that it is transparent, can contain scroll bars, and can support dynamic visibility.

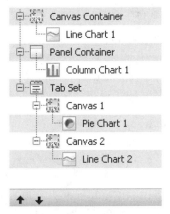

Figure 25-2   Container components in the Object Browser

Panel Container

Panel containers contain a canvas for components, but also include a title and color options for the background. Panel containers are useful when components need to be dynamically displayed together with a title to explain their purpose. Depending on the theme that is used, one to three panel containers are available.

Tab Set

The tab set container is one of the most popular components, as it is very intuitive and easy for end users to understand. Unlike the other container components, the tab set is usually visible on the canvas during the entire use of the model.

Tab set containers can contain multiple tabs, each displaying a separate canvas. These tabs usually represent different subjects or features for a Dashboard Design model. This allows for one dashboard to contain multiple subject areas in one file. For example, an executive dashboard might contain tabs for Sales, Finance, HR, and Marketing. Each of these tabs can contain its own set of properties for background color and scroll bars.

You can work with tab set containers as follows:

- **Select a tab set** Click an existing tab or select the tab set container in the Object Browser.

- **Add and remove tabs** Click the add button (plus sign) or remove button (minus sign) at the top-left corner of the component. These buttons will be visible only if the tab set container is selected. Selecting the canvas in a tab set will not display the add and remove buttons.

- **Delete a tab** Select a tab and click the remove button (minus sign). Alternatively, select and delete the tab's canvas in the Object Browser.

- **Move a tab** In the Object Browser, select the canvas in the tab set and use the up or down arrow to move the tab canvas, or right-click the tab canvas and select Bring to Front, Send to Back, Bring Forward, or Send Back. Alternatively, right-click the canvas for the tab and select Bring to Front, Send to Back, Bring Forward, or Send Back.

Selectors

Selectors are primarily used to make selections or interact with the data. Much of the interactivity that is available within Dashboard Design is attributed to these components. Selector components basically move data from a source to a destination depending on the label item selected. This data can be used to display filtered data, trigger an event like dynamic visibility, or supply a prompt value for a query.

Types of Selectors

Many different selector components are available within Dashboard Design. Some selectors are simple, like the check box, while others can be very sophisticated, like the scorecard selector. Dashboard Design also includes selectors that allow users to scroll through several images to select items. Remember that selector components move data based on selected items in the component.

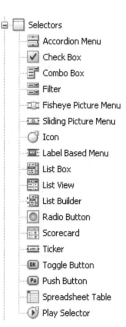

Accordion Menu

An accordion menu is a two-level menu that lets users first select a category and then select from items within that particular category. This selector is useful for organizing values into different categories.

Check Box

A check box component allows users to either check or uncheck the box to make a selection. When a check box is selected, it inserts a value in the target cell. When the check box is unselected, it inserts a different value in the target cell. Check boxes can be particularly useful when combined with other components using the dynamic visibility function.

Combo Box

A combo box is a combination of a drop-down list and a text box that contains the selected value from the drop-down list. A combo box can be used with other components to filter the values displayed based on the value selected in the combo box.

Filter

A filter selector displays a cascading filtered list. If two or more filters are displayed, then the value selected in the first filter item will limit the values of the second item. This is useful for filtering hierarchical type data.

Fisheye Picture Menu

A fisheye picture menu is a visual selector that displays images (embedded or from a URL) as items to be selected. The pictures get larger as your mouse approaches the center of the picture, much like the effect of a fisheye lens. The number of pictures in the selector should be limited to conserve space on the canvas. When a selection from the fisheye picture menu is made, data is inserted into the corresponding target range in the spreadsheet. The fisheye picture menu is often used with the dynamic visibility options to provide navigation for your dashboard and works similarly to the other menu components, but it is more visually engaging.

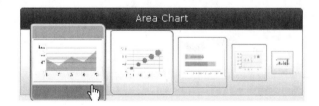

Sliding Picture Menu

A sliding picture menu is another type of menu component that uses image files as menu options. The sliding picture menu only displays a few images at a time with an arrow or scroll bar to scroll to the next set of images. Users can view the other images by sliding the displayed images to the side or by using the left and right navigation buttons. When a selection from the sliding picture menu is made, data is inserted into the corresponding target range in the spreadsheet. The sliding picture menu is often used with the dynamic visibility options to provide navigation for your dashboard and works similarly to the other menu components.

Icon

An icon selector is generally used to display an indicator, for example, a green sphere indicating a positive numeric value. An icon selector can also be used as a selector component. When the user clicks the icon, it passes a value to a destination cell in the spreadsheet, which can be used to filter data in other components. For example, icon selectors could be used to display and/or filter values that fall in specific data ranges defined as green (i.e., the top 33 percent), yellow (i.e., the middle 33 percent), or red (i.e., the bottom 34 percent).

Label Based Menu

A label based menu displays labels either horizontally or vertically. The number of labels in this component should be limited to conserve space on the dashboard. The label-based menu is often used with the dynamic visibility options to provide navigation in your dashboard.

North	South	East	West

List Box

A list box is similar to a label based menu, except the number of labels displayed depend on the size of the component. Scroll bars are automatically added to the component if the number of labels exceeds the height of the component. A list box is often used to filter data displayed in a chart or other components in your dashboard. When the user selects a value from the list box, data from the selected value (a source range) will be updated in the target range of the spreadsheet.

Regions

North
South
East
West

List View

A list view is a table-like view of a range of data. Users can click the headers in the table to sort the data in ascending or descending order. The list view component allows you to display data in a grid-like interface.

Region	Sale ↓	Margin
East	2,908	723
North	2,482	663
West	2,181	468
South	1,159	606

List Builder

A list builder component allows users to build a list of selected values from a source list. Values are either added or removed from the destination panel. Once the list has been built, the user clicks the Update button to make the selection. The list builder component provides a way for users to create their own sets of data.

Radio Button

Choosing the radio button component creates a list of labels with radio buttons that can be selected to enable one item from the list. Radio buttons can be displayed either vertically or horizontally. Radio buttons are often used to filter data in charts or other components in your dashboard.

Scorecard

A scorecard selector displays a continuous range of data in a table view with visual indicators that are based on the alert values. This selector can include traffic light-type indicators, trend indicators, or other icons as indicators. The scorecard selector is used to display red, yellow, and green or up and down arrows as visual indicators of, for example, whether or not values are acceptable/unacceptable or rising/falling.

Region	Sales	Margin		Inventory
North	2482	⇨	663 ●	234
South	1159	⇨	606	324
East	2908	⤢	723	543
West	2181	⬊	468	254

Ticker

A ticker component displays a set of data as a scrolling ticker, like a stock ticker. When the user hovers the mouse pointer above the ticker selector, the movement stops. Clicking a ticker value selects the value for an action. The ticker component is often used to filter data, but can also be useful for navigation in conjunction with the dynamic visibility options.

North   2,482 | **South**   1,159 | **East**   2,9

Toggle Button

A toggle button toggles between two values. This is useful for enabling and disabling dynamic visibility. Some themes have multiple toggle button components.

Off

Push Button

A push button sends a range of values to a destination when it is selected. This range can include multiple rows and columns, as long as they are contiguous. The push button component can be useful as a restore or reset button as it can copy a source range of values back to a target range in the spreadsheet.

Push

Part IV

Spreadsheet Table

A spreadsheet table displays a range of data in the embedded spreadsheet as it is formatted in the spreadsheet. This is useful for displaying a table of data that is highly formatted or has formatting that can't be shown using the other selector components.

Region	Sales	Margin
North	2,482	663
South	1,159	606
East	2,908	723
West	2,181	468

Play Selector

A play selector looks similar to a control on a video player. It contains play, forward, backward, skip to beginning, and skip to end buttons. This selector allows users to scroll through a list of values in a set time interval. This can be useful for scenario testing or as a slide show-type selector.

Single-Value Components

Single-value components are mapped to a single cell and are commonly used to display progress or to accept a new value. By default, all single-value components are output components, meaning that they can display a value, but they may also be an input component, meaning that they can accept a new value. For example, a dial will display a default value, but the user can change the dial value. To prevent a single-value component from being used as an input component, the single-value component needs to be mapped to a cell in the Excel spreadsheet, containing a formula. Or you need to check the Enable Interaction property on the component Properties Pane on the Behavior | Common tab.

Users interact with single-value components by selecting a slider or clicking in the component and dragging up or down to increase or decrease the value. The increment at which the movement occurs is defined within the behavior properties of the component. The properties of single-value components also allow you to define minimum and maximum values that can be selected. Be careful when working with percentages. A maximum value of 1 for a component that represents a percentage will equal 100 percent, not 1 percent. For 1 percent, use the value 0.01 in the component's properties.

Types of Single-Value Components

The Single Value category includes horizontal and vertical sliders, dual sliders, dials, gauges, progress bars, spinners, and play control components.

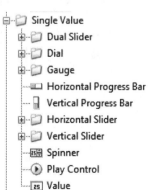

Horizontal and Vertical Sliders

Horizontal and vertical sliders map to a single cell in the Excel spreadsheet. These single-value sliders can be used to create what-if scenarios. For example, the slider can allow for input of values representing a forecasted change in percent that can be used to calculate a forecasted sales amount.

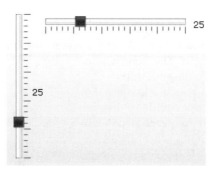

Dual Sliders

One exception to the single-cell mapping rule for single-value components is the dual sliders component. Dual sliders are mapped to two cells within the Excel spreadsheet. Users interact with these components by moving one of the sliders along the horizontal axis. This will select a high value and a low value. A dual slider can be used to set variables that affect other components. For example, you could set a start and end date used to only display data in a line chart between those two dates, or a minimum and maximum value to display only data that is between the range.

Dial

A dial is often used as an input component that allows the user to interact with the dashboard. The dial is linked to a single cell with a defined minimum and maximum value. The user can change the value of the single cell, much like the dial on your stereo, which affects any other component, such as a chart, that is linked to that cell.

Gauge

Gauges are very similar to dials, but they are often used as an output component only. Think of the gauge as a speedometer in your car, and a dial as an input device on your stereo.

Progress Bar

Progress bars display a value between minimum and maximum values in a horizontal or vertical bar. As the value increases, the progress bar fills with a selected color.

Spinner

A spinner contains a single value that is mapped to a single cell, and includes up and down buttons to change the value. The user can also click the displayed value and drag up or down to increase or decrease the value.

Play Control

A play control component incrementally increases the value displayed from a defined minimum to a defined maximum value. Auto play, auto rewind, and auto replay can be used with this component. This component can be used in conjunction with other components to display data like a movie. For example, the play control could flip through a list of products, displaying each product in a chart for a period of time.

Value

The value component allows the end user to increase or decrease the value by selecting the value in the component and by double-clicking inside the component and typing in a new value.

Maps

Dashboard Design contains roughly 100 maps, which represent confidence, countries, regions, and states. These are used to display data for various geographical regions.

As with other components within Dashboard Design, a map component can also be used as a selector. For example, users can view a map containing sales by state and click a state to see a detailed chart representing monthly sales for that state.

Text Components

Text components display text, and in some cases, accept input, such as a password. These components are very common in Dashboard Design models. They may be used to show information such as data labels, headers, the date of the last data refresh, and comments. These components can contain either static data, such as hard-coded values, or linked to a cell to display the data it contains. Some of these components can also display HTML code for additional formatting options or provide hyperlinks to other web sites.

Types of Text Components

Three types of text components are available: input text area, label, and input text.

Input Text Area

An input text area allows multiple lines of text to be displayed or input in a single component. For example, an input text area may be used for paragraphs describing the usage of the dashboard, comments stored in a database, or a list of values that the user needs to modify.

Label

Label components are commonly used to create headers or labels within a dashboard. Labels can only display values; they do not accept new input.

Input Text

Input text components are like input text area components, except the values are represented on a single line. This component is useful for entering a single value, such as a password, or to display brief text. The input text component has special features when dealing with passwords.

Other Components

The Other component category contains more specialized components that can enhance a Dashboard Design model. Most of these components have unique functionality that may require some practice to master.

Types of Other Components

The components in the Other category include the calendar, local scenario button, trend icon, history, panel set, source data, trend analyzer, print button, reset button, and grid.

Calendar

The calendar component provides a calendar-like interface to select dates in the Dashboard Design model. The component allows the end user to select a date and easily navigate to a specific month and year.

Local Scenario Button

Users might like to return to a specific point of analysis without reselecting specific values and components. Adding a local scenario component to the model allows users to save the current analysis (the selected items that are being displayed) to their local machine. After saving a scenario, users can use this component to reload that scenario or set it as the default. This is a very powerful option for users who requently use a model and need to make several selections to do their analysis.

NOTE Scenarios are loaded from the local Excel spreadsheet. These are not saved on the server.

Trend Icon

The trend icon component is an indicator that shows the trend of the data, as follows:

- A positive value will appear with an upward-pointing arrow.
- A negative value will appear with a downward-pointing arrow.
- A value of zero will appear with a horizontal dash.

History

The history component captures changed values in a cell by creating a historical list of the values. For example, if the user selects different values from a combo box each time a new value is selected, the old value is appended to a list of values. This list of values can be used by other components or as a list of values for a prompt. The history component is used to create a historical list of values in the Excel spreadsheet and the component itself is not visible at runtime.

Panel Set

The panel set component offers more than 20 layout templates that can be used to display images (JPEG) or Flash files (SWF). These images or SWF files can be embedded or linked to a URL. Dashboard Design-based SWF files cannot be imported into the panel set component, and SWF files that use a live-data connection will not accept new data loads.

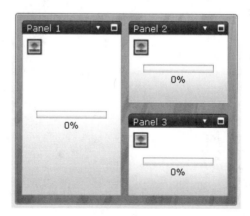

Source Data

The source data component can be used to move data based on a cell changing values. This cell will contain a value that is used as an index value to the source data to a destination. The insertion type can be a single value, a row, or a column. The source data component is not visible at run time. The index cell acts as a trigger for data movement.

Trend Analyzer

The trend analyzer component is used to analyze trends based on historical data. These trends are based on a regression analysis, which can be fine-tuned through the component's properties. This component is useful for creating forecast and trend values. It is not visible at run time.

Print Button

The print button component allows the user to print the dashboard model during run time.

Reset Button

The reset button sets the model back to its original state when it was first opened by the user. This will reset any components in the model back to their original values. If your dashboard has a lot of input components such as dials and sliders that allow users to forecast or manipulate the data in the dashboard, a reset button will return the dashboard to its original state.

Grid

The grid component is used to display multiple rows and columns of data from the embedded Excel spreadsheet. Users can modify the values within the grid by double-clicking a cell and entering a new value, or by clicking in the cell and dragging up or down to increase or decrease the value. The grid component is also very useful during development to show which values are in a range of cells.

1	2	3	4	5
2	4	6	8	10
3	6	9	12	15

To prevent a grid component from being used as an input component, the grid component needs to be mapped to a cell in the Excel spreadsheet containing a formula or the Enable Interaction property in the Property Pane Behavior | Common tab needs to be unchecked.

Art and Backgrounds Components

The components in the Art and Backgrounds category are used to provide additional visual effects to the model. Items such as lines, rectangles, circles, and backgrounds are available in this category.

Types of Art and Background Components

The Art and Backgrounds category includes background, ellipse, image, vertical and horizontal line, and rectangle components. These components are used to make your dashboard model more visually appealing.

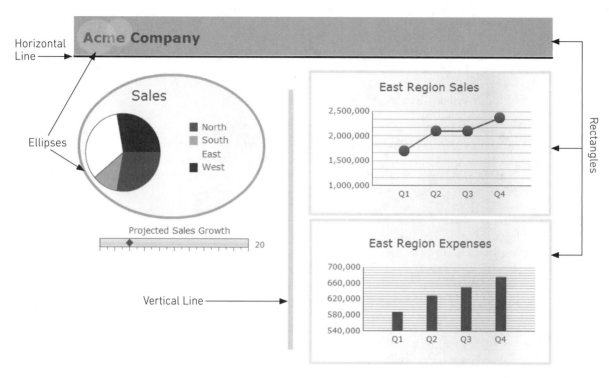

Figure 25-3 Dashboard model with art and background components

Background
Backgrounds are theme-dependent images and graphics that are used in a model as a background or as a way to visually divide content on the canvas.

Ellipse
The ellipse component is used to draw circles or ovals in a model.

Image Component
The image component displays images or Flash files in the model. These images can be embedded or referenced using a URL. The image component is typically used to add a logo to a model. You can use other Dashboard Design SWF files in the image component, but they will not be embedded.

Vertical and Horizontal Line Component
The vertical and horizontal line component is used to create lines within the model. This is useful to divide content visually or to provide additional visual effects.

Rectangle
The rectangle component creates squares and rectangles in a model. These can be used to outline a set of components.

Web Connectivity

The Web Connectivity category includes components that are used to manage data, dynamic images, and Flash files, along with URLs. These components predominantly rely on external web sites, images, data connections, and other information that is not stored in the Dashboard Design model. Many of the items that are referenced by these components are created outside of Dashboard Design.

Types of Web Connectivity Components

The Web Connectivity category includes URL button, reporting services button, slide show, SWF loader, and connection refresh button components.

URL Button

The URL button component opens a new URL either in the current window or in a new window. The URL can be hard-coded, or it can be made dynamic by referencing a cell. The URL that is referenced can be triggered by a cell changing values or becoming a specific value. This component is often used to link a dashboard to a Web Intelligence or a Crystal Reports document.

Reporting Services Button

The reporting services button is used to retrieve information from a reporting services report. This is similar to using the data manager connection options, but information retrieval is managed within this component instead of the data manager section.

Slide Show

The slide show component uses URL-based images and Flash (SWF) files to create a slide show. Unlike the image component, this component does not contain any embedded images. The images and Flash files are referenced within a cell. As the URL in the cell changes, so does the image within the slide show component. The URL needs to be accessible at run time. The component also has several transition options for additional effects, such as fade, split, wedge, and wide.

SWF Loader

The SWF loader component is like the slide show component, but only for SWF files. As with the slide show component, the URL needs to be accessible at run time for users to be able to view the SWF file. This component supports using SWF files based on Dashboard Design models, which will retain their interactivity. Dashboard Design models that are located on the BusinessObjects Enterprise server can be referenced using the OpenDocument URL.

Connection Refresh Button

The connection refresh button component is used to refresh existing data connections. All connections defined in the data manager can be refreshed by this button. You can select one or multiple connections in the component's properties. When a user clicks the connection refresh button, all the selected connections in the component will be refreshed. This component can also use a cell in the Excel Spreadsheet to trigger the connection refresh.

Universe Connectivity

The components in the Universe Connectivity category are used to refresh and manage prompts for universe queries defined in the Dashboard Design Query Browser (as discussed in Chapter 27).

Types of Universe Connectivity Components

Two Universe Connectivity components are available: the query refresh button and the query prompt selector.

Query Refresh Button

The query refresh button refreshes the queries defined in the Query Browser. These are all universe-based queries. The queries in the Query Browser are based on the IDT universes, not the legacy universes. This component is nearly identical to the connection refresh button in the Web Connectivity category.

Query Prompt Selector

The query prompt selector component maps prompts from a universe query to a component that can be used by the end users to refresh and select prompt values for query. These can be existing prompts or prompts new to the universe. Each prompt requires a dedicated query prompt selector component; for example, if five prompts are used, then five query prompt selection components are needed. A prompt with a between filter actually uses two prompts, so it requires two query prompt selector components.

These interactive query selection components can be mapped to query prompts where different options are available, depending on the prompt options selected (such as a list of values or an optional prompt) and the operator used (such as equal to, in list, or greater than). In-list prompts have multiple options available to perform actions, such as select all, deselect all, show all values, show selected values, and search. Prompts that require a single value, such as an equal-to or a greater-than value, also provide the ability to search, but they allow selection of only one value.

Summary

Hundreds of Dashboard Design components are available to create very rich, interactive, and useful visualizations. Depending on the data, audience, and interactivity needed, some components are more useful than others. Selecting the right component takes planning, and you may need to use mock-ups or prototyping. Components are what the end users are going to see and interact with, so taking time to plan which components to use and where to use them will save time later during development.

CHAPTER

26

Properties, Excel, and Colors

The previous chapters have been about navigating within Dashboard Design and the capabilities of its components. The components are the building blocks within Dashboard Design, but how do they work?

This chapter covers two critical topics related to how components work: properties and the embedded Excel workbook. The components have properties, and the properties are bound to cells within the embedded workbook.

The last part of this chapter discusses how to customize the appearance of the dashboard using themes and colors. Themes can dictate which components are available to be used in the model. Using themes with color schemes can help save development time. Using a consistent color scheme, such as a set of corporate-defined colors, across all dashboards helps to ensure a consistent user experience as well.

Properties Overview

A component's properties tell it what to display, how to display it, and what to do upon some action. This allows the components and the model to be dynamic. All components have properties, and many of these properties are common across several components.

Typically, the Properties panel appears on the right side of the Dashboard Design workspace. If the Properties panel is not visible, you can display it by pressing ALT-ENTER or selecting View | Properties from the Menu toolbar. When a component is selected, the properties of that component are displayed. You can also access properties by selecting the component in the Object Browser. If multiple components are selected in either the Object Browser or the canvas, then only their common properties will be available. This is useful when you need to update these common properties for several components.

The Properties panel is divided into different tabs depending on the selected component, such as General, Insertion, Behavior, Appearance, and Alerts.

Properties can be set as hard-coded values, bound to cells, or bound directly to data sources. Some properties are selection items, such as fonts, colors, and behavior; others are settings that can be enabled or disabled.

Hard-coded values are commonly used for properties that will not be changing within the model—those that are not dynamic—such as labels, titles, and series names. Properties that can accept hard-coded values have a white input box. You can click in the input box and enter a value. As the values are entered, they are visible in the component.

Most properties are bound to cells to allow the components to be dynamic. Properties that can be bound to cells have gray backgrounds.

General Properties

The General tab of the Properties panel contains properties that are typically used to define what will be displayed, including titles, labels, axis values, and the data that is visible in a component. These properties should be defined first before proceeding to the other property tabs. Defining the data is one of the most important tasks; otherwise, nothing will be displayed.

Some properties link to a single cell, and others are for a range of cells. Properties that are bound to a single cell are typically those that allow for hard-coded values as well. Binding these single cell properties to cells, rather than hard-coding them, allows for a more dynamic visualization. Often, a single chart component can be used multiple times for different purposes depending on some selection criteria. For example, a chart might represent sales by month, but can also be used to display margin by week.

You can map data to a component by range or by series. If the data is in a continuous set of rows or columns, then the By Range option is recommended. If data is not continuous, then the By Series option should be used. Both options will create series of data. By Range is an easier option to use.

Mapping Data by Range

The By Range option is used to bind a set of continuous rows or a column to a component's properties. This option also includes the ability to create a range of values where data is in rows or columns. The first row or column should include the desired label value for each series of data. The first selected row or column should also include the category label values. The By Range option will create multiple data series that includes the name of the series, the data, and the category labels. By default, these options are grayed out until the By Series option is selected, as described next.

To bind a property to cells, select the component and click the Bind button in the Properties panel.

This displays the Select a Range dialog box.

Select the cells in the workbook that are to be bound to that specific component property. These cells must be continuous and within some defined range. For example, the range D:D cannot be used, because this will exceed the defined row limit.

Remember that Dashboard Design is used to display aggregated data. The maximum number of rows defined in the document properties applies to the ranges defined in component properties. Selecting too many rows can also cause performance issues.

Figure 26-1 shows how Dashboard Design maps the selected range of data for the series name, values, and category labels when either the data in columns or the data in rows is chosen. Table 26-1 shows which properties are mapped in the example.

Mapping Data by Series

Most of the time, the By Range option will be used, but the By Series offers more flexibility when the data is not continuous or if category labels are not located in the first column or row. Selecting the By Series option requires a few more steps to bind the data to different series, as shown in Figure 26-2. Because the series name, values, and category labels need to be bound one by one, the location of each of these properties can be in noncontinuous

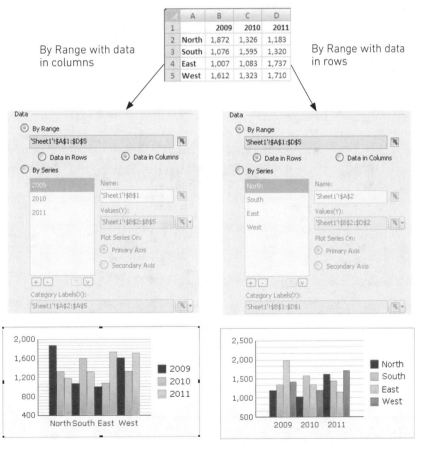

Figure 26-1   Using columns versus rows for a range of data

Setting	By Columns	By Rows
Name(s)	Three series created for each year (B1, C1, D1)	Four series created for each region (A1, A2, A3, A4)
Value(s)	Three value ranges for the columns (B2:B5, C2:C5, D2:D5)	Four value ranges for the columns (B2:D2, B3:D3, B4:D4)
Category Labels	Column range from A2:A5 and used by all series	Row range from B1:D1 and used by all series

Table 26-1 Mapping Properties for the By Range Column and Row Options

cells, or even on a different worksheet. The series name can also be hard-coded (recall that property cells with a white background will accept hard-coded values), which is useful if this value does not change.

Along with binding each property for the By Series option, you can also create multiple series by clicking the plus sign (+). You can use a secondary axis on certain components, and also define the order of the series.

NOTE If you originally selected the By Range option, selecting the By Series radio button will convert the selected range to a series. This is a common workflow if the range of data needs a little more customization before it is displayed.

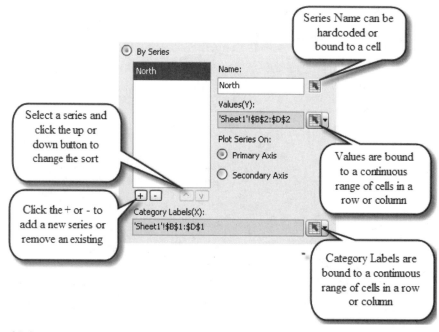

Figure 26-2 Options for mapping data by series

General Properties for Selectors

Selector components are used to perform an action when a selection is made. The values (labels) that are available to be selected are defined in the General tab. What happens when the selection is made depends on what is defined in the Data Insertion section of the General tab.

Data insertion refers to the process of taking data from a source and putting it into a destination. How Dashboard Design does this is defined by the Insertion Type property.

Multiple Data Insertion options are available and listed in Table 26-2. Their use depends on the source data and what needs to happen when the data is inserted.

Insertion Properties

The Insertion tab is available for certain components, including some charts, and is used to define how the component moves data based on a selection. When these properties are set for a chart, the chart will act as a selector when a user selects a series within it. This is sometimes referred to as *drill-down* because it can allow the user to drill from a high-level set of data to a more focused set of data in another component. For example, you might select sales for a specific year, and then see sales by month for the selected year in another component.

NOTE Data insertion does have a limitation in that a component can't have a different series with the same destination.

Table 26-2 describes the properties on the Insertion tab.

Property	Description
Enable Data Insertion	Enables data insertion. This must be selected to set the other data insertion properties.
Series Name Destination	Sets the cell that will contain the series name that was selected for the data insertion.
Insertion Type	Sets how the source data is organized for the data insertion (see Table 26-3).
Series	Sets the series in the component. This is defined in the General tab.
Source Data	Sets the source of the data. This is enabled for only some insertion types. For example, if the Row insertion type is selected, the Source Data setting does not need to be the same as what was defined in the General tab.
Destination	Sets where the data defined for data insertion will go. The selection here depends on the insertion type. For example, if you select the Position option, just one cell is needed. If you select the Column option, a column destination is needed.
Interaction Option	Sets the interaction as a click or a mouse-over.
Default Selection	Sets the default for a series and the item. Choose No Selection to have no default.

Table 26-2 Data Insertion Properties

Knowing how and when to use the different data insertion types will take some practice. The tool tips (little callouts next to the Insertion Type options) are a great way to see these different options in action. Table 26-3 briefly describes the Data Insertion Type options.

Behavior Properties

The Behavior tab defines how the component will behave based on the data and other events. It is also where dynamic visibility is defined. Almost all visible components that contain data have behavior properties.

The Behavior tab can contain three subtabs to organize the different properties: Common, Scale, and Animations and Effects.

Common Properties

The properties in the Common subtab vary greatly from component to component. Some common settings include Ignore Blank, Enable Range Slider, Enable Sort, Enable Run-Time Tools, and Dynamic Visibility. Of these, the Ignore Blank and Dynamic Visibility settings are the most commonly used.

Ignore Blank   During the development process, you need to anticipate the data that will be available to know which cells to bind. In some cases, cells at the end of a range will be blank and will likely represent the maximum, or last, rows or columns needed for a component.

Data Insertion Type	Description
Position	Inserts the position of the value selected into the destination. For example, if the fifth item is selected, then a 5 is entered into the destination. No source data exists for this.
Value	Inserts the value of the item selected into the destination. For example, if the value 125 is selected, then a 125 is entered into the destination. No source data exists for this.
Row	Inserts a row of data into the destination based on the item selected. This type does allow a different row to be used as a source, instead of the row defined in the General tab. For example, if the fifth item is selected, then the fifth row defined in the data insertion source will be entered into the destination row. The source and target should have the same number of columns.
Column	Inserts a column of data into the destination based on the item selected. This type does allow a different column to be used as a source, instead of the column defined in the General tab. For example, if the fifth item is selected, then the fifth column defined in the data insertion source will be entered into the destination column. The source and target should have the same number of rows.
Status List	A true/false setting that contains a series or rows or columns that match the rows or columns in the component. Whenever an item is selected, a 1 will be added to the Status List, and all other items will have a zero (0).

Table 26-3 Data Insertion Types

When these blank cells are bound in Dashboard Design, the component will have blanks at the end, which may not be what should be displayed in the component. To avoid this, select the Ignore Blank setting so the blank cells at the end of a range will not be displayed.

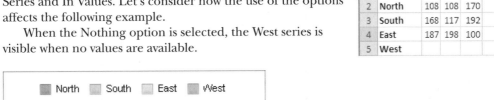

Ignore Blank has two options that can be used together: In Series and In Values. Let's consider how the use of the options affects the following example.

When the Nothing option is selected, the West series is visible when no values are available.

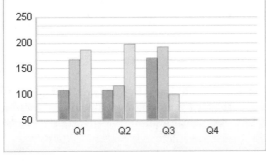

When the In Series option is selected, the West series is no longer visible.

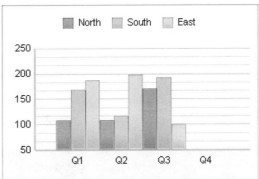

When the In Values option is selected, Q4 is not visible because it contains no values.

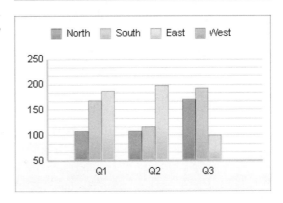

With both In Series and In Values selected, both Q4 and West are no longer visible.

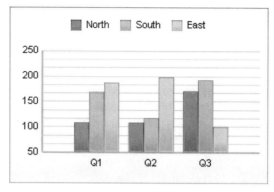

Enable Run-Time Tools Choosing the Enable Run-Time Tools setting will show some additional buttons and options at run time to allow the users to change the scale, scale behavior, and focus options.

Enable Range Slider Enable Range Slider is a great option to use if not all the values can be displayed at once, such as if 100 days need to be displayed on a chart, but it makes sense to show only 20 days at a time. The Enable Range Slider option will create an interactive slider that can be used to focus on a different range of data. Because the range slider can be based on the position or category label, and the values can be bound, the range can be dynamic as well.

The range slider contains both beginning and ending values. If the slider is based on position, and the beginning value is 1, then the first value will be visible. For the first and tenth values to be visible, use 1 and 10. The ending value should be greater than or equal to the beginning value, or all of the values will be visible.

When a chart with a range slider is used, the values between the beginning and ending values are visible by default, but the user has the ability to select a different range (larger or smaller), or slide the range to view a different series of values. The range slider will show a small representation of the chart. The following example shows a line chart with a range slider with a beginning value of 1 and an ending value of 10.

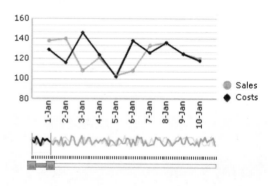

The range can be increased or decreased by clicking the begin or end points and dragging on the range slider.

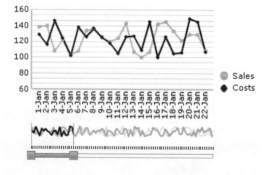

Users can move the range by clicking the middle of the range slider and sliding left or right.

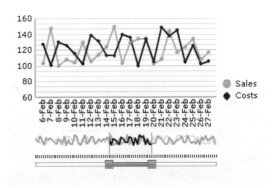

Enable Sorting   The Enable Sorting option allows the data that is selected to be sorted based on the data or category labels. The By Data sort option will sort data based on a series in ascending or descending order. The By Category option will sort data based on the category labels.

Dynamic Visibility   Dynamic visibility is a powerful feature used in most models to hide or display components based on the values of a certain cell. Dynamic visibility is often used to allow users to determine what information (components) that they want to see and when. This is done using the Dynamic Visibility options of a chart or other data display component combined with a selector component that sets the value of a cell as a trigger to either hide or show the chart or data display component if the Status cell matches the Key value. Both the Status and the Key values can be bound to a cell, or the key can be a hard-coded value.

A simple example is a chart and a table placed in the same spot, with only one visible at a time. This visibility can be controlled by another component, like radio buttons to show the table or chart, as in the following examples. In the first example, the Chart radio button is selected, and in the second example, the Table radio button is selected.

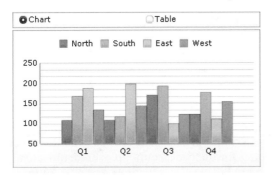

	Q1	Q2	Q3	Q4
North	108	108	170	123
South	168	117	192	177
East	187	198	100	111
West	134	143	123	154

Dynamic Visibility has a wide range of uses because it provides the ability to set the Status cell and Key value dynamically.

Scale Properties

The properties on the Scale subtab are used to set the scale within components, like charts, along with labels and scale divisions. These properties can make the visualization easier to use and also can affect the performance. These properties are also dependent on the properties set in the Appearance tab.

Scale   Most of the time, the Auto Axis option is used for the Scale setting, but the values can be set manually either by hard-coding the values or by binding to cells (for example, the minimum or maximum values can be bound to cells with MIN or MAX Excel formulas).

The scale on the axis can also be linear or logarithmic. You can set the Label Size option to Fixed Label Size. This can help optimize performance and space on the visualization. For example, 100,000 can be shown as 100K.

Divisions   If the Auto Axis setting is used, only the Minor Division option is enabled. Choosing the Manual Axis option for the Scale setting enables the Number of Divisions and Size of Divisions options. Both of these options can be hard-coded or bound to a cell.

NOTE If too many divisions are on a chart (such as when the size of the division is 100, and the values are in the 100,000 or higher range), then performance can suffer.

Animations and Effects Properties

Animation and effects can be used to give the visualization a more custom look and feel. These properties can be useful when dynamic visibility is used—an animation can draw attention to the components that are changing.

The data can be animated as well to gradually show data changes instead of the data changing instantaneously. Entry effect properties include fade-in, wipe right, and wipe right-down, along with the duration of the effect.

Appearance Properties

Appearances are important in life and in visualizations. The visualization needs to be engaging, easy to read, and well organized. It also needs to provide the correct content. But even if the content is correct and well organized, using the wrong fonts, distracting colors, or a cluttered display will reduce a visualization's usability.

Dashboard Design offers some great features that can be used to enhance the visualization and add additional interactive options to keep the users engaged and able to easily perform additional analysis.

Dashboard Design contains several options for the Appearance properties—Layout, Series, Axes, Text, Color, and Alerts, to name a few. As with other properties, the settings available depend on the selected component.

Layout

Appearances can be tricky at times, but a simple rule should be used when choosing to make elements visible. Does the element have a purpose, or does it distract from the purpose? The Layout properties include options for the background, plot area, title area, and legend. Some of these elements are useful to see in some situations, but not all the time. If these elements are not necessary, they should be disabled to avoid unnecessary clutter in the component.

One property that is somewhat unusual is the ability to use the legend as a selector. The Enable Hide/Show Chart Series at Run-Time property lets the user click different series in the legend to hide or show them, as shown in Figure 26-3. This interaction with the legend can be done by using either check boxes or mouse clicks. (If the click option is used, then some sort of help or training should be available so the users are aware of this feature.)

Series

The Series properties are used to set options such as series colors, marker size, line thickness, and transparency. Again, these properties depend on the components selected.

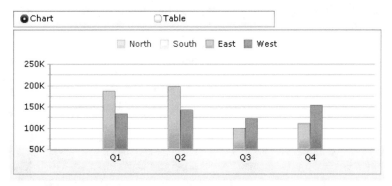

Figure 26-3 The Enable Hide/Show Chart Series at Run-Time property allows the legend to be used as a selector to show or hide a series. In this example, North and South were unselected.

As with other color properties, the default colors for series are based on the selected themes and color schemes. The individual series colors can be set to specific colors. They can also be bound to a cell color code.

Components such as line charts have properties to set the marker size, shape, and color. Marker sizes need to be a number between 1 and 100. Markers can also be disabled to show only lines within a line chart.

Axis

The Axis properties are used to set how the axis looks. This includes the vertical axis, horizontal axis, and grid lines. Their size, color, and thickness can be set.

Text

The Text properties are used to control which text items to display, fonts, alignment, font style, color, position, offsets, and even number formats. Text properties are generally in two areas: what to show and how to show it.

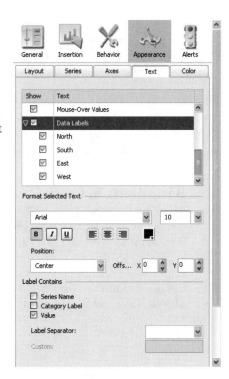

The top section of the Text properties contains a series of check boxes to show or hide specific text items. This includes items such as titles, labels, and legends. It is good practice to uncheck text items that will not be used in the component.

Depending on which text item is selected, the properties for the selected text item will be selected in the Format Selected Text section at the bottom of the Text properties.

Using these properties, you can also add some text items to the component that are not available through the other properties. The Data Labels option allows the inclusion of other properties to show the series value, name, and/or category label in a chart. The following examples show setting data labels for the series values and the resulting display.

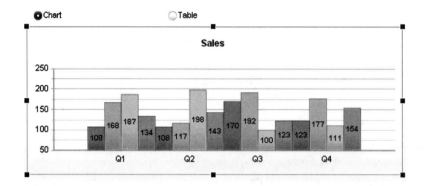

Color

Color properties are used to set some of the colors for components. Some of these are redundant (for example, the series colors can be set in the Series properties and in the Color properties), but others are unique. The series, background, title area, plot area, legend area, axis, and grid line colors can all be independently set.

Alerts Properties

Alerts are visual indicators to help manage and display data by exception, by drawing attention to the data suggesting that an action needs to be taken. Typically, when alerts are mentioned, people think that a user is notified, via e-mail or another means, but this is not the purpose of these alerts. Alerts are used to highlight certain events visually, such as when sales hit or miss a certain target.

Alerts are available for most of the chart and selector components where values and targets are both used. Targets can be used to trigger the alert or to calculate a percentage of targets for the alert. The alert will also have a threshold range to allow for multiple ranges to be used. Alerts can also be set up so low values are good, high values are good, or middle values are good.

Alerts are not available for all components and will not work with components with multiple series.

Basic Alerts in Charts

Alerts need to have values to begin with; targets are optional. Using an alert with only values can be useful in situations where the target is a percentage (for example, if the component is showing a percentage, and anything over 90 percent is always good).

If the value in the series needs to be compared to something, then this will be the target. From the target, Dashboard Design will calculate the percentage difference between the two and use this for the alert. Alert thresholds can then be added or removed to create different alert colors per range, as shown in the following examples.

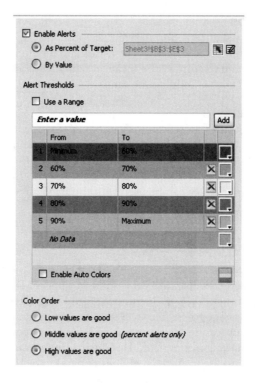

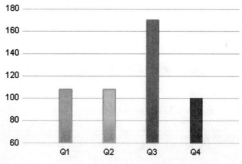

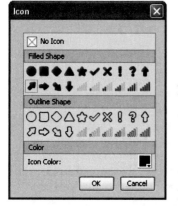

Alerts with the Scorecard Component

The scorecard component offers several other features when it comes to alerting. This component also contains visual icon indicators along with the colors. These can be selected by clicking the leftmost color range selector (in the Alert Threshold area).

　　You can select a color for the icon and a different color for the background and font. The background and font colors are selected in the color drop-down list to the right of the icon selector.

Alerts with Maps

Alerts with maps are slightly different from the other alerts. The Display Data option in the General tab contains a location name (or code) and a value. Alerts for maps work in the same way, as they need to contain the location name (or code) and a target value. The location name (or code) should be the same as what is used for the display data values.

Alerts with Selectors

Selectors can also contain alerts. This is a good way to indicate to the users which label should be selected. The selector might show regions, but can also include a red dot to alert that sales are below expectations.

Because selectors do not have values, the alert has another option for alert values. These values can be used with the By Value option, or another range of values can be selected as the target.

Dashboard Design and Excel

Excel Dashboard Design was created to build data visualizations from Excel data, hence the original product name: Xcelsius. Excel is still a key part of Dashboard Design. It is used for storing static data, functions, and documentation. Using Excel allows users without any programming knowledge to be able to create data visualizations.

Excel is used only for the development and design process of Dashboard Design. It is not needed when viewing a completed Dashboard Design model. Once a model is exported, Excel is not needed to use it. And Excel doesn't need to be installed on the server either.

When Dashboard Design is launched, Excel is also launched in the background. The embedded spreadsheet is a fully functional version of Excel, but it does not support the following features in Dashboard Design:

- Macros
- Conditional formatting
- Pivot tables
- Links to external workbooks
- Some functions (see the "Excel Functions" section later in this chapter)
- Filters

When starting a new model, a blank Excel workbook is already embedded in Dashboard Design, but you can also import a workbook or select one with a new model. This can help jump-start the design process.

Importing Spreadsheets

You can import a spreadsheet into a new model or one that has already been created by clicking the Import Spreadsheet button on the Standard toolbar (or pressing CTRL-SHIFT-I). If you're importing a spreadsheet into an existing model with components, that spreadsheet must contain the same worksheet names and cell locations for the components that have already been mapped in the properties. If they are not the same, the components will be mapped to the wrong cells and will not work. If you're using an existing data connection, such as SAP BusinessObjects Live Office, and import a new workbook, then these connections need to be redefined. Data connections are discussed in Chapter 27.

It is important to remember that once a workbook has been imported into Dashboard Design, it is now a copy of the original. Changes to the original Excel workbook will not be reflected in the Dashboard Design embedded workbook. In some cases, copying data, rather than importing it, is a better solution for moving data into Dashboard Design.

Opening multiple Excel workbooks can sometimes cause issues with Dashboard Design. To avoid Excel session issues when Dashboard Design is running, any other Excel workbook should be opened from Windows Explorer, rather than by launching a new session of Excel (Program Files | Excel). When you go through Windows Explorer, the current Excel instance launched from Dashboard Design will be used to open the other workbook. If Excel was started before Dashboard Design, it is best to end the Excel session, open Dashboard Design, and then reopen the Excel workbook.

> **NOTE** If Dashboard Design does not respond or closes without being prompted, or Excel is unable to start, you may need to close the Dashboard Design and Excel applications using the Task Manager (launch Task Manager, select the Processes tab and select EXCEL.EXE process, and click End Process).

Exporting Spreadsheets and Snapshots

You can work with the spreadsheet embedded in Dashboard Design in much the same way as you work with a workbook in Microsoft Excel. Cells can be sorted, copied, pasted, cut, and deleted, and most of the standard Excel functionality is available. However, functionality that requires add-ins and most of the Excel File menu options (such as Save, Print, and Open) are not available. If you need this other functionality, you can export the embedded Excel workbook into an Excel file.

To export a spreadsheet, select Data | Export (or press CTRL-SHIFT-E) and select a location and filename. This will export the workbook to a new Excel file. This is useful if the workbook requires a lot of modifications and the full version of Excel is needed.

When testing and troubleshooting a model, you may want to export a snapshot of it. You can export a snapshot of the model with data in preview mode, which will contain the data within the model that is supporting the current preview.

Model Design Considerations

Working within the embedded Excel workbook can make or break the Dashboard Design model. It's important to plan the location of the data, where data-insertion cells will be located, functions that are needed (discussed in the next section), and the amount of data that will be loaded into the Excel workbook.

Data within Dashboard Design should be continuous rows or columns for the same data source (avoid gaps in data when possible). The logic within the model should flow from the top-left corner to the lower-right corner. This can also help improve performance.

Values within the Dashboard Design model can be used to supply data to the components or for formulas to be used by the components. Dashboard Design is used to display an aggregated set of data, so the amount of rows and columns needs to be considered. By default, Dashboard Design has a 512 row limit, but this can be changed via File | Preferences | Excel. The number of rows set for the maximum also applies for formulas. When a model is exported as a Flash file, all the embedded data, up to the maximum row, is exported as well. You should remove any data you don't need before exporting a model.

Part IV

The location of the data is also important, especially when components have already been mapped. When data is added to the model, either by live data sources or manually entered, that data is likely to grow or shrink as the model is developed. If the data will grow, then the cells to the right and below should not be used.

While designing a model, you may find that you need to insert a new row or column in the middle on an existing row or column. If components are mapped to the range of cells, then the component will automatically adjust as needed. However, you must consider whether ranges of cells above or below or to the left or right will be negatively affected. It is often a good idea to plan ahead and design the worksheet to suit the data that will be consumed. Sometimes this is best done with additional spreadsheets.

You can use multiple spreadsheets to organize the data, formulas, component properties, and documentation of a Dashboard Design model. You might start out with three or four worksheets, each with a different purpose. Whether you'll need more worksheets than that depends on the complexity of the model being created. If several live data sources are being used, it is often useful to separate these into dedicated worksheets. Giving the worksheets meaningful names that describe their purpose will help with the model development and future enhancements.

The coloring of cells in the embedded Excel workbook is another consideration. It can help you understand and document the use of the cells within the model. For example, you might use yellow cells (with a yellow background) for labels, blue cells for data from live data sources, gray cells for formulas, and green cells for data-insertion ranges. Using colors will help avoid confusion and errors during development. It is also useful to begin using colored cells before adding any data or components to the model. The coloring can act as a placeholder to organize the layout in Excel. Add a legend that defines the purpose of the colors to the worksheet that contains documentation or development notes, as shown in the example in Figure 26-4.

Excel Functions

In Dashboard Design, Excel functions are used to aggregate, modify, and perform lookups, and as triggers. Because Dashboard Design uses Excel functions, developers do not need to learn another programming language to build an interactive dashboard.

Dashboard Design supports nearly 200 Excel functions, as listed in Table 26-4. These range from advanced mathematical and financial functions to simple functions to perform if-then-else logic.

Some functions—such as SUMIF, COUNTIF, and to some extent VLOOKUP and HLOOKUP— should be used with caution. These can cause some significant performance issues if they are used with a large number of cells. You can achieve the same functionality using a combination of other functions (such as IF, LOOKUP, MATCH, INDEX, and SUM). These slow-performing functions can be used, but with a limited set of cells.

Legend
The spreadsheet contains color coded sections for metrics, analytics, data and formulas:

Variables - do not edit
Formulas - do not edit
Dashboard labels - user defined
Data entry - user input
Data entry - user input

Figure 26-4   A legend of the cell colors used in the Balance Sheet template

NOTE To see the latest list of available functions, in Dashboard Design, select Help | Working with Data | Understanding the embedded spreadsheet | Supported Excel functions.

ABS	FIXED	PMT
ACOS	FLOOR	POWER
ACOSH	FORECAST	PPMT
ADDRESS	FV	PRODUCT
AND	GE	PV
ASIN	GEOMEAN	QUARTILE
ASINH	GT	QUOTIENT
ASSIGN	HARMEAN	RADIANS
ATAN	HLOOKUP	RAND
ATAN2	HOUR	RANDBETWEEN
ATANH	IF	RANGE_COLON
AVEDEV	Index	RANK
AVERAGE	INDIRECT	RATE
AVERAGEA	INT	REPLACE
AVERAGEIF	INTERCEPT	REPT
BETADIST	IPMT	RIGHT
CEILING	IRR	ROUND
CHAR	ISBLANK	ROUNDDOWN
CHOOSE	ISERR	ROUNDUP
COLUMNS	ISERROR	ROW
COMBIN	ISEVEN	ROWS
CONCATENATE	ISLOGICAL	RSQ
CORREL	ISNA	SECOND
COS	ISNONTEXT	SIGN
COSH	ISNUMBER	SIN
COUNT	ISODD	SINH
COUNTA	ISTEXT	SLN
COUNTBLANK	KURT	SLOPE
COUNTIF	LARGE	SMALL
COVAR	LE	SQRT
DATE	LEFT	STANDARDIZE
DATEVALUE	LEN	STDEV
DAVERAGE	LN	STDEVA
DAY	LOG	STDEVP

Table 26-4   Excel Functions Supported by Dashboard Design

Part IV

DAYS360	LOG10	SUBTOTAL
DB	LOOKUP	SUM
DCOUNT	LOWER	SUMIF
DCOUNTA	MATCH	SUMPRODUCT
DDB	MAX	SUMSQ
DEGREES	MAXA	SUMX2MY2
DEVSQ	MEDIAN	SUMX2PY2
DGET	MID	SUMXMY2
DIVIDE	MIN	SYD
DMAX	MINA	TAN
DMIN	MINUS	TANH
DOLLAR	MINUTE	TEXT
DPRODUCT	MIRR	TIME
DSSTDEVP	MOD	TIMEVALUE
DSTDEV	MODE	TODAY
DSUM	MONTH	TRUE
DVAR	NE	TRUNC
DVARP	NETWORKDAYS	TYPE
EDATE	NORMDIST	VALUE
EFFECT	NORMINV	VAR
EOMONTH	NORMSINV	VARA
EVEN	NOT	VARP
EXACT	NOW	VARPA
EXP	NPER	VDB
EXPONDIST	NPV	VLOOKUP
FACT	OFFSET	WEEKDAY
FACTDOUBLE	OR	WEEKNUM
FALSE	PEARSON	WORKDAY
FIND	PERCENTRANK	WXYZ
FISHER	PERMUT	YEAR
FISHERINV	PI	YEARFRAC

Table 26-4   Excel Functions Supported by Dashboard Design *(continued)*

Lookup Functions

Looking up values in Excel is a common practice that is performed using a few Excel functions. A *lookup* is the process of finding a value based on another value that is located in a range of cells. For example, if a user selects Region 1 from a selector, a lookup can return values located in a row or column to display monthly sales for the selected region.

Several functions can be used to perform a lookup. The most popular are VLOOKUP and HLOOKUP, but as noted earlier, these functions can cause performance issues. Other functions that can be used for a lookup include MATCH, INDEX, and OFFSET. Table 26-5 summarizes these functions.

Using the MATCH and INDEX functions together, rather than VLOOKUP or HLOOKUP, can be a better choice when performing a lookup, even though you need to use two functions instead of just one. MATCH is used to find a value in a range of cells. When the value is located, an index value is returned. The INDEX function is used to return a value based on an array (a range of cells) and an index value. The INDEX array can be a single row/column or multiple rows/columns. If multiple rows and columns are used, then two index values are needed: one for the row and the other for the column. Think of these as the X and Y axes, where the coordinates need to be supplied to return a value.

Consider the following spreadsheet data:

	A	B	C	D	E
1		Q1	Q2	Q3	Q4
2	Region 1	2,589	2,145	4,461	4,633
3	Region 2	1,080	2,919	2,156	3,430
4	Region 3	2,075	2,655	1,426	3,998
5	Region 4	1,519	4,218	1,190	2,667
6	Region 5	1,429	4,772	2,479	2,851
7	Region 6	4,016	2,662	4,832	3,934

Using VLOOKUP, you could look up the value in cell H2 (Region 5), in the range (A2:E7), and when the value Range 5 is found, return the value in the second column.

`=VLOOKUP(H2,A2:E7,2,FALSE)`

	H	I	J
	Region 5	1,429	

Excel Function	Syntax	Description
VLOOKUP	VLOOKUP(lookupvalue, range, indexnumber, false)	Returns a value in a vertical range using a lookup value as a key
HLOOKUP	HLOOKUP(lookupvalue, range, indexnumber, false)	Returns a value in a horizontal range using a lookup value as a key
MATCH	MATCH (lookupvalue, range, match type)	Finds a value in a range of cells and returns an index value (match type should be set to 0)
INDEX	INDEX(range, row number, [column number])	Returns a value based on an array (a range of cells) and an index value
OFFSET	OFFSET(reference cell, row number, column number)	Returns a cell based on a reference cell (a starting point) and a row and column number (row and column can be positive or negative)

Table 26-5   Excel Lookup Functions

Using HLOOKUP, you could look up the value in cell H2 (Q2), in the range (B2:E7), and when the value Q2 is found, return the value in the second column.

=HLOOKUP(H2,B1:E7,2,FALSE)

H	I	J
Q2	2,145	

Using MATCH, you could look up the value in cell H2 (Region 5), in the range (A1:A7), and when the value Region 5 is found, return the index value.

=MATCH(H2,A2:A7,0)

H	I
Region 5	5

Using INDEX, for the range (A1:E7), you could return the value in the row defined in cell H2 (5) and column 3.

=INDEX(A1:E7,H2,3)

H	I
5	4,218

Using MATCH and INDEX together, you could look up the value in cell H2 (Region 5), in the range (A1:A7), and when the value Region 5 is found, return the index value. In the range (A1:E7), return the value in row defined in cell H2 (5) and column 3.

=INDEX(A1:E7,MATCH(H2,A2:A7,0),3)

H	I	J	K
Region 5	4,218		

This might look more complicated than using VLOOKUP, but it offers more flexibility and better performance.

NOTE When using MATCH and INDEX together, make sure that the ranges (arrays) are the same rows or columns.

An alternative to using MATCH and INDEX is pairing MATCH and OFFSET. OFFSET is similar to INDEX, except an array is not defined. The OFFSET function uses a single cell as a start location (reference cell), and offset values are supplied to select a cell vertically and horizontally offset from the start, or reference, cell. The offset values can be zero, positive, or negative integers. Because an array does not need to be defined in an OFFSET function, Dashboard Design doesn't need to read multiple cells for a lookup, but only points to the cell. Thousands of rows can be used with significant performance gains when using OFFSET. For example, you could use OFFSET from cell A1 to return the value in the cell down 4, across 3.

=OFFSET(A1,4,3)

H	I
1190	

OFFSET and MATCH can be used together to perform a lookup of a cell without the need to define a range, as with the LOOKUP and INDEX functions. In the following example, a MATCH function is used to find the row and column of values selected by a component. The row and column values are used in the OFFSET function to find the value based on a reference cell.

	H	I	J
1			
2	Selection	Index Value	Formula
3	Q2	2	=MATCH(H3,B1:E1,0)
4	Region 3	3	=MATCH(H4,A2:A7,0)
5	Value	2,655	=OFFSET(A1,I4,I3)

Other Common Functions

Other common Excel functions include CONCATENATE, IF, OR, AND, and ISBLANK.

CONCATENATE   Within Excel, cells can be concatenated together using an ampersand (&), but for longer strings like URL, use the CONCATENATE function.

`CONCATENATE(text1,text2,...)`

	A	B	C
	fx	=CONCATENATE(A1," ",B1)	
1	Test	this.	Test this.

IF   IF is used for logical expressions to see if something is true or false. If the logical test is true, the first value is returned; if it is false, the second value is returned. The results for true or false can be other functions or nested IF statements.

`IF(logical_test,value_if_true,value_if_false)`

	A	B	C	D
	fx	=IF(A1=1,B1,C1)		
1	2	A	B	B

OR   OR returns true if one of the logical arguments is true. Used primarily in conjunction with the IF function.

`OR(logical1,logical2,...)`

	A	B	C	D
	fx	=IF(OR(A1=1,A1=2),B1,C1)		
1	2	A	B	A

AND   AND returns true if all of the logical arguments are true. Used primarily in conjunction with the IF function.

`AND(logical1,logical2,...)`

	A	B	C	D
	fx	=IF(AND(A1=1,A1=2),B1,C1)		
1	2	A	B	B

ISBLANK   ISBLANK returns true if a cell is blank.

`ISBLANK(cell)`

	A	B	C
	fx	=ISBLANK(A1)	
1	2	FALSE	

Using Themes and Colors in Dashboard Design

With every visualization, selections of the appropriate colors and styles are key ingredients. Colors and styles should be used to convey the same message, along with guiding the users to use the visualization. The number of colors used will greatly depend on the data and the number of series (dimensions) that will be visible at one given time. Titles, URL links, help buttons, and other common components should be consistent not only across the visualization, but also across the organization.

Dashboard Design has several options to change the look and feel of visualizations. Here, we will discuss the use of themes and color schemes, as well as binding colors to component properties. Each of these options has its own purpose and features that can greatly enhance the look of a visual (or make it difficult to understand). Designing visualization is part art and part science.

Dashboard Design Themes

Themes are what determine the style of the components and default colors in a model. You should decide which theme you will use early in the design process.

Dashboard Design contains ten themes:

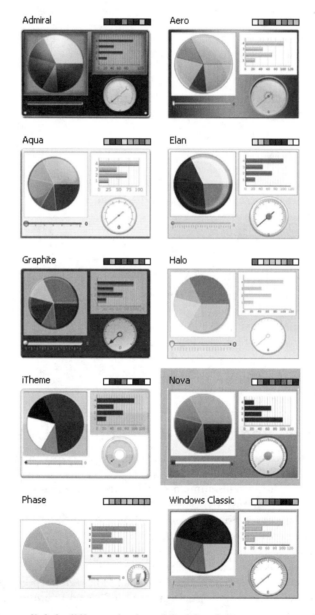

Each theme has a slightly different look and feel for the components, along with a certain number of components available and its own color scheme. For example, the Areo theme has only two components, while the Nova theme has ten.

NOTE Themes are delivered with Dashboard Design and cannot be updated or created.

To apply a theme, select one from the Theme drop-down menu on the Themes toolbar or select Format | Theme. From the drop-down menu, you'll see the selected theme's name, color scheme, and a thumbnail showing its appearance.

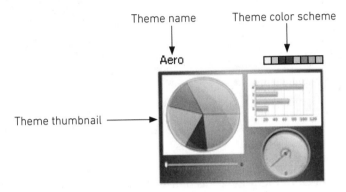

Once the theme has been selected, Dashboard Design will update the components on the canvas with the new theme style, update nonexisting components from the original theme to a similar style, and apply the theme's default color scheme.

NOTE You should save your model prior to selecting a different theme, because once the theme is selected, undo will not revert to the previous theme. So use caution!

Color Schemes

Color schemes are used to customize the colors that are applied within the component properties. Two types of color schemes are available: built-in and custom. Built-in color schemes are predefined schemes created by SAP. These can't be updated, but they can be used as templates to create custom color schemes.

To apply a color scheme, select one from the Change Color Scheme drop-down menu (next to the Theme drop-down in the Themes toolbar) or select Format | Color Scheme.

When a color scheme is selected, by default, the color properties for the components on the canvas will be updated. For example, if blue was selected for the title text with a green background, these properties will be repopulated when a new color scheme is selected. This can be avoided by disabling the Apply to Existing Components option, located at the bottom of the Change Color Scheme drop-down menu (or the Format | Color Scheme menu).

If colors in a component property use the Bind to a Color option (discussed in the next section), then the color will remain bound to the defined cell, even when the color scheme or theme is updated. Creating a custom color scheme allows developers to use the same color scheme across all Dashboard Design models. The process of creating a new color scheme starts with the selection of an existing color scheme and selecting the Create New Color Scheme option at the bottom of the Change Color Scheme drop-down menu (or right-clicking an existing color scheme and selecting Create New). This will open the Custom Color Scheme dialog box, as shown in Figure 26-5.

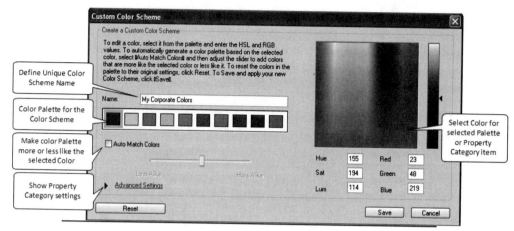

Figure 26-5 Custom color scheme options

Table 26-6 shows the defaults that can be customized by selecting each item in the color palette (as numbered in the following illustration) one by one.

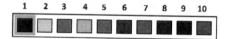

Custom color schemes are saved to the developer's computer in the Xcelsius customThemes folder. On a Windows XP system, the path is C:\Documents and Settings*Windows User*\Application Data\XcelsiuscustomThemes. On a Windows 7 system, the path is C:\Users*Windows User*\AppData\Roaming\XcelsiuscustomThemes. When a custom color scheme is saved, an XML file with the same name is saved in this location. This XML file can be shared with other developers.

NOTE The Application Data or AppData folders might be hidden or restricted, depending on the computer's security policies.

Color Binding Properties

The Theme and Color Scheme options are very useful when a color is constant and doesn't need to change. But what if a color does need to change depending on some action or value? Conditional formatting within the embedded Excel workbook is not supported, but Dashboard Design does have the ability to bind a property color to a cell. This allows the color to be truly dynamic!

Binding a property to a cell is done within the properties for items with colors. Not all components have this feature; for example, the canvas needs a nonbinding color. Color properties that do use this feature have the Bind to a Color option when a color is selected, as shown in Figure 26-6. When you use this option, you must select a cell to be used to define the property color.

Components and Colors			Palette Color Position										
			1	2	3	4	5	6	7	8	9	10
Backgrounds	Background components	Background color				X						
	Canvas backgrounds	Background color 1			X							
		Background color 2			X							
Text		All	X									
Buttons		Default color		X								
		Mouse-over		X								
		Pressed color			X							
		Selected color			X							
		Disabled color										X
Charts	Background	Chart background color		X								
	Text	Title text color	X									
		Subtitle text color	X									
		Other text color	X									

Table 26-6 Advanced Settings for Color Scheme Defaults

Components and Colors			Palette Color Position									
			1	2	3	4	5	6	7	8	9	10
Selectors	Labels	Default tex	X									
		Mouse-over text	X									
		Selected text		X								
	Label background	Default		X								
		Mouse-over				X						
		Selected					X					
Single value	Sliders and progress bars	Marker color					X					
		Track color										X
		Tick color	X									
	Dials and gauges	Needle color					X					
		Grip/frame color										X
		Center color		X								
		Background color										X
		Tick color	X									

Table 26-6 Advanced Settings for Color Scheme Defaults (*continued*)

Components and Colors			Palette Color Position									
			1	2	3	4	5	6	7	8	9	10
Maps	Regions	Default color		X								
		Mouse-over color		X								
		Selected color					X					
		Selectable color				X						
	Region border	Border color	X									
Scroll bars		Track		X								
		Thumb				X						
		Buttons		X								
		Button symbol	X									

Table 26-6 Advanced Settings for Color Scheme Defaults *(continued)*

Part IV

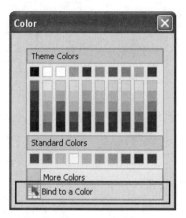

Figure 26-6 Color selector with the Bind to a Color option

The cell that has been selected for the color can contain one of the following color definitions:

- RGB
- HEX
- VGA color names
- Decimal color equivalent

Table 26-7 shows examples of five different colors and the color values for the supported binding options.

Of these four options, the easiest to use is RGB, because most developers can understand it. The RGB color code can be created with a simple formula, which can read the red, green, or blue color from other cells. The cells that contain the individual red, green, or blue can be the results of other formulas or components.

	f_x	="("&B1&", "&B2&", "&B3&")"	
A	B	C	D
Red	211		(211, 64, 33)
Green	64		
Blue	33		

NOTE When using RGB, make sure the parentheses and spaces after the commas have been entered.

Option	Black	White	Red	Blue	Green
RGB	(0, 0, 0)	(255, 255, 255)	(255, 0, 0)	(0, 0, 255)	(0, 128, 0)
HEX	000000	FFFFFF	FF0000	0000FF	008000
VGA	Black	White	Red	Blue	Green
Decimal	0	16777215	16711680	255	32768

Table 26-7 Sample Colors and Color Values for the Supported Binding Options

Using the Bind to a Color option is very useful when colors should be consistent across all components in visualization. Properties such as title, axis, and other items can be controlled fairly well from the color scheme options.

Different colors for chart series are not managed within the color scheme, but can be handled with the Bind to a Color option. For example, you could make all the Sales, Cost, Margin, and Quantity series the same color in all components. This can be done be creating a new worksheet called Colors with measures across the top and the RGB codes with the individual color values (a row for red, green, and blue) underneath.

▲	A	B	C	D	E
1		Sales	Costs	Margin	Quantity
2	RGB Code	(211, 64, 33)	(211, 211, 56)	(33, 33, 33)	(255, 126, 5)
3	Red	211	211	33	255
4	Green	64	211	33	126
5	Blue	33	56	33	5

Now when a new chart component is added and it contains a series of data (like Sales) in another component, the color can be bound to the same cell. If the color of the series needs to be changed and ten chart components are affected, the color value will need to be updated only in the cell used for the binding. This can save a lot of development time and also keep colors consistent.

Summary

Properties are what make the components work. Without the properties, the components will be basically an empty picture. Most of the components have the same options, but many have several differences. These differences do take some time to understand, but the basic principles of the properties are the same across all the components. Along with the data within the components being bound, interactive and formatting options are also set within the Properties panel.

Understanding the features and supported functions of the embedded Excel workbook is necessary to make the components work via the properties and to avoid potential performance issues. With basic Excel knowledge, you can quickly and easily create intuitive and interactive models using Dashboard Design.

The following are several considerations for designers before beginning a new Dashboard Design model:

- Planning the layout of your Excel model is necessary before beginning development.
- Using color coding, multiple worksheets, and organizing your data to be in continuous ranges will help development.
- Limiting the data can avoid performance issues and large Flash files.
- Selecting the right functions is always important.

Part IV

Remember that Excel is being used to store data, perform calculations with functions, and to bind component properties.

Managing colors and the styles used within the visualization does take some initial planning, but this can save future redevelopment tasks. Dashboard Design has several options to customize the look and feel of the visualization by using themes, color schemes, and color binding options.

Themes should be selected early to avoid using components that are not available in certain themes. Color schemes should be chosen to set the standard colors to be used within visualization and also to create custom schemes to be consistent across dashboards created by other developers. The use of color binding can make colors more dynamic during run time or by creating a defined list of colors for specific component parts or chart series.

Data Sources

SAP BusinessObjects Dashboards 4.0 offers a variety of ways to connect to your data sources. In Xcelsius 2008 and prior versions, most of the data for your components was loaded into the embedded spreadsheet. In Dashboards 4.0, the new Query Browser allows you to connect directly to your BusinessObjects enterprise environment to access data directly through a universe or BEx query.

In this chapter, we will discuss the different categories of data sources used to connect data to your components:

- Embedded spreadsheets
- Universe and BEx queries
- Live Office
- External data connections

Embedded Spreadsheets

The embedded spreadsheet within Dashboard Design is an Excel spreadsheet—actually, an Excel workbook with multiple Excel spreadsheets—that contains the data that you want to link to the components in your dashboard. You can work with data in the embedded spreadsheet within Dashboard Design in much the same way as you work with data in Excel outside Dashboard Design.

The embedded spreadsheet should be displayed beneath the canvas for your dashboard. If it is not displayed, select the Quick Views drop-down from the toolbar and select Show My Workspace.

The embedded spreadsheet includes the Excel menu and toolbars (Excel 2003) or ribbon toolbars (Excel 2007). However, some of the buttons and options normally available in Excel that are not related to working with data in the Excel spreadsheets are not available in the embedded spreadsheet. Figure 27-1 shows an example of an embedded spreadsheet.

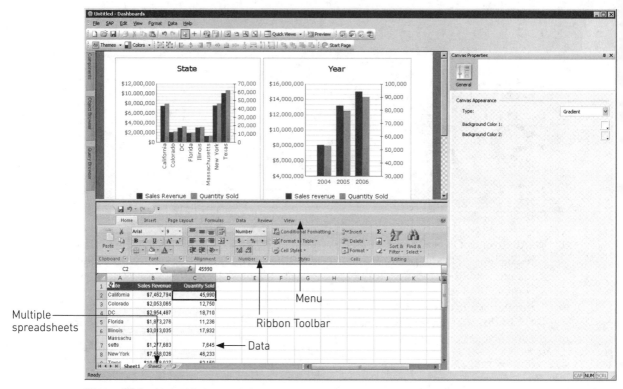

Figure 27-1 Embedded spreadsheet

Adding Data to the Embedded Spreadsheet

The data in the embedded spreadsheet is entirely contained within the dashboard model. Data can be added to the embedded spreadsheet by one of the following methods:

- Importing a spreadsheet from Excel
- Copying and pasting data into the embedded spreadsheet
- Manually entering data into the embedded spreadsheet
- Linking a query into the embedded spreadsheet

Once the data is contained within the embedded spreadsheet, you can add, modify, or delete the data within the embedded spreadsheet.

Using Functions in the Embedded Spreadsheet

One of the reasons that the embedded spreadsheet is such a powerful data source is that many of the Excel functions are supported in Dashboards 4.0. However, not all functions are supported. You will want to make sure that your embedded spreadsheet contains only supported functions. See Table 26-4 for a list of Excel functions supported by SAP BusinessObjects Dashboards 4.0.

Setting Preferences for the Embedded Spreadsheet

Dashboard Design provides preference settings when working with embedded spreadsheets as a data source for your models. Excel preferences were covered in Chapter 24.

To set preferences for the embedded spreadsheet, do the following:

1. Select File | Preferences from the menu bar. The Preferences dialog box will display.

2. Select Excel Options from the left panel. The Excel Options preferences will display.

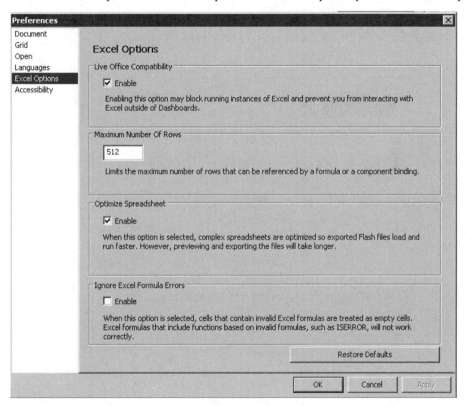

3. Set your desired preferences and then click OK.

Binding Components to Embedded Spreadsheets

Once your data has been added to your embedded spreadsheet, you need to link it to components on your dashboard canvas. In our simple example, we will create a spreadsheet of data containing Sales Revenue and Quantity Sold data by State in our embedded spreadsheet, as follows:

	A	B	C
1	**State**	**Sales Revenue**	**Quantity Sold**
2	California	$7,462,794	45,990
3	Florida	$1,873,276	11,236
4	Illinois	$3,013,035	17,932
5	Massachusetts	$1,277,683	7,645
6	New York	$7,558,026	46,233
7	Texas	$10,078,027	62,150

You can now start creating dashboard components that are linked to this data. To bind data to an embedded spreadsheet, do the following:

1. Select the Components panel from the left side of Dashboard Designer. The Components list will display. From the Tree view, select the Charts folder.

2. Select and drag the column chart component to the canvas.

3. In the Column Chart 1 Properties panel, select the Data | By Series radio button, and then click the + button to add a series.

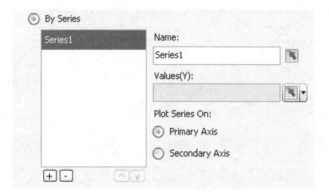

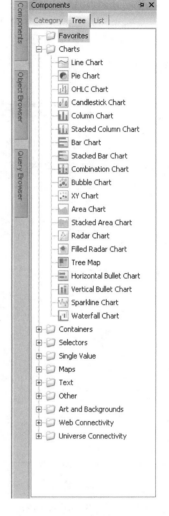

4. For Values(Y), select the drop-down data binding selector button, and then select Spreadsheet.

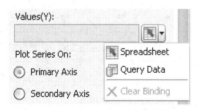

5. The Select a Range dialog box will display. Select the embedded spreadsheet range that represents the Sales Revenue data values to be the first series in the column chart. You can either click and drag on the values in the embedded spreadsheet or type them into the Select a Range dialog box.

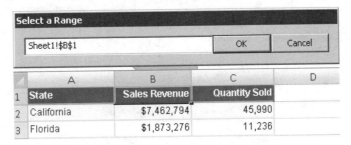

6. Click OK. You will see the values in the column chart update.

7. Click the Name drop-down data binding selector button and select Spreadsheet. You will now select the embedded spreadsheet range that represents the column heading for the Sales Revenue data values.

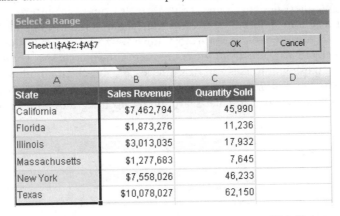

8. Click OK. You will see the Series Name update to Sales Revenue.

9. Click the Category Labels(X) drop-down data binding selector button and select Spreadsheet. You will now select the embedded spreadsheet range that represents the X-axis data value names to be displayed in the column chart.

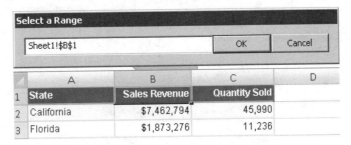

10. Click OK. Dashboard Designer should look like Figure 27-2. You may need to resize the chart.

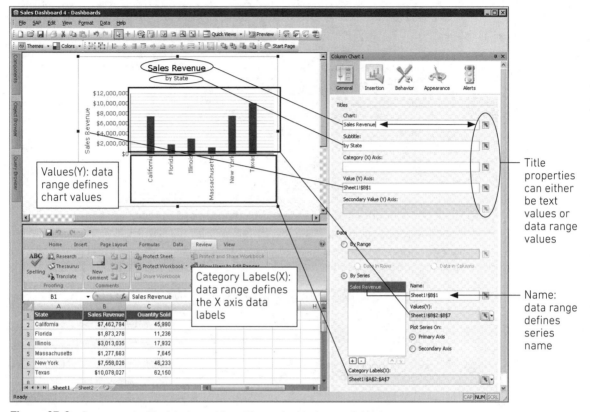

Figure 27-2 Component with data bound from the embedded spreadsheet

Universe and BEx Queries

Universe and BEx queries are new to SAP BusinessObjects Dashboards 4.0. Using the Query Browser and query designer to bind data directly from your universes to the components in your dashboard, including the pros and cons, was covered in Chapter 23.

The data returned in a query from a universe can be bound to the embedded spreadsheet and also directly to the components on your canvas. There are still some limitations to using universes and BEx queries as a direct data binding source to your components. You will find that some of the properties of your components, such as title properties, range sliders, and alerts, are still tightly integrated with the embedded spreadsheet only. So, for now, while you will start to use the Query Browser to retrieve some of the data for direct binding to your components, you will continue to use the embedded spreadsheet concepts discussed in the prior section.

To create a universe or BEx query from the Query Browser, do the following:

1. Select the Query Browser panel from the left side of Dashboard Designer. Click the Add Query button.

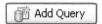

2. The Add Query dialog box will display, with the choices Universe and BEx. Select Universe for this example, and then click Next.

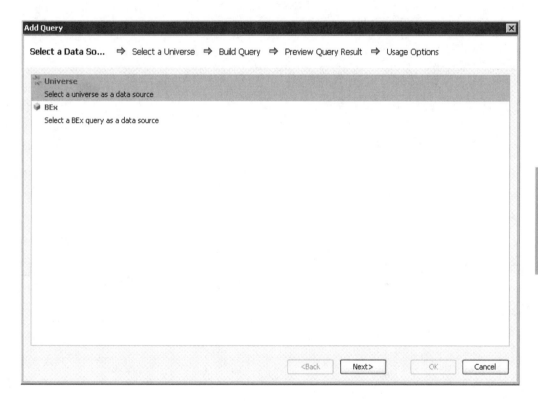

3. Navigate through the universe folder structure and select the universe from which you would like to create a query for data to include in your dashboard component. In this example, select eFashion. Click Next.

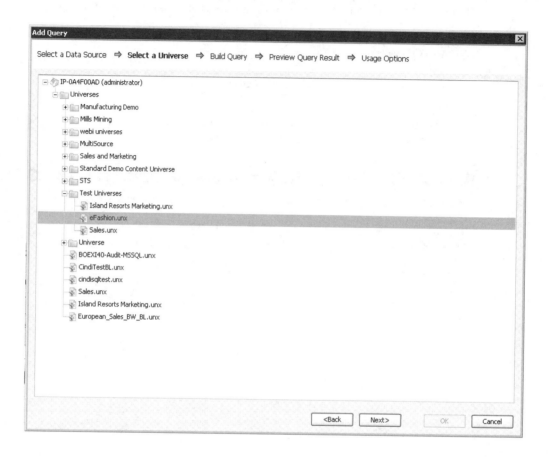

4. The Build Query window will display. Create the desired query to return data for your dashboard component. In this example, select the Year, Sales revenue, and Quantity sold objects. Click Next.

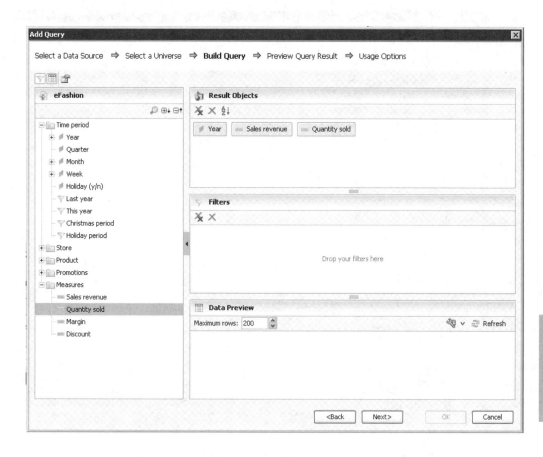

5. The query will run and return the data in the Preview Query Result window. Click Next.

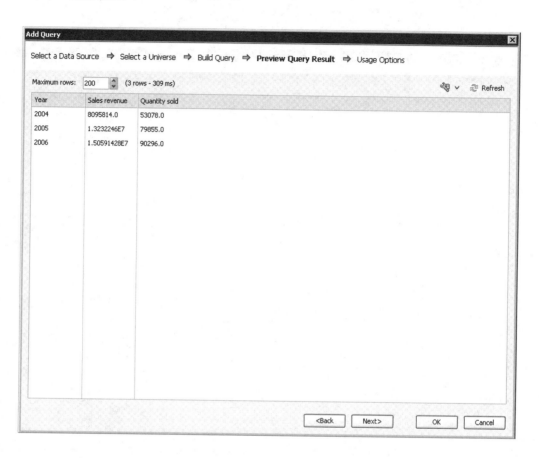

6. The Usage Options window will display, as shown in Figure 27-3. Usage options are optional and default to Refresh Before Components are Loaded.

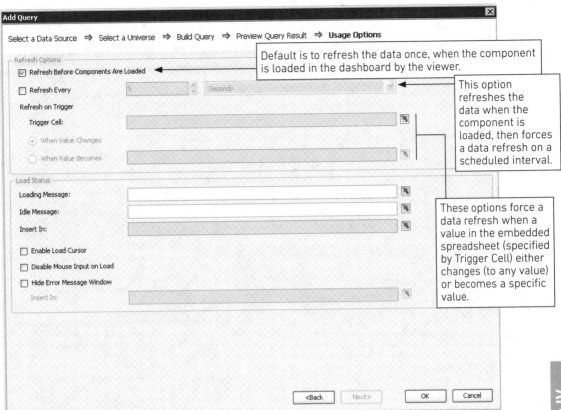

Figure 27-3   Query Browser Usage Options

Binding Components to Universe or BEx Queries

Once your data is retrieved in your query, you can bind the data to components in your dashboard. Data binding to queries was covered in Chapter 23. Figure 27-4 shows a column chart component bound to the query returned in the prior section.

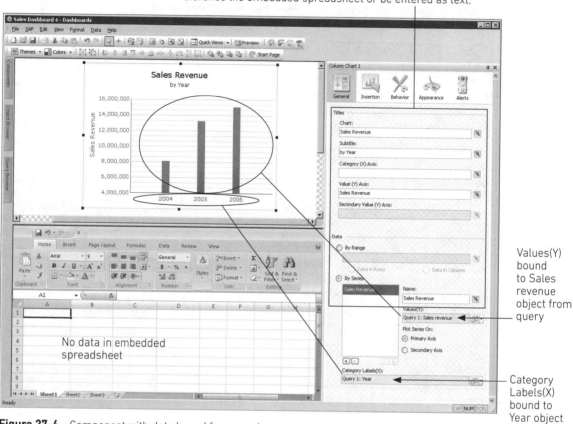

These property values cannot reference query data. They must reference the embedded spreadsheet or be entered as text.

Values(Y) bound to Sales revenue object from query

Category Labels(X) bound to Year object from query

Figure 27-4   Component with data bound from a universe query

Inserting Query Data into the Embedded Spreadsheet

Data can be retrieved in the query and inserted into the embedded spreadsheet also. To insert query data into the embedded spreadsheet, do the following:

1. Select the Query Browser panel from the left side of Dashboard Designer. Your query should display. Select Result Objects.

   ▼ **Result Objects**

2. From the Result Objects list, select the object that you would like to insert into the embedded spreadsheet and enter the data range where you would like to place the data. Note that the range can be larger than the number of rows in the query.

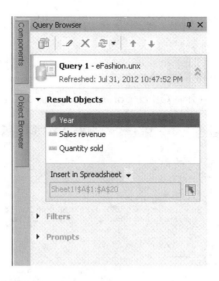

3. Repeat step 2 for each result object you would like to have inserted in the embedded spreadsheet.

The data will not display in the embedded spreadsheet, but will be available for reference in component properties, and will be populated when the dashboard is rendered and previewed.

Live Office Connections

The SAP BusinessObjects Live Office add-in for Microsoft Office (Excel, Word, Outlook, and PowerPoint) allows you to insert data into Microsoft Office from Crystal Reports reports, Web Intelligence reports, and universe queries. Before SAP BusinessObjects Dashboards 4.0 allowed for data to be queried directly from a universe or BEx query, the data in the embedded spreadsheet was kept fresh by using Live Office.

Creating the Live Office Object

The embedded spreadsheet can contain many Live Office objects. These Live Office objects have several advantages over other data connection methods:

- The Live Office objects can use data from a scheduled Crystal Reports or Web Intelligence report. Therefore, the scheduled instance of the report can run during off-peak hours, and the dashboard does not need to query the database every time a user is viewing the dashboard.

- When Live Office objects are based on Crystal Reports or Web Intelligence reports, you get all the benefits of the report design tools themselves, such as formulas, formatting, layout, and block formats.

- The Live Office objects populate the embedded spreadsheet with data, which makes development easier.

To add a Live Office-enabled embedded spreadsheet to your dashboard, do the following:

1. Create a new, blank dashboard model. Select File | Preferences and select Excel Options from the left pane.

2. Make sure that Live Office Compatibility Enable check box is selected. Click OK.

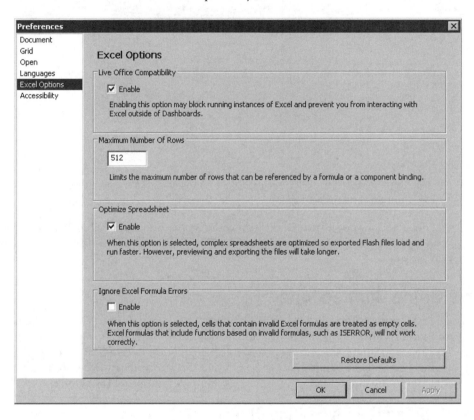

3. View the embedded spreadsheet menu bar. You should see the Live Office menu option. Click Live Office to display the ribbon toolbar.

4. Click Crystal Reports, Web Intelligence, or Universe Query to insert data into your embedded spreadsheet. For this example, select Web Intelligence. You will be prompted to log on to your BusinessObjects environment. Enter your user ID and password, and then click OK.

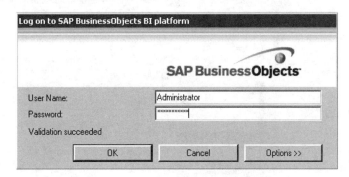

5. The Live Office Insert Wizard dialog box will display. Navigate to the folder that contains the Web Intelligence document and select it. In this example, select Sales and Quantity by State Dashboard. Click Next.

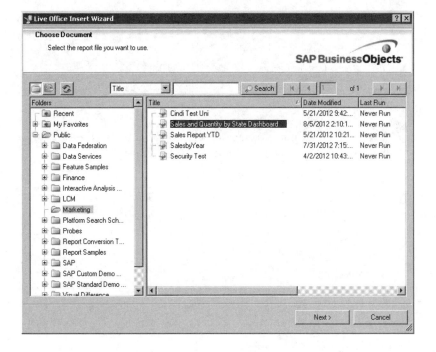

6. The report will display. Select the block from the Web Intelligence report that contains the data to return to the embedded spreadsheet. Click Next.

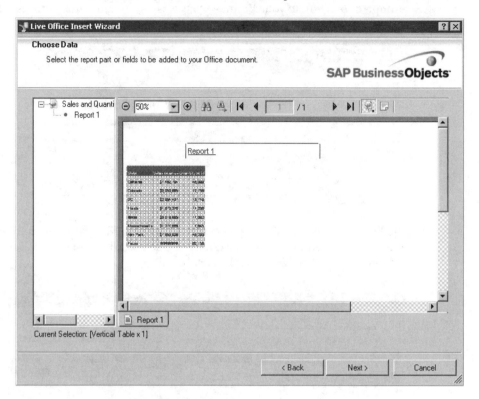

7. The Summary displays. You can accept the default for the Live Office object name or provide a more meaningful name. Click Finish.

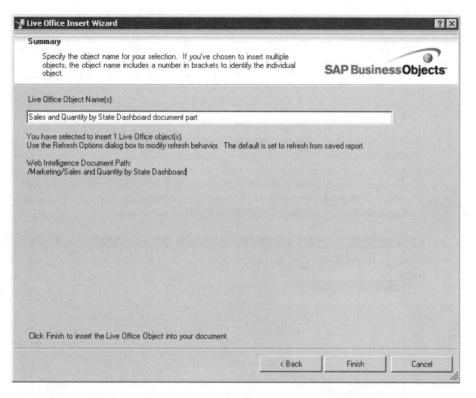

8. The Live Office object is created, and the embedded spreadsheet is now populated with data from the Web Intelligence report.

Setting Live Office Object Properties and Refresh Options

Once you have created a Live Office object, you can set and modify the object properties.
To modify the Live Office object properties, do the following:

1. Select the Live Office object you wish to work with. You can do
   this by clicking the data in the embedded spreadsheet or by
   selecting the Go To Object drop-down list and selecting the object.

2. Select the Object Properties button from the Live Office
   ribbon toolbar.

3. The Live Office Object Properties dialog box will display. From the General tab,
   you can change the name of the object or update the report name and folder path
   location from your BusinessObjects Enterprise system.

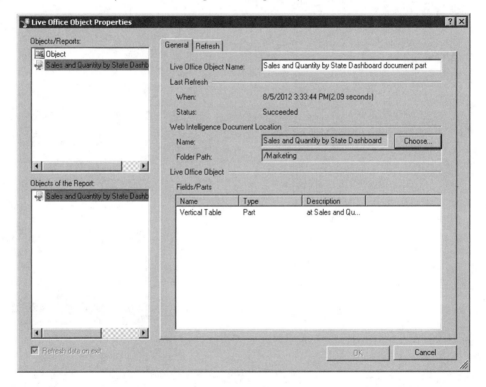

4. Click the Refresh tab. From the Refresh tab, you can apply any report formatting
   (numeric, date, and so on) to the data in the embedded spreadsheet and choose to
   save the model with the embedded spreadsheet data concealed. You can also access
   the Refresh Options dialog box by clicking the Edit button.

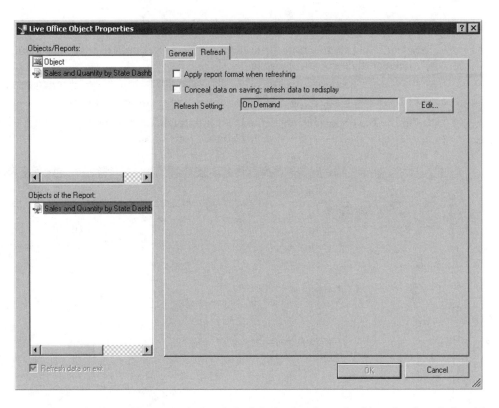

5. The Refresh options specify the default behavior for refreshing the data defined in the Live Office object. You can specify the following:

- **Latest Instance**   The last instance in the BusinessObjects Enterprise environment that was scheduled by a specific user.

- **On Demand**   Forces the user to manually refresh the data when new data is desired. You can refresh the data manually by clicking the Refresh All Objects button in the Live Office ribbon toolbar.

- **Use Report Saved Data**   Uses the data found in the saved report.

- **Specific Instance**   Uses the data found in a specific instance specified.

Creating a Live Office Data Connection

Live Office data connections allow you to refresh data from a Live Office-enabled embedded spreadsheet that has been created using a Crystal Reports report, Web Intelligence report, or universe as a data source. The data connection will allow users from within BI Launch Pad or from outside BI Launch Pad to connect to the BusinessObjects Enterprise system to refresh the data defined in the Live Office objects.

Part IV

To create a Live Office data connection, do the following:

1. Select Data | Connections from the Dashboard Designer toolbar. The Data Manager dialog box will display.

2. Click the Add drop-down list and select Live Office Connections. If there is only one Live Office object in the current document, that object will be added by default.

3. On the Data Manager dialog box Definition tab, update the Session URL to contain the web server name for your BusinessObjects Enterprise environment.

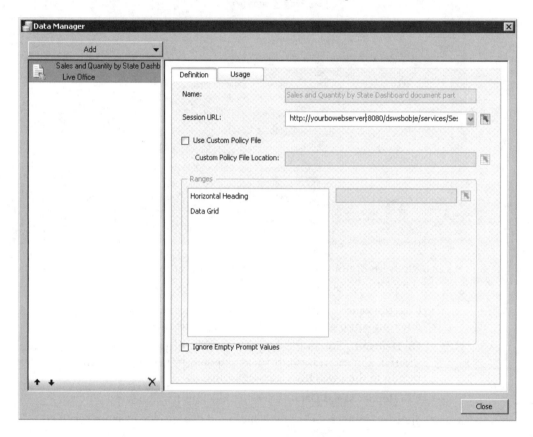

4. On the Usage tab, you can specify how often the data is refreshed and provide messages to display to the users.

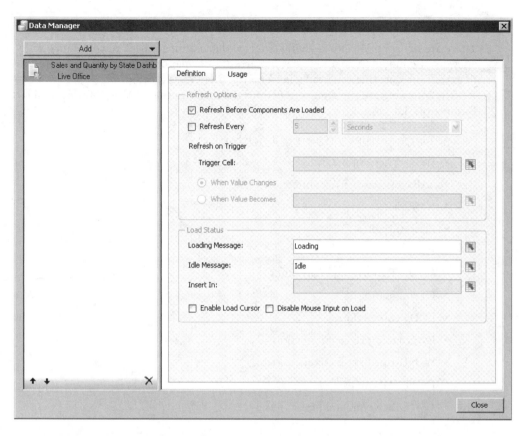

5. When you have made the changes, click Close.

6. To test the data connection, click the Preview button on the Dashboard Designer toolbar. You should be prompted with a login dialog box from your BusinessObjects Enterprise environment.

External Data Connections

There are many options for creating external data connections. External data connections allow for the model to be updated with current information when the model runs, rather than with the data that was available when the model was created.

The following are the data connections that can be created in SAP BusinessObjects Dashboards 4.0.

- Web service query (Query as a Web Service)
- Web service connection
- SAP NetWeaver BW connection
- XML data
- Flash variables
- Portal data
- Crystal Reports data consumer
- FS command
- LCDS connection
- External interface connection
- Web Dynpro Flash Island
- Excel XML maps
- Live Office connections

Creating a Query as a Web Service Connection

To create a Query as a Web Service (QaaWS) data connection, do the following:

1. Select the Query as a Web Service Designer from the SAP BusinessObjects BI Platform 4 | SAP BusinessObjects BI platform Client Tools folder.

2. The login dialog box displays. Enter your user ID and password. The Query as a Web Service Designer displays.

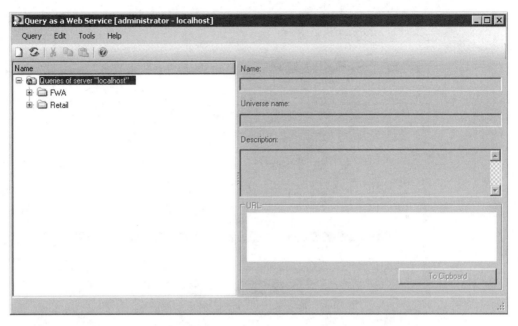

3. Select Query | New | Query from the menu.

4. Type a name in the Web Service Name field and optionally add a description. Click Next.

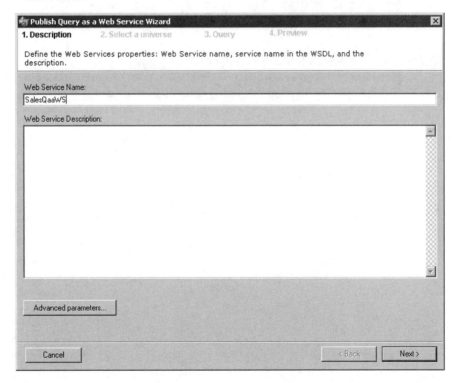

5. Select the universe from which you want to create your query. In this example, select eFashion. Click Next.

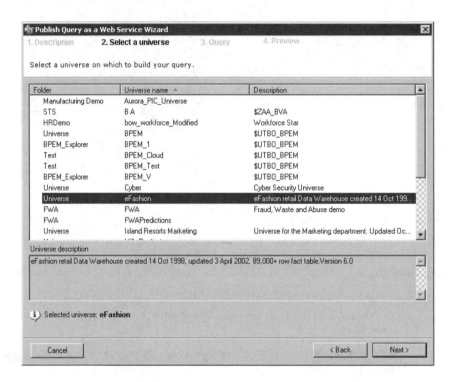

6. The next window looks like the Query Panel from a Web Intelligence query. Select the result objects and any filter objects to add to your query. In this example, add the State, Sales revenue, and Quantity sold objects. Click Next.

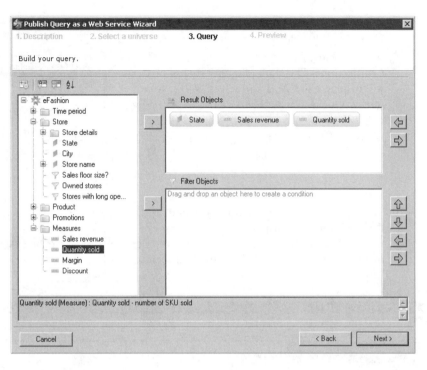

7. The preview window displays with the results from your query. Click Publish.

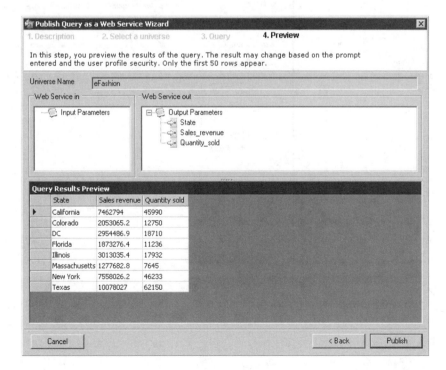

8. Click the To Clipboard button to copy the URL to your clipboard.

9. In Dashboard Designer, select Data | Connections. The Data Manager dialog box will display. Click Add and select Web service query (Query as a Web Service).

10. The QaaWS Data Connection is created, and the Definition tab displays. Type in a name for the data connection, copy the URL (copied in step 8) into the WSDL URL field, and click Import.

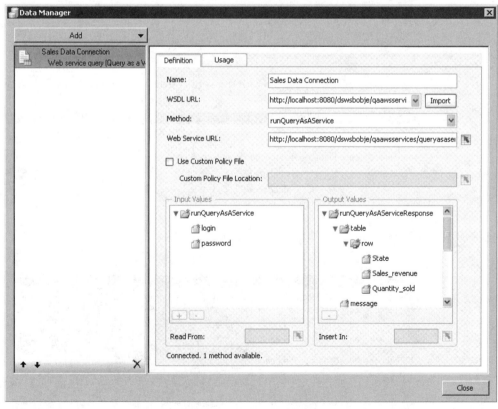

11. Select the row folder in the Output Values list. Since there are three columns of data in the web service query, you need to bind to three columns in the embedded spreadsheet. In this example, bind the web service query to Sheet1!$A$1:$C$30.

12. On the Usage tab, select Refresh Before Components are Loaded.

13. Click Close.

14. Notice the data from the QaaWS connection is not displayed in the embedded spreadsheet. To display the data retrieved from the QaaWS data connection, add a component to the dashboard canvas, such as a spreadsheet table component and bind it to the data in Sheet1!$A$1:$C$30.

15. Click Preview. You will be prompted to enter your user ID and password. The component will be filled with data from the QaaWS data connection.

Summary

SAP BusinessObjects Dashboards 4.0 has been enhanced to allow direct data connections to the BusinessObjects Enterprise universes and BEx queries. Dashboard Design continues to work with data in the embedded spreadsheet, and the data can be populated from Live Office or through a data connection such as QaaWS.

Part IV

28 Explorer

SAP BusinessObjects Explorer is a visual data discovery tool that allows casual users to interact with sets of data visually. It can be used as a native iPad application or invoked from the BI Launch Pad in a browser. This chapter introduces the main Explorer features.

Explorer Concepts

This section discusses concepts and terminology you should be familiar with before using Explorer:

- **Visual data discovery** Visual data discovery is a new category within the BI market that uses best practices in visualization to help users more readily find the patterns in the data. It uses either in-memory processing or pre-indexing to ensure speed-of-thought response time. At the time of this writing, SAP also released a new visual discovery tool, Visual Intelligence, which is more positioned for power users.

- **Information Space** Information Spaces are pre-indexed sets of data that users can access with Explorer. An Information Space can be created based on a universe, HANA data model, or spreadsheet. Creating an Information Space is described in the next section.

- **Search** Many BI vendors have been trying to apply some of the simplicity that Google provides for web searches to BI. In Explorer, the starting point is a simple search box. Here, you can enter keywords that appear anywhere within a range of Information Spaces. These keywords will then serve as the starting point for an exploration *within* an Information Space.

- **Facet** Facets in Explorer are similar in concept to dimensions within a universe, but unlike dimensions, facets are not hierarchical. Facets are made up of values, similar in concept to members of a dimension. For example, the *Year* facet may contain values of 2012, 2011, 2010, and so on.

- **Measure** Measures within a universe are also designated as measures within the Information Space in Explorer.

Creating an Information Space

When you create the Information Space, the SAP BusinessObjects Enterprise server will pre-calculate and pre-aggregate data so that users can quickly find, explore, and navigate with the Information Space. This is in contrast to a Web Intelligence query, for example, in which a user is querying the relational data source directly. It's important to keep in mind that the data within the Information Space is not real time. As an administrator, you can schedule the Information Space to be re-indexed on an automatic basis. In generating the index, both the metadata and the data values are indexed. For example, if your universe contains a dimension *Product*, with the data values of Dresses, T-shirt, and so on, the terms Product, Sweatshirt, T-shirt, and so on are all indexed.

As HANA is an in-memory appliance, the size of the data in the Information Space can be quite large, based on millions or billions of rows of granular data. However, when the universe is the data source, the upper limit may be only in the hundreds of thousands of rows to ensure speed-of-thought query performance. Much depends on the back-end server infrastructure, degree that distributed servers are used, and number of concurrent users. Customers should consult the *Sizing SAP BusinessObjects Explorer* guide when creating Information Spaces.

To create an Information Space on a SAP BW InfoCube, you must first create a universe layer on top of that cube, as described in Chapter 10.

To create an Information Space on a universe, follow these steps:

1. From BI Launch Pad, select Applications | Explorer. The Explorer Home page appears, as shown in Figure 28-1.

2. From the menu bar at the top, select Manage Spaces.

3. The Manage Spaces dialog box displays a list of universes and public spreadsheets, as shown in Figure 28-2. Navigate to the desired folder and universe, and then click New.

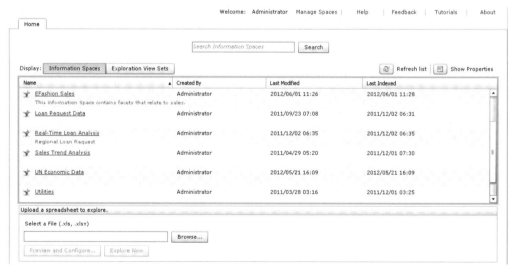

Figure 28-1 Explorer displays a search box and Information Spaces.

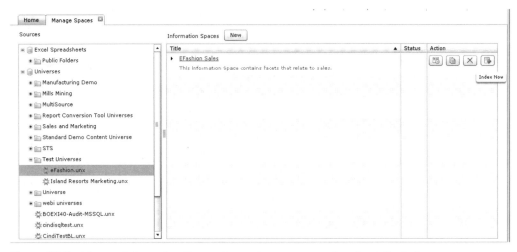

Figure 28-2 Manage Information Spaces to create new ones or to refresh the index.

NOTE You can create an Information Space only on a universe created with the IDT that has a .unx extension. You cannot create an Information Space on a 3.x universe created with the Universe Design Tool.

4. From the Properties tab of the Create Information Space dialog box, enter a name for the Information Space. This is the name that users will see from the Explorer Home page. Optionally, enter a description and keywords.

5. Select the folder where the Information Space should be stored.

6. Select regional settings.

7. Select the Objects tab to choose which dimensions and measures to index as part of the Information Space. By default, Explorer will create a measure *Occurrences*, which is a count of the number of records for that particular facet. Drag-and-drop the additional measures to add to this Information Space, such as *Sales*, *Margin*, *Discount*, and *Quantity Sold*. You may optionally create a new calculated measure as a simple calculation between two columns.

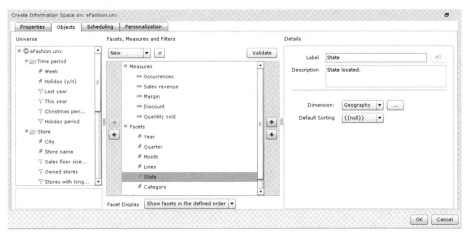

8. Select the dimension objects that you would like to create as facets. For each dimension, you can specify the type in the Details panel on the right. For example, *State* should be specified as Geography. Names of months should be designated as Months so that the sort order is by calendar month. You also may want to set the sort order for numeric months and years to A to Z; otherwise, Explorer will sort them according to the measure values (for example, month with the highest sales).

Geography	▼	...
Day (Mon..Sun)		
Geography		
Months (Jan..Dec)		
Standard		

9. Optionally, add any relevant filters if you do not wish to index all query results in the universe.

10. Click OK to return to the Manage Spaces dialog box.

11. From the Action column, click Index Now.

Exploring the Data

To explore the data, you may either explicitly choose an Information Space or enter keywords to find the most applicable Information Space. In the following example, the search term "sales New York 2006 dresses" has been entered in the search box.

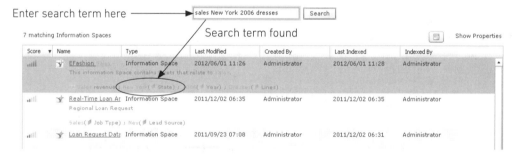

Similar to a Google search, the search terms are not case-sensitive. Explorer will search the name of the Information Space, keywords you defined when creating the Information Space, and facet and measure names, as well as the values for those facets. Based on the number of matches found in the keywords, the most relevant Information Space appears first in the list. So, for example, the search term "New York" is found in the *State* facet. Note that the score for the eFashion Sales Information Space is the highest.

Figure 28-3 shows the initial exploration of an Information Space. Measures appear in the top left; facets are in the panel on the right. Any search terms that you used to access this Information Space appear in orange. Notice that each facet has a precalculated grand total. For example, Q1 Sales revenue across all products and regions is $9,697,584, while the grand total for the T-Shirts category is $11,855,971. To view totals by other measures, click the desired measure in the Measures panel on the left.

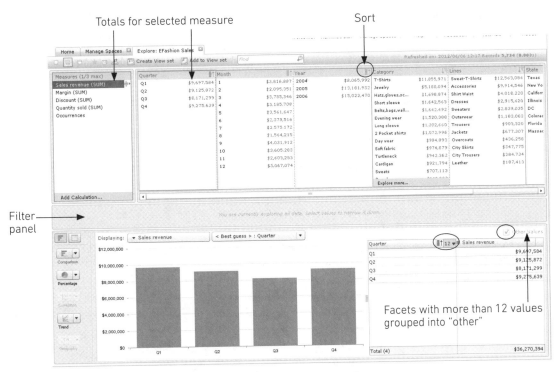

Figure 28-3   Exploration of the eFashion Sales Information Space

The bottom panel will display a chart, referred to as an *analysis type*. This uses a best guess at the measure and facet you wish to appear based on keyword search terms.

Filtering

To filter the information displayed in the chart and table, click any facet in the exploration panel. Use CTRL-click to select multiple values. For example, to filter by the lowest performing categories, follow these steps:

1. Click the sort icon for the *Category* facet to sort in ascending order.

2. From the drop-down menu, select Right Column Ascending. This option uses the measure column on the right as the sort criteria. Choosing Left Column Ascending sorts the list of categories alphabetically.

3. CTRL-click to select Pants, Night wear, and Shirts. These three categories will now appear in the filter panel.

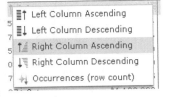

4. To remove the filter, click the X in the filter panel.

Part IV

Working with Charts

As noted earlier, each exploration is automatically displayed as a chart, referred to as an analysis type. Explorer supports five analysis types: comparative, percentage, correlation, trend, and geographic. Explorer will automatically pick the best chart to use for the data displayed.

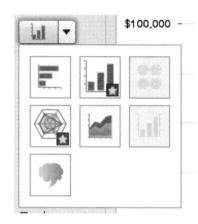

To change the chart type used, click the category of the chart type first. For example, comparison chart choices include vertical bar chart, horizontal bar chart, radar chart, surface chart, and tag cloud. Explorer will recommend a chart by displaying a gold star next to the most suitable visualization.

A tag cloud will display the names of the items in a size that relates to the measure. In the following example, the tag cloud chart shows that T-Shirts have the highest sales, whereas Day wear generates significantly less revenue.

Percentage charts show parts related to the whole, and include pie charts and tree maps. The following tree map for product lines uses a larger box for those lines that have higher revenues. Smaller boxes have lower revenues. Mouse-over to see the details for any individual box.

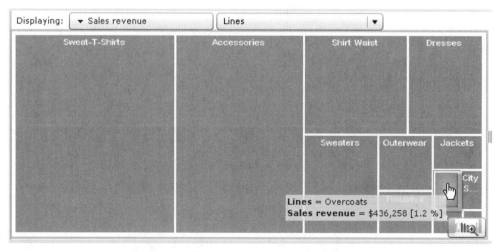

To change either the measures displayed or the facets displayed in the chart, click the appropriate drop-down arrow. You can select up to three measures to chart at one time.

By default, Explorer will chart data for the top 12 facet values. Values beyond this can be grouped into an "other" bucket. You can also increase the number of values to display, which may be useful for certain visualizations, such as tag clouds and maps, but not for bar charts.

Creating Exploration Views

Exploration views are new in Feature Pack 3 and allow you to create a collection of saved views. A view is a visualization that includes both the filters and chart settings.

To create an exploration view, follow these steps:

1. Create your desired visualization.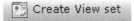

2. Select Create View Set from the main toolbar.

3. Specify the properties and name of the view. The properties name will appear as the title in the list of documents within BI Launch Pad. The name of the view will appear in the drop-down list within that view collection.

4. Select Save, and then specify a filename and location.

5. Explorer confirms the view was created. Click OK.

To open an existing exploration view, from the Explorer Home page, select Exploration View Sets. You can also copy the URL of the view to add directly to a workspace. Multiple views can be saved in one file.

Exporting Data

You can export either all the data from the Information Space or the filtered data to a comma-separated values (CSV) file, an Excel file, or a Web Intelligence document, or as a PNG image.

To export the data, follow these steps:

1. Select Export from the main toolbar.

2. Choose the desired format: Data, Excel, Web Intelligence, or Image. For this
example, choose Web Intelligence.

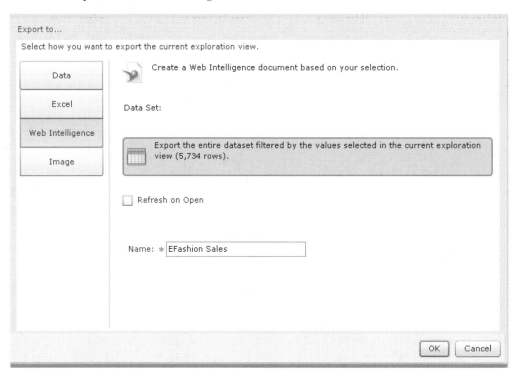

3. Specify a filename when prompted.

If you choose Web Intelligence as the export format, the document will be sent to the
BI Launch Pad inbox and will open in a new browser session. A tabular report similar to the
exploration view is automatically created with a query based on the underlying universe.

NOTE Explorer does not automatically assign a .png file extension when you export to an image. For ease
in opening the file, we recommend you explicitly append this extension to the filename.

Explorer on the iPad

Explorer can also be used as a native application on either the iPad or the iPhone. As
shown in Figure 28-4, the panes and actions on the iPad are similar to those available from
a web browser, bur rather than mouse clicks, you use touches and swipes to explore the
data. Explorer can be installed from the Apple iTunes store and then connected to your
Enterprise server.

Figure 28-4   Explorer can be used on the iPad.

Summary

Explorer is a user interface ideal for iPad users and casual users who want visual explorer subsets of data and don't need to create highly formatted reports or complex calculations. Explorer allows users to begin their exploration using a familiar search box, similar to Google's approach, to look for keywords in the Information Spaces and facets within those Information Spaces. Information Spaces can be based on universes, spreadsheets, and text files, as well as data loaded into HANA.

Index